D0214634

DATE DUE

National City Public Library
200 East 12th Street
National City, California 92050

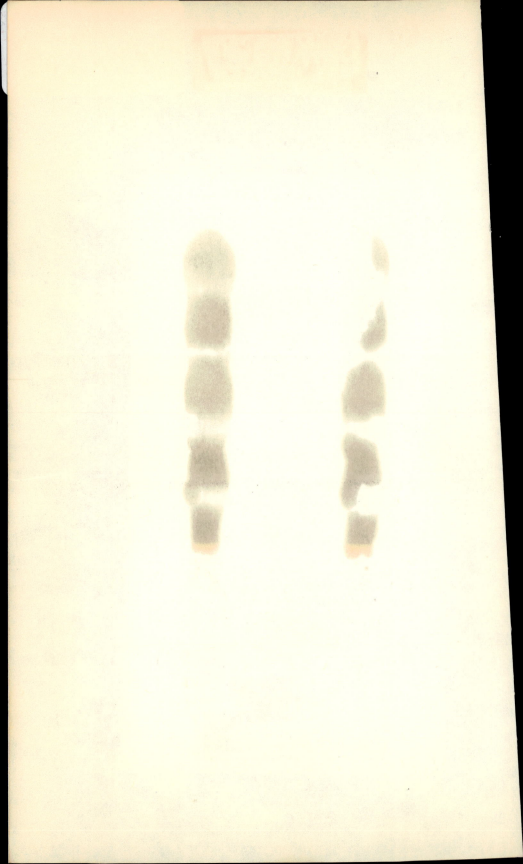

VOLUME 12 begins in the early part of August 1787 and continues through the end of March 1788, a time when Jefferson, as minister to France, was continuing his persistent efforts not only to secure the enforcement of the favorable trade regulations (especially for tobacco) already conceded to the United States but also to widen their scope to other imports from America.

In this volume, too, are letters from America with reports of the Federal Convention which met in Philadelphia in 1787 and adopted a proposed Constitution for the United States, the ensuing letters between Jefferson and his friends discussing the merits and defects of the proposed plan of government.

During this period, John Adams was arranging for his departure for America and Jefferson prepared to shoulder the responsibility—hitherto carried chiefly by Adams—of the American loans abroad. In order to have the benefit of Adams' counsel on the subject, Jefferson hastily left Paris and spent most of March conferring with Adams and bankers in Amsterdam on the Dutch loans; these negotiations resulted in arrangements designed to sustain American credit in Europe down to the end of 1790, at which time it was expected that the new government would have become stabilized.

Among Jefferson's personal but semi-official duties was the entertainment and instruction of young Americans travelling abroad. One

THE PAPERS OF
THOMAS JEFFERSON

of the most promising was Thomas Lee Shippen of Philadelphia, whom Jefferson presented at court. Young Shippen sent home to his father a graphic account of a day spent at Versailles with Jefferson (published in this volume for the first time), in which he wrote: "I observed that although Mr. Jefferson was the plainest man in the room, and the most destitute of ribbands crosses and other insignia of rank that he was most courted and attended to (even by the Courtiers themselves) of the whole Diplomatic corps."

Jefferson's personal letters in this volume—to Abigail Adams, Maria Cosway, John Trumbull, William Stephens Smith, Mme. de Bréhan, Peter Carr, Mme. de Corny, and others—present delightful pictures of his family and social life. The volume includes the first letters exchanged with the charming Angelica Schuyler Church, whom Jefferson met in the winter of 1787-1788.

THE PAPERS OF
Thomas Jefferson

Volume 12
7 August 1787 to 31 March 1788

JULIAN P. BOYD, EDITOR

MINA R. BRYAN AND FREDRICK AANDAHL
ASSOCIATE EDITORS

PRINCETON, NEW JERSEY
PRINCETON UNIVERSITY PRESS

1955

65377

Copyright © 1955, by Princeton University Press
London: Geoffrey Cumberlege, Oxford University Press
L.C.CARD 50-7486

Printed in the United States of America by
Princeton University Press, Princeton, New Jersey

DEDICATED TO THE MEMORY OF

ADOLPH S. OCHS

PUBLISHER OF THE NEW YORK TIMES

1896-1935

WHO BY THE EXAMPLE OF A RESPONSIBLE

PRESS ENLARGED AND FORTIFIED

THE JEFFERSONIAN CONCEPT

OF A FREE PRESS

ADVISORY COMMITTEE

DAVID K. E. BRUCE, *CHAIRMAN*

FRANCIS L. BERKELEY, JR.

SOLON J. BUCK

L. H. BUTTERFIELD

GILBERT CHINARD

HENRY STEELE COMMAGER

HAROLD W. DODDS

LUTHER H. EVANS

A. WHITNEY GRISWOLD

BRECKINRIDGE LONG

ARCHIBALD MAC LEISH

DUMAS MALONE

BERNARD MAYO

RICARDO A. MESTRES

SAMUEL E. MORISON

HOWARD W. SMITH

DATUS C. SMITH, JR.

IPHIGENE OCHS SULZBERGER

WILLIAM J. VAN SCHREEVEN

LAWRENCE C. WROTH

JOHN C. WYLLIE

CONSULTANTS AND STAFF

PROFESSOR ARCHIBALD T. MAC ALLISTER, *Consultant in Italian*

PROFESSOR RAYMOND S. WILLIS, *Consultant in Spanish*

FRANCE C. RICE, *Consultant in French*

HOWARD C. RICE, JR., *Consultant*, Princeton University Library

DOROTHY S. EATON, *Consultant*, The Library of Congress

LAURA B. STEVENS, *Assistant Editor*

GUIDE TO EDITORIAL APPARATUS

1. TEXTUAL DEVICES

The following devices are employed throughout the work to clarify the presentation of the text.

[. . .], [. . . .]	One or two words missing and not conjecturable.
[. . .]¹, [. . . .]¹	More than two words missing and not conjecturable; subjoined footnote estimates number of words missing.
[ ]	Number or part of a number missing or illegible.
[roman]	Conjectural reading for missing or illegible matter. A question mark follows when the reading is doubtful.
[*italic*]	Editorial comment inserted in the text.
⟨*italic*⟩	Matter deleted in the MS but restored in our text.
⟦ ⟧	Record entry for letters not found.

2. DESCRIPTIVE SYMBOLS

The following symbols are employed throughout the work to describe the various kinds of manuscript originals. When a series of versions is recorded, *the first to be recorded is the version used for the printed text.*

Dft	draft (usually a composition or rough draft; later drafts, when identifiable as such, are designated "2d Dft," &c.)
Dupl	duplicate
MS	manuscript (arbitrarily applied to most documents other than letters)
N	note, notes (memoranda, fragments, &c.)
PoC	polygraph copy
PrC	press copy
RC	recipient's copy
SC	stylograph copy
Tripl	triplicate

All manuscripts of the above types are assumed to be in the hand of the author of the document to which the descriptive symbol pertains. If not, that fact is stated. On the other hand, the follow-

[vii]

ing types of manuscripts are assumed *not* to be in the hand of the author, and exceptions will be noted:

FC   file copy (applied to all forms of retained copies, such as letter-book copies, clerks' copies, &c.)

Tr   transcript (applied to both contemporary and later copies; period of transcription, unless clear by implication, will be given when known)

3. LOCATION SYMBOLS

The locations of documents printed in this edition from originals in private hands, from originals held by institutions outside the United States, and from printed sources are recorded in self-explanatory form in the descriptive note following each document. The locations of documents printed from originals held by public institutions in the United States are recorded by means of the symbols used in the National Union Catalog in the Library of Congress; an explanation of how these symbols are formed is given above, Vol. 1: xl. The list of symbols appearing in each volume is limited to the institutions represented by documents printed or referred to in that and previous volumes.

CLU   William Andrews Clark Memorial Library, University of California at Los Angeles

CSmH   Henry E. Huntington Library, San Marino, California

Ct   Connecticut State Library, Hartford, Connecticut

CtY   Yale University Library

DLC   Library of Congress

DNA   The National Archives

G-Ar   Georgia Department of Archives and History, Atlanta

ICHi   Chicago Historical Society, Chicago

IHi   Illinois State Historical Library, Springfield

MB   Boston Public Library, Boston

MH   Harvard University Library

MHi   Massachusetts Historical Society, Boston

MHi:AMT   Adams Family Papers, deposited by the Adams Manuscript Trust in Massachusetts Historical Society

MdAA   Maryland Hall of Records, Annapolis

MdAN   U.S. Naval Academy Library

MeHi   Maine Historical Society, Portland
MiU-C   William L. Clements Library, University of Michigan
MoSHi   Missouri Historical Society, St. Louis
MWA   American Antiquarian Society, Worcester
NBu   Buffalo Public Library, Buffalo, New York
NcU   University of North Carolina Library
NHi   New-York Historical Society, New York City
NK-Iselin Letters to and from John Jay bearing this symbol are used by permission of the Estate of Eleanor Jay Iselin.
NN   New York Public Library, New York City
NNC   Columbia University Libraries
NNP   Pierpont Morgan Library, New York City
NNS   New York Society Library, New York City
NcD   Duke University Library
NjP   Princeton University Library
PBL   Lehigh University Library
PHC   Haverford College Library
PHi   Historical Society of Pennsylvania, Philadelphia
PPAP   American Philosophical Society, Philadelphia
PPL-R   Library Company of Philadelphia, Ridgway Branch
PU   University of Pennsylvania Library
RPA   Rhode Island Department of State, Providence
RPB   Brown University Library
Vi   Virginia State Library, Richmond
ViHi   Virginia Historical Society, Richmond
ViRVal   Valentine Museum Library, Richmond
ViU   University of Virginia Library
ViW   College of William and Mary Library
ViWC   Colonial Williamsburg, Inc.
WHi   State Historical Society of Wisconsin, Madison

4. OTHER ABBREVIATIONS

The following abbreviations are commonly employed in the annotation throughout the work.

Second Series   The topical series to be published at the end of this edition, comprising those materials which are best suited to a classified rather than a chronological arrangement (see Vol. 1: xv-xvi).

[ix]

TJ Thomas Jefferson

TJ Editorial Files Photoduplicates and other editorial materials in the office of *The Papers of Thomas Jefferson*, Princeton University Library

TJ Papers Jefferson Papers (applied to a collection of manuscripts when the precise location of a given document must be furnished, and always preceded by the symbol for the institutional repository; thus "DLC: TJ Papers, 4:628-9" represents a document in the Library of Congress, Jefferson Papers, volume 4, pages 628 and 629)

PCC Papers of the Continental Congress, in the National Archives

RG Record Group (used in designating the location of documents in the National Archives)

SJL Jefferson's "Summary Journal of letters" written and received (in DLC: TJ Papers)

SJPL "Summary Journal of Public Letters," an incomplete list of letters written by TJ from 16 Apr. 1784 to 31 Dec. 1793, with brief summaries, in an amanuensis' hand (in DLC: TJ Papers, at end of SJL)

V Ecu

ƒ Florin

£ Pound sterling or livre, depending upon context (in doubtful cases, a clarifying note will be given)

s Shilling or sou

d Penny or denier

₶ Livre Tournois

℔ Per (occasionally used for pro, pre)

5. SHORT TITLES

The following list includes only those short titles of works cited with great frequency, and therefore in very abbreviated form, throughout this edition. Their expanded forms are given here only in the degree of fullness needed for unmistakable identification. Since it is impossible to anticipate all the works to be cited in such very abbreviated form, the list is appropriately revised from volume to volume.

Atlas of Amer. Hist., Scribner, 1943 James Truslow Adams and R. V. Coleman, *Atlas of American History*, N.Y., 1943

Barbary Wars Dudley W. Knox, ed., *Naval Documents Related to the United States Wars with the Barbary Powers*

Betts, *Farm Book*   Edwin M. Betts, ed., *Thomas Jefferson's Farm Book*

Betts, *Garden Book*   Edwin M. Betts, ed., *Thomas Jefferson's Garden Book*

Biog. Dir. Cong.   Biographical Directory of Congress, 1774-1927

B.M. Cat.   British Museum, *General Catalogue of Printed Books*, London, 1931—. Also, *The British Museum Catalogue of Printed Books 1881-1900*, Ann Arbor, 1946

B.N. Cat.   Catalogue général des livres imprimés de la Bibliothèque Nationale. Auteurs.

Burnett, *Letters of Members*   Edmund C. Burnett, ed., *Letters of Members of the Continental Congress*

Cal. Franklin Papers   Calendar of the Papers of Benjamin Franklin in the Library of the American Philosophical Society, ed. I. Minis Hays

CVSP   *Calendar of Virginia State Papers . . . Preserved in the Capitol at Richmond*

DAB   *Dictionary of American Biography*

DAE   *Dictionary of American English*

DAH   *Dictionary of American History*

DNB   *Dictionary of National Biography*

Dipl. Corr., 1783-89   The Diplomatic Correspondence of the United States of America, from the Signing of the Definitive Treaty of Peace . . . to the Adoption of the Constitution, Washington, Blair & Rives, 1837, 3 vol.

Elliot's *Debates   The Debates of the Several State Conventions on the Adoption of the Federal Constitution . . . together with the Journal of the Federal Convention . . . Collected and Revised from Contemporary Publications by Jonathan Elliot.* 2d. ed., Philadelphia, 1901

Evans   Charles Evans, *American Bibliography*

Ford   Paul Leicester Ford, ed., *The Writings of Thomas Jefferson*, "Letterpress Edition," N.Y., 1892-1899.

Freeman, *Washington*   Douglas Southall Freeman, *George Washington*

Fry-Jefferson Map   *The Fry & Jefferson Map of Virginia and Maryland: A Facsimile of the First Edition*, Princeton, 1950

Gottschalk, *Lafayette, 1783-89*   Louis Gottschalk, *Lafayette between the American Revolution and the French Revolution (1783-1789)*, Chicago, 1950

Gournay *Tableau général du commerce, des marchands, négocians, armateurs, &c., . . . années 1789 & 1790*, Paris, n.d.

HAW Henry A. Washington, ed., *The Writings of Thomas Jefferson*, Washington, 1853-1854

Hening William W. Hening, *The Statutes at Large; Being a Collection of All the Laws of Virginia*

Henry, *Henry* William Wirt Henry, *Patrick Henry, Life, Correspondence and Speeches*

JCC *Journals of the Continental Congress, 1774-1789*, ed. W. C. Ford and others, Washington, 1904-1937

JHD *Journal of the House of Delegates of the Commonwealth of Virginia* (cited by session and date of publication)

Jefferson Correspondence, Bixby *Thomas Jefferson Correspondence Printed from the Originals in the Collections of William K. Bixby*, ed. W. C. Ford, Boston, 1916

Johnston, "Jefferson Bibliography" Richard H. Johnston, "A Contribution to a Bibliography of Thomas Jefferson," *Writings of Thomas Jefferson*, ed. Lipscomb and Bergh, xx, separately paged following the Index.

L & B Andrew A. Lipscomb and Albert E. Bergh, eds., *The Writings of Thomas Jefferson*, "Memorial Edition," Washington, 1903-1904

L.C. Cat. *A Catalogue of Books Represented by Library of Congress Printed Cards*, Ann Arbor, 1942-1946; also *Supplement*, 1948

Library Catalogue, 1783 Jefferson's MS list of books owned and wanted in 1783 (original in Massachusetts Historical Society)

Library Catalogue, 1815 *Catalogue of the Library of the United States*, Washington, 1815

Library Catalogue, 1829 *Catalogue. President Jefferson's Library*, Washington, 1829

MVHR *Mississippi Valley Historical Review*

OED *A New English Dictionary on Historical Principles*, Oxford, 1888-1933

PMHB *The Pennsylvania Magazine of History and Biography*

Randall, *Life* Henry S. Randall, *The Life of Thomas Jefferson*

Randolph, *Domestic Life* Sarah N. Randolph, *The Domestic Life of Thomas Jefferson*

Sabin Joseph Sabin and others, *Bibliotheca Americana. A Dictionary of Books Relating to America*

[xii]

Sowerby *Catalogue of the Library of Thomas Jefferson*, compiled with annotations by E. Millicent Sowerby, Washington, 1952-53

Swem, *Index* E. G. Swem, *Virginia Historical Index*

Swem, "Va. Bibliog." Earl G. Swem, "A Bibliography of Virginia," Virginia State Library, *Bulletin*, VIII, X, XII (1915-1919)

TJR Thomas Jefferson Randolph, ed., *Memoir, Correspondence, and Miscellanies, from the Papers of Thomas Jefferson*, Charlottesville, 1829

Tucker, *Life* George Tucker, *The Life of Thomas Jefferson*, Philadelphia, 1837

Tyler, *Va. Biog.* Lyon G. Tyler, *Encyclopedia of Virginia Biography*

Tyler's Quart. *Tyler's Quarterly Historical and Genealogical Magazine*

VMHB *Virginia Magazine of History and Biography*

Wharton, *Dipl. Corr. Am. Rev.* *The Revolutionary Diplomatic Correspondence of the United States*, ed. Francis Wharton

WMQ *William and Mary Quarterly*

CONTENTS

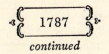

1787

continued

CONTENTS

[xvi]

CONTENTS

[xvii]

CONTENTS

CONTENTS

CONTENTS

[xx]

CONTENTS

[xxi]

CONTENTS

CONTENTS

[xxiii]

CONTENTS

[xxiv]

CONTENTS

[xxv]

CONTENTS

CONTENTS

1788

CONTENTS

CONTENTS

CONTENTS

[xxx]

CONTENTS

CONTENTS

CONTENTS

ILLUSTRATIONS

FACING PAGE

DEMOLITION OF HOUSES ON THE PONT NOTRE-DAME, PAINTING BY HUBERT ROBERT, 1786 — 34

Reporting on the "wonderful improvements" taking place in Paris, Jefferson wrote to David Humphreys, 14 August 1787, that "one of the old bridges has all its houses demolished, and a second nearly so." The first of the bridges referred to by Jefferson—the Pont Notre-Dame, connecting the Ile de la Cité with the Right Bank—is shown in the painting by Hubert Robert reproduced here. The view is taken from the Right Bank looking west. Beneath the arches of the Pont Notre-Dame can be seen the Pont au Change, the second of the bridges mentioned by Jefferson (painted by Hubert Robert, during the demolition of its houses, in 1788, in another canvas also in the Musée Carnavalet). The third bridge visible here is the Pont Neuf. The removal of the houses from the old bridges was generally considered one of the important urban improvements of the reign of Louis XVI: Sébastien Mercier, for example, in his *Tableau de Paris*, referred triumphantly to the "unshackled bridges," cleared of their "Visigothic" obstructions. (Courtesy of the Musée Carnavalet, Paris, through Howard C. Rice, Jr.)

THE SALON OF 1787 — 35

Engraving by P. A. Martini. The public exhibitions of the Académie Royale de Peinture et Sculpture were held every two years, opening on Saint Louis' Day (August 25), in the Salon Carré of the Louvre—hence the extended meaning of the word "salon." In his letter of 30 Aug. 1787 to John Trumbull, Jefferson urged the young American artist to come from London to see the Salon, enclosing a catalogue and commenting on several of the works shown. The "best thing," according to Jefferson, was David's "Death of Socrates," painted for M. de Trudaine (acquired in 1931 by the Metropolitan Museum of Art, New York), visible here in the bottom row, left of center. On the walls at right and left can be seen Hubert Robert's series of the Roman antiquities of Provence (commissioned by the King for the Palace at Fontainebleau, now in the Louvre)—the Maison Carrée, the Pont du Gard, and other "remains of Roman grandeur" that Jefferson had admired during his journey into Southern France several months earlier. Madame Vigée-Lebrun's portrait of Queen Marie-Antoinette and her three children is in the very center of the engraving, while the "crucifixion by Roland [de la

[xxxiv]

ILLUSTRATIONS

Porte]," mentioned by Jefferson, hangs in the bottom row, extreme left. Historical canvases by such artists as David, Vien, Doyen, La Grenée and others—a genre also practiced in London by Benjamin West and his pupil John Trumbull—predominated in this Salon, as they did in 1785 and 1789. Many of the visitors depicted by Martini in this engraving are holding the *livret* of the exhibition; the tiny numerals inscribed in the corners of the paintings correspond to the numbers in this catalogue. (Courtesy of the Cabinet des Estampes, Bibliothèque Nationale, through Howard C. Rice, Jr.)

PRELIMINARY SKETCH OF COL. DEUX-PONTS FOR TRUMBULL'S "SURRENDER OF LORD CORNWALLIS AT YORKTOWN"   66

Trumbull's sketch for the figure of Col. Deux-Ponts and his notes concerning the military dress of the French soldiers for his painting of the surrender at Yorktown were doubtless made in Jefferson's house in Paris, where the portraits of the French officers were painted. See overleaf illustration; also John Trumbull to TJ, 28 Aug., 17 Sep. and 7 Dec. 1787; TJ to Trumbull, 13 Nov. 1787. (Courtesy of The Yale Gallery of Fine Arts.)

DETAILS FROM TRUMBULL'S PAINTING OF THE "SURRENDER OF LORD CORNWALLIS AT YORKTOWN"   67

These enlarged details from Trumbull's painting, which he completed in London before 1797, depict the heads of Rochambeau (upper left), Lafayette (upper right), Chastellux, Vioménil, Barras, and De Grasse (below, left to right), taken from the portraits and sketches "painted from life, in Mr. Jefferson's house" in the winter of 1787-1788. Trumbull considered his work in Paris that winter "as the best of my small portraits." See *The Autobiography of Colonel John Trumbull*, ed. Theodore Sizer, p. 152; John Trumbull to TJ, 28 Aug.; and references mentioned for the preceding illustration. (Courtesy of The Yale Gallery of Fine Arts.)

THE HERMITAGE ON MONT CALVAIRE, OR MONT VALERIEN, SEEN FROM THE BOIS DE BOULOGNE   482

This engraving by De Monchy, after a drawing made in 1766 by Simon Mathurin Lantara, shows Mont Calvaire (also known as Mont Valérien) substantially as it was in 1786-1788 when Jefferson went there for week-end visits. See TJ to Mme. de Corny, 18 Oct. 1787; Frémin de

ILLUSTRATIONS

Fontenille to TJ, 23 Oct. 1787; TJ to Frémin de Fontenille, 24 Oct. 1787; TJ to John Adams, 31 Dec. 1787. On the top of the hill, rising above the village of Suresnes and across the Seine from Longchamps and the Bois de Boulogne, were situated the church of the Priests of Calvary, a popular pilgrimage, and also buildings housing a community of lay brothers known as the Hermits of Mount Calvary. The latter cultivated their vineyards (producing *vin de Suresnes*), manufactured excellent silk stockings, and received paying guests who, according to Sébastien Mercier in his *Tableau de Paris*, "enjoyed good air, a magnificent view, and found comfort for body as well as for soul." Although Martha Jefferson was not strictly accurate when she referred, in her latter-day reminiscences of her father's life in Paris, to this spot as a Carthusian monastery, it was nevertheless a "chartreuse," or retreat, in the extended meaning of the word (OED). During the nineteenth century Mont Valérien was used for military purposes, a fort replacing the shrine and hermitage. For further discussion and reproduction of a page from the Hermits' account book recording Jefferson's visits, see H. C. Rice, Jr., "Jefferson in Europe a Century Later, Notes of a Roving Researcher," *Princeton University Library Chronicle*, XII (1950), 19-35; and his "Les Visites de Jefferson au Mont-Valérien," *Bulletin de la Société Historique de Suresnes*, III, 13 (1953-54), 46-49. (Courtesy of M. René Sordes, Suresnes, through Howard C. Rice, Jr.)

AN ACT FOR THE ENCOURAGEMENT OF THE COMMERCE
OF FRANCE WITH THE UNITED STATES   483

First page of the corrected proof sheets of the arrêt of 29 Dec. 1787 which William Short enclosed in his letter to John Jay, 1 Jan. 1788, q.v. See also Lambert to TJ, 29 Dec. 1787, where the English text of this arrêt is printed in full as an enclosure and this copy described in note. (Courtesy of the National Archives.)

RECEIPT OF THE POLYGRAPHIC SOCIETY FOR A PICTURE
PURCHASED BY JOHN TRUMBULL FOR JEFFERSON   483

Jefferson first saw and became interested in the copying of oil paintings by a mechanical process when he was in England in the spring of 1786—at about the same time that he was investigating the possibilities of "polytype" printing (Vol. 6: 316-24). Jefferson was naturally interested in this process, described as one which "without any injury whatever to the original painting . . . produces

[xxxvi]

ILLUSTRATIONS

such an exact copy, or likeness, as cannot, without difficulty and close attention, be distinguished from the archetype . . . while the price . . . to the public is a trifle." The promise of economy as well as improvement appealed to Jefferson: in asking Trumbull to procure one of the prints, he said, "like the rest of the world, I like to have good things at a small price." See TJ to Trumbull, 13 Nov. 1787, for a note concerning *An Address . . . on the Polygraphic Art* from which the above description is taken; also Trumbull to TJ, 7 Dec. 1787, 22 Feb. and 6 Mch. 1788. (Courtesy of the Massachusetts Historical Society.)

JOHN ADAMS. PORTRAIT BY MATHER BROWN, 1788   514

This portrait of Adams was painted at Jefferson's request, and was sent to him in Paris in the spring of 1788, together with one of the portraits of himself painted by Brown in London in the spring of 1786, the other copy of which was painted for Adams. See Vol. 1, facing p. 3; TJ to W. S. Smith, 31 Dec. 1787 and 2 Feb. 1788; from W. S. Smith, 16 Jan. 1788; from Trumbull, 22 Feb., 6 Mch., 23 May, 20 June 1788; to Trumbull, 18 May 1788. (Courtesy of The Boston Athenaeum.)

BIRTHDAY ILLUMINATIONS FOR THE PRINCE OF ORANGE, ROTTERDAM, 8 MARCH 1788   515

"The illuminations were the most splendid I had ever seen and the roar of joy the most universal I had ever heard," Jefferson wrote to William Short (10 March 1788) after his passage through Rotterdam on the evening of 8 March. The engraving reproduced here, by F. Sansom after A. Boon, comes from a commemorative volume of plates issued at the time: Nicolaas Cornel, *Verheerlijkt en verlicht Rotterdam, of beschryving der plechtige illuminatien en decoratien, welken binnen voornoemde Stad hebben plaats gehad, den 8sten Maart 1788*, Rotterdam, [1788]. The legend of the engraving reads: "Picture of the Illumination and Decoration on the House of the True Patriotic Society on the Westnieuwland in Rotterdam on the first joyful Birthday of His Illustrious Highness after the long-desired and successful Reestablishment of the Country's old and blessed Constitution on the 8th of March 1788, [executed] under the direction of . . . Johan Philip de Monte . . . and . . . Matthius Theodorus Peypers, both directors of this Society." The birthday celebration in Rotterdam symbolized the Orangist triumph in the civil strife of the previous autumn—events that, because of France's failure to support the Patriot cause, filled Jef-

ILLUSTRATIONS

ferson with none of the joy felt by the burghers of Rotterdam. The triumph of the Stadtholder's party, supported by England and Prussia, had a direct bearing, in different ways, upon the personal lives of several of Jefferson's correspondents. Van Hogendorp, with whom he had corresponded so warmly until the autumn of 1786, had linked his fortunes to the Orangist cause, and indeed, as *Raadpensionaris*, had conveyed to Their Illustrious Highnesses the official greetings of the City of Rotterdam at this 8 March celebration. (There is no evidence that Jefferson saw Van Hogendorp, or made any effort to do so, as he passed through Rotterdam on this festive occasion.) The Orangist victory, on the other hand, had brought threats of violence and great uneasiness of mind to C. W. F. Dumas, the American agent at The Hague; sent many Dutch patriots into exile in France (see Van der Capellen to TJ, 29 Feb. 1788); and caused others, such as Van der Kemp (see TJ to Madison, 8 March 1788), to set out for America. (Courtesy of the Rijksarchief, The Hague, through Howard C. Rice, Jr.)

[xxxviii]

Volume 12

7 August 1787 to 31 March 1788

JEFFERSON CHRONOLOGY

1743 · 1826

1743.	Born at Shadwell.
1772.	Married Martha Wayles Skelton.
1775-76.	In Continental Congress.
1776-79.	In Virginia House of Delegates.
1779-81.	Governor of Virginia.
1782.	His wife died.
1783-84.	In Continental Congress.
1784-89.	In France as commissioner and minister.
1790-93.	U.S. Secretary of State.
1797-1801.	Vice President of the United States.
1801-09.	President of the United States.
1826.	Died at Monticello.

VOLUME 12

7 August 1787 to 31 March 1788

ca. 3 Sep. 1787. Began conferences with French officials to improve the status of French-American trade.

17 Sep. Federal Convention agreed on a proposed Constitution for the United States, and adjourned.

1 Oct. Sent Buffon specimens of American animals.

12 Oct. Was reappointed minister to France for three years from 10 Mch. 1788.

29 Dec. French Council of State passed an Act for the encouragement of commerce between France and the United States.

13 Jan. 1788. Sent Egyptian rice to South Carolina for experimentation.

4 Mch. Left Paris to negotiate funding plans in Holland with John Adams.

6 Mch. At Antwerp.

8 Mch. At Rotterdam.

9 Mch. At The Hague.

10 Mch. Arrived in Amsterdam.

31 Mch. Left Amsterdam.

THE PAPERS OF
THOMAS JEFFERSON

To Langlade

Monsieur   à Paris ce 7me. Aout. 1787.

Le nom de Mr. Jaques Tourny m'est tout à fait inconnu. Je crois pouvoir vous assurer qu'aucune personne de ce nom n'a pas commandé une fregate des etats unis d'Amerique, qu'il n'y a point de ville de Petersburgh dans le comté d'Essex en Virginie, que jamais l'etat de Virginie n'a pas fait des expeditions à Livourne ni eu aucunes affaires avec aucun negotiant de cette ville, que consequement personne ne m'a informé de ses demarches auprès de ce negociant supposé, ni reçu des reponses de moi sur ce sujet.

J'ai l'honneur d'etre avec bien de consideration Monsieur votre tres humble et tres obeissant serviteur,   Th: Jefferson

PrC (MHi).

To St. Victour

à Paris ce 7me. Aout 1787.

J'ai la satisfaction de vous faire part, Monsieur, que le Gouverneur de Virginie vient de m'avertir qu'on a trouvé les bayonettes qui faisoient partie de vos envoye d'armes, et qu'au premier moment on avoit craint d'avoir eté omis. Il faudra attendre les ordres de l'Etat pour les fournitures ulterieures. On n'en a pas parlé du tout dans les dernieres lettres. J'ai l'honneur d'etre Monsieur avec beaucoup de consideration votre très humble et très obeissant serviteur,   Th: Jefferson

PrC (ViWC). See Randolph to TJ, 4 May 1787, note.

To Frederick Soffer

Sir   Paris Aug. 7. 1787.

Immediately on the receipt of your letter of July 14. I took measures to obtain the information you desired as to the terms on

[3]

which American vessels are received in the Isle of France. They are precisely the same on which other foreign vessels are admitted, there having been no peculiar favor granted us. American vessels may carry thither the productions of the United states which are favorably received.

I am with much respect Sir Your most obedient humble servant,

TH: JEFFERSON

PrC (DLC); at foot of text: "Monsr. Fred. Soffer chez M. Pre. Changeur Negt. rue Rousselle à Bordeaux."

The MEASURES TO OBTAIN THE IN-FORMATION that TJ took followed the familiar course of utilizing the good offices of Lafayette. In response to Lafayette's inquiry the intendant-general of the colonies, De Vaivre, wrote: "Jusqu'à présent les américains ne sont admis à l'isle de France, que pour des besoins de relâche, et il ne leur a été accordé aucune faveur particulière. Mais, le ministre est occupé de la proposition qui lui a été faite d'établir un port-franc au port Louis. Si ce port-franc a lieu, alors les américains,

comme les autres nations, pourront y avoir un commerce libre d'Echanges" (ViWC; dated at Versailles, 4 Aug. 1787). Two days later Rayneval also wrote the marquis: "On a fait prévenir les américains, que leurs Vaisseaux destinés pour la Chine seroient admis à l'isle de France, et qu'ils y trouveroient tous les sucres dont ils pourroient avoir besoin; s'ils y conduisent des productions de leur pays, elles seront favorablement accueillies" (same; dated at Versailles, 6 Aug. 1787; endorsed by TJ: "Rayneval"). As in so many other instances of their collaboration, TJ in this case evidently made the appeal and Lafayette the response without having to resort to written communication.

To Stael de Holstein

SIR   Paris Aug. 7. 1787.

I have transmitted to the Secretary for foreign affairs [of] the United states of America, the letter which your excellency [did] me the honour to write me on the 3d. inst. on the subject of the Mary Elizabeth, a Swedish vessel, pyratically carried of by the master and crew, and supposed to be in some of the harbors of the United states. You may be assured that due search will be made for them, that whatever can be recovered of the vessel and cargo [will] be restored to the owners, and that the offenders, if they can be found and proved guilty, will be punished there, our laws inflicting death for the offence of pyracy, but permitting in no case the surrender of persons claimed for whatever cause by any other n[ation.] I shall have the honour of communicating to you the result of this enquiry, and have now that of assuring you of the sentiments of profound esteem and respect with which I have the honor to be Your Excellency's Most obedient & Most humble servant,   TH: JEFFERSON

PrC (DLC); at foot of text: "H.E. The Ambassador of Sweden."

[4]

To William Frederick Ast

SIR   Paris Aug. 8. 1787.

I am honoured with your favor of the 3d. inst. and am sorry to be obliged to inform you that no late remittances having arrived from the board of treasury of the U.S. and Mr. Grand being unwilling to extend his advances beyond their present amount, Mr. Barclay's bills in your favor must lie awhile unpaid. I have reason to expect that remittances would be on the way before they receive my letter by the June packet in which I informed them that their funds here were then exhausted. The moment they arrive your demands shall be answered. I am with much respect Sir Your most obedt. humble servt,   TH: JEFFERSON

PrC (DLC).
YOUR FAVOR OF THE 3D. INST.: Not found, but recorded in SJL as received 7 Aug. 1787, together with a letter of Zachariah Loreilhe, [ca. 3 Aug.] in which it was probably enclosed.

To John Churchman

SIR   Paris Aug. 8. 1787.

I have duly received your favor of June 6. and immediately communicated it's contents to a member of the Academy. He told me they had received the other copy of your memorial which you mention to have sent thro' another channel, that your ideas were not conveyed so explicitly as to enable them to decide finally on their merit, but that they had made an entry in their journals to preserve to you the claim to the original idea. As far as we can conjecture it here, we imagine you make a table of variations of the needle for all the different meridians whatever. To apply this table to use in the voiage between America and Europe, suppose the variation to increase a degree in every 160 miles, two difficulties occur. 1. A ready and accurate method of finding the variation of the place. 2. An instrument so perfect as that (tho' the degree on it shall represent 160 miles) it shall give the parts of the degree so minutely as to answer the purposes of the navigator. The variation of the needle at Paris actually is 21°. W. I make no doubt but you have provided against the doubts entertained here, and I shall be happy that our country may have the honour of furnishing the old world what it has so long sought in vain. I am with much respect Sir Your most obedient humble servt.,

TH: JEFFERSON

[5]

PrC (DLC); at foot of text: "Mr. John Churchman Philadelphia." The RC is described in the *Catalogue of the Alfred Morrison Autograph Collection* (NN), but has not been found.

To Richard Claiborne

Sir   Paris Aug. 8. 1787.

I am of opinion that American tenants for Western lands could not be procured, and if they could, they would be very unsure. The best as far as I have been able to judge are foreigners who do not speak the language. Unable to communicate with the people of the country they confine themselves to their farms and their families, compare their present state to what it was in Europe, and find great reason to be contented. Of all foreigners I should prefer Germans. They are the easiest got, the best for their landlord, and do best for themselves. The deed in which you were interested having been sent to me the other day to be authenticated, I took the inclosed note of it's particulars for you. I am with much esteem Sir Your most obedient & most humble servt.,

Th: Jefferson

PrC (DLC). Enclosure missing.

To Francis Coffyn

Sir   Paris Aug. 8. 1787.

I was informed in the course of the last year that there was in the prison of Dunkirk a person of the name of Alexander Gross confined as hostage for the ransom of the sloop Charlotte taken by the privateer Countess d'Avaux, Capt. Carry, in Feb. 1782. I learn that his owners refused to release him, and that the owners of the privateer have since stopped paiment and become bankrupt. I will be obliged to you if you will inform me whether he be still in prison, and if it be true that the owners of the privateer have failed; because tho this be a case of private property in which their hostage should not be released against their consent, yet seeing that his imprisonment is useless, and a continued expence, I would wish to obtain an order for his discharge. I will beg of you to make these enquiries without naming me, as it might give a false hope to the owners that my interfering was by public authority, and might produce to them the paiment of the ransom money. I do not

[6]

move in it by public authority nor is it consistent with our laws to take the discharge of any such contract on themselves in any case. Your answer as soon as you shall have obtained information will much oblige Sir Your most obedt. humble servant,

TH: JEFFERSON

PrC (DLC).
TJ's memorandum to Montmorin concerning ALEXANDER GROSS is to be found under 7 Jan. 1788.

To R. & A. Garvey

GENTLEMEN   Paris Aug. 8. 1787.

Having reason to believe that the harpsichord I expected from England will arrive soon at Rouen addressed to your care, I have obtained a passport for it to prevent it's being opened at Rouen, as I have directed it to be very well packed. I now inclose the passport and will beg the favor of you to have the harpsichord sent up by water. I am sorry I could not save the necessity of an Acquit a caution, but you may be assured I shall be very careful to withdraw it and return it to you. I have the honour to be with much respect, Gentlemen, Your most obedient humble servt.,

TH: JEFFERSON

PrC (MHi). Enclosure missing.

To Zachariah Loreilhe

SIR   Paris Aug. 8. 1787.

I have the honour to acknowlege the receipt of your favour dated Lorient Aug. 1787. together with the packets accompanying, and of returning you my thanks for your care of them. I have now that of assuring you of the sentiments of esteem and regard with which I am Sir Your most obedient & most humble servt.,

TH: JEFFERSON

PrC (MHi). YOUR FAVOUR: Printed above under 3 Aug. 1787.

To Benjamin Putnam

SIR   Paris Aug. 8. 1787.

I received in Sep. last your favor on the subject of your claim against this government for a sloop taken from you in the island

[7]

of Guadeloupe. As it contained no documents which could enable me to stir in the business, as you supposed Mr. Ridley had turned it over to Mr. Barclay and I was in the immediate expectation of his return from Marocco, I let the matter rest till I could see him. On his return however, he took the resolution of embarking for America, and I received last night information that he had sailed from Lorient the 2d. instant. I seize the first moment therefore to apprize you of this. Mr. Ridley and Mr. Barclay being both now in America you can get from them the state in which your matter is. If any thing remains yet to be done, in which I can be serviceable to you, I shall be so chearfully. I will only desire of you in that case to furnish every document necessary, and to engage some person here to follow the details of the business, as my occupations could not permit me to do that. But in counsel to your agent here, and every other service which may be performed by me I shall be ready. Your letter being without date of time or place, but your name inducing a presumption that you are of some one of the Eastern states, I put this letter into the hands of Mr. Derby of the Massachusets who will endeavor to find you. I am Sir your very humble servant, TH: JEFFERSON

PrC (DLC). Putnam's FAVOR, here acknowledged, is printed above under 11 Oct. 1786. This letter, according to the entry in SJL, was carried to America by Elias Hasket Derby.

To David Ramsay

DEAR SIR   Paris Aug. 8. 1787.

I have duly received your favor accompanying that of Mr. Van bram Houckgeete on the subject of a cask of snuff sent by him to Bordeaux. The importation of that article is prohibited by the laws of France on pain of fine and forfeiture of the article to the Farmers general. His snuff was seized and condemned on due process of law. He sais he was ignorant of the law, and I believe it: his captain having reported the article on his entry is a proof. But ignorance of the law is a plea in no country and in no case. The snuff is become the property of the Farmers general, who will not cede it, nor can the king take it from them to give back to the shipper. Were he to do any thing, it must be to repay it's value to the shipper. But you are too good a reasoner not to see that I could not ask this of the king at any time, much less at this when from the distresses of their finances they are obliged to discontinue the pensions and bounties to their own best citizens. I must take the liberty of asking you to communicate this answer to Mr. Houckgeest. I wish with all my heart his case had admitted my serving him: it would have yet been an additional gratification to me as you interest yourself for him. But you will be sensible it did not admit of it. I beg you to be assured of my dispositions to do whatever you would wish, and of the sentiments of sincere esteem with which I have the honor to be Sir your most obedient & most humble servant, TH: JEFFERSON

PrC (DLC).

From Viel

Paris, 8 Aug. 1787. Acknowledges receipt of a letter from Derieux, transmitted by TJ.

RC (ViWC); 2 p.; in French; endorsed by TJ: "de Rieux." Not recorded in SJL. The letter acknowledged was transmitted in Derieux to TJ, 1 June 1787, q.v.

To Burrill Carnes

SIR   Paris Aug. 9. 1787.

I am now to acknolege the receipt of your favor of July 19. By a letter of this day to Messrs. Schweighauser & Dobree I have asked the favor of them to put into your hands one of the good muskets, bayonets and sabres which came from Holland, and to inform you what they think they would sell for, if they should be sold. This information I will ask you to communicate to the Commissioners of the treasury of the U.S. sending them at the same time the musket &c. by way of sample, together with my letter to them herein inclosed. My object in this is to have their instructions ready at the time of the decision, that if it be in favor of Messrs. Schweighauser & Dobree, and the arms be to be sold, I may not be obliged to delay the sale for want of instructions whether to purchase or not. Be so good as to drop me a line of information when you shall have forwarded these articles, which will oblige Sir Your most obedient humble servt.,   TH: JEFFERSON

PrC (DLC); at foot of text: "Mr. Cairnes." Enclosure: TJ to Commissioners of the Treasury, same date, q.v.

To C. W. F. Dumas

Sir   Paris Aug. 9. 1787.

The departure of a packet boat from Havre for New York occasioning me always a great deal of previous writing, I have not been able sooner to acknowlege the receipt of your Note of June 8. on Warneck's succession, letter of June 30. Extract of letter of July 9. to Mr. Adams, and letters of July 10. and 12. to myself. Your last dispatches to Mr. Jay go by the Packet-boat which sails tomorrow. As these vessels sail regularly the following days Feb. 10. Mar. 25. May 10. June 25. Aug. 10. Sep. 25. Nov. 10. Dec. 25. you will always be able to avail yourself of them for your dispatches, only taking care that they reach me four days beforehand. I commit my packet always to a trusty passenger, so that it never enters a post-office. I communicated to Mr. Adams the information that Mr. Grand refused all further advances for our Treasury board till he should receive remittances from them.—From America there is nothing new and very interesting. The Federal Convention is sitting at Philadelphia, General Washington being president of it. Their proceedings will not be made known till they rise. So many of the members of Congress are of that body, that Congress could not continue it's sessions. They have therefore adjourned for some weeks. Your affairs and those of your neighbors now occupy all tongues and minds. Whether they will produce a general war or not seems still undecided. I have the honour to renew the assurances of esteem and respect with which I am Sir your most obedient & most humble servant,

Th: Jefferson

RC (NN). PrC (DLC). The LAST DISPATCHES TO MR. JAY were those enclosed in Dumas to TJ, 30 June and 12 July 1787.

From Ferdinand Grand

Paris, 9 Aug. 1787. William Frederick Ast, ignorant of the present status of the account of the United States, has presented two drafts on TJ, one for 495.^{tt} 17 for Barclay and another for 1,800^{tt} for himself. Grand asks TJ to write to Ast on this subject; he will refer to such a letter in his own to Ast.

RC (DLC); 2 p.; in French, in a clerk's hand, signed by Grand; endorsed. Not recorded in SJL.

To Jeudy de l'Hommande

SIR   Paris Aug. 9. 1787.

At the time you honored me with your letter of May 31. I was not returned from a journey I had taken into Italy. This circumstance, with the mass of business which had accumulated during my absence must apologize for the delay of my answer. Every discovery which multiplies the subsistence of men, must be a matter of joy to every friend to humanity. As such I learn with great satisfaction that you have found the means of preserving flour more perfectly than has been done hitherto. But I am not authorized to avail my country of it by making any offer for it's communication. Their policy is to leave their citizens free, neither restraining nor aiding them in their products. Tho' the interposition of government in matters of invention has it's use, yet it is in practice so inseparable from abuse, that they think it better not to meddle with it. We are only to hope therefore that those governments who are in the habit of directing all the actions of their subjects by particular law, may be so far sensible of the duty they are under of cultivating useful discoveries, as to reward you amply for yours which is among the most interesting to humanity. I have the honour to be with great consideration and respect Sir your most obedient & most humble servant,

TH: JEFFERSON

PrC (DLC).

From André Limozin

Le Havre, 9 Aug. 1787. Acknowledges TJ's letter of 6 Aug. and a small box of seeds. Dr. Gibbons has visited him, is dining with him, and has promised to take care of the seeds and TJ's dispatches. Limozin thanks TJ for continuing to inform him of the political situation; his transactions are "larger than I could wish them to be in such a dangerous time." Packet will sail tomorrow without fail.

RC (MHi); 2 p.; endorsed. Recorded in SJL as received 12 Aug. 1787.

To Schweighauser & Dobrée

GENTLEMEN   Paris Aug. 9. 1787.

The departure of a packet boat for America, which gives me always a great deal of previous writing, has prevented my sooner acknoleging the receipt of your favor of July 19. inclosing the opinion of a lawyer on the questions existing between the United states and yourselves. Mr. Barclay's settlement of your account having been made on view of copies of your vouchers only, I mentioned to you that these copies should be put into the hands of Mr. Burrell Cairnes to be verified by the originals. He writes me that some progress is made in this, but that some originals are not yet on the spot in readiness for examination. The moment that he shall certify to me that all the copies exhibited to Mr. Barclay correspond with their originals, it will leave us nothing but the legal questions to settle, which, so far as shall depend on me shall meet with no delay. I should be glad to know from you at what prices you think the muskets, and sabres could be sold each, because I would write to America to know whether they could chuse they should be sold at these prices or sent to America. I will also be obliged to you to deliver one of them to Mr. Cairnes to be sent to the war-office in America to enable them to decide whether they will suit them. I have the honor to be Gentlemen your most obedient & most humble servant, Th: Jefferson

PrC (DLC).

No letter from Schweighauser & Dobrée of july 19 has been found. The only letter from that firm recorded in sjl as received during July is one of 3 July 1787, received on 6 July, but it has not been found. It would have been possible for TJ to have replied to this missing letter and for Schweighauser & Dobrée to have responded on 19 July. But this is unlikely in view of the fact that no copy of such letters has been found and none is recorded in sjl. The reference to a letter of 19 July is evidently an error of transference from burrell cairnes' letter, which *was* dated 19 July 1787.

To the Commissioners of the Treasury, with Enclosure

Gentlemen   Paris Aug. 9. 1787.

Agreeable to the desire expressed in your letter of Feb. 16. 1787. I now send you a rough state of the articles attached by Messrs. Schweighauser & Dobree, and actually remaining in the warehouse at Nantes. You will perceive that it is only an estimate made by myself on the spot, as an exact account could not be obtained without unpacking the whole. My estimate is followed by some Notes on the several articles sent me lately by Mr. Dobreé giving an historical account of them. I have desired him, by a letter of this day, to deliver one of the muskets and sabres to Mr. Cairnes to be forwarded to you, at the same time saying at what price they would probably sell at Nantes. If the matter is decided in favor of these gentlemen, these arms will be sold: my object therefore in sending you the sample is to receive your instructions, whether, in that event, the U.S. would wish to become purchasers at any, and what price? The war office, on view of the sample, will tell you whether they will suit them at all, and at what price, and yourselves will determine whether you can pay for them, or chuse to abandon them to sale. If the question is determined in favor of the U.S. I shall have time to take their commands whether to sell, or to send them to America. I have the honor to be with sentiments of the most perfect respect, Gentlemen, your most obedient & most humble servant, TH: JEFFERSON

ENCLOSURE

24. casks of gun locks
  6. cases of gun barrels
65. cases of old bayonets.
Locks and furniture of 3100 firearms of various kinds taken from the peasantry of Bordeaux when they were deprived of the droit de chasse, and purchased by Mr. Deane. The above are broken, eaten up with rust, and worth nothing.
15,000 pieces of walnut for gunstocks, very good.
30. cases of muskets from Holland; about 27. in each case: say about 700 muskets with their bayonets: good of their form but not of the best form: in such condition that they will need only such a cleaning as the soldier himself can give.
21. cases of sabres from Holland, about 63. in each case, say about 1300. in good condition.
18 hogsheads of gun flints.
10. anchors weighing on the whole about 21,500 ℔.
But we must deduct about a fifth from the muskets and sabres, because these use in the warehouse five tier of cases; the bottom one of which having been partly under water during an inundation of the Loire, that whole tier may be considered lost. Another deduction will be warehouse rent, 600^{lt} a year from the year 1782.

The 6. chests of rampart barrels and the 24. hogsheads of gun locks &c. are from the old arsenal bought of M. de Monthieu. The muskets of which they belonged were so bad that they never were found worth mending or cleaning and it was a long time questioned whether they should be sent over to America or not. But as it would have been difficult to sell them, Dr. Franklin ordered that the stocks which were mostly broke or worm-eaten, should be taken off to save freight, and that the barrels and furnitures should be packed as they are.
The 65. chests of Bayonets are mostly from these.
The 3100. Paysan muskets are also of M. Monthieu's arsenal. We have

[13]

been told that they were taken from the peasantry in the neighbourhood of Bordeaux. They have always been looked upon of little or no value.

The 30. chests of arms from Holland
The 21. chests of sabres   idem } were received from
The 18. hhds. gun flints
The 10 anchors   } Mr. Jonathan Williams
and the 16,000 gun and pistol stocks

PrC (DLC); enclosed in TJ to Burrill Carnes, same date, q.v. Enclosure (PrC in DLC); in the hand of William Short.

To Peter Carr, with Enclosure

DEAR PETER   Paris Aug. 10. 1787.

I have received your two letters of Decemb. 30. and April 18. and am very happy to find by them, as well as by letters from Mr. Wythe, that you have been so fortunate as to attract his notice and good will: I am sure you will find this to have been one of the most fortunate events of your life, as I have ever been sensible it was of mine. I inclose you a sketch of the sciences to which I would wish you to apply in such order as Mr. Wythe shall advise: I mention also the books in them worth your reading, which submit to his correction. Many of these are among your father's books, which you should have brought to you. As I do not recollect those of them not in his library, you must write to me for them, making out a catalogue of such as you think you shall have occasion for in 18 months from the date of your letter, and consulting Mr. Wythe on the subject. To this sketch I will add a few particular observations.

1. Italian. I fear the learning this language will confound your French and Spanish. Being all of them degenerated dialects of the Latin, they are apt to mix in conversation. I have never seen a person speaking the three languages who did not mix them. It is a delightful language, but late events having rendered the Spanish more useful, lay it aside to prosecute that.

2. Spanish. Bestow great attention on this, and endeavor to acquire an accurate knowlege of it. Our future connections with Spain and Spanish America will render that language a valuable acquisition. The antient history of a great part of America too is written in that language. I send you a dictionary.

3. Moral philosophy. I think it lost time to attend lectures in this branch. He who made us would have been a pitiful bungler if he had made the rules of our moral conduct a matter of science.

[14]

For one man of science, there are thousands who are not. What would have become of them? Man was destined for society. His morality therefore was to be formed to this object. He was endowed with a sense of right and wrong merely relative to this. This sense is as much a part of his nature as the sense of hearing, seeing, feeling; it is the true foundation of morality, and not the το χαλον truth, &c., as fanciful writers have imagined. The moral sense, or conscience, is as much a part of man as his leg or arm. It is given to all human beings in a stronger or weaker degree, as force of members is given them in a greater or less degree. It may be strengthened by exercise, as may any particular limb of the body. This sense is submitted indeed in some degree to the guidance of reason; but it is a small stock which is required for this: even a less one than what we call Common sense. State a moral case to a ploughman and a professor. The former will decide it as well, and often better than the latter, because he has not been led astray by artificial rules. In this branch therefore read good books because they will encourage as well as direct your feelings. The writings of Sterne particularly form the best course of morality that ever was written. Besides these read the books mentioned in the inclosed paper; and above all things lose no occasion of exercising your dispositions to be grateful, to be generous, to be charitable, to be humane, to be true, just, firm, orderly, couragious &c. Consider every act of this kind as an exercise which will strengthen your moral faculties, and increase your worth.

4. Religion. Your reason is now mature enough to receive this object. In the first place divest yourself of all bias in favour of novelty and singularity of opinion. Indulge them in any other subject rather than that of religion. It is too important, and the consequences of error may be too serious. On the other hand shake off all the fears and servile prejudices under which weak minds are servilely crouched. Fix reason firmly in her seat, and call to her tribunal every fact, every opinion. Question with boldness even the existence of a god; because, if there be one, he must more approve the homage of reason, than that of blindfolded fear. You will naturally examine first the religion of your own country. Read the bible then, as you would read Livy or Tacitus. The facts which are within the ordinary course of nature you will believe on the authority of the writer, as you do those of the same kind in Livy and Tacitus. The testimony of the writer weighs in their favor in one scale, and their not being against the laws of nature does not

weigh against them. But those facts in the bible which contradict the laws of nature, must be examined with more care, and under a variety of faces. Here you must recur to the pretensions of the writer to inspiration from god. Examine upon what evidence his pretensions are founded, and whether that evidence is so strong as that it's falshood would be more improbable than a change of the laws of nature in the case he relates. For example in the book of Joshua we are told the sun stood still several hours. Were we to read that fact in Livy or Tacitus we should class it with their showers of blood, speaking of statues, beasts &c., but it is said that the writer of that book was inspired. Examine therefore candidly what evidence there is of his having been inspired. The pretension[1] is entitled to your enquiry, because millions believe it. On the other hand you are Astronomer enough to know how contrary it is to the law of nature that a body revolving on it's axis, as the earth does, should have stopped, should not by that sudden stoppage have prostrated animals, trees, buildings, and should after a certain time have resumed it's revolution, and that without a second general prostration. Is this arrest of the earth's motion, or the evidence which affirms it, most within the law of probabilities? You will next read the new testament. It is the history of a personage called Jesus. Keep in your eye the opposite pretensions. 1. Of those who say he was begotten by god, born of a virgin, suspended and reversed the laws of nature at will, and ascended bodily into heaven: and 2. of those who say he was a man, of illegitimate birth, of a benevolent heart, enthusiastic mind, who set out without pretensions to divinity, ended in believing them, and was punished capitally for sedition by being gibbeted according to the Roman law which punished the first commission of that offence by whipping, and the second by exile or death *in furcâ*. See this law in the Digest Lib. 48. tit. 19 § 28. 3. and Lipsius Lib. 2. de cruce. cap. 2. These questions are examined in the books I have mentioned under the head of religion, and several others. They will assist you in your enquiries, but keep your reason firmly on the watch in reading them all. Do not be frightened from this enquiry by any fear of it's consequences. If it ends in a belief that there is no god, you will find incitements to virtue in the comfort and pleasantness you feel in it's exercise, and the love of others which it will procure you. If you find reason to believe[2] there is a god, a consciousness that you are acting under his eye, and that he approves you, will be a vast additional incitement. If that there be a future state, the hope of a happy existence in that increases the appetite to deserve it; if that Jesus was also a god, you will be comforted by a belief of his aid and love. In fine, I repeat that you must lay aside all prejudice on both sides, and neither believe nor reject any thing because any other person, or description of persons have rejected or believed it. Your own reason is the only oracle given you by heaven, and you are answerable not for the rightness but uprightness of the decision. —I forgot to observe when speaking of the New testament that you should read all the histories of Christ, as well of those whom a council of ecclesiastics have decided for us to be Pseudo-evangelists, as those they named Evangelists, because these Pseudo-evange-lists pretended to inspiration as much as the others, and you are to judge their pretensions by your own reason, and not by the reason of those ecclesiastics. Most of these are lost. There are some however still extant, collected by Fabricius which I will endeavor to get and send you.

5. Travelling. This makes men wiser, but less happy. When men of sober age travel, they gather knowlege which they may apply usefully for their country, but they are subject ever after to recollections mixed with regret, their affections are weakened by being extended over more objects, and they learn new habits which cannot be gratified when they return home. Young men who travel are exposed to all these inconveniences in a higher degree, to others still more serious, and do not acquire that wisdom for which a previous foundation is requisite by repeated and just observations at home. The glare of pomp and pleasure is analogous to the motion of their blood, it absorbs all their affection and attention, they are torn from it as from the only good in this world, and return to their home as to a place of exile and condemnation. Their eyes are for ever turned back to the object they have lost, and it's recol-lection poisons the residue of their lives. Their first and most delicate passions are hackneyed on unworthy objects here, and they carry home only the dregs, insufficient to make themselves or any body else happy. Add to this that a habit of idleness, an in-ability to apply themselves to business is acquired and renders them useless to themselves and their country. These observations are founded in experience. There is no place where your pursuit of knowlege will be so little obstructed by foreign objects as in your own country, nor any wherein the virtues of the heart will be less exposed to be weakened. Be good, be learned, and be industri-ous, and you will not want the aid of travelling to render you

precious to your country, dear to your friends, happy within yourself. I repeat my advice to take a great deal of exercise, and on foot. Health is the first requisite after morality. Write to me often and be assured of the interest I take in your success, as well as of the warmth of those sentiments of attachment with which I am, dear Peter, your affectionate friend, TH: JEFFERSON

P.S. Let me know your age in your next letter. Your cousins here are well and desire to be remembered to you.[3]

ENCLOSURE

Antient history. Herodot. Thucyd. Xenoph. hellen. Xenoph. Anab. Q. Curt. Just.
Livy. Polybius. Sallust. Caesar. Suetonius. Tacitus. Aurel. Victor. Herodian.
Gibbons' decline of the Roman empire. Milot histoire ancienne.
Mod. hist. English. Tacit. Germ. & Agricole. Hume to the end of H.VI. then Habington's E.IV.—Sr. Thomas Moor's E.5. & R.3.—Ld. Bacon's H.7.—Ld. Herbert of Cherbury's H.8.—K. Edward's journal (in Burnet) Bp. of Hereford's E.6. & Mary.—Cambden's Eliz. Wilson's Jac.I. Ludlow (omit Clarendon as too seducing for a young republican. By and by read him) Burnet's Charles 2. Jac.2. Wm. & Mary & Anne.—Ld. Orrery down to George 1. & 2.—Burke's G.3. Robertson's hist. of Scotland.
American. Robertson's America.—Douglass's N. America.—Hutcheson's Massachusets, Smith's N. York.—Smith's N. Jersey.—Franklin's review of Pennsylvania. Smith's, Stith's, Keith's, & Beverley's hist. of Virginia.
Foreign. Mallet's Northn. Antiquities by Percy.—Puffendorf's histy. of Europe & Martiniere's of Asia, Africa & America.—Milot histoire Moderne. Voltaire histoire universelle.—Milot hist. de France.—Mariana's hist. of Spain in Spa[nish.]—Robertson's Charles V.—Watson's Phil. II. & III.—Grotii Belgica.
Mosheim's Ecclesiastical history.
Poetry. Homer—Milton—Ossian—Sophocles—Aeschylus—Eurip.—Metastasio—Shakesp.—Theocritus—Anacreon [. . .]
Mathematics. Bezout & whatever else Mr. Madison recommends.
Astronomy. Delalande &c. as Mr. Madison shall recommend.
Natural Philosophy. Musschenbroeck.
Botany. Linnaei Philosophia Botanica—Genera Plantarum—Species plantarum—Gronovii flora [Virginica.]
Chemistry. Fourcroy.
Agriculture. Home's principles of Agriculture—Tull &c.
Anatomy. Cheselden.
Morality. The Socratic dialogues—Cicero's Philosophies—Kaim's principles of Natl. religion—Helvetius de l'esprit et de l'homme. Locke's Essay.—Lucretius—Traité de Morale & du Bon[heur]
Religion. Locke's Conduct of the mind.—Middleton's works—Boling-

broke's philosoph. works—Hume's essays—Voltaire's works—Beattie. Politics & Law. Whatever Mr. Wythe pleases, who will be so good as to correct also all the preceding articles which are only intended as a ground work to be finished by his pencil.

PrC (DLC). Fragment of RC (ViU). Enclosure (PrC in DLC).

This letter was not sent until 28 May 1788; see TJ to Peter Carr of that date.

[1] The preceding two words interlined in substitution for "it," deleted.
[2] Fragment of RC begins at top of page with "lieve there is."
[3] Fragment of RC ends at this point.

From Bourdon des Planches

MONSIEUR   Paris, le 10. aoust 1787. rüe de l'Echelle, N. 12.

Dans le courant du mois de novembre dernier, Votre Excellence a bien voulu se charger d'une lettre pour le Général Washington, à laquelle j'avois joint un certificat de M. Le Comte de Grasse, dont l'objet etoit d'affirmer que j'avois été premier Sécrétaire de l'armée qu'il commandoit lors de la prise d'York-Town et de Glocester. Mon but, Monsieur, etoit d'obtenir des Etats unis, une concession, et Votre Excellence, sans me donner aucun espoir de succès, eut cependant la bonté de me promettre d'Envoyer mon paquet. Permettés moy, Monsieur, de vous demander si vous y avés recû reponse et daignés croire que tel sort qu'ait pû avoir ma demande, il ne peut influer en rien sur les sentiments de reconnoissance et de respect avec lesquels j'ai l'honneur d'etre, Monsieur De Votre Excellence Le trés humble et trés obéissant serviteur,

BOURDON

RC (DLC). Recorded in SJL as received 12 Aug. 1787.
On 8 Jan. 1788 George Washington acknowledged a letter from Bourdon des Planches of 8 Dec. 1786 (*Writings*, ed. Fitzpatrick, XXIX, 363); Bourdon again wrote TJ on this matter on 29 Mch. 1788, q.v.

From André Limozin

Le Havre, 10 Aug. 1787. After writing on 9 Aug., Limozin learned that Dr. Gibbons "found him self in Such distress for want of Money" that Limozin feared "he Should be obliged to remain here, and could never go forward." Gibbons applied to Limozin for funds, but the latter, "having never seen him before . . . did not chuse to comply with his beseech." Apparently Gibbons "met with some generous friend" for he is setting out this day; the packages delivered by TJ's servant have been turned over to him and he has given a receipt for them.

RC (MHi); 2 p.; endorsed. Recorded in SJL as received 12 Aug. 1787.

[19]

From Vaudreuil

au chateau de vaudreuil par castelnaudarry, le 10e. août 1787

J'ai l'honneur de m'adresser à vous, Monsieur, avec une entière confiance pour de pauvres gens auxquelles je prens beaucoup d'interêt, et dont le bien est situé dans une de mes terres. Le petit mémoire ci-joint vous apprendra leurs noms et l'objet de leur demande: il s'agit d'une succession qui leur appartient, qui leur serait toujours chère, et qui est encore plus prétieuse à raison de leur peu de fortune. J'ai l'honneur de vous envoyer aussi, Monsieur, les papiers qui peuvent être nécessaires dans cette circonstance. La justice de leur demande, leur étroite position, et la perspective d'un sort plus heureux qui semble les attendre me font desirer que cette succession leur parvienne, et qu'il en soit distrait le moins de fraix possible. J'ai cru, Monsieur, ne pouvoir mieux venir à bout de ces deux objets qu'en m'adressant à vous. Je conserverai une reconnaissance infinie des soins que va vous donner cette affaire, et j'ajouterai ce sentiment à celui de l'attachement vrai et respectueux avec lequel j'ai l'honneur d'être, Monsieur, votre très humble et très obéïssant serviteur,   LE MIS. DE VAUDREUIL

RC (DLC). Tr and PrC (DLC); in the hand of William Short. Recorded in SJL as received 20 Aug. 1787. The enclosed papers (missing) were forwarded by TJ to John Langdon in a letter of 18 Sep. 1787, q.v.

From Wilt, Delmestre & Cie.

L'Orient, 10 Aug. 1787. Acknowledge TJ's letter of 14 July; have just found a safe opportunity for forwarding the "paccan nuts"; Bisson, who sets out for Paris tomorrow, has taken charge of the box and has been requested to deliver them himself. The box in which they arrived was so large that for convenience and safety they have been repacked; the quantity of nuts is considerably less than was "Juged at first by the Size of the Case They came in."

RC (DLC); 2 p.; endorsed. Recorded in SJL as received 22 Aug. 1787.

To Thomas Mann Randolph, Sr.

DEAR SIR   Paris Aug. 11. 1787.

Mr. Ammonit sent me your favor of May 7. which you expected he would have brought. He furnished me with the name of the family to whose property he supposes himself entitled, and the name of the town where it lies. I have endeavored to have them searched out, but as yet neither family nor town is discovered: if they can be found, the estate will then be to be searched for; the laws for limitation of actions will form the next opposition to him, and probably the laws of forfeiture against the protestants who were the subject of the revocation of the edict of Nantes, which laws have never been repealed, nor probably ever will be, even should the future condition of Protestants here be mitigated. I shall proceed in the enquiry for him and let him know the result.

Your son Thomas, at Edinburgh has done me the favor to open a little correspondence with me. He has sometimes asked my advice as to the course of his studies, which I have given to him the more freely as he informed me he was not tied down to any particular plan by your instructions. He informed me in his last letter that you proposed he should come to Paris this fall, stay here the winter and return to Virginia in the spring. I understand him as proposing to study the law, so that probably on his return you will place him at Williamsburgh for that purpose. On this view of his destination I venture to propose to you another plan. The law may be studied as well at one place as another; because it is a study of books alone; at least till near the close of it. Books can be read equally well at Williamsburg, at London, or Paris. The study of the law is an affair of 3. years, the last of which should be spent in attending Mr. Wythe's lectures. Upon the plan he has now in expectation, his residence here 6. months as a traveller must cost him 100 guineas, and 3 years study at Williamsburg 450. guineas more, making 550. guineas in the whole. My proposition is that he shall pass his two first years of legal study in some one of the villages within an hour's walk of Paris, boarded with some good family wherein he may learn to speak the language, which is not to be learned in any other way. By this means he will avoid the loss of time and money which would be the consequence of a residence in the town, and he will be nigh enough to come to dine, to make acquaintances, see good company, and examine the useful details of the city. With very great oeconomy he may do this on 100. guineas a year, but at his ease for 150 guineas. At the end of 2. years I would propose him a journey through the Southern parts of France, thence to Genoa, Leghorn, Florence, Rome, Naples, Venice, Milan, Turin, Geneva, Lyons and Paris. This will employ him 7. months and cost him 300. guineas if he goes alone, or 230. guineas if he finds a companion. Then he should return to Virginia and pass his third year of legal study in attending Mr. Wythe's lectures. This whole plan would take 3. years and 7. months and cost from 700. to 750. guineas which would be one month longer, and 150 or 200 guineas dearer than the one proposed. The advantages of this would be his learning to speak French well, his acquiring a better acquaintance here with men and things, and his having travelled through the most interesting parts of Europe, advantages which he will for ever think cheaply purchased for 150. or 200 guineas, even were a deduction of that sum to be made from the establishment you mean to give him. But in every case, whether you decide that he shall return to study in Virginia, or remain here for that purpose, I would recommend that he should not be tied down to quit Edinburgh this fall precisely, but only when he shall have finished his courses of lectures in those sciences with which he should not be unacquainted. I have taken the liberty of noting these to him. I perceive by his letters that he has good genius, and every body bears witness to his application, which is almost too great. It would be a pity therefore he should miss of giving them full improvement. I must beg your pardon for thus intruding myself into a business belonging to yourself alone, and hope you will find it's excuse in the motives from which it proceeds, friendship for yourself, for Mrs. Randolph, and your son, a wish to see you gratified and to be gratified myself in seeing him act the advantageous part which will naturally result from his talents, his merit, and the favorable ground from which he will start, a fear of seeing this endangered by a too early return to our own country where the examples of his cotemporaries may so possibly lead him from the regular pursuits his friends may chalk out for him, all these considerations have impelled me to take this liberty and to rely for pardon on the assurance of the sincere attachment and respect with which I am, dear Sir, your affectionate friend & servant, TH: JEFFERSON

PrC (DLC).

YOUR FAVOR OF MAY 7: Not found but recorded in SJL as received 30 June 1787. See John Ammonet to TJ, 10 May 1787. I WOULD PROPOSE HIM A JOURNEY: The following undated memorandum (ViWC), entirely in TJ's hand, undoubtedly represents the calculations on which TJ based the estimates of time and money necessary for the journey he proposed (the superscript numerals attached to place names are in MS and indicate the number of days allocated to each):

"Plan of journey for TMR.

Paris. Orleans. Nantes.[2] Bordeaux.[4] Thoulouse. Cette. Montpelier. Nismes.[2] Avignon. Marseilles.[4] Toulon. Hieres. Nice.[1] Genoa.[7] Pisa.[1] Leghorn.[3] Florence.[14] Rome.[30] Naples.[30] Rome. Ancona. Bologna. Padua. Venice.[7] Padua. Mantua. Verona. Milan.[7] Turin.[7] M. Cenis. Chamberri. Geneva.[7] Lyon.[2] Dijon.[3] Paris.

[22]

	days	Louis
4000. miles @ 50. miles a day & 16s a mile	80	133
80 days travelling expences @ 6^{lt}		20
131 days residence in the cities @ 12.^{lt}	131	65
	211 = 7. months	
Disbursemt. of money to servants		10
Theaters		10
purchase of Cabriolet		30
repairs of do.		6
⟨servant 131 days @ 2^{lt}		11⟩
Contingencies		26
		300
	days	
If a twelvemonth employed it adds	154	77
If he has a companion it will lessen the sum £70."		

To Bourdon des Planches

〚*Paris, 12 Aug. 1786.* Recorded in SJL as written on this date. Not found.〛

To Wilson Miles Cary

DEAR SIR   Paris Aug. 12. 1787.

Your favor of Mar. 28. has been duly received and I thank you for the kind enquiries after my health and that of my daughter, still more for the information that the several members of your family are well. The distance to which I am removed renders that kind of intelligence more interesting, more welcome, as it seems to have given a keener edge to all the friendly affections of the mind. Time, absence, and comparison render my own country much dearer, and give a lustre to all it contains which I did not before know that it merited. Fortunatus's wishing cap was always the object of my desire, but never so much as lately. With it I should soon be seated at your fireside to enjoy the society of yourself and family. I congratulate you on the additions to it which my neice is making; but tell her she has chosen a bad model for their heads. Neither the outside nor the in is worth her copying. I am in hopes therefore to hear that the hair of the next will indicate a better taste in the choice of the original from which she copies. You ask if we know a merchant in Bourdeaux who may be recommended for a consignment of tobacco. My acquaintance there is not extensive. There is a Mr. John Bondfeild of whom I

[23]

have a good opinion. He is an American, and is Agent there for the United states. If wine is your object, he is a good judge of that. He supplies me, as he had before done Doctr. Franklin, with very good. They cost now 30 sous a bottle, and 2 livres when 3. years old, which is the age before which they should not be drank. If you like white wines, ask for Sauterne which is the best in that country, and indeed is excellent. Mrs. Oster is arrived here, and is gone to settle herself among her friends in Lorraine. My younger daughter is arrived also, tho by a different route, and is in good health as well as her sister. It is difficult to say which of them is most anxious to get back to their own country.—We are here in a crisis of unknown issue. All the indications are of war, yet the desperate state of finances in the two principal parties, England and France, renders it so impossible for them to furnish supplies for a war, that we still presume they will come to an arrangement. They are endeavouring to do it, this country heartily, England thro' compulsion from the voice of the nation and the wisest part of her ministry. A war between those two powers would, at the first blush, promise advantage to us. But it might perhaps do us more injury on the whole by diverting us from agriculture, our wisest pursuit, by turning us to privateering, plunging us into the vortex of speculation, engaging us to overtrade ourselves, and injuring our morals and in the end our fortunes. A steady application to agriculture with just trade enough to take off it's superfluities is our wisest course. I beg leave to be presented to Mrs. Cary the elder and younger, to Mr. Cary, and the young ladies in the most affectionate terms, and that you will be yourself assured of the sentiments of esteem and respect with which I have the honour to be Dear Sir your most obedient humble servant,

TH: JEFFERSON

PrC (DLC).

YOUR FAVOR OF MAR. 28.: Not found but recorded in SJL as received 22 June 1787 and as dated at "Caley's," Elizabeth City co. MY NEICE: Jane Carr, daughter of Martha Jefferson Carr, married Wilson Cary, son of Wilson Miles Cary, in 1782 (Randolph, *The Randolphs*, p. 119).

To George Gilmer

DEAR DOCTOR   Paris Aug. 12. 1787.

Your letter of Jan. 9. 1787. came safely to hand in the month of June last. Unluckily you forgot to sign it, and your hand writing is so Protean that one cannot be sure it is yours. To increase the causes of incertitude it was dated *Pen-park*, a name which I only knew as the seat of John Harmer. The hand writing too being somewhat in his style made me ascribe it hastily to him, indorse it with his name, and let it lie in my bundle to be answered at leisure. That moment of leisure arriving, I set down to answer it to John Harmer, and now for the first time discover marks of it's being yours, and particularly those expressions of friendship to myself and family which you have ever been so good as to entertain, and which are to me among the most precious possessions. I wish my sense of this, and my desires of seeing you rich and happy may not prevent my seeing any difficulty in the case you state of George Harmer's wills: which as you state them are thus.

1. A will dated Dec. 26. 1779. written in his own hand and devising to his brother the estates he had received from him.

2. Another will dated June 25. 1782. written also in his own hand, devising his estate to trustees to be conveyed to such of his relations J.H. J.L. or H.L. as should become capable of acquiring property, or, on failure of that, to be sold and the money remitted them.

3. A third will dated Sep. 12. 1786. devising all his estate at Marrowbone and his tracts at Horsepasture and Poison feild to you, which will is admitted to record and of course has been duly executed. You say the learned are divided on these wills. Yet I see no cause of division, as it requires little learning to decide that 'the first deed, and last will must always prevail.' I am afraid therefore the difficulty may arise on the want of words of inheritance in the devise to you: for you state it as a devise to 'George Gilmer' (without adding 'and to his heirs') of 'all the *estate* called Marrowbone' 'the *tract* called Horsepasture' and 'the *tract* called Poisoned feild.' If the question is on this point, and you have copied the words of the will exactly, I suppose you take an estate in fee simple in Marrowbone, and for life only in Horsepasture and Poisoned feild, the want of words of inheritance in the two last cases being supplied as to the first by the word 'estate' which has been repeatedly decided to be descriptive of the quantum of interest devised, as well as of it's locality. I am in hopes however you have not copied the words exactly, that there are words of inheritance to all the devises, as the testator certainly knew their necessity, and that the conflict will be only between the different wills, in which case I see nothing which can be opposed to the last. I shall

[25]

be very happy to eat at Pen-park some of the good mutton and beef of Marrowbone, Horsepasture and Poisoned feild, with yourself and Mrs. Gilmer and my good old neighbors. I am as happy no where else and in no other society, and all my wishes end, where I hope my days will end, at Monticello. Too many scenes of happiness mingle themselves with all the recollections of my native woods and feilds, to suffer them to be supplanted in my affection by any other. I consider myself here as a traveller only, and not a resident. My commission expires the next spring, and if not renewed, I shall of course return then. If renewed, I shall remain here some time longer. How much I cannot say; yet my wishes shorten the period. Among the strongest inducements will be that of your society and Mrs. Gilmer's, which I am glad to find brought more within reach by your return to Pen-park. My daughters are importunate to return also. Patsy enjoys good health, and is growing to my stature. Polly arrived here about a month ago, after a favorable voiage, and in perfect health. My own health has been as good as ever, after the first year's probation. The accident of a dislocated wrist, badly set, has I fear deprived me for ever of almost every use of my right hand. Nor is the extent of the evil as yet known, the hand withering, the fingers remaining swelled and crooked, and losing rather than gaining in point of suppleness. It is now eleven months since the accident. I am able however to write, tho for a long time I was not so. This inability was succeeded by a journey into the Southern parts of France and Northern of Italy, which added to the length of the chasm in my correspondence with my friends. If you knew how agreeable to me are the details of the small news of my neighborhood, your charity would induce you to write frequently. Your letters lodged in the post office at Richmond (to be forwarded to N. York) come with certainty. We are doubtful yet whether there will be war or not. Present me with warm affection to Mrs. Gilmer and be assured yourself of the unvarying sentiments of esteem and attachment with which I am Dear Doctor your sincere friend & servant,

TH: JEFFERSON

PrC (DLC). Gilmer's letter of JAN. 9. 1787 is endorsed "Gilmer George" and there is no evidence on it that TJ had first endorsed it with the name of JOHN HARMER. This may have been done on the address cover, but probably was not—TJ habitually removed the address covers of letters as received and placed his endorsements on what remained.

To Lewis Littlepage

Sir   Paris Aug. 12. 1787.

I had the honour to inform you in a former letter that until we should know whether your uncle should have replaced to the Governor of Virginia the money you had desired him to replace, we would decline availing ourselves here of the bill of exchange you have been pleased to forward to the M. de la Fayette on Messrs. Tourton & Ravel. Having lately received a letter from the Governor informing me that your uncle refused to replace it in Virginia, I presented the bill on Messrs. Tourton & Ravel, who duly honoured it, paying the sum of five thousand three hundred livres tournois into the hands of Mr. Grand for the state of Virginia, of which I have now the pleasure to inform you.

You have heard doubtless of disturbances in Massachusets which had taken place the last year. These are all happily terminated. A federal convention is now sitting at Philadelphia, of which Genl. Washington is President. It's object is to amend the confederation by strengthening more the hands of Congress. Much good is hoped from it. It is composed of the greatest characters in America, every state having appointed to it except Rhode-island. They will go on without her. Congress are beginning the sale of our Western lands, which I hope will pay our debts. I have the honour to be with much esteem and respect Sir, your most obedient & most humble servant,

Th: Jefferson

PrC (DLC).

To John Blair

Dear Sir   Paris Aug. 13. 1787.

I received the letter with which you were pleased to honor me by Mrs. Oster, and immediately waited on her with a tender of my services. She had however so far got her matters arranged as to be no longer in fear of any disagreeable measure, and is since gone to establish herself with her friends in Lorraine. I wish she may not there have alarms of a different nature. We have hitherto been in hopes that the desperate state of the finances of France and England would indispose those powers to war, and induce them by an armed mediation to quiet the affairs of Holland. The actual march however of the Prussian troops, the departure of the British squadron

[27]

somewhere Westwardly, and the preparations for a naval armament at Brest and a land one in the neighborhood of the Netherlands render war at present more expected than it has been. Still we look to the necessities of the two principal powers as promising efficacy to the negotiations not yet broken off. Tho we shall be neuters, and as such shall derive considerable pecuniary advantages, yet I think we shall lose in happiness and morals by being launched again into the ocean of speculation, led to overtrade ourselves, tempted to become sea-robbers under French colours, and to quit the pursuits of Agriculture the surest road to affluence and best preservative of morals. Perhaps too it may divert the attention of the states from those great political improvements which the honourable body of which you are a member will I hope propose to them. What these may be I know not, but I am sure they will be what they should be. My idea is that we should be made one nation in every case concerning foreign affairs, and separate ones in whatever is merely domestic. That the Federal government should be organized into Legislative, executive and judiciary as are the state governments, and some peaceable means of enforcement devised for the federal head over the states. But of all these things you are a better judge. I have delivered your message to Mr. Mazzei who is still here. Be so good as to present me respectfully to Mrs. Blair and to be assured yourself of the sentiments of esteem and respect with which I have the honor to be, dear Sir your most obedient & most humble servant,   TH: JEFFERSON

PrC (DLC).

From Thomas Blanchard

Bordeaux, 13 Aug. 1787. Hopes that being presented by Mr. Barclay is sufficient excuse for writing; if not, "being an american may; for we are told that your Excellency's goodness and attention, extend to the most inconsiderable of your Countrymen." Has established himself at Bordeaux as an American ship broker with the advice and approval of Bondfield who vouches for him and suggested that he write; hopes TJ will give him his approbation.

RC (DLC); 2 p.; endorsed. Recorded in SJL as received 22 Aug. 1787.

From John Bondfield

Bordeaux, 13 Aug. 1787. Introduces "Mr. Lennox," of Charleston, S.C., who has been in Bordeaux, is now proceeding to Paris, and is an

American travelling as a private citizen with a view to enlarging his commercial connections.

RC (DLC); 2 p.; endorsed. Recorded in SJL as received 12 Sep. 1787, "by Lenox."

To Richard Cary

DEAR SIR   Paris Aug. 13. 1787.

I am to acknolege the receipt of your favor of Mar. 21. and to correct a most unfortunate error in mine of Dec. 26. 1786. wherein I have written the word Lorient instead of Havre, praying you to send plants and seeds to *Lorient* only, to the care of M. Limozin, instead of *Havre* only to the care of M. Limozin, for it is at Havre he lives, and that is much the surest port for me. Plants especially come best by that port because from thence they come up the Seine, whereas from the other ports they must come by land. By the packet which will sail from Havre the 20th. of September I shall be sending a box of books, directed to Mr. Wythe. In this I will put the seeds and bulbs which I was disappointed in sending you the last year, as well as a repetition of those I sent. They will go to Mr. Madison at New York, and if you know of any particularly sure conveiance from thence to your river you would do well to drop him a line on the subject. I will send you also some plants of the Melon Apricot, a variety of fruit obtained in France only 8. or 10. years ago and as yet known no where else. It is an Apricot with the high flavor of a muskmelon, and is certainly the best fruit in this country. You have never yet told me what seeds &c. you wish for most, so I am obliged still to go on the old edition in Mazzei's hands. Peace and war have for some time hung in equal balance. A late movement of England and Prussia seem to give a momentary preponderance to the scale of war, but the state of finances both in England and France induce a presumption that they will still find some other mode of settling the Dutch differences. I am with very great esteem Dear Sir your friend & servant,

TH: JEFFERSON

PrC (DLC).

To the Rev. James Madison

DEAR SIR   Paris Aug. 13. 1787.

I have been long, very long, without answering your favor of Mar. 27. 1786. and since that I have received those of Dec. 28. and by Mrs. Oster. The reason of this has been that the genius of invention and improvement in Europe seems to be absolutely taking a nap. We have nothing to communicate to you but of the small kind, such as the making the axle tree turn with the wheel, which has been proposed here, adopted by some, and thought to be proved best by experiment, tho' theory has nothing to urge in it's favor. A hydrostatic waistcoat is lately announced, which a person puts on either above or below his cloaths in a minute and fills with air by blowing with the mouth in 12. seconds. It is not yet shewn however, so I cannot tell you either the manner or matter of it's construction. It may be useful when the loss of a vessel is foreseen. Herschel's discovery of two satellites to his planet you have heard of ere this. He first saw them in January last. One revolves round it's principal in about a week, the other in about a fortnight. I think your conjecture that the periodical variation of light in certain fixed stars proceeds from Maculae is more probable than that of Maupertuis who supposes those bodies may be flat, and more probable also than that which supposes the star to have an orbit of revolution so large as to vary sensibly it's degree of light. The latter is rendered more difficult of belief from the shortness of the period of variation. I thank you for the shells you sent me. Their identity with marine shells and their vicinity to the sea argue an identity of cause. But still the shells found in the mountains are very imperfectly accounted for. I have lately become acquainted with a Memoire on a petrification mixed with shells by a Monsr. de la Sauvagere giving an exact account of what Voltaire had erroneously stated in his Questions Encyclopediques, article Coquilles, from whence I had transferred it into my notes. Having been lately at Tours I had an opportunity of enquiring into de la Sauvagere's character, and the facts he states. The result was entirely in his and their favor. This fact is so curious, so circumstantially detailed, and yet so little like any known operation of nature, that it throws the mind under absolute suspense. The Memoire is out of print. But my bookseller is now in search of it, and if he can find it I will put a copy of it into a box of books I shall send by the September packet addressed to Mr. Wythe. In the same box I will put for you the Bibliotheque Physico oeconomique for 1786. 1787. the Connoissance des tems, Fourcroy's chemistry, wherein all the later discoveries are digested, and a number of my Notes on Virginia, a copy of which you will be pleased to accept. It is a poor crayon, which yourself and the gentlemen who issue from your school must fill up.—We are doubtful here whether we are to have peace or war. The movements of Prussia and England indicate war, the finances of England and France should indicate peace. I think the two last will endeavor to accomodate the Dutch differences. Be pleased to present me respectfully to Mrs. Madison, and after repeating the recommendations of my nephew to you, I take the liberty of assuring you of the sincerity of that esteem with which I am Dear Sir your friend & servant,

TH: JEFFERSON

PrC (DLC). The MEMOIRE ... BY A MONSR. DE LA SAUVAGERE was Felix François de la Sauvagère's *Recueil de Dissertations ... avec de nouvelles assertions sur la végétation spontanée des coquilles du chateau des Places, des dessins d'une* *collection de coquilles fossiles de la Touraine et de l'Anjou, de nouvelles idées sur la Falunière de Touraine et plusieurs lettres de M. de Voltaire, relatives a ces différents objets,* Paris, 1776 (Sowerby, No. 647).

To Marbois

DEAR SIR   Paris Aug. 13. 1787.

Mr. Derby, a citizen of Massachusets, thinking he has just grounds to complain of the condemnation of a vessel in your island, proposes to institute a suit against the persons by whose fraud he supposes the cause for that condemnation was contrived. Knowing the embarrassments of a stranger when entering the lists of law in any country against a native, I take the liberty of recommending him to such good offices as you can render him consistently with the justice due to the adverse party. To protect him against combination, to see that he has fair play, is so consistent with your dispositions to justice, that the recommending his case to your notice with this view will need no apology. I do it with the more readiness as it gives me a new occasion of assuring you of those sentiments of esteem and respect with which I have the honor to be Sir your most obedient & most humble servant,

TH: JEFFERSON

PrC (DLC). For the complaint of MR. DERBY, see Elias Hasket Derby to TJ, 1 Mch. 1787. This letter was carried by Derby himself.

[31]

To David Humphreys

DEAR SIR   Paris Aug. 14. 1787.

I remember when you left us, it was with a promise to suppl
all the defects of correspondence in our friends, of which we com
plained, and which you had felt in common with us. Yet I have
received but one letter from you which was dated June 5. 1786
and I answered it Aug. 14. 1786. Dropping that however and
beginning a new account, I will observe to you that wonderful im
provements are making here in various lines. In architecture the
wall of circumvallation round Paris and the palaces by which we
are to be let in and out are nearly compleated, 4 hospitals are to
be built instead of the old hotel-dieu, one of the old bridges has
all it's houses demolished and a second nearly so, a new bridge is
begun at the Place Louis XV. the Palais royal is gutted, a considerable part in the center of the garden being dug out, and a sub-
terranean circus begun wherein will be equestrian exhibitions &c.
In society the habit habillé is almost banished, and they begin to
go even to great suppers in frock: the court and diplomatic corps
however must always be excepted. They are too high to be reached
by any improvement. They are the last refuge from which etiquette,
formality and folly will be driven. Take away these and they would
be on a level with other people. The assemblée des Notables have
done a great deal of good here. Various abolitions of abusive laws,
have taken place and will take place. The government is allotted
into subordinate administrations, called Provincial assemblies, to
be chosen by the people; great reductions of expence in the trappings of the king, queen, and princes, in the department of war &c.
Notwithstanding this, the discovery of the abuses of public money,
some expences of the court not in unison with the projects of
reform, and the new taxes, have raised within a few weeks a spirit
of discontent so loud and so general as I did not think them susceptible of. They speak in all companies, in coffee-houses, in the
streets, as if there was no Bastile: and indeed to confine all offenders
in this way, the whole kingdom should be converted into a Bastile.
The parliament of Paris puts itself at the head of this opposition.
The king has been obliged to hold a bed of justice to enforce the
registering the new taxes. The parliament proposes to forbid their
execution, and this may possibly be followed by their exile. The
mild and patriotic spirit of the new ministry, and the impossibility
of finding subjects to make a new parliament, may perhaps avoid

[32]

his extremity. It is not impossible but that all the domestic disturbances may be calmed by foreign difficulties. War has within a few days past become more probable. Tho the kings of England and Prussia had openly espoused the views of the Stadholder, yet negotiations were going on which gave hopes of accomodation. But the stoppage of the Princess of Orange, on her way to excite commotions at the Hague, kindled the kingly pride of her brother, and without consulting any body, he ordered 20,000 men to march instantly to revenge this insult. The stoppage of the sister of a king then is sufficient cause to sacrifice the lives of hundreds of thousands of better people and to lay the most fertile parts of Europe in ashes. Since this hasty movement, which is pertinaciously pursued, the English squadron has sailed Westwardly, and will be followed by a squadron from Brest, while a land army moves on to the confines of Holland. Still however the negociations are continued, and it is thought that the fiscal distresses of the principal powers may yet prevent war. So much for the blessings of having kings, and magistrates who would be kings. From these events our young republics may learn many useful lessons, never to call on foreign powers to settle their differences, to guard against hereditary magistrates, to prevent their citizens from becoming so established in wealth and power as to be thought worthy of alliance by marriage with the neices, sisters &c. of kings, and in short to besiege the throne of heaven with eternal prayers to extirpate from creation this class of human lions, tygers and mammouts called kings; from whom, let him perish, who does not say 'good lord deliver us,' and that so we may say, one and all, or perish is the fervent prayer of him who has the honor to mix with it sincere wishes for your health and happiness, and to be with real attachment and respect dear Sir your affectionate friend & humble servant,

TH: JEFFERSON

P.S. Aug. 15. The Parliament is exiled to Troyes this morning.

PrC (DLC). The WALL OF CIRCUMVALLATION was the new wall of the farmers-general; see Map of Paris, Vol. 10: xxviii and facing p. 211. For the HOUSES . . . DEMOLISHED, see illustration in this volume.

To Joseph Jones

DEAR SIR   Paris Aug. 14. 1787.

I have never yet thanked you, but with the heart, for the act of assembly confirming the agreement with Maryland, the pamphlet and papers I received from you a twelvemonth ago. Very soon after their receipt I got my right wrist dislocated which prevented me long from writing and as soon as that was able to bear it took a long journey from which I am but lately returned. I am anxious to hear what our federal convention recommends, and what the states will do in consequence of their recommendation. I wish to see our states made one as to all foreign, and several as to all domestic matters, a peaceable mode of compulsion over the states given to Congress, and the powers of this body divided, as in the states, into three departments legislative, executive, and judiciary. It is my opinion the want of the latter organization has already done more harm than all the other federal defects put together, and that every evil almost may be traced to that source. But with all the defects of our constitutions, whether general or particular, the comparison of our governments with those of Europe are like a comparison of heaven and hell. England, like the earth, may be allowed to take the intermediate station. And yet I hear there are people among you who think the experience of our governments has already proved that republican governments will not answer. Send those gentry here to count the blessings of monarchy. A king's sister for instance stopped in the road, and on a hostile journey, is sufficient cause for him to march immediately 20,000 men to revenge this insult, when he had shewn himself little moved by the matter of right then in question. I apprehend this hasty movement of the king of Prussia may perhaps decide the crisis of Europe to war, when it was before doubtful. The English squadron has sailed Westwardly: the French will doubtless do the same, and they are moving an army into the neighborhood of Holland. Still however the negociations are not broken off, and the desperate state of finances both in England and France give a hope they will yet arrange matters. In this country a great and sudden discontent has arisen, since the separation of the assemblee des Notables. It is not easy to fix the causes, since it is certain that great improvements of their laws and constitution have actually taken place and others are promised; great reforms in expence have been effected and are effecting. But the investigation of the horrid depredations in the late administration of their finances, some new and inconsiderate expences of the court, and the new taxes have probably excited this discontent. The opposition of the parliament to the new taxes is carried to it's last point, and their exile is a measure which may very possibly take place. The principal security

Demolition of houses on the Pont Notre-Dame. (See p. xxxiv.)

LAUDA-CONATUM

EXPOSITION AU SALON DU LOUVRE EN 1787.

against it is the mild and patriotic character of the new ministry. From all these broils we are happily free, and that god may keep us long so, and yourself in health and happiness is the prayer of, dear Sir, your most obedient & most humble servant,

Th: Jefferson

P.S. Aug. 15. The Parliament is exiled to Troyes this morning.

PrC (DLC).

To John Stockdale

Sir   Paris Aug. 14. 1787.

The books you have last sent me are this moment come to hand, and all right except that the 'Historical remarks on the taxation of free states' printed by Richardson 1781. is not among them. I will still trouble you therefore to send it by some opportunity. I thank you for the dozen copies of the Notes on Virginia. The remaining 34. shall be sold so as to pay the 8d. sterl. a vol. their transportation costs, the commission for selling and your 5/4. Upon the whole they must be sold at about 7.^{tt} 15s. Unless you are very sure of your information of the printing the Notes on Virginia in America, I doubt it. I never sent but six copies to America, and they were in such hands as I am sure would not permit them to be published. I have letters from Philadelphia as late as the 6th. of June, and certainly no such publication was then suspected by my friends. On the contrary Mr. Hopkinson, one of those to whom I had given a copy, and who is concerned in compiling the Columbian magazine, tells me he hopes I will not object to his publishing a few extracts from it, particularly the passages in which M. de Buffon's work is controverted. So that unless you are very certain on the point, I shall disbelieve it. I am Sir your very humble servant,

Th: Jefferson

PrC (DLC).
Actually there were more than six copies of *Notes on Virginia* in America at the time this letter was written. Three of these—those belonging to Franklin, Humphreys, and Otto—had been presented in France and subsequently carried to America by their recipients. Also, TJ erred in thinking that he had sent only six, for it is certain that copies belonging to James Currie, Francis Hopkinson, James Monroe, James Madison, John Page, David Rittenhouse, and Charles Thomson had been sent before mid-August 1787. TJ was right in thinking that a separate edition had not appeared in America in 1787; Stockdale had probably been misinformed as a result of the appearance of some parts of *Notes on Virginia* in American newspapers (see Barlow to TJ, 15 June 1787).

[35]

To George Washington

DEAR SIR   Paris Aug. 14. 1787.

I was happy to find by the letter of Aug. 1. 1786. which you did me the honour to write me, that the modern dress for your statue would meet your approbation. I found it strongly the sentiment of West, Copeley, Trumbul and Brown in London, after which it would be ridiculous to add that it was my own. I think a modern in an antique dress as *just* an object of ridicule as an Hercules or Marius with a periwig and chapeau bras.

I remember having written to you while Congress sat at Annapolis on the water communications between ours and the Western country, and to have mentioned particularly the information I had received of the plain face of the country between the sources of Big beaver and Cayohoga, which made me hope that a canal of no great expence might unite the navigations of L. Erie and the Ohio. You must since have had occasion of getting better information on this subject and, if you have, you would oblige me by a communication of it. I consider this canal, if practicable, as a very important work.

I remain in hopes of great and good effects from the decisions of the assembly over which you are presiding. To make our states one as to all foreign concerns, preserve them several as to all merely domestic, to give to the federal head some peaceable mode of enforcing their just authority, to organize that head into Legislative, Executive, and Judiciary departments are great desiderata in our federal constitution. Yet with all it's defects, and with all those of our particular governments, the inconveniencies resulting from them are so light in comparison with those existing in every other government on earth, that our citizens may certainly be considered as in the happiest political situation which exists.—The assemblée des Notables has been productive of much good in this country. The reformation of some of the most oppressive laws has taken place and is taking place. The allotment of the state into subordinate governments, the administration of which is committed to persons chosen by the people, will work in time a very beneficial change in their constitution. The expence of the trappings of monarchy too are lightening. Many of the useless officers, high and low, of the king, queen, and princes are struck off. Notwithstanding all this the discovery of the abominable abuses of public money by the late comptroller general, some new expences of the

[36]

court, not of a piece with the projects of reformation, and the imposition of new taxes, have in the course of a few weeks raised a spirit of discontent in this nation, so great and so general, as to threaten serious consequences. The Parliaments in general, and particularly that of Paris put themselves at the head of this effervescence, and direct it's object to the calling the states general, who have not been assembled since 1614. The object is to fix a constitution, and to limit expences. The king has been obliged to hold a bed of justice to enforce the registering the new taxes: the parliament on their side propose to issue a prohibition against their execution. Very possibly this may bring on their exile. The mild and patriotic character of the new ministry is the principal dependance against this extremity.

The turn which the affairs of Europe will take is not yet decided. The Emperor, on his return to Vienna, disavowed the retrocessions made by his governors general in the low countries. He at the same time called for deputies to consult on their affairs. This, which would have been the sole measure of a wise sovereign, was spoiled by contrary indications resulting from his Thrasonic character. The people at first refused to send deputies. At last however they sent them without powers, and go on arming. I think there is little doubt but the Emperor will avail himself of these deputies to tread back his steps. He will do this the rather that he may be in readiness to take part in the war likely to be produced by the Dutch differences. The kings of England and Prussia were abetting the cause of the Stadholder, France that of the Patriots: but negotiations were going on to settle them amicably, when all of a sudden, the Princess of Orange, undertaking a secret journey to the Hague to incite an insurrection of the people there, is stopped on the road, writes an inflammatory letter to her brother, he without consulting England, or even his own council, or any thing else but his own pride, orders 20,000 men to march into the neighborhood of Holland. This has been followed by the sailing of the English squadron somewhere Westwardly, and that will be followed by a squadron from Brest, and an army to the confines of Holland from this country. Appearances therefore are within a few days past more like war than they had been. Still however the negotiations are going on, and the finances both of France and England are so notoriously incompetent to war, that the arrest of hostile movements and an amicable adjustment are not yet altogether despaired of. A war, wherein France, Holland and England should be parties, seems primâ facie to promise much advantage to us. But in the first place no war can be safe for us which threatens France with an unfavourable issue. And in the next, it will probably embark us again into the ocean of speculation, engage us to overtrade ourselves, convert us into Sea-rovers under French and Dutch colours, divert us from Agriculture which is our wisest pursuit, because it will in the end contribute most to real wealth, good morals and happiness. The wealth acquired by speculation and plunder is fugacious in it's nature and fills society with the spirit of gambling. The moderate and sure income of husbandry begets permanent improvement, quiet life, and orderly conduct both public and private. We have no occasion for more commerce than to take off our superfluous produce, and tho people complain that some restrictions prevent this, yet the price of articles with us in general shew the contrary. Tobacco indeed is low, not because we cannot carry it where we please, but because we make more than the consumption requires. Upon the whole I think peace advantageous to us, necessary for Europe, and desireable for humanity. A few days will decide probably whether all these considerations are to give way to the bad passions of kings and those who would be kings. I have the honour to be with very sincere esteem and respect dear Sir Your most obedient & most humble servant,

Th: Jefferson

P.S. Aug. 15. The Parliament is exiled to Troyes this morning.

RC (DLC: Washington Papers); endorsed in Washington's hand. PrC (DLC).

To Gaudenzio Clerici

Sir   Paris Aug. 15. 1787.

I cannot express to you how great was my concern on returning here to find a letter of your's dated Novara, March 5. I had passed thro' Novara the 20th. of April, and surely if I had had the least suspicion of your being there I should have found you out. Since that I have also received your favor of July 14. by which I presume you are fixed in the neighborhood of Ticino in the Milanese. I congratulate you on your happy return to your family. Your acquaintance also with the Count del Verme is a subject of congratulation. I was indeed under extreme obligations to him at Milan. Being restricted to pass a very short time there, he directed my attention to those objects precisely which merited most attention. Milan was the spot at which I turned my back on Rome and Naples. It was a moment of conflict between duty which urged me to return, and inclination urging me forwards. I do not despair altogether of finding yet some favorable interval when I may be able to go on to those renowned places.—My last advices from America inform me of a perfect tranquillity there. Deputies from all the states are occupying themselves at Philadelphia with amending some defects in the instrument of our confederation. General Washington is President of that Convention and Doctor Franklin a member of it. I send to the Count del Verme the books which I had mentioned to him when at Milan. I put into the same package for you a copy of some Notes on the state of Virginia which I wrote in the year 1781. and which have been lately printed in London. A careless translation of them has been published here, which I hope will not make it's way to your country. The subjects are too uninteresting and too imperfectly treated to be worth translating into your language. Mr. Mazzei is still here. His book is in the press. He proposes going on to Florence in the winter, where I imagine he will print his work in Italian. I shall always be happy to hear from you, being with sincere wishes for your success, and with sentiments of perfect esteem Sir your most obedient & most humble servant,   TH: JEFFERSON

PrC (DLC).
MY LAST ADVICES FROM AMERICA INFORM ME OF A PERFECT TRANQUILLITY THERE: Compare this observation —typical of TJ's remarks made for the benefit of Europeans—with those in, for example, his letters to Carrington, Currie, and Hay of 4 Aug. 1787.

To John Jay

SIR   Paris Aug. 15. 1787.

An American gentleman leaving Paris this afternoon to go by the way of Lorient to Boston furnishes me the rare occasion of a conveiance, other than the Packet, sure and quick. My letter by the packet informed you of the bed of justice for enregistering the stamp tax and land tax. The parliament, on their return, came to an Arreteé (a Resolution) which, besides protesting against the enregistering, as done by force, laid the foundation for (an Act) an Arret de defence against the execution of the two new laws. The question on the final Arret was adjourned to the day before yesterday. It is beleived they did not conclude on this Arret, as it has not appeared. However there was a concourse of about 10,000 people at the Parliament house, who on their adjournment received them with acclamations of joy, loosened the horses of the most eminent speakers against the tax, from their carriages, and drew them home. This morning the parliament is exiled to Troyes. It is believed to proceed principally from the fear of a popular commotion here.

The officer charged by this court to watch the English squadron which was under sailing orders, returned about a week ago with information that it was sailed, having shaped it's course Westwardly. This is another step towards war. It is the more suspicious as their minister here denies the fact. Count Adhemar is here from London by Congé from his court. The Duke of Dorset, the British Ambassador here, is lately gone to London on Congé. Neither of these Ambassadors have the confidence of their courts on the point of abilities. The latter merits it for his honesty. The Minister of the British court, resident here, remains, but Mr. Eden, their Ambassador to Spain, under pretence of taking this in his route, is in truth their factotum on the present emergency. Nothing worth noting has occurred since my last either in the Dutch or Austrian Netherlands. I have the honour to be with the most perfect esteem & respect Sir Your most obedient & most humble servant,

TH: JEFFERSON

PrC (DLC).

To James Madison

DEAR SIR   Paris Aug. 15. 1787.

A gentleman going from hence by Lorient to Boston furnishes me an opportunity of recommending to your care the inclosed letters which I could not get ready for the last packet. Pray inform me in your next whether letters directed to your foreign ministers or franked by them are free of postage. That they ought to be so, is acknoleged substantially by the resolution of Congress allowing us to charge postages. I have sometimes suspected that my letters stagnate in the post-offices.—My letters by the last packet brought down the domestic news of this country to the day in which the bed of justice was held. The day before yesterday the parliament house was surrounded by ten thousand people, who received them, on their adjournment, with acclamations of joy, took out the horses of the principal speakers and drew their chariots themselves to their hotels. The parliament not having taken the desperate step (as far as is known yet) of forbidding the execution of the new tax laws by an Arret de defense sur peine de mort, we presume it is the fear of a popular commotion which has occasioned the king to exile them to Troyes. This is known only this morning. The ministry here have certain information that the English squadron has sailed, and took it's course Westwardly. This is another move towards war. No other important fact has taken place since my letters by the packet. Adieu. Yours affectionately,

TH: JEFFERSON

RC (DLC: Madison Papers). PrC (DLC). The enclosed "letters which I could not get ready for the last packet" have not been identified, but they must have included most of those written after 8 Aug. and destined for America; those to Putnam (8 Aug.) and Marbois (13 Aug.) were carried by Elias Hasket Derby, according to entries in SJL. The fact that these two were specifically mentioned as being carried by Derby would seem to indicate that all of the others were carried by someone else, though the description of A GENTLE-MAN GOING FROM HENCE BY LORIENT TO BOSTON would seem to fit Derby.

To John Sullivan

SIR   Paris Aug. 15. 1787.

I have duly received your favor of April 27. wherein you advise me of having drawn on me for £46-17-10 sterl. and refer me to an explanation sent by Capt. Samuel Pierce, which explanation and the captain also have probably miscarried, as I have as yet heard nothing of them. Supposing that this must be for the bones and skin of the Moose which your Excellency had been so kind as to undertake to get for me, or for some other good cause of which I may be unapprized, I remitted the money for your bill immediately to Mr. Adams, Colo. Smith being absent in Portugal. Should the bones and skin of the Moose have miscarried I would decline repeating the expence or giving your Excellency the trouble of a second sample.

Europe is at this moment in a crisis of very doubtful issue. The hopes of accomodating the Dutch differences were good, till the K. of Prussia, on hearing of the stoppage of the Princess of Orange, ordered 20,000 men to march immediately to revenge the insult. Since this the British squadron is sailed Westwardly, and probably a French one will follow them immediately, and a French army will move into the confines of Holland on this side. Still the notorious incompetence of the French and English finances for war, and the continuance of the negotiations leave some hope of accomodation. I have the honour to be with sentiments of the most perfect esteem and respect, your Excellency's most obedient & most humble servant, TH: JEFFERSON

PrC (DLC). The EXPLANATION . . . BY CAPT. SAMUEL PIERCE, as contained in Sullivan to TJ, 26 Apr. 1787, was received by TJ on 2 Sep. 1787.

To Francis dal Verme

SIR   Paris Aug. 15. 1787.

In consequence of the permission you were so kind as to give me, when I had the honour of seeing you at Milan, I shall sometimes take the liberty of troubling you with a line. I cannot begin with an act of greater justice than that of expressing to you all my gratitude for your attentions and services while in your capital, and to which I am indebted for the best informations I received there. I then mentioned some late publications on the subject of America which I would do myself the honour of sending you, one because it was my own, and two others because worth reading. Mine are some Notes only on the state of Virginia, the others are Ramsay's history of the war, and Soulé's history. The first is very authentic, there being no fact in it which may not be relied on: but it is confined to the war in the Southern states. The last is a general history, of which we can only say it is the best of those written in Europe. There is a history of the same period now printing in London, tho written in America by an English clergyman of the name of Gordon. He had access to some collections of papers not known to any other writer. But I am unable to say as yet what may be the merit of his work.

You must have observed when in America that time and trial had discovered defects in our federal constitution. A new essay, made in the midst of the flames of war, could not be perfect. The states have appointed deputies, who are now sitting at Philadelphia, to consider what are these defects, and to propose new articles to be added to the instrument of confederation, for amending them. The articles to be proposed by them will be to be confirmed by Congress and by the legislature of every state before they will be in force. As yet their proceedings are not known. Probably they go to the following points. 1. To invest Congress with the exclusive sovereignty in every matter relative to foreign nations and the general mass of our Union, returning to the states their individual sovereignty in matters merely domestic. 2. To devise some peaceable mode whereby Congress may enforce their decisions. 3. To organize Congress into three branches Legislative, Executive and Judiciary. I had the honour of informing you of the commotions which had taken place in Massachusets, the only ones which had ever taken place since the declaration of Independance. I have now that of informing you that those commotions have been entirely quieted. General Washington is well, and is president of the federal convention sitting at Philadelphia as beforementioned. Doctor Franklin and other the greatest characters of America are menbers of it.—I do not give you European news: you have that from other quarters: after adding therefore that the books beforementioned are delivered to Messieurs Cathalan of Marseilles who will send them to their correspondent at Genoa, with instructions to forward them to you at Milan, I shall only repeat very sincere assurances of the esteem and respect with which I have the honor to be, Sir, your most obedient & most humble servant,

TH: JEFFERSON

PrC (DLC).

Count Francis dal Verme had been IN AMERICA shortly after the war, having gone there with impressive recommendations. John Adams introduced him as "a Nobleman of Milan in Italy, and a near Relation of Prince Carminico, an Ambassador at the Court of London. He is very highly Recommended by Dr. Franklin, Messrs. Adams and Laurens. I beg your polite Attention to this Illustrious Traveller, who wishes much to see and know whatever is worthy of Notice in each State" (Adams to John Langdon, 14 Aug. 1783; *Letters by Washington, Adams, Jefferson, and Others, written during and after the Revolution to John Langdon* [Philadelphia, privately printed, 1880]).

From Anthony Vieyra

MOST EXCELLENT SIR   Trinity Coll. Dublin 15 of Augt. 1787

My return to this College has been so sudden, and hurried that I could not comply with my duty and wishes by calling on your Excellency's house and receiving your Commands. The bearer of this gives me the opportunity of offering you my Services in this City. He is a Bookseller, that has collected a great quantity of valuable and rare books, as you may see from his Catalogue. If you should choose any of them, I would be glad of having made him known to your Excellency. My precipitated departure from Paris hindred me from obtaining from the most Christian King the permission of dedicating to him the Etymological Enquiry which I had made upon the name of Paris, and which I have shown to your Excellency; And as it should not be so proper to dedicate it to any body else in this Country; I could wish your Excellency should take the trouble of geting the same permission, for which favor, I shall not be able to return my most sincere thanks otherwise, than by presuming a Copy to be sent to you by Yr. Excellency's Most humble Servant, ANTHONY VIEYRA

RC (MoSHi). Recorded in SJL as received 2 Sep. 1787.

From Francis Coffyn

SIR   Dunkerque Augst. 17th. 1787.

In answer to your Excellencys letter of 8 inst. I have the honnor to inform him that Allexander Cross [Gross] hostage for the ransom of the sloop Charlotte of Southampton McGriger master taken by the privateer Countess Davaux in february 1782, is still confined in the prison of this Town. Agreable to your Excellencys request I have made all possible inquiry respecting the cause of the hostages long detention, and have [been] told that the Sloop Charlotte was lost at Sea the voyage after she was ransom'd, that Captn. McGriger (who was the owner) with all hands on board were drowned; that the privateer was fitted out from Boulogne by a M. A. Butay of that place, and that his agent here was M. Michelon. The latter stop'd payment about three years ago, but I have not been able to learn wether M. Butay fail'd. The loss of the Sloop Charlotte, and the death of the owner leaves no hopes that the ransom ever will be paid; yet I find that the concerned in the privateer detain the hostage in expectation that somebody will soon or late offer to pay his expences since his confinement in prison, which allready amounts to £.3052 french money. By the steps I have taken, to obtain these informations, nobody can suspect that Your Excellency has order'd me to procure them. It would be an act worthy of your Excellencys humanity if he could procure an order for the discharge of the poor hostage. If any further illucidation should be requisite, I shall be very ready to give them, and think myself happy if I can be instrumental in the execution of your Excellencys charitable exertions.

I have been twice at Paris last spring, and call'd several times during my stay there at the Barrière de Chailliot to pay my respects to your Excellency, but was told that you was in the Country.

I have the honnor to remain very respectfully Sir Your Excellencys most obedient and most humble Servant,

F. Coffyn

P.S. Two american ships, one from Rhode Island with pitch Tar and Lumber, and the other from Nantuckett with whale oil, arrived here this week.

RC (DLC). Recorded in SJL as received 20 Aug. 1787.

From Thomas Paine

Dear Sir   Sunday Augt. 18th[1]

I am much obliged to you for the Book you are so kind to send me. The second part of your letter, concerning taking my picture, I must feel as an honor done to me, not as a favour asked of me, but in this as in other matters I am at the disposal of your friendship.

The Committee have among themselves finally agreed on their report which I saw this morning. It will be read in the Academy on Wednesday. The report goes pretty fully to support the principles of the Construction with their reasons for that opinion. Your's Affectionately,   Thomas Paine

RC (DLC); endorsed. Not recorded in SJL.

TJ's LETTER CONCERNING TAKING MY PICTURE, which evidently accompanied a copy of the Stockdale edition of *Notes on Virginia* (the BOOK), has not been found and is not recorded in SJL. The COMMITTEE of the Académie des Sciences did not read its report on Paine's plan for an iron bridge until

Wednesday, 29 Aug. 1787; the reading may have been postponed from Wednesday, 22 Aug., the date that Paine seems to have had in mind. On Paine's PICTURE, see Trumbull to TJ, 19 Dec. 1788; TJ to Trumbull, 12 Jan. 1789.

[1] Thus in MS; Paine erred in writing the date, for Sunday fell on the 19th.

To William Frederick Ast

Sir   Paris Aug. 19. 1787.

I learn with great concern the difficulties of your situation, and with the more as it is entirely out of my power to aid you, my own situation being precisely yours. I have informed Mr. Grand of the reason we have to expect some remittances daily, and considerable ones ere long. But he is decided to await their arrival before he increases his advances. With respect to the monies in Holland, I wrote to Mr. Adams, who alone has the direction of them, to know whether I could draw on them for my own salary. This was a month ago. I have received no answer, which I consider as a negative one, either that there is no money of ours in Holland, or that he has no authority to furnish me from that fund. If you have any personal interest with Mr. Grand, perhaps you may prevail on him to pay your bill. It is impossible for me to ask it after what has passed between him and me on the subject. If you cannot obtain it from him, all I can do is to assure you that whenever any remittances arrive, if they shall be subjected to my direction, your wants shall be among the first supplied. I am with very great esteem Sir Your most obedient humble servt.,

TH: JEFFERSON

PrC (DLC).
This letter is, doubtless, a reply to Ast's (missing) letter of 14 Aug., recorded in SJL as received 19 Aug. 1787.

From André Limozin

MOST HONORED SIR   Havre de Grace 19th august 1787.

Since my former of the 10th instant, I am deprived of your most honored favors. Since I think it my duty to inform your Excellency of every thing passing relating the welfare, or interest of America, I take the Freedom to acquaint your Excellency that there is a Scheme in view which the author designs to lay under the Eyes of the French Minister. If that scheme should take place, it would be very much against the advantage of the American Planters, and surely as much so as Mr. Robt. Morris's Contract was.

The Scheme is to establish a French House in America to purchase alone all the Tobacco wanted by the Farmers Generals, on the account of whom the purchase and Shipment would be made, and the House would charge only $2\frac{1}{2}$ ⅌ Cent Commission. The author of that Scheme Saith that the Said house having alone the Commission of the Farmers Generals, he can assure that he might become Master of the prices of Tobacco which he would be certain to get it reduced of 25 ⅌ Ct. It is certain that the number of purchasers of a commodity being very much lessend, the prices of it must decline: he assures that if the Farmers will accept his offer, he will give them good Security, and that they will find an advantage every year on their purchases for about 1500, thousand Lyvers. It [is] needless for me to write to your Excellency fuller on that Matter because your Excellency can feel at least as well as I do the consequences of Such a Scheme, which should distroy intirely the Liberty of trade.

I have the honor to be with the highest regard Your Excellency's most obedient & very Humble Servant, ANDRE LIMOZIN

RC (MHi); addressed and endorsed, with seal intact; postmarked: "HAVRE." Recorded in SJL as received 21 Aug. 1787.

From James Madison

[*Philadelphia*, *19 Aug. 1787*. Recorded in SJL as received 13 Dec. 1787, "(recommendation of Tenche Cox)." Not found.]

From Percey

[*Paris*, *20 Aug. 1787*. Recorded in SJL as received 21 Aug. 1787. Not found.]

From Adam Walker

SIR   London Augst. 20th. 1787

I have seen Your Harpsichord safe Packed and hope it will arrive safe to you.

The Instrument remaining so long in my hands, has given me time to observe where the chief defects of the Celestina stop lay, and also of the machine that moved it. I am sorry to say that altho it answerd in some degree better than the common Fly Wheel, yet I found by use and time it was very liable to be out of order, and particularly as it had to go by Sea. In short I cou'd not safely trust it, to give you satisfaction on the arrival. I therefore judged it best to take it off, and apply a Fly Wheel (on an improved Plan) in its stead. The Motion of this is so exceedingly easy, it can be no objection to the performer and giving it a few quick impulses at will the Wheel will continue to move two or three Minutes. If, at any future period I succeed in the construction of a Machine for the above purpose, I shall most certainly send one of them to you, without any additional Expence.

Directions for the Celestina

When this Stop is used, 1st. draw the outside Knob (on the right hand of the Instrument) quite out, and move the middle Knob (which is the 2d. Unison) towards the right. 2d. Press down the Left Pedal, or let the Stay, which is connected with it, hold down the Pedal, and so disengage the Foot, then the Left foot applied to the Center Pedal, or Traddle will put the Wheel in Motion. The first action of the foot on the Traddle gives the Wheel an impulse in the right direction, and in which it shoud be continued. N.B. The Loudest Effect of the Celestina is producd, by increasing the Speed of the Wheel, with the pressure of the Keys. The Right Pedal for the Swell Lid has a good affect with the Celestina, observing that the pressure of the Fingers and the Pedal correspond. When the above position of the Stops has been formed, the Celestina affect is on the Upper Keys, and a soft additional Stop, as an accompaniment to it, is on the Lower. This will be found a great improvement of the Celestina, adding great variety to its affects, for by this divice may Two performers accompany each other, the Rapid Lesson on the Lower, and the Viola or Sostenuto accompaniment, on the Upper. Or a performer may accompany a soft Cantabile Air, with an Harpeggio or running Bass on the Lower Keys, and may change positions by playing fine holding Notes like the Violoncello with the left hand on the Upper keys, and a Rapid movement with the right, on the Lower Keys. When the Full Harpsichord is required, Let the Stops and Pedal be in their first Position, viz, the Celestina Knob Slid inwards, the Center Knob on the right, moved towards the Left hand, this puts the 2d. Unison on. The Pedal being Up, the full Tone of the Instrument is produced.

A Quantity of Silken Bands, Knotted to a proper measure and ready Rosin'd, are sent, with a Vial of the Liquid Rosin, which is prepared by mixing about $\frac{1}{3}$ in Bulk of Powder'd Black Rosin to the best Rectified Spirit of Wine. A New Band may be put on once pr. Month or oftener, if much used, and Rosin'd in 4 or 5 days, or when the Sound appears lower than usual. The manner of Rosining, is by holding the piece of Cloth dip'd in the Liquid to the Band, whilst it circulates once or twice over it, and then leave it ten Minutes to dry.

The Stop is easily disingaged from the Harpsichord, by first taking off the Rulers, and drawing out the two small brass Pins which fasten the Stop to each side of the Instrument.

RC (DLC); unsigned; endorsed by TJ: "Walker." Recorded in SJL as received 20 Nov. 1787.

To the Georgia Delegates in Congress

GENTLEMEN   Paris Aug. 21. 1787.

The bearer hereof, Mr. Auckler, proposing to settle himself in the Western parts of Georgia, I take the liberty of recommending him to your patronage and counsel. You will see by his papers that he has been an advocate in this country, of distinction and of good character, and he seems to have taken the resolution of removing to America from a desire of living in a land of freedom. These certificates of his worth as well as his character of a stranger will recommend him to your friendly reception and guidance, while they are my apology for the present liberty, an additional motive to which is the desire of availing myself of every occasion of assuring you of those sentiments of perfect respect with which I have the honour to be Gentlemen Your most obedient & most humble servant,   TH: JEFFERSON

PrC (DLC).

From St. Victour

MONSIEUR   rue des menars paris le 21 aoust 1787.

J'ignore s'il croit a la virginie ou dans quelqu'autres provinces des etats unis des noÿers ou d'autres especes de boïs qui, par sa legereté et sa solidité fut comme le bois de noÿer propre a la monture des fusils, mais vous le sçavés surement, et alors il pourroit s'etablir une correspondance également utile aux etats et a la manufacture de tulle, en lestant les batimens qui sont expediés des divers ports de l'amerique pour celuÿ de bordeaux, de planches de bois de noÿer ou d'autres bois propres a la monture des fusils; nous pourrions prendre jusques a trente mille planches et par preferance seches dans l'espace de trois ans, dans les dimensions et aux prix que je vais avoir l'honneur de vous etablir, rendues au port de bordeaux, et si nous nous trouvions bien de cet approvisionement nous le continuerions les années suivantes.

[49]

Les planches doivent avoir deux pouces trois lignes d'epaisseur
sept pieds six pouces de longeur
onze ou douze pouces de largeur, le tout mesure de france.
Nous pourrions paÿer ces planches rendues a bordeaux quarante
sols, et si elles etoient bien seches et bien saines, sans noeud ni autre
avaries, jusques a cinquante sols.

J'aÿ l'honneur d'etre avec les sentimens les plus respectueux
Monsieur votre très humble et très obeissant serviteur,

ST. VICTOUR

RC (ViWC); endorsed. Recorded in SJL as received 23 Aug. 1787.

From William Carmichael

DEAR SIR   Madrid 22 Augt. 1787

I inclose a copy of a Letter which I had the honor to address you
the 9th of July. I hope I may be permitted to say that your correspondence gives me too much pleasure and Instruction to regard
the privation of it with Indifference. This I cannot do untill convinced that my inclination to merit your confidence is not accompanied by proofs arising from public Duty which may in some degree
claim it.

Since my last you will have seen by the public prints the changes
that have taken place in the Administration in this Country. Much
has been said of the motives and Intrigues which gave rise to this
new System. I may venture to Assure you that the Ct. de F/B
directed every thing agreable to his own desire. A New counsel of
State has been established of the Ministers of the various Departments of Government, to which council others may occasionally be
admitted. The Ct. De F.B. will have it in his power, to defeat
their resolutions in council if contrary to his own or by his Influence on the Kings mind or to prevent their Effect and certainly
he has more discernment than all the Junta for I know their
Characters well enough to form this opinion.

The Object of this Junta is principally extended to Ways and
Means and a new system of Government of their foreign possessions. It meets every monday and its deliberations are as secret
as possible so that you will conclude that I rather form my opinion
of the nature of their deliberations from the knowledge of some
minute and particular circumstances, than from authenticated facts.
It is necessary that the Assembled wisdom of the Nation should be

employed to correct Abuses and restore that energy to Government which certainly it cannot without great extraordinary and even unexpected Effects exert at present. At the same time I must tell you that there are Little Intrigues in the Interior of the Palace which cannot but give uneasiness to a Minister whose principal Object has been the Aggrandisement of his Nation. I enter not into his System. I only speak of what I believe to be his Intentions. Perhaps he may see an approaching Storm and desire to enjoy otium cum dignitate. The King has had several Slight Attacks which in spite of a robust constitution, denote some approach to decadence. At present He is well, but one Day or other he may be brought dead from his favorite Amusement, the chase.

I have nothing from Algiers except that the Dey makes the Spanish Consul responsible for the American Prisoners who are under his protection and will exact the same price for them as if they Made their escape, even should they die by the Plague. I have writ[ten] to the Consul that I had no orders to consent to his protecting them on this footing, because It was impossible to know to what amount the Dey Might value them. Two are dead of the Plague. I have forwarded the Letters I have received to Mr. Jay. The Duc de Vauguyon delivered me the packet you intrusted to his care. It came late to my hands and I find that the Ambassador seems to wish to leave me to sollicit the recompense for services demanded by the State of South Carolina. I wish you to favor me in detail of all you know on this subject, for from what I perceive by your Letters, it appears that the affair has taken a different aspect. If the Court of France is interested, the Ct. de Montmorin will explain decisively to you the Instructions the Ambassador may have received on this Subject. You will please to mention to that Minister, whose friendship and partiality I rely on, that I am at a loss how to proceed, until I can positively know the wishes and Intentions of the Court of France. There are some rumors of Arming at Darel. The Prussian Minister Communicated last Saturday week the Intentions of his Sovereign to send an Army to Cleves, in order to accelerate the Satisfaction for the Insult received by the Princess of Orange in being stopped in her way to the Hague. As this communication was general you must have seen it. I have sent a copy of the Extract of the Kings Letter to his Minister here to Mr. Jay. I beleive the Answer made was in general terms. The Commercial Treaty with England will not be concluded by the Present Minister and I doubt much whether Mr.

Edens Abilities will succeed better. This Letter is intrusted to a Spanish Cabinet courier and My Notice of his Departure is short. If you wish that I should write you regularly make use of the Cypher. Nothing can give me greater pleasure and assuredly you will never have reason to complain of the confidence which you may repose in one who has the honor to be with the highest Esteem & respect Your Excellencys Most Obedt & obliged Hble. Sevt,

WM. CARMICHAEL

RC (DLC); endorsed. Recorded in SJL as received 29 Aug. 1787. Enclosure: Copy of Carmichael to TJ, 9 July 1787.

From Burrill Carnes

Nantes, 23 Aug. 1787. In accordance with TJ's letter of 9 Aug., has procured from Dobrée one each of the muskets, bayonets, and sabres; has had them cleaned and will send them to New York, together with TJ's letter to the Commissioners of the Treasury and an estimate of the value of the muskets if sold locally. The muskets should be worth from 6 to 8 livres each, the sabres about 40 sols each; if sold at Nantes they would be sent to the coast of Guinea. Has examined several chests of muskets and found them of "indifferent Quality . . . considerably damaged," and if not cleaned in a short time "must be entirely lost." "The price for Cleaning is twenty Sols each Musket, Bayonet and Sabre"; but some rebate might be obtained at present; the cost will be greater "some months hence." Encloses a list of American ships arrived at Nantes since the beginning of 1782, as TJ requested. The list cost one guinea. Can obtain a list of ships previous to 1782 if desired. Has just heard from Dobrée "respecting the examination of the other Accounts with Mr. Schweighauser," and hopes to complete this business in time to send a report by Barclay's secretary who is expected to arrive from L'Orient on his way to Paris.

RC (DLC); 4 p.; endorsed. Recorded in SJL as received 28 Aug. 1787. Enclosure (DLC: TJ Papers, 36:6204-5): "Liste de tous les Navires arrivés des Etats Unis depuis 1782 Jusqu'a Aout 1787"; giving the date of arrival, the name of the ship, name of captain, port of departure, and cargo.

From Madame de Colmare

Paris, [*23 Aug. 1787*]. Holds a "Billet de banque de Philadelphie" which she wishes to redeem, although she can ill afford to suffer the loss which the depreciation on the note occasions; since TJ expressed an interest in helping her and inasmuch as he is best informed on this matter, she encloses the note and asks to be informed of the exact value at which it can currently be redeemed.

RC (DLC); 2 p.; in French; endorsed; date supplied from entry in SJL of the receipt of a letter from Mme. de Colmare on this date and TJ's reply. Enclosure returned in TJ's reply of this date, following.

To Madame de Colmare

à Paris ce 23me Aout 1787.

Je suis très faché, Madame, de ne pouvoir pas repondre à la lettre que vous me faites l'honneur de m'ecrire en vous faisant toucher la somme qui vous pourroit etre due pour le billet de papier-monnaie des etats unis que vous m'avez envoyé et que je vous renvoye ci-dedans. Mais premierement la valeur dependra de l'epoque à laquelle votre mari l'a recu. Le billet au moment de sa date (Sep. 1778) valoit environ 73.^{tt} Après la fin de l'année 1780 il n'a valu plus de 4.^{tt} 4s. Si on l'a recu entre ces deux termes il aura une valeur moyenne selon le moment. De plus ce n'est qu'en Amerique que ces billets seront payés. C'est là seulement qu'il y a des personnes qui connoissent les veritables des faux. On en a fait la contrefaçon en Angleterre, et ce sont des billets contrefaits pour la plupart qui circulent chez l'etranger, parce que c'est là qu'on ne s'y connoit pas. Le conseil que j'ai donné toujours aux personnes qui m'ont adressé de ces billets, c'est de les envoyer au Consul de France en Amerique, ayant soin de lui bien constater l'epoque ou on les a reçu: et c'est le seul conseil, Madame, que je suis dans le cas de vous donner. J'ai l'honneur d'etre, avec bien de regrets de ne pouvoir pas vous mieux servir, et avec des sentiments très respectueux, Madame, votre tres humble et tres obeissant serviteur, TH: JEFFERSON

PrC (DLC).

From Le Pommereux

[Rouen, 23 Aug. 1787. Recorded in SJL as received 24 Aug. 1787. Not found.]

From R. & A. Garvey

SIR   Rouen the 24 August 1787

We differed answering the letter your Excellency honored us with the 8 Inst., Inclosing a passport for a harpsicord, which when here shall be sent you by water, untill we received tiding of it, but getting none, we deem it necessary to own receipt. Mr. Woodmason sent us par the Rouen Packet a Case for your Excellency, we got it Corded and Plombed and sent by acquit a Caution No. 94 which you have Inclosed, we beg you'll have it presented at the Douane and when it is charged returned us on the other side.

Note of our Charges importing Do.	£21-10-6
also note of Charges on your Wine	46-14-6
Togeather	£68 5

Which have valued on you at sight order of Perregaux & Co. and we beg you will Own same on presentation. We are with respectful & true regard Sir Your Excellency's most humble & very obed. Servts.,

by procn. of RT. & AT. GARVEY
PLOWDEN W. GARVEY

RC (MHi); addressed and endorsed; with appended statement of expenses for receiving and expediting "quatres Caisses Contenantes Chaques 45 Bouteilles de Vin de Bordeaux d'Envoy de Mrs. fregen Grammont & Cie" and another "Caisse reçue de Londres d'Envoy de M. Js. Woodmason" (containing a copying press for Chastellux, as evidenced by an entry in Account Book under 27 Aug. 1787). The sight draft on TJ payable to Perregaux & Cie. in the amount stated is in MHi.

From André Limozin

Le Havre, 24 Aug. 1787. Has forwarded a package from Francis Hopkinson and encloses a letter from the same source.

RC (MHi); 2 p.; addressed and endorsed. Recorded in SJL as received 26 Aug. 1787. Enclosure: Hopkinson to TJ, 8 July 1787.

From Valade

[Paris], 24 Aug. 1787. Offers TJ a portrait of Louis XVI, dressed in ceremonial garb. The picture is 5 by 4 feet, in a gilded frame ornamented by the arms of the king; was executed by a fine artist "pour une Salle d'audience ou pour orner un Sallon. Il seroit bien proportionne pour le Cabinet de Votre Excellence." Hopes TJ will be interested in acquiring it or will tell his friends about it. Recalls that he procured for TJ the portrait of Dr. Franklin.

RC (MoSHi); 2 p.; in French; endorsed.

From John Adams

DEAR SIR   Grosvenor Square, London Aug. 25. 1787

On my return from an Excursion to Devonshire with my Family, where we have been to fly from the Putrefaction of a Great City in the Summer heat, I had the Pleasure to find your favours of 17. and 23. of July.

A Million of Guilders are borrowed on a new Loan in Holland, and I went over lately to Subscribe the obligations, a Punctillio which the Brokers were pleased to think indispensible, to gratify the Fancies of the Money Lenders. But as I had no fresh Authority from Congress, nor any particular new Instructions, I have been and am Still under Serious Apprehensions of its meeting with obstacles in the way of its Ratification.—If it is ratified, Congress may if they please, pay the Interest and Principal too, out of it, to the French officers.—I presume that if Mr. Grand Should refuse your Usual draughts for your Salary Messrs. Willinks and Vanstaphorsts, will honour them to the amount of yours and Mr. Short's Salaries, without any other Interposition than your Letter. But if they Should make any difficulty, and it Should be in my Power to remove it, you may well Suppose, I shall not be wanting. To be explicit, I will either advise or order the Money to be paid, upon your Draught as may be necessary, So that I pray you to make your Mind perfectly easy on that Score.

Mr. Barclay, I agree with you, took the wisest Course, when he embarked for America, tho it will lay me under Difficulties in Settling my affairs finally with Congress.

The French Debt, and all the Domestic Debt of the United States might be transferred to Holland, if it were judged necessary or profitable, and the Congress or Convention would take two or three preparatory Steps. All the Perplexities, Confusions and Distresses in America arise not from defects in their Constitutions or Confederation, not from a want of Honour or Virtue, So much as from downright Ignorance of the Nature of Coin, Credit and Circulation.—While an annual Interest of twenty, thirty and even fifty Per Cent, can be made, and a hope of augmenting Capitals in a Proportion of five hundred Per Cent is opened by Speculations in the Stocks, Commerce will not thrive. Such a State of Things would annihilate the Commerce, and overturn the Government too in any nation in Europe.

I will endeavour to Send you a Copy, with this Letter of the

Second volume of the Defence &c. If Frouillé the Bookseller has a Mind to translate it he may, but it may not Strike others as it does Americans. Three Editions of the first volume have been printed in America. The Second volume contains three long Courses of Experiments in Political Philosophy, every Tryal was intended and contrived to determine the Question whether Mr. Turgots System would do. The Result you may read. It has cost me a good deal of Trouble and Expence to Search into Italian Rubbish and Ruins. But enough of pure Gold and Marble has been found to reward the Pains. I shall be Suspected of writing Romances to expose Mr. Turgots Theory. But I assure you, it is all genuine History. The vast Subject of Confederations remains: but I have neither head, heart, hands, Eyes, Books, or Time, to engage in it. Besides it ought not to be Such an hasty Performance as the two volumes already ventured before the Public.

With perfect Esteem, your Sincere Friend,   JOHN ADAMS

RC (DLC); addressed and endorsed. FC (MHi: AMT); in Abigail Adams Smith's hand there is at the foot of the text (which is in her husband's hand): "Copy sent 8th of octor. p. post." Tr (DLC); in Smith's hand, incorporated in his letter to TJ, 8 Oct. 1787, q.v. Recorded in SJL as received 11 Sep. 1787.

It will be noted that Adams, perhaps pointedly, failed to acknowledge TJ's letter of 28 July 1787 in which he had enclosed a bill of exchange as a remittance for the draft drawn on William Stephens Smith by John Sullivan that Adams had accepted. Both Adams and Smith thought in mid-October that TJ had not, in turn, acknowledged the present letter or THE SECOND VOLUME of Adams' *Defence of the Constitutions of Government of the United States of America*, London, 1787 (Sowerby, No. 3004). TJ did not in fact acknowledge the present letter until 13 Nov. 1787. According to Smith, this letter and the copy of *Defence* were carried by Madame de Corny. Evidently, then, Adams sent a second copy of that volume by Cutting with his letter of 16 Sep. 1787 q.v. See also Adams to TJ, 9 Oct. 1787; Smith to TJ, 8 Oct. 1787; and TJ to Adams, 28 Sep. 1787, in which he acknowledged the "favours by Mr. Cutting." But Smith could have been mistaken and the "favours by Mr. Cutting" could have been those of 25 Aug. and 16 Sep. 1787.

From Thomas Blake, Jr.

Ostend, 25 Aug. 1787. Asks whether United States colors and passes for voyages may be granted for vessels fitted out in Ostend for the East Indies; and, if so, what the conditions and expenses are. Danish and other colors are granted under these circumstances. He would prefer those of the United States.

RC (DLC); 2 p.; endorsed. Recorded in SJL as received 8 Sep. 1787.

From Jonathan Jones

Sir   Bordeaux 25. august. 1787.

The Protection you are pleased to give, to every object that Interests the American Trade, encourages me to address you the Present: and will Serve to hand you Copy of a Memorial that the Merchants of Bordeaux have this day addressed Mr. Villedeuil Comptroleur General, stateing the Number of Hogsheads Tobacco now in Store, and what is further expected to arrive shortly; by which you will please to observe, that the quantity is but Small, Considered as an object for the fermiers Generaux; but which falls heavy on the Particulars, who have made Large advances on the Tobaccos recieved, or are under acceptances for near the full Value.

The Merchants of Bordx. Look up to your Excellency with Confidence, for Support in this affair; and beg Leave to Sollicit your warm interest, by representing to the Comptroleur General all the hardships we Lay under at this moment, occasioned by the fermiers Generaux ceasing at once their purchases of Tobacco, under pretext that they have Complied with the orders of the Comitée of Berni; but which appears to us rather Dubious, seeing that the Trade of Bordeaux has not been able to place more than 800 to 900 hogsheads at the prices fixed by the Comitée.

Begging Leave to be referred to the enclosed for further particulars, I have the honor to be with the most Perfect Consideration Sir Your most obedient & most humble Servant,

JONA: JONES

RC (MoSHi); endorsed. Recorded in SJL as received 29 Aug. 1787. Enclosure (MoSHi): Copy of a memorial of the merchants of Bordeaux to Villedeuil, Controller General, dated 14 Aug. 1787, stating that they have benefited very little from the regulations set forth in Calonne's letter to TJ of 22 Oct. 1786 because, when their tobacco began arriving from America, the farmers-general ceased buying that commodity under the pretext that they had bought their quota; they ask that Villedeuil require the farmers to comply with the agreement of Berni; if this is not done, the merchants will suffer a considerable loss; a statement of tobacco received and expected by the various merchants of Bordeaux is attached showing that such firms as Marois, Galway & Carré, French & Neveu, and others—there were nine in all—had received 2,871 hogsheads and were expecting 1,200 more.

From Robert Montgomery

Alicante, 25 Aug. 1787. Last wrote TJ on 24 July and has had no reply. Has letters from Algiers of 17 Aug. "which mention that the fury

[57]

of the Plague was much Mitigated . . . Scarce two Persons were daily carried off by it whereas Some months ago the deaths frequently ascended to two hundred and twenty." Deaths since 1 Jan. are estimated at 16,000 Mohammedans, 1,800 Jews, and 640 Christian slaves, including "only three of our Wretches." Four of their group are working in the dockyard, remainder as servants in the king's house, except captains and mates who are "Supported by the Bounty of Congress." Some small corsairs are now at sea. Many seamen having succumbed to the plague, it is believed the Algerines will not be able to man their vessels for summer cruising—but American ships should be on guard. Hopes to be appointed consul at Alicante; has only written to some of his friends about this; but asks TJ's advice whether he should send a memorial to Congress.

RC (DLC); 2 p.; endorsed. Recorded in SJL as received 8 Sep. 1787.

From Abbé de Reymond de St. Maurice

MONSIEUR   Rue de Bourbon près les Théatins Le 26. aoust 1787.

N'aiant pu avoir L'honneur de vous Rencontrer Lorsque j'ai pris la liberté de me présenter à votre hotel, je prens La précaution de mettre sous Envéloppe Les papiers que vous voules Bien faire passer au Consul françois près d'Edenton, afin de procurer à M. de Mainville La Satisfaction qu'il a droit d'attendre de Mrs. Cabarrus Peyrinault et Compe.

Ces papiers Consistent, 1°. En une Coppie des Billets, Ensemble de Douze mille Sept Cents vingt huit livres, cette Coppie est Collationnée par un procureur au chatelet de paris, et Légalisée par quatre de Mrs. Les Echevins de La même Ville, qui me l'ont Beaucoup fait Languir, c'est Ce qui m'a privé de l'avantage de vous La Remettre pour Les jours que vous avies Eu La Bonté de me fixer, pour En faire une Expédition plutot. 2°. Un mémoire instructif Sur La Cause de cette créance, afin que M. Le Consul françois puisse Etre En Etat de Répondre à tout, Et terminer Lui-même La Conclusion, Et Le paiement de cette créance. 3°. Enfin une Lettre à Monsieur Le Consul françois qui, jointe à celle que vous aures La Bonté de Lui Ecrire, accelerera Surement Le Succès de cette négotiation. Je vous Supplie d'En aggréer d'avance mes Remerciements Les plus Réspectueux avec Lesquels j'ai L'honneur d'Etre Monsieur Votre très humble Et très obeissant serviteur,

L'ABBÉ DE REYMOND DE ST. MAURICE
Vic. Gnal de Baionne

RC (MHi); endorsed. Recorded in SJL as received 27 Aug. 1787. Enclosures not found, but see Mainville to TJ, ca. July 1787.

From Lafayette

MY DEAR FRIEND　　　　　　　Chavaniac August the 27th 1787

Notwithstanding the Advantage of Your Situation in the busy Center of public Affairs, I know that our Country News will not be Quite Uninteresting to You, particularly when they Are Mixed with the Personal News of a family Most sincerely Attached to You. Our Preliminary Assembly is at an End, the journal of which I Have directed to be sent to You. We Had No details to Enter into, but it Has Been pleasing for me to Remark at the first Glance, that the Assembly were disposed to Act with zeal, and Good Harmony, whereby Many abuses May be destroied, liberal principles Be adopted, and Great deal of Good Be done. There is in the *tiers Etat* more self dignity than You perhaps imagine, and altho' they are not well disposed towards the New Nobles, a disgust which May produce some Embarassiments, there is a Very Good Understanding Between the Ancient Noblesse and the last order. Our Parish Assemblies Have Succeeded tolerably well for the first time.

We are Very Anxious to Hear the News from the Northward. Tomorrow I set out on a journey throughout the Mountaneous part of Auvergne—a Country which in a phisic, and in a Moral point of View is Very interesting. I Expect, My dear Sir, as Has Been Settled Between Us to pay You a short visit on the twentieth of the Next Month. I must Be Back for the Assembly of the Election, By the Eighth of October, and wish very much that the Ministry will Give Us a Hearing on our Commercial Affairs during that time. M. de la Boulaie Cannot But Have Collected Every thing He May stand in Need of to Meet us with Efficacy, and an Hour's Conversation with the Arch Bishop de Toulouse and M. de Montmorin would settle our Treaty Admirably well, provided You Can find out some Conciliatory Scheme Respecting tobacco. With My Best Compliments to Mr. Short and our American Acquaintances in Paris, and Requesting that My Particular Respects Be Presented to the Young ladies, I Have the Honour to be, My dear friend Yours,　　　　　　　LAFAYETTE

RC (DLC); endorsed. Recorded in SJL as received 4 Sep. 1787. The JOURNAL that Lafayette had been directed to send (and possibly enclosed) was the pamphlet *Proces verbal des séances de l'Assemblée Provinciale d'Auvergne, tenue à Clermont-Ferrand, dans le mois d'Août 1787* (see Sowerby, No. 2460; Gottschalk, *Lafayette, 1783-1789,* p. 332-4).

From John Trumbull

DR. SIR   London August 28th. 1787.

When I first receiv'd your letter about the Harpsichord, I was out of the way. It is now compleated packed shipp'd, and I hope saild for Rouen. I enclose you a Bill of Lading.

I have paid Mr. Walker for adding the Stop, thirteen Guineas; and Mr. Kirkman for porterage &c. 14/. in all £14-7-0. The Instrument was pack'd by Mr. Kirkman in the usual way, and which he says he has never known to fail of perfect security. For this He makes no charge. It is a very fine instrument, and I hope will come safe to you.

Will you do me the favor to inform me at what season I shall most probably meet the principal Officers who serv'd in America, at Paris. I shall soon be ready to paint my picture of the surrender of York Town, and must then come to paris. I suppose the winter is the most certain time of meeting them in Town. I shall wish to see the Marquis L Fayette, Count Rochambeau, Chatellux, the two Viomenils, De Grass and D Bar[ras]. I will thank you to mention my intention to the Marquis, and he can probably answer my Question.

Before this reaches you, Mrs. Cosway will be with you. I am very sorry I cannot be there at the same time. The Salon would be doubly interesting seen in such company.

With the sincerest Respect & Esteem I am Sir Your Gratefull friend,
                                                    JNO. TRUMBULL

Compliments to Mr. Short.

RC (DLC); endorsed. Recorded in SJL as received 2 Sep. 1787. Enclosure (DLC): Bill of lading, dated 22 Aug. 1787, signed by James Dunn, master of the ship *James*, for "One Case Containing a Harpsichord," shipped by Abraham Kirkman for TJ "To the Care of Mr Garvey Mercht at Rouen."

"In the autumn of 1787," Trumbull wrote in his *Autobiography*, "I again visited Paris, where I painted the portrait of Mr. Jefferson in the original small Declaration of Independence, Major General Ross in the small Sortie from Gibraltar, and the French officers in the Surrender of Lord Cornwallis . . . . I regard these as the best of my small portraits; they were painted from the life, in Mr. Jefferson's house"

(Theodore Sizer, ed., *Autobiography of Colonel John Trumbull*, New Haven, 1953, p. 152). On 6 Feb. 1788 Trumbull wrote to his brother, Jonathan Trumbull, Jr.: "I have been in this capital of dissipation and nonsense near six weeks for the purpose of getting the portraits of the French Officers who were at York Town, and have happily been so successfull as to find all those whom I wished in town. I have almost finished them, and shall return to London in a few days:—they are Rochambeau, DeGrasse, De Barras, Viomenil, Chastellux, St. Simon, the young Viomenil, Choizy, Lauzun, de Custine, de Laval, Deuxponts, Pherson, & Damas, besides the Marquis La Fayette" (quoted in same, p. 152, note). See illustration in this volume.

[60]

From Madame de Colmare

[*Paris*], *29 Aug.* 1787. Has received TJ's letter informing her that the value of paper money in America depends on the date on which it was received. The bill in her husband's possession must have been received in the summer of 1779 because he left America in September of that year and never returned; therefore, even though the bill might not be worth more, it certainly would not be valued at less than the 73.^{tt} mentioned by TJ as its worth in 1780. In reply to TJ's suggestion that she apply to the French consul in America, she has no acquaintance there to assist her and time does not permit this procedure; asks TJ to take charge of the bill and to advance her 73.^{tt}, an amount which, though modest, is necessary to meet her obligations.

RC (DLC); 2 p.; in French. At the foot of the first page are calculations by TJ converting the value of the bill into livres according to some depreciation scale: he divided 60.0 by [1]6.7, arriving at a figure of 3.6 which he multiplied by 5.25, obtaining a total of 18.^{tt} 18s., a value which he neglected to indicate in his to Mme. de Colmare, 23 Aug. 1787.

To Madame de Colmare

à Paris ce 29e Aout 1787.

J'ai l'honneur, Madame, de vous renvoyer encore le billet de papier-monnoye. L'arrangement de ces billets est tout-a-fait etranger aux objets qui me sont confiés içi. C'est du ressort d'une commission particuliere etablie en Amerique, et dans les affaires de laquelle je ne peux pas me meler. Je pense toujours que le meilleur parti à prendre seroit de le confier au Consul François à Philadelphie. Je m'aurois chargé tres volontier de cette commission pour vous, Madame, mais je n'ai pas l'honneur de la connoissance de ce Monsieur. J'ai celui de vous temoigner tous mes regrets de l'impuissance ou je suis de vous etre utile dans cette occasion, et de vous repeter les assurances de la consideration avec laquelle je suis Madame votre tres humble et tres obeissant serviteur,

TH: JEFFERSON

PrC (DLC).

To the Editor of the *Journal de Paris*

SIR   Paris Aug. 29. 1787.

I am a citizen of the United states of America, and have passed in those states almost the whole of my life. When young, I was

[61]

passionately fond of reading books of history, and travels. Since the commencement of the late revolution which separated us from Great Britain, our country too has been thought worthy to employ the pens of historians and travellers. I cannot paint to you, Sir, the agonies which these have cost me, in obliging me to renounce these favorite branches of reading and in discovering to me at length that my whole life has been employed in nourishing my mind with fables and falshoods. For thus I reason. If the histories of d'Auberteuil and of Longchamps, and the travels of the Abbé Robin can be published in the face of the world, and can be read and believed by those who are cotemporary with the events they pretend to relate, how may we expect that future ages shall be better informed? Will those rise from their graves to bear witness to the truth, who would not, while living, lift their voices against falshood? If cotemporary histories are thus false, what will future compilations be. And what are all those of preceding times? In your Journal of this day, you announce and criticize a book under the title of 'les ligues Acheenne, Suisse, and Hollandoise, et revolution des etats unis de l'Amerique par M. de Mayer.' I was no part of the Achaeen Swiss or Dutch confederacies and have therefore nothing to say against the facts related of them. And you cite only one fact from his account of the American revolution. It is in these words, 'Monsieur Mayer assure qu'une seule voix, un seul homme, prononça l'independance des Etats unis. "Ce fut, dit il, John Dickinson, un des Deputés de la Pensilvanie au Congrés. Le veille, il avoit voté pour la soumission. L'egalité des suffrages avoit suspendu la resolution; s'il eut persisté, le Congrés ne deliberoit point. Il fut foible: il cede aux instances de ceux qui avoient plus d'energie, plus d'eloquence, et plus de lumieres; il donna sa voix: l'Amerique lui doit une reconnoissance eternelle; c'est Dickinson qui l'a affranchie." ' The modesty and candour of Mr. Dickinson himself, Sir, would disavow every word of this paragraph, except these 'il avoit voté pour la soumission.' These are true, every other tittle[1] false. I was on the spot, and can relate to you this transaction with precision. On the 7th. of June 1776. the delegates from Virginia moved, in obedience to instructions from their constituents, that Congress should declare the 13. united colonies to be independant of Great Britain, that a Confederation should be formed to bind them together, and measures be taken for procuring the assistance of foreign powers. The house ordered a punctual attendance of all their members the next day at ten o'clock, and then resolved themselves into a Committee of the whole and entered on the discussion. It appeared in the course of the debates that 7. states, viz. N. Hampshire, Massachusets, Rhodeisland, Connecticut, Virginia, North Carolina and Georgia were decided for a separation, but that 6. others still hesitated, to wit, New York, New Jersey, Pennsylvania, Delaware, Maryland and South Carolina. Congress, desirous of unanimity, and seeing that the public mind was advancing rapidly to it, referred the further discussion to the 1st. of July, appointing in the mean time a Committee to prepare a declaration of independance, a second to form Articles for the confederation of the states, and a third to propose measures for obtaining foreign aid. On the 28th. of June the Declaration of Independance was reported to the house, and was laid on the table for the consideration of the members. On the 1st. day of July they resolved themselves into a committee of the whole, and resumed the consideration of the motion of June 7. It was debated through the day, and at length was decided in the affirmative by the votes of 9. states, viz. New Hampshire, Massachusets, Rhode island, Connecticut, *N. Jersey, Maryland*, Virginia, North Carolina and Georgia. Pennsylvania and South Carolina voted against it. Delaware, having but two members present, was divided. The delegates from New York declared they were for it, and their constituents also: but that the instructions against it, which had been given them a twelvemonth before, were still unrepealed; that their convention was to meet in a few days, and they asked leave to suspend their vote till they could obtain a repeal of their instructions. Observe that all this was in committee of the whole Congress, and that according to the mode of their proceedings the Resolution of that Committee to declare themselves independant was to be put to the same persons re-assuming their form as a Congress. It was now evening, the members exhausted by a debate of 9 hours, during which all the powers of the soul had been distended with the magnitude of the object without refreshment, without a pause;[2] and the delegates of S. Carolina desired that the final decision might be put off to the next morning that they might still weigh in their own minds their ultimate vote. It was put off, and in the morning of the 2d. of July they joined the other nine states in voting for it. The members of the Pennsylvania delegation too, who had been absent the day before, came in and decided the vote[3] of their state in favor of Independance, and a 3d member of the state of Delaware, who, hearing of the division of the sentiments of his two

collegues, had travelled post to arrive in time, now came in and
decided the vote of that state also for the resolution. Thus twelve
states voted for it at the time of it's passage, and the delegates
of New York, the 13th. state received instructions within a few
days to add theirs to the general vote: so that, instead of the
'egalité des suffrages' spoken of by Mr. Mayer, there was not a
dissenting voice. Congress proceeded immediately to consider the
Declaration of Independence which had been reported by their
committee on the 28th. of June. The several paragraphs of that
were debated for three days. viz. the 2d. 3d. and 4th. of July.
In the evening of the 4th. they were finally closed, and the instrument approved by an unanimous vote, and signed by every member, *except Mr. Dickinson.* Look into the Journals of Congress of
that day, Sir, and you will see the instrument, and the names of
the signers, and that Mr. Dickinson's name is not among them.
Then read again those words of your paper. 'Il (Mr. Mayer) assure
qu'une seule voix, un seul homme, prononça l'independance des
etats unis. "Ce fut John Dickinson. L'Amerique lui doit une reconnoissance eternal; c'est Dickinson qui l'a affranchie." ' With my
regrets, and my Adieus to History, to Travels, to Mayer, and to
you, Sir, permit me to mingle assurances of the great respect with
which I have the honor to be, Sir, your most obedient & most
humble servant,   AN AMERICAN

MS (ViWC); at head of text: "To
the Editor of the Journal de Paris";
entirely in TJ's hand; with numerous
deletions, interlineations, and corrections, the more important of which are
noted below. PrC of the preceding
(DLC); lacks five words that are in MS
(see note 2, below). Despite the numerous alterations made by TJ in MS,
it is evident that this text is a fair copy
and not a rough draft; a rough draft
must have preceded it, but it has not
been found.

All of the evidence indicates that TJ
wrote the present MS in a burst of
indignation over the mistaken account
of the adoption of the Declaration of
Independence that he had read in the
Journal de Paris OF THIS DAY; then,
with customary prudence, permitted
himself a cooling-off period; and finally,
on reflection, decided not to dispatch
the document. This evidence may be
summarized as follows: (1) Being
generally averse to newspaper contro-
versy, TJ usually sent his remarks

intended for publication to some third
person who could be depended upon to
make a good translation and also to
conceal the source effectively (see, for
example, Vol. 9: 4-7); there is no
evidence that he did so in the present
instance. (2) The letter was never published in the *Journal de Paris.* (3) It
is not recorded in SJL as having been
sent. (4) Both the MS and the PrC
were retained among TJ's papers, as
proved by the fact that the former was
used by Henry A. Washington for his
edition of TJ's *Writings* (HAW, IX,
309-12). Finally, (5) TJ was known
in Paris as the author of the Declaration of Independence, and his account
of the events leading up to its adoption
is so circumstantial and detailed as to
point directly to him as the one who
WAS ON THE SPOT, a consequence that
he clearly would have wished to avoid
as is indicated by his choice of pseu-
donym.—The article in the *Journal de
Paris* that aroused him so keenly appeared on 29 Aug. 1787; it was an un-

signed review of Mayer's two-volume *Les Ligues Achéenne, Suisse et Hollandoise, et Révolution des Etats-Unis de l'Amérique comparés ensemble.* The reviewer criticized Mayer for allotting scarcely 200 pages to the great events of the American revolution and the causes leading up to them, and then stated: "Il a cependant resserré dans le petit espace des particularités qui sont peu connues et des observations qui lui appartiennent. Par exemple, il assure qu'une seule voix, un seul homme, prononça l'indépendance des Etats-unis. Ce fut dit-il, *John Dickenson . . .'* "

&c. (as quoted above by TJ).—For an account of the signing and adoption of the Declaration and the sources used by TJ in compiling the present letter, see Editorial Note, Vol. 1: 304-8.

[1] TJ deleted the words "of the paragraph."
[2] The preceding five words were inserted in MS after the PrC had been made, and are not in the latter.
[3] TJ first wrote: "turned the votes" and then altered the phrase by overwriting and deletion to read as above.

To Abigail Adams

DEAR MADAM   Paris Aug. 30. 1787.

I have omitted writing sooner to you in expectation that Colo. Smith would have taken this in his route: but receiving now information from him that he embarks from Lisbon, I avail myself of the opportunity by Mr. Payne of thanking you for the disbursements you were so kind as to make for my daughter in London, and of stating to you our accounts as follows.

	£	s	d
Disbursements of Mrs. Adams as summed up in her state of them	10	15	8
Error in addition to her prejudice	1	0	6
	11	16	2
Cash paid by Petit to Mrs. Adams, viz. 6. Louis d'ors @19/6	5	17	
Paid by do. for black lace 75.^{tt} which at the same exchange is	3	1	
Do. for 2. doz. pr. gloves 37^{tt} – 12s	1	10	6
Balance due to Mrs. Adams	1	7	8
	11	16	2

which balance I will beg the favor of Colo. Smith to pay you, and to debit me with.   I am afraid, by the American papers, that the disturbances in Massachusets are not yet at an end. Mr. Rucker, who is arrived here, gives me a terrible account of the luxury of our ladies in the article of dress. He sais that they begin to be sensible of the excess of it themselves, and to think a reformation necessary. That proposed is the adoption of a national dress. I fear however they have not resolution enough for this. I rejoice in the character of the lady who accompanies the Count de Moustier to America, and who is calculated to reform these excesses as far as her example can have weight. Simple beyond example in her dress, tho neat, hating parade and etiquette, affable, engaging, placid, and withal beautiful, I cannot help hoping a good effect from her example. She is the Marquise de Brehan, sister in law to the Count de Moustier, who goes partly on account of a feeble health, but principally for the education of her son (of 17. years of age) which she hopes to find more masculine there and less exposed to seduction. The Count de Moustier is of a character well assorted to this. Nothing niggardly, yet orderly in his affairs, genteel but plain, loving society upon an easy not a splendid tone, unreserved, honest, and speaking our language like a native. He goes with excellent notions and dispositions, and is as likely to give satisfaction as any man that could have been chosen in France. He is much a whig in the politics of his own country. I understand there is a possibility that Congress will remove to Philadelphia.— My daughter talks of you often and much, still fancies she is to pay you the visit she promised. In the mean time she is very contented in the Convent with her sister. Both join me in compliments to Mrs. Smith and in assurances to yourself of the attachment and respect which I have the honour to proffer for them as well as for, dear Madam, your most obedient & most humble servant,

TH: JEFFERSON

RC (MHi: AMT); addressed and endorsed. PrC (DLC).

TJ's sanguine hopes for THE MARQUISE DE BREHAN and THE COUNT DE MOUSTIER were doomed to disappointment. The latter soon changed his NOTIONS AND DISPOSITIONS about America and the nature of the relation of the former to her brother-in-law became the subject of gossip soon after their arrival in New York, in which the interpretation varied greatly from that here given by TJ. For a good account of TJ's miscalculation in this instance (which revealed an uncharacteristic departure from his generally realistic appraisal of all persons who were likely to have an effect upon Franco-American relations), see Malone, *Jefferson*, II, 197-8, and the authorities there cited.

To John Adams

DEAR SIR   Paris Aug. 30. 1787.

Since your favor of July 10. mine have been of July 17. 23 and 28. The last inclosed a bill of exchange from Mr. Grand on Tessier for £46-17-10 sterl. to answer Genl. Sullivan's bill for that sum.

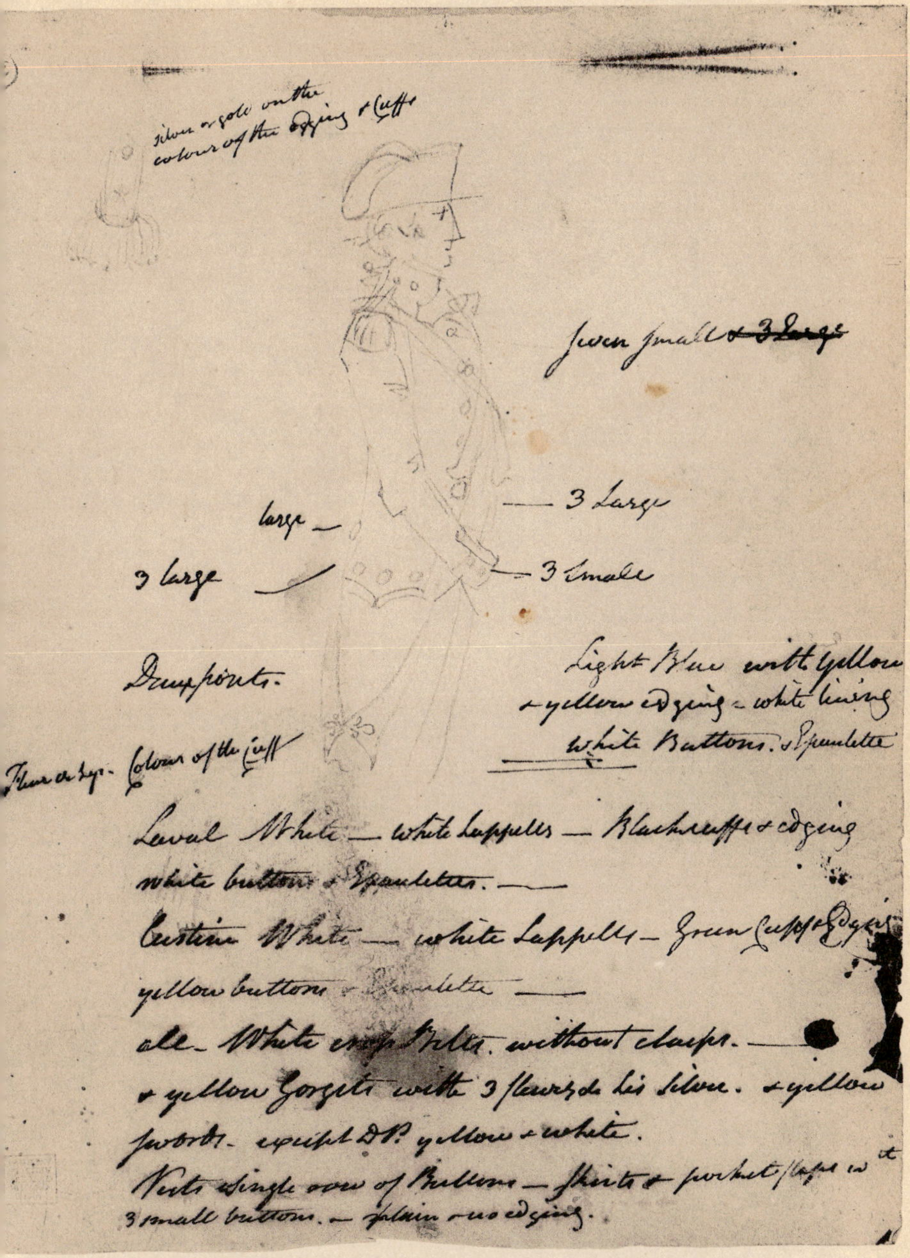

Trumbull's sketch of Col. Deux-Ponts. (See p. xxxv.)

Rochambeau

Lafayette

Chastellux   Vioménil   Barras   De Grasse

Details from Trumbull's "Surrender of Lord Cornwallis at Yorktown."
(See p. xxxv.)

I hope it got safe to hand, tho' I have been anxious about it as it went by post and my letters thro' that channel sometimes miscarry.

From the separation of the Notables to the present moment has been perhaps the most interesting interval ever known in this country. The propositions of the Government, approved by the Notables, were precious to the nation and have been in an honest course of execution, some of them being carried into effect, and others preparing. Above all the establishment of the Provincial assemblies, some of which have begun their sessions, bid fair to be the instrument for circumscribing the power of the crown and raising the people into consideration. The election given to them is what will do this. Tho' the minister who proposed these improvements seems to have meant them as the price of the new supplies, the game has been so played as to secure the improvements to the nation without securing the price. The Notables spoke softly on the subject of the additional supplies, but the parliament took them up roundly, refused to register the edicts for the new taxes, till compelled in a bed of justice and prefered themselves to be transferred to Troyes rather than withdraw their opposition. It is urged principally against the king, that his revenue is 130. millions more than that of his predecessor was, and yet he demands 120. millions further. You will see this well explained in the 'Conference entre un ministre d'etat et un Conseiller au parlement' which I send you with some other small pamphlets. In the mean time all tongues in Paris (and in France as it is said) have been let loose, and never was a license of speaking against the government exercised in London more freely or more universally. Caracatures, placards, bon mots, have been indulged in by all ranks of people, and I know of no well attested instance of a single punishment. For some time mobs of 10; 20; 30,000 people collected daily, surrounded the parliament house, huzzaed the members, even entered the doors and examined into their conduct, took the horses out of the carriages of those who did well, and drew them home. The government thought it prudent to prevent these, drew some regiments into the neighborhood, multiplied the guards, had the streets constantly patrolled by strong parties, suspended privileged places, forbad all clubs, &c. The mobs have ceased: perhaps this may be partly owing to the absence of parliament. The Count d'Artois, sent to hold a bed of justice in the Cour des Aides, was hissed and hooted without reserve by the populace; the carriage of Madame de (I forget the name) in the queen's livery was stopped by the populace under a belief that it was Madame de Polignac's whom they would have insulted, the queen going to the theater at Versailles with Madame de Polignac was received with a general hiss. The king, long in the habit of drowning his cares in wine, plunges deeper and deeper; the queen cries but sins on. The Count d'Artois is detested, and Monsieur the general favorite. The Archbishop of Thoulouse is made Ministre principale, a virtuous, patriotic and able character. The Marechal de Castries retired yesterday notwithstanding strong sollicitations to remain in office. The Marechal de Segur retired at the same time, prompted to it by the court. Their successors are not yet known. M. de St. Prist goes Ambassador to Holland in the room of Verac transferred to Switzerland, and the Count de Moustier goes to America in the room of the Chevalier de la Luzerne who has a promise of the first vacancy. These nominations are not yet made formally, but they are decided on and the parties are ordered to prepare for their destination. As it has been long since I have had a confidential conveiance to you, I have brought together the principal facts from the adjournment of the Notables to the present moment which, as you will perceive from their nature, required a confidential conveyance. I have done it the rather because, tho' you will have heard many of them and seen them in the public papers, yet floating in the mass of lies which constitute the atmospheres of London and Paris, you may not have been sure of their truth: and I have mentioned every truth of any consequence to enable you to stamp as false the facts pretermitted. I think that in the course of three months the royal authority has lost, and the rights of the nation gained, as much ground, by a revolution of public opinion only, as England gained in all her civil wars under the Stuarts. I rather believe too they will retain the ground gained, because it is defended by the young and the middle aged, in opposition to the old only. The first party increases, and the latter diminishes daily from the course of nature. You may suppose that under this situation, war would be unwelcome to France. She will surely avoid it if not forced by the courts of London and Berlin. If forced, it is probable she will change the system of Europe totally by an alliance with the two empires, to whom nothing would be more desireable. In the event of such a coalition, not only Prussia but the whole European world must receive from them their laws. But France will probably endeavor to preserve the present system if it can be done by sacrifising to a certain degree the pretensions of the patriotic party in Holland. But of all these matters you can judge, in your position, where less secrecy is observed, better than I can. I have news from America as late as July 19. Nothing had then transpired from the Federal convention. I am sorry they began their deliberations by so abominable a precedent as that of tying up the tongues of their members. Nothing can justify this example but the innocence of their intentions, and ignorance of the value of public discussions. I have no doubt that all their other measures will be good and wise. It is really an assembly of demigods. Genl. Washington was of opinion they should not separate till October. I have the honour to be with every sentiment of friendship and respect Dear Sir Your most obedient & most humble servant, TH: JEFFERSON

PrC (DLC). Enclosure: *Conférence entre un Ministre d'etat et un Conseiller au Parlement* (Sowerby, No. 2453); the other pamphlets have not been identified.

The CONFIDENTIAL CONVEIANCE in this instance was Thomas Paine, who also carried to London the letters to Mrs. Adams and to Trumbull of this date.

To John Trumbull

DEAR SIR   Paris Aug. 30. 1787.

My last to you were of the 16th. and 17th. of July on the subject of my harpsichord. I imagine Colo. Smith is now arrived in London and can aid you in that trouble. The Salon has been open four or five days. I inclose you a list of it's treasures. The best thing is the Death of Socrates by David, and a superb one it is. A crucifixion by Roland in imitation of Relief is as perfect as it can be. Five peices of antiquities by Robert are also among the foremost. Many portraits of Madme. Le Brun are exhibited and much approved. There are abundance of things in the stile of mediocrity. Upon the whole it is well worth your coming to see. You have only to get into the Diligence and in 4. days you are here. The whole will be an affair of 12. or 14. days only and as many guineas; and as it happens but once in two years, you should not miss it. Come then and take your bed here. You will see Mrs. Cosway who arrived two days ago, Madme. de Brehan before her departure &c. &c. I will expect you. Adieu. Your's affectionately,

TH: JEFFERSON

PrC (DLC). Enclosure: *Explication des peintures, sculptures et gravures, de Messieurs de l'Académie Royale* . . . Paris 1787 (copy in Bibliothèque Nationale, Cab. Est. Yd² 980 [1787]). See illustration in this volume.

From François Baudin

St. Martin, Ile de Ré, 31 Aug. 1787. Wrote Barclay, when Barclay was at Bordeaux, asking for appointment as American consul or agent for the Ile de Ré; he replied that, on the basis of information he had received concerning Baudin, he was disposed to grant his request. Having no further news on this matter, and being informed that TJ is responsible for all such appointments, he now makes the same request to him. His firm is well established and has served a number of American ships, both during the war and since the peace. A consul or agent at that place is essential. If TJ wishes it, he will send him monthly reports of imports and exports; trade between the island and America would be mutually advantageous.

RC (DLC); 4 p.; in French; endorsed. Recorded in SJL as received 12 Sep. 1787.

To André Limozin

SIR   Paris Aug. 31. 1787.

I have duly received your favors of the 19th. and 24th. of August and the box of papers mentioned in the last are at the Syndic chamber from which I shall receive them to-day. Appearances for a little while had taken more the aspect of war, but the hopes of a continuance of the peace prevail at this moment, and are perhaps stronger than when I wrote you last. The approach of autumn and winter will add a further security, and give another winter for arranging differences. You have doubtless heard that the Archbishop of Toulouse is appointed principal minister. M. de Castries and M. de Segur are retired, and their places not yet filled. M. de Villedeuil is transferred to the Council of finance, M. de Lambert appointed Comptroller general and M. de la Borde Directeur de la tresorerie royale. I think the changes of ministry will stop here, and that Monsieur de Breteuil and M. de Montmorin will remain in office.

I shall take the liberty of sending to your address in a few days 3. boxes of books, one for New York, one for Williamsburg and one for Richmond, but all to be forwarded by the Packet to New York to the care of Mr. Madison a member of Congress, unless direct opportunities to Richmond and Williamsburgh should offer. I have the honor to be with much esteem Sir your most obedient humble servant,   TH: JEFFERSON

PrC (DLC).
On the three BOXES OF BOOKS, see TJ to Wythe, 16 Sep. 1787; TJ to Alexander Donald and to James Madison, 17 Sep. 1787.

From André Limozin

Le Havre, 31 Aug. 1787. Is forwarding a box of seeds which arrived from Philadelphia on the American ship *Rising Sun*. This ship brought some pearl ash, on which the customs officers require "a very great duty." Has spoken to them about the promises made to TJ in Calonne's letter of 22 Oct. 1786, but they refuse "to pay the least attention to it." Suggests that TJ "make necessary application about the infraction."

RC (MHi); 2 p. Recorded in SJL as received 2 Sep. 1787.

To William Stephens Smith

DEAR SIR   Paris Aug. 31. 1787.

In your favor of June 30. from Madrid is the following paragraph. 'Mr. Jay sais 562. 163. 449. 350. 92. 213. 479. 609. 57. 189. 547. 407. 407. 642. 186. 48. 449. 186. 72. 290. 136. 92. 368. 38. 582. 518. 48. 186. 149. 327. 48. 186. 92. 547. 324. 290. 82. 518. 72. 393. 525. 371. 407. 82. 570. 189. 339. 380.' I have four cyphers, two of which it was possible you might have copies of, and two impossible. I tried both the possible and impossible; but none would explain it. I presume you have mistaken the cypher you meant to make use of. I did not write to you from Bordeaux on Mr. Barclay's affair, because it must have past through the post offices of France and Spain. The erroneous decision of the parliament in his favor was fortunate for him. His adversaries applied to the ministry who declared he was under no protection against his creditors. The evening before the parliament of Bourdeaux were in consequence of this to revoke their decision, he left Bordeaux for l'Orient where he was detained a month by contrary winds before he could sail for America. He sailed about the 2d. or 3d. of Aug. leaving his family here. Before the receipt of your favor of Aug. 3. Mr. Short had communicated to me your intentions of passing by water from Lisbon to London. This has increased my misfortune of missing you in your way to Spain. I wish the Salon which is now open, or the pleasures or tumults of Paris, could excite a desire in you to visit it. The first circumstance will I expect bring Trumbul, and you might as well be of the party. I have taken the liberty of telling Mrs. Adams you will pay her for me a small balance of 27/8 sterling. Understanding that my harpsichord was finished, I wrote to Mr. Trumbul, in your absence,

[71]

to be so good as to forward it to me. I have not heard whether he did so. This being sent off, will enable you to give me a final state of my account, which I will thank you for, that I may remit you any balance due, or employ it for you here as you shall think proper. I am particularly desirous to have Woodmason's accounts, because for want of them I have not been able to settle with the Marquises Fayette and Chatellux. Mrs. Smith was so good as to give me notice of the draught Genl. Sullivan had made on you in my behalf. In a letter of July 28. therefore I inclosed to Mr. Adams a bill of exchange from Mr. Grand on Lewis Teissier, which I calculated would get to hand two days before the draught on you became due. It was paiable on sight. That Genl. Sullivan should have incommoded you with this draught was more unaccountable, than that he should have made it on me without apprising me of the cause. There does not exist as far as I know, and never did exist an article of account between us. I did indeed, when in America, ask him to send me the skin and some of the bones of a Moose, which I imagined would have been bought of some hunter for a guinea or two. But I have never heard that he has got these for me, and much less expected, or can yet suppose any body would have asked, or he have given such a sum for them. However I have no doubt he will explain the matter to me. We are here in a terrible pickle. Mr. Grand, being about 1000 guineas in advance for the U.S. chuses to advance no more till he receives remittances from America: and Mr. Rucker tells me he thinks there are none coming from thence. Carmichael and Dumas used to be paid from hence.— Since my letter of yesterday to Mr. Adams, Villedeuil, the comptroller general is transferred to the council of finance (i.e. decently cashiered) and Monsr. de Lambert appointed to his office, but Monsieur de la Borde is named Directeur de la Tresorerie royale. This last is the office into which Mr. Neckar came first, and after a while, that and the Comptrol general were united in his person and have not been since separated till now. No nomination yet in the room of de Castries and Segur. I think the changes in the ministry will now stop. There remains no body of the former set but Breteuil and Monmorin. The first is too firmly supported by the queen to be removed, and the latter enjoys a very general esteem of all parties. Having exhausted the feild of news in my letter to Mr Adams, I will only add, what is no news, that I am with sentiments of the most sincere friendship and attachment Dear Sir your most obedient & most humble servant,

Th: Jefferson

RC (MHi); endorsed, in part: "Ansr. Septr. 18th." PrC (DLC).
For a decoding of the passage that TJ was unable to decode, see Smith to TJ, 30 June 1787.

From John Stockdale

SIR   Piccadilly 31st. Augt. 1787.

I duly received yours of the 14th. Instant, and am exceedingly obliged to you for the trouble you have taken with the Bookseller for the Sale of the Notes on Virginia.

I have seen Mr. Dilly Bookseller in the Poultry, who positively assures me that your Book is printed at Philidelphia, and that his authority, is, Mr. Bury, Bookseller at New York, Mr. Dilly believes what he has asserted, tho' I must confess I agree with you, and doubt it. I have sent a small number to Dr. Ramsay and Mr. Laurens at Charleston. Mr. Dilly has sent a few copies to New York. I have received by your favor Vol. 1 to 9 of Mr. Berquin's friend of Youth and Vol. 2, of Little Grandison, and shall esteem it a particular favor if you'll be so good as to give directions, that all after Vol. 9, of the friend of Youth and Vol. 1, 3, &c. of Little Grandison may be sent by the first oppertunity.

I have sent to Mr. Richardson at the Royal Exchange, I believe at least a dozen times by his appoinment, for the "Remarks on the Taxation of free states." And tho' he his[1] sensible he has got many copies he has not yet been able to find one. If I can meet with one, you will receive it thro' the chargé des affairs of France hands. I am with great respect Your much obliged & very hble. Servt.,

                                          JOHN STOCKDALE

RC (MHi); endorsed. Recorded in SJL as received 5 Sep. 1787.

[1] Thus in MS.

[73]

To Moustier

[1 Sep. 1787]

Packets sail at present	
from Havre	from N. York
Feb. 10	Jan. 25
Mar. 25.	Mar. 10
May 10	Apr. 25.
June 25	June 10.
Aug. 10.	July 25.
Sep. 25.	Sep. 10
Nov. 10.	Oct. 25
Dec. 25.	Dec. 10

Passages from France to America are almost always under 7. weeks, those from America to France under 5. weeks. Not above one passage in a year, of the eight performed by the packets, will exceed these terms. If a letter is sent by the packet which sails from Havre Mar. 25. it will arrive at New York before May 15. It must then wait 25. days to wit to June 10. before a packet will be sailing to bring the answer. And so upon every other packet that sails in the year, it will be found that allowing 7. weeks for the passage, there will be 25 days more before the sailing of any packet to bring the answer.

If a letter is sent from New York by the packet which sails Mar. 10. it will arrive at Havre before Apr. 15. It must then wait 25. days, to May 10. before a packet will sail to carry the answer.

Packets sail at present	
from Havre	from N. York
Jan. 20.	Jan. 25.
Mar. 5.	Mar. 10
Apr. 20.	Apr. 25.
June 5.	June 10
July 20.	July 25
Sep. 5.	Sep. 10
Oct. 20	Oct. 25
Dec. 5	Dec. 10

It is proposed to alter the sailing days from Havre, so that the packets shall sail from thence 20 days sooner than they do now; this will allow 5. days for the letters to come from Havre and the answer to be returned to that place, and will save all other delay. Thus, a packet shall sail from Havre the 5th. of March, as in the Margin (instead of the 25, as at present); it arrives at N. York in 7. weeks, viz. before the 22d. of Apr. and a packet sails from thence with the answer the 25th of April. So a packet sails from New York the 10th. of March as at present, and arrives at Havre in 5. weeks, that is, before the 14th. of April; and a packet shall sail from Havre the 20th.

[74]

of Apr. (instead of the 10th. of May as at present) allowing just time for the letter to come from Havre to Paris, and the answer to get back to Havre. This quick notice is of great consequence to commerce. If it was thought better to keep the sailing days from Havre the same and to change those of New York, they should be Jan. 1. Feb. 15. Apr. 1. May 15. July 1. Aug. 15. Oct. 1. Nov. 15. but this brings the packet of Feb. 15. and Aug. 15. on the coast in the moment of the equinox.

PrC (DLC); at foot of text: "M. le Comte de Moustier"; unsigned and undated. Date has been assigned on the basis of an entry in SJL for 1 Sep. 1787 reading "Moustier le Cte. de." This may refer to a missing letter covering the present memorandum or it may refer only to the memorandum itself.

From Madame de Bréhan

[*Paris, ca. Sep. 1787?*] Accepts TJ's invitation "for Monday"; if it is a family affair "the satisfaction shall be greater"; wishes she could speak English "the whole time" but in spite of her efforts TJ will find "very little progress"; hopes some months in America will help her; in the meantime, she will avail herself of TJ's lessons if he will give her any so that she may carry on a correspondence with him.

RC (DLC); addressed and endorsed; without date and not recorded in SJL; written sometime between Moustier's appointment as minister to the United States and his departure with Mme. de Bréhan early in October 1787.

To André Limozin

SIR   Paris Sep. 2. 1787.

By the inclosed paper I presume there are arrived for me on board the packet three small boxes of seeds or plants, and a large box, the contents of which I know not. I will beg the favor of you to pay for me the freight and other expences, and to send the three small boxes by the Diligence. As to the large one, I conjecture it may contain bones and other objects of Natural history which should come by water, as the motion of a carriage would destroy them. I will therefore pray you to send the large box up here by water, taking such precautions as are necessary to prevent their being stopped at Rouen. Perhaps the plumbing the box may be necessary; in which case I will take particular care to return any Acquit á caution you may be so kind as to enter into for me.

As to news, every thing stands as in my letter of the day before yesterday, except that M. de la Borde's appointment seems not yet firm. I have the honor to be with much esteem, Sir, your most obedient & most humble servant, TH: JEFFERSON

PrC (MHi). The enclosed paper has not been found.

Documents on the American Tobacco Trade

I. JEAN JACQUES BERARD & CIE. TO THE FARMERS-GENERAL, 14 JULY 1787

II. BERARD'S OBSERVATIONS ON THE TOBACCO TRADE, [CA. 3 SEP. 1787]

III. FURTHER OBSERVATIONS ON THE TOBACCO TRADE, [CA. OCT. 1787]

EDITORIAL NOTE

The documents in this group reveal what a powerful ally Jefferson had in Simon Bérard and the mercantile firm to which he belonged in the effort to make the farmers-general live up to the agreement reached at Berni in May 1786 and given the approval of the ministry in Calonne's letter to Jefferson of 22 Oct. 1786. The blunt, forthright challenge here presented to the farmers-general to meet their obligation or to declare their disavowal of it in writing was scarcely the line that the American minister could take. But he could and did lend all of the assistance in his power to Bérard and his able associate, Jacob Vernes, in the preparation of their impassioned statements. Lafayette, of course, continued his invaluable work, but even the letter that he wrote from Chavaniac on 10 Sep. 1787 bears traces of the argument that Bérard had put into his appeal to Vergennes on 10 Jan. 1786, and both of these documents clearly owe something to Jefferson's letter to Vergennes of 15 Aug. 1785 (see Lafayette to Lambert, 10 Sep. 1787, printed as an enclosure to Lafayette to TJ, 18 Sep. 1787; see also Vol. 8: 385-93; Vol. 9: 458-9; Gottschalk, *Lafayette, 1783-89*, p. 336). Lafayette thought that two hours of the controller-general's time would be sufficient to clear up the issue, but Lambert was very different from Villedeuil. Throughout the autumn of 1787, the controller-general, Jefferson, Bérard, Vernes, Dupont, and, to a lesser extent than usual, Lafayette, struggled with the vexing tobacco problem and the evasive farmers-general. Lambert insisted on finding out the situation for himself and —according to a statement that Jefferson caused to be printed late in 1788 and distributed privately to all members of the French ministry (Lambert asked for two extra copies)—the controller-general "with a patience and assiduity almost unexampled, went through all the investigations necessary to assure himself that the conclusions of the Committee [at Berni] had been just" (*Observations on the Whale-Fishery*).

[76]

EDITORIAL NOTE

It is no disparagement of Lafayette to suggest that Bérard was a more vigorous coadjutor on the tobacco problem in the autumn of 1787 than he. Lafayette had performed prodigiously in the spring and summer of 1786 and was a tower of strength in the work of the American Committee that led up to the decision at Berni and the letter from Calonne. But in 1787 the situation was different. For one thing, the threat of war in Holland caused Lafayette to make a mad dash northward in the expectation that he might be made commander of the Dutch Republican army—an expectation that was doomed to disappointment when events marched rapidly and when the post was given to the man whom Jefferson called "a prince without talents, without courage, and without principle," the Rhingrave de Salm. For another thing, Lafayette spent most of the autumn in Auvergne, deep in matters of constitutional reform, returning to Paris only in time for the new year (Gottschalk, *Lafayette, 1783-89*, p. 338-46, 351-63). Even if these circumstances had not placed Lafayette toward the edge of the little circle that wrestled with the tobacco problem, the nature of the issue would undoubtedly have placed Bérard nearer the center than either Lafayette or Dupont— and Jefferson, naturally, was content to let others occupy the central position and drive home points that he could not make as effectively as they. In 1786 the issue had been to get the ministry to break or at least modify the "double monopoly" enjoyed by the farmers-general and Robert Morris; in 1787 the issue was to get the ministry to honor its own regulations governing both the monopoly and private merchants. Among the latter, none in France was so deeply committed in the tobacco trade as the firm of Jean Jacques Bérard & Cie., a house that had had several thousand hogsheads of tobacco lying in the warehouses of L'Orient since October of 1786 while other shipments continued to arrive in that and other ports of France and while the farmers-general appeared to discriminate both against the port of L'Orient and against the house of Bérard. This fact alone is sufficient to explain the vigor of language used in the accompanying documents and the assiduity with which Simon Bérard and Jacob Vernes worked with the American minister during the summer and autumn of 1787 (see Vernes to TJ, 30 June, 13 Nov. 1787; 10 Apr. 1788; TJ to Dupont, 6 Oct. 1787, note; TJ to La Boullaye, 18 July and 24 Sep. 1787). Bérard's interest in the issue was immediate, direct, and vital.

Lafayette could, however, bring to bear influences that even the leading merchant of France could not exercise. In the autumn of 1786, when twenty-three mercantile houses of Baltimore expressed their gratitude to Bérard & Cie. for the work of the American Committee in bringing about the new regulations, they said they experienced a greater pleasure in the opportunity this afforded them of "confirming the obligations that they have for the Marquis de la Fayette's gracious services which they have so often experienced" (dated 30 Sep. 1786; Arch. Aff. Etr., Corr. Pol., E.-U., xxxii; Tr in DLC). It was also Lafayette who in the spring of 1787 had initiated the move to enforce the regulations announced in Calonne's letter: "Cette Lettre," he declared, "avoit produit les meilleurs effets dans L'Amerique; mais on a negligé de lui donner la Sanction convenable dans les Ports Soit par un Arrêt du

Conseil, soit de toute autre maniere efficace; et les inconvenients de cet oubli sont aisés à prévoir" (Lafayette to Montmorin, 17 Mch. 1787; same; he also wrote to LeNoir, president of the committee, at the same time; see Short to TJ, 4 Apr. 1787). Montmorin passed this on to Villedeuil, with the comment that Otto had informed him of the excellent effect Calonne's letter had produced in America. But Villedeuil thought that the formality desired by Lafayette was unnecessary, unprecedented, and even incompatible with the nature of the usages and constitution of the Council: the simple letter of instructions was sufficient in itself to fulfill the object for which it was destined, and if it were otherwise, it would be necessary to take other steps than a decree in Council (Montmorin to Villedeuil, 7 May 1787; Villedeuil to Montmorin, 14 May 1787; Arch. Aff. Etr., Corr. Pol., E.-U., xxxii; Tr in DLC). Lambert, his successor, took a very different attitude in response to the appeals of Jefferson and the pressure of such merchants as Bérard (TJ to La Boullaye, 18 and 24 Sep. 1787; Lambert to La Boullaye, 23 Oct. 1787; Lambert to TJ, 29 Dec. 1787).

I. Jean Jacques Bérard & Cie. to the Farmers-General

MESSIEURS   Paris le 14 Juillet 1787

Nous avons eu l'honneur de vous écrire le 25 du mois dernier pour vous prier de faire recevoir à l'Orient par votre preposé le restant d'environ quatre mille Boucauds de Tabac venus a notre consignation depuis le mois d'octobre 1786. dans les termes de la décision de Bernis, et dont sur une autre lettre de nous du 13e may vous avés fait recevoir mille Boucauds dans le mois de Juin.

Vous ne nous avés pas repondu par ecrit; mais Mr. Delaville votre Directeur nous a dit de votre part que vous ne prendriez point actuellement ces tabacs.

Nous ne devions pas nous attendre à ce refus. Vos preposés ont immédiatement reçu les tabacs arrivés dans tout autre Port de france jusqu'au mois de Juin dernier. Nous ne voyons aucune raison qui pût justifier le refus fait à l'Orient de tabacs venus dans le meme tems et depuis l'epoque assés reculée du mois d'octobre 1786.

Nous vous avons réiterativement exposé la position de notre Maison; ses avances considérables aux Americains, propriétaires des tabacs; la confiance de ceux cy dans la décision de Bernis qui seule a déterminé leurs expeditions. Nous avons pris la liberté de vous rappeller les engagements contractés par la Ferme Générale en conséquence de cette décision, ne pouvant croire que vous attachiés peu d'importance a des engagements aussi solemnels.

Une nouvelle répetition de ces détails semble inutile. Mais il ne l'est point. Nous croyons même honnête et convenable de vous mettre sous les yeux les suites que va avoir le sistème que vous adoptés, et de nous expliquer avec franchise sur la conduite que nous allons être obligés de suivre.

La Ferme Générale s'est engagée à Bernis envers le Gouvernement à recevoir environ trente mille boucauds de tabac des particuliers, à raison de quinze mille par an pendant les deux dernières années du traité de M. Robert Morris, pourvû qu'ils fussent expediés directement des Etats-Unis sur Navires François ou Americains. Le Commerce n'a pû ni dû refuser une entière confiance à cet engagement deux fois et ministeriellement annoncé et rendu public dans nos Ports et en Amerique, d'abord à l'époque de la decision et ensuite le 22 8bre dernier par la lettre du Ministre des Finances à Mr. de Jefferson.

Quelle a êté la suite de cette confiance? D'un coté les Americains ont achetté et expedié dans nos Ports des tabacs propres à la consommation de la France de la maniere et sur les Navires prescrits, éxigeant de fortes avances dés l'arrivée des tabacs et de promts comptes de vente. De l'autre Notre Maison a fait tout ce qu'elle a pu pour faire réussir les vües du Gouvernement et encourager les Planteurs et les Negotiants Americains. Elle s'est livrée aux fortes avances exigées sur leurs cargaisons, sure que par leur promte vente a la ferme elle verroit rentrer ses fonds sans retard.

Cette attente est maintenant déçüe. Nos avances sont considérables, et durent depuis assés longtems. Nous ne devons pas les augmenter, puisqu'il n'y a plus d'espoir prochain et assuré de rentrées.

Il n'y a qu'un achetteur de tabacs en France. Dès que cet acheteur refuse de recevoir les tabacs ils deviennent un fonds mort sans valeur sur lequel nous ne pouvons sans imprudence faire des avances d'une étendüe et d'une durée aussi indeterminées. Il n'est en France aucune Maison Prudente et Jalouse de son credit qui voulut en courir les risques, malgré tout le desir possible de faire reussir les vües du Gouvernement en attirant le Commerce des Etats-Unis et malgré l'interét qu'ont d'ailleurs les Negociants à étendre leurs afaires.

Nous nous trouvons en conséquence forcés pour notre propre sureté de suspendre toute avance aux Americains aprés beaucoup de tems et de peine. Ils commençoient à s'acoutumer a consommer des Marchandises de France. Nous allons être obligés de contremander les ordres que nous avions, et de ne point éxécuter ceux que nous pourrons recevoir pour des envois d'objets de France en retour de partie de leurs tabacs. De plus nous laisserons protester en y refusant notre acceptation toutes les traittes des Americains qui nous seront présentées de même pour avances sur de nouveaux chargemens de tabac et dont plusieurs nous sont annoncées.

Nous ne pourrons non plus nous dispenser de rendre compte de tout ceci au Ministre Americain et de remplir d'ailleurs toutes les formes qui seront les plus propres ici ou à l'Orient pour constater le refus que vous feriés des tabacs à établir les dommages resultants pour leurs proprietaires et la non-éxecution de la décision de Bernis, ainsi qu'à leur assurer leurs reccours pour les indemnités que très certainement ils se croiront très fondés à prétendre. A ces Indemnités ils joindront sans doute leurs reclammations de la perte de vingt pour cent que coutera aux tireurs des lettres protestées, selon les loix d'Amerique, le retour de leurs traites; un effet de 100£. de Capital protesté, obligeant chez eux à un remboursement de 120£.

Répondrés vous Messieurs que vous avés recu assés de tabacs des Negotiants Americains pour paroitre avoir satisfait à l'engagement d'une année? Mais vous n'ignorés pas Messieurs, que le commerce connoit très bien le détail de ces receptions? Au reste sans entrer dans ces détails, sans repéter notre juste surprise d'avoir vû recevoir au Havre, à Morlaix, à Bordeaux sans retard les tabacs arrivés jusqu'en Mai dernier pendant que vous refusiés encore les Cargaisons arrivées à l'Orient dés le mois d'octobre de l'année passée, sans examiner à quelle époque doivent commencer et finir les deux années ennoncées par la décision de Bernis votre engagement, en le suposant même accompli pour la première année, n'en subsiste pas moins d'une manière aussi pressante pour la seconde.

Nous ne présumons pas non plus que vous pussiés refuser les tabacs de l'Orient sous le pretexte d'atteindre ceux qui pourroient venir des autres ports. Car outre qu'ils viennent dans une beaucoup plus petite proportion en ces autres ports la décision de Bernis loin d'établir une distinction défavorable a celui de l'Orient vous a acordé une diminution de 30 sols par quintal de tabac qui n'arriveroit pas dans les Ports ou sont vos Manufactures; elle a ainsi prévenus les préferences desavantageuses aux Commerce que sans cette compensation votre interet eut pu vous porter à établir, et elle n'a

[80]

certainement pas entendu laisser rejetter des tabacs arrivés en faveur de tabas non-arrivés.

Comme le parti extrême que nous venons de vous exposer, Messieurs, aura certainement de très facheuses suites par l'éclat de mécontentement général qui s'élevera aux Etats-Unis, tant par l'inéxécution des ordres de marchandises en retour et le renvoi des vaisseaux a vuide, que par les embarras et la défiance produits dans le commerce par les protets et remboursemens des lettres de change et par les pertes que les Américains éprouveront sur leurs envois à raison des fraix, dechets, magazinages et Interets de fonds; Nous répugnons éxtrémement à une telle résolution, et ne pouvons nous résoudre à l'éxécuter sans vous mettre à même de la prevenir en vous en donnant connoissance.

Encore une fois Rappellés vous de grace Messieurs, les engagemens de la Ferme Générale; l'esprit et les intentions qui ont dirigé la décision de Bernis, ses éxpréssions même, la manière dont elle a été annoncée, la lettre du Ministre des Finances du 22. 8bre dernier au Ministre Americain. Veuillés vous représenter en conséquence combien le Gouvernement et le commerce ont dû s'attendre que vous attireriés sinon par des traitemens prévenans du moins par une éxacte et égale éxecution de vos Engagemens, les Navires et les Negotians des Etats-Unis. Enfin considerés la position de ceux qui ont envoyés leurs Navires et qui loin d'éprouver le traitement promis, voyent leurs fonds arretés et leurs cargaisons diminuées par les retards parmi lesquels d'autres verront encore leurs traites protestées détruire leur crédit et les surcharger d'un retrait de 20 pour cent. Trés certainement si un Particulier eut pris un engagement pareil à celui que vous avés contracté le commerce d'Amérique croiroit pouvoir faire retomber sur lui en France les pertes et indemnités causées par son inéxecution.

Nous ne pouvons croire que ces refléxions ne vous frappent, Messieurs, mais si cependant il en etoit autrement, Nous venons vous demander de vouloir bien nous marquer par écrit votre refus. Nous ne sommes en tout cecy que simples Commissionnaires des Propriétaires de tabac dont aucune Cargaison ne nous apartient. Nous sommes comptables de notre conduite, d'abord à ces Négotiants, et ensuite d'aprés leurs ordres à leur Ministre en France. Il faut que nous puissions leur prouver que si leurs tabacs ne sont pas vendus il n'y'a pas de notre faute; et que nous ne nous sommes décidés à laisser sans éxécution leurs ordres en Marchandises, et à laisser protester leurs traittes qu'aprés avoir infructueusement tenté auprés de vous toutes les démarches possibles pour vous engager a prendre leurs tabacs. Or nous croions que la copie de la présente lettre et votre refus par ecrit, si reellement vous y persistés, renfermeroit tout ce qui est nécessaire à notre justification.

Les Américains etoient bien loin de s'attendre au refus de leurs tabacs. Mais ils nous avoient prévenus de nous adresser à leur Ministre pour les petites contrariétés que nous pourrions eprouver dans le cours des livraisons. Nous n'avons pas voulu jusqu'à présent reclammer son intervention; mais actuellement nous serons forcés de lui rendre compte de la situation des choses et de la necessité ou nous sommes de prendre le parti que nous vous indiquons. Nous lui remmettrons en même tems les nottes des tabacs et les copies des factures et connoissemens et nous attendrons pour continuer ces operations qu'il ait pu obtenir un changement plus favorable aux Interets du Commerce.

Nous avons dû, Messieurs, vous prevenir des suites que va necessairement entrainer le refus des tabacs venus a L'Orient. Nous avons cru en nous expliquant ainsi, faire ce que nous prescrivoient l'honneteté et la considération que nous vous devons. Nous serions trés fachés que vous trouvassiés aucune autre disposition dans notre conduite. Mais il est telle position ou l'on n'a point le choix du parti à prendre, et vous trouverés certainement, Messieurs que nous sommes dans cette position. Nous désirons plus que toute autre chose que vous veuillés bien avoir égard à nos observations et donner ordre a M. Bard de recevoir nos tabacs. Nous vous prions d'etre persuadés des sentiments distingués de consideration avec lesquels Nous avons l'honneur d'être, Messieurs, Vos trés humbles et trés Obeissants Serviteurs

J. J. BÉRARD ET CIE. VERNES

Tr (DLC); evidently in the hand of Vernes.

II. Bérard's Observations on the Tobacco Trade

[ca. 3 September 1787]

Observations sur l'état actuel du Commerce du Tabac des Etats Unis avec La france.

On croit nécessaire de rapeller ce qui s'est passé depuis la paix, jusqu'au moment où la conduite de la ferme générale a obligé le ministère d'interposer son autorité, pour rassurer un commerce quelle éloignoit.

Les Tabacs étoient fort chers en 1782, ils se vendoient 75.^{tt} le Quintal et au delà. Dès le commencement de La paix la ferme générale crut pouvoir faire rapidement baisser les prix. Elle ne voulut payer que 45.^{tt} le Tabac de Virginie et 42.^{tt} pour Le Maryland avec 15. p%. de Tare.

Mais comme la guerre avoit détruit beaucoup de Tabacs et dérangé la culture, L'équilibre entre les besoins de l'Europe et les récoltes d'Amérique ne put être rétabli par la récolte de 1783. Le prix des Tabacs resta donc élevé en Angleterre et en Hollande jusqu'à La fin de 1784. au dessus du Taux de 45.^{tt} et 42.^{tt} fixé par la ferme.

Il vint en france peu de chargements dont plusieurs même furent réexpédiés à Londres ou à Amsterdam. La ferme générale ne fit rien pour rapeller les américains. Au lieu d'augmenter les prix jusqu'à un taux équivalent aux cours étrangers, Elle suppléa leurs tabacs par une très grande consommation de Tabacs de flandres, de Hollande et d'Alsace: elle y gagnoit beaucoup, par le bas prix de ces sortes de feuilles. Elle se trouva si bien d'une telle économie qu'en Juillet ou Août 1784, elle n'offrit plus que 40.^{tt} du Tabac Virginie et 38.^{tt} du Maryland: offres que peu de tems après elle baissa de 2.^{tt} par Quintal.

Les Américains s'étoient dégoutés de nos ports. La ferme générale étoit sans tabacs des états unis, ou étoit alors en Septembre 1784.

On se plaignoit généralement de l'infériorité du tabac débité par la ferme. En Bretagne particulierement la police fit vérifier la qualité de quelques Tabacs, qui furent brulés par son Ordre. La ferme craignit sans doute d'être obligée de rendre Compte de ses approvisionnements, et de laisser voir au ministère et au public qu'elle se trouvoit absolument dépourvuë de Tabacs des états unis.

Elle ordonna sur le Champ des achats de Tabacs en Angleterre et en Hollande qui remplirent ses premiers besoins. Les difficultés de Bretagne s'arrangerent.

A cette Epoque M. Robert morris avoit en france, ou en route pour y arriver, 2000. Boucauds de Tabacs d'une qualité si inférieure qu'ils étoient invendables partout aillieurs qu'en france. Il les fit offrir à la ferme générale à 36.^{tt} le Quintal, Tare réelle (Elle est d'environ 10 p.cent.) et proposa de fournir au même Taux 60. mille Boucauds en 3. ans.

On accepta les 2000. Boucauds et le Traité fut conclu à 36.^{tt} tare réelle: on preta un million de Livres tournois à M. Morris en avance sur ce traité.

Ces conditions égaloient, et passoient même 40.^{tt} Tare 15. p%, qu'on eut payées à d'autres particuliers sans avances et sans d'autres avantages accordés à M. Morris.

Elles étoient trop fortes pour un traité, qui devoit durer 3. ans: car la récolte de 1784, ou au moins celle de 1785, devoient rétablir l'Equilibre entre la culture et la consommation du Tabac, et ramener les anciens prix de paix. Mais la ferme n'eut pas la prévoyance de cette possibilité.

Cette révolution n'arriva pas en 1785. Les Tabacs furent encore assez chers en Amérique pendant cette année pour rendre le prix du traité peu avantageux à M. Morris; aussi n'expedia-t-il à la ferme que 4700. B[ouc]auds de Tabacs, au lieu de 20,000. B[ouc]auds à quoi il étoit engagé. La majeure partie même ne fut chargée qu'en Automne, lorsque l'assurance de la belle récolte de 1785. donna celle d'une baisse dans les prix d'Amérique.

Alors la ferme vit bien que M. Morris alloit éxécuter son traité. Elle voulut se dedommager avec les autres particuliers des conditions avantageuses accordées à ce Négotiant; la baisse des prix d'achat avoit attiré en france quelques cargaisons américaines, que les propriétaires avoient compté de vendre aux mêmes conditions accordées à M. Morris: Les fermiers généraux en refusoient l'achat au dessus des prix quelle fixoit tous les mois plus bas; d'abord 35.^{tt} puis 34.^{tt} puis 33.^{tt} pour Les premieres qualités: Elle a même profité des besoins de quelques vendeurs pour acheter au dessous de ce dernier prix.

Les Américains qui avoient crû trouver au moins le même prix que recevoit leur compatriote étoient fort rebutés d'une loi si dure et dont le terme n'étoit même point fixé. On annoncoit que la ferme vouloit réduire les prix des tabacs à 30.^{tt}

Plusieurs ne voulurent pas vendre; il s'accumula ainsi 6. à 7. mille Boucauds à l'orient, dont une partie fut par les besoins des Vendeurs, livrée au taux offert par la ferme.

Ce fut alors, au commencement de 1786, que le Commerce se plaignit au ministère.

Il representa que la Conduite de la ferme générale alloit écarter pour toujours les Américains; qu'on ne pouvoit les rassurer qu'en faisant cesser les retards et mauvais traitements dont on les accueilloit, à l'Orient surtout, Le port même qui avoit été affranchi pour eux et qui leur convenoit le plus.

Que les négocians des états unis étoient ulcérés de la différence que la ferme mettoit entr'eux et un de leurs compatriotes. Qu'au reste le Traité étoit contraire aux vrais principes du commerce, aux intérêts du royaume, à ceux de la ferme elle même. On trouva même que ce contrat étoit informe, sans réciprocité d'obligations, et nul par son essence et par sa forme.

Toutes ces choses furent amplement et longuement discutées devant le comité choisi à cet effet, et dans le quel se trouverent toujours appellés MM. Les fermiers généraux. Ils defendirent leur traité, mais sans succès. Les arrêtés du comité anéantirent ces défenses et consacrèrent en entier ces amères plaintes du Commerce.

Il falloit un nouvel ordre de choses. Ce même comité fut assemblé à Bernis le 24. may 1786. en présence de M. de Vergennes et du ministre des finances. Le premier, après avoir hautement désapprouvé la conduite de la ferme générale, ouvrit l'avis qu'on devoit mettre tous les négociants américains de Niveau avec M. Robert Morris; et si la ferme désiroit ne pas voir casser le traité, payer leurs tabacs au prix de ce traité. Elle s'obligea solemnellement à recevoir 15. mille Boucauds des autres particuliers par an, jusqu'à l'expiration du traité de M. Morris, et aux mêmes conditions.

Cette décision porta de plus que le traité ne seroit pas renouvellé. Elle fut ministériellement annoncé à son Exc. Mr. de Jefferson, et confirmée par la lettre que lui adressa M. de Calonne le 22. 8bre. 1786.

Mais comment a-t-elle été éxécutée?

Il faut rappeller les détails de cette décision.

Elle Ordonnait

1° Que le traité ne seroit plus renouvellé ni avec M. Morris, ni avec toute autre personne.

2° Que pour éviter un denuement de tabacs qui ramenat le pretexte d'un traité, la ferme en auroit constamment un approvisionnement suffisant.

3° Que la ferme s'engageoit à prendre des particuliers 12. à 15. mille Boucauds de Tabacs par an, jusqu'à l'Expiration du Traité du Sr. Morris, *aux mêmes prix et Conditions* Stipulés par ce traité.

4° Quand les Chargements ne seroient pas assortis selon le traité on payeroit

38.^{tt} du Quintal net. du Tabac James et York river

36.^{tt} du Tabac de Potoumack ou Rappahanock et autres crûs de Virginie.

34.^{tt} du Tabac de Maryland le tout:

1ere. qualité de chaque espèce propre pour france.

5.º En cas de difficultés sur les qualités, elles devoient être jugées par une commission sur des échantillons envoyés au Conseil:

6.º Il devoit être diminué 30.s par Quintal sur ces prix ci-dessus pour les tabacs Livrés ailleurs que dans les ports de manufacture, qui sont *Sette, Bordeaux, Morlaix, Dieppe* et le *Havre.*

7.º Qu'il Seroit donné communication aux Américains des articles ci-dessus convenus.

On a vû par le récit que nous venons de faire, que l'esprit et l'intention du prononcé de Bernis étoient de placer les Tabacs des particuliers éxactement dans la même position où se trouveroient ceux du traité. Les expressions de l'arte. 3e. ne laissoient à la ferme aucun doute sur ce point. Elle porte . . . *aux mêmes prix et conditions stipulés par le traité.*

Cependant et dans les *conditions* et dans *les prix* la ferme a blessé cette égalité qui lui étoit prescrite.

Quant aux Conditions

Vue des principales, qui tient le plus à cœur aux américains, et qui est le plus nécessaire pour les cultiver dans nos ports c'est que leurs Cargaisons soyent livrées à leur arrivée. Les Tabacs du Sr. Morris sont reçus dès qu'ils peuvent être déchargés, et entrent tout de suite dans les magazins de la ferme.

Elle a bien reçu sans de très longs retards les Tabacs arrivés dans les ports de Manufacture pour les particuliers; Mais elle a suivi une toute autre marche à Lorient qui reçoit seul plus de Tabacs que les autres ports ensemble.

En may 1786. époque de la décision, il y avoit à L'orient plus de 4000. B[ouc]auds invendus parceque la ferme n'offroit que 32. à 33.^{tt} pour le Virginie et 31 à 32.^{tt} du Maryland Tare 15. p%.

L'on attendoit environ 2400. B[ouc]auds.

Il sembloit qu'après la décision elle devoit donner Ordre de recevoir ces 6400. B[ouc]auds.

Elle en reçut 1500. en Juillet
           1500. en Août
et déclara qu'elle n'enprendroit plus de quelque temps.

II. BERARD'S OBSERVATIONS

Cependant un particulier lui ayant offert en septemb. de recevoir son payement à 3. mois de terme, au lieu d'un mois fixé ci devant, on prit ses tabacs sans examiner l'ordre de leur arrivée avec ceux des autres particuliers. Ceux ci se plaignirent; et enfin en 8bre. seulement, la ferme se décida à recevoir les tabacs arrivés jusqu'au 10. d'Octobre, à condition de payer aussi à 3. mois.

Cette livraison a duré jusqu'en février, la mauvaise saison l'ayant rendue difficile et chere dailleurs pour les Vendeurs et pour la ferme.

Depuis le mois d'Octobre, les américains ayant eu connoissance de la décision, ont envoyé environ 5000. Boucauds à L'Orient. La ferme générale n'en a encore voulu recevoir dans le mois de may que 1000. Boucauds payables, toujours à 3. mois. Elle a refusé le reste, sans même fixer de terme à ce refus, sous pretexte qu'elle a remplis et au dela ses engagements pris au Comité de Bernis.

Les Américains souffrent étrangement de ces delais inattendus, par le retard de leurs fonds, les frais de Magasinage et l'intérêt d'argent; ils accusent leurs correspondants de négligence. La confiance donnée par le Comité de Bernis se change en éloignement et défiance, et plusieurs expéditions ont été arrêtées par le retard des Comptes de Vente. Les frais seront encore augmentés, si l'on attend les jours courts et le mauvais temps pour recevoir ces tabacs.

Dans les ports de manufactures on a reçu les Tabacs particuliers peu après leur arrivée; mais c'est qu'il y en est venu fort peu. Les importations à Bordeaux montent à 1600. B[ouc]auds. de may 1786. à may 1787. A Morlaix elles ne vont qu'à 825. B[ouc]auds. Au Havre elles ne vont pas à 400. Boucauds.—Si l'on en retranche les Cargaisons venuës par Vaisseaux étrangers que proscrit La décision de Bernis.

L'on n'a pas encore les états de Sette et de Dieppe.

La prolongation du terme de payement à 3 mois, forme une différence de conditions entre M. Morris et les particuliers, très onereuse pour ceux ci. Il paroit que c'est réellement une véxation arbitraire, qui porte l'empreinte d'une lésinerie de principe, et au caractère de mauvaise volonté envers le Commerce, sans utilité pour les fermes généraux.

Le retard de deux mois sur le payement est très imposant pour les américains, surtout après en avoir éprouvé de beaucoup plus long pour les livraisons. Il devient au Contraire d'une très petite importance, et peut être même d'une importance absolument nulle

[87]

pour la ferme générale, qui est obligée d'avoir toujours dans sa Caisse de très gros fonds Lesquels ne rapportent pas d'Intérêt.

Elle a avancé un million sans Intérêts au S. Robert Morris; elle paye ses tabacs en papier à Usance à la livraison; pourquoi ne paye-t-elle les particuliers qu'à 3. Usances?

Evaluons en Argent la perte résultante pour les particuliers des différences de traitement ci dessus.

Un Boucaud de tabac coute au commerce
pour magazinage, par mois   £ — 10s. —
Le déchet sur le poid ne peut être estimé
moins de ½ p% par mois soit   1. 15. —
   (un Boucaud vaut environ 350.)
L'interêt des fonds pour un envois
coute aussi ½ p.cent.   1. 15. —
            _____

Perte par mois   £ 4. — —

Les 4000. Boucauds qui étoient à Lorient invendus en may 1786. arrivés dans les mois précédents depuis 7bre. 1785. n'ont été livrés l'un dans l'autre qu'en Août.

Le Retard commun peut être évalué depuis le mois de février 1786.—C'est jusqu'au mois d'août 6. mois à 4.^{tt} par Boucauds
               24,000^{tt} —

Les 5000 B[ouc]auds qui sont à lorient et qu'on offre à la ferme, arrivés depuis 8bre. 1786. ne pourront, si on les reçoit tout de suite, être livrés qu'en 3. mois; c'est à dire au mois d'Août pour terme moyen. Prenons le mois de mars pour le terme moyen de leur arriveé, le retard sera encore de 5. mois à 4.^{tt} par mois 5000. Boucauds.   20,000 —
            _____
           £ 44,000 —

Transport
La ferme a payé à 3. mois environ 4500. B[ouc]auds.
Livrés l'année derniere c'est 1.p%. ou   15,750 —
Elle éxige le même terme pour la suite, et
sure les 5000. B[ouc]auds actuel c'est encore
1.p%. ou   17,500 —
            _____
          £ 77,250 —

Ces divers Calculs qui sont au dessous de la réalité présentent une somme de £95250.—de perte effective.

Mais l'on ne peut assigner la perte qui résulte du retard de rentrées des fonds des négociants Américains, chez qui l'argent est très rare, et ne peut jamais être supplée par le Crédit.

Quant aux prix.

La ferme générale a acheté dans divers ports de manufacture à prix inférieurs au Traité, et ces Achats ne devront pas être comptés pour l'éxécution de la décision. Mais à Lorient qui plus recherché par les Américains semble avoir été pris en inimitié particulière par la ferme, elle a fait faire par son Directeur de telles diminutions de prix pour les diverses gradations de Qualité, que loin de rendre 34.^{tt} 10.s du Quintal, les Chargements souvent mieux assortis que ceux de M. Morris, ne rendent que de 33.^{tt} 10.s à 33.^{tt} 15.s. Cette différence est très forte parcequelle vient à la suite d'une diminution de 1.^{tt} 10.s par Quintal accordée par la décision.

Voici par quel moyen elle opere la diminution ci dessus.

Le Traité portoit que le Sr. Morris
Livreroit ses Cargaisons assorties de
 ¼. en James ou Yorck-River
 ½. en Virginie, de Potowmack ou Rappahanock
 ¼. en tabac de Maryland
 Le tout en premieres Qualités propres pour la france.

Or, ces premieres Qualités propres pour *La france* ne sont pas les premieres qualités des crûs. La ferme Generale n'ayant jamais consommé les premieres qualités des crûs, Le Commerce a pris l'habitude d'apeller *sortes francoises* les Qualités moyennes et inférieures des crûs: car les premieres Qualités de chaque crû, consommées en Hollande, en Angleterre et dans le Nord, se vendent bien plus cher que les prix que paye la ferme. Cependant en vertu du terme *1er. qualité* que renferme L'arte. 4e. de la décision ses agents ne mettent aux prix fixés que les premieres sortes des Crûs, et placent en 2de. et 3me. sorte les qualités moindres qui devroient cependant être reçues comme *1eres Qualités propres pour la ferme.*

Ainsi à L'orient la premiere sorte de James river est payée 36.^{tt}–10s. La seconde seulement 34.^{tt}–6s.

Ainsi la premiere sorte de Virginie est payée à 34.^{tt}–10s. La seconde seulement 33.^{tt}–6s. La 3me. 31.^{tt}–6s. Or, il y a Beaucoup de secondes sortes puisqu'on ne met que le très beau en premieres.

C'est ainsi que s'opere la différence de prix contraire au vœu de la décision. La ferme n'éxige pas les mêmes choses des tabacs de M. morris, qui, à moins d'une très grande infériorité de Qualité, ou d'avaries sont toujours reçus comme bien assortis et payés l'un dans l'autre à 36.^{tt}

Telle est la position de ce commerce. Il est evident que soit rancune, soit vuës particulières pour l'avenir, la ferme générale a pris à tâche de maltraiter et de dégouter les Américains, et de leur oter toute la Confiance que les dispositions du Ministère leur avoit inspirée.

Les retards surtout sont désolants pour Les négociants de cette Nation. La ferme les a portés au dernier periode; Elle refuse même d'en annoncer le terme. Elle se couvre de faux prétextes,—oppose le deffaut de magasins, d'argent, et l'éxécution, à ce qu'elle dit, complettement faite à ce jour de l'engagements pris au comité de Bernis: Elle veut faire commencer ces engagements qu'à la datte de La décision, ce qui jusqu'à la fin de 1787. ne leur donneroit qu'un an et demi pour durée au lieu de deux, et diminueroit d'un quart la quantité de 24. à 30. mille Boucauds quelle doit prendre.

En même temps cependant, elle veut faire entrer dans l'accomplissement de ses engagements les 4000. Boucauds de Tabac qui se trouvoient arrivés depuis longtems à L'orient avant la décision.

Cependant encore ses objections pour les tabacs au prix du traité ne subsistent plus pour des tabacs à bas prix. Elle a acheté au Havre des Tabacs venus sur Vaisseaux Anglois et impériaux parcequ'on les a donnés à bon marché: Elle fait offrir à Bordeaux de prendre à des prix inférieurs deux Cargaisons refusées à ceux de la décision.

Il n'est pas décent de supposer qu'une telle conduite soit l'effet d'un moment de mauvaise humeur contre le commerce d'un corps tel que la ferme générale ou doit lui donner plustôt pour motif un plan d'assurer le ministère à lui permettre un nouveau Traité.

Les négociants maltraités n'enverront plus de Tabacs en france. La ferme manquera d'approvisionnement: elle représentera que le commerce, auquel on s'étoit fié pour fournir aux besoins de La ferme, n'y a point pourvû, *malgré Les faveurs accordées*; que l'on va être obligé de recourir à l'Angleterre et à la Hollande et que pour éviter cette mesure il vaut mieux faire un nouveau traité.

Ce résultat est inévitable si l'on n'arrête pas sur le champ la marche qui le prépare: et ce doit être l'objet des démarches du ministre américain.

La Conduite de la ferme générale a été assez adroite. Comme il n'est pas arrivé beaucoup de tabacs dans les ports de manufacture, elle leur a fait moins éprouver de retards et de diminutions; sans doute pour éviter par là des plaintes trop nombreuses. Elle a porté toute son attention à Lorient qui est le port de Choix des Américains et où ils affluent davantage. Elle a reussi en partie à les détourner de nouveaux envoys. L'on peut montrer au ministre plusieurs lettres de maisons américaines qui L'annoncent.

MS (DLC); in clerk's hand; endorsed by TJ: "Berard."

III. Further Observations on the Tobacco Trade

[ca. Oct. 1787]

Oservations sur L'Etat des Tabacs d'Amérique, Achetés du Commerce à L'Orient, depuis le 1er. Janvier 1786 Jusqu'au 3 Septembre 1787.

L'Etat des Tabacs livrés à l'Orient depuis cette Epoque et paiés, suivant la décision de Berny, monte, en effet, à 8700 Boucauds environ. Tous ces Tabacs sont arrivés sur Navires français ou Américains, à l'exception de 5 à 600 Boucauds qui se trouvaient déjà à l'Orient lorsque la décision de Berny fut connue; par cette raison et que les chargements étaient pour Compte Américain, ils ont joui des prix convenus à Berny.

La vente de ces 8700 Boucauds a été faite aux prix suivants

Le James River divisé en trois Classes paié

$$36^{tt}\text{--}10/\ 34^{tt}\text{--}6/\ 33^{tt}\text{--}16/$$

Le Potoumak et Rapahanock . . idem . .

$$34^{tt}\text{--}10/\ 34^{tt}\text{--}2/\ 33^{tt}\text{--}10/$$

ditto de plus inférieur

$$31^{tt}\text{--}6/$$

Le Maryland en deux Classes $\quad 32^{tt}\text{--}10/\ 32.^{tt}$

Le tout a été livré à la tarre réelle que, d'après quelques épreuves faites, on a fixée à 102^{tt} par Boucaud.

La totalité des tabacs invendus éxistante à l'Orient peut s'élèver à 3700 Boucauds que la ferme refuse sèchement, sous prétexte que les prix sont beaucoup trop chers, que ses Magasins sont pleins et qu'elle a rempli l'engagement de la convention de Berny; mais dans le vrai, il parait qu'elle traiterait dans les prix de 30 à $31.^{tt}$ mais avec la tarre de 15 p% sur laquelle ils insistent.

Il peut y avoir d'invendu à Bordeaux env. 4000. Boucauds
au Havre   1000.   "
à Morlaix   150.   "
à Marseille   300.   "

5450. Boucauds

Mais tous ces Tabacs ne sont arrivés dans ces Ports que depuis Mai et Juin 1787, tandis que ceux à l'Orient y sont depuis Janvier jusqu'en mai dernier pour la majeure partie, et sont tous venus sur Navires Américains ou Français. Il y a eu trois autres chargements sous Pavillon Anglais contenant 991 Boucauds; mais ils n'y ont pas été déchargés et ont relevé pour Rotterdam et Londres.

Il sera donc de toute justice de demander que la ferme générale donne ordre à ses préposés d'acheter dans chaque Port les tabacs du Commerce par datte d'arrivée, et que dans ce moment elle commence par le Port où ses refus d'acheter depuis long-tems et sa conduitte véxatoire ont accumulé des tabacs depuis Janvier 1787. sur lesquels les propriétaires Américains éprouveront des pertes tant par les intérêts qu'ils païent sur les avances qu'ils ont reçu, que par le déchet de leurs tabacs, les Magasinages et surtout l'éloignement qui doit s'ensuivre pour de nouvelles opérations.

La Ferme prétend avoir rempli son engagement de Berni par l'achat du Commerce de 15000. Boucauds mais elle doit recevoir cette quantité chaque Année jusqu'à l'expiration du Contrat avec M. Moris, qui va jusqu'en Avril 1788: il faudrait donc, pour se dispenser de continuer ses Achats, qu'elle prouvat avoir acheté depuis le 1er. Juin 1786. aux conditions de la convention de Berny, 28000 Boucauds et tous venus sur Navires Français ou Américains. Or c'est ce qu'elle ne peut prouver. On lui prouvera au contraire que dans les achats qu'elle a fait faire particulièrement au Havre, à Dunkerque et à Morlaix: depuis cette même convention elle a acheté, depuis le moi de mai 1786 Jusqu'en mai 1787. 7871 Boucauds de tabacs venus sur Navires Anglais, à des prix et tarre de sa convenance et au dessous de la convention de Berni.

Donc 2712. Boucauds au Havre
1159.   ditto   à Morlaix
et 4000.   ditto   à Dunkerque

7871 Boucauds

d'une seule maison (Messieurs De Bagnes freres) cette dernière, il est vrai, avec l'Agrément de M. De Calonne; mais tous ces tabacs venus par Vaisseaux Anglais ou étrangers ne doivent pas être compris dans les 15000. Boucauds que la ferme s'est engagée d'acheter annuellement du Commerce particulier jusqu'à la fin du traité avec M. Morris.

Il est indispensable que la ferme s'explique sur les quantités de tabacs qu'elle compte encore recevoir du Commerce jusqu'á la fin du traité et le prix qu'elle compte etablir sur ceux qui arriveront après que le traité avec M. Morris sera terminé, et que par suite la convention de Berny n'aura plus d'Effet, afin que les Américains sachent d'avance sur quoi ils pourront compter pour regler leurs envois en conséquence.

MS (DLC); in clerk's hand. This document was probably prepared by Bérard and certainly was compiled after the first of October when the state of tobacco purchases by the farmers-general, covering the period 1 Jan. 1786 to 3 Sep. 1787, was made available to TJ (see note to TJ to Dupont, 6 Oct. 1787).

From Tench Coxe

[*Philadelphia, 3 Sep. 1787.* Recorded in SJL as received 13 Dec. 1787. Not found.]

From Fanny Delagarde

HONOURED SIR   Versills Sepepember 3th[1] 1787

I take the liberty to write to you, to beg the favour of you to send me if you have any opportunity to Boston those two letters, that I have took the liberty to send to you, as I have not heard any news this year from my famely, and the late fier that I have been informed has been in Boston of several hundred houses and many people also that makes me very anxcious about my friends and my not hearing makes me quit sure that somthing has happined sencn my departur from Amercai. If Mr. jefferson has heard in what part of Boston the fier took if you would be so Kind as send me a line to inform me you will do me the greatest pleasur. If Madam de lafayete had been in paris I should a beged her Sir, to have disired of you to send those letters for me but as not I hope youill be so good as to send them for me. My famely lost all their fourtain in the last war my father lost his welth and life and my mama has for her all a house and a litel land and six yong children to Bring

[93]

up and if she has lost her house out of five wee oned at Boston she is ruind. But I hope she is not in the number. I have felt the smarts of my not beeing rich sencn I am in france. Mrs. Delafayette informed you Sir of my unhappy selavation and my not haveing any fortain in amercai is the reson of my not returning back.

I am honoured sir with the greatest Respects your most obedent servant,
FANNY DELAGARDE

hotel Noaille rue de la pompe a versills

RC (MHi); endorsed: "Garde, Madme de la." Recorded in SJL as received 3 Sep. 1787. Enclosures not identified.

1 Originally dated "4th," then "4" was changed to "3."

To Fanny Delagarde

MADAM
Paris Sep. 3. 1787.

I this moment receive your letter, inclosing those which you wish to have sent to America. I will put them under cover to the Delegates of Massachusets in Congress and will send them by the packet which sails the 25th. of this month, so that you may be assured of their going safe. A packet goes to New York from Havre every six weeks. Whenever you chuse to write to your friends therefore, send your letters to me and they shall be safely conveyed. In like manner if you will desire your friends to send letters for you to the Massachusets delegates in Congress, they can put them under cover to me, and you shall be sure to receive them. I well know Madame de la Fayette's friendship for you; but there will never be any occasion to trouble her for the conveiance of your letters, as I shall always be ready to receive them from yourself directly, and to convey them, or render you any other service I can.

The fire in Boston happened on the 27th. of April. It broke out in a malt house belonging to William Patten near the Liberty pole at the South end of the town. The wind was at North East and blew the sparks to the spire of Wight's meeting house (fifty rods from where the fire began) which was consumed, and from which it spread twenty rods wide and went on in the direction of the wind across the main street, destroying the buildings on one side from Mr. Knapp's to Mr. Bradford's, and on the other from Mr. Inches to Mr. Osborne's, about a hundred buildings in all. No lives were lost. I shall sincerely rejoice if you find that your friends were not of that quarter of the town, and that this imperfect description of the fire may relieve your mind from anxiety on their account: being with every possible wish for your happiness, Madam your most obedient and most humble servant,

TH: JEFFERSON

PrC (DLC).

To R. & A. Garvey

GENTLEMEN   Paris Sep. 3. 1787.

I have this day received from the Douane the box with the copying press you were so kind as to forward to me from Mr. Woodmason of London. I take the first moment therefore to inclose to you the Acquit a caution No. 94. which you were so kind as to enter into for me. I inclose at the same time a bill of lading for the harpsichord I took the liberty of having addressed to your care. I had before forwarded to you the passport, and wished you to send it up by water. Your disbursements for freight and other purposes shall be paid to your order on sight. I have troubled you with so many letters on affairs which did not concern you that their postage must by this time have become an object. If you will be so good as to add the amount of it to your bill on me, I shall reimburse it with pleasure, and gratitude, no matter whether you can state it exactly, if you can conjecture nearly what it was, making the amount fully sufficient to cover what you may have paid. I am, with constant thanks for your attentions, Gentlemen your most obedient & most humble servant,

TH: JEFFERSON

PrC (DLC). Enclosures not found.

From John Paul Jones

SIR   New-York Septr. 4th. 1787.

Some time after your departure for the South of France I set out to go to Copenhagen; expecting to receive, at Bruxelles, the necessary Funds for my Journey and transactions in the North. I had the mortification to be disappointed; which induced me to turn about and embark in the Packet at Havre de Grace, as the method the most sure and expeditious to procure the necessary supply. I should have returned by the July Packet, but was unexpectedly detained by the Treasury; and notwithstanding my continual pressing application since that time the Board has not yet reported to Congress on my Business done with the Court of France. There is no Congress at this moment; but as the grand Convention is expected to rise about the 20th. there is little doubt but that Congress will be full soon afterwards. The Board, I understand, is now ready to report. I expect to obtain from Congress a Letter of Thanks to the King, for the Force he put under my command, and supported under the Flag of the United-States, and my Promotion has been talked of to be dated from the day I took the Serapis. I am much obliged to you for the Letter from Madame T——— which you forwarded by the June Packet. I now take the liberty to enclose a Letter for that worthy Lady; and as I had not the happiness to introduce you to her, (because I wished her Fortune to have been previously established) I shall now tell you *in Confidence* that she is the Daughter of the late King and of a Lady of Quality, on whom his Majesty bestowed a very large Fortune on her Daughter's account. Unfortunately the Father Died while the Daughter (his great favorite) was very young; and the Mother has never since shewn her either Justice or natural Affection. She was long the silent Victim of that injustice; but I had the pleasure to be instrumental in putting her in a fair way to obtain redress. His present Majesty received her last year with great kindness. He gave her afterwards several particular audiences, and said he charged himself with her Fortune. Some things were, as I have understood, fixed on, that depended solely on the King; and he said he would dictate the Justice to be rendered by the Mother. But the Letter you sent me, left the feeling Author all in Tears! Her Friend, Her Protectoress, Her introductoress to the King, was suddenly Dead! She was in dispair! She lost more than a Mother! A loss, indeed, that nothing can repair; for Fortune and Favor are never to be compared to tried Friendship. I hope, however, she has gone to visit the King in July, agreeable to his appointment given her in the Month of March. I am persuaded that he would receive her with additional kindness, and that her loss would, in his Mind, be a new claim to his protection; especially as he well knows and has acknowlidged her superiour Merit and just pretentions. As I feel the greatest concern for the situation of this worthy Lady, you will render me a great favor by writing her a Note *requesting her to call on you, as you have something to communicate from me.* When she comes, be so good as to deliver her the within Letter, and shew her this; that she may see, both my confidence in you and my advice to her. The lateness of the Season will oblige me to seek a Passage as directly as Possible for Copenhagen, where I pray you to write me (Poste Restante) or by the Courier of the Count de Montmorin, aux soins de Monsieur le Baron de La Houze. I am, with the highest esteem, Sir, Your most Obedient and most humble Servant,

J Paul Jones

RC (MdAN); at head of text: "*Private*"; endorsed. Recorded in SJL as received 13 Oct. 1787. Enclosure: John Paul Jones to Mme. T. Townsend, 4 Sep. 1787, which reads: "No language can convey to my fair mourner the tender sorrow I feel on her account! The loss of our worthy friend is indeed a fatal stroke! It is an irreparable misfortune which can only be alleviated by this one reflection, that it is the will of God, whose providence has, I hope, other blessings in store for us. She was a tried friend, and more than a mother to you! She would have been a mother to me also had she lived. We have lost her! Let us cherish her memory, and send up grateful thanks to the Almighty that we once had such a friend. I cannot but flatter myself that you have yourself gone to the king in July as he had appointed. I am sure your loss will be a new inducement for him to protect you, and render you justice. He will hear you, I am sure; and you may safely unbosom yourself to him, and ask his advice, which cannot but be flattering to him to give you. Tell him you must look on him as your father and protector. If it were necessary, I think, too, that the Count d'A[rtois] his brother, would, on your personal application, render you good offices by speaking in your favour. I should like it better, however, if you can do without him. Mr. Jefferson will show you my letter of this date to him. You will see by it how disgracefully I have been detained here by the board of treasury. It is impossible for me to stir from this place till I obtain their settlement on the business I have already performed; and as the season is already far advanced, I expect to be ordered to embark directly for the place of my destination in the north.

Mr. Jefferson will forward me your letters. I am almost without money, and much puzzled to obtain a supply. I have written to Dr. Bancroft to endeavour to assist me. I mention this with infinite regret, and for no other reason than because it is impossible for me to transmit you a supply under my present circumstances. This is my fifth letter to you since I left Paris. The two last were from France, and I sent them by duplicates. But you say nothing of having received any letters from me! Summon, my dear friend, all your resolution! Exert yourself, and plead your own cause. You cannot fail of success; your cause would move a heart of flint! Present my best respects to your sister. You did not mention her in your letter; but I persuade myself she will continue her tender care of her sweet godson, and that you will cover him all over with kisses from me; they come warm to *you both* from the heart!" (This letter was among the personal papers of John Paul Jones which were sent to his family in Scotland after his death and were subsequently brought to America by his niece, Janette Taylor; their present whereabouts is unknown. The above text is taken from *Life and Correspondence of John Paul Jones*, Robert Sands, ed., New York, 1830, p. 373-4.)

THE LETTER FROM MADAME T——— WHICH YOU FORWARDED BY THE JUNE PACKET: This first mention to TJ of the mysterious "Madame T———," about whom Jones's biographers have made so many and so diverse conjectures, implies that it was she who took the initiative in informing TJ of the relationship which existed between herself and Jones. Whether Jones's rather detailed explanation of the lady's situation was occasioned by a desire to explain why he had not previously mentioned her or because he desired TJ's cooperation in her interest, he was, at least, willing to have TJ continue to act as intermediary. In that position, TJ wrote to Mme. Townsend the day after he received Jones's letter; Mme. Townsend replied when she returned from the country, signing her name "Townsend" in her first letter and "T. Townsend" in the next (see TJ to Mme. Townsend, 15 Oct., 6 and 7 Nov.; Mme. Townsend to TJ, 5, 7, and 13 Nov. 1787). This exchange of correspondence between TJ and "Madame T———" invalidates various conjectures that have been made about her identity; but her full name and identity and the information which Jones gave TJ about her cannot apparently be verified. A survey of the genealogies of the House of Bourbon which identify the illegitimate children of Louis XV does not disclose any facts which substantiate Mme. Townsend's claim. Henri Vrignault, in *Les Enfants de Louis XV. Descendance illégitime* (Paris, 1954), lists eleven "certain," five "prob-

able," and four "possible" illegitimate children of Louis XV, none of whom seems to relate to Mme. Townsend. Whatever her background or identity, it is possible that she had manufactured a story by which she hoped, through Jones's influence in court circles, to profit. In any case, Jones's last mention of her to TJ throws some doubt on her integrity: "I pray you to inform me, if you possibly can, what is become of Mrs. T———. I am astonished to have heard nothing from her since I left Paris. . . . You must know, that besides my own purse, which was very considerable, I was good-natured, or, if you please, foolish enough to borrow for her, four thousand four hundred livres. . . . When that affair is cleared up, I shall be better able to judge of the rest" (Jones to TJ, 29 Aug./9 Sep. 1788). The reference to the "sweet godson" of the sister of Madame Townsend in Jones's letter to the latter of 4 Sep. 1787 has led some scholars to suppose that Madame Townsend bore Jones a son—a plausible supposition in the context in which the allusion was made.

From C. W. F. Dumas

The Hague, 5 Sep. 1787. Thanks TJ for the information in his letter of 9 Aug.; asks to be informed when news arrives from America concerning Congress, the Federal Convention, and the treasury department. Encloses a letter which contains all the information he has concerning affairs in The Netherlands.

RC (DLC); 2 p.; in French; endorsed. FC (Dumas Letter Book, Rijksarchief, The Hague; photostats in DLC). Recorded in SJL as received 9 Sep. 1787. Enclosure: Dumas to Jay, 5 Sep. 1787, giving an account of the political situation in Holland for the preceding two months, during which he had "had neither courage nor strength to write . . . any connected account of the state of things in this agitated country"; enclosing a copy of the declaration of

the "Provincial Assembly of the Corps of Armed Volunteers of Holland, held at Leyden . . . on the 4th of August, 1787"; again urging attention to arrearages due him; and stating that for his half year's salary due in Oct. he would soon be obliged to draw on the U.S. account in Amsterdam "unless I soon receive from Mr. Jefferson orders to draw upon him as formerly" (translations of letter and enclosure printed in *Dipl. Corr., 1783-89*, III, 582-9).

From John Adams

DEAR SIR   Grosvenor Square Sepr. 6 1787

I am Sorry to give you the trouble of this Commission: but I fear it will not be effectually done but by you, and therefore let me beg the favour of you to send for Mr. de La Blancherie and withdraw my Subscription to the Society of whose affairs he has the direction, and put a stop to his sending me the Nouvelles de la Republique des Lettres et Des Arts. He persuaded me at the Hague to Subscribe and I paid him a years Subscription. The society continued One year and then ceased and I thought I had done with it forever: but since I have been in England now and then a Bundle of those Gazettes are pourd in upon me. I have no use for them, and sometimes I am put to an enormous expence of Postage. I am now determined at all Events to put a stop to it forever and pray you to take Measures for that purpose by paying him off and taking his Receipt, and by delivering him the inclosed Letter which Contains a Renunciation of my Subscription.

With great Esteem I am &c. &c.

P.S. When I subscribed I understood it to be for one year only, and accordingly paid him the four Guineas. But I suppose he will now pretend that I am bound by that Subscription to pay for the Subsequent years. I will not dispute this with him, tho I am not bound in Law or Honour. One year the Society and Paper ceased since which it has been revived two years, or nearly so that he may pretend that I am eight Louis D'ors in Arrear. Pay him this if you please and no more, and I will repay you immediately. But at all Events I will be cleared from all Connection with this Man and his society and Nouvelles for the future.   J A

FC (MHi: AMT); in hand of Abigail Adams Smith. Recorded in SJL as received 23 Sep. 1787. Enclosure: Adams to La Blancherie, same date, asking that his subscription be cancelled, and adding: "His Excellency Mr Jefferson, will pay, the Arrears, if any are due from me, and take your Receipt, after which you will be pleased to cease sending me, that Paper, and to erase my Name from the List of Subscribers" (in Adams' hand, in DLC: TJ Papers; addressed by TJ: "A Monsieur Monsieur De La Blancherie Quai des Theatins No. 13.").

From William Carmichael

DEAR SIR   Madrid 6th Septr. 1787

I have, since I had the honor to address you by the last courier of the Cabinet from hence, made various Attempts to Induce the French Ambassador to explain how far he would cooperate with me to support the Claim of the State of S.C. for a recompence for the Services the Frigate of that State, commanded by Commodore Gillon, rendered to this Government, in the reduction of the

Bahama Islands. I find ultimately that he has no ministerial Instructions on the Subject and of course I must make my representations without any prospect of being supported except perhaps by his *personal* Interference. I shall therefore instantly address the Minister by reminding him of the Answer he gave to my sollicitations on this Subject in the month of October 1784, of which answer I have the honor to inclose you a copy and which I forwarded to Congress the 9th of Decr. the same year. After having put this business in what I thought a proper train; I cannot conceive the reason, why it has for so long a period been left unnoticed by Congress and the State of S.C., to the negotiation of the Delegates of which State, its interests, by the measures as you will see by his Excy. the Ct. de F. B. that I induced the court to take, were in some degree committed. I know that the finances of this court are in such a Situation, that there can be little expectation of a speedy decision of this Affair unless for *particular* reasons, the good will of that State at the present crisis may be desirable. I shall have the honor to inform you of my future proceedings and Intreat you to favor me with your sentiments thereon. I am informed that Spain has consented to pay 24000 Dollars to the Algerines for the restitution of the two Spanish vessels taken since the signature of the Treaty and that 700000 Dlls. are sent to complete the redemption of the Captives, which with other additional presents will procure a precarious peace. The actual appearance of Affairs in Europe gives much uneasiness here. Should a war be the consequence, this Country is ill prepared to take a part in it. I have no advice officially from America. The Perusal of a Foreign Ministers Letter from New York dated the 3d of July informs me that Congress was not then Assembled and of course will not Assemble till Late in Autumn. By this Letter it appears various conjectures were formed respecting the plans agitated by the Convention assembled at Philadelphia. Colonel Smith is I suppose at this period in London. I know generally that he had reason to be pleased with his recep[tion.] I have taken the Liberty of recommending Sir Alexander Monro late British Consul here and Mr. Bonelli who accompanies him to your Notice and for Many Reasons, I wish that these gentlemen should be distinguished by you. I beg you to excuse Innacuracies for I have had but short Notice and the Moment is at hand when I must despatch this and My other Letters.

I have the honor to be with great Esteem & Respect Your Excellencys Most Obedt. & Hble. Sevt,   WM. CARMICHAEL

RC (DLC). Recorded in SJL as received 16 Sep. 1787. Enclosure (DLC): Tr, in Carmichael's hand, of a letter in Spanish from Floridablanca to Carmichael, 16 Oct. 1784, stating that, having insufficient information on hand to judge the claim of South Carolina, he has, by order of the king, instructed Galvez, governor of Havana, to inform Gardoqui about the claim so that he may conduct the affair with the South Carolina delegates in Congress (translation printed in *Dipl. Corr.*, *1783-89*, III, 290-1; there is a PrC of Short's Tr of this enclosure in MHi).

From William Gordon

SIR   London Sepr. 6. 1787.

When last in town for a few days, I received your very obliging letter; and, notwithstanding my numerous engagements, should have given an immediate answer, had I not attended to some circumstances which rendered it unnecessary, upon observing that during the summer the readers are in the country, and being in no such forwardness as to admit of my going directly to the press, saw that I might safely delay till I returned, which was the last tuesday. Though you do not mention it, I flatter myself that your tour was equally safe and pleasant. No particular damage can arise from the papers having lain by till your return. I shall not begin to print till the end of the next month; when, health and strength permitting, I mean to continue it, till the whole work is finished, which will not be before March or April. You have done me great honor by entertaining so good an opinion of me, wish you may not be disappointed: but I shall endeavour to approve myself a faithful and impartial historian as far as my powers extend.

Am sorry that but few read English in France. Translations can seldom retain that pointedness which is to be met with in the original, through a difference in idiom, and the translator's not being equally master of both languages.

I embrace your offer with the warmest gratitude. In my situation such a gratuity is an object, more especially should the bookseller increase it proportionable to that number of volumes: but that is a matter which I shall readily submit to your judgment. In case of an agreement propose sending the three first volumes soon after the fourth goes to the press, that so the translator may get in the greater forwardness. Shall go again into the country on the morrow, and not return before the middle of October. Should you have any inducement to write sooner, let the letter be directed for me at Mr. Mollyner's Orange Street Red Lion Square. Request your mentioning the wanton damage done to your estate and property by Tarleton in order for insertion in its proper place.

[101]

Your condescension and friendship render me incapable of expressing how much I am Sir your most obedient humble servant,

WILLIAM GORDON

My most respectful compliments to the Marquis de la Fayette; have not yet received a line from him.

RC (DLC); endorsed. Recorded in SJL as received 11 Sep. 1787. TJ's VERY OBLIGING LETTER was that of 2 July 1787.

From James Madison

DEAR SIR   Philada. Sepr. 6. 1787.

My last was intended for the Augst. Packet and put into the hands of Commodore Paul Jones. Some disappointments prevented his going, and as he did not know but its contents might be unfit for the ordinary conveyance, he retained it. The precaution was unnecessary. For the same reason the delay has been of little consequence. The rule of secrecy in the Convention rendered that as it will this letter barren of those communications which might otherwise be made. As the Convention will shortly rise I should feel little scruple in disclosing what will be public here, before it could reach you, were it practicable for me to guard by Cypher against an intermediate discovery. But I am deprived of this resource by the shortness of the interval between the receipt of your letter of June 20. and the date of this. This is the first day[1] which has been free from Committee service both before and after the hours of the House, and the last that is allowed me by the time advertised for the sailing of the Packet.

The Convention consists now as it has generally done of Eleven States. There has been no intermission of its Sessions since a house was formed; except an interval of about ten days allowed a Committee appointed to detail the general propositions agreed on in the House. The term of its dissolution cannot be more than one or two weeks distant. A Government will probably be submitted to the *people*[2] *of* the *states* consisting of a [President][3] *cloathed* with *executive power*; a *Senate chosen* by the *Legislatures*,[4] and another *house chosen* by the *people of* the *states* jointly *possessing* the *legislative power* and a regular[5] *judiciary* establishment. The mode of constituting the *executive* is among the few points not yet finally settled. The *Senate* will consist of two *members* from each *State* and *appointed sexennially*: The other, of *members appointed bien-*

[102]

nially by the *people of* the *states* in proportion to their number. The Legislative power will *extend to taxation, trade* and sundry other general matters. The powers of Congress will be *distributed* according to their *nature among the several departments.* The States will be *restricted from paper money* and in a *few other instances.* These are *the outlines.* The extent of them may perhaps surprize you. I hazard an opinion nevertheless that the *plan should* it *be adopted* will neither effectually *answer* its *national object* nor prevent the local *mischiefs* which every where *excite disgusts* against the *state governments.* The grounds of this opinion will be the subject of a future letter.

I have written to a friend in Congress intimating in a covert manner the necessity of deciding and notifying the intentions of Congress with regard to their foreign Ministers after May next, and have dropped a hint on the communications of Dumas.

Congress have taken some measures for disposing of their public land, and have actually sold a considerable tract. Another bargain I learn is on foot for a further sale.

Nothing can exceed the universal anxiety for the event of the Meeting here. Reports and conjectures abound concerning the nature of the plan which is to be proposed. The public however is certainly in the dark with regard to it. The Convention is equally in the dark as to the reception which may be given to it on its publication. All the prepossessions are on the right side, but it may well be expected that certain characters will wage war against any reform[6] whatever. My own idea is that the public mind will now or in a very little time receive any thing that promises stability to the public Councils and security to private rights, and that no regard ought to be had to local prejudices or temporary considerations. If the present moment be lost it is hard to say what may be our fate.

Our information from Virginia is far from being agreeable. In many parts of the Country the drouth has been extremely injurious to the corn. I fear, tho' I have no certain information, that Orange and Albemarle share in the distress. The people also are said to be generally discontented. A paper emission is again a topic among them. So is an instalment of all debts in some places and the making property a tender in others. The taxes are another source of discontent. The weight of them is complained of, and the abuses in collecting them still more so. In several Counties the prisons and Court Houses and Clerks offices have been wilfully burnt. In Green Briar the course of Justice has been mutinously stopped, and associations entered into against the payment of taxes. No other County has yet followed the example. The approaching meeting of the Assembly will probably allay the discontents on one side by measures which will excite them on another.

Mr. Wythe has never returned to us. His lady whose illness carryed him away, died some time after he got home. The other deaths in Virga. are Col. A. Cary, and a few days ago, Mrs. Harrison, wife of Benjn. Harrison Junr. and sister of J. F. Mercer. Wishing you all happiness I remain Dear Sir Yrs. affecty.,

Js. MADISON Jr.

Give my best wishes to Mazzei. I have received his letter and book and will write by next packet to him. Dorhman is still in Va. Congress have done nothing further in his affair. I am not sure that 9 states have been assembled of late. At present it is doubtful whether there are seven.

RC (DLC: Madison Papers); partly in code; endorsed. Recorded in SJL as received 13 Dec. 1787.

[1] This word interlined in substitution for "meeting," deleted.
[2] This and subsequent words in italics are written in code, unless otherwise indicated, and were decoded interlineally by Madison late in life; his decoding has been verified by the editors, employing Code No. 9.
[3] Madison failed to encode the word "president," but, late in life, interlined this word in brackets.
[4] This word is not encoded and is underlined in MS.
[5] Madison wrote this word and then repeated it in code, but late in life failed to decode the repetition.
[6] At this point Madison first wrote and then deleted "effectual innovations."

From André Limozin

Le Havre, 7 Sep. 1787. Acknowledges letters of 31 Aug. and 2 Sep; asks permission to send the boxes of books for Richmond and Williamsburg to Philadelphia because the freight would be less than to ship to New York; is sorry the second letter did not arrive in time to carry out the instructions therein; the one large and three small boxes from New York and the box from Philadelphia had all been forwarded by wagon at the rate of 4^{tt} per 100; asks TJ to inform Luzerne that a pipe of Madeira wine which arrived for his account from Philadelphia has been forwarded by water.

RC (MHi); 4 p.; addressed; endorsed; postmarked. Recorded in SJL as received 9 Sep. 1787.

From Anthony Gerna

Paris, Friday [8 Sep. 1787]. Has arrived from Dublin and is charged by Mr. Vierya to deliver some books to TJ; will leave the next day at noon for Lyon on his journey to Leghorn; will return to Paris in six weeks; will execute any commissions given him.

RC (DLC); 1 p.; endorsed. Date supplied from TJ's letter to Anthony Vieyra, 10 Sep. 1787, 8 Sep. being the Friday before that date. Not recorded in SJL.

From John Jay

DR. SIR   New York 8th. September 1787

I had flattered myself that Chevalier Jones would have been prepared to go in the french Packet which is to sail the Day after Tomorrow, but certain Circumstances make it necessary for him to postpone his Departure to some future Opportunity. It seems also that Mr. Jarvis who had given me Notice of his Intention of taking his Passage in the Packet, finds it convenient to remain here until the first of next Month.

On the 24th. July last I had the Honor of writing you that further Dispatches on Subjects touched in your Letters should soon be transmitted, and I flatter myself that the Reasons which have hitherto delayed them will soon cease. Your Letters of the 4th. May and 21st. June have since arrived, and been communicated to the President of Congress. Since their Arrival a Quorum of the States has not been represented, so that as yet they have not been laid before Congress, and consequently have not given Occasion to any Acts or Instructions. I read them with Pleasure, for in my Opinion they do Honor to the Writer.

You will find herewith enclosed an Act of Congress of the 27th. July, containing the Instructions you requested respecting the Medals, and also a Copy of a Letter from me to the President of Congress, covering one I had received from the Governor of Rhode Island, respecting the Seizure and Condemnation of a Vessel of that State at Tobago. These Papers speak for themselves, and therefore do not require Explanation or Comments. The enclosed Letter for Mr. Pauly is from Genl. Varnum on that Subject.

The Convention will probably rise next Week, and their Proceedings will probably cause not only much Consideration, but also much Discussion, Debate, and perhaps Heat; for as docti indoctique scribimus, so docti indoctique disinterested Patriots and interested Politicians will sit in Council and in Judgment, both within and without Doors. There is nevertheless a Degree of Intelligence and Information in the Mass of our People, which affords much Room for Hope that by Degrees our Affairs will assume a more consistent and pleasing Aspect. For my own part, I have long found myself in an awkward Situation, seeing much to be done and enabled to do very little. All we can do is to persevere—if Good results our Labor will not be in vain, if not we shall have done our Duty, and that Reflection is valuable.

With the best Wishes for your Health and Happiness, and with very sincere Esteem and Regard, I am &c., JOHN JAY

FC (DNA: PCC, No. 121). Dft (NK-Iselin). Recorded in SJL as received 13 Oct. 1787. Enclosures: (1) Order of Congress accepting the report of Jay on that part of TJ's letter of 9 Jan. 1787 concerning medals, that it "would be proper to instruct Mr. Jefferson to present in the name of the United States one silver Medal of each denomination to every Monarch (except His Britannic Majesty) and to every Sovereign and independent State without exception in Europe and also to the Emperor of Morocco; that he also be instructed to send fifteen silver Medals of each set to Congress to be by them presented to the thirteen United States respectively and also to the Emperor of China with an explanation and a Letter and one to General Washington; that he also be instructed to present a copper Medal of each denomination to each of the most distinguished Universities except the British in Europe and also to Count de Rochambeau, to Count d'Estaing and to Count de Grasse. And lastly that he be instructed to send to Congress two hundred copper ones of each set together with the dies." (2) Copy of Jay's letter to Congress, 27 July 1787. (3) Copies of its enclosures: John Collins to Jay and the papers relating to the sloop *Sally* which was seized, condemned, and sold in Tobago in March 1787. Texts of enclosures are printed in JCC, XXXIII, 420-3.

To Montmorin

SIR   Paris Sep. 8. 1787.

I had the honor of addressing to your Excellency on the 3d. of July some observations on the letter of Monsieur de Calonnes of Octob. 22. 1786. relative to the commerce of France with the United States of America; of proposing to it some small amendments; and of expressing a wish that it might be put into such form as would secure it's execution. Monsieur de Villedeuil, then Comptroller general, was pleased to inform me that the Farmers general had received orders on the 1st. of April 1787. to conform themselves to the decisions notified in that letter, and that on the 5th. of the same month they had given orders not to levy 'sur les *huiles* et autres produits de la *peche Americaine* que les droits mentionnés dans la lettre.' This expression, restrained to the produce of the *fisheries*, with recent information received from the American agent at Havre, make me apprehensive that the antient duties are still demanded on all other objects and induce me to repeat to your Excellency my request that the letter of M. de

Calonnes may be put into such form as will ensure it's execution and stability.

In my letter of July 23. I took the liberty of proposing that timely measures might be adopted for encouraging the direct importation of the tobaccoes of the United States into this kingdom when the order of Bernis should be expired, and that in the mean time that order might be strictly executed. A great accumulation of tobaccoes in the sea-ports of France, and a refusal of the Farmers general to purchase any more, on the pretence that they have purchased the whole quantity required by government, excites discontent among the merchants. It is their opinion that the Farms have not complied with the order of Bernis. As the government was pleased to desire the publication of that order to induce the merchants to bring tobaccoes here, it would be very satisfactory to make known also the execution of that order. If the Farms can verify that they have strictly executed it, all discontents will cease, and the merchants become sensible that the present glut is occasioned by their importing too much. On the other hand, if it shall appear, from the list of purchases made by the farms, or from other evidence, that they have not purchased the whole quantity on the conditions prescribed by government, they will doubtless be instructed to do it, and that too without delay, as the duration of the contract of Mr. Morris, and of the order of Bernis founded on that will soon expire.

A parcel of gazettes and magazines sent to me from America, for my own use, and detained in the Syndic chamber, obliges me to trouble your Excellency for an order for their delivery.

I have the honor to be with sentiments of the most perfect esteem and respect Your Excellency's Most obedient & most humble servant, TH: JEFFERSON

PrC (DLC).

To Thomas Blake, Jr.

SIR   Paris Sep. 9. 1787.

Congress do not grant their sea letters for the East-Indies but to ships belonging to citizens of the united states, and navigated by officers and seamen of the United states. Even the cargo must also belong to their own citizens. Nor can these letters be obtained but on an application to Congress themselves, whereupon they appoint a committee of their own body to enquire into the circumstances relative to the vessel, cargo, and crew, and on their report of the fact they grant or refuse the passport.

I am with much respect Sir Your most obedient humble servant,

TH: JEFFERSON

PrC (DLC).

To Thomas Blanchard

SIR   Paris Sep. 9. 1787.

I am honoured with your favor of Aug. 13. and shall always be glad to render you any service I can in your commerce and to hear of your success. Supposing that it may be interesting to you to be well informed on the question of war and peace, I take the liberty of informing you that tho' the affairs of the Dutch had left hopes of accomodation, yet that the commencement of a war between the Turks and Russians, leaves now little hope of the continuance of peace. Such is the present state of Europe that a war begun in any part of it must extend over the whole. We may hope that the advanced season will prevent the other European powers from engaging till the ensuing spring: yet this cannot be depended on. I have the honor to be with much respect Sir Your most obedient humble servt.,   TH: JEFFERSON

PrC (DLC).
This letter was never delivered, for reasons set forth in Bondfield to TJ, 21 Sep. 1787. See also TJ's letters to Bondfield, Carnes, Limozin, and Loreilhe of this date in which he cautions them against indiscreet use of the information contained therein—a caution that he himself appears to have violated in the present letter to one who was, presumably, a stranger.

To John Bondfield

SIR   Paris Sep. 9. 1787.

The affairs of Holland, tho' at one moment they had threatened a war, had got again into a hopeful train of accomodation, when all of a sudden a war is kindled between the Russians and Turks. The latter have imprisoned the Russian Ambassador resident with them, which you know is their manner of declaring war; and tho no news of actual hostilities is yet arrived, every body considers them as inevitable. In the present state of Europe a spark dropped any where must kindle the whole. The only thing to be hoped is that the advance of the season may prevent the other powers from being drawn into the vortex of hostilities till the next spring. But this cannot be depended on. Government here would still wish for peace, and may see disagreeably the publication of any opinion unfriendly to their wish. I will beg of you therefore to make use of this for your own information only and that of the persons concerned in our commerce for your port. My duty leads me to the care of them, and my desire to give no offence makes me wish to give no further alarm. I make the same communication to the ports of Nantes, Lorient and Havre. I am with much esteem Sir your most obedient humble servt.,   TH: JEFFERSON

PrC (DLC). Although no enclosure is mentioned, this letter covered the preceding one to Blanchard (see Bondfield to TJ, 21 Sep. 1787).

To Burrill Carnes

SIR   Paris Sep. 9. 1787.

I am to thank you for the list of American ships inclosed in your favor of Aug. 23. and to desire your orders for the reimbursement of what it cost you.   The affairs of Holland which for some time had threatened a war, were in a promising course of negotiation, when suddenly a war is kindled between the Russians and Turks. The latter have imprisoned the Russian Ambassador resident with them, and I think there is no hope of preventing the war. In the present situation of Europe, a spark dropped any where must necessarily kindle the whole. The utmost that can be hoped is that the other powers of Europe may not be drawn into the vortex of hostilities till the ensuing spring. But this is not certain. As the desire of this government to continue the peace might render the publication of this opinion disagreeable to them, I wish you to make use of this only for the information of the persons concerned in the commerce of the United states from your port, my duty carrying me to the care of them, and my desire of doing nothing disagreeable to government preventing me from wishing this communication to go further. I am with much esteem, Sir, Your most obedient & most humble servt.,   TH: JEFFERSON

PrC (DLC).

[109]

To André Limozin

SIR   Paris Sep. 9. 1787.

Immediately on the receipt of your favor of the 31st. of August I waited on the person who is charged with the superintendance of the conduct of the farms, and informed him that the Custom house officers had required the antient duties on a cargo of pearlash arrived at Havre. He observed to me that the duties promised to be abolished by the king were only those due to himself or the farms; but that there were droits locaux, which he could not abolish; that the officers of the customs might have demanded the droits locaux, but that it was impossible they should have demanded any other duties. If they have done so, I will beg the favor of you to send me such evidence of the demand as will enable me to press a proper notice of the farms if they have failed to give orders, or a punishment of the officer if he has failed to obey them.

The box from Philadelphia, which you were so kind as to forward, is not yet come to my hands. I should be glad to know by what conveyance it was sent, that I may have necessary enquiries made from time to time.

No further changes in the government since my last. The office of Directeur du tresor royal was offered to M. de la Borde and refused by Him.—Had no accident intervened, I think the affairs of the Dutch would have been arranged without producing any war immediately. They are even at this moment in a train of negociation. But in the mean time a war has broke out between the Russians and Turks. We have no news yet of any action, but the Turks have imprisoned the Russian Ambassador at Constantinople, and no hope is entertained of preventing hostilities. Considering the situation of things in Europe, it seems inevitable that this fire must spread over the whole of it. The utmost that can be hoped in my opinion is that the season is so far advanced as that the other powers of Europe may not be drawn into the vortex of hostilities till the ensuing spring. The desire of government to prevent a war, might make it disagreeable to them to see this opinion published; I will pray you therefore to make use of it only for your own government, and that of the Americans concerned in commerce with your port. I shall make the same communication to our agents at Nantes and Bordeaux. I have the honour to be with much esteem, Sir, your most obedient & most humble servant,   TH: JEFFERSON

P.S. Just as I was going to seal this letter, I received yours of the 7th. instant. With respect to the two boxes of books for Williamsburg and Richmond, I would rather they should go to New York, because they will there be in the hands of a friend who will forward them very surely and without delay. I thank you for your care of the boxes of seeds &c. which you have forwarded. I have no doubt they will all come safe, and the information you now give of the conveiance by which they come answers that part of the present letter which asks for that information. I will give the notice you desire to the Chevalier de la Luzerne.

PrC (DLC).

To Zachariah Loreilhe

Sir   Paris Sep. 9. 1787.

The affairs of Holland, tho' they had at one moment threatened war, had lately got into a good train of accomodation. But a war is suddenly kindled between the Turks and Russians. The latter[1] have imprisoned the Russian Ambassador at Constantinople, which is their manner of declaring war. Such is the present state of Europe that a spark kindled any where must spread over the whole. Accordingly every one now considers a general war as inevitable. Perhaps the advance of the season may prevent the other powers from engaging till the spring. This government no doubt wishes for the continuance of peace and might view disagreeably any opinion unfriendly to their wish. For this reason I will desire you to make use of my information only for your own government and that of the persons of your port concerned in the commerce of the United states. My duty leads to the care of them; my desire of giving no offence induces me to wish to give the alarm no further. I have the honor to be with much esteem Sir Your most obedient humble servt.,   TH: JEFFERSON

PrC (DLC).   [1] Thus in MS.

From Abigail Adams

Dear Sir   London Septr. 10th

Your obliging favours of july and August came safe to Hand. The first was brought during my absence on an excursion into the

[111]

Country. I was very happy to find by it, that you had received your daughter safe, and that the dear Girl was contented. I never felt so attached to a child in my Life on so short an acquaintance. Tis rare to find one possessd of so strong and lively a sensibility. I hope she will not lose her fine spirits within the walls of a convent, to which I own I have many, perhaps false prejudices.

Mr. Appleton deliverd my Lace and gloves safe. Be so good as to let petit know that I am perfectly satisfied with them. Col. Smith has paid me the balance [which] you say was due to me, and I take your word for it, but [I do] not know how. The Bill which was accepted by Mr. Adams [in] the absence of Col. Smith, I knew would become due, in our absence, and before we could receive your orders. The money was left with Brisler our Servant, who paid it when it was presented. On our return we found the Bill which you had drawn on Mr. Tessier, but upon presenting it he refused to pay it, as he had not received any letter of advise tho it was then more than a month from its date, but he wrote immediatly to Mr. Grand, and by return of the next post, paid it.

With regard to your Harpsicord, Col. Smith who is now returnd, will take measures to have it sent to you. I went once to Mr. Kirkmans to inquire if it was ready. The replie was, that it should be ready in a few days, but [that he had] no orders further than to report when it [was done. I told him] to write you, but he seemd to think he had done all [that was] required of him. The Canister addrest to Mr. Drayton [was] delivered to Mr. Hayward with special directions, and he assured me he would not fail to deliver it.

The ferment and commotions in Massachusetts has brought upon the surface abundance of Rubbish; but still there is some sterling metal in the political crusible. The vote which was carried against an emission of paper money by a large majority in the House, shews that they have a sense of justice; which I hope will prevail in every department of the State. I send a few of our News papers, some of which contain sensible speculations.

To what do all the political motions tend which are agitating France Holland and Germany? Will Liberty finally gain the ascendency, or arbitrary power strike her dead.

Is the report true that is circulated here, that Mr. Littlepage has a commission from the King of poland to his most Christian Majesty?!

We have not any thing from Mr. Jay later than 4th of july. There was not any congress then, or expected to be any untill the convention rises at Philadelphia.

Col. Smith I presume will write you all the politicks of the Courts he has visited, and I will not detain you longer than to assure you that I am at all times Your Friend and Humble Servant,

A A

RC (DLC); endorsed: "Adams Mrs." Recorded in SJL as received 23 Sep. 1787. No enclosure is mentioned, but the present letter covered one from Mrs. Adams to Mary Jefferson, which has not been found (see TJ to Mrs. Adams, 4 Oct. 1787).

From William Duer

[New York], 10 Sep. 1787. Asks TJ to forward an enclosure which missed the British packet.

RC (MHi); 2 p.; signed by Duer as secretary of the "Board of Treasury." Recorded in SJL as received 15 Oct. 1787. Enclosure not identified.

To C. W. F. Dumas

SIR   Paris Sep. 10. 1787.

I am honoured with your favor of the 5th. instant and will forward the letter to Mr. Jay by the packet boat which sails the 25th. of this month. I am sorry for the situation in which Mr. Grand's refusal to make further advances has placed you. I know it's pain, because I participate of it.   The aspect of your public affairs has also been discouraging. Perhaps the war kindled between Russia and Turkey may engage your friends of necessity in measures they wished to avoid, and may ultimately relieve you.

Our Federal convention is likely to sit till October. There is a general disposition through the states to adopt what they shall propose, and we may be assured their propositions will be wise, as a more able assembly never sat in America. Happy for us, that when we find our constitutions defective and insufficient to secure the happiness of our people, we can assemble with all the coolness of philosophers and set it to rights, while every other nation on earth must have recourse to arms to amend or to restore their constitutions. The sale of our Western lands begins this month. I hope from this measure a very speedy reduction of our national debt: it can only be applied to pay off the principal, being irrevocably made a sinking fund for that purpose. I have the honor to be with much esteem and respect Sir your most obedient & most humble servt.,   TH: JEFFERSON

RC (PHi); addressed and endorsed. PrC (DLC).

To John van Heukelom & Son

GENTLEMEN   Paris Sep. 10. 1787.

The purpose of the present is to acknowlege the receipt of your letter of March 1786. and to assure you that it never came to my hands till last night. You will probably have thought me guilty of a neglect of which I beg you to be assured I am incapable towards you.—Probably by this time you have arranged your matter with Mr. Barclay. He is gone to America with the express view of selling his property and making good his engagements. It was the best step he could take for himself and his creditors. From what I have heard of his debts and of his property, I think there is no danger of any body losing by him. I was not acquainted with Mr. Barclay till I came to Europe, but have had much acquaintance with him since that. His embarrassments may have compelled him to disappoint his creditors, but I believe him as honest a man as can be. I am persuaded he will do for you every thing possible, and that for that purpose nothing more will be necessary than to address a letter to him at Philadelphia, unless you have already done it. I have the honor to be with much respect Gentlemen your most obedient humble servant,

TH: JEFFERSON

PrC (MoSHi).

To Jonathan Jones

SIR   Paris Sep. 10. 1787.

I am to acknolege the receipt of your favor of Aug. 25. covering the memoire to the Comptroller general. I am doing every thing in my power on that business; tho' I do not promise myself great success. The new Comptroller general, Monsr. Lambert is put in possession of what has been done and promised hitherto. The unsettled state of things is a difficulty the more added to those which had before embarrassed our measures. If nothing is obtained, it shall not be my fault. I have the honour to be with much respect Sir Your most obedient & most humble servt.,

TH: JEFFERSON

PrC (DLC).

To Robert Montgomery

SIR   Paris Sep. 10. 1787.

I am honoured with your letter of August 25, and think that a letter addressed to Mr. Jay on the subject of the consulate at your port will suffice. If you have already written to him, nothing more will be necessary.   I really deplore the situation of our prisoners at Algiers. If they could have been redeemed at the prices formerly paid by the nations of Europe, I think it probable they would have been redeemed: but beyond this I understand our people are not disposed to go lest it should make it too much the interest of the Pyratical states to cruize in quest of American vessels. So that on the whole it appears doubtful whether they will redeem the prisoners now in captivity at Algiers, and certain they will never redeem any taken afterwards.

I am with much respect Sir Your most obedient & most humble servt.,   TH: JEFFERSON

PrC (DLC).

To John Stockdale

SIR   Paris Sep. 10. 1787.

Perceiving by your favor of Aug. 31. that the 1st. vol. of le Petit Grandison has miscarried I went to the bookseller's and have got it supplied. You will receive therefore with this letter the 1st. and 3d. vols. of le Petit Grandison, and the 10th. of the Friend of youth, which are the last. What comes out hereafter shall be forwarded as soon as it appears.—You may remember that some numbers of Andrews's history, which you sent me, miscarried, a year or 18. months ago. My servants found them lately at the Syndic chambers. You had sent them by some traveller, I suppose. They had been sent at the barrier of Paris (where the baggage of travellers is searched) to the Syndic chamber, according to rule. The person gave me no notice of it. You, trusting to him, had not written to me. And thus they had escaped. When I was in England you replaced them to me. I therefore now send them to you, to wit, Nos. 4. 6. 7. 8. 9. I suppose No. 5. has been lost at the Syndic chamber.—I shall be glad if you will keep in view the 'Remarks on the taxation of free states.'—On your informing me you should decline sending any copies of the 'Notes on Virginia' to America I sent 40. which remained of the original edition, to Richmond. I am morally sure it had not been printed in America so late as July, and equally so that some copies would sell in Boston, N. York, Philadelphia and Baltimore. I am with much esteem, Sir, your very humble servt., TH: JEFFERSON

P.S. Would you take the trouble for me to send and ask of Lackington whether he has not lately published a catalogue of [books]? He has sent me no copy.

PrC (DLC).

To Vaudreuil

à Paris ce 10me Sept. 1787.

Je viens de reçevoir, Monsr. le Marquis, la lettre que vous m'avez fait l'honneur de m'ecrire, avec les papiers relatives à la reclamation de l'heritage d'Antoine Monset, mort à Portsmouth dans la Nouvelle Angleterre. Je me charge très volontier de les faire passer à Portsmouth, de les adresser à Monsieur Langdon ancien President de cet etat, qui est de mes amis, et de le prier de faire ce qui pourroit etre le mieux pour en faire le recouvrement. Je serois charmé si je pourrois etre utile aux honnetes gens dont vous daignez proteger l'interet, et d'autant plus que ce me donnera l'occasion de faire ce qui vous sera agreable, et de vous donner des preuves de l'attachement et des sentiments de respect avec lesquels j'ai l'honneur d'etre, Monsieur le Marquis votre tres humble et tres obeissant serviteur, TH: JEFFERSON

PrC (DLC).

To Anthony Vieyra

SIR Paris Sep. 10. 1787.

I am to thank you for your letter of Aug. 15. and for the acquaintance of the person who was the bearer of it, and whom I shall engage to send me some books. I would gladly have served you in asking leave to make the dedication to the king of the article you desire but that it might appear an officious intrusion into the department of another. We are known to him only as charged with the affairs of our respective states, and this business would of course be naturally expected to pass thro' the hands of the British Ambassador here, or in his absence thro' the hands of Mr. Hales the minister for that country.

I have the honour to be with much respect Sir Your most obedient & most humble servant, TH: JEFFERSON

PrC (DLC).

From John Bondfield

SIR   Bordeaux 11 Sept. 1787.

The fermentation has spread from the Capital to the Provinces who in return furnish fresh heat to animate the Capital. Our Parlement is translated to an inland Town, their Arets and resolves as also them of other Parlements are pointed to Capital reforms, this parlement attack directly the illegality and undue presumption in administration Issueing of Lettres de Cachets in any case whatever, the Language of every Aret indicates a new and entire Change of Sentiments. Royalty is no longer the main spring. The People appear ripe to Espouse a new Doctrine, the eagerness of every Individual to purchase the Antiministerial publications as they appear are not less, if not more than ever appeard in America. The Assembly of the States are the General conclusions, but it is not pointed out the special Business to which they are to attend. It is therefore probable the States may be assembled, meet, and disolve, and the Nation remain in the same Lyberynth.

Europe appears preparing for revolution, a general Caos, without a permanent system Universally prevails, the New World has begun what the Old one may finish and posibly arrive earlier to a higher degre of perfection.

You receiv'd some Posts past a memorial from the Importers of Tobacco, who solicite your engaging Government to releive them of burthens, by changing hands. I have been attentive to our Imports and Exports. It is with regret I am obliged to observe to you that france is the Dupe of her political Indulgences. In the Article of Tobacco, of 18 millions the Amount of Mr. Morris's contract, 17 at least has served to pay England for imports to America of her Manufactures. The Exports from hence to the United States for three years past have not amounted to Three hundred Thousand Livres, how therefore can it equitably be expected that france can be brought to continue prices so much above the Standard of other

Nations as she has invariably done to engage commercial conections on liberal and equal correspondent terms. Trade will work its natural Channel. All attempts by indirect or corrupted measures (for I look upon Gouvernment encouragement a specie of Bribery) has no other influence than the momentary continuance of the Bounty. Protection and fredom is a very different case. France continueing her protection to a free Import and Export will give every Bias in her favor without any privation of her National Tresor and she appears at this day in colours that in lieu of soliciting an application to the injury of her revenu ought to draw from America every exertion to the releif of her wants. If by purchasing of Tobacco on the footing of other Nations, her Tobacco farm could be raised two Million ℔ annum, the difference would fall on the English and Scotch merchants of the 5000 hhds. now in this port. The proceeds of 4700 at least are to be remitted to England, not a single Cargoe is to be laid out in produce or Manufactures of the Country or to pay outstanding debts in france, nor is the Virginia planter anyways benifited the prices in Virginia being kept down by the Monopolizers. To correspond with this Kingdom, Virginia has taken of her Duties on french Wines and Brandys. These measures be assured will operate every commercial advantage and which are the sole Sacrifices Nations can mutually make. My Views may posibly be contracted, my sentiments differing, from the Subscribers to the memorial before you, I deferd writing you on the subject being unwilling to counteract private pursuits, but that my silence might not appear to spring from inattention I give you my Ideas on the Subject.

I could wish to see some regulations take place in the Consular department. The Limits of Mr. Barclays powers to me do not permit such exertions as I esteem essential to shew the real consiquence of American Trade. With due Respect I have the honor to be Sir Your most Obedient hble. Servant,

JOHN BONDFIELD

RC (DLC); endorsed. Recorded in SJL as received 15 Sep. 1787.

From Jean François Lesparat

[*Paris*] *11 Sep. 1787.* Sends a copy of his *Réflexions*; hopes the United States will avoid the abyss into which the principal powers of Europe have fallen because of their accumulation of a permanent debt; if the advice in his pamphlet will be of use to the citizens of the United States, as he hopes it will, now or later, be of use in France, his labors will not have been in vain.

RC (ViWC); 1 p.; in French. Recorded in SJL as received 11 Sep. 1787. Enclosure: *Réflexions sur la nécessité d'assurer l'amortissement des dettes de l'Etat, ainsi que les ressources nécessaires en temps de guerre; avec l'indica-* *tion des plus sûrs moyens d'y parvenir. Memoire expositif & justificatif des operations, procedes & formules proposés.* . . . (London [1787]; Sowerby, No. 2459).

From Bouébe

Paris, 12 Sep. 1787. Asks for an appointment to discuss a subject of interest to the United States which was first brought to the attention of Dr. Franklin by Vergennes.

RC (DLC); 2 p.; in French; endorsed. Recorded in SJL as received 12 Sep. 1787. See TJ to Bouébe, 2 Oct., and TJ to Jay, 8 Oct. 1787.

From Fanny Delagarde

HONOURED SIR   Versills Sep. the 13 1787

By the liberty you gave me I send you hear inclosed a letter that I have wrote to my mama to give her the conveyance of her letters to me as you was so kind as to offer me and mine to my friends. I beg Sir you will except my sinscer thanks for your goodness, and am very sincible of your kind wishis towards my wellfare. I was very happy to hear that the fire happened in the south end of the town for my famely lives near the mill Bridg and as the fire did not Extend to our Building I Can asur you sir that my mind is greatly relived from the greatest anxiety by the news you was so kind as to give me and wish to have been in paris been to thank you my self but sence I had the honour to hear from you I have had a fit of a fever that lasted me several days but am now quit well and Expect to return to paris at the later End of this month. I ricived a letter las week from Mrs. Delafayet. She was in parfect health. She has found great Benefit from the warters. She as you know sir has the greatest friendship for me and all her famely and wee are unhappy Enugh to be this three years in franc without my husband having any place. Wee Expected last july to have a place and at the moment that wee Expected to injoy it the king sold the hotel Bogion and that flung us again in our old grief, wee was allmost two years after getting the promis from Mr. Ctt. Dangivelr and wee had it and now wee are a waiting for som new thing to present and I am afraid that wee shall have none this winter. I hope Sir you enjoy your health. I am Sir your obedent Servant, FANNY DELAGARDE

RC (MHi); endorsed. Recorded in SJL as received 13 Sep. 1787.

From Boutin

Paris Le 14e. Septembre 1787

J'ay reçu, monsieur, en meme temps que Le Billet que vous m'avés fait L'honneur de m'Ecrire, votre Interessant ouvrage sur la virginie, Et La greine de Juniperus que vous avés eu L'Extreme Bonté de m'Envoyer. J'ay L'honneur de vous en faire mes plus sinceres Remerciments.

Je vais m'occuper de trouver Le ris sec de La cochinchine, s'il y en a a Paris, Et Je serois charmé de pouvoir contribuer au succes de vos recherches a cet Egard, ainsy qu'au But utile Et remply D'humanité qui vous engage a substituer cette plante a La culture du ris ordinaire si Funeste aux Pays qui La pratiquent.

Je desirerois fort, Monsieur, que vous voulussiés Bien me faire L'honneur de venir disner *Lundy prochain a ma maison de La rüe de clichy* avec M. Le comte Du moutier, Et quelques autres personnes dont quelques unes seront, a ce que J'espere, de votre connoissance. Je seray charmé de recevoir de votre part cette marque D'amitié, Et de vous y renouveller Les assurances de L'Inviolable Et respectueux attachement avec lequel J'ay L'honneur d'Estre, Monsieur, Votre tres humble Et tres obeïssant serviteur,

BOUTIN

RC (DLC); endorsed. Recorded in SJL as received 14 Sep. 1787.

The BILLET from TJ, here acknowledged, is missing and is not recorded in SJL. Boutin, who was "Trésorier Général de la Marine et des Colonies" (*Almanach Royal*, 1787, p. 569), possessed a cabinet of natural history and also one of the most famous gardens just outside the center of Paris: "Ce jardin, le premier de ce genre qui ait été fait à Paris, réunit des parties bien peignées à des promenades agrestes, où serpente une petite rivière et des ruisseaux qui en rendent la promenade délicieuse: un Pavillon quarré contient une belle statue de marbre blanc. . . . Auprès, et dans le voisinage des basse cours, est une

jolie petite Laiterie.—Le Cabinet d'Histoire naturelle de M. Boutin . . . consiste en une collection de Minéralogie, rassemblée avec goût, et disposée pour en faire un Cabinet d'Etude, plutôt qu'un objet de luxe, ce qui prouve suffisament les connoissances du Proprietaire.—Le Pavillon . . . est à l'extrémité de cette rue [rue de Clichy], à droite. Cet édifice à la Romaine, bâti au milieu d'un vaste jardin . . . est d'ordonnance ionique. Le porche, par lequel on arrive aux appartemens, d'où l'on jouit d'une vue très-agréable, est soutenu par quatre colonnes du même ordre, élevées sur un magnifique perron" (Thiéry, *Guides des Amateurs*, 1787, I, 140). It was a setting that TJ would have found congenial.

From Le Mesurier & Cie.

SIR   Le Havre 14th. September 1787

We have the honor to acquaint you that the Brig Jenny Captn. David Peoples arrived here with a Cargo of Two Hundred and Thirty five Hogsheads of Tobacco belonging to Messrs. Willing Morris & Swanwick of Philadelphia, which those gentlemen trusted would be sold to the Farmers General at the price which they had fixed for Tobaccos of the same quality; but after getting the quality ascertained by the Directors of the Manufactury here, and offering this Cargo at an inferior price, we find that the Company refused to take them. We now therefore take the liberty of applying to Your Excellency on behalf of the Owners of this Tobacco, persuaded that you will assist them in procuring a sale, which they flattered themselves would admit of no difficulty, and that you will induce the Farmers General to put themselves to a temporary inconvenience, rather than throw the exportation of Tobaccos from America into other channels, which must infallibly be the case if a ready Sale for them is not found here.

Besides these 235 Hhds., there are Four more belonging to the Captain and Mate of the Brig. Those have likewise been refused; but we hope the Company will take this trifling parcel, of no further consequence than as it belongs to an Individual who cannot afford to leave his venture behind him.

Mr. Stephen Cathalan, now at Paris, is desired by us to do for this Cargo as he is now doing for a larger quantity he has in his possession belonging to the same Owners, and he will no doubt consult Your Excellency upon what is most for Messrs. Willing Morris & Swanwick's interest.

We have the honor to be with great respect, Sir, Your Excellency's most obedient and most humble Servants,

HAV. LEMESURIER & COMP.

RC (ViWC); endorsed. Recorded in SJL as received 16 Sep. 1787.

To Francisco Chiappe

SIR   Paris September 15. 1787.

I have lately received from Mr. Jay, secretary for foreign affairs to the United states of America, [the inclosed letter from Congress to his majesty the emperor (whom god preserve) and their ratification of the treaty between his majesty (whom god preserve) and the United states; together with an instruction to forward them to you to be delivered into the hands of his majesty (whom god preserve.) I am at the same time to ask the favor of you to deliver the inclosed letter to Taher Ben Abdelhack Fennish.

Mr. Jay also informs me][1] that Congress had confirmed Mr. Barclay's appointment of yourself to be their Agent at Morocco, of Don Joseph Chiappi to be their Agent at Mogador, and Don Girolamo Chiappi to be their agent at Tangier, with which agents it was their desire that their ministers at Versailles and London should regularly correspond; that want of time prevented his having and sending to me the certified copies of these acts by that opportunity, but that he would do it by the next. It will be with singular pleasure that I shall be instrumental in forwarding to you these testimonies of the sense which Congress entertain of your personal[2] merit, and of your dispositions[3] to be useful to the citizens of America.

In the mean time I shall be very happy to receive from you such communications from time to time as may be interesting to either nation, and will avail myself of every occasion of making communications of the same nature to you, and of assuring you of those sentiments of esteem and respect with which I have the honour to be, Sir, Your most obedient and most humble servant,

TH: JEFFERSON

Minister plenipotentiary for the United states of America at the court of Versailles.

P.S. Our letters to each other had better be put under cover to Messrs. Cathalan merchants at Marseilles. Be so good as to inform me what address I should put on my letters to you.

PrC (DLC). Enclosures: (1) Congress to the Emperor of Morocco, 23 July 1787. (2) Ratification by Congress of the treaty with Morocco. (3) Jay to Taher Fennish, 24 July 1787. All of these were enclosed in Jay to TJ, 24 July 1787, q.v.

With the exception of that portion of the letter relating to the enclosures listed above, TJ sent almost identical letters to Girolamo and Giuseppe Chiappe on this date (PrC in DLC).

[1] The text in brackets (supplied) is included only in the letter to Francisco Chiappe; the rest of the text is almost identical, with the substitution of "yourself" for the name of the addressee in each case.

[2] The letters to Girolamo and Giuseppe Chiappe both read: "general."

[3] The letters to Girolamo and Giuseppe Chiappe both read: "particular dispositions."

From Malesherbes

à Versailles Le 15 7bre. 1787.

Je ne suis, Monsieur, presque Jamais à Paris. J'ai profité d'un seul Jour où J'y ai été pour aller vous faire mes remercimens de la prodigieuse quantité de Graines de Cedre rouge que vous m'avez envoyés, et Je n'ai pas été assez heureux pour vous trouver. J'espere être plus heureux la premiere fois que J'irai, mais Je ne veux pas attendre Jusques là à vous exprimer ma reconnoissance.

Ces Graines seront semées dans deux Jours en Pépiniere à côté d'un vaste Terrein de Sable noir très propre à la Végétation des Arbres verts, où on pourra en semer au moins une douzaine d'Arpens, ce qui revient à autant d'acres de votre Pays.

Je crois qu'il n'y aura nulle part en Europe d'aussi grande Plantation de cet arbre précieux.

Vous connoissez l'inviolable attachement avec lequel J'ai l'Honneur d'être, Monsieur, Votre très humble et très obéissant Serviteur,

MALESHERBES

RC (NNP); in a clerk's hand, signed by Malesherbes; endorsed. Recorded in SJL as received 17 Sep. 1787.

To Willink & Van Staphorst

GENTLEMEN   Paris Sep. 15. 1787.

During my absence from this place, on a journey of three or four months, the funds placed here by the Board of Treasury for support of the American legation at this court, and for other ordinary expences, became exhausted. It was not known to me till my return and I immediately gave notice to the Board of treasury. But as it would necessarily be three or four months before I could get an answer, and some money would be wanting in the mean time, I wrote to Mr. Adams to know whether I could venture to draw on the funds in Holland. He answered me in these words. 'I presume Messrs. Willinks and Van Staphorsts will honour your draughts for the purposes you mention, without any other interposition than your letter. But if they should make any difficulty, and it should be in my power to remove it, you may well suppose I shall not be wanting. To be explicit, I will either advise or order the money to be paid upon your draught as may be necessary.'   Before I draw however, in consequence of this advice from Mr. Adams, I

[123]

would wish to be assured from yourselves that my draughts will be honored. The first would be immediately for between 6. and 7000 livres, and afterwards about 5000. livres a month till I hear from the board of Treasury. Your answer by the first post will much oblige, Gentlemen, your most obedient and most humble servant, TH: JEFFERSON.

PrC (DLC).

From John Adams

DEAR SIR London Septr. 16, 1787

Give me Leave to introduce to you Mr. John Brown Cutting, who will need no other Recommendation, than his own Genius. Let me beg your acceptance, too of a Sett of my Defence &c. and let me know your Opinion of the Second volume, and whether it is worth my while to write a third upon Confederations &c. Yours most Sincerely, JOHN ADAMS

RC (DLC); endorsed. Recorded in SJL as received 23 Sep. 1787. MY DEFENCE &c.: See Adams to TJ, 25 Aug. 1787.

From Madame Plumard de Bellanger, with Enclosure

ce 16 septembre 1787

Voici Monsieur la lettre que j'ecris a Mr. Derieux, puisque vous voulés bien la mettre dans vos paquets pour lui faire tenir. Je lui marque que vous avés la bonté de répondre de ma sureté vis a vis des Négocians qui lui donneront l'argent que je lui destine: que c'est une somme de quinze mille livres qu'il touchera. Il convient Monsieur puisque vous voulés bien vous avancer ainsi pour que Mr. Derieux touche plutot, que je vous envoye un engagement par lequel je promets de vous remettre la ditte somme de quinze mille livres a la fin de Novembre de cette année. Cette promesse est cy jointe.

Je vous fais mille remerciemens Monsieur de ce que vous voulés bien vous interresser a mon malheureux Cousin. J'espère que vous voudrés bien le recommander a Mr. le Colonnel Nic Loüis [Nicholas Lewis] pour qu'il lui donne les conseils dont il a besoin pour tirer le meilleur parti de la somme que je lui envoye.

Vous avés eu bien beau tems pour retourner a Paris. Je desire qu'il soit tel encore assés de tems pour que vous reveniés a st Germain faire la partie de dés chés moi. J'ay étté enchantée des momens que vous avés bien voulu me donner.

J'ay l'honneur d'être Monsieur Votre tres humble et tres obeissante servante, PLUMARD BELLANGER

ENCLOSURE

Monsieur Jefferson voulant bien avoir la bonté de se charger de faire toucher a Monsr. Plumard Derieux mon Cousin actuellement en Virginie une somme de quinze mille livres que je veux lui faire passer

Je soussigné m'engage et promets de remettre a Monsieur Jefferson Ministre Plénipotentiaire des Etats Unis d'Amérique la ditte somme de quinze mille livres a la fin de Novembre pour être payées sur les traittes que fournira sur Monsieur Jefferson le dit sieur Derieux, lesquelles lettres aquittées me seront remises pour ma décharge envers Monsieur Jefferson. A St Germain ce 16 septembre 1787.

PLUMARD VE. BELLANGER, Conser. D Etat[1]

RC (DLC). Recorded in SJL as received 16 Sep. 1787. Enclosure (DLC). The letter from Mme. Bellanger to Derieux, also enclosed, has not been found.

[1] Both documents are in the same hand; Mme. Bellanger's husband had been a "Conseiller au Châtelet" (*Almanach Royal*, 1787, p. 402-5; TJ to Lewis, 17 Sep. 1787).

To J. P. P. Derieux

SIR   Paris Sep. 16, 1787.

I availed myself of the letter of June 1 with which you were pleased to honor me to wait on Madame Bellenger, and to begin an acquaintance which I have found perfectly agreeable, and the more so as it has enabled me to be useful to you. I found in her all the good dispositions possible towards you, but not seeing clearly in what way her bounties would relieve you. I made her sensible that by furnishing you with a sum of money to purchase half a dozen working negroes, with all the appendages necessary, it would be a most sensible assistance. I shewed her that this would require fifteen thousand livres. She had made up her mind for ten thousand, but in fine has authorised you in the inclosed letter to draw on her for fifteen thousand. That your draughts may command the best exchange I write the inclosed letter, to satisfy the merchants that they shall be secure in purchasing your bills. It will remain with you to determine whether you will lay out the whole sum in negroes, or partly in negroes, partly in a small peice of good land. You so well know the judgment and honesty of our worthy neighbor Colo. Nicholas Lewis, that you will not think his councils to be neglected in the disposal of this money. It was a considerable encouragement to Madame Bellenger, when I undertook to engage him to advise with you on this subject, and to avail you of the benefit of his experience. Madame Bellenger was so kind as to enter into some details on the disposition she intended to make of her estate after death. By this you will come in on that event for about twelve thousand guineas from her. She even supposed it possible she might be able to give you more. You will be too wise to count on this as a certainty, because there are so many accidents which might disappoint you, but I take the liberty to mention it to you merely to shew you how worthy the good dispositions of this lady are of being cultivated by you. Nothing shall be wanting on my part to encourage and increase them. I beg the favor of you to present me in the most friendly terms to Madame de Rieux, and to be assured of the sentiments of respect and esteem with which I have the honor to be Sir your most obedient and most humble servant, TH: JEFFERSON

PrC (DLC). Enclosures: (1) Mme. Bellanger to Derieux, not found. (2) TJ to Derieux, following.

To J. P. P. Derieux

SIR   Paris Sep. 16. 1787.

Madame de Bellanger having informed me that she has authorized you to draw on her for fifteen thousand livres Tournois, the purpose of the present letter is to assure those who may be disposed to purchase your bills to that amount that they will be certainly and punctually paid, and, as a further satisfaction to the purchaser, to authorize Colo. Nicholas Lewis to write my name on the back of the bills, which shall oblige me, as endorser, as effectually as if I had written it myself. The bills should be paiable at 30. days sight. Should a paiment in London instead of Paris enable you to obtain a more favorable exchange upon the whole, I will undertake to have the paiment made in London: but in that case you must allow about 15. days more for paiment and leave so much of the whole sum as will pay the difference of exchange. The merchants will be best able to inform you what the exchange between London and Paris shall be at the time. I have the honor to be with sentiments of the most perfect esteem and respect Sir your most obedient and most humble servant,

TH: JEFFERSON

PrC (DLC).

To George Wythe, with Enclosure

DEAR SIR   Paris Sep. 16. 1787.

I am now to acknowlege the receipt of your favors of Dec. 13. and 22. 1786. and of Jan. 1787. These should not have been so long unanswered, but that they arrived during my absence on a journey of between 3. and 4. months through the Southern parts of France and Northern of Italy. In the latter country my time allowed me to go no further than Turin, Milan, and Genoa; consequently I scarcely got into classical ground. I took with me some of the writings in which endeavors have been made to investigate the passage of Annibal over the Alps, and was just able to satisfy myself, from a view of the country, that the descriptions given of his march are not sufficiently particular to enable us at this day even to guess at his tract across the Alps. In architecture, painting, sculpture, I found much amusement; but more than all in their agriculture, many objects of which might be adopted with us to great advantage. I am persuaded there are many parts of our lower country where the olive tree might be raised, which is assuredly the richest gift of heaven. I can scarcely except bread. I see this tree supporting thousands in among the Alps where there is not soil enough to make bread for a single family. The caper too might be cultivated with us. The fig we do raise. I do not speak of the vine, because it is the parent of misery. Those who cultivate it are always poor, and he who would employ himself with us in the culture of corn, cotton &c. can procure in exchange for that much more wine, and better than he could raise by it's direct culture.—I sent you formerly copies of the documents on the Tagliaferro family which I had received from Mr. Fabroni. I now send the originals. I have procured for you a copy of Polybius, the best edition; but the best edition of Vitruvius, which is with the commentaries of Ficinus, is not to be got here. I have sent to Holland for it. In the mean time the Polybius comes in a box containing books for Peter Carr and for some of my friends in Williamsburg and it's vicinities. I have taken the liberty of addressing this box

[127]

to you. It goes to New York in the packet boat which carries this letter, and will be forwarded to you by water by Mr. Madison. It's freight to New York is paid here. The transportation from thence to Williamsburgh will be demanded of you, and shall stand as the equivalent to the cost of Polybius and Vitruvius if you please. The difference either way will not be worth the trouble of erecting and transmitting accounts. I send you herewith a state of the contents of the box, and for whom each article is. Among these are some as you will perceive, of which I ask your acceptance. It is a great comfort to me that while here I am able to furnish some amusement to my friends by sending them such productions of genius, antient and modern, as might otherwise escape them; and I hope they will permit me to avail myself of the occasion, while it lasts.— This world is going all to war. I hope ours will remain clear of it. It is already declared between the Turks and Russians, and considering the present situation of Holland, it cannot fail to spread itself all over Europe. Perhaps it may not be till the next spring that the other powers will be engaged in it; nor is it as yet clear how they will arrange themselves. I think it not impossible that France and the two empires may join against all the rest. The Patriotic party in Holland will be saved by this, and the Turks sacrificed. The only thing which can prevent the union of France and the two empires, is the difficulty of agreeing about the partition of the spoils. Constantinople is the key of Asia. Who shall have it is the question? I cannot help looking forward to the re-establishment of the Greeks as a people, and the language of Homer becoming again a living language as among possible events. You have now with you Mr. Paradise, who can tell you how easily the modern may be improved into the antient Greek.—You ask me in your letters what ameliorations I think necessary in our federal constitution. It is now too late to answer the question, and it would always have been presumption in me to have done it. Your own ideas and those of the great characters who were to be concerned with you in these discussions will give the law, as they ought to do, to us all. My own general idea was that the states should severally preserve their sovereignty in whatever concerns themselves alone, and that whatever may concern another state, or any foreign nation, should be made a part of the federal sovereignty. That the exercise of the federal sovereignty should be divided among three several bodies, legislative, executive, and judiciary as the state sovereignties are; and that some peaceable means should be continued for the federal head to enforce compliance on the part of the states.—I have reflected on your idea of wooden or ivory diagrams for the geometrical demonstrations. I should think wood as good as ivory; and that in this case it might add to the improvement of the young gentlemen, that they should make the figures themselves. Being furnished by a workman with a peice of vineer, no other tool than a penknife and a wooden rule would be necessary. Perhaps pasteboards, or common cards might be still more convenient. The difficulty is, how to reconcile figures which must have a very sensible breadth, to our ideas of a mathematical line, which, having neither breadth nor thickness, will revolt more at these than at simple lines drawn on paper or slate. If after reflecting on this proposition you would prefer having them made here, lay your commands on me and they shall be executed.

I return you a thousand thousand thanks for your goodness to my nephew. After my debt to you for whatever I am myself, it is increasing it too much to interest yourself for his future fortune. But I know that, to you, a consciousness of doing good is a luxury ineffable. You have enjoyed it already beyond all human measure, and that you may long live to enjoy it and to bless your country and friends is the sincere prayer of him who is with every possible sentiment of esteem and respect, dear Sir, your most obedient & most humble servant, TH: JEFFERSON

ENCLOSURE

Contents of the box marked G.W.

For Mr. Wythe.

Polybius. Gr. Lat. 3. vols. 8vo.
Coluthi raptus Helenae. 8vo.
Fabulae Homericae de Ulixe. 8vo.
Guys. voiage literaire en Grece. 4. v. 8vo.
Savary sur l'Egypte. 3. vols. 8vo.
Volney sur l'Egypte. 2. vols. 8vo.
Code de l'humanité. 13. vols. 4to.

For Peter Carr.

Diccionario de la lingua Castellana. fol.
Gronovii Flora Virginica. 4to.
Linnaei Systema naturae. 4. vols. 8vo.
    Philosophia Botanica. 8vo.
    Genera plantarum. 8vo.
    Species plantarum. 4. vols. 8vo.
    Mantissa plantarum. 8vo.

Millot. histoire ancienne 4. vols. 12mo.
             moderne. 5. vols. 12mo.
             de la France. 3. v. 12mo.
Codex pseudepigraphus veteris testamenti. Fabricii. 12 mo.
Codex apocryphus novi testamenti. Fabricii 12mo.

For Mr. Madison of the college.

Bibliotheque physico-œconomique 1786. 1787. 4. vols. 12mo.
Connoissance des tems. 1788. 1789. 2. vols. 8vo.
Chymie de Fourcroi. 4. vols. 8vo.
Dissertation de la Sauvagere.

For Mr. Page of Rosewell.

Bibliotheque physico-œconomique. 1786. 1787. 4. vols. 12mo.
Connoissance des tems. 1788. 1789. 2. vols. 8vo.
Dissertation de la Sauvagere. 8vo.
Troubles de l'Amerique par Soulés. 4 vols. 8vo.

A pair of reading glasses for Mr. Bellini.

10. copies of the Notes on Virginia for Mr. Wythe, P. Carr, Mr
Madison, Mr. Page, Mr. Bellini, Genl. Nelson, Mr. D. Jamieson, Colo
Innes, Colo. Richd. Cary of Warwick, and Colo. Wilson Miles Cary
37.[1] copies for such young gentlemen of the college as Mr. Wythe
from time to time shall think proper, taking one or more for the colleg
library.

RC (DLC). PrC (DLC). Enclosure
(PrC in DLC); there is also in MHi a
Dft in TJ's hand of all the books listed
here as being included in the box for
Wythe, together with the items in
the boxes for Alexander Donald and
James Madison (see letters to Donald
and Madison, 17 Sep. 1787); this agrees
in substance with the list here printed
and the items mentioned in the letters
to Donald and Madison, but varies in
spelling, order of titles, and names (see

note 1).

I NOW SEND THE ORIGINALS: thes
were doubtless included in the box o
books (see also Fabbroni to TJ, 2
July 1786; TJ to Wythe, 13 Aug
1786).

[1] Dft reads: "37 ⟨40⟩ do. to be give
to such young gentlemen of the Colleg
from time to time as Mr. Wythe sha
think proper, except one or more copie
as he pleases for the library."

To Thomas Barclay

DEAR SIR   Paris Sep. 17. 1787.

I have duly received your favor of July 30. covering Mr. Hunt
ington's papers on the subject of the claim for depreciation o
money advanced by him for some French prisoners. That the clain
is substantially just is certain, but at the same time it is one whicl
I cannot urge. You know it is established in practice with us no
to give an account once settled and discharged, merely on a clain
of depreciation. This is the answer I have been obliged to give t

the numberless applications made to me for French subjects for indemnification of losses sustained by depreciation in their transactions with the public or with individuals in America. If any thing can be done with it, it would only be in the way you suggest, to wit by a negotiation between Mr. Huntington and the French Consuls. I therefore return you the papers, and am with sentiments of sincere esteem and respect Dear Sir, Your most obedient & most humble servt., TH: JEFFERSON

PrC (DLC). The papers which were returned to Barclay in this letter have not been identified.

From Burrill Carnes

Tours, 17 Sep. 1787. Has communicated the information in TJ's letter of 9 Sep. only to those interested in U.S. commerce; asks to be informed how far America would be involved in the event of a general European war. Before leaving Nantes he forwarded the case containing the musket, bayonet, and sabre for the treasury commissioners to L'Orient to be shipped on the first vessel bound for New York or that vicinity; the ship he previously reported as bound from Nantes for Philadelphia is sailing, instead, for Virginia; will be glad to place any commissions TJ may have for that place in the hands of the captain of the vessel.

RC (DLC); 2 p.; endorsed. Recorded in SJL as received 20 Sep. 1787.

From Stephen Cathalan, Jr.

SIR   Paris 17th. 7ber. 12 O'Clock of the morning

The Estate of the Purchases of Tobacco is ready. I had it in my hands this morning for a moment, and has been Brought to the Commity of the Farmers, where they have sent it I believe to the Minister; it is inside exactly as you desire, but you will observe that it begins, the 1st. of January 1786 and the treaty of Berni is of the 24th. May. You will observe also, of the larger parcels bought at Lower Prices than the Treaty, of the Tare of 15 pr. ct.

Marseilles has furnished 3540 hogsd. in that Period; all the tobacco purchased in France before the 24th. May must be deducted, and the Tobacco bought since at an under Price or cannot be included, or they must pay the difference;

By what I have seen of the Purchases of Marseilles, I really believe the Estate is very accurate, and free of errors for the numbers and prices; but they have not fullfilled the conditions of the Treaty nor they will not continue to do so, if not forced.

It appears that their actual language is that this treaty being made under Calonne, being not their advantage to continue it, they have paid no regard to it, and are at liberty to Breake it.

If they can continue with impunity there is no further refflexion on the Subject.

Every day they receive lower offers from the northern Ports, their plan is to make any [none?] for Purchasing, and as the olders [holders?] want to make money of their cargoes, when their low proposals will agree with their rappacity, then perhaps they will buy.

It appears to me that if the Ministers will help you and the olders, some proper means could take place, which would be agreable to both parties, amicably.

I remain with respect Sir Your most obedient humble Servant,

STEPHEN CATHALAN Junr.

When you will have the estate in your Power if you find it convenient, we will together make on it our observations.

RC (DLC); addressed and endorsed. Recorded in SJL as received 17 Sep. 1787.

To Alexander Donald

DEAR SIR   Paris Sep. 17. 1787.

I had the honor of writing to you on the 28th. of July, when appearan[ces] rather threatened a war in Europe from the quarter of Holland. Since that the affairs of that country have continued to become more and more incapable of reconciliation. In the mean time a war has actually broken out between the Turks and Russians. It has been formally declared by the former against the latter, and accompanied by such circumstances as seem to render accomodation impossible. That this will become general, and will involve every power in Europe I think certain, or at least every one of note. Particularly it appears to me that France, the two Empires, Turkey, Prussia, England Spain and the United Netherlands will be engaged. How they will take sides is not yet known. Probably that will all be settled during the winter, and that it may be the Spring before the war becomes general. We I hope shall remain neuter. The only danger is that England by harrassing our merchant ships may oblige us to become parties. If we remain neutral our commerce must become considerable; and particularly the carrying business must fall principally into our hands. The West Indian islands of all the powers must be opened to us.— Nothing is yet concluded on the subject of our tobacco trade with this country after the expiration of the order of Bernis. Perhaps the prospect of war may be favorable to that arrangement.

You made me a very unlucky offer of service in Richmond. Probably you did not know how troublesome I should be to you. And if you had known, I still doubt whether it would have deterred you from the offer, for I well remember that it was a part of your character to serve others tho you suffered yourself by it. I have taken the liberty to send to the care of Mr. Madison at New York a box addressed to you which contains 100 maps of Virginia, Maryland, Pennsylvania and Delaware, and 57 copies of a bad book called Notes on Virginia, the author of which has no other merit than that of thinking as little of it as any man in the world can. 17. of these copies are destined for yourself, Govr. Randolph, Genl. Washington, Colo. Monroe, Doctr. Mc.lurg, Doctr. Turpin, Richard Henry Lee, Colo. Mason, Mr. Jo. Jones of King George, Mr. Smith, president of the P. Edwd. College, F. Eppes, H. Skipwith, C. H. Harrison, John Bolling junr. Mr. Zane, Mr. Stuard of Rockbridge, and Mr. Brown nephew to Colo. Preston. As you will probably see all these gentlemen, sooner or later in Richmond, you will have no other trouble than the delivery of the books with my request to accept of them. The remaining 40 copies, if any body will buy, at 10/ Virginia money apiece and the maps at half that, it may refund to me a part of the expences of impression. To save both to you and myself the trouble of accounts, part with them only for the cash in hand. The sums would not be worth the trouble of collecting. I have taken the liberty of desiring Colo. N. Lewis of Albemarle to send some seeds to your care to be forwarded for me to Havre, where Mr. Limozin, agent for the United states will take care of them for me. Perhaps he may add to them a dozen or two of hams, which the captain, who brings them, must pretend to be a part of his private stores, or they will be seised. Perhaps too the object may not be worth the trouble. Of this the captains are the best judges. I have it in contemplation to write to Mr. Eppes for some of a particular kind of cyder which he makes, and in like manner to trouble you with it. Judge now if you acted wisely in offering me your services, or whether you can contrive to indemnify yourself by entrusting me with the execution of any commissions on your part, which I chearfully offer, and will faithfully execute. Particularly I can undertake to procure for you in the cellars of the persons who make it, any wines of [this country] which you may desire. I have visited all the most celebrated wine cantons, have informed myself of the best vignobles and can assure you that it is from them alone that genuine wine is to be got, and not from any winemerchant whatever; for this or any other purpose make what use of me you please, being with sentiments of real esteem and attachment Dear Sir your most obedient friend and servant, TH: JEFFERSON

PrC (DLC).

TJ's memorandum in MHi (see note to TJ to George Wythe, 16 Sep.) lists the contents of the box for Donald in abbreviated form; in that memorandum TJ states that the 40 copies of the *Notes* are "to be sold @ 1⅔ dollars," the "100 maps to be sold @ ⅚ of a dollar."

To Nicholas Lewis

DEAR SIR   Paris Sep. 17. 1787.

I wrote you last on the 29th. of July. It appeared probable at that time that the affairs of Holland would involve Europe in war. They have become more difficult since, and to render this issue still more inevitable war has been actually declared by the Turks against the Russians, and that under such circumstances as render all accomodation hopeless. How the powers of Europe will arrange themselves depends on negotiations actually carrying on, and probably it will not be till spring that we shall see them generally engaged. I think France must certainly take a part, and in that event I hope, and believe, that England will also be engaged in it.

I take the liberty of putting under your cover the inclosed letter for Monsr. de Rieux. It is from a relation of his, widow to one of the king's counsellors, who is very wealthy, and much disposed to assist him. This letter from her authorizes him to draw on her for fifteen thousand livres, equal to about six hundred pounds sterling with which it is her expectation he will purchase negroes and necessaries to stock his farm. She was more encouraged to make this advance to him, on my assuring her that you would be so good as to aid him with your counsel in laying it out to greatest advantage. Perhaps a part of it might be well employed in buying a small peice of good land so situated as that it might be enlarged in case of any future aids from the same quarter. In general I will take the liberty of recommending him to your friendly offices. His connections here are not only respectable but splendid; and the lady who sends him the present sum, tells me that in the disposition of her estate after her death she allots him about twelve thousand guineas certainly, and perhaps more. She is between 50. and 60. years of age. That he may be able to obtain a favourable exchange for his bills, I have inclosed to him a letter, wherein I undertake to ensure the punctual paiment of his bills, by authorizing and desiring you to indorse my name on them; which I am now to ask the favor of you to do to the amount of 15000 livres.

I cultivate in my own garden here Indian corn for the use of my own table, to eat green in our manner. But the species I am able to get here for seed, is hard, with a thick skin, and dry. I had at Monticello a species of small white rare ripe corn which we called Homony-corn, and of which we used to make about 20. barrels a year for table use, green, in homony, and in bread. Great George will know well what kind I mean. I wish it were possible for me to receive an ear of this in time for the next year. I think too it might be done if you would be so good as to find an opportunity of sending one to Mr. Madison at New York, and another to Mr. A. Donald at Richmond. More at your leisure I would ask you to send me also an ear of two of the drying corn from the Cherokee country, some best watermelon seeds, some fine Cantaloupe melon seeds, seeds of the common sweet potato (I mean the real seeds and not the root which cannot be brought here without rotting) an hundred or two acorns of the willow oak and about a peck of acorns of the ground oak or dwarf oak, of the kind that George gathered for me one year upon the barrens of buck island creek. As these will be of some bulk, I will ask the favor of you to send them to Mr. Donald at Richmond who will find a conveiance for them to Havre. Perhaps I should do better to trouble Mrs. Lewis with this commission; I therefore take the liberty of recommending myself to her. The failure of the former attempt to send bacon hams to me discouraged me from proposing the attempt again. Yet I should think Mr. Donald could get them to me safely. A dozen or two would last me a year, would be better than any to be had on this side the Atlantic, which, inferior as they are, cost about a guinea apiece.

I shall be anxious to hear from you the prospect of renting my estate. I look forward to it as my only salvation. My daughters are well and desire to be remembered to your family whom they recollect with affection. Be so good as to join me also in assurances of respect and esteem to Mrs. Lewis, your son, and the young ladies, and to believe me to be with much sincerity dear Sir your friend and servant, TH: JEFFERSON

PrC (DLC). Enclosure: TJ to Derieux, 16 Sep. 1787, with its enclosures.

To James Madison

DEAR SIR   Paris Sep. 17. 1787.

My last to you were of Aug. 2. and 15. Since that I have sent to Havre to be forwarded to you by the present packet 3. boxes marked I.M. G.W. and A.D. The two last are for Mr. Wythe in Williamsburgh, and Mr. Alexr. Donald merchant in Richmond. The first contains the books for yourself which shall be noted at the close of my letter, together with the following for Mr. Rittenhouse; viz. la Chymie de Fourcroi 4 vols. 8vo. Connoissance des Tems 1788-1789. and Dissertation de la Sauvagere. I have put into the same box 9. copies of the Notes on Virginia. That of the English edition, and one of the others are for yourself. The 7. remaining are for Mr. Jay, Mr. Thomson, Mr. Hopkinson, Mr. Mercer (late of Congress) Mr. Rittenhouse, Mr. Izard and Mr. Ed. Rutledge, which I will pray of you to have delivered in my name to those gentlemen. I have also put into the box 100 copies of the map of Virginia Pennsylvania &c. which be so good as to put into the hands of any booksellers you please in New York and Philadelphia to be sold at such price as you think proper, ready money only. I have sent some to Virginia to be sold at 5⁄6 of a dollar. If it should appear that a greater number might be sold, I would have the plate re-touched, and any number struck off which might be desired. It may serve to refund a part of the expences of printing the book and engraving the map.—In my letter of Aug. 2. I troubled you on the case of John Burke. I now inclose you a letter lately received, by which it will appear that Mr. Broom (not Groom) of New York paid into the hands of a Capt. William S. Browne of Providence in Rhode island a balance of £56. The property of John Burke deceased, brother to Thos. Burke who writes the letter: that possibly there may be more of his property in Brown's hands: and that it is Brown for whom your enquiries must be directed, and of whom the money must be demanded. If he will pay it on this letter of Thomas Burke, (in real money) it might be placed in the bank of Philadelphia till called for by T. B. If he requires more regular authority, be so good as to inform me what may be necessary and I will give notice to Mrs. Burke the wife of Thomas who lives in France and to whom he has confided the pursuit of this object.   I have received the box you were so kind as to send me with paccans. There were 13. nuts in it, which I mention, because I suspect it had been pillaged. Your situation at New York, and the packets coming from thence to Havre, where Mr. Limozin, agent for the U.S. will take care of any thing for me, may enable you to send me a few barrels of Newtown pippins and cranberries. If you could send me also 50. or 100 grafts of the Newtown pippin they would be very desireable. They should be packed between layers of moss, a layer of moss and a layer of plants alternately, in a box, and the box nailed close, with directions to Limozin to forward them by the Diligence. Red birds for the ladies, and Opossums for the naturalists would be great presents, if any passenger would take charge of them. I must either refer you to my public letter for news, or write you a letter of news if my time will permit. I am with sincere esteem, dear Sir, your friend and servant,   TH: JEFFERSON

J. Madison esq. to Th: Jefferson Dr.

To paid Frouille for the box marked J.M. No. 1. and packing	20^{tt}- 0
Memoires sur les impositions de l'Europe 4. v. 4to.	36-
Loisirs d'Argenson. 2 v. 8vo.	8-10
Charlevoix histoire de la nouvelle France. 3. v. 4to.	27
American traveller 4to.	3
Pollucis onomasticon. 4to.	5
Buffon Mineraux. 5th. 6th. 7th. 8th. volumes	12
Pieces interessantes. 5th. vol.	3
Dissertation de la Sauvagere 8vo.	4-12
	119-2

Your watch is done, and is in my possession. She costs 3. guineas more than I had told you she would. Two were owing to a mistake of mine in the price of my own, and the other to that of the workman who put that much gold into the case more than he had into mine. Yours costs therefore 600.^{tt} I have worn it a month during which, tho new, it is impossible for a watch to go better. I shall send her by the French minister, Monsieur le comte de Moustier. I wish the step-counter may be done in time to go by the same conveiance. I have been almost tempted to buy for you one of the little clocks made here mounted on marble columns. They strike, go with a pendulum, a spring instead of a weight, are extremely elegant and can be had for 10. guineas. But I shall wait your orders.   TH: J.

P.S. Will you be so good as to pay Mr. C. Thomson 86.35 dollars for me, and to apologize to him for my not writing, the bearer going off a day sooner than he had told me. The letter to N. Lewis is of great consequence.

RC (DLC: Madison Papers); endorsed; on verso of last page, in the hand of Charles Thomson: "New York. Decr. 27. 1787. Recd. from James Madison Jr. the within mentioned Eighty six and 35/90 Dollars. Chas Thomson." PrC (DLC: TJ Papers). Enclosures: (1) Copy of a letter from Thomas Burke to his wife, dated 4 Aug. 1787, transmitting a copy of a letter from John Broom to Thomas Burke, 16 May 1787, stating in detail the facts concerning the property of John Burke, which TJ summarizes briefly in the present letter (DLC: Madison Papers, 7: 111). (2) TJ to Nicholas Lewis, preceding.

TJ's draft memorandum in MHi (see note to TJ to George Wythe, 16 Sep.) lists the contents of the box for Madison in abbreviated form.

From John Trumbull

DR. SIR   London 17th. Septr. 1787.

Several days ago I had the pleasure to receive your favor of the 30th. Augt. by which I suppose you had not at that time mine of the 25th.[1] in which I acquainted you that I had fulfill'd your commission respecting the Harpsichord. It was put on board a ship for Rouen the 22d. (the first which saild after I had your request) and a bill of Lading was enclos'd in the Letter. I now send a duplicate lest that should have miscarried. I likewise informed you that I had paid Mr. Walker for the Stop thirteen Guineas, and Kirkman for sending it on board 14/.

This letter you will unquestionably receive safe, as I give it in charge to Mr. Cutting, an old friend and military acquaintance of mine, who makes now his first visit to France, after having resided for the last year in this place to compleat his legal studies. You will find him very well informed and conversible and will do me a particular favor in shewing him every Civility.

I owe you a thousand Thanks for the very friendly manner in which you repeat your invitations to me for the Salon. I am mortified that I must not accept them; but I have undertaken a picture of the Sortie made by the Garrison of Gibraltar which I exceedingly wish to finish immediately; and I find it so difficult a subject that I can spare no time for amusement &c. I am not quite prepared to make my Journey to Paris a matter of Business. I wish to have decided exactly in my own Mind and even in a Sketch, the composition for the Surrender at York; that I may have no embarrassment and lose no time when I do come to you.

Mr. Cutting will give you the politics of the day, and I hope by his return to be honor'd with a line.

You of course see Mrs. Cosway. Pray tell her that *three* posts have pass'd in which no one of her friends has receivd a single line from her, that Lady Lyttleton, Mr. C., her sister and all the world are not only angry at her for not writing, but suffer all the distress of anxiety least illness or accident of any kind should have occasiond her silence. I am commissioned to scold her heartily. Will you permit me to transfer the commission and to beg that you will execute it with all due severity and Elegance. From you I am sure of its effect.

Do the Count de Moutier and Madame Brehan go out to America this year? I am so selfish as almost to wish them a little longer detaind. Their absence from Paris will be most sensibly felt by me, and if they were detaind till next spring I should not only enjoy Paris this winter, but should even indulge myself with a hope of going out with them. I am afraid Madame De Brehan thinks me a most ungallant wretch. I promised to copy a part of my picture of Bunkers Hill for her; but I have an excuse—I have not seen the picture since I left it in Germany, and I have not forgotten the promise, which shall most faithfully be fulfilld the moment I possess the Picture. I beg you to make this apology and to say that I should have written it to herself, if I had dar'd, and say both to her and the Count that I shall never forget their friendship to me; or think that I have sufficiently acknowledged their kindness. Whenever they sail may they have a pleasant Voyage, and find themselves happy in America beyond their expectations.

I beg your pardon for so many commissions, yet they cannot be disagreeable as they are to two whom you esteem.

I am most gratefully Dr. Sir Your friend & Servant,

JNO. TRUMBULL

My compliments to Mr. Short.

RC (DLC); endorsed. Recorded in SJL as received 23 Sep. 1787. Enclosure missing.

1 Trumbull's letter is dated 28 Aug., and is printed above under that date.

To Mantel Duchoqueltz

SIR   Paris Sep. 18. 1787.

Immediately on the receipt of your favor of July 25. informing me that you had forwarded to me by the packet some boxes of plants &c. and that you had disbursed for me 23^{tt}-12-6, I wrote to M. Limozin at Havre to repay this sum with the other charges which might have been incurred. I thank you for your attention, Sir, to those articles, and beg you to be assured that any disbursements you may be so good as to make for me on any other similar occasion shall always be pointedly replaced, with many thanks for your attentions from him who has the honour to be with much respect Sir your most obedient & most humble servt.,

TH: JEFFERSON

PrC (MHi).

To Francis Hopkinson

DEAR SIR   Paris Sep. 18. 1787.

The bearer hereof, Mr. Burgoin, is recommended to me as a worthy and ingenious artist, skilled in drawing and engraving. Being desirous of establishing himself in America, and preferably in Philadelphia, I know I cannot do better for him than by recommending him to your patronage and counsels. One who loves the arts, must be well disposed to those who practice them. I am with great and sincere esteem Dear Sir Your friend & servant,

TH: JEFFERSON

PrC (MHi).

From Lafayette, with Enclosure

MY DEAR FRIEND   Fontainebleau September the 18th

Thus far I Have Come down from My Mountains, and Hope I will not Be sent Back without some decision or other Respecting American affairs. Inclosed is the Copy of a letter to M. Lambert which I Have writen as soon as I Knew His Appointement. I also inform M. de la Boulaïe that I will Be Ready to Meet Him Every day in the Next week, But that I am obliged to set out Again on the fifth of October for an Assembly of Departement wherein I

[140]

Have Accepted a seat. Now I am Going to Visit the duke du chatelu, and Marchal de Castries at their Country seats, from thence to Marchal de Mouchy's and then on a Visit to the Archbishop whose order I will take Respecting our affairs. The Moment I Get to Paris I shall let You Know. My Respects to the Young ladies, and Compliments to M. Short and all friends. Most affectionately Yours, LAF.

ENCLOSURE

Lafayette to Lambert

Chavaniac ce 10. 7bre. 1787.

L'Honneur que j'ai eu d'être votre confrere, Monsieur, m'a mis à portée d'applaudir à la confiance que le Roi vous témoigne et je joins à ce sentiment celui de mon attachement particulier. La place qu'on vient de vous donner n'est pas dans le moment actuel exempte de difficultés; mais l'immensité du travail ne vous effraie pas, et l'on sait depuis longtems que vous savez faire beaucoup et bien faire. C'est dans une douzaine de jours que j'espere avoir le plaisir de vous voir, mais je n'ai pas voulu tarder à me rappeller à votre souvenir dans cette occasion, et j'en profite pour vous parler d'une affaire qui, quoique etrangere, n'en Est pas moins très pressante même au milieu des Circonstances intérieures où nous nous trouvons.

La France a fait une guerre glorieuse, mais chère, pour séparer les Etats-unis de l'Angleterre. Parmi les avantages sans nombre de cette révolution, un des principaux etoit sans doute d'attirer ici le Commerce des Etats-unis, commerce essentiel à la Politique, puisque les Négociants de ces républiques influeront beaucoup sur les décisions de chaque Etat et du Corps fœdératif; commerce bien avantageux en lui-même puisqu'il s'agit de payer des produits Bruts avec nos productions façonnées et les ouvrages de nos manufactures, et d'obtenir la plus grande part dans un Négoce d'environ Quatre-vingt millions, favorable à la navigation parcequ'il est de grand encombrement; bien moins précaire que nos liaisons avec le Nord et le levant, et croissant rapidement avec la population de ce pays nouveau et fortuné. J'ajouterai que les avantages de ce Commerce doivent être comptés au double pour nous, puisque chacun de nos gains dans les Etats-unis est une perte politique et mercantile pour une nation rivale.

La Guerre avoit donné des occasions et du tems pour engager ce commerce, on en a peu profité. Les premières années de la paix etoient favorables, on les a négligées. Il faut en accuser les prejugés ou l'avidité de quelques corps ou compagnies, quelques fautes particulières de Négociants dans les deux nations; la révolution du papier monnoye, trop longue à expliquer ici, et qui l'est fort bien dans la Nouvelle encyclopédie; mais par dessus tout le funeste Esprit de la finance et le courant d'affaires qui emp[loyent] journellement l'attention des ministres. C'est par ignorance ou mauvaise foi qu'on allègue la différence de Religion et l'attachement aux Anglois, dans un pays où toutes les Religions sont égales et où l'Angleterre est haïe par les trois quatre et demi des Citoyens. Et s'il est moins absurde de parler des inconvenients d'une langue différente, de l'habitude des Americains pour les manufactures Anglaises, des Liens qu'entraïnent nécessairement une ancienne dette, on ne doit pas croire que ces difficultés tiennent contre un peu de tems et de Soins, et surtout contre la seule et grande règle de tout Négoce, *Le profit*; et à moins que le Gouvernement ne barre le cours naturel du Commerce Américain, il appartiendra principalement à la Nation qui, pouvant avoir presque tous les articles Anglais, en a beaucoup que le Climat refuse à l'Angleterre et dont la position offre à peu de fraix des dépots pour toutes les mers d'Europe.

Il est vrai que l'Angleterre, en même tems qu'elle sembloit négliger l'Alliance des Etats-unis, a fait les plus grands efforts, et même des Sacrifices considerables, pour se les attacher par tous les liens du Commerce. L'Amérique est inondée de facteurs, de Correspondances et de marchandises Britanniques. Les Gouverneurs des Isles ont souvent fermé les yeux. Tous les moyens d'augmenter la dette des Americains ont été multipliés. Les Credits qu'ils obtenoient étoient sans bornes et même sans distinctions, et l'on n'a pas été intimidé par les Banqueroutes. Enfin, les marchandises francaises ont été déguisées sous des noms anglais, et nos Rivaux ont usé de tous les moyens populaires qui leur sont connus pour décrier nos manufactures.

Pendant ce tems, les Négociants francais usoient d'une prudence que je ne puis blâmer dans l'Etat d'incertitude où ils se trouvoient, et les productions americaines étoient repoussées de nos ports. Tantôt, Messieurs de la Marine prononçoient sur les munitions navales, et le resultat est toujours qu'il n'y a rien de bon qu'à Riga, où nous payons à peu près tout en Or. Tantôt, les agens du fisc ont réclamé les droits sur les Huiles de baleine, et sur toutes les marchandises d'Amerique; ou bien, ils ont établi des vexations, des discussions, de longueurs pires que les droits. Il n'y a pas jusqu'aux Arbres d'Amérique dont l'Introduction n'ait été gênée, et quand l'Américain a voulu se fournir en France, les barrières intérieures, la langue financiere qu'il falloit apprendre en outre de la langue française, ont contrarié sa bonne volonté. Les fermiers généraux de France ont cru devoir acheter en Ecosse les Tabacs d'Amérique, ou lorsqu'on a voulu changer le cours de leurs emplettes, ils ont imaginé un monopole d'achat par addition à celui de la vente et, donnant un privilège exclusif à M. Moriss dans l'autre Hemisphere, comme ils en ont un dans celui-ci, ils l'ont de plus payé, non pas en marchandises françaises, mais en lettres de changes sur Londres. Et l'on dit ensuite *qu'il faut que les Américains n'aiment pas la France puisqu'il y a si peu de leurs Vaisseaux dans nos ports!*

M. De Calonne, qui a souvent rendu service au Commerce, sentit qu'il étoit ridicule de ne pas trouver sur quatre-vingt millions d'Exportations Américaines un seul objet qui convint aux intérêts de nos Compagnies exclusives, ou aux Loix de notre fiscalité. Il nomma un Comité presidé d'abord par M. De Boullongne et ensuite par Mr. LeNoir. Il etoit composé de membres du Conseil, Intendants du Commerce, négociants, fermiers generaux, Messrs. Boyetet et Dupont et moi. Ce fut après un long examen que nous Convïnmes de différents points etablis dans une lettre de M. De Calonne à Mr. Jefferson, ministre des Etats-unis. Elle ne prononce sur aucun Sacrifice de la France, mais seulement sur les objets qui lui sont evidement avantageux. Cette lettre, signée par le Controleur général, envoyée officiellement par le Ministre des affaires étrangeres, presentée au Congrès par les Ministres respectifs et imprimée partout, produisit un si bon effet que plusieurs etats americains accordèrent sur le champ des avantages à notre Commerce et qu'elle a occasionné de vifs debats au parlement d'Angleterre.

Mais, par une Negligence étrange, on oublia de donner dans les ports les ordres nécessaires. La Ferme en profita pour vexer le Commerce. Les Navires Americains n'arrivèrent que pour voir la lettre sans effet, les engagements violés et pour rapporter dans leur pays cette singulière nouvelle; M. De Calonne se contenta de promettre qu'on rembourseroit les droits injustement perçus. L'Assemblée des Notables est survenüe et depuis la nouvelle administration on n'a pû encore que mettre la lettre en vigueur, et il reste à donner à cette convention une forme Stable et l'Extension dont elle est susceptible.

M. De La Boullaye a pris des renseignements. M. Jefferson s'est fort occupé de cet objet, il est très familier à M. LeNoir et aux autres membres du Comité dont l'opinion est consacrée dans le proces Verbal. Je ne vous propose pas d'entrer à present dans l'Examen des grands partis à prendre, ou des petits details à suivre pour le Commerce Gallo-Americain, mais les objets de la lettre sont simples, excepté Celui du Tabac qui est très urgent. Nous en aurions quelques autres à vous présenter, et si vous accordiez une Conference à Mr. Jefferson, M. De La Boullaye, M. Le Noir, moi, et telles autres personnes qui vous Conviendront, deux heures Suffiroient pour fixer un arrangement Solide, dont le delay nous est Extremement préjudiciable.

Je vous demande pardon, Monsieur, de ma longue epitre. Elle porte sur un Interet bien important, et qui le deviendra plus encore lorsque les Etats-unis auront la voix préponderante qui leur est destinée.

Je suis à portée de voir que le tems presse et c'est ce qui m'engage à joindre ces Reflexions à l'hommage des Sentiments que vous me Connoissez pour vous et que Je m'empresse de vous Renouveler à cette occasion, ainsi que le Sincere attachement Etc.

RC (DLC). Recorded in SJL as received 19 Sep. 1787. Enclosure (Tr in hand of a clerk, unsigned, DLC).

To John Langdon

DEAR SIR   Paris Sep. 18. 1787.

The Marquis de Vaudreuil, who I believe had the honour of being known to you in America, sent me the inclosed papers, whereby it appears that a certain Anthony Monset, a native of Languedoc, and merchant of Portsmouth in New Hampshire, died at Portsmouth in September or October 1786. and that William

Monset and Mary Monset his brother and sister, inhabitants of Revel in Languedoc are entitled to his inheritance. I beg the favor of you to inform me what he has left, and to take measures for receiving and depositing it where it may be subject to the order of the claimants. The Marquis de Vaudreuil interests himself much for these people; of course, besides the charity to them, your assistance will confer an obligation on him as well as on Dear Sir Your most obedient and most humble servant,

TH: JEFFERSON

PrC (DLC). Enclosures not found.

To David Rittenhouse

DEAR SIR   Paris Sep. 18. 1787.

I am now to acknolege the receipt of your favors of April 14. and June 26.[1] as also of the 2d. vol. of the transactions you were so kind as to send me. It would have been a grateful present indeed could you have accompanied them with a copy of your observations on our Western country. Besides the interest I feel in that country in common with others, I have a particular one as having ventured so many crudities on that subject. A copy of these with some late corrections I have put into a box of books sent to Mr. Madison, and another for Mr. Hopkinson. I hope he will forward them to you from New York. I have also put into the same box for you a dissertation by de la Sauvagere on the spontaneous growth of shells. When I was at Tours this summer, I enquired into the character of de la Sauvagere from a gentleman who had known him well. He told me he was a person of talents, but of a heated imagination, however that he might be depended on for any facts advanced on his own knolege. This gentleman added that he had seen such proofs of this growth of shells in many parts of the country round Tours, as to convince him of the truth of the fact, and that he had never seen any person, even the most incredulous, quit those Falunieres but under the same conviction. After all I cannot say I give faith to it. It is so unlike the processes of nature to produce the same effect in two different ways, that I can only bring myself to agree it is not impossible. I have added for you the Connoissance des temps for 88. and 89. and a copy of Fourcroi's chemistry which is the best and most complete publication in that line which we have had for some time past. I shall be happy to receive an account of your improvement in time pieces, as well as the 3d. vol. of the transactions when published. There are abundance of good things in the 2d. vol. but I must say there are several which had not merit enough to be placed in such company. I think we should be a little rigid in our admission of papers. It is the peculiar privilege derived from our not being obliged to publish a volume in any fixed period of time.—A person here pretends to have discovered the method of rendering sea-water potable, and has some respectable certificates of it's success. He has contrived a varnish also for lining biscuit barrels, which preserves the biscuit good, and keeps it free from insects. He asks money for his secrets, so we are not to know them soon.

The affairs of Holland had got so far entangled as to leave little hope that war could be avoided. In this situation the Turks have declared war against the Russians. This I think renders a general war inevitable. Perhaps the European powers may take this winter to determine which side each shall take. There is a possibility that an alliance between France and the two empires may induce England and Prussia to tread back their steps. In that case the Patriotic party in Holland will be peaceably placed at the head of their government, the Turks will be driven out of Europe, their continental possessions divided between Russia and the Emperor, and perhaps their islands and Egypt be allotted to France. These events seem possible at present. Small circumstances however may baffle our expectations. I hope the British will permit us to keep clear of the war, if it should become general. Peace should be our plan, and the paiment of our debts, improvement of our constitutions and extension of agriculture our principal objects.

My daughters are well. The elder one joins me in a friendly recollection of Mrs. Rittenhouse, yourself, and daughters: and I am with very sincere esteem Dear Sir your most obedient & most humble servant, TH: JEFFERSON

PrC (DLC).

1 That is, 26 June 1786.

From William Stephens Smith

DEAR SIR   London Septr. 18th. 1787.

In the first place I must introduce my very particular friend Mr. J. B. Cutting as a Gentleman of genius and merit. There may one or two lines shew themselves, which at first will be rather apt to prejudice against him, at least I was sensible of it, and have not been able to obliterate them from his Countenance and motion, but they are really only superficials. I know you will put them aside. You will find him a Gentleman remarkably well informed, of an inquisitive mind and possessing very good sentiments on the subjects which interest our Country. He passess only a few day in Paris to wonder and Gap (as he say's) and returns here to embark for America &c. &c.

Your Letter of 31st. Ulto. I have received, the Cypher which put you to so much trouble I copied from Mr. Jay's Letter to Mr. Adams which I had with me and was intended to convey this Idea—that Congress expected that the polite manner in which they appear to have intended forwarding their Letter of thanks to her most faithful majesty, might produce agreable effects relative to the conclusion of the pending treaty—and I may now inform you that I went to that Court under a Commission from Mr. Adams, as Mr. Jay did not forward any, tho' Congress voted that I should be commissioned for that purpose. Of Course I could not present the Letter in person; it was conveyed thro' the Minister of State to the Queen. I had two long interviews with him, in which we conversed very freely on the situation and commerce of the 2 Countries. You doubtless will carry the Idea with you, that I talked only as a private Gentleman, but he as Minister told me, that there were several points which her majesty thought required alteration and he fully agreed with her that the Chevalier de Pinto had been a long time absent from his Country and did not seem to be sufficiently acquainted with some little internal arrangements which it was always necessary should be attended to in the establishment of a Commercial intercourse, but that at the first Leisure he would revise it, and forward to London a Counter-project. But Sir (said he) this mode of conducting our affairs by ministers residing in London is subject to great inconvenience and delay and does not promise much success. If the United States would send a minister to Portugal the Queen would immediately dispatch one to reside with Congress, an agreable foundation would then be laid for an intimacy and the United States would soon from the disposition of her Majesty and her ministers relative to them find every facility in their negotiations that they could wish. Indeed her majesty has been a little displeased that she has not been attended to on this subject and as she felt herself rather interested in the Career of my Country she wished to be well and regularly informed of its present State and future prospects, which on the exchange of ministers would be the case. He proceeded in a very complimentary Strain and was answered with as great civility as possible, without committing myself on the subject. When my business was compleatly finished and I had made some preparations for my departure I informed the minister of it and requested to know whether her majesty had any Commands. I was informed by the deputy secretary of State the next day, that Her majesty would see me the day following at ½ past 4 tho' not a Court day. This was a very particular mark of civility and from whence it sprung I cannot say. But it put an agreable period to my business. I made a small speach to her on the occasion and she returned a polite answer, and I left her territories tolerably sick but glad it was no worse. I thank you for the invitation to the noise of Paris, but I cannot visit it this season unless *By order*. I have paid Mrs. Adams 27/8. agreable to your request, and find that Trumbull has sent the harpsicord before my return. Why I do not send a statement of our account Current is because it is not regularly made out and I am apprehensive the balance is against me, but you shall have it the first leisure morning. You shall have it by post or a private hand before the Marquis returns from the south. I am very sorry that you should have occasion to be astonished at Genl. Sullivan's draught. Shall I in answer to his Letter to me say any thing on the Subject? And what. At this distance from the Board of Treasury I do not see clearly how we shall get out of the pickle you mention. Dumas has got an order from Mr. Adams to receive his salary at Amsterdam and your Letter puts me on the project of endeavouring to obtain a similar one for Carmichael. I will watch for a pleasant favourable moment to bring it forward. I am much obliged by the political note in your Letter and attended to its reference with pleasure and instruction. We look with anxiety to the youthful movements of the Prussian. I think he appears to be in a fair way to be ducked, and that may make him *Madder*, but European wars will do no hurt to us. We shall have sense enough to keep ourselves cool and perhaps may profit by the folly of others. I am almost ashamed of the 2 last lines, least it should convey an Idea, that I was capable of deriving pleasure from the misfortunes of others, if from their errors I (or my Country) could be benifitted, and, had I time to write another letter, I would throw this in the fire on their account. But you will put the best construction on them they will bear. I feel myself always safe with you and will let them go.

Mrs. Adams would be obliged if you will send her 5 ells of Cambric at 12 Livers pr. ell. She says she will pay me, so charge it. She joins Mrs. Smith in sincere wishes for your health and happiness, in which they appear equally interested with your obliged friend & humble Servt., W. S. SMITH

RC (DLC); endorsed. Recorded in SJL as received 23 Sep. 1787.

From William Stephens Smith

London, 18 Sep. 1787. Introduces Benjamin Parker, nephew of Daniel Parker, a student at "Cambridge Colledge in Massachusetts," who will spend three months in Paris before returning to America; "being hard of hearing . . . prevents him from seeking society with that goût which might be expected from his age and situation."

RC (MHi); 2 p.; endorsed. Recorded in SJL as received 23 Sep. 1787.

To the South Carolina Delegates in Congress

GENTLEMEN   Paris Sep. 18. 1787.

I take the liberty of sending to your care the third and last parcel of Piedmont rice, addressed to Mr. Drayton, and will beg the favor of you to have it forwarded. I divided it into separate parcels that the chances of some one of them getting safely to hand might be multiplied.

You will find by my letter to Mr. Jay that the claim by your state against Spain for the use of the Indian frigate is remitted by that count to be settled between yourselves and Mr. Gardoqui. I am in hopes it may be effected to your satisfaction.

I have the honor to be with sentiments of the most perfect esteem & respect Gentlemen Your most obedient & most humble servant,

TH: JEFFERSON

PrC (DLC).

[148]

To the Commissioners of the Treasury

GENTLEMEN   Paris Sep. 18. 1787.

Congress having thought proper by their vote of July 18. to instruct me to take measures for the redemption of our captives at Algiers, and to desire you to furnish the money necessary, it is proper to state to you some data whereby you may judge what sum is necessary. The French prisoners, last redeemed by the order of Mathurins, cost somewhat less than 400 dollars; but the General of the order told me that they had always been made to pay more for foreign prisoners than their own. The smallest sum then at which we can expect ours, including redemption, cloathing, feeding and transportation, will be 500 dollars each. There are twenty of them. Of course 10,000 dollars is the smallest sum which can be requisite. I think a larger sum should be set apart, as so much of it as shall not be wanting for the prisoners, will remain for other uses. As soon as you shall have notified me that the money is ready, I will proceed to execute the order of Congress. I must add the injunctions of the General of the Mathurins that it be not made known that the public interest themselves in the redemption of these prisoners, as that would induce the Algerines to demand the most extravagant price. I have the honour to be with sentiments of the most profound respect, Gentlemen, your most obedient & most humble servant,   TH: JEFFERSON

PrC (DLC).

CONGRESS . . . VOTE OF JULY 18: Enclosed in John Jay to TJ, 24 July 1787, q.v.

From George Washington

DEAR SIR   Philadelphia Sept. 18th. 1787.

Yesterday put an end to the business of the Fœdral Convention. Inclosed is a copy of the Constitution, by it agreed to. Not doubting but that you have participated in the general anxiety which has agitated the minds of your Countrymen on this interesting occasion, I shall be excused I am certain for this endeavor to relieve you from it, especially when I assure you of the sincere regard and esteem with which I have the honor to be Dr. Sir Yr. Most Obedt and Very Hble Servant,   G. WASHINGTON

FC (DLC: Washington Papers). Recorded in SJL as received 19 Dec. 1787.   Enclosure: A copy of the official edition of the final report of the Federal Convention, consisting of (1) the text of the proposed Constitution; (2) the resolution of the Convention; and (3) the letter from Washington to the president of Congress transmitting the report. On 17 Sep. 1787 Dunlap and Claypoole printed 500 copies of this edition, but, although TJ received other copies of this and other editions from American correspondents, no copy has been found among the books left by him (communication of E. Millicent Sowerby to the Editors, 18 Jan. 1954), nor has the Editors' canvas of copies preserved in the Library of Congress and other repositories turned up any text of this edition definitely identifiable as having been TJ's. Copies owned by Washington, Madison, and Pendleton are in the Library of Congress (JCC, XXXIII, 760, No. 592).

On this same date Washington sent Lafayette a copy of the report of the Convention, saying: "It is the production of four months deliberation. It is now a child of fortune, to be fostered by some and buffeted by others" (*Writings*, ed. Fitzpatrick, XXIX, 276-7; see also Lafayette to TJ, 25 Dec. 1787).

From Mary Barclay

SIR   St. Germain-en-Laye 19 Sept 1787

I have not been able to get the Books you were so good as to say you would forward for me, and only trouble you at present with my letter.

The sum due Mr. Barclay for Balance of account I shall not want for some time therefore beg you will not send it till perfectly convenient to you. I was too sensible of the friendly offer you made me to thank you as I wished to do but beg you will [believe] I shall ever retain the most lively sense of your politeness and attention to me and that I am with sincere esteem Sir your most obedient humble Servant,   MARY BARCLAY

RC (MHi); endorsed. TJ recorded the receipt of a letter from Mrs. Barclay on 20 Sep. 1787, entering its date only as "Sep."—doubtless a reference to this letter.

To John Jay

SIR   Paris Sep. 19. 1787.

My last letters to you were of the 6th. and 15th. of August: since which I have been honoured with yours of July 24. acknoleging the receipt of mine of the 14th. and 23d. of February. I am anxious to hear you have received that also of May 4. written from Marseilles. According to the desires of Congress expressed in their vote confirming the appointments of Francis, Giuseppe and Girolamo Chiappi their agents in Marocco, I have written letters to these gentlemen to begin a correspondence with them. To the first I have inclosed the ratification of the treaty with the emperor of

Marocco, and shall send it either by our agent at Marseilles, who is now here, or by the Count D'aranda who sets out for Madrid in a few days, having relinquished his embassy here. I shall proceed on the redemption of our captives at Algiers as soon as the Commissioners of the treasury shall enable me, by placing the money necessary under my orders. The prisoners redeemed by the religious order of Mathurins cost about 400 dollars each, and the General of the order told me that they had never been able to redeem foreigners on so good terms as their own countrymen. Supposing that their redemption, clothing, feeding and transportation should amount to 500. dollars each, there must be at least a sum of 10,000 dollars set apart for this purpose. Till this is done I shall take no other step than the preparatory one of destroying at Algiers all idea of our intending to redeem the prisoners. This the General of the Mathurins told me was indispensably necessary, and that it must not on any account transpire that the public would interest themselves, for their redemption. This was rendered the more necessary by the declaration of the Dey to the Spanish consul that he should hold him responsible, at the Spanish price, for our prisoners, even for such as should die. Three of them have died of the plague. By authorizing me to redeem at the prices *usually* paid by European nations, Congress, I suppose, could not mean the Spanish price, which is not only unusual but unprecedented, and would make our vessels the first object with those pyrates. I shall pay no attention therefore to the Spanish price, unless further instructed. Hard as it may seem, I should think it necessary not to let it be known even to the relations of the captives that we mean to redeem them.

I have the honor to inclose you a paper from the Admiralty of Guadeloupe, sent to me as matter of form, and to be lodged I suppose with our marine records. I inclose also a copy of a letter from the Count de Florida Blanca to Mr. Carmichael, by which you will perceive they have referred the settlement of the claim of South Carolina for the use of their frigate, to Mr. Gardoqui and to the delegates of South Carolina in Congress.

I had the honour to inform you in my last letter of the parliament's being transferred to Troyes. To put an end to the tumults in Paris, some regiments were brought nearer, the patroles were strengthened and multiplied, some mutineers punished by imprisonment; it produced the desired effect. It is confidently beleived however that the parliament will be immediately recalled, the stamp tax, and land tax repealed, and other means devised of accomodating their receipts and expenditures. Those supposed to be in contemplation are a rigorous levy of the old tax of the deux vingtiemes, on the rich, who had in a great measure withdrawn their property from it, as well as on the poor on whom it had principally fallen. This will greatly increase the receipts, while they are proceeding on the other hand to reform their expences far beyond what they had promised. It is said these reformations will amount to 80 millions. Circumstances render these measures more and more pressing. I mentioned to you in my last letter that the officer charged by the ministry to watch the motions of the British squadron had returned with information that it had sailed Westwardly. [The fact was] not true. He had formed his conclusion too hastily and has led the ministry into error. The King of Prussia, urged on by England, has pressed more and more the affairs of Holland, and lately has given to the states general of Holland four days only to comply with his demand. This measure would of itself have rendered it impossible for France to proceed longer in the line of accomodation with Prussia. In the same moment an event takes place which seems to render all attempt at accomodation idle. The Turks have declared war against the Russians, and that under circumstances which exclude all prospect of preventing it's taking place. The king of Prussia having deserted his antient friends, there remains only France and Turkey, perhaps Spain also, to oppose the two empires, Prussia and England. By such a peice of quixotism France might plunge herself into ruin with the Turks and Dutch, but would save neither. But there is certainly a confederacy secretly in contemplation, of which the public have not yet the smallest suspicion: that is between France and the two empires. I think it sure that Russia has desired this, and that the Emperor, after some hesitation has acceded. It rests on this country to close. Her indignation against the king of Prussia will be some spur. She will thereby save her party in Holland, and only abandon the Turks to that fate she cannot ward off, which their precipitation has brought on themselves by the instigations of the English Ambassador at the Porte, and against the remonstrances of the French Ambassador. Perhaps this formidable combination, should it take place, may prevent the war of the Western powers, as it would seem that neither England nor Prussia could carry their false calculations so far as, with the aid of the Turks [only,] to oppose themselves to such a force. In that case the Patriots of Holland would be peaceably established in the powers of their government, and the war go on against the Turks only, who would probably be driven from Europe. This new arrangement would be a total change of the European system, and a favourable one for our friends. The probability of a general war in which this country would be engaged on one side and England on the other has appeared to me sufficient to justify my writing to our agents in the different ports of France to put our merchants on their guard against risking their property in French or English bottoms. The Emperor, instead of treading back his steps in Brabant as was expected, has pursued the less honourable plan of decoying his subjects there by false pretences to let themselves be molested by his troops, and this done, he dictates to them his own terms. Yet it is not certain the matter will end with that.

The Count de Moustier is nominated minister plenipotentiary to America; and a frigate is ordered to Cherburg to carry him over. He will endeavor to sail by the middle of next month, but if any delays should make him pass over the whole of October, he will defer his voiage to the spring, being unwilling to undertake a winter passage. Monsr. de St. Priest is sent Ambassador to Holland, in the room of Monsr. de Verac appointed to Switzerland. The Chevalr. de la Luzerne might I beleive have gone to Holland, but he preferred a general promise of promotion, and the possibility[1] that it might be to the court of London. His prospects are very fair. His brother the Count de la Luzerne (now governor in the West Indies) is appointed minister of the marine in the place of Monsr. de Castries who has resigned. The Archbishop of Toulouse is appointed Ministre principale, and his brother Monsr. de Brienne minister of war in the place of Monsr. de Segur. The department of the Comptroul has had a very rapid succession of tenants. From M. de Calonnes it passed to M. de Fourqueux, from him to Villedeuil, and from him to Lambert, who holds it at present, but divided with a M. Cabarrus (whom I beleive you knew in Spain) who is named Directeur de tresor royal, the office into which Mr. Neckar came at first. I had the honour to inform you that before the departure of the Count de la Luzerne to his government in the West Indies, I had pressed on him the patronage of our trade with the French islands, that he appeared well disposed, and assured me he would favor us as much as his instructions and the laws of the colonies would permit. I am in hopes these dispositions will be strengthened by his residence in the islands, and that his acquaintance among the people there will be an additional motive to favor them. Probably they will take advantage of his appointment to press indulgences in commerce with us. The ministry is of a liberal complection, and well disposed to us. The war may add to the motives for opening their islands to other resources for their subsistence, and for doing what may be agreeable to us. It seems to me at present then, that the moment of the arrival of the Count de la Luzerne will be the moment for trying to obtain a freer access to their islands. It would be very material to do this, if possible, in a permanent way, that is to say by treaty. But I know of nothing we have to offer in equivalent. Perhaps the paiment of our debt to them might be made use of as some inducement, while they are so distressed for money. Yet the borrowing the money in Holland will be rendered more difficult by the same event, in proportion as it will increase the demand for money by other powers.

The gazettes of Leyden and France to this date are inclosed, together with some pamphlets on the internal affairs of this country.

I have the honor to be, with sentiments of the most perfect esteem and respect, Sir, Your most obedient & most humble servant,

TH: JEFFERSON

PrC (DLC). Enclosures: (1) Copy of letter from Floridablanca to Carmichael, 16 Oct. 1784, enclosed in Carmichael to TJ, 6 Sep. 1787, q.v. (2) Extract of the minutes of the admiralty of Guadeloupe concerning the affair of the American traders in Guadeloupe (see their letter to TJ, 3 May 1787); in transmitting this and other letters to Congress on 23 Jan. 1788, Jay excepted this enclosure, "which being lengthy and in the french Language the Interpreter has not yet made a translation of it" (JCC, XXXIV, 23). It evidently has not survived in the Papers of the Continental Congress and may have disappeared along with the RC of the present and other dispatches from TJ to Jay during 1787. Congress was very familiar with the difficulties of the American traders at Guadeloupe. Early in 1787 Otto had transmitted to Vergennes a copy of the traders' memorial complaining of having been assailed at night by armed people without any provocation—a memorial that Otto said some ill-designing persons had printed in all of the American newspapers and had thereby created "beaucoup de bruit en Amérique," though he also reported that Calonne's letter to TJ on American

trade had done much to offset this effect and that TJ's official dispatches on this had produced "la plus grande sensation" (Otto to Vergennes, 13 Aug. 1786, 5 Jan. 1787; Arch. Aff. Etr., Corr. Pol., E.-U., XXXII; Tr in DLC).

Also on 19 Sep., William Short wrote Jay a letter that must have been with TJ's acquiescence if not under his guidance; it thanked Jay for his of 5 July 1787 and added: "I immediately mentioned, sir, to Mr. Jefferson the reports you had made to Congress, and I am sure no circumstance could attach him more to his own sentiments on these subjects than to find that you concurred in them.—I do not venture to importune your Excellency by information on a variety of matters which you will receive so much better from your minister here. You will see, sir, that the great dispute in this country is, whether the annual deficit of 140 millions, which exists in the public revenues, shall be made up by the oeconomies of the crown, or by additional taxes on the people—that the Parliament of Paris insists on the former, and has preferred banishment to the latter—that the Ottoman Porte has unexpectedly declared war against Russia; and that after their manner they have emprisoned the Rusian Ambassador residing at Constantiople—that affairs have come to a crisis in Holland which must very soon decide whether the States of that country are the sovereign or not—in fine that Europe is generally supposed in this moment at the eve of a general war" (DNA: PCC, No. 87, II). Short erred in supposing that Jay had concurred with TJ's "own sentiments on these subjects"; see note to Jay to Short, 5 July 1787.

1 This word interlined in substitution for "prospect," deleted.

To François Baudin

SIR   Paris Sep. 20. 1787.

I have duly received the letter of Aug. 31. which you did me the honour to write me. The power of appointing Consuls for the United states of America rests with Congress alone. As yet they have made but one appointment in France, which was that of Mr. Barclay. Perhaps it may yet be some time before any such appointments are made, as the convention for defining the Consular powers is not yet settled. I shall by the first occasion transmit your letter to Congress, and have no doubt that if they should appoint a Consul for your island they will pay to your application that just attention which your services and your character merit. I have the honour to be with much respect Sir Your most obedient & most humble servant,   TH: JEFFERSON

PrC (DLC); at foot of text: "M. Baudin. negociant à St. Martin. Isle de Rhé." I SHALL BY THE FIRST OCCASION TRANSMIT YOUR LETTER TO CONGRESS: TJ had received Baudin's letter on 12 Sep. and he wrote Jay only a week afterward, but presumably he did not then (or ever) transmit the application.

To Madame Plumard de Bellanger

[20 Sep. 1787]

Monsieur Jefferson a bien reçu la lettre que Madame Bellanger lui a fait l'honneur de lui ecrire, avec celle pour Monsieur de Rieux. Il l'a envoyé avec ses depeches, et a pris des mesures pour qu'elle soit rendue trés surement. Comme les négociants la-bas n'ont pas l'honneur de connoître Madame Bellanger, M. Jefferson a autorisé M. le Colonel Lewis de mettre sa signature sur les lettres de change de Monsieur de Rieux pour rassurer les negociants qu'elles seront payées au jour, et pour mettre par là M. de Rieux dans le cas d'exiger l'échange la plus favorable.—M. Jefferson est très sensible aux politesses de Madame de Bellanger. Le prix qu'il mette à l'honneur de sa connoissance l'engagent toujours de profiter des bonnes dispositions que Madame Bellanger a la bonté de temoigner pour lui, et de lui faire sa cour, ou à St. Germain ou à Paris, dans toutes les occasions convenables. Il la prie d'agreer l'hommage de ses respects, et de son attachement inviolable.

PrC (DLC); without date, which has been supplied from internal evidence and an entry in SJL under this date of a letter to Madame de Bellanger.

From André Limozin

MOST HONORED SIR   Havre de Grace 20th Septber. 1787

I have postponed answering to the Letter your Excellency hath honored me with in expectation to hear that the Boxes forwarded were deliverd in a good order, for I am very uneasy about it. [I have waited upon the Comptroler of our Customs, he shewd me the Copy of the orders forwarded to him by the Director of the Customs at Rouen by which there is not the least thing mentionned neither of Pearl ash nor of the Furs: in consequence where of I have desired the Comptroller to write again to the Director and to mentionn him that he had seen M. DeCalonne's Letter to Your Excellency by which it was said that Potash and Pearl ash, and likewise Furrs coming from America imported by French or American ships would be lyable to no duty. I knew very well that the said freedom granted was only for the Kings Duties, and not for the Droits Locaux. I have begd of our Comptroller to transmitt me the Letter of the Director but hath refused it; observing that the Farmers General have the Copy of the orders they have sent the 5th April last to the Director of Rouen, that these Farmers Generals could not refuse to deliver to your Excellency a Copy of these orders and duly certifyed by their Committee because if that Copy was not conform to what they wrote this new Copy would be lookd upon in the Customs House as a new order and would be directly and punctually complyd with. I must beg of your Excellency to observe that the Freedom of duties upon the Furrs is of the greatest importance for the American trade, which already is lyable to very great losses by the behavior of the Farmers Generals who will hardly pay now 33. Lvers. for the very first quality Virginia Tobbacco; and require still very heavy allowances for tare, whilst they continue to receive immense parcells arriving every day on account of the Contract for which they pay 38 Lvers. with no other allowance but the real Tare of the hhd. If representations on that Matter are not taken in Consideration by the Farmers Generals I am sory to foresee the intire ruin of the American trade in this Kingdom.][1] As long as I shall be considerd upon as Agent of the United States for this Port, I shall make it my duty to trouble your Excellency with my frequent observations for all whatever may be usefull for the greatest advantage of your Nation, for I dont know to whom I can apply beter to procure redress to the nation. If I should be too troublesome I hope your Excellency will have the indulgence to forgive my Zeal. It would be indeed very unhappy for the Nation if no body should take her interest in hands. The very same day your Excellency's said Letter reached me, an American Ship Saild for Philada. I had happily time enough to give hint thither that the Turks had declared War to Russia and that Politick Matters were in an alarming Situation; that there was more room to think that war would be the consequence there of, than to hope that Peace should continue.

In order that the Magistrates should pay a more speedy attention to my Care for the interest of the American Nation, would your Excellency give a petition to the Ministers exposing them the matter and the necessity which obligeth Your Excellency in these Circumstances to beg of them to write to the Intendant of the Marine in this Port, and to the Judge of the admiralty to grant me their assistance on every occasion when the interest of your Nation shall require it, because till such times as Congress hath apointed Consuls or agents in France, your Excellency hath desired me to act for such in this Port, observing that I am not for that reason intitled to require the least Salaries, proemiums, reward nor the least thing, but that the American Masters will be obliged to shew me their papers, to prove that they are truely Americans, and that I shall be obliged to Certify (gratis) that I have found them in a due form, in order to prevent all Frauds. I believe your Excellency's application will meet with a cheerfull approbation from the French Ministers, and from Congress.

I have observed by the Court Gazetes that the Court of Versailles had at last appointed an Ambassador for America. I wish the choice may be agreable to the American Nation, and that the French Government may find means to Ciment a real and Sincere Friendship and confidence between the two Nations. I believe the only mode to Succeed in that Point is to give more incouragement than hitherto hath been done to the american trade in this Kingdom; but unhappily incouragement to Commerce is not or at least very little known in this Country. We have received yesterday great many Letters from Amsterdam acquainting us that they had received hint that the Prussian Army had liberty to inter into the Province of Gueldern, in consequence the States of Holland had taken the Resolution to drownd the Country, thus they begd to make no further purchase for their account, nay even to not let the Goods shipped to sail. These advices are very alarming, and makes one fear that all hopes of reconciliation are lost. I beg of your Excellency to do me the Kindness to continue me your good advices. I expect that an American Ship will sail very soon from hence for New York. We have several waiting only for a fair wind bound for Philadelphia. On board of these Sundry valuable bales of Cambrick and St. Quintin, fine Linnens and Lawns have been shipped. I have the Honor to be with the highest regard Your Excellency's Most obedient & very Humble Servant,

ANDRE LIMOZIN

RC (MHi); endorsed; at the foot of the last page TJ's younger daughter wrote her name, "Mary Jefferson," practicing in the manner of the young and incidentally affording evidence (1) that she preferred this spelling and (2) that TJ's love of system and order did not cause him to exclude his nine-year-old and beloved Polly from his official archives. Tr of an extract (DLC); this extract was enclosed in TJ to La Boullaye, 24 Sep. 1787. Recorded in SJL as received 22 Sep. 1787.

¹ The text in brackets, supplied, is the whole of the extract in Short's hand.

To Le Mesurier & Cie.

GENTLEMEN   Paris Sep. 20. 1787.

I have duly received the letter of the 14th. instant with which you have been pleased to honor me, and should cheerfully do any thing in my power to aid you in the disposal of your tobaccoes. I have asked of the Minister an order to the Farmers general to make out a report of all their purchases since the date of the order of Bernis, that we may see whether they have complied with that order. I expect daily a communication of their return. If it should appear from that, or from other evidence that they have not purchased the whole quantity required by the order of Bernis and on the terms therein specified, I shall ask an immediate injunction on them to purchase what they are deficient. These measures will require some little time, and in the mean while you might do well perhaps to be treating with the Farmers yourselves. Should any thing favourable take place, I shall immediately communicate it thro the agents at the several ports. M. Limozin is invested with that character at Havre.

[158]

I have the honor to be Gentlemen Your most obedient & most humble servant, TH: JEFFERSON

PrC (DLC).

To Charles Thomson

DEAR SIR   Paris Sep. 20. 1787.

Your favor of April 28. did not come to my hands till the 1st. inst. Unfortunately the boxes of plants, which were a day too late to come by the April packet, missed the packet of June 10. also, and only came by that of July 25. They are not yet arrived at Paris, but I expect them daily. I am sensible of your kind attention to them, and that as you were leaving New York you took the course which bade fair to be the best. That they were forgotten in the hands in which you placed them, was probably owing to much business and more important. I have desired Mr. Madison to refund to you the money you were so kind as to advance for me. The delay of your letter will apologize for this delay of the repaiment. I thank you also for the extract of the letter you were so kind as to communicate to me on the antiquities found in the Western country. I wish that the persons who go thither would make very exact descriptions of what they see of that kind, without forming any theories. The moment a person forms a theory, his imagination sees in every object only the tracts which favor that theory. But it is too early to form theories on those antiquities. We must wait with patience till more facts are collected. I wish our philosophical society would collect exact descriptions of the several monuments as yet known, and insert them naked in their transactions, and continue their attention to those hereafter to be discovered. Patience and observation may enable us in time to solve the problem whether those who formed the scattering monuments in our Western country, were colonies sent off from Mexico, or the founders of Mexico itself? Whether both were the descendants or the progenitors of the Asiatic red men. The Mexican tradition mentioned by Dr. Robertson is an evidence, but a feeble one, in favor of the one opinion. The number of languages radically different, is a strong evidence in favor of the contrary one. There is an American of the name of Ledyard, he who was with Capt. Cook on his last voiage and wrote an account of that voiage, who is gone to Petersburg, from thence he was to go to Kamschatka, to cross over thence to the Northwest coast of America, and to penetrate through the main continent to our side of it. He is a person of ingenuity and information. Unfortunately he has too much imagination. However, if he escapes safely, he will give us new various, and useful information. I had a letter from him dated last March, when he was about to leave St. Petersburgh on his way to Kamschatka.

With respect to the inclination of the strata of rocks, I had observed them between the Blue ridge and North Mountain in Virginia to be parallel with the pole of the earth. I observed the same thing in most instances in the Alps between Nice and Turin: but in returning along the precipices of the Appennines where they hang over the Mediterranean, their direction was totally different and various; and you mention that in our Western country they are horizontal. This variety proves they have not been formed by subsidence as some writers of theories of the earth have pretended for then they should always have been in circular strata, and concentric. It proves too that they have not been formed by the rotation of the earth on it's axis, as might have been suspected had all these strata been parallel with that axis. They may indeed have been thrown up by explosions, as Whitehurst supposes, or have been the effect of convulsions. But there can be no proof of the explosion, nor is it probable that convulsions have deformed every spot of the earth. It is now generally agreed that rock grows, and it seems that it grows in layers in every direction, as the branches of trees grow in all directions. Why seek further the solution of this phaenomenon? Every thing in nature decays. If it were not reproduced then by growth, there would be a chasm.—I remember you asked me in a former letter whether the steam mill in London was turned by the steam immediately, or by the intermediate agency of water raised by the steam. When I was in London, Boulton made a secret of his mill. Therefore I was permitted to see it only superficially. I saw no waterwheels, and therefore supposed none. I answered you accordingly that there was none. But when I was at Nismes, I went to see the steam mill there, and they shewed it to me in all it's parts. I saw that their steam raised water, and that this water turned a wheel. I expressed my doubts of the necessity of the inter-agency of water, and that the London mill was without it. But they supposed me mistaken; perhaps I was so; I have had no opportunity since of clearing up the doubt.

We are here on the eve of great events. The contests in Holland seemed to render war probable. But it has actually begun in another quarter, between the Turks and Russians. The desertion of antient riends by the king of Prussia seems to render it necessary for them to seek new connections. New ones offer themselves, and I really suppose the offer will be accepted. A confederacy between France and the two empires may give law to the world. If it takes place the patriots of Holland will be saved, and the Turks expelled Europe. Constantinople, it is thought, will fall to the Empress of Russia, who, it is said, does not mean it as a dependance on her empire, but to make a separate kingdom of it for a younger son. Thus we may live to see the Greeks re-established as a people, and the language of Homer again a living language. Little will be wanting to amend the modern into antient Greek. It is whispered that the Mediterranean islands and Egypt would suit France well, the latter as the means of drawing the trade of the East Indies through the Red sea. Learning and civilisation will gain by the success of these projects, but it is first to be doubted whether they are seriously proposed, and then whether they may not be baffled by some event too small to be foreseen.

I had a letter from Mr. Churchman, but not developing his plan of knowing the longitude fully. I wrote him what was doubted about it so far as we could conjecture what it was.

I am with very great & sincere esteem Dear Sir Your friend & servant,
TH: JEFFERSON

RC (DLC: Thomson Papers). PrC (DLC: TJ Papers).

From John Bondfield

Bordeaux, 21 Sep. 1787. Acknowledges TJ's letter of 9 Sep.; is returning a letter sent under his cover for Thomas Blanchard, who was first employed, at Bondfield's request, by a French firm "and that with a view of drawing the Americans from the British line in which throu the influence of the English ship Broker who they all apply too as speaking their Language confounds and makes appear as one Nation." Blanchard, however, is now employed by an English firm, a change in employment that may alter the kind of information which TJ might wish to send him. Bondfield lacks sufficient authority to obtain the information TJ desires concerning the arrival of American ships in that port; has applied repeatedly for this information to the English broker without success.

RC (DLC); 4 p.; endorsed. Recorded in SJL as received 29 Sep. 1787. Bondfield forgot to enclose TJ's letter to Blanchard of 9 Sep. 1787 (see Bondfield to TJ, 6 Oct. 1787).

[161]

To André Limozin

SIR Paris Sep. 21. 1787.

I must beg the favor of you to put the inclosed letter into the hands of Monsr. Bourgoin who is going passenger in the packet to America. He has received my other dispatches, but this was not ready when he left Paris. The boxes of plants are not yet arrived, which I mention lest sickness or some other accident should detain the carter at Havre still.—With respect to war, appearances are still the same.—Monsr. de Brienne, brother of the Archbishop of Toulouse is appointed minister of war; the Count de la Luzerne governor of St. Domingo, and brother to the Chevalier de la Luzerne, is minister of the marine, M. Cabarrus (of the banque St Charles) Directeur du tresor royal instead of M. de la Borde who refused; le Comte de Moustier Minister plenipotentiary to America in the room of the Chevalier de la Luzerne. I am with much esteem, Sir, your most obedient humble servant,

TH: JEFFERSON

PrC (DLC). Enclosure: TJ to Thomson, 20 Sep. 1787 (see Limozin to TJ 23 Sep.).

From Montmorin, with Enclosure

à Versles. le 21. 7bre. 1787

J'avois communiqué, Monsieur, à Mr. de Villedeuil les observations que vous m'aviez fait l'honneur de m'adresser le 23. Juillet dernier relativement à différens objêts de Commerce à l'egard desquels vous demandéz que le Roi fasse joüir les Etats Unis des avantages du Traité Anséatique. Mr. Lambert, Successeur de Mr de Villedeuil, vient de me faire la réponse dont vous trouverez cijoint la copie. Vous y verrez, Monsieur, une preuve bien sensible du desir que nous avons de concourir à tout ce qui peut contribuer à la prospérité du Commerce des Etats Unis.

J'ai l'honneur d'être très sincérement, Monsieur, votre très humble et très obéissant Serviteur,

LE CTE DE MONTMORIN

ENCLOSURE

Copie de la lettre de Mr. Lambert à Mr. le Comte de Montmorin.
Paris le 6. 7bre. 1787.

Il m'a été représenté, Monsieur, avec la lettre que vous avés adressé

[162]

à M. de Villedeüil, un exemplaire imprimé de celle de M. de Calonne écrite le 22. 8bre. dernier à M. Jefferson, et copie des observations faites par ce Ministre Plenipotentiaire des Etats-Unis sur divers articles qu'elle renferme. Il résulte du Compte que je me suis fais rendre à cet égard, qu'il est question, entre autres choses, de faire jouir les Etats-Unis des avantages du traité Anséatique, pour les huiles de poisson étrangers, d'admettre les poils et peaux de Castor et les Cuirs verds en exemption de droits, et de les reduire sur la thérébentine, le Goudron et la poix.

Quoique ce traité soit nuisible aux progrès de la Peche nationale, et qu'elle doive éprouver encore plus d'obstacles dans la concurrence en faisant participer les américains à cette convention, il n'en faut pas moins tenir les engagemens pris sur ce point avec eux: ainsi je donnerai les ordres nécéssaires pour en procurer l'éxécution. Les droits sur la thérébentine, la poix et les goudrons seront réduits, et ceux sur les poils et peaux de Castor et les Cuirs verds presque entièrement supprimés.

On se plaint d'un droit sur la Potasse, perçu dans la Ville de Rouen; mais ce droit étant local il n'admet pas d'exception. Cependant s'il est possible de le modérer, je concourrai avec plaisir à donner encore ce nouveau temoignage d'encouragement au Commerce des Etats Unis. J'ai l'honneur d'être &c.

RC (DLC); in a clerk's hand, signed by Montmorin. FC (Arch. Aff. Etr., Paris, Corr. Pol., E.-U., XXXII, 357; Tr in DLC). Tr (DLC); in the hand of William Short. Not recorded in SJL but received on 22 Sep., in time for a copy to be enclosed in TJ to Jay of that date, q.v. Enclosure (DLC). Filed with the enclosure are two Tr in Short's hand; the RC of Lambert's letter to Montmorin (Arch. Aff. Etr., Paris, Corr. Pol., E.-U., XXXII, 352-3; Tr in DLC) has the following note at head of text: "Envoyé copie à M. Jefferson le 21

7bre. 1787."

Montmorin on 25 July had forwarded to Villedeuil TJ's OBSERVATIONS, with this comment: "Je ne puis, M. que m'en remettre a la forme que vous croirez devoir adopter; mais ce que j'ai à desirer c'est qu'il ne soit porté aucune atteinte aux avantages qui ont été promis aux Etats unis et que l'engagement qui a été pris a cet effet, ait son entière execution" (Arch. Aff. Etr., Paris, Corr. Pol., E.-U., XXXII, 352-3; Tr in DLC).

From John Stockdale

Sir   Piccadilly London 21st. Sepr. 1787.

I duly received yours of the 10th. Inst. and return you my sincere thanks for your kindness in sending the little Volumes wanted, which I received by favor of Mr. ———— of Hatton Garden, and for your attention in forwarding the continuation.

Mr. Lackington informed me that he had sent you a Catalogue a fortnight since, but for fear you should not have received it, I have sent another together with some other articles this day.

I this morning called upon Mr. Faden Map Engraver &c. at Charing Cross, he is a tradesman of the strictest honor and in-

[163]

tegrity in his line of business. I put the question candidly to him, "what would be a fair Price for me to pay for the use of the Plate of Virginia" when he gave it as his opinion that "Thirty Guineas was betwixt Man and Man a fair price for working 1,000." Mr. Coxe Printer in Quality Court Chancery Lane is the person that I employed to work your Plate; he has workt exactly 1,000 and 25, to supply any accidents that might happen by tearing, &c. Notwithstanding Mr. Faden's opinion I now leave it to you to deduct whatever you think proper for your Bill, and also be so good as to deduct for Mr. Berquins works and the other Books you have been so kind as to send. I will endeavour to find out some method to send your Books to different parts of America, as speedily as possible. I am with great Respect, Sir, Your much obliged and very hble. Servt.,   JOHN STOCKDALE

P.S. I have sent again this day to Richardson's for the "Historical Remarks on free States," but they say they have not got one left, but I will endeavour to get one from some private Gentleman.

RC (MHi); endorsed. Recorded in SJL as received 25 Sep. 1787.

From Bouébe

[*Paris, 22 Sep. 1787.* Recorded in SJL as received 23 Sep. 1787. Not found; enclosed in TJ to Jay, 8 Oct. (1st letter); see also Bouébe to TJ, 12 Sep. 1787; TJ to Bouébe, 2 Oct. 1787.]

To Burrill Carnes

SIR   Paris Sep. 22. 1787.

I am honored by your favor of the 17th. instant. A war between France and England does not necessarily engage America in it; and I think she will be disposed rather to avail herself of the advantages of a neutral power. By the former usage of nations the goods of a friend were safe tho taken in an enemy bottom, and those of an enemy were lawful prize tho found in a free bottom. But in our treaties with France &c. we have established the simpler rule that a free bottom makes free goods, and an enemy bottom enemy goods. The same rule has been adopted by the treaty of armed neutrality between Russia, Sweden, Denmark, Holland and Portugal, and assented to by France and Spain. Contraband goods however are always excepted, so that they may still be seized, but the same powers have established that naval stores are not contraband: and this may be considered now as the law of nations. Tho' England acquiesced under this during the late war, rather than draw on herself the neutral powers, yet she never acceded to the new principle, and her obstinacy on this point is what has prevented the late renewal of her treaty with Russia. On the commencement of a new war this principle will probably be insisted on by the neutral powers, whom we may suppose to be Sweden, Denmark, Portugal, America, and perhaps Spain. Quaere if England will again acquiesce. Supposing these details might be useful to you, I have taken the liberty of giving them, and of assuring you of the esteem with which I am, Sir, your very humble servant,

TH: JEFFERSON

PrC (DLC).

To John Jay

SIR   Paris Sep. 22. 1787.

The letters of which the inclosed are copies, are this moment received, and as there is a possibility that they may reach Havre before the packet sails, I have the honor of inclosing them to you. They contain a promise of reducing the duties on tar, pitch and turpentine, and that the government will interest itself with the city of Rouen to reduce the local duty on Potash. By this you will perceive that we are getting on a little in this business, tho', under their present embarrasments, it is difficult to procure the attention of the ministers to it. The parliament has enregistered the edict for a rigorous levy of the deux vingtiemes. As this was proposed by the king in lieu of the impot territorial, there is no doubt now that the latter, with the stamp tax, will be immediately repealed. There can be no better proof of the revolution in the public opinion as to the powers of the Monarch, and of the force too of that opinion. Six weeks ago we saw the king displaying the plentitude of his omnipotence, as hitherto conceived, to enforce these two acts. At this day he is forced to retract them by the public voice; for as to the opposition of the parliament, that body is too little esteemed to produce this effect in any case where the public do not throw themselves into the same scale. I have the honour to be with the most perfect esteem and respect, Sir, your most obedient & most humble servant,   TH: JEFFERSON

PrC (DLC). Tr (DLC); in an unidentified hand. Enclosures: Montmorin to TJ, 21 Sep. 1787, and its enclosure.

To John Jay

SIR   Paris Sep. 22. 1787.

When I had the honor of addressing you this morning, intelligence was handing about which I did not think well enough authenticated to communicate to you. As it is now ascertained, I avail myself of the chance that another post may yet reach Havre before the departure of the packet. This will depend on the wind which has for some days been unfavorable. I must premise that this court about 10. days ago declared, by their Chargé des affaires in Holland, that if the Prussian troops continued to menace Holland with an invasion, his Majesty was determined, in quality of ally, to succour that province. An *official* letter from the Hague, of the 18th. inst. assures that the Prussian army entered the territory of Holland on the 15th. that most of the principal towns had submitted, some after firing a gun or two, others without resistance: that the Rhingrave de Salm had evacuated Utrecht, with part of the troops under his command, leaving behind him 144. peices of cannon, with great warlike stores: that the standard of Orange was hoisted every where: that no other cockade could be worn at the Hague: that the States general were to assemble that night for reinstating the Stadtholder in all his rights. The letter concludes 'we have this moment intelligence that Woerden has capitulated, so that Amsterdam remains without defence.' So far the letter. We know otherwise that Monsr. de St. Priest, who had set out on his embassy to the Hague, has stopped at Antwerp, not chusing to proceed further till new orders. This court has been completely deceived, first by it's own great desire to avoid a war, and secondly by calculating that the king of Prussia would have acted on principles of common sense, which would surely have dictated that a power, lying between the jaws of Russia and Austria, should not separate itself from France, unless indeed he had assurances of dispositions in those two powers which are not supposed to exist. On the contrary I am persuaded that they ask the alliance of France, whom we suppose to be under hesitations between her reluctance to abandon the Turks, her jealousy of increasing, by their spoils, the power of the two empires, and her inability to oppose them. If they cannot obtain her alliance, they will surely join themselves to England and Prussia.

Official advices are received that the first division of the Russian army has passed the Borysthenes into the Polish Ukraine and is marching towards the frontiers of Turkey.—Thus we may con-

[166]

sider the flames of war as completely kindled in two distinct parts of this quarter of the globe, and that tho' France and England have not yet engaged themselves in it, the probabilities are that they will do it. I have the honor to be with the most perfect esteem and respect Sir Your most obedient & most humble servant,

TH: JEFFERSON

PrC (DLC). Tr (DLC); in an unidentified hand.

TJ's emphasis upon the phrase OFFICIAL LETTER served to inform Jay that Dumas had not provided the information and that it must, therefore, have come either from the French minister at The Hague (the Marquis de Verac) or from the Dutch minister at Versailles (De Berkenroode), the latter was indubitably TJ's informant (see TJ to Jay, 24 Sep. 1787; TJ to Abigail Adams, 4 Oct. 1787).

To André Limozin

Paris Sep. 22. 1787.

Mr. Jefferson begs the favor of Monsieur Limozin to deliver the inclosed to the same Monsr. Bourgoin, passenger on board the packet, to whom he desired his last to be delivered. This contains the copy of a letter from the minister promising the reduction of duties on tar pitch and turpentine, which Mr. Jefferson had sollicited, and to interest himself with the city of Rouen to reduce the local duty on Potash which Monsr. Limozin had written to Mr. J. about, and which he had also sollicited from the minister.

PrC (DLC). Enclosure: TJ to Jay of this date (1st letter).

To André Limozin

SIR Paris Sep. 22. 1787.

I must trouble you with another letter to Mr. Jay, to be delivered to Monsr. Bourgoin on board the packet, which I hope will not be sailed before it gets to your hands, as the latter is of extreme importance. It is to inform Congress that *official* advice is just received here that the Prussian troops entered the territory of Holland on the 15th. instant, that most of the principal towns had submitted, that Utrecht was evacuated by the Rhingrave de Salm, and Woerden capitulated, so that Amsterdam remained without defence. M. de St. Priest had stopped at Antwerp and waited further orders.— We know also that the first division of the Russian army has passed the Borysthenes into the Polish Ukraine, and is marching towards the frontiers of Turkey. War then is well kindled in those two quarters.

Monsr. Cabarrus is arrived at Paris, but will not accept the appointment offered him unless they will adopt his plans. On this there is hesitation; so that it is not certain he will come in.

I have received your favor of the 20th. and shall make proper use of it's contents. Should the packet be sailed, I will pray you to send my letter by the first of the vessels which you mention bound for Philadelphia. I am with great esteem Sir your most obedient humble servant, TH: JEFFERSON

PrC (DLC). Enclosure: TJ to Jay of this date (2nd letter).

From Zachariah Loreilhe

Bordeaux, 22 Sep. 1787. Acknowledges TJ's letter of 9 Sep., which arrived only the day before, since it was addressed to L'Orient; will use the information therein as TJ requested. Has gone to Bordeaux on business for Barclay and will remain there and at Bergerac until he hears from Barclay. Tenders his services, at Barclay's suggestion in the "affair of the disputed Inssurance bettween Messrs. Geraud & Rolland of Amsterdam and Mr. Barclay as Consul General"; is willing to go to Amsterdam if his going would bring the matter to a speedy conclusion.

RC (DLC); 2 p.; endorsed. Recorded in SJL as received 26 Sep. 1787.

From C. W. F. Dumas

MONSIEUR   La Haie 23e. 7bre. 1787

L'état où je suis avec mon Epouse et fille est affreux. Le désordre est dans la province et dans ce lieu, le bras civil obéit à la Haie au militaire, et à la populace écumante de rage. Tout cela n'est peut-être pas encore à son comble. Nous avons sauvé notre vie foible, en nous réfugiant à l'hôtel de France, dénués de tout le nécessaire à l'entretien de nos personnes, sans pouvoir parvenir à nos hardes et linge, sauvés ça et là précipitamment, en divers lieux, où nous ne pouvons les réclamer que Dieu sait quand, de peur d'exposer les gens qui nous les gardent peut-être. Notre maison a été sauvée jusqu'ici par des sentinelles qui y vivent à discretion. Je ne puis y aller, de peur d'être assailli en chemin et assommé impunément comme cela pensa m'arriver hier où je fus hué et poursuivi. J'ai eu beau me constituer prisonnier; on ne veut pas de moi, mais, à ce qu'il paroît, que je périsse au milieu d'une meutte, ou par quelque autre piege ou coup que l'on puisse ensuite déguiser ou colorer comme on voudra.

Mr. l'Ambassadeur doit arriver ce soir. J'implorerai la protection, les secours et l'assistance à tous égards de Sa Majesté, les plus prompts, sans quoi [nous périssons de] désolation et de misère, car personne ne peut ni n'ose nous rendre le moindre service, même mercenaire, de peur qu'on ne crie haro sur lui aussi. Je supplie [Votre Excellence de] vouloir faire connoître préalablement ce triste Cas aux Etats Unis et de prévenir les impressions sinistres que dans la suite on pourroit vouloir faire naître contre moi, uniquement pour avoir été ami fidèle du Souverain qui vient de succomber à la conquête, et d'avoir fait de mon mieux pour y bien servir les Etats Unis, mes maîtres, et la France, ses bons Alliés. Je ne sais si je pourrai vous donner, Monsieur, ultérieurement de mes nouvelles, savoir, si je vivrois. [Au nom du ciel] ayez, Monsieur, une conférence au moins personnelle si ce n'est Ministérielle, ou avec Mr. de Montmorin ou avec Mr. de Rayneval, sur mon horrible situation, et sur les prompts secours du Roi en tout [sens] dont j'ai besoin. Si je vis et puis être un peu plus calme, dans la suite, je donnerai à Votre Excellence une idée juste de toute ma propriété [ici] et en Gueldre, en biens et immeubles, dont mon malheur et la confusion qui s'ensuivit [doivent me] faire perdre plus des ¾ de leur valeur, [. . . lisent] forcément, et pendant ces troubles. [Dieu ait] pitié de moi, et benisse votre Excellence, les Etats Unis et le Roi, mes uniques ressources dans [la] détresse De votre Excellence l'excessivement infortuné [. . . .]

RC (DLC); unsigned; MS faded; illegible words supplied from FC (Dumas Letter Books, Rijksarchief, The Hague; photostats in DLC). Recorded in SJL as received 1 Oct. 1787.

On the day before this letter was written, Dumas wrote to the Marquis de Verac, asking him to inform TJ of "l'état affreux où je me trouve plongé avec ma pauvre famille" in order that he might bring it immediately to the attention of Congress (same; this text, serving as FC for both the letter to Verac and that to TJ, is dated 22 Sep. 1787).

From André Limozin

MOST HONORED SIR   Havre de Grace 23rd Septber 1787

Since my former of the 20th instant, I have received this day the Letter your Excellency hath honored me with the 21st. instant, inclosing me one for M. Charles Thomson Secretary of Congress which I shall deliver into the hands of Mr. Burgoin, if I can find out his Lodgings. The Carters left this Town the 4th. inst. with the Boxes, and was bound to deliver them unto your Excellency the 15th. instant under the Fine to be deprived of one third of his freight. I beg of your Excellency to make him Stand to his agreement, and upon no consideration whatsoever to pay that Carrman, agreable to his terms, because it is the only way to make these Fellows diligent and punctuall. I am assured by Mr. Cabarus' oncle that he thinks that his nephew shall not accept of the imployment offerd to him, that he will not prefer an uncertainty to a very agreable Condition that he injoys now, and wherein he may look himself fixed upon a very solid footing.

We are here reduced to a very alarming situation if War should take place before the insuing May.

I have the honor to be with the very highest regard Your Excellency's Most obedient & very Humble Servant,

ANDRE LIMOZIN

RC (MHi); addressed and endorsed. Recorded in SJL as received 25 Sep. 1787.

To La Boullaye

à Paris ce 24me. Septembre. 1787.

J'ai eu l'honneur, Monsieur, de vous communiquer l'information que j'avois reçu de l'Agent des etats unis au port du Havre, de ce que les employés des fermes demandoient les droits anciens sur une cargaison de pot-asse qui venoit d'y arriver. Sur les soupçons que vous avez bien voulu m'exprimer que ce pourroient etre les droits locaux qu'on demandoit, j'ai écrit à l'Agent, et j'ai actuellement l'honneur de vous faire passer sa reponse. Vous le jugerez peut etre à propos, Monsieur, de demander aux fermes la copie des ordres qu'ils ont donné pour l'execution de la lettre de M. de Calonnes.

Je prends la liberté, en meme temps, de vous renouveller la demande que j'ai eu l'honneur de vous faire, d'avoir communication du rapport des fermes sur l'execution de l'ordre de Bernis.

Je vous prie, Monsieur, de me pardonner les importunités que je vous fais sur ces objets. Les interets du commerce des deux pays, et le desir de les voir se rapprocher de plus en plus m'en imposent le devoir.

J'ai l'honneur d'etre avec des sentiments d'estime et d'attachement très distingués, Monsieur, votre tres humble et très obeissant serviteur,

TH: JEFFERSON

PrC (DLC). Enclosure: Extract of Limozin to TJ, 20 Sep. 1787, q.v. On the subject of this letter, see Limozin to TJ, 31 Aug. 1787; TJ to Limozin, 9 Sep. 1787; La Boullaye to TJ, 12 Nov. 1787.

To John Jay

SIR   Paris Sep. 24. 1787.

The times are now so critical that every day brings something new and important, not known the day before. Observing the wind still unfavorable, I am in hopes that the packet may not sail tomorrow, and that this letter may be at Havre in time for that conveiance. Mr. Eden has waited on Count Montmorin to inform him officially that England must consider it's convention with France relative to the giving notice of it's naval armaments as at an end, and that they are arming generally. This is considered here as a declaration of war.—The Dutch Ambassador told me yesterday that he supposed the Prussian troops probably in possession of the Hague. I asked him if it would interrupt the course of business, commercial or banking, in Amsterdam; and particularly whether our depot of money there was safe. He said, the people of Amsterdam would be surely so wise as to submit, when they should see that they could not oppose the Stadholder: therefore he supposed our depot safe, and that there would be no interruption of business. It is the hour of the departure of the post: so I have only time to add assurances of the respect and esteem with which I have the honour to be Sir Your most obedient humble servt.,

                                                     TH: JEFFERSON

PrC (DLC). Tr (DLC); in an unidentified hand.

To André Limozin

                                                    Paris Sep. 24. 1787.

Yet another letter Sir to go by the packet. It conveys information that the British Minister here has formally notified the court that they are arming generally for the present war. I am Sir Your most obedt. servt.,   TH: JEFFERSON

PrC (DLC). Enclosure: TJ to John Jay, preceding.

From André Limozin

Le Havre, 24 Sep. 1787. Since his letter of 23 Sep., has received TJ's letter of 22 Sep. and will try to place its enclosure in Bourgoin's hands; will be happy if TJ's application for the reduction of duties on tar, pitch, and turpentine, and the local duty at Rouen on potash succeeds.

RC (MHi); 2 p.; endorsed.

From Willink & Van Staphorst

Amsterdam 24 September 1787

We are honored with Your Excellency's respected favor of 15th Inst. desiring our Concurrence to your drawing immediately upon us £6000 to £7000. We say between Six and Seven Thousand Livres; To which request our personal Esteem for your Excellency, and the Regard we at all times pay to the Credit of the United States induces our ready Acquiesence, begging your Bill may be at Sight, as we do not choose to come under Acceptances, during the present critical situation of public affairs here. We are confidant his Excellency John Adams Esqr. will chearfully assent to this and every other disposal you might make on us for account of the United States, but for the present we cannot assume to discharge the Monthly Amount, you wish our Authorization to value upon us for on their Account. However we hope the Credit of America from the Proceedings of the Convention now assembled at Philadelphia, will speedily rise so as to justify our Compliance, and in the mean time if your Excellency will please advise whenever you find it necessary to pass a Bill upon us, you may depend upon our best disposition to prevent any inconveniency to your Excellency.

With great respect We have the Honor to be Your Excellency's Most obedient and very humble Servants,

WILHEM & JAN WILLINK
NIC: & JACOB VAN STAPHORST

RC (DLC); endorsed. Recorded in SJL as received 29 Sep. 1787.

To William Carmichael

DEAR SIR   Paris Sep. 25. 1787.

The copy of your letter of July 9. and that of Aug. 22. came to hand together. The original of the former I never received. My last to you was dated June 14. I heard indirectly that Mr. *Grand*[1] had refused to *pay a bill* of *yours*, but he never said a word to me on

[172]

the subject, nor mentioned any *letter of yours* in consequence of it. I have stated the matter to the *board of treasury*. I also wrote to Mr. Adams a state of the same fact. There are at Amsterdam *100,000 florins at his disposal*. Colo. Smith will endeavor to get *for you an order* to *draw on* that *fund*. The subject of *Smith's mission to Portugal* appeared to me so *causeless* as *given out* that I imagined it was only the *ostensible* one, the *real cause remaining a secret between him and Congress*. Yet I never heard *any other hinted*. With respect to the reimbursement to the Count d'Expilly for the maintenance of our prisoners at Algiers, I wrote to Mr. Jay what you had formerly communicated to me, but am not authorised to give any answer. I think it important to destroy at Algiers every idea that Congress will redeem our captives there, perhaps at any price, much less at that paid by Spain. It seems to be the general opinion that the redeeming them would occasion the capture of greater numbers by increasing the incitements to cruise against us. We must never make it their interest to go out of the streights in quest of us, and we must avoid entering into the streights, at least till we are rich enough to arm in that sea. The Spanish consul therefore cannot too soon withdraw himself from all responsibility for our prisoners. As to the affair of the frigate of South Carolina, I communicated to you every thing I knew on the subject, by inclosing you all the papers which had come to my hands.   I have received letters and gazettes from America to the 25. of July. The federal convention was likely to sit to the month of October. A thin Congress was sitting at the same time. They had passed an Ordinance dividing the Country North of Ohio into three states, and providing both a present and future form of government for them. The sale of their lands commences this month. An idea had got abroad in the Western country that Congress was ceding to Spain the navigation of the Missisipi for a certain time. They had taken flame at it, and were assembling Conventions on the subject, wherein the boldest and most dangerous propositions were to be made. They are said to be now 60,000 strong, and are more formidable from their spirit than numbers. This is the only bone of contention which can arise between Spain and us for ages. It is a pity it could not be settled amicably. When we consider that the Missisipi is the only issue to the ocean for five eighths of the territory of the U.S. and how fast that territory peoples, the ultimate event cannot be mistaken. It would be wise then to take arrangements according to what must happen.

There had been a hope that the affairs of Holland might be accomodated without a war. But this hope has failed. The Prussian troops have entered the territories of the republic. The Stadtholder is now at the Hague, and there seems to be no force capable of opposing him. England too has notified this court by her envoy, two days ago, that she is arming. In the mean time *little provision* has been *made here* against such an *event*. M. de *Segur declares* that six *weeks ago* he *proposed in council* to *march 24,000 men into Holland*. The *archbishop* is *charged* principally with having *prevented this*. He seems to have been *duped by his* strong desire for peace, and by calculating that the K. of Prussia would have acted on principles of common sense. To complicate the game still more, you know of the war which has arisen between Russia and the Turks. You know also that it was excited there, as well as at Berlin by the English. Former alliances thus broke, Prussia having thrown herself into the scale opposed to France, Turkey having abandoned her councils and followed the instigations of her enemies, what remains for this country to do? *I know* that *Russia proposed a confederation* with *this court* but *this court* without committing *itself wished* to know the *final determination* of the *emperor, that he* came *into the proposition*, has formed a line from the Prussian to the Turkish confines by 4. camps of 30,000 men in one, and 50,000 in each of the others. *Yet* it does *not seem that France has closed* the *proposal* in *favor of* which every principle of common sense enlists itself. *The queen, Breteuil and Monmorin* have been for some time *decidedly for* this *triple alliance* which, especially if *aided by Spain*, would give *law to the world*. The *premier* is still *accused with hesitation*. They begin to say that *tho he is* a patriotic *minister and an able one for peace he* has not *energy enough for war*. *If* this *takes place* the consequences to Prussia and the *Stadholder* may be easily foreseen. *Whether it* does *or not* the Turks must *quit Europe*. Neutrality should be our plan: because no nation should without urgent necessity begin a second war while the debts of the former remain unpaid. The accumulation of debts is a most fearful evil. But ever since the accession of the present king of England, that court has unerringly done what common sense would have dictated not to do. Now common sense dictates that they should avoid forcing us to take part against them, because this brings on them a heavy land war. Therefore they will not avoid it: they will stop our ships, visit and harrass them, seise them on the most frivolous pretexts and oblige us to take from them Canada and Nova Scotia, which it is not our interests to possess. Mr. Eden sets out in a few days for Madrid.

You will have to oppose in him the most bitter enemy against our country which exists. His late and sudden elevations makes the remembrance of the contempt we shewed to his mission in America rankle the more in his breast. Whether his principles will restrain him to fair modes of opposition, I am not well enough acquainted with him to say. I know nothing of him but his parliamentary history, and that is not in his favor. As he wishes us every possible ill, all the lies of the London papers are true history in his creed, and will be propagated as such, to prejudice against us the mind of the court where you are. You will find it necessary to keep him well in your eye, and to trace all his foot-steps.—You know doubtless that M. de Brienne has been appointed minister of war, and the Count de la Luzerne minister of marine. He is brother of the Chevalier, and at present in St. Domingo of which he is Commandant. The Count de Moustier goes minister to America, the Chevalier de la Luzerne preferring the promise of the first vacant embassy. Lambert is Comptrolleur general. De la Borde and Cabarrus have successively refused the office of Directeur du tresor royal.—Having now got the maps for the Notes on Virginia, I will send by the Count d'Aranda two copies, one for yourself, and one for Monsr. de Campomanes. By the same conveyance I will forward the Ratification of the treaty with Marocco, and ask the favor of you to contrive it to that court. Mr. Barclay is gone to America. I am with great esteem, Dear Sir, your most obedient humble servant,

Th: Jefferson

PrC (DLC); partly in code; the text *en clair* for the coded passages is on a separate sheet in TJ's hand. Tr (ViRVal); in H. A. Washington's hand, with coded passages decoded interlineally, but with several omissions.

This letter represents the first use of a coded message in the correspondence between TJ and Carmichael. Ironically, the most significant passage in it—the assertion that the Mississippi Question was the ONLY BONE OF CONTENTION WHICH CAN ARISE BETWEEN SPAIN AND US FOR AGES and that it would therefore be wise TO TAKE ARRANGEMENTS ACCORDING TO WHAT MUST HAPPEN—was one that TJ must have intended Carmichael to pass on to Floridablanca but, to make doubly sure, left uncoded. These facts and this letter can only assume their proper perspective in the light of Carmichael's insistence through more than two years that he could not safely or fully discuss

international affairs or the domestic policies and court intrigues of Madrid without being possessed of a cipher. Carmichael first broached the subject in June, 1785, and it is perhaps significant that he then suggested to TJ that Congress would do well to send "a common cypher . . . to each of their Ministers and Chargé Des Affaires"; he continued to urge the need of a code and thought that it might be "useful to give Mr. Adams a copy of the same" (Carmichael to TJ, 27 June, 28 July, 2 Sep., 29 Sep., 24 Oct., and 6 Nov. 1785; Jay appears to have originated the suggestion, however, that Carmichael should be enabled to correspond in code with him; see Jay to Carmichael, 14 Mch. 1786, *Dipl. Corr., 1783-89*, III, 306). TJ promised to send a copy of the cipher he had given Adams, and assured Carmichael that Lamb would bring one possessed in common by TJ, Lamb, Barclay, and

Adams (TJ to Carmichael, 18 Aug., 18 and 25 Oct., and 4 Nov. 1785). The letter containing this assurance was handed to Carmichael by Lamb shortly after the latter arrived in Madrid on 4 Dec. 1785. But Lamb, after remaining in Madrid for almost two months, departed for Africa without fulfilling Carmichael's expectations: during this time he neither turned over to Carmichael the cipher that he was supposed to have brought nor permitted him to take a copy of the duplicate in his own possession. It was not until after Lamb had departed from Madrid that Carmichael explained to TJ how Lamb, on examining his papers, found "that he had but one Copy of the Cypher and . . . that he recollects that Mr. Barclay has the one Destined for me"; accordingly, Carmichael stated, he would have to await Barclay's arrival before sending TJ "any confidential Communications" (Carmichael to TJ, 17 Dec., ca. 26 Jan. and 4 Feb. 1786). Lamb's explanation was certainly evasive and possibly not true. He must have known, as Carmichael did, that a cipher was intended for Carmichael and that it would be one possessed by the Commissioners, by their agents (Barclay and himself), and by Carmichael, thus enabling all of them, in TJ's words, "to keep up such correspondencies with each other as may be requisite" (TJ to Carmichael, 4 Nov. 1785). If this was so, it is remarkable that Lamb, awaiting over a course of weeks the results of Carmichael's effective but somewhat reluctant intercession for him at the court of Madrid, should not have allowed Carmichael to take a copy of his own duplicate. If the explanation that Lamb gave Carmichael was correct—that he did not have Carmichael's copy of the cipher among his papers—then several explanations are possible: (1) TJ retained it in order to send it later by Barclay; (2) Lamb carried it but lost it or misplaced it among his papers; (3) Lamb disposed of it elsewhere or retained it for the purpose of doing so —a serious supposition but not beyond the bounds of possibility in view of Lamb's proved failure to meet his responsibilities as a public agent; or (4) Lamb actually had the duplicate cipher with him and accessible, but deliberately avoided giving it up for some unknown reason—possibly out of pique, possibly because he felt some distrust

of Carmichael (evidently a mutual feeling), possibly because he thought an improper use might be made of the code. It does not seem likely that TJ failed to send the cipher by Lamb; the reference to it was the first matter to be touched upon in his letter of 4 Nov. 1785, and the opening words were: "At length a confidential opportunity arrives for conveying to you a cypher; it will be handed you by the bearer Mr. Lambe." Lamb's refusal in 1787 to surrender to Carmichael his own copy of the cipher, even on the specific direction of TJ and after Lamb had suffered the ignominy of being recalled, would seem to support the conjecture that he carried the duplicate but declined, for some undisclosed reason, to hand it over while he was in Madrid in 1786. It is perhaps even more significant that TJ refrained from commenting upon Carmichael's explanation for the failure of Lamb to turn over the cipher and the supposition of the latter that it was Barclay who was expected to bring a copy. It is also worth noting that, on his return from England and after receiving Carmichael's explanation, TJ began furnishing him with particularly favorable accounts of American affairs, even quoting the calculated optimism of Franklin (TJ to Carmichael, 5 May, 20 June, and 7 July 1786; Franklin to TJ, 20 Mch. 1786, note).

Meanwhile, Barclay had turned up in Madrid and remained there several weeks in the spring of 1786. But neither he nor Carmichael in their letters mentioned the cipher that the latter had been awaiting so anxiously and that Lamb had said Barclay was bringing. Lamb himself returned to Madrid soon after Barclay's departure. He was even more distant toward Carmichael than before and the latter, still without a cipher, remained strangely silent on the subject. Perhaps fearing that TJ would think this silence required some explanation in the light of his earlier insistence on the need of a means of secret communication, he ventured the following observation possibly as an excuse: "I mention nothing of the Foreign or even interior politics of this court, because I have remarked that in your answers to my letters, you appeared not disposed to enter into any observations on such subjects" (Carmichael to TJ, 15 July 1786). The premise was sound, but its conclusion was scarcely convincing in view of the fact that Carmichael followed this with three letters in quick succession that surpassed most of his previous communications in revealing his familiarity with the policies of Floridablanca's administration, in containing probing questions about diplomatic subjects, and in setting forth indiscreet hints and suggestions. In one of these Carmichael went so far as to remark that if TJ chose "to be acquainted with two Amiable Ladies," he might deliver two enclosed letters himself. TJ ignored such crude hints in his replies, and silently deleted as many as four indiscreet passages in a single copy of one of Carmichael's letters that he forwarded to Jay (Carmichael to TJ, 18 and 31 July, 17 Aug., and 4 Sep. 1786; see Vol. 10: 330, note). But Carmichael's observation gave TJ the opportunity of reopening the question of a cipher: "You observe that I do not write to you on foreign subjects. My reason has been that our letters are often opened; and I do not know that you have yet received the cypher Mr. Barclay was to leave with you. If you have not, be so good as to ask a copy of his. . . . Indeed I wish you could get the one from Mr. Lamb, which is a copy" (TJ to Carmichael, 22 Aug. 1786). TJ knew that letters going to Spain by post were opened not often but always, and almost invariably he sent letters to Carmichael by private hands; the reason for his failure to write on foreign subjects lay deeper. Carmichael acted promptly on receiving TJ's renewed authorization, but, presumably because Barclay had not yet returned from Morocco, he applied to Lamb "expressing a wish . . . of having the original of the paper in question to be sent to me by a safe conveyance." Lamb remained intransigent: "That Gentleman," Carmichael informed TJ, "thinks without a peremptory order, he ought not send it" (Carmichael to TJ, 29 Sep. 1786). Lamb told TJ that "By post all my letters are broke," but he made no mention of his correspondence with Carmichael concerning the cipher (Lamb to TJ, 10 Oct. 1786). Shortly after this Barclay and Franks arrived back in Madrid, and Carmichael arranged an interview with Floridablanca. Immediately after this interview Carmichael wrote TJ, mentioned an audience the French ambassador had had with the

king on the subject of a letter written by Marie Antoinette concerning the differences between the courts of Madrid and Naples, and promised in a few days to find out the effect of the queen's communication (Carmichael to TJ, 15 Nov. 1787). Carmichael's letter was conveyed by Franks, who departed from Madrid the next day. The remarkable fact is that, in a letter touching on foreign affairs of a fairly secret nature, Carmichael made no use of the cipher that Franks had already given him, nor did he mention the fact that he possessed such a cipher. A month later Carmichael reported on matters of some importance—continued proofs of Floridablanca's good will, the Portuguese ambassador's hint that the present was a good moment to press for the conclusion of the treaty, and the same ambassador's suggestion that "mutual arrangements" might be made for suppressing the Barbary piracies (the last is a certain indication that Carmichael had learned through the Portuguese ambassador at Madrid of the proposed confederation against the Barbary powers that TJ had given to the Portuguese ambassador in Paris only two weeks earlier; see Vol. 10: 562)—but still he felt no need to discuss such matters in code or to mention the fact that he was then in a position to do so (Carmichael to TJ, 17 Dec. 1786). Late in December, TJ forwarded to Carmichael "a note desiring Mr. Lambe to deliver you his cyphers." The use of the plural may or may not be significant, but TJ's direction to Lamb shows that Franks, who was then in Paris, had not told TJ a copy of Barclay's cipher had been left with Carmichael. It is also noteworthy that TJ made no comment on the hints given Carmichael by the Portuguese minister, that he supplied him with favorable news from America, and that he sent him a present of a copying press (TJ to Carmichael, 26 Dec. 1786). Eight months passed after Carmichael received a cipher from Franks before it was mentioned again (he had written only one letter during that time), and then it was TJ who brought the subject up: on returning to Paris from his southern tour, TJ resumed "immediately the correspondence with which you have been pleased to honour me," and then casually asked at the end of his letter: "Have you yet the cypher of which I formerly wrote to you, or any copy of it?" (TJ had seen

Barclay in Bordeaux and may have learned from him that Carmichael had received a copy from Franks; italics supplied). In response to this direct and carefully phrased inquiry, Carmichael, two years after he had begun to await anxiously the arrival of a cipher, wrote simply: "I have the cypher you mention and you may make use of it when you think proper. By your manner of employing it I shall judge of what I ought to do" (Carmichael to TJ, 9 July 1787). As if to support this remarkably equivocal statement, Carmichael wrote: "I enter into no details of the Politics of this Court. In the present situation of Europe, you are at the fountain head and can better develop than myself the Catastrophe. I own I cannot plunge thro' the chaos." Six weeks later he wrote again: "If you wish that I should write you regularly make use of the Cypher, Nothing can give me greater pleasure and assuredly you will never have reason to complain of the confidence" (Carmichael to TJ, 22 Aug. 1787). In response to this, TJ wrote the present letter with its coded passages, and then, in the next few months, there emerged the discovery that "Colonel Franks must have made some mistake in the delivery of the Cypher": the code that Carmichael had obtained—or at least the one that he returned to TJ for verification—was not the Adams-TJ-Barclay-Lamb copy but one that TJ did not possess. Carmichael sent this erroneous code to TJ "in order that you may have it in your power by seeing the paper to discover the reason of this extraordinary *mistake*"—a remark clearly intended to convey the impression that the mistake had been calculated. TJ acknowledged the letter enclosing the copy, but made no allusion to the enclosure or to the alleged mistake (he had already stated that the "cyphered words in your letter of Apr. 14 prove to me that Mr. Barclay left you a wrong cypher," a fact that scarcely needed proof; see Carmichael to TJ, 6 Sep., 15 Oct., 5 and 15 Nov. 1787; 14 and 29 Apr., 8 and 18 May, 24 July 1788; TJ to Carmichael, 15 Dec. 1787; 1 Feb., 3 June, and 12 Aug. 1788).

The foregoing summary of Carmichael's effort to obtain a code raises a number of questions for which there appear to be no satisfactory answers. It is profitless to speculate on some of these questions, but it is worth noting that, in mid-summer of 1787, when Carmichael finally acknowledged that he had the cipher, he was reluctant to begin its use. Did he know then that it was an erroneous cipher? Had a mistake been made, real or calculated? Or had Carmichael received the correct cipher and did not *at that moment* have it in his possession? The answer to the last may appear in Carmichael's friendship and correspondence at this precise moment with another lover of intrigue who occupied a place at the center of Europe's current trouble spot—the ever-scribbling Dumas at The Hague. Dumas, who was a pensioner of France, shared with Carmichael a close friendship with the Chevalier de Bourgoing, secretary of the French legation at Madrid. Bourgoing was probably even more adept than Carmichael and Dumas at court intrigue; he was, by Carmichael's account, better informed about affairs at Madrid than any other foreigner and "the most intimate friend I have had in this Country" (Carmichael to TJ, 18 July 1786). TJ had been favorably impressed by Bourgoing when Carmichael introduced them in 1786, and the chevalier had excited TJ with news of a secret survey made by Spain of the Isthmus of Panama for a possible canal—a survey that Campomanes said was only an idea in prospect, but TJ, evidently placing greater reliance on Bourgoing's report, pressed Carmichael to procure a copy, stating that it was a "vast desideratum for reasons political and philosophical" (TJ to Carmichael, 3 June 1788; Carmichael to TJ, 14 Apr. 1788; see also Vol. 10: 287). Bourgoing had also been able to give TJ "an ample detail" of the suppressed Cruz Cano map of South America (Carmichael to TJ, 29 Sep. 1786; see Vol. 10: 213-7). During the summer of 1787 Bourgoing saw Dumas and read to him a letter he had received from Carmichael—as perhaps the latter had intended him to do. Dumas thanked Carmichael for the passages "trés obligeants à mon égard"; complained about the failure of Congress to insure payment of his salary ("N'est-on donc devenu libre que pour etre indolent et laisser périr de fideles serviteurs?"); pressed Carmichael to let him know the moment a final arrangement was to be made concerning the finances of the United States, especially the foreign debt; and then put this revealing question to Carmichael: "Expliques-moi, je vous prie, clairement ces dernières lignes de votre Lettre à Mr. le Chev. de Bourgoing: *We shall soon have an order and a cypher, which will oblige us par force to write to each other*" (Dumas to Carmichael, 31 Aug. 1787; Rijksarchief, The Hague, Dumas Letter Books; photostats in DLC). Dumas may not have transcribed the sentence correctly ("oblige" would seem to be Dumas' interpretation of Carmichael's "enable"), but the implication is clear: Carmichael expected to procure a cipher from some other source, not to produce one common to themselves alone (which would have been possible at any time). The cipher referred to in this revealing letter may have been the one that Carmichael had been expecting to receive from John Jay (Jay did send it by a trusted sea captain a few weeks after Carmichael wrote to Bourgoing (Jay to Carmichael, 17 Aug. 1787; DNA: PCC, No. 121; see also *Dipl. Corr., 1783-89*, III, 369). Or it may have been the one that Carmichael received from Franks in Nov. 1786. If it was the latter, the Carmichael-Bourgoing-Dumas correspondence may indicate that this cipher was temporarily out of Carmichael's possession and this, in turn, would indicate why Carmichael was reluctant to be the first to use code in his correspondence with TJ. Carmichael's letter to Bourgoing was written about the same time that he urged TJ to take the initiative in using coded messages.

Perhaps the best evidence that Carmichael wanted the code for some such purpose as that indicated in his letter to Bourgoing is to be found in his own letters. In 1785-1787 he wrote fully and sometimes informatively about important political matters; he undoubtedly had access to persons of consequence in the Spanish government; and Floridablanca (or someone close to him) seems occasionally to have deliberately furnished him with information. Yet, upon acknowledging after so long and strange a silence that he had a code, Carmichael not only showed a sudden disinclination to use it (his first use of it in the letter of 8 May 1788 was trivial and generally unnecessary), but he began writing letters of a different character: he no longer seemed to have such access to state secrets as he formerly enjoyed. Possibly the death on 14 June 1787 of José de Gálvez, Marqués de Sonora, the shepherd boy who had risen to power in the reign of Charles III as colonial secretary, may have had something to do with this. It is worth noting that Gálvez was more familiar with America than any other minister and that he had risen to high office and to noble rank largely through the influence of various mid-century French ambassadors at Madrid who had possibly taken an interest in him because his second wife was French (H. I. Priestley, *José de Gálvez*, Berkeley, Cal., 1916, p. 2-11). Gálvez' death certainly brought about important ministerial changes, and one of the inconsequential results of his passing may have been the fact that Carmichael no longer had as much to say at the very time that he had finally achieved the means of saying it safely and secretly. But it is very doubtful whether this had been Carmichael's whole object, after all.

¹ This and subsequent words in italics are written in code and have been supplied by the Editors from the text *en clair* in TJ's hand.

From André Limozin

Most Honored Sir   Havre de Grace 25th Septber 1787.

I had the honor of writing your Excellency the 21st. and 22nd.¹ instant; I made it my duty to send yesterday all over the Town to find out Mr. Burgoin but one found that he arrived into Town the 22nd. instant. Nevertheless it was impossible to know his Lodgings. When the Packet saild for New York, I sent a Clarke on board of her and your two first inclosed were delivered to him. He promised to take the greatest care of them.

[179]

I received too late for the New York's Packet your Excellency's Letter of the 22nd. instant inclosing me a letter for the Honble. Jay, which I have delivered directly to Captn. Blair of Ship Rising Sun which saild just now for Philadelphia.

Mr. Cabarus's Uncle received yesterday advice of his nephews arrival at Paris. He advised his Nephew to not accept the imployment offerd to him.

I am very thankfull for your very necessary and usefull information.

I am very glad to hear that your Excellency will take the trouble to procure incouragement to the American trade in this Kingdom. I have the honor to be with the highest regard Your Excellency's Most obedient and very Humble S[ervt.],

ANDRE LIMOZIN

RC (MHi); addressed and endorsed. Recorded in SJL as received 27 Sep. 1787.

1 Thus in MS; Limozin meant to refer to his letters of 23 and 24 Sep., which acknowledged TJ's of 21 and 22 Sep. 1787.

From Richard O'Bryen

Algiers 25 Sep. 1787. Has had no reply to his many letters since Lamb was in Algiers; reviews the circumstances of his capture; wrote previously about the plague; in this "melancholy situation," all "surrounded by the messengers of death and the piercing shrieks or cries of our brother slaves," three of their countrymen died, eighteen survived.

Concerning a treaty with Algiers: before negotiations are begun, the foundation should be laid and conditions known "by some unbiassed man of good repute and character in Algiers"; it is important to know the negotiator, "for it is well known that it is a very lucrative and much desired negotiation"; frauds occur and the negotiator, especially if he is a consul of a commercial nation, could "baffle and upset" the proceedings, or, if successful, might enrich himself and "obtain a more favourable understanding between his own nation and the Dey and regency." A "sensible man that is well acquainted with the ways of these people . . . might obtain a peace for one half the sum that would be asked the unpolitical consul, for it is not every consul in Algiers that is acquainted with the proper chanels for business of this nature." Even in the best weather "navigation is difficult and requires a skilled pilot, for there are many dangerous shoals"; but when the foundation is laid and the conditions of the treaty known, the American ambassador should come to finish the negotiations. "The French Consul [De Kercy], Mr. Favre, or Mr. Woulfe would be very proper men that is if you could confide in them. They certainly know the policy of this country better than any Christian Monsieurs in Algiers."

Has learned the following from Mr. Wolfe concerning the mission of Lamb and Randall: The day after they arrived, Lamb asked the French consul to go personally to present the letter from Congress to the Dey, but the consul declined, saying it would be better to send the French interpreter to inquire whether the Dey would accept the letter. Being recommended by the courts of Spain and France to their representatives, Lamb was bound to follow their advice; Lamb had also been recommended to Wolfe by Carmichael, but Wolfe did not have sufficient authority to recommend measures which were in opposition to those recommended by De Kercy and D'Expilly. Prior to the meeting of D'Expilly, De Kercy, Lamb, Randall, and Wolfe at the home of the French Consul, Wolfe informed Lamb and Randall "what would be requisite for them to propose in this assembly"; they met and debated. "The Count and French consul said it was their opinion that the most effectual plan was to begin with the Dey; that the Dey was very arbitrary and that if he did not chuse to make a peace with America that it would not be in the power of any of his ministers or great men to influence the Dey to it." Lamb, Randall, and Wolfe thought it more "expedient to adopt some plan with the Dey's ministers." Randall said he had been informed in Spain that the only means of doing business was to begin with the prime minister, admiral of the marine, and lord chamberlain, the men of greatest influence. When the Count and French consul insisted on beginning with the Dey, Randall and Wolfe reminded him that "was not the way the Count took himself" for "laying the foundation of the Spanish peace"; D'Expilly and De Kercy insisted that the case of America was different; that "Spain had expended larger sums of money"; Randall asked Wolfe, who spoke better French, to explain their position, but D'Expilly and De Kercy refused to alter their opinion; Lamb, therefore, followed their advice.

O'Bryen's "remarks": It is well known in Algiers that the Dey never accepts any letter unless letters have previously passed between him and the "crowned heads of the Christian nations and between their ministers"; since this had not been done in the case of America, the Dey refused Congress' letter, being busy with Spanish affairs and not knowing "the minds of his ministery, or what would be the voice of his people." The "Dey is not so arbitrary as is generally thought or considered by the Christian nations"; has a parliament "that he must pay great attention to"; if he made a peace "contrary to the voice of his ministry and soldiery" it might be the means of dethroning him; had the prime minister, admiral of marine, and lord chamberlain "been consulted and palmed" previously, they would have influenced the Dey in favor of America; "they are the only chanel for all negociations with him"; to obtain their influence requires "money and presents"; special attention must be paid to the admiral of the marine because he advises the Dey on matters of war and peace with the Christian nations and "arranges all maritime affairs." He believes a peace can be secured with Algiers for £60,000 sterling, including the ransom of prisoners; if negotiations were made through Spain the demand would be "very great and exorbitant" for "these people well know that the Spaniards could well afford to help America with large sums"; the Spaniards having given such a large sum for their peace, the Algerines and other Barbary States expect more money from other nations which have to make peace with them. Although it cost Spain two and a half millions for their peace with Algiers, including presents, expences and ransoming, "their treaty is of no use"; if "they were to give all the value of Peru and Mexico, the Spaniards would never be liked in Algiers"; he thinks the Algerines would be justified in making war against Spain, "for at present there are 700 sail of foreign vessels sheltered under the Spanish colours and having Spanish passeports." The Dey refused to make peace with Spain unless they "would change both merchant and King's flag," which was a "national dishonour" to Spain. "About 17. years past the Danes obtained a peace with the Algerines for the sum of 160,000 dollars and every two years they send a ship with naval stores and make consulary presents. The Dutch tribute this year amounted to 14,000 dollars in naval and military stores and 6,000 dollars in presents. The Venetian tribute in cash and presents amounted this year to upwards of 26,000 dollars and more under hand. What the French give is not very considerable, but is very difficult to ascertain. For I must need say that the French do their public business in a very masterly manner, which adds much to their national character for being politicians; and if the French were sincere or wished America to obtain a peace with Algiers the French Consul would be a very proper person to negotiate."

Does not believe France wants America to make peace with the Barbary states because it is not to their interest; "they have ⅘ths of the commerce of Barbary, and are the chief carriers of its produce." Believes England has made attempts to prejudice Algiers against America; England will do all she can to "prevent America from becoming formidable or being a commercial nation." Has letters from Lord Fife and members of the British parliament concerning two of his crew, stating that they will not ransom British subjects taken under American colors but that if they had been captured under any other colors they would be redeemed; the British members of the crew died of the plague, but from this it is apparent that Britain would obstruct an American peace with the Barbary States unless they secured concessions in commerce in return which would not be "consistent with the honor and dignity of the United States of America and as becoming a free and independent people." As to France being a mediator for America, they would be of "no weight or influence with Algiers without money and presents, for the French are considered in Algiers to be a knowing artful and deceitful nation"; any consideration they receive is "through their alliance with the Grand Seignor"; unless letters from the King of France or his ministers are accompanied "with a valuable present they are not even read"; a letter from a French official could only serve as a passport, "which is customary for an Ambassador to have in coming to Algiers." Letters from the French king are "generally wrote in the Turkish stile and language and a copy thereof given or sent by the minister to the consul"; hopes the next letter from Congress for the Dey will be so written. America is losing a favorable opportunity to make peace; if Portugal makes a peace with the Algerines, the latter "would go a great distance out of the streights towards the western islands and chanel of England." The Spaniards are considered in Algiers as a "conquered nation and a cowardly and dastardly people." France did not wish Spain to make a peace and "Spain baffled and obstructed the Portuguese and Neapolitans, notwithstanding they are all four linked together in family connexions"; it is well known that it is "by the jealousies of the Christian nations relative to commerce that the Algerines have been so enriched as to become the terror of all Europe." The English are "much esteemed and venerated," especially if what they say is "accompanied with good and valuable English watches and clocks"; but their prestige fell after the war. At present there are 40,000 British Mediterranean passports issued at £3, a great revenue; Spain gets 70 dollars for each passport; America could defray the expence of the peace by taxing passports. A letter "from the Grand Seignor has some weight with the Algerines"; however the emperor of Germany had difficulty in spite of his intervention. One-third of what the Americans pay for insurance each year would obtain a peace with all Barbary; America leaving her subjects in slavery increases the amount paid for insurance; the underwriters propagate falsehoods about frequent captures. Since July 1785 there have been only "two Algerine cruisers which have attempted to go beyond the Streights of Gibralter." The present Dey is very old and there will be great changes when he dies, but "much depends on having a good Consul here." The capture of an American vessel, particularly if valuable, would convince the Algerines of what they have been told, that a war with America would be profitable; but the distance of America is in her favor in making a peace. A war with the Barbary states is a war of honor but most unprofitable; the regency of Algiers is rich and powerful and much dreaded; having no commercial vessels, Algiers has nothing to lose; if a cruiser is captured, it will not be redeemed, and if a peace is made, captured cruisers must be returned for nothing. If the United States fitted out a fleet to cruise against the Algerines it would cost a vast amount; estimates that it would take 10 cruisers, mounting 236 guns, and manned by 2140 men, to oppose the Algerine force of 13 ships, mounting 200 guns, and manned by 2412 men; that it would cost $637,200 to build the American fleet; calculating pay for the crew at $9 per month and provisions at $4 per month per man, the total cost of building and maintaining the fleet for one year would be $961,040.;[1] in contrast to this, Algerine officers and men are advanced only about 6 shillings for a two-month cruise, and provisions cost about 4s.6d. per man per month; the expense for bounty and provisions for the Algerines for a two-month cruise would be 10,500 Spanish dollars compared with 55,640 dollars to maintain the American fleet for two months. No country can fit out a fleet as cheaply as the Algerines; the American fleet would have to be "fitted in the completest manner," come into the straits about March, form in two divisions and wait for the Algerine cruisers to come out, taking the risk of having many ships destroyed or taken when they encounter the cruisers. If this were a war that could be decided in a summer, or the Algerines a people who could be "frightened by the empty parade of a fleet," a "patched up fleet" would be sufficient, but the Spanish have found this is not true. In his opinion, therefore, America should try for a peace first, having the way prepared for it by someone in Algiers; if this does not work, fit out the squadron and "act with vigilance." The plague is over; during the seven months it continued, 616 Christian slaves, 1,850 Jews, and 14,420 Mohammedans died. There are now 490 slaves belonging to the public. Believes that the Americans can be ransomed for less than the amount the Dey mentioned to Lamb; Lamb told him, when he was in Algiers, that he only had $6,000 and could not redeem the captives even if the Dey were willing to release them at the price he offered; but O'Bryen still relies on TJ's letter and believes it is TJ's intention to have them redeemed. When Lamb was in Algiers the Dey had a great number of slaves on hand and "made a precedent for all nations by setting so exorbitant a price on the Americans." When Lamb made the offer of $30,000, O'Bryen advised him that this was sufficient and not to make a further offer; does not know why Lamb had further audiences with the Dey; at that time he did not doubt Lamb's veracity; but now thinks he was unsuitable for the mission and his behavior "by no means political, or to the honor of the United States." Lamb wrote him from Minorca that, not being in agreement with the ministers, he could not return to Algiers to redeem the captives, indicating that "the ministers retard our redemption." Hopes TJ understands that there is no connection between their redemption and the making of a peace, and that leaving them in slavery "can answer no public good." Expresses gratitude for the provision made for them; Carmichael writes that a subscription has been "set on foot in America" for their redemption; hopes this is true; asks TJ to allow monthly provisions for all of his crew. Is informed the Dey told Lamb that he would not make a peace with America without the consent of Great Britain. Is writing to Carmichael about their situation and hopes TJ will write De Kercy about their future protection.

He was in the state service, serving as a lieutenant on the brig *Jefferson*, when TJ was governor of Virginia; James Maxwell can give information about him; if the United States fits out a fleet he hopes he can be redeemed to serve his country. Asks that parts of his letter be kept secret; may be addressed through De Kercy, Favre, or Wolfe. Spanish affairs are unsettled; the Spanish consul is leaving for Madrid; the Spanish treaty is void; the French are endeavoring to renew theirs. "If there is any good policy in getting money you may rely the Algerines are very clever, a brave knowing political nation."

Tr (DLC); 17 p.; in the hand of William Short. Fragment of a Tr in the hand of H. A. Washington (MHi) and another part of the same Tr (ViU: Smith Deposit). Recorded in SJL as received 15 Oct. 1787; enclosed in TJ to Jay, 3 Nov. 1787.

1 O'Bryen erred; according to his calculation, this figure should have been $971,000.

From Louis Guillaume Otto

MONSIEUR   A Newyork le 25. 7bre. 1787

Je profite du depart d'un Batiment Marchand pour vous adresser plusieurs exemplaires de la nouvelle Constitution proposée par l'Assemblée federale de Philadelphia. On espere assés généralement que les peuples ratifieront ce nouveau plan de Gouvernement; du moins les patriotes et les amis de l'Amerique le desirent avec ardeur.

Je suis avec respect Monsieur, de Votre Excellence le très humble et très obeissant serviteur

OTTO

RC (DLC); endorsed. Recorded in SJL as received 15 Nov. 1787. Enclosure: The copies of the Federal Constitution that Otto sent may have been newspaper reprints from the first public text—that which appeared in the *Pennsylvania Packet and Daily Advertiser* for 19 Sep. 1787—or they may have been one of the pamphlet editions that appeared in Philadelphia and elsewhere almost immediately.

The present letter and its enclosures preceded by five days the similar one that Otto wrote Montmorin, perhaps because the copy of the Constitution sent the latter was in translation; both letters were received in Paris on 15 Nov. 1787 and both evidently went by the same merchant vessel (Otto to Montmorin, 10 and 30 Sep. 1787; Arch. Aff. Etr., Paris, Corr. Pol., E.-U., XXXII; Tr in DLC). The official copy of the Constitution that Washington sent TJ on 18 Sep. arrived more than a month after the present communication. Otto's copies were the first that TJ received directly from America, but he had already received a copy forwarded by Adams some two days before the present letter and its enclosures arrived (see TJ to Smith, 13 Nov. 1787).

From André Limozin

MOST HONORED SIR   [26 Sep. 1787]

I am very sory that your Excellency's last dispatch of the 24th instant arrived too late for the Packet and for the Ship bound for Philada., they having Saild both yesterday. The accounts your Excellency is pleas'd to give me are most alarming for our trade.

We have been informed yesterday by the Packet arrived from Portsmouth that there is now a general Press for the Sailors thro all England, that Seven Dutch Ships are already taken, Sailors Confined amongst these Ships. There are 3 Men of War. Your Excellency's inclosed shall be forwarded to New York in the Course of ten days.

I am with the highest regard your Excellency's Most Obedient & very Humble Servant,

ANDRE LIMOZIN

[185]

RC (DLC); endorsed; without date, but written in reply to TJ's letter of 24 Sep. 1787, q.v., and the day after the packet and the ship bound for Philadelphia sailed (see Limozin to TJ, 25 Sep.). Recorded in SJL as received 29 Sep. 1787.

From George Washington

MY DEAR SIR   Phila. Sept. 26th –87

The merits of Mr. Shippen, Son of Doctr. Shippen of this City, will be the best apology I can offer for introducing him to your attention and civilities whilst he is in Paris. He is a young Gentleman of Talents and improvement—these I am sure you love. I shall only add therefore how much and how sincerely I am Yours &c.,

G. WASHINGTON

FC (DLC: Washington Papers).

From D'Aranda

[*Paris, ca. 27 Sep. 1787*] Formal note of farewell.

RC (DLC); 2 p.; addressed and endorsed; without date and not recorded in SJL but acknowledged in TJ to D'Aranda of this date.

To D'Aranda

Jeudi. ce 27me. de Septembre 1787.

Monsieur Jefferson profite de la permission de Son excellence Monsieur l'Ambassadeur d'Espagne en lui envoiant un paquet pour Monsr. Carmichael, ou il y a deux volumes in 8vo. Il ose meme de le prier de vouloir bien se charger encore d'une lettre pour Monsieur Carmichael qui contient la ratification du traité entre le Congrès et l'empereur de Maroc, et qui est trop consequent pour etre confié à la poste ordinaire, ou à une personne dont les bonnes dispositions sont moins connues que celles de Monsieur le comte d'Aranda.

Monsieur Jefferson a reçu avec bien de regrets l'honneur des Adieux de Monsieur l'Ambassadeur. Sans pretensions à celui de sa connoissance particuliere, il n'a pas moins sçu respecter son extreme merite. C'est une rude perte que subira le corps diplomatique, dont il n'y aura personne qui sera plus sensible que Monsieur Jefferson. Il prie Monsieur l'Ambassadeur de daigner agreer l'hommage de ses respects et de son attachement, et de lui permettre d'y meler des prieres très sinceres pour sa santé.

PrC (DLC). Enclosure: TJ to Carmichael, 25 Sep. 1787, together with two copies of *Notes on Virginia*, one for Carmichael and one for the Count de Campomanes (see TJ to Carmichael, 26 Dec. 1786, 15 Dec. 1787; Carmichael to TJ, 15 Oct. 1787).

From D'Aranda

à Paris ce 27 7re. 1787.

Le Comte d'Aranda presente ses hommages à Mr. Jefferson et il a l'honneur de lui dire que si ses deux Paquets pour Mr. Carmichael etoient venus avant hier, ils seraient partis par un voyageur de toute Confiance qui alloit en Porte. Le Comte n'a point nulle difficulté de s'en charger personnellement; mais comme, quoiqu'il partira d'ici a peu de jours, il ne sera rendu à Madrid qu'a moitié de Novembre, parceque passant par quelques unes de ses terres il y perdra du tems. Il desire savoir de Monsieur Jefferson s'il y a de l'inconvenient à ce retard, autrement il faudra que le Comte les remette à son sucesseur pour la premiere occasion de courier-Extraordinaire, ou que Monsieur Jefferson les retire. Tout depend des Ordres de Monsieur Jefferson, comme aussi la personne du Comte qui en tout tems et lieu sera très flatté de meriter son souvenir et d'avoir des occasions de pouvoir se dire son vrai et tres humble serviteur.

RC (DLC); endorsed. Recorded in SJL as received 27 Sep. 1787.

From John Banister, Jr.

Battersea [Dinwiddie co., Va.] 27 Sep. 1787. Thanks TJ for his letters; asks for a description of the machines for cleansing rice and preparing hemp mentioned therein. The political situation is unchanged since his last letter; the "proceedings of the convention will not transpire untill a meeting of the different assemblies"; he heard a letter read from the governor to Col. Harrison in which he said "it would be a degree of weakness in one to censure transactions which had not yet been laid before the public. From thence we may collect his opinion in general. Singular as it is, the Southern States were republicans whilst the Eastern leaned towards a monarchy." Corn crop is generally bad because of dry weather; Eppes family are well; he had hoped to follow TJ's "advice in every particular" and also had expected to be married but the "mother of the young lady" says she is too young. Will send TJ the plants he desires as soon as possible. Encloses a letter at the request of Miss Blair.

RC (DLC); 4 p.; endorsed. The enclosed letter has not been identified.

From Madame Oster

Nancy, 27 Sep. 1787. Asks pardon for using "so freely" TJ's services in transmitting her letters to her friends in America, by whom she wants always to be remembered and who are always in her mind; writes "with a great dificulty thir language if can't do it often"; asks that letters for her be forwarded to Nancy.

RC (MHi); 2 p.; signed: "Oster"; endorsed: "Oster Mde." The enclosed letters have not been identified.

To Jean Vautelet

à Paris ce 27me. Septembre 1787.

Vous savez, Monsieur, [sans doute] que Monsr. Jean Batiste Vautelet votre fils, a fait un etablissement dans l'etat de la Nouvelle Hampshire en Amerique. Monsieur John Sullivan, l'homme du premier respect et puissance dans cet etat, a bien voulu proteger votre fils, et lui preter des secours pour son etablissement; de sorte qu'il y a due de votre fils à Monsieur Sullivan de deux à trois mille francs, argent de France. Ce Monsieur, croyant qu'il etoit tems d'exiger un commencement de remboursement, votre fils lui a donné une lettre de change sur vous pour mille francs, laquelle lettre de change M. Sullivan a envoyé à moi, me priant de recevoir et de lui remettre l'argent. Cette somme payée, il se propose de donner pour le reste le tems convenable à votre fils pour que ses etablissements prennent de la consistance. Je ferai presenter la lettre de change, ou à vous meme, Monsieur, à Sedan, ou à telle personne à Paris que vous chargerez d'en faire le paiment, si vous jugerez à propos de preter la main à votre fils sur cette occasion. J'aurai l'honneur de charger quelqu'un à Sedan de vous presenter la lettre de change, à moins que vous ne me faites celui de m'indiquer dans quelques jours d'ici la personne à Paris que vous chargerez de la payer. Les paquebotes qui partent de Havre touts les six semaines vous pretent d'occasions d'ecrire à votre fils. Je vous donne mon adresse; si vous me ferez l'honneur de m'adresser vos lettres, je les ferai passer toujours avec mes depeches. J'ai l'honneur d'etre, Monsieur, votre tres humble et tres obeisst. servitr.,   TH: JEFFERSON

PrC (MoSHi); at foot of text: "M. Jean Vautelet, negociant à Sedan"; in left-hand margin: "Monsieur Jefferson, ministre plenipotentiare des etats unis d'Amerique, à Paris." See TJ to Sullivan, 5 Oct. 1787.

To John Adams

DEAR SIR   Paris Sep. 28. 1787.

I received your favors by Mr. Cutting, and thank you sincerely for the copy of your book. The departure of a packet-boat, which always gives me full emploiment for some time before, has only permitted me to look into it a little. I judge of it from the first volume which I thought formed to do a great deal of good. The first principle of a good government is certainly a distribution[1] of it's powers into executive, judiciary, and legislative, and a subdivision of the latter into two or three branches. It is a good step gained, when it is proved that the English constitution, acknowleged to be better than all which have proceeded it, is only better in proportion as it has approached nearer to this distribution of powers. From this the last step is easy, to shew by a comparison of our constitutions with that of England, how much more perfect they are. The article of Confederations is surely worthy of your pen. It would form a most interesting addition to shew what have been the nature of the Confederations which have existed hitherto, what were their excellencies and what their defects. A comparison of ours with them would be to the advantage of ours, and would increase the veneration of our countrymen for it. It is a misfortune that they do not sufficiently know the value of their constitutions and how much happier they are rendered by them than any other people on earth by the governments under which they live.—You know all that has happened in the United Netherlands. You know also that our friends Van Staphorsts will be among the most likely to become objects of severity, if any severities should be exercised. Is the money in their hands entirely safe? If it is not, I am sure you have already thought of it. Are we to suppose the game already up, and that the Stadtholder is to be reestablished, perhaps erected into a monarch, without this country lifting a finger in opposition to it? If so, it is a lesson the more for us. In fact what a crowd of lessons do the present miseries of Holland teach us? Never to have an hereditary officer of any sort: never to let a citizen ally himself with kings: never to call in foreign nations to settle domestic differences: never to suppose that any nation will expose itself to war for us &c. Still I am not without hopes that a good rod is in soak for Prussia, and that England will feel the end of it. It is known to some that Russia made propositions to the emperor and France for acting in concert; that the emperor consents and has disposed four camps of 180,000 men from the limits of Turkey to those of Prussia. This court hesitates, or rather it's premier hesitates; for the queen, Monmorin and Breteuil are for the measure. Should it take place, all may yet come to rights, except for the Turks, who must retire from Europe; and this they must do were France Quixotic enough to undertake to support them. We I hope shall be left free to avail ourselves of the advantages of neutrality: and yet much I fear the English, or rather their stupid king, will force us out of[2] it. For thus I reason. By forcing us into the war against them they will be engaged in an expensive land war as well as a sea war. Common sense dictates therefore that they should let us remain neuter: ergo they will not let us remain neuter. I never yet found any other general rule for foretelling what they will do, but that of examining what they ought not to do.—You will have heard doubtless that M. Lambert is Comptroller general, that the office of Directeur general du tresor royal has been successively refused by Monsr. de la Borde and Monsr. Cabarrus; that the Conte de Brienne, brother of the Archbishop, is minister of war, and the Count de la Luzerne minister of Marine. They have sent for him from his government in the West Indies. The Chevalier de la Luzerne has a promise of the first vacant Embassy. It will be that of London if Adhemar can be otherwise disposed of. The Chevalier might have had that of Holland if he would. The Count de Moustier will sail about the middle of next month. Count d'Aranda leaves us in a few days. His successor is hourly expected.—I have the honor to be with my best respects to Mrs. Adams, and sentiments of perfect esteem and regard to yourself dear Sir your most obedient & most humble servant,

TH: JEFFERSON

P.S. Since writing the above, I learn through a *very*[3] good [*channel*] *that this court is deci*[*ded*] and is ar[*ran*]*ging with the* [*two empires*]. Perhaps as a proof of this we may soon *see them recall their officers in the* [*Dutch serv*]*ice.*

RC (MHi:AMT); partly in code. PrC (DLC).

[1] This word interlined in substitution for "division," deleted.

[2] These two words interlined in substitution for "into," deleted.

[3] This and subsequent words in italics are written in code and have been decoded by the Editors, employing a partly-reconstructed key. TJ must have confused Adams, as he did the Editors, by one minor error in encoding and by his surprising use of the Barclay-Lamb code (Code No. 11) instead of the one regularly employed in correspondence with Adams (Code No. 8). Syllables and words in brackets (supplied) are conjectural readings.

From Burrill Carnes

Nantes, 28 Sep. 1787. Acknowledges TJ's letter of 22 Sep.; had hoped to send by Ast, who brings this, the account of the United States with Schweighauser & Dobrée, but illness of Dobrée has prevented, and will for some time, completion of examination of that account. Wishes to present the "difficulty American vessels labour under here, on their return home for want of Salt provisions"; the provisions they get in France will not keep; if "they could be permitted to take Irish Provisions, like the French West India Ships, it would be esteemed a very great favour."

RC (DLC); 2 p.; endorsed. Recorded in SJL as received 4 Oct. 1787.

From C. W. F. Dumas

[*The Hague, 28 Sep. 1787*]. Encloses letter with several papers addressed to Jay; leaves them open; asks TJ to read, seal, and forward immediately.

RC (DLC); 2 p.; in French; endorsed. This letter, without place or date, was evidently written as a covering letter for one from Dumas to Jay, 28 Sep. 1787; on 29 Sep. Dumas added a postscript to the letter to Jay, informing him of the capitulation of Amsterdam, and sent another (dated) covering letter to TJ, q.v. Dumas informed Jay of his distressing situation, saying that he and his "family have every moment expected to be destroyed," and enclosed copies of his correspondence with General Kratchmar, commandant of the garrison at The Hague, and with other authorities, in which he set forth his claim under the law of nations for protection to his person, his family, and his property against all damage or violence (Dumas Letter Book, Rijksarchief, The Hague; photostats in DLC; translations of both letter and enclosures are printed in *Dipl. Corr., 1783-89*, III, 589-94). TJ recorded receipt of letters from Dumas of 28 and 29 Sep. in SJL under 3 Oct. 1787.

From Jan Ingenhousz

SIR   Vienna Sept. 28 1787

Recieve my harty thanks for your kind offers to take under your care any parcel, which my old venerable friend Dr. Franklin may direct to me or I to him. Permit me to begg you one favour, viz. to send to the Imperial Ambassadour such parcels (if there should be sent any to you) which by their bulk or weight should exceed much a common letter, or of a weight above 2 or three ounces, but I should be very much obliged to you if you would send any small parcels, such as letters, immediately to Messrs. Tourton & Ravel, who will immediately send them to me by the post office, as such letters may be of too much importance for me

[191]

to be retained at the Ambassadour till a messenger goes to Vienna, which may become very irregular and uncertain in time of warr, when the Emperour will probably be at the head of his army.

I am very respectfully Sir your most obedient humble servant,

J. INGEN HOUSZ

I take the liberty to recommend to your protection this parcel directed to Dr. Franklin which will be sent to you by my bankers Messrs. Tourton & Ravel.

RC (DLC); endorsed. Recorded in SJL as received 9 Oct. 1787. Enclosure: Ingenhousz to Franklin, 28 Sep. 1787 (PPAP; see Ingenhousz to TJ, 23 Jan. 1788).

From Moustier

Ce 28.7bre. 1787.

Mr. Le Coulteux a assuré au Cte. de Moustier qu'il y avoit ordre de recevoir toutes les lettres qui arriveroient au Havre pour l'A.S. [Amérique Septentrionale] toutes les fois que les Paquebots auroient été detenus par les vents contraires. L'ordre est même que les paquets soient renouvellés de quatre heures en quatre heures dans tous les cas de retard, si dans un pareil intervalle il arrivoit des lettres à la poste du Havre pour l'A.S.

A l'égard des passagers il n'y a d'autres raisons d'en refuser que lorsque le nombre de 23. fixé par l'arrêt du Conseil est complet. Ceux qui se presenteroient pour passer, dans le cas où le paquebot auroit été detenu au delà de l'epoque fixée, doivent etre reçus.

Le Cte. de Moustier s'empresse de faire passer cet avis à Monsieur Jefferson qu'il a l'honneur de prier d'agreer ses très sinceres complimens.

RC (DLC); endorsed.

To William Stephens Smith

DEAR SIR   Paris Sep. 28. 1787.

I have duly received your favor by Mr. Cutting. I had before had a transient acquaintance with him, and knew him to be sensible. Your recommendation is always a new merit. I really think, and had taken the liberty some time ago of hinting to Congress that they would do well to have a diplomatic character at Lisbon. There s no country whose commerce is more interesting to us. I wish Congress would correspond to the wishes of that court in sending a person there, and to mine in sending yourself, for I confess I had rather see you there than at London, because I doubt whether it be honourable for us to keep any body at London unless they keep some person at New York. Of all nations on earth they require to be treated with the most hauteur. They require to be kicked into common good manners.—You ask if you shall say any thing to Sullivan about the bill. No—only that it is paid. I have within these two or three days received letters from him explaining the matter. It was really for the skin and bones of the Moose, as I had conjectured. It was my fault that I had not given him a rough idea of the expence I would be willing to incur for them. He had made the acquisition an object of a regular campaign, and that too of a winter one. The troops he employed sallied forth, as he writes me, in the month of March—much snow—a herd attacked—one killed—in the wilderness—a road to cut 20 miles—to be drawn by hand from the frontiers to his house—bones to be cleaned &c. &c. &c. In fine he put himself to an infinitude of trouble more than I meant, he did it cheerfully, and I feel myself really under obligations to him. That the tragedy might not want a proper catastrophe, the box, bones and all are lost: so that this chapter of natural history will still remain a blank. But I have written to him not to send me another. I will leave it for my successor to fill up whenever I shall make my bows here. The purchase for Mrs. Adams shall be made and sent by Mr. Cutting. I shall always be happy to receive her commands. Petit shall be made happy by her praises of his last purchase for her. I must refer you to Mr. Adams for the news. Those respecting the Dutch you know as well as I. Nor should they be written but with the pen of Jeremiah. Adieu mon ami! Yours affectionately,

TH: JEFFERSON

RC (MHi: DeWindt Collection); addressed; endorsed by Smith in part: "Ans. Octr. 8th." PrC (DLC). Not recorded in SJL.

From C. W. F. Dumas

The Hague, 29 Sep. 1787. An express for France, departing at this moment, permits him only to ask that the enclosed be added to his first dispatch to Congress; TJ knows his sad state; is very unhappy.

RC (DLC); 2 p.; in French; endorsed. Recorded in SJL as received 3 Oct. 1787. For the enclosure, see note to Dumas to TJ, under 28 Sep. 1787.

To Ferdinand Grand

Sir   Paris Sep. 30. 1787.

Desirous of not abusing the good dispositions you were pleased to express as to myself and your willingness to advance monies for my particular use, I wrote to Messrs. Willinck & Van Staphorsts to know whether my draught on them for six or seven thousand livres would be honored on account of the United states. They answer me by letter of Sep. 24. that they will pay it on sight, desiring however that it may not be delayed as they could not answer long against the effect of the present circumstances of their country. If it should be perfectly agreeable to you to furnish me with 7000.ᵗ on my bill on those gentlemen, I will take the liberty of asking you to have such a bill prepared, paiable on sight, which I will sign. Having occasion for a bill on London for fourteen pounds seven shillings sterling, I should thank you for such a one, to be deducted from the money paiable for my bill on Messrs. Willink & Van Staphorsts. I will thank you for an answer to this immediately, and if you chuse to take my bill, I will call at your bureau early tomorrow morning, as I shall be going into the country for several days to come. I have the honor to be with much respect Sir your most obedient humble servant,   Th: Jefferson

PrC (DLC).

To Buffon

Sir   Paris Octob. 1. 1787.

I had the honour of informing you some time ago that I had written to some of my friends in America, desiring they would send me such of the spoils of the Moose, Caribou, Elk and deer as might throw light on that class of animals; but more particularly to send me the complete skeleton, skin, and horns of the Moose, in such condition as that the skin might be sowed up and stuffed on it's arrival here. I am happy to be able to present to you at this moment the bones and skin of a Moose, the horns of [another] individual of the same species, the horns of the Caribou, the el[k,] the deer, the spiked horned buck, and the Roebuck of America. They all come from New Hampshire and Massachusets. I give you their popular names, as it rests with yourself to decide their real names The skin of the Moose was drest with the hair on, but a great deal

[194]

of it has come off, and the rest is ready to drop off. The horns of the elk are remarkeably small. I have certainly seen of them which would have weighed five or six times as much. This is the animal which we call elk in the Southern parts of America, and of which I have given some description in the Notes on Virginia, of which I had the honour of presenting you a copy. I really doubt whether the flat-horned elk exists in America: and I think this may be properly classed with the elk, the principal difference being in the [horns.] I have seen the Daim, the Cerf, the Chevreuil of Europe. But the animal we call Elk, and which may be distinguished as the Round-horned elk, is very different from them. I have never seen the Brand-hirtz or Cerf d'Ardennes, nor the European elk. Could I get a sight of them I think I should be able to say to which of them the American elk resembles most, as I am tolerably well acquainted with that animal. I must observe also that the horns of the Deer, which accompany these spoils, are not of the fifth or sixth part of the weight of some that I have seen. This individual has been of three years of age, according to our method of judging. I have taken measures particularly to be furnished with large horns of our e[lk] and our deer, and therefore beg of you not to consider those now sent as furnishing a specimen of their ordinary size. I really suspect you will find that the Moose, the Round horned elk, and the American deer are species not existing in Europe. The Moose is perhaps of a new class. I wish these spoils, Sir, may have the merit of adding any thing new to the treasures of nature which [have] so fortunately come under your observation, and of which she seems [to] have given you the keys. They will in that case be some gratification to you, which it will always be pleasing to me to have procured, having the honor to be with sentiments of the most perfect esteem and respect, Sir, your most obedient & most humble servant,

TH: JEFFERSON

PrC (DLC).

To L. J. M. Daubenton

Oct. 1. 1787.

Mr. Jefferson, being informed that Monsieur le Comte de Buffon is absent, takes the liberty of recommending to the care of Monsieur D'Aubenton the objects of Natural history which accompany this letter. He leaves the letter to Monsieur de Buffon open, that Monsieur D'Aubenton may see under what names these objects have come, and he will beg the favor of him to seal and forward the letter when he shall have read it. He has the honour of presenting his respects to Monsieur Daubenton.

PrC (DLC). Enclosure: TJ to Buffon, preceding.

From Jean Vautelet

[*Sedan, 1 [Oct.] 1787.* Recorded in sJL as dated 1 Sep. and received 4 Oct. 1787. TJ obviously made an error in his entry and must have intended 1 Oct. because the letter in question is a reply to TJ to Vautelet, 27 Sep. 1787, and was enclosed in TJ to John Sullivan, 5 Oct. 1787, qq.v.]

To Willink & Van Staphorst

GENTLEMEN   Paris Octob. 1. 1787.

This serves to advise you that I have drawn on you this day in favor of Mr. Grand, banker of Paris, for three thousand two hundred and one florins one sol de banque paiable at one day's sight on account of the United states of America, which I depend on your honouring and am with great respect gentlemen Your most obedient & most humble servant,   TH: JEFFERSON

PrC (MHi).

To Bouébe

à Paris ce 2me Octobre 1787.

Je suis très sensible, Monsieur, de l'utilité majeure des procès, des machines &c. que vous avez imaginés et j'en rendrai conte au Secretaire du Congrès. Mais la justice, qui ne permet pas de donner de fausses esperances, me fait un devoir de vous observer que l'encouragement des projets, tellement utiles qu'ils peuvent etre, n'est pas du ressort du Congrès. C'appartient tout-a-fait aux legislations differentes des treize etats. Ce rendroit necessaire une application à chacune d'eux qui seroit embarrassante. Et encore leur maniere d'encourager est, comme en Angleterre, de donner une privilege exclusive de se servir de ces projets pour 14. ans. Ainsi il ne me semble pas qu'on peut conter beaucoup sur le parti qu'on pourroit

[196]

tirer de ces decouvertes en Amerique. J'ai l'honneur d'etre, avec beaucoup de consideration, Monsieur, votre tres humble et tres obeissant serviteur, TH: JEFFERSON

PrC (DLC); at foot of text: "M. Bouebé rue de Bourbon à coté des Théatins. No. 31."

From Richard Claiborne

London, 2 Oct. 1787. Thanks TJ for his letter of 8 Aug. and the "paper which was inclosed, specifying the substance of Colo. Blackden's transaction with Mr. De L'Ormiere"; has not heard from Blackden for two months and does not know the addresses of Appleton and Barrett, to whom TJ referred him; encloses a letter for Blackden and has sent a duplicate to Amsterdam. Has acquired a property in England which, he is told, will provide a "permanent and hansome income"; has formed a good mercantile connection in London; expects to go soon to settle in Jamaica where he will manage the estates of "a very worthy and respectable Gentleman, whose Estates in Jamaica amount to at least between 2 and 300,000£," and who will also establish him in business. His business between London, Jamaica, and America should enable him "to live comfortably, and with industry, acquire a competancy. . . . The most that I fear which may alter my prospects is, the war," of the effects of which TJ is a better judge than he.

RC (MoSHi); 4 p.; addressed and endorsed. Recorded in SJL as received 6 Oct. 1787. Enclosure missing.

From L. J. M. Daubenton

a Paris le 2 octobre 1787

M. Daubenton a l'honneur d'assurer Monsieur Jefferton de ses respects. Il a reçu La lettre et la caisse; demain il en donnera avis a M. Le Cte. de Buffon en lui envoyant la lettre. Il paroit que cette caisse contient des depouilles fort interressantes d'animaux peu connus; c'est un present qui fera grand plaisir a M. de Buffon et grand bien au cabinet d'histoire naturelle.

RC (DLC); endorsed.

To Theresa Murphy

MADAM   Paris Oct. 2. 1787.

I have duly received the letter you did me the honor to inclose for America, but you have omitted to write the address on it, so that I do not know who it is for. If you will be so good as to inform me what address to put on it, I will forward it by an occasion which offers in six or eight days. I have the honour to be with much respect Madam Your most obedt & most humble servt,

TH: JEFFERSON

PrC (MHi).

From Stephen Cathalan, Jr.

[Paris] the 3th. october 1787—11 o.Clock

Messrs. Cathalan presents their respects to his excelency Ths. Jefferson Esqr. and wait on him to take leave and his orders for Marseilles he has after great deal of Pains Sold his two Cargoes of Tobacco lately arived at 34. the Virginia and 31 the Maryland, payable 3 Months after delivery at Cette.

Mr. Cathns. will leave this place next friday evening, or Saturday before dinner.

RC (DLC); in the hand of Stephen Cathalan, Jr. Not recorded in SJL.

From Stephen Cathalan, Sr.

SIR   Wednesday 4 o.Clock after noon

I extremly regret that your departure for the Country prevents me and my Son to have the honor of seeing you again, perhaps never I will enjoy that pleasure again!

I would have desired to tell you by how many sollicitations, intrviews &a. I could obtain a Sale of my cargoes MM. Ant. de Montcloux was for me in the Commitée.

I wish with all my heart you may succeed, in Shewing them in a fair light toward the Ministers. They are alltogether very bad Sett of People; and I must yet appear Satisfied and acknowledge them my thanks.

I keep with me your Packet for the Count del Vermé at Milan, hoping to find room in my Carriage; the Charges from Marseilles to Milan say to Genoa will be but very triffling, and will be always compensable between you and me.

Our ladies and Eulalie will be always very gratefull of your remaimbrance, and with pleasure we Bear them your Compliments.

Your wishes for our Journey are received by us with the greatest gratude, we ask from you the Continuation of your Friendship and Beg you to be perfectly assured of our respectfull regard, being always at your command, and for life very respectfully Sir of your excellency and america the most obedient and Devoted Servant,

STEPHEN CATHALAN

RC (DLC); in the hand of Stephen Cathalan, Jr.; assigned to this date from internal evidence and the letter preceding, which was evidently written the same day. Not recorded in SJL.

TJ must have replied to the preceding letter with one in which he sent his compliments to the LADIES AND EULALIE and also his best wishes to Cathalan and his son for their journey, but no such letter has been found. It also evidently explained that TJ was on the point of DEPARTURE FOR THE COUNTRY. There is nothing in the Account Book to indicate a departure on Wednesday the 3rd; but an entry under 5 Sep. 1787 shows that TJ "took possession of apartments at Mont Calvaire" and it is likely that he visited, or expected to visit, the hermitage kept by the lay brothers on Mont Calvaire (or Mont Valérien) beyond the Bois de Boulogne, where the hermits tended vineyards, manufactured stockings of a superior quality (see TJ to Abigail Adams, 2 Feb. 1788), and maintained apartments for some forty guests who were permitted to walk in the gardens but not talk there (see Malone, *Jefferson*, II, 137-8). On 12 Oct. 1787 another entry in the Account Book reads: "paid at Mont Calvaire 60f. viz @ 2f10 myself and 1f my horse," showing that this covered several visits to the retreat between 5 Sep. and 12 Oct. 1787. TJ usually went to Mont Calvaire on Fridays or Saturdays, but not always (see TJ to Grand, 30 Sep. 1787; TJ to Barrett, 8 Oct. 1787; Fontenille to TJ, 23 Oct. 1787; TJ to Fontenille, 24 Oct. 1787). See illustration in this volume.

To C. W. F. Dumas

SIR   Paris Octob. 3. 1787.

I had received your favor of the 23d. of September two days ago. That of the 28th. and 29th. was put into my hands this morning. I immediately waited on the Ambassadors, ordinary and extraordinary of the United Netherlands, and also on the Envoy of Prussia, and asked their good offices to have an efficacious protection extended to your person, your family, and your effects, observing that the United states know no party, but are the friends and allies of the United Netherlands as a nation, and would expect from their friendship that the person who is charged with their affairs until the arrival of a minister should be covered from all insult and injury which might be offered him by a lawless mob, well assured that their minister residing with Congress would on all occasions receive the same. They have been so good as to promise me, each, that he will in his first despatches press this matter on the proper power, and to give me reason to hope that it will be efficacious for your safety. I will transmit your letter to Mr. Jay by the Count de Moustier who sets out within a week for New York as Minister plenipotentiary for France in that country. I sincerely sympathize in your sufferings, and wish that what I have done may effect an end to them, being with much respect & esteem, Sir, your most obedient & most humble servant, TH: JEFFERSON

RC (PHi); after date, in Dumas' hand: "reçue le 9e."; endorsed. PrC (DLC).

TJ's immediate appeal to THE AMBASSADORS and his report on Dumas' situation in his letter to Jay of 8 Oct. 1788 (which Jay never commented upon) rested the matter squarely on the principle of diplomatic immunity without implying that Dumas was anything more than a PERSON . . . CHARGED WITH American affairs pending the appointment of a minister. John Adams had been requested by the States General to dismiss Dumas forthwith, but, while clearly regarding Dumas as an American agent, and recognizing that his difficulties proceeded from his activities as a Patriot and as a supporter of France, Adams could only transmit the formal complaint to Congress (Adams to TJ, 28 Oct. 1787). This he did with a blunt statement of the implications: "I am sorry for his embarrassed situation, but know not the cause of it but by conjecture. One thing I know, that the United States may very easily be involved in a war by indiscreet intimacies between their servants and foreign Powers and national parties. Congress have but two ways to take upon this occasion—either to dismiss Mr. Dumas at the requisition of the States General, or to write a letter, or order one to be written, desiring their High Mightinesses to articulate the particulars of their exceptions and displeasure against Dumas." In a subsequent letter to Jay, Adams conjectured that the British ambassador at The Hague was the instigator of the attack on Dumas and stated that the British, conscious of the importance of The Netherlands in the balance against France, had suspected him of directing Dumas' course; that, as Dumas had a pension from France reversible to his daughter, it would be better for the United States to pay this pension or to dismiss him rather than to have in their service a person receiving pay from two powers; that he hoped Congress would, nevertheless, take time to deliberate upon the subject—in fact, he hoped that they

would "take so much [time] that the present passions may cool, and the present scene be shifted" (Adams to Jay, 25 Oct. and 15 Nov. 1787, the first enclosing his correspondence with Fagel, secretary of the States General, and all printed in *Dipl. Corr.*, *1783-89*, II, 811-7). The injunction to proceed slowly was scarcely needed; in another month Dumas was hoping to escape his difficulties and to enhance his standing by negotiating a treaty at Brussels, but it was not until the following March that Jay, having received Dumas' and Adams' letters from Congress with directions to report, began to struggle with an incident that had already passed the critical stage. As to the two courses suggested by Adams, Jay rejected the first on the ground that it would be "improper to dismiss any of the public servants on the complaint of a foreign court without a previous Hearing, it being of great Importance that the Ministers and officers of the united States should have nothing to hope for or to fear from foreign Courts." He also rejected Adams' suggested alternative as being open to other objections: "In whatever Light Mr. Dumas may be considered at the Hague, the fact is that he never was regularly charged with the affairs of the united States at that court, nor does he hold any *official* place of any kind under them. Hence it follows that Congress cannot on that Principle take cognizance of his Conduct or institute any Inquiries relative to it.—It is true that Mr. Dumas has for many years been (tho rather indirectly than otherwise) employed as a political agent, in which Capacity he has been zealous and useful, and that Congress in Consideration of his services have allowed him a Pension themselves, and consented to his receiving another from the King of France. They have also continued to treat and consider him as being in some sort in their service for they have permitted him to live in their House at the Hague, and his Correspondence with them and their ministers still proceeds as heretofore. These and similar circumstances have probably led their high

[200]

Mightinesses into some Mistake relative to this Gentleman, and yet they seem to be apprized that no Appointment from Congress has in the usual and regular form been communicated to them; for Mr. Fagel in the letter before mentioned seems to consider him as deriving his appointment from Mr. Adams, and it is from Mr. Adams and not from Congress that he requests and expects his Dismission." Jay therefore thought that it would be "most prudent to avoid all Questions relative to the Conduct of Mr. Dumas or the Treatment he has met with, as on the one hand he was not restrained or discouraged, so on the other he was not Instructed nor requested nor stimulated by Congress or by any Letters from this office, to intermeddle in the domestic Quarrels of the Dutch, and holding no office under Congress they are not accountable to their High Mightinesses for his Conduct, nor to him for the Consequences of his having acted according to his own private Judgment and wishes, or according to the wishes and Desires of others." At the same time, Jay thought it was not prudent to ignore the matter and to leave the States General in doubt as to Dumas' relation to Congress, for "if the complaints against him should continue unnoticed, they will naturally be led to conclude that his conduct had been dictated by their Instructions," especially since Adams' reply to Fagel had pointed out that " 'all the authority by which Mr. Dumas acts under the United States, is derived directly from Congress.' " Jay thought the least objectionable method of communicating this view was that he "should be *permitted*," not directed, to express regret on behalf of Congress that Dumas had incurred the displeasure of the States General to such an extent that they had requested "his Dismission from what they apprehend to be an Employment under Congress," and to say that Dumas' zeal and services during the Revolution had won Congress' confidence and good will; that it was not owing to any change in their sentiments that he had not been since the peace

charged with the care or direction of the affairs in The Netherlands; that "from that period he had constantly been regarded by Congress as a gentleman who deserved well of them, and to whom, tho holding no Place under them, it would always give them Pleasure to shew marks of kindness and Regard"; that, "altho it would be improper for Congress to enter into any Inquiries relative to the political conduct of a Gentleman not in their Services yet . . . they cannot forbear to wish that Mr. Dumas may experience all that magnanimity which honest men who in civil commotions take different sides, should shew to each other" (Dft, dated "March 1788" in NK-Iselin). Jay was correct in thinking Dumas had never been regularly appointed, but he was wrong in regarding Dumas' annual stipend as a pension: according to the resolution of 14 Oct. 1785 approving the report on Dumas' status that Jay himself had drawn, it was a "salary of thirteen hundred dollars per Annum," retroactively begun on 19 Apr. 1775 and to "continue till the further order of Congress, he continuing his services" (JCC, XXIX, 835). The dilemma posed for the secretary for foreign affairs was inherently an impossible one, and though Congress on 14 Feb. 1788 had directed Jay to report on the matter, he never complied: his attempt to carry out the direction, while completed in rough form, remained among his private papers and bore this endorsement by him: "Draft of an unfinished Report respecting Mr. Dumas' conduct."

The direct and immediate course adopted by TJ was perhaps based on doubtful assumptions concerning Dumas' status and it must have led to the demand by the States General for Dumas' dismissal (see note to Dumas to TJ, 26 Oct. 1787), but it effectively averted the threat posed against Dumas as a person. The real danger that Adams pointed out continued to stand unconfronted by Congress, the only authority that had both the responsibility and the power to face it.

To Abigail Adams

DEAR MADAM   Paris Octob. 4. 1787.

By Mr. Cutting I have an opportunity of acknoleging the receipt

[201]

of your favor of Sep. 10th. inclosing one for my daughter Polly. When she received it she flushed, she whitened, she flushed again, and in short was in such a flutter of joy that she could scarcely open it. This faithful history of her sensibility towards you must stand in lieu of her thanks which she has promised me she will write you herself: but at this moment she is in the convent where she is perfectly happy. By Mr. Cutting you will also receive the 5. aunes of cambric which Colo. Smith desired me to have purchased for you at 12. livres the aune. I am sorry you were put to the trouble of advancing the money for Mr. Sullivan's bill. I thought myself sure that Mr. Grand's bill would reach you in time, and did not know he had omitted to advise Mr. Teissier of it. He is always afraid to give to any body a complete power to call on him for money. Mr. Littlepage is here under a secret commission from the King of Poland. Possibly it may become a permanent one. I thank you for the American newspapers, and am glad to find that good sense is still uppermost in our country. Great events are I think preparing here: and a combination of force likely to take place which will change the face of Europe. Mr. Grenville has been very illy received. The annunciation by Mr. Eden that England was arming, was considered as an insult: after this and the King of Prussia's entrance on the territories of Holland, Mr. Grenville's arrival with conciliatory propositions is qualified with the title of 'une insulte tres gratuite.' I am not certain that the final decision of this country is yet taken. Perhaps the winter may be employed in previous arrangements unless any thing takes place at sea to bring on the rupture sooner. The Count de Gortz told me yesterday that the Prussian troops would retire from Holland the moment the states of Holland should make the expected reparation of the insult to the Princess. May not the scene which is preparing render it necessary for Mr. Adams to defer the return to his own country?   I have the honor to be with very sincere sentiments of esteem & respect Dear Madam your most obedient & most humble servant,

TH: JEFFERSON

RC (MHi: AMT). PrC (DLC).

From Fantin Latour

MONSIEUR   À Grenoble ce 4 8bre 1787

La Bonté avec laquelle vous avés repondu à La lettre que j'ai eu L'honneur De vous écrire L'année Derniere pour un jeune homme qui Desiroit s'aller établir en amérique, m'engage à vous en écrire une seconde pour vous prier De vouloir Bien vous intéresser à un jeune homme De mes parens.

Je vous Dirai D'abord, monsieur, que Le jeune homme pour qui je vous avois écris n'a pas encore pu executer son projet. Quand il a voulu vendre sa légitime, son frere Lui a élévé Des Difficultés qu'il n'a pu surmonter jusqu'à présent.

Mon parent Dont j'ai à vous entretenir est Dans une position Différente. Il a Deux freres et une soeur. Son pere âgé de 68 ans peut lui laisser à sa mort une legitime De 6000.^{tt} Ce jeune homme a Depuis long tems le Dessein De passer Dans votre patrie. Son unique But, monsieur, est D'y acquerir Des terres, De se marier et De se nourrir lui et sa famille Du travail De ses mains. Il veut mener une vie champêtre Dont on ne peut goûter Les vrais Douceurs que Dans un pays Libre et De Bonnes mœurs.

Etant en ceci, monsieur, le seul confident De mon parent, il m'a très bien observé que le seul tems favorable pour L'execution D'un pareil projet étoit celui De La jeunesse. Il voudroit Dans ce cas trouver Dans votre patrie quelques moyen De subsister jusqu'à La mort De son pere; alors, monsieur, il s'y etabliroit D'autant plus facilement qu'il sauroit La langue angloise, les coutumes et Les usages De votre patrie.

Mon parent seroit au comble de ses vœux, monsieur, si vous pouvies Lui procurer ce qu'il Desire. Je crois qu'il pourroit se rendre utile Dans une maison De commerce; il écrit passablement et sait bien L'arithmétique. Il est âgé de 28 ans, D'une constitution robuste; il professe la religion protestante. Je n'entre pas Dans De plus grands Détails à son égard parceque je n'ai point L'honneur D'être connu De vous, mais j'ose vous Dire qu'il ne perdra rien à se faire connoitre.

Je croirois, monsieur, ma Lettre imparfaite, si pour vous prouver L'envie qu'il a De passer Dans votre patrie, J'oubliois De vous Dire qu'il a Le Dessein D'y passer en qualité D'engagé s'il ne trouvoit pas L'argent nécessaire pour son passage. Il vous prieroit Dans ce cas Là De lui indiquer le port De mer Le plus fréquenté par Les Batimens américains et De L'addresser s'il est possible à quelque cessionnaire connu de vous.

J'ai L'honneur D'être avec le plus profond Respect Monsieur votre très humble et très obeissant serviteur,

FANTIN LA TOUR

Demeurant cour De chaulne grande [rue] à grenoble

RC (MHi); endorsed. Recorded in SJL as received 9 Oct. 1787.

To the Governor of South Carolina

SIR   Paris Oct. 4. 1787.

I am informed that the persons having claims against the state of South Carolina on account of the frigate of the same name have appointed Mr. Cutting their attorney for settling those claims with the state. It becomes my duty therefore to inform you that a claim of the state against the court of Spain for services performed by that frigate was transmitted to me the last spring by Mr. Jay, together with the papers on which it was founded, and that I was instructed to forward the same to Mr. Carmichael at Madrid to be sollicited by him, and at the same time to confer with the Prince of Luxemburg on the subject and engage the assistance of the French Ambassador at Madrid in the sollicitation. All this was done, and I have lately received a letter from Mr. Carmichael, inclosing the copy of one from the Count de Florida Blanca by which it appears that the Court of Spain has referred the adjustment of your claim to Mr. Gardoqui and your delegates at New York, where perhaps the whole business may be most conveniently settled. In my conference with the Prince of Luxemburg I undertook to quiet his mind by assurances, which I knew I might make with truth, that the State of South Carolina would settle his claim finally with justice and honor, and would take measures for paying it as soon as their situation would permit. A recent instance of arrangements taken in a like case by the state of Maryland has had a good effect in counteracting those calumnies against us which our enemies on the other side the channel disseminate industriously through all Europe.

I have the honour to be with sentiments of the most perfect esteem & respect, Your Excellency's most obedient & most humble servant,   TH: JEFFERSON

PrC (DLC).

From William Stephens Smith

DEAR SIR   London October 4th. 1787.

The Bearer Mr. Stewart was an officer in our troops during the war and some time under my immediate command. He proposes returning to America in the French Packet of November. Permit me to introduce him to your Excellency and recommend him to

[204]

your civilities during his stay at Paris. Any Letters you may commit to his care when he departs for America will be taken care of, and he will be able to give you some information relative to the num[bers,] situation and expectation of the People on the Western Waters. Every thing here looks like war and Count or Comte Sarsefield told me last night, that from what he could now learn and discover, he should not be surprised to hear of immediate captures in or attacks upon the West Indies on the part of England. If the British Cabinet are anxious for a war and are determined to take the lead in it, I must confess I cannot see any other object they can have in view, but to put themselves in the way of the smiles of fortune, under whose auspices they may stand a chance to retrieve the losses of the last war or make the present relieve them of the weight of the national debt, by a National banckruptcy. Their prospects are without doubt Gloomy, and I really believe they are satisfied they cannot by regular means surmount the difficulties that press them and therefore they feel themselves qualified to make daring experiments.

It is not worth while to attempt a description of the situation of affairs in the United Netherlands, for I do not wish to put myself in a Meloncholy habit of mind. I have a letter from Amsterdam of the 28th. uto. at 7 in the evening. The Patriots still held it and felt themselves competent to the defence of it if there was any hope of assistance from the quarter they once were lead to expect it, or in case that should decidedly fail them, untill they could obtain tollerable terms. But what terms can be even tolerable to men who fail in an attempt to be free and establish the rights of human Nature? I wish North Holland could be removed and connected with North America. From some secret springs which are in motion here, I think it would be worth our while in case the War should break out soon, to keep one eye fixed on the movements of England and another glancing at the internal affairs of South America. It is a subject that I am pretty clear some wise men in the Cabinet here dream of. If you discover anything pointed on this subject, I should be happy to have it communicated.—Mr. A has received a Letter from Richard Henry Lee from New York of the 3d. of September. As from a particular part of it, you may be informed what projects are likely to come forward, I forward it. In the mean time with the most perfect submission to clear and more brilliant heads, I must confess to me it casts "shadowy clouds and darkness" on the subject, and I am apprehensive if too great a refinement is attempted in the

Principles of Government in the formation of a new fœdral system, we shall risk the existence of the fœdral head and furnish grounds for a few discontented Demagogues to step forward and attempt to destroy the fabric—*but God forbid.*

"On my arrival here I met with and read with great pleasure your book on the American Governments. The Judicious collection that you have made, with your just reflections thereon, have reached America at a great crisis, and will probably have their proper influence in forming the fœdral Government now under consideration. Your Labour may therefore have its reward in the thanks of this and future generations. The present fedral system, however well calculated it might have been for its designed ends, if the States had done their duty, under the almost total neglect of that duty has been found quite inefficient and ineffectual. The government must be both Legislative and Executive, with the former powers paramount to the State Legislatures in certain respects essential to fœdral purposes. I think there is no doubt but that this Legislature will be recommended to consist of the triple ballance, if I may use the expression to signify a compound of the three simple forms acting independently, but forming a joint determination. The Executive (which will be part of the legislative) to have more duration and power enlarged beyond the present. This seems to be the plan expected and generally spoken of."

Will you be so good as to enlighten me by some observations on this subject, and let me know of what fœdral power is to consist which is to aid the executive in carrying into effect the decissions of the Legislative in case of particular States objecting?

I am dr. Sir with great esteem & affection your obliged Humble Servt.,   W. S. SMITH

RC (DLC); endorsed. Recorded in SJL as received 13 Oct. 1787.

To John Trumbull

DEAR SIR   Paris Octob. 4. 1787.

So many infidelities in the post offices are complained of since the rumors of war have arisen that I have waited a safer opportunity of inclosing you a bill of exchange to reimburse you what you had paid on account of my harpsichord. Mr. Cutting now furnishes that conveiance, and you have inclosed a bill drawn by Mr. Grand on Mr. Teissier of London for £14-7 sterling. One trouble more will close those you have had with this business. It is, to know whether the ship has certainly sailed for Rouen: because I have not yet heard of her arrival and I have had things kept a twelvemonth in their passage from London to Rouen. The immediate danger of war renders it the more urging. Receive my thanks for all the pains this instrument has cost you. I showed to Mrs. Cosway the part of your letter respecting her, and begged her to consider the scold as hanging over her head till I could get a machine for scolding invented, because it is a business not fit for any human heart, and especially when to be directed on such subjects as her. Madme. de Brehan also read so much as concerned her, and was pleased to find you still recollected her and your promise to her. She and the Count de Moustier set out for America in Tuesday next. I should suppose a few days before and after Christmas the most likely to assemble all the officers here whom you wish to see. Will you execute another commission for me? It is to ask the favor of Mr. Brown to draw a picture for me of Mr. Paine, author of common sense, now in London. I asked his permission, and it will be necessary to do it immediately lest he should quit London sooner than he expects. I would wish it of the size of the one he drew of myself, and both may be sent to me together when you come, if you will take the trouble to bring them with you. I hope there is no gaucherie in charging you with this commission to a brother painter: if there is, put it on Colo. Smith, who will not be under the same difficulties. Adieu. Your's affectionately,

TH: JEFFERSON

PrC (DLC).

From Stephen Cathalan, Jr.

friday morning [5 Oct. 1787]

Mr. Cathalan's respects to his Excy. Th. Jefferson Esqr. The State of the Purchase appears to me Just, for the quantity of hogshds. bought at Marseilles; for the prices they appear right, excepting the parcels at 39—of which I was not informed, but I dear Say they were paid so.

They say that those prices alltogether are more than the Treaty, but they don't mention that 15 p.ct. Tare makes a difference of 5 p.ct. with that of Berny which makes 1s. p. each french livre on the prices.

Yesterday I went to Versailles, to take leave of abbé de Loménie, nephew of M. de Toulouse, who lodges with him, and has a part of the travail of his Bureau; he told me that he had spoke to Monsr. de Montmorin about my affair; I answered that I had finished at length with the Farmers, in mentioning them,[1] that he and Monsr. de Toulouse were informed, and would act in my Behalf.

When you will go to Versailles, would advise you to become acquainted with him, you will pleased to know him, and if you have some plan for the Insuing he will be usefull to you; he and M. de Toulouse are the greatest ennemys of exclusive priviledges.

I wish you a good health, happiness and injoyment. And have the honour to be very respectfully your most obedient humble servant,   STEPHEN CATHALAN Jr.

RC (DLC); endorsed; undated and not recorded in SJL, but probably written just before the Messrs. Cathalan left Paris for Marseilles (see letters from the Cathalans to TJ, 3 Oct., Wednesday, 1787).

[1] Thus in MS; Cathalan may have intended to write: ". . . in mentioning them, he said that," &c.

To John Sullivan

SIR   Paris Oct. 5. 1787.

I have now before me your several favors of Apr. 16. 26. and 30. and of May 9. and 29. and received also a few days ago the box containing the skin, bones and horns of the Moose and other animals which your Excellency has been so kind as to take so much trouble to obtain and forward. They were all in good enough condition except that a good deal of the hair of the Moose had fallen off. However there remained still enough to give a good idea of the animal, and I am in hopes Monsieur de Buffon will be able to have him stuffed and placed on his legs in the king's cabinet. He was in the country when I sent the box to the Cabinet, so that I have as yet no answer from him. I am persuaded he will find the Moose to be a different animal from any he had described in his work. I am equally persuaded that our elk and deer are animals of a different species from any existing in Europe. Unluckily, the horns of them now received are remarkeably small: however I have taken measures to procure some from Virginia. The Moose is really a valuable acquisition: but the skeletons of the other animals would not be worth the expence they would occasion to me, and still less the trouble to you. Of this you have already been so kind as to take a great deal more than I intended to have given you, and I beg you to accept my sincere thanks. Should a pair of large horns of the elk or deer fall into your way by accident I would thank you to keep them till some vessel should be coming directly from your nearest port to Havre. So also of very large horns of the Moose, for I understand they are sometimes enormously large indeed. But I would ask these things only on condition they should occasion you no trouble, and me little expence.

I have also lately received your Excellency's letter inclosing the bill on Vautelet. I immediately wrote to him to know whether he would pay it, and here or at Sedan. I inclose you his answer. Immediately on receiving it I had the bill sent to Sedan to be regularly protested. I doubt whether it will come back in time to be returned to you by this conveiance. If it does not I will send it by the first packet.

You will have known that war is commenced between the Turks and Russians, and that the Prussian troops have entered Holland and reinstated the Stadtholder. It is said that even Amsterdam has capitulated. Yet it is possible, and rather probable, this country will engage in a war to restore the Patriots. If they do, it will be the most general one long known in Europe. We I hope shall enjoy the blessings of a neutrality, and probably see England once more humbled. I am with great esteem and respect your Excellency's most obedient & most humble servant,

TH: JEFFERSON

PrC (DLC). Enclosure (missing): Vautelet to TJ, 1 Oct. 1787 (see entry under that date).

To the Agents for the United States in France

SIR   Paris Octob. 5. 1787

The government having at my request called on the farmers general for a state of their purchases of tobacco agreeable to the conditions of the order of Berni, and just now furnished me with a copy of it, I send you an extract of that part which concerns your port in hopes you will do me the favor to examine whether it be just and to certify any errors you may discover in it on unquestionable certainty. Be pleased also to note whether the tobaccoes came in American or French bottoms, and whether their real tare only was deducted, these circumstances being omitted in the state of the farmers.

[209]

I must ask you too to do this without the loss of a moment, as the term of the order is so nearly expired as scarcely to leave time to complete its execution. The impossibility of my knowing whether their state be true or not will I hope be a sufficient apology for my giving you this trouble. I have the honor to be with much respect Sir, your most obedient & most humble Servant,

TH: JEFFERSON

PrC (DLC); in Short's hand, signed by TJ. TJ's REQUEST was made in his to La Boullaye, 18 July and 24 Sep. 1787. See note to TJ to Dupont, 6 Oct. 1787.

From Nathaniel Barrett

Paris, 6 Oct. 1787. Encloses a communication he has received from La Boullaye; is ignorant of "the Terms imposed in this Decision"; asks TJ to learn what they are so that he may comply "or represent to him the necessity of any Alterations to be made."

RC (DLC); 1 p. Recorded in SJL as received 8 Oct. 1787. Enclosure missing (but see TJ to Barrett, 8 Oct. 1787).

From John Bondfield

SIR   Bordeaux 6 October 1787

At my return from the Country I found the inclosed letter on my Desk which I omitted in mine of the 21st. Ulto.

Every appearance here bespeaks preparatives for offensive or deffensive measures. All the workmen in the different branches of the Marine Service are took up and sent to the different arsenals and orders are come to the Marine Board not to grant any more seamen leave to embark til further orders.

Should hostilities take place the American Navigation if Neutre will reap great advantages but great abuses will take place which it will be difficult to prevent. The conections betwixt England and America will facilitate the means to obtain Cover for British bottoms under American Registers. France cannot enjoy the like advantages. Difference of Language and other striking objects will make any attemps of false papers subject to more rigourous scrutin. The Courts of both Nations will have employment from the contests that will arise. Nothing less than an Act of Navigation carrying protection to *American Built* ships only with other partial cloggs can free the Americans from lending their names and transfering to other Nations the advantages which circumstances would give them exclusively.

[210]

We have many arrivals of late from America the wharehouses fill and little prospect of being spe[edily] emptied. I am assured from good authority that the Farmers at this day have upwards of two Year's consumation in Store. By what I can learn all or the greatest part of the Tobaccos here are for account of London and Glasgow Houses who speculated in Virginia and that the Virginia planter will be but little affected by the result of this market. It is true Tobaccos had got up a few shillings in Virginia but the Exchange was at forty on London which ballanced the advance, and the new Crop will bring the prices to the former level. In England and Holland Tobaccos are at 22.2¾ and 3d. At both markets heavy charges attend. Our charges are very moderate, and at equal prices ours is a better market. I could wish to see a steddy intercourse established betwixt Virginia and this City but the repeated retard that all consignments meet with in having returns, deters us from speculating, and all the consignments from Virginia having fallen on the English line, where conections have another tendance, I do not find a single House established in a respectable solid line. The measures taking in the Convention at Philadelphia appear to be conducted with secrecy or at least the arrivers are entirely unacquainted of any diliberations resolved on.

With due respect I have the honor to be Sir Your very hble Servant, JOHN BONDFIELD

RC (DLC); addressed and endorsed. Recorded in SJL as received 10 Oct. 1787. Enclosure: TJ to Blanchard, 9 Sep. 1787 (see Bondfield to TJ, 21 Sep. 1787).

To Pierre Samuel Dupont

Paris Oct. 6. 1787.

Mr. Jefferson has the honour of sending to Monsieur Dupont a copy of the Statement of purchases of tobacco made by the Farmers general. According to this it would seem that they have purchased 16573 hogsheads on the conditions prescribed by the order of Berni. That order was for about 12, or 15,000 hogsheads. M. de Vergennes, in his letter, fixes it at 15,000 hogsheads absolutely. But take the middle term 13,500 hogsheads, and it gives 1125. per month, which in 19 months (to wit, from May 24. 1786 to Dec. 31. 1787.) amounts to 21,375 hogsheads, so that there remain to be purchased 4802. hogsheads before the close of the year.

But as to the 16,573 hogsheads which they consider as purchased according to the order of Berni, they do not state 1. The bottoms in which they came, to wit, French and American, or foreign: 2. The tare allowed, viz. the *real tare*, which is about 10. per cent, and is stipulated to Mr. Morris, or the *legal tare* which is 15. per cent, and which being taken from the other venders, has been a deduction of 34, 36, and 38 sous the quintal from the prices ordered at Berni: 3. The times of paiment. Mr. Morris's contract was that they should pay for every cargo of tobacco within a month after it's delivery. It has been confidently said that the farmers took longer periods of paiment with the other merchants, tho' the order of Berni was that they should have all the conditions of Mr. Morris's contract.

PrC (DLC). Enclosure (DLC: TJ Papers, 36: 6214-8): "Etat des Tabacs d'Amérique achetés du Commerce depuis Le 1er. Janvier 1786. jusques au 3 Septembre 1787." This was the report of purchases of tobacco that TJ had requested La Boullaye to oblige the farmers-general to submit (see TJ to La Boullaye, 18 July and 24 Sep. 1787), but the various categories of information that he had suggested were not precisely followed. The report was divided into six columns giving information on eleven ports of entry: name of the port; name of the ships bringing tobacco (but not designating the flag as TJ had requested); date of entry (but not the time of purchase and payment); name of the venders of the tobacco (not requested by TJ); quantity in hogsheads; and "Conditions des ventes," reciting the price save in those items that bore the general designation "suivant la Décision de Berny." A "Récapitulation par Port" contained the following:

	Boucauds
"Bordeaux	1919
L'Orient	9947
Le havre	3137
Morlaix	1215
Marseille	3540
Nantes	477
Bayonne	217

	Boucauds
Cette	110
Dunkerque	12
Dieppe	1445
Rochefort	105
Total Général	22,124."

Of this grand total, 16,573 hogsheads were imported and sold ON THE CONDITIONS PRESCRIBED BY THE ORDER OF BERNI. L'Orient received 8,783 hogsheads under the order of Berni and more than half of these were consigned to the firm of Jean Jacques Bérard & Cie., who imported 5,584 hogsheads. This was more than five times the amount brought in by any other mercantile firm in France (Macarty of L'Orient and Haller of Dieppe, the next largest shippers, brought in 1,000 hogsheads each under the order of Berni). The detailed reports of which the foregoing report is a summary are to be found in Arch. Aff. Etr., Mémoires et Documents, E.-U., Vol. IX; photostats in DLC. TJ sent copies of extracts of the report to all agents of the United States in France on 5 Oct. 1787, asking them to verify the statements for the ports in which they resided; see also Coffyn to TJ, 9 Oct. 1787; Limozin to TJ, 11 Oct. 1787; and note to Bérard to TJ, 6 May 1786.

To Victor Dupont

Paris Oct. 6. 1787.

Mr. Jefferson has the honour of presenting his compliments to Monsieur Dupont le fils, and begs the favor of him to deliver the inclosed letter personally, to it's address, as he would wish to make Monsieur Dupont acquainted with this gentleman whom he will find an agreeable and useful acquaintance.

RC (NN); endorsed. Not recorded in SJL. Enclosure: TJ to Robert R. Livingston, same date.

To Robert R. Livingston

DEAR SIR   Paris Oct. 6. 1787.

The bearer hereof is a Mr. Dupont son to a gentleman of my acquaintance here of great worth and knowlege, and holding a very distinguished office in the department of Commerce. He was the friend of the late M. Turgot and wrote his life, which perhaps you may have seen. He sends his son to America to finish his education under the patronage of the Count de Moustier, believing that he may im[bibe there republican][1] principles and habits and be [less exposed to seduction. I beg][2] leave to recommend this you[ng gentleman to your car]e and good offices, and in case he [should go to] other parts of America, will pray your letter[s of] introduction for him to your friends, which will be considered as a particular favor done to him who has the honour to be with sentiments of the most perfect esteem and respect Dear Sir your most obedient and most humble servant,   TH: JEFFERSON

PrC (DLC); MS mutilated, the center part of leaf being torn away. Enclosed in TJ to Victor Dupont, this date.

[1] Two or three words missing, but parts of the ascenders remain and con-

firm the conjectural reading.

[2] Four or five words missing; this conjectural reading is supported by the similar expression that TJ used respecting Mme. de Bréhan's son (see TJ to Abigail Adams, 30 Aug. 1787).

From André Limozin

Le Havre [7 Oct. 1787]. Has reports that all disputes between England and France "are almost entirely Settled," but will believe only what he learns through TJ, especially while he hears that "they are continuing to press People in England to fitt out their Fleet." Feels it his duty to observe that it would be to the advantage of the commerce of the United States to solicit from the French government permission to transfer goods which cannot be sold on their arrival in France, except at a great loss, to ships bound for other ports, under the supervision of customs officers, without landing the goods, paying only a small duty such as one-half of one per cent; the customs officers now require not only full import duties but also very heavy export duties, the two amounting to one-fourth of the value of the goods. Asks pardon for his "frequent and troublesome observations." Encloses statement of account for the expenses of "la Reception et Expedition d'une grande Caisse Contenant Curiosité naturelle et trois Caisses Graines" which arrived for TJ on the last packet from New York, amounting to £160 7s. Will ship on the American vessel, the *Juno*, Captain Jenkins, the four boxes of books TJ forwarded to him; she is a fast-sailing, three-masted ship of 240 tons and will depart in two or three weeks, in case TJ has anything else to forward; or, if there are any passengers that TJ wants to go by her, she "hath an exceeding good Cabbin."

RC (MHi); 4 p.; addressed and endorsed. Recorded in SJL as "no date," received 9 Oct. 1787. The date has been taken from the statement of account.

To Nathaniel Barrett

DEAR SIR   Paris Octob. 8. 1787.

Your letter is put into my hand in the moment of my departure into the country. Mr. Short will translate the decision and send it with this. What are the conditions of the several dates referred to therein I cannot tell, having never meddled with the contract of Sangrain. I expect the sum of their requisition is that if you claim a total reimbursement under Sangrain's contract you must comply with the conditions annexed to that contract, and that if you claim only as an American by the extension to us of the Hanseatic conditions, then such titles or formalities only are to be produced as are required in that case. What these formalities are I know not, these being details of execution which belong to the captains of ships. I am with much respect Dear Sir Your friend & servant,

TH: JEFFERSON

PrC (DLC). Enclosure not found.
MY DEPARTURE INTO THE COUNTRY: TJ was evidently at the hermitage at Mont Calvaire from the 8th to the 12th when he settled his account for an extended period there (see note to Cathalan to TJ, under 3 Oct. 1787, second letter).

To John Jay

SIR   Paris Oct. 8. 1787.

I had the honor of writing you on the 19th. of Sep. twice on the 22d. and again on the 24th. The two first went by the packet, the 3d. by a vessel bound to Philadelphia. I have not yet learned by what occasion the last went. In these several letters I communicated to you the occurrences of Europe as far as they were then known.

[214]

Notwithstanding the advantage which the emperor seemed to have gained over his subjects of Brabant by the military arrangements he had been permitted to make under false pretexts, he has not obtained his ends. He certainly wished to enforce his new regulations; but he wished more to be cleared of all domestic difficulties that he might be free to act in the great scenes which are preparing for the theatre of Europe. He seems therefore to have instructed his governor general of the Netherlands to insist on compliance as far as could be insisted without producing resistance by arms, but at the same time to have furnished him with a sufficiently complete recantation to prevent the effects of insurrection. The governor pressed; the people were firm; a small act of force was then attempted, which produced a decided resistance in which the people killed several of the military; the last resource was then used, which was the act of recantation. This produced immediate tranquillity, and every thing there is now finally settled by the emperor's relinquishment of his plans. My letter of the evening of Sep. 22. informed you that the Prussian troops had entered Holland, and that of the 24th. that England had announced to this court that she was arming generally. These two events being simultaneous, proved that the two sovereigns acted in concert. Immediately after, the court of London announced to the other courts of Europe that if France entered Holland with armed force, she would consider it as an act of hostility and declare war against her; sending Mr. Grenville here at the same time to make what she called a conciliatory proposition. This proposition was received as a new insult, Mr. Grenville very coolly treated and he is now gone back. It is said he has carried the ultimatum of France. What it is particularly, has not transpired: it is only supposed in general to be very firm. You will see in the Leyden gazettes one of the letters written by the ministers of England to the courts of their respective residence, communicating the declaration before mentioned. In the mean time Holland has been sooner reduced by the Prussian troops than could have been expected. The abandonment of Utrecht by the Rhingrave of Salm, seems to have thrown the people under a general panic, during which every place submitted except Amsterdam. That had opened conferences with the Duke of Brunswic; but as late as the 2d. instant no capitulation was yet concluded. The king of Prussia, on his first move, demanded categorically of the king of Poland what part he intended to act in the event of war. The latter answered that he should act as events should dictate: and is, in consequence of this species of menace from Prussia, arming himself. He can bring into the feild about seventy thousand good cavalry. In the mean time, tho' nothing transpires publicly of the confederation between France and the two empires, mentioned in my letter of Sep. 19. it is not the less sure that it is on the carpet, and will take place. To the circumstances beforementioned, may be added, as further indications of war, the naming a Generalissime of their marine on the Atlantic, Monsr. de Suffrein on the Mediterranean Monsr. Albert de Rioms, the recalling Monsr. de St. Priest their Ambassador, from Antwerp, before he had reached the Hague, and the activity of their arming by sea. On the other hand, the little movement by land would make one suspect they expected to put the king of Prussia into other hands. They too, like the Emperor, are arranging matters at home. The rigorous levy of the deux vingtiemes is enregistered, the stamp act and impot territorial are revoked, the parliament recalled, the nation soothed by these acts, and inspired by the insults of the British court. The part of the council still leaning towards peace are become unpopular, and perhaps may feel the effects of it. No change in the administration has taken place since my last, unless we may consider as such Mr. Cabarrus's refusal to stand in the lines. Thinking he should be forced to follow, too servilely, plans formed by others, he has declined serving. Should this war take place, as is quite probable, and should it be as general as it threatens to be, our neutrality must be attended with great advantages. Whether of a nature to improve our morals or our happiness is another question. But is it sure that Great Britain, by her searches, her seizures, and other measures for harrassing us will permit us to preserve our neutrality? I know it may be argued that the land war which she would superadd to her seawar by provoking us to join her enemies, should rationally hold her to her good behavior with us. But, since the accession of their present monarch, has it not been passion, and not reason, which, nine times out of ten, has dictated her measures? Has there been a better rule of prognosticating what he would do, than to examine what he ought not to do? When I view his dispositions, and review his conduct, I have little hope of his permitting our neutrality. He will find subjects of provocation in various articles of our treaty with France which will now come into view in all their consequences, and in consequences very advantageous to the one and injurious to the other country. I suggest these doubts on a supposition that our magazines are not prepared for war, and on the opinion that provisions for that event should be thought of.

The inclosed letter from Mr. Dumas came to me open, tho directed to you. I immediately waited on the Ambassadors ordinary and extraordinary of Holland, and the envoy of Prussia, and prayed them to interest themselves to have his person, his family, and his goods protected. They promised me readily to do it, and have written accordingly: I trust it will be with effect. I could not avoid inclosing you the letter from Monsr. Bouebé, tho' I have satisfied him he is to expect nothing from Congress for his inventions. These are better certified than most of those things are: but if time stamps their worth, time will give them to us. He expects no further answer. The gazettes of Leyden and France to this date accompany this, which will be delivered you by the Count de Moustier, Minister plenipotentiary from this country. I have the honour to be with sentiments of the most perfect esteem & respect Sir, Your most obedt. & most humble servt.,

TH: JEFFERSON

PrC (DLC). Enclosures: (1) Dumas to Jay, 28 Sep. 1787, with postscript of 29 Sep. (see Dumas to TJ, 28 and 29 Sep. 1787). (2) Bouébe to TJ, 22 Sep. 1787 (missing).

To John Jay

DEAR SIR   Paris Octob. 8. 1787.

The Count de Moustier, minister plenipotentiary from the court of Versailles to the United states will have the honour of delivering you this. The connection of your offices will necessarily connect you in acquaintance: but I beg leave to present him to you on account of his personal as well as his public character. You will find him open, communicative, candid, simple in his manners, and a declared enemy to ostentation and luxury. He goes with a resolution to add no aliment to it by his example, unless he finds that the dispositions of our countrymen require it indispensably.—Permit me at the same time to sollicit your friendly notice, and thro you, that also of Mrs. Jay, to Madame la Marquise de Brehan, sister in law to Monsieur de Moustier. She accompanies him in hopes that a change of climate may assist her feeble health, and also that she may procure a more valuable education for her son, and safer from seduction, in America than in France. I think it impossible to find a better woman, more amiable, more modest, more simple in her manners, dress, and way of thinking. She will deserve the friendship of Mrs. Jay, and the way to obtain hers is to receive her and trust her without the shadow of etiquette.

[217]

The Count d'Aranda leaves us in a day or two. He desired me to recall him to your recollection and to assure you of his friendship.—In a letter which I mean as a private one, I may venture details too minute for a public one, yet not unamusing nor unsatisfactory. I may venture names too, without the danger of their getting into a newspaper. There has long been a division in the council here on the question of war and peace. M. de Montmorin and M. de Breteuil have been constantly for war. They are supported in this by *the[1] queen. The king goes for nothing. He hunts one half the day, is drunk the other, and signs whatever he is bid.* The Archbishop of Thoulouse desires peace. Tho brought in by the queen he is opposed to her in this capital object, which would produce an alliance with her brother. Whether the archbishop will yield or not, I know not. But an intrigue is already begun for ousting him from his place, and it is rather probable it will succeed. He is a good and patriotic minister for peace, and very capable in the department of finance. At least he is so in theory. I have heard his talents for execution censured.

Can I be useful here to Mrs. Jay or yourself in executing any commissions great or small? I offer you my services with great cordiality. You know whether any of the wines of this country may attract your wishes. In my tour last spring I visited the best vineyards of Burgundy, Cote-rotie, Hermitage, Lunelle, Frontignan, and white and red Bordeaux, got acquainted with the proprietors, and can procure for you the best crops from the Vigneron himself. Mrs. Jay knows if there is any thing else here in which I could be useful to her. Command me without ceremony, as it will give me real pleasure to serve you, and be assured of the sincere attachment and friendship with which I am, Dear Sir, your most obedient humble servt., TH: JEFFERSON

RC (NK-Iselin); addressed to Jay as "Secretary for foreign affairs to the United states in Congress"; marked "Private" on address cover and so recorded in SJL; partly in code. PrC (DLC); accompanied by coded passage *en clair* in TJ's hand.

On the future relations between the Jays and the COUNT DE MOUSTIER and the MARQUISE DE BREHAN, see Malone, *Jefferson*, II, 197-8, and note to TJ to Abigail Adams, 30 Aug. 1787.

[1] This and the following words in italics are written in code and were decoded interlineally by Jay in RC, employing Code No. 10.

To James Madison

DEAR SIR   Paris Oct. 8. 1787.

The bearer hereof the count de Moustier, successor to Monsr.

de la Luzerne, would from his office need no letter of introduction to you or to any body. Yet I take the liberty of recommending him to you to shorten those formal approaches which the same office would otherwise expose him to in making your acquaintance. He is a great enemy to formality, etiquette, ostentation and luxury. He goes with the best dispositions to cultivate society without poisoning it by ill example. He is sensible, disposed to view things favorably, and being well acquainted with the constitution of England, it's manners and language, is the better prepared for his station with us. But I should have performed only the lesser, and least pleasing half of my task, were I not to add my recommendations of Madame de Brehan. She is goodness itself. You must be well acquainted with her. You will find her well disposed to meet your acquaintance and well worthy of it. The way to please her is to receive her as an acquaintance of a thousand years standing. She speaks little English. You must teach her more, and learn French from her. She hopes by accompanying M. de Moustier to improve her health which is very feeble, and still more to improve her son in his education and to remove him to a distance from the seductions of this country. You will wonder to be told that there are no schools in this country to be compared to ours, in the sciences. The husband of Madame de Brehan is an officer, and obliged by the times to remain with the army. Monsieur de Moustier brings your watch. I have worn her two months, and really find her a most incomparable one. She will not want the little re-dressing which new watches generally do, after going about a year. She costs 600 livres. To open her in all her parts, press the little pin on the edge, with the point of your nail. That opens the chrystal. Then open the dial plate in the usual way. Then press the stem, at the end within the loop, and it opens the back for winding up or regulating. *De Moutier*[1] *is remarkably communicative. With adroitness he may be pumped of any thing. His openness is from character not from affectation. An intimacy with him will on this account be politically valuable.* I am Dear Sir Your affectionate friend & servant, TH: JEFFERSON

RC (DLC: Madison Papers); partly in code; endorsed. PrC (DLC: TJ Papers); accompanied by coded passage *en clair* in TJ's hand.

are written in code, and have been decoded by the Editors, employing Code No. 9. RC has been decoded interlineally in a later hand, probably that of one of Madison's editors.

1 This and subsequent words in italics

From William Stephens Smith

London, 8 Oct. 1787. Acknowledges TJ's letter of 28 Sep.; would be "much flattered if Congress would join you in opinion relative to the appointment you mention"; agrees "fully respecting the proper conduct which ought to be pursued relative to *the Island*"; thinks "it would be fortunate for U.S. if we could see it once fairly entered upon." Sends copy of John Adams' letter of 25 Aug. which TJ has not acknowledged; fears it and the book sent with it have gone astray; it was sent by Mme. de Corny when she returned to Paris the first of September.

RC (DLC); 4 p. (including Tr of Adams letter); addressed. Recorded in SJL as received 15 Oct. 1787.

From John Adams

DEAR SIR   Grosvenor Square Oct. 9. 1787

I sent you a copy of my second volume by Mr. Barthelemy the French Chargé here now Minister, with a Letter about Money matters. In your favour of Sept. 28. you dont mention the receipt of them.—I have indeed long thought with Anxiety of our Money in the hands of our Friends, whom you mention, and have taken the best Precaution in my Power, against Accidents. I do not consider the Game as up. But a disgrace has happened, which is not easy to get rid of.—Disgrace is not easily washed out, even with blood. Lessons my dear Sir, are never wanting. Life and History are full. The Loss of Paradise, by eating a forbidden apple, has been many Thousand years a Lesson to Mankind; but not much regarded. Moral Reflections, wise Maxims, religious Terrors, have little Effect upon Nations when they contradict a present Passion, Prejudice, Imagination, Enthusiasm or Caprice. Resolutions never to have an hereditary officer will be kept in America, as religiously as that of the Cincinnati was in the Case of General Greens son. Resolutions never to let a Citizen ally himself with things will be kept untill an Opportunity presents to violate it. If the Duke of Angoleme, or Burgundy, or especially the Dauphin should demand one of your beautiful and most amiable Daughters in Marriage, all America from Georgia to New Hampshire would find their Vanity and Pride, so agreably flattered by it, that all their Sage Maxims would give way; and even our Sober New England Republicans would keep a day of Thanksgiving for it, in their hearts. If General Washington had a Daughter, I firmly believe, she would be demanded in Marriage by one of the Royal Families of

[220]

France or England, perhaps by both, or if he had a Son he would be invited to come a courting to Europe.—The Resolution not to call in foreign Nations to settle domestic differences will be kept untill a domestic difference of a serious nature shall break out.— I have long been settled in my own opinion, that neither Philosophy, nor Religion, nor Morality, nor Wisdom, nor Interest, will ever govern nations or Parties, against their Vanity, their Pride, their Resentment or Revenge, or their Avarice or Ambition. Nothing but Force and Power and Strength can restrain them. If Robert Morris should maintain his Fortune to the End, I am convinced that some foreign Families of very high rank will think of Alliances with his Children. If the Pen Family should go to America, and engage in public affairs and obtain the Confidence of the People, you will see Connections courted there. A Troop of Light Horse from Philadelphia meeting Dick Pen in New Jersey, will strike the Imaginations of Princes and Princesses. How few Princes in Europe could obtain a Troop of Light Horse to make them a Compliment of Parade. In short my dear Friend you and I have been indefatigable Labourers through our whole Lives for a Cause which will be thrown away in the next generation, upon the Vanity and Foppery of Persons of whom we do not now know the Names perhaps.—The War that is now breaking out will render our Country, whether she is forced into it, or not, rich, great and powerful in comparison of what she now is, and Riches Grandeur and Power will have the same effect upon American as it has upon European minds. We have seen enough already to be sure of this. A Covent Garden Rake will never be wise enough to take warning from the Claps[1] caught by his Companions. When he comes to be poxed[1] himself he may possibly repent and reform. Yet three out of four of them become even by their own sufferings, more shameless instead of being penitent.

Pardon this freedom. It is not Melancholly: but Experience[2] and believe me without reserve your Friend, JOHN ADAMS.

O tempora—*oh mores*

RC (DLC); endorsed. FC (MHi: AMT); in the hand of William Stephens Smith; with slight variations in spelling and punctuation. Recorded in SJL as received 15 Oct. 1787.

I SENT YOU . . . BY MR. BARTHELEMY: In Smith's letter to TJ of 8 Oct. he said the letter and book were sent by Mme. de Corny; Adams apparently sent another copy of his book by John Brown Cutting on 16 Sep. (see Adams to TJ, of that date) which TJ acknowledged in his letter of 28 Sep. TJ did not acknowledge Adams' letter of 25 Aug. until 13 Nov. 1787.

1 This word blotted out in FC.
2 This word underlined in FC.

To Madame de Bréhan

Paris Octob. 9. 1787.

Persuaded, Madam, that visits at this moment must be trouble-some, I beg you to accept my Adieus in this form. Be assured that no one mingles with them more regret at separating from you. I will ask your permission to enquire of you by letter some-times how our country agrees with your health and your expecta-tions, and will hope to hear it from yourself. The imitation of European manners which you will find in our towns will I fear be little pleasing. I beseech you to practice still your own, which will furnish them a model of what is perfect. Should you be singular, it will be by excellence, and after a while you will see the effect of your example.

Heaven bless you, Madam, and guard you under all circum-stances: give you smooth waters, gentle breezes, and clear skies, hushing all it's elements into peace, and leading with it's own hand the favored bark, till it shall have safely landed it's precious charge on the shores of our new world.

PrC (DLC).

From Burrill Carnes

[*Nantes, ca. 9 Oct. 1787.*] In answer to TJ's inquiry of the 5th, he has called upon the twelve individuals and firms in the appended list, and gives a state of their sales of tobacco to the farmers-general: eight of them sold lots ranging in size from 2 to 203 hogsheads, at prices ranging from 28^{tt} for a lot of 3 hogsheads to 34^{tt} for a lot of 203 hogs-heads, all paid 15 per cent tare, three lots were in American vessels, and five in French; four of the merchants could not be found, but they had sold a total of 35 hogsheads. "There is Tobacco now for sale here, but the farmers will not purchase at the fix'd prices." Asks for informa-tion about the prospects of war.

RC (DLC); 2 p.; endorsed; without date which has been assigned from internal evidence and an entry in SJL of a letter of Carnes, "no date," which was received on 12 Oct. 1787.

From Francis Coffyn

Dunkerque, 9 Oct. 1787. In accordance with TJ's letter of 5 Oct., has ascertained that, in addition to the 12 hhds. listed in the enclosed statement as sold by Mr. A. Tresca in Sep. 1786, 1,000 hhds. of Vir-

[222]

ginia tobacco were sold by Debacque Frères, in the same month, the latter being sent by French coasting vessels to Dieppe and should be checked with the Dieppe returns to see if the amount was included there; both sales met the conditions of the order of Berni. "The Merchants here have made many applications to the Farmers general to Sell to them the Tobaccos they receive from America but they Seem averse to accept their proposals"; this he attributes to jealousy because the farmers cannot exercise a monopoly in that town. Tobacco is a considerable item of trade there, 6,000 hhds. yearly are "consumed by the Fabricants besides a great quantity Sol'd to the English Smugglers"; estimates the latter at 150 hhds. per month. "The greatest part is received from America and the rest from Glasgow London and other ports in England." Returns the statement TJ sent him, having added the sale of Debacque Frères.

RC (DLC); 2 p.; endorsed. Recorded in SJL as received 13 Oct. 1787. Enclosure: Statement sent to Coffyn in his copy of TJ's letter to American agents in France, 5 Oct. 1787.

To Fantin Latour

MONSIEUR   à Paris ce 9me. 8bre. 1787.

Il y a en Amerique des maisons de commerce François ou votre parent pourroit bien peut-etre trouver de l'occupation. Dans le cas qu'il en manqueroit, et qu'il voulut se nourrir du travail de ses mains, il trouveroit de l'occupation dans ce genre partout, et à très bonnes gages. Bordeaux seroit le port d'ou il pourroit esperer le plus probablement de passer en qualité d'engagé. J'ai l'honneur d'etre avec beaucoup de respect, Monsieur, votre tres humble et tres obeissant serviteur,   TH: JEFFERSON

PrC (MHi).

To André Limozin

SIR   Paris Octob. 9. 1787.

I have duly received your favor with my account, balance 180.ᵗᵗ 7s which shall be paid to your order. I observe it supposed with you that the differences between the courts of London and St. James[1] are nearly settled. But be assured on the contrary that no accomodation is expected, and that war is as certain as it can be, without being actually commenced or declared. There remains indeed a possibility of preventing it, but it is very feeble. This court would be disposed to do it, but they beleive that of London

[223]

decided on war. We cannot foresee the moment it will commence, but it is not distant, according to present appearances. M. de Suffrein is appointed to command on the ocean, and M. Albert de Riom on the Mediterranean.

I have the honour to be with much respect Sir Your most obedient humble servant, TH: JEFFERSON

PrC (DLC). ¹ Thus in MS.

To Zachariah Loreilhe

SIR Paris Oct. 9. 1787.

Your favor of Sep. 22. is now before me. Mr. Barclay, just before his departure, wrote to me on the affair of Geraud and Rolland. I have written to him in answer that I thought the management of it would be better placed in the hands of Mr. Dumas who does our business in Holland, and is on the spot: that he can take the orders of the Treasury board on the subject, and act accordingly. So that I am not authorized to take any step in that business at present.

War is reduced almost to a certainty. There remains but a weak possibility of accomodation between this country and England. It may not commence till the spring, but it may commence also at every moment.

I have the honor to be with much respect Sir Your most obedient humble servant, TH: JEFFERSON

PrC (DLC).

To Moustier

Paris Octob. 9. 1787.

Mr. Jefferson has the honour of presenting his respects to Monsieur le conte de Moustier, and of taking leave of him by letter, which he is prevented doing in person by an unexpected visit to Versailles today. He will hope to have the pleasure of sometimes hearing from him, and will take the liberty occasionally of troubling him with a letter. He considers the count de Moutier as forming with himself the two end links of that chain which holds the two nations together, and is happy to have observed in him dispositions to strengthen rather than to weaken it. It is a station of importance, as, on the cherishing good dispositions and quieting bad ones will depend in some degree the happiness and prosperity of the two countries. The Count de Moustier will find the affections of the Americans with France, but their habits with England. Chained to that country by circumstances, embracing what they loathe, they realize the fable of the living and dead bound together. Mr. Jefferson troubles the Count de Moutier with two letters to gentlemen whom he wishes to recommend to his particular acquaintance and to that of Madame de Brehan. He bids Monsieur de Moustier a most friendly Adieu, and wishes him every thing which may render agreeable his passage across the water and his residence beyond it.

PrC (DLC). Enclosures: (1) TJ to Madison, 8 Oct. 1787. (2) TJ to Jay, 8 Oct. 1787 (second letter).

From Moustier

à Paris le 9. 8bre. 1787.

Le Cte. de Moustier conservera pretieusement le billet que Monsieur Jefferson lui a fait l'honneur de lui adresser ce matin, afin de s'en servir comme de souvenir des sentimens de Monsieur Jefferson à son egard. Il tachera de remplir en Amerique l'espoir qu'il a bien voulu former de lui et il peut l'assurer que personne en France et depuis plus longtems que lui, n'a formé de desirs plus ardens et plus sinceres pour la prosperité des Etats Unis, qu'il est persuadé qui depend beaucoup de celle d'un Pays qui doit avoir les raports les plus constans avec les Etats Unis après avoir eû ceux qui etoient les plus critiques. Le Comte de Moustier prie Monsieur Jefferson d'etre convaincu de sa vive reconnoissance ainsi que des sentimens d'estime et d'attachement qu'il lui a voués et qu'il se trouvera bien heureux de pouvoir cultiver dans le nouveau monde comme dans l'ancien.

RC (DLC); endorsed. Recorded in SJL as received 9 Oct. 1787.

To Edward Rutledge

DEAR SIR   Paris Oct. 9. 1787.

This will be delivered you by Mr. Cutting, with whom I had a small acquaintance in America, and who brought me letters of good recommendation from Mr. Adams and Colo. Smith in London. On these foundations I am authorized to recommend him to you as a gentleman of merit, worthy of your acquaintance. He comes to sollicit a settlement of the affairs of the Indian frigate and provision for a paiment of the balance. In all this you will do of your own motion what is just, and you would not do more were I so injust as to ask it. Any attentions and civilities you will be so good as to shew him, will be considered as favours done to Dear Sir Your most obedient & most humble servant,

TH: JEFFERSON

PrC (DLC).

From John Bondfield

Bordeaux, 10 Oct. 1787. All workmen in the public dockyards "are taken up and put forward"; 3,000 seamen have been ordered from that place; war appears "not far distant"; many private American ships are in Europe; their seamen will be pressed into service "on one side or other"; few will be "found for the American Navigation." Has been advised by an inhabitant of Quebec who arrived two days past that Gen. Carleton "keeps the Canadians to a strickt Militia Dicipline."

RC (DLC); 2 p.; endorsed. Recorded in SJL as received 13 Oct. 1787.

From Cavelier

Dieppe, 10 Oct. 1787. In accordance with TJ's request of 5 Oct. he has obtained, not without difficulty, a statement of tobacco received, which, however, does not include the shipments which have arrived for the account of Le Normand and Le Couteulx. Is unable to give an exact count of American and French ships. There are very few of these, but there are a large number of English ships flying the American flag. If, in the future, TJ wishes a detailed report on the number, nationality, &c. of ships carrying tobacco from North America he has only to give the order and he will receive the most complete and detailed information. It appears that nothing further has been decided as to preference to be granted to American ships. Lists the quantity of tobacco received on 16 ships, totalling 1,445 hhds., of which 434 hhds. were sold at 33.^{tt} and 34.^{tt} and 1,011 hhds. at 36.^{tt} and 38.^{tt}

RC (DLC); 4 p.; in French; endorsed. Recorded in SJL as received 12 Oct. 1787.

From Dr. Lambert

Frontignan, 10 Oct. 1787. Has been informed by his banker, Cabanis, that he called on TJ to present Parent's bill for 374.^{tt}14s. and while he was there TJ praised the wine he had received from Parent to a nobleman who was also present; Cabanis offered to transmit an order for the gentleman but the latter refused, wishing to order direct; urges TJ's friend to order at once because there is little left of the vintage TJ procured and it will not be equalled by the next crop. As TJ has observed, he enjoys a considerable income in addition to the revenue from his vineyard and is thus enabled to practice his profession with ease; however, he desires to improve his technical knowledge in medicine by serving in an army hospital; there are rumors of war; asks TJ to assist him in securing a post in the medical service.

RC (MHi); 2 p.; in French; endorsed; at foot of text there are calculations in TJ's hand, apparently showing the cost per bottle of wine purchased. Recorded in SJL as received 21 Oct. 1787.

To John Stockdale

SIR   Paris Oct. 10. 1787.

Your favor of Sep. 21. inclosing your account came safely to hand. I observe one error in it, a History of Philip 3d. charged as a quarto edition 25/. whereas it was the 8vo. edition in 2. volumes which I presume was cheaper. Also the 34. copies of the Notes on Virginia £9-1-4. for which I have no objections to be answerable when the bookseller shall have sold them, but not before.

With respect to the use of the plate for the map, I am allowed 10d. sterling a peice here for those annexed to the French edition, and no objection to it from the bookseller, and those things are dearer in England than here. I could not abate to you, without, in honor, doing the same to him, and then I should not be reimbursed the money I paid for engraving the plate in London, and correcting it in Paris, with charges of transportation &c. so that I could not without loss let them go at less than 10d. a peice, making on the 1025 struck for you £42-14-2.

I inclose an extract from Lackington's last catalogue, of the articles I should be glad to have, and will beg the favor of you to send me. Send me also

Martin's Philosophical grammar
Linnaeus on the sexes of Plants
Linnaeus's reflections on the study of nature } in English.

These new additions being made to my account, and the preceding corrections, be so good as to state to me the balance, and I will immediately remit it to you. I suppose it will be under £14. The last books you sent me were very much rubbed, which I mention,

[227]

that these may be well packed. Be so good as to send me also the copper plate of my map. I am Sir Your very humble servant,

TH: JEFFERSON

PrC (DLC). The enclosed extract from Lackington's catalogue has not been identified.

From Guiraud & Portas

Cette, 11 Oct. 1787. Appeal for aid and protection in their claim for loss caused by barratry of John Ferriere, of Sijean, who had command of their brig, *The David*. On 1 July 1787 Ferriere took freight, against their will or orders, at Cape St. Domingo and set sail for Nantes, without paying duties or signing part of the bills of lading; a "Kings frigate was dispatched after him without Success." They have just learned by letters from Norfolk, Va., dated 11 Aug., that the ship came into that port on 26 July; that, after plundering the cargo, Capt. Ferriere and his crew, excepting one boy, deserted. Having no acquaintance in Norfolk and "Knowing said harbour dangerous for Vessels to lay in there any long time on account of the Worms," they ask that the ship be provided with a new crew by authority of Congress to return her and the cargo to Nantes at the expense of the owners; if this is not practicable they ask that the ship and cargo be sold at auction, the returns to be held by the admiralty at Norfolk for the account of the insurers and the rightful owners, excepting some wood and cacao for which there are no bills of lading but are mentioned in Capt. Ferriere's accounts as bought for the ship's owners; if these articles exist they may also be sold and the proceeds forwarded for their or their insurer's account. Regret putting TJ to the trouble of writing to Congress but trust his "upright goodness" to assist them in recovering their cargo and taking "such Steps so as the guilty Captain Ferriere and his crew may be brought to proper Justice, in order to deter in future other french Seamen from the Thoughts of running away with safety to the american shores, with their owners and Loaders propriety."

RC (DLC); 2 p.; endorsed. Recorded in SJL as received 19 Oct. 1787.

[William Lewis to Thomas Lee Shippen]

Philadelphia 11. Oct. 1787.

I have given ⟨*your father*⟩ two or three papers which contain the substance of what has passed here respecting the federal convention. The connecting thread is all I shall send, except a few minutes of the proceedings of the convention.

After four months session the house broke up. The represented

[228]

states, eleven and a half, having unanimously agreed to the act handed to you, there were only three dissenting voices; one from New England, a man of sense, but a Grumbletonian. He was of service by objecting to every thing he did not propose. It was of course more canvassed, and some errors corrected. The other two are from Virginia: but Randolph wishes it well, and it is thought would have signed it, but he wanted to be on a footing with a popular rival. Both these men sink in the general opinion. No wonder they were opposed to a Washington and Madison. Dr. Franklin has gained much credit within doors for his conduct, and was the person who proposed the general signature. He had prepared his address in writing. The exertion of speaking being too great, they allowed another to read it. The day previous he sent for the Pennsylvania delegates; and it was reported that he did it to acquaint them of his disapprobation of certain points, and the impossibility of agreeing to them. His views were different. He wanted to allay every possible scruple, and make their votes unanimous. Some of the sentiments of the address were as follows.

'We have been long together. Every possible objection has been combated. With so many different and contending interests it is impossible that any one can obtain every object of their wishes. We have met to make mutual sacrifices for the general good, and we have at last come fully to understand each other, and settle the terms. Delay is as unnecessary as the adoption is important. I confess it does not fully accord with my sentiments. But I have lived long enough to have often experienced that we ought not to rely too much on our own judgments. I have often found I was mistaken in my most favorite ideas. I have upon the present occasion given up, upon mature reflection, many points which at the beginning, I thought myself immoveably and decidedly in favor of. This renders me less tenacious of the remainder. There is a possibility of my being mistaken. The general principle which has presided over our deliberations now guides my sentiments. I repeat, I do materially object to certain points, and have already stated my objections. But I do declare that these objections shall never escape me without doors; as, upon the whole, I esteem the constitution to be the best possible, that could have been formed under present circumstances; and that it ought to go abroad with one united signature, and receive every support and countenance from us. I trust none will refuse to sign it. If they do, they will put me in mind of the French girl who was always quarelling and finding fault with every one around her, and told her sister that she thought it very extraordinary, but that really she had never found a person who was always in the right but herself.'

Our assembly was on the point of breaking up, and it was immediately brought on the carpet. Our back-county men, who have had much pains taken with them by those whose places will become less lucrative, opposed it being agitated: not because they objected: (for the thing was good:) but because it came not from Congress. They thought it impossible it could come in time. A vote was carried 43. to 19. They were to meet to fix a time of election. The 19. absconded, so as to prevent there being a house. The resolution of Congress was sent forward by express (by Bingham) and was here 12. hours after signature. They now still refused to attend. A Serjeant at arms and some citizens went for them, and two were obliged to attend. The prints tell the rest. 16. of the 19 addressed, and will render themselves infamous by their wicked and abominable lies. All parties (except the few interested) are for it. It meets with general approbation, and we have no doubt of it's adoption.

Our Assembly election has passed without any opposition. Constitutionalists and Anti-Constitutionalists are lost in Federal and Anti-federal: and we expect no opposition but from those abovementioned, and the lawless banditti on the frontiers whose depredations would be then put an end to, and they obliged to be under regular government.

The attempt is novel in history; and I can inform you of a more novel one; that I am assured by the gentlemen who served, that scarcely a personality, or offensive expression escaped during the whole session. The whole was conducted with a liberality and candor which does them the highest honor. I may pronounce that it will be adopted. General Washington lives; and as he will be appointed President, jealousy on this head vanishes. The plan once adopted, difficulties will lessen. 9. states can alter easier than 13 agree. With respect to Rhode island, my opinion is that she will join speedily. She has paid almost all her debts by a sponge, and has more to gain by the adoption than any other state. It will enable us to gain friends, and to oppose with force the machinations of our enemies. Yours &c.

Tr (DLC); entirely in TJ's hand; endorsed by him late in life: "Constitution of United States." PrC of Tr (DLC); lacks one page. The deletion (unusually heavy and clearly intended to obscure) in the first line appears in both Tr and PrC, and was therefore made by TJ shortly after he had completed the Tr (or while copying) and before the PrC was executed.

This letter has been printed a number of times from the copy made by TJ

—the original evidently has disappeared —but it is not to be found in any previous edition of his writings. At different times it has been described as being a letter to him or as one written by him. Among the various printings are: *Documentary History of the Constitution*, IV, 324-7; Farrand, *Records of the Federal Convention*, III, 104-5; Benjamin Franklin, *Works*, ed. Bigelow, IX, 417-8. In the first two it is described as a letter to TJ; in the last, as one by him; in none is the other correspondent identified. Because of its history and implications it is necessary to print it again and to discuss briefly TJ's known or conjectured relations with it. The date-line and internal evidence make it apparent at once that it was impossible for TJ to have written it, and almost equally so for it to have been addressed to him. It is also evident that the author was a Pennsylvanian and probably a Philadelphian; that he was presumably a member of the state legislature; that he was not himself a member of the Federal Convention, but certainly enjoyed the confidence of one or more members of the delegation from his state to that body (Benjamin Franklin, Thomas Mifflin, Robert Morris, George Clymer, Thomas FitzSimons, Jared Ingersoll, James Wilson, and Gouverneur Morris). It is evident, too, that the recipient was someone who arrived in Paris late in 1787 or early in 1788; that he may possibly have left America after the Federal Convention adjourned, otherwise a copy of its ACT could not have been handed him; that he was probably young; and that his father, who was living, may or may not have been a Pennsylvanian.

The identification of the writer and recipient cannot be certainly established in the absence of the original letter, but the most plausible conjecture would seem to indicate that William Lewis, a rising young member of the Philadelphia bar, a representative in the legislature, and an ardent supporter of the Constitution, was the writer. He was, of course, well known to the Shippens and to most if not all of the Pennsylvania delegates to the Federal Convention. He was a friend of Dr. William Shippen, Jr., the father of Thomas Lee Shippen, with whom he also corresponded and who the Editors believe was the recipient. Thomas Lee Shippen, nephew of Arthur and Richard Henry

Lee, was studying law in England and in his correspondence with his father and his uncles in the summer and autumn of 1787 frequently discussed the Constitution and its reception in America and abroad. A good example of this correspondence is R. H. Lee's letter to young Shippen of 22 July 1787 (*Letters of Richard Henry Lee*, ed. Ballagh, II, 427). Dr. Shippen agreed with R. H. Lee about the need of a bill of rights and, in discussing this with his son, said: "I am thus particular because I suppose you wish to know all on political development. . . . Prager at last fixes his departure on Saturday, and I am making a packet for my young Barrister. In it you will find the Debates of our last session of A[ssembly] taken by T. Lloyd, an American Museum for October, and all the papers Against and for the New Constitution.—Brutus said to be by R. H. Lee or Jay—Cincinnatus by A Lee—Old Whig and Centinel by a Club—Bryan, Smilie, Hutchn, &c." As the Pennsylvania ratifying convention was completing its labors, Dr. Shippen again wrote his son: "Lloyd will publish the whole debates as soon as possible and they will be a treat to you and Mr. Jefferson. . . . I hope it [the Constitution] will be amply commented upon by the learned and unprejudiced on your side of the water. —Your observations I think should be confind to me or your uncle R. H. L. unless you think 'tis a good and safe System; I confess I am not enough versed in matters of Government to give a wellfounded judgment" (Dr. William Shippen, Jr., to Thomas Lee Shippen, 18-22 Nov. 1787, 12 Dec. 1787; Shippen Family Papers, DLC). It is clear from these and other letters that Dr. Shippen was in the habit of making up packets of documents for his son pertaining to political affairs in America, such as the author of the present letter had given to the father of the recipient evidently for the purpose of having them forwarded. In a letter of 4 June 1787 Dr. Shippen referred to the meeting of the Federal Convention, said that he was sending a packet via the *Ruby*, Captain Smith, and added: "Lewis thanks you for your letter and promises to answer it." In another letter of 19 Jan. 1788 he remarked that Lewis held young Shippen in high esteem—an opinion shared, evidently, by many others, including TJ and the young man's well-known uncles (same).

If it is assumed that the writer of the letter was William Lewis and its recipient was Thomas Lee Shippen, then all of the major conditions—especially that the father and the writer were on friendly terms, but that the former was less *au courant* of political affairs than the latter, while his son shared the writer's political interests—are met. The combination of circumstances is so strong as to be almost conclusive, particularly in connection with the deleted words of the first line (discussed below), but there is one difficulty—that is, the implications of the words THE ACT HANDED TO YOU. Young Shippen was in England during the summer and autumn of 1787 and no copy of the Constitution could have been "handed" to him there so early as 11 Oct. 1787. The difficulty posed by this phrase must be admitted, yet there are various possible explanations: (1) that TJ erred in transcribing—an unlikely explanation in any case, but particularly so in view of the fact that he interlined the preposition "to" in the phrase in question; (2) that a copy of the Constitution had been given to someone late in Sep. or early in Oct. to "hand" to young Shippen when the vessel arrived some time after the present letter was written—a plausible but improbable explanation; (3) that the words were not meant literally; or (4) that the writer of the present letter *was himself transcribing from another letter*. The last, while not fully convincing, is made plausible by the fact that the writer set out to present a few MINUTES of the proceedings of the Convention—a word possibly implying that he was copying from a letter he himself had received. The writer certainly obtained from a member of the Pennsylvania delegation all of the information in the paragraph in which the phrase occurred and in that containing the present version of Franklin's speech. He may have obtained this information orally or he may have obtained it in writing, but there is at least a probability that Lewis was copying some MINUTES that had been sent to him in writing. There are others who could possibly be considered as the recipient of this letter—for example, James Jarvis, who left New York soon after it was written, who carried a copy

of the Constitution with him, and to whom TJ was referred for news about the general subject of the Convention and its work, though various other factors eliminate him as a possibility—but the Editors conclude that, despite the difficulty posed by the phrase referred to, William Lewis wrote the letter and Shippen received it. The conclusive evidence for them appears in the deletion of the two words YOUR FATHER.

The significance of this deletion lies primarily in the fact that, as indicated above, it was done during or immediately after TJ had transcribed the letter, otherwise he could not have obtained so clear a press-copy containing the deletion. From this fact two conclusions follow: (1) the deletion was made in order to conceal the identity of the recipient, a conclusion also supported by the fact that TJ (contrary to habit) omitted the signature of the writer and gave the letter no endorsement until many years later, as the handwriting of the endorsement shows; (2) the transcription was made with some purpose in mind that involved showing it to another person, a conclusion confirmed by the fact that he made both a Tr and a PrC. The question at once arises: What was that purpose and who was the person that it concerned? Certainly TJ did not intend this letter for publication, since, despite the note struck in the concluding paragraph, most of its MINUTES OF . . . PROCEEDINGS tended to reveal the extent of divisiveness in American councils. It would have been wholly out of keeping with TJ's career as a minister to reveal to the public anything of this nature. If not intended for publication, then, the copy must have been made for some individual—not, obviously, for Lafayette, for he received information of the Constitution from Washington and others; and also, though TJ fully shared American news with him, the Marquis usually obtained this in consultation or by reading letters and documents shown to him: he was such a close ally of the American minister that TJ would not have had to delete YOUR FATHER or to omit the signature or endorsement if the letter were intended for him. But the unknown person for whom the transcript was made must have been one who would have been able, *by means of the deleted words*, to identify the recipient. This again points to young Shippen as the recipient, for early in 1788 TJ extended many civilities to the young man, invited him to dine twice a week at Hôtel de Langeac, introduced him to the De Cornys and others, and even presented him at court. Hence, with young Shippen known to intellectual, political, and social circles in Paris to a degree probably not equalled by any other young American who visited TJ early in 1788, it may have seemed to TJ merely a good precaution to delete from the letter anything that might reveal the identity of its recipient. The person for whom the transcript was made was also someone who must have had a special interest in the contents of the letter or in a part thereof. Now if the revealing comments of the writer about divisive opinions in the Federal Convention and about the machinations of the Federalist majority of the Pennsylvania legislature—matters which TJ clearly would not have wanted to spread about—are eliminated, the remaining matter of paramount interest is Franklin's speech. Indeed, that speech, because it was Franklin's and because it had great influence in the Convention and during the course of the ratification of the Constitution, is the principal element in the letter even if nothing is eliminated. This letter evidently contains the earliest version of the speech, which may have been paraphrased from memory merely in order to present SOME OF THE SENTIMENTS OF THE ADDRESS or it may actually have been transcribed from a text or from notes taken by one of the members of the Pennsylvania delegation. The speech began to be the subject of conversation in America from the time Franklin invited the Pennsylvania delegates to meet with him on Sunday, 16 Sep. 1787, for a preliminary reading. On 30 Oct. 1787 Nathaniel Gorham of Massachusetts asked Franklin for a copy to be employed "to correct that possitive attachment which men are too apt to have for their own ideas" and also "for the purpose of publishing it, provided you do not think it improper." Franklin complied and Gorham caused the version of the speech that he had received to be published in a Boston paper "excepting a few lines" (Gorham to Franklin, 30 Oct. and 3 Dec. 1787; quoted in Farrand, *Records of the Federal Convention*, IV, 78-80). Franklin freely gave copies of the speech to Daniel Carroll of Maryland and to

others, and it was reprinted in the *American Museum* for December, possibly with his consent (Carl Van Doren, *Benjamin Franklin*, p. 756). The *New York Journal* for 10 Dec. also printed the text (doubtless that sent to Gorham with its exceptions) from a Boston paper of 3 Dec. 1787.

Now if, as seems plausible, the transcript was made by TJ because of the Franklin speech and because he thought someone in Paris wished to see it, the evidence points inevitably to Franklin's friend Le Veillard, with whom TJ had already been exchanging information about Franklin (see note to TJ to Le Veillard, 9 May 1786). This is wholly conjectural, but inherent plausibilities support the possibility. Moreover, the presence of both Tr and PrC in TJ Papers would seem to indicate that TJ failed to make use of the copy for the purpose for which it was intended. If this were the case, it could have been because he thought it would have been indiscreet to reveal so much of American politics—or it could have been because the object which the copy was intended to achieve had already been met. If TJ made the copy in order to give Le Veillard a text of the Franklin speech, the need to do so disappeared when Le Veillard received Franklin's letter of 17 Feb. 1788 which included the following remarks: "I attended the business of the convention faithfully for four months. Enclosed you have the last speech I made in it" (*Works*, ed. Bigelow, IX, 459).

But the presence of both Tr and PrC in TJ Papers does not necessarily prove that TJ failed to carry out his purpose. It will be observed from the descriptive note above that the PrC lacks one page. The page missing is one that contains *no part of the text of the letter save the speech by Franklin*, with the exception of the single catch-word OUR which is separated from the text and is at the extreme lower right-hand corner and therefore easily torn away, obliterated, or (as was possible the case) simply not copied when the PrC was being made. The speech by Franklin is so centered in the page as to make it appear that TJ purposely transcribed the letter in order to have its text easily separable. If so, then TJ transcribed the whole of this interesting letter primarily for his own files and, in doing so, performed the typically Jeffersonian feat of making a part of it adaptable to some secondary use. If this other use was that of giving the text to Le Veillard, then the transcript must have been made before Le Veillard received Franklin's letter with its longer version of the speech—that is, it must have been made around Feb. or Mch. 1788, or, in other words, while young Shippen was in Paris and seeing much of the one whom he considered "the wisest and most amiable man I have seen in Europe."

From André Limozin

MOST HONORED SIR   Havre de Grace 11th October 1787.

Since my former of the 7th of this Month, I have received two days after the Letter your Excellency hath honored me with. It is impossible to examine perfectly and exactly wheter the note furnished to your Excellency by the Farmers Generals is very exact or not, because to do it with punctuality would be to desire their Manufacturers to shew me the agreements they have made with the houses mentioned in that note. But should I try such a proceeding, they would refuse surely all the light I should require. I being not intitled nor having the least legal appointement to force them to give me such informations, I dont find any means to procure them.

You cant conceive how many Frauds are committed by the British ships when they come from America in order to injoy the priviledges of the Americans, altho so small that they are scarcely worth taking notice of. But the British Master, paying a very great attention to the least thing which can procure him some advantage, the most of them come in to our Port and hois American Colors, and declare them americans and Their Ships American Properties. The united States having here no body legally apointed to prevent such frauds which are intirely to the detriment of their nation and of its trade, it is very easy to the English Master to make our Customhouse officer believe that they are Americans. I have observed it very often and have offerd to prevent such fraud as soon as I shall be legally appointed agent. I dont require a farthing of salary. I am thank God above a reward. I require nothing else but thanks from the nation and I am certain to Succeed in preventing such frauds. I return here annexed a Note with my observations. I could not get informations neither upon the quantity of Tobacco sold to the Farmers Generalls nor upon the terms. I am very sory that it is not in my power to do beter.

I have the honor to be with the highest regard Your Excellencys Most obedient & very Humble Servant,

ANDRE LIMOZIN

[234]

RC (MHi); addressed and endorsed. Recorded in SJL as received 13 Oct. 1787. Enclosure not found.

To John Trumbull

DR SIR   Paris Octob. 11. 1787.

Mr. Cutting has for some days been in possession of a letter for you, but finding his departure put off from day to day, I take the liberty of repeating by post a request which is in that letter. It is to enquire whether the ship James (Capt. Dunn) with my harpsichord is actually sailed from London. The appearances of an immediate rupture between the two nations make me anxious that it should arrive here as immediately as possible. I will also be obliged to you to enquire the price of a good harmonica, the glasses fixed on an axis, to comprehend 6 octaves, if they ever comprehend as much, in a plain mahogany case.

Mr. Cutting was the first private opportunity that occurred of sending you a bill of exchange for the money you had been so kind as to advance for me. The bill is enclosed in the letter he has for you, and I am chagrined that you should be kept from receiving it. If any private hand goes before him I will send the letter by such private hand. I am with much esteem Dear Sir Your friend & servant,   TH: JEFFERSON

PrC (DLC).

From John Bondfield

Bordeaux, 12 Oct. 1787. Finds the return made by the farmers-general, enclosed in TJ's letter of 5 Oct., accurate; the register of the farmers does not indicate the nationality of the ships in which tobacco was imported so he cannot ascertain how much came in French or American ships, only that "the whole has been brought from America"; the "Tare is taken net the Hogsheds being stript as prescribed by the regulations"; will send, "in a post or two," a general return of all tobacco imported from 1 Jan. 1786 to 24 Sep. 1787; 18,062 hhds. have been received under Morris' contract, 6,279 hhds. on private account; four or five ships have arrived since 24 Sep. which will add about 2,000 hhds. Has seen a proclamation in one of the English papers "that all British seamen in foreign Service taken by the Algerines and Turks shall not be redeem'd. This can only alude to American Ships . . . a counter proclamation on the part of America might prevent American seamen entering into the British service." In the event of a war more British will "serve in the American Navigation" and, based on the experience of the last war, "there will be a most extraordinary mellange" in every prison in France.

RC (DLC); 2 p.; endorsed. Recorded in SJL as received 18 Oct. 1787.

From Le Mesurier & Cie.

SIR   Havre 13th. October 1787

We have been honored by Your Excellency's Letter of the 20th. last month, and are sensible of your attention to the Trade of America by obtaining an Order to the Farmers General to make a Report of all the Tobacco they have purchased since the date of the Order of Bernis. As however their report may turn out unfavorable, we have followed the intimation you have been pleased to give us, and have been in treaty with them for 474 Hhds. Tobacco we had in our warehouses, but without success, although we offered the Virginia at 32^{lt} the Hundred weight. The Margaretta is just arrived with 568 Hhds. more, so that we have now upwards of 1000 Hhds. lying on hand, without any prospect of Sale unless the Farmers General will take them off our hands. In this predicament we have thought it prudent to send one of our House to Paris, the Bearer Mr. Delamotte, who signs by Procuration, and who will have the honor of delivering this Letter. He will have it in his power to convince the Farmers, that if they reduce the prices of Tobacco to too low a rate, they will check the direct importation from America, and in a very little while be reduced to the same state they were before the Independency of the United States.

We have the honor to be with the greatest respect Sir, Your Excellency's most obedient and most humble Servants,

HAV. LE MESURIER & COMP.

RC (ViWC); endorsed. Recorded in SJL as received 16 Oct. 1787.

From Benjamin Franklin

DEAR SIR   Philada. Oct. 14. 1787

I take this Opportunity of sending you another Copy of the propos'd new federal Constitution, and of acquainting you that the Box containing the Encyclopedia for me and Mr. Hopkinson is just come to hand in good Order. With great Respect and Esteem I am, Your Excellency's most obedient & most humble Servant,

B. FRANKLIN

RC (DLC). Not recorded in SJL but entered in SJL Index and, therefore, probably received early in 1788, for which year the pages are lacking in SJL. Enclosure: Probably one of the official copies of the Constitution (see note to Washington to TJ, 18 Sep. 1787).

From André Limozin

Le Havre, 14 Oct. 1787. Thinks it his duty to report all matters which affect American trade, especially since America is not concerned in the differences between England and France. A British ship arrived on 25 Sep. with tobacco from Virginia, under the command of a Thomas Crawford, a lieutenant of the British navy; the ship has an American crew, or so they declare under oath; they also say that the articles they signed specify an immediate return to Virginia; but the master, hearing that all British officers are called home, intends to proceed to London and threatens "when in Liquor (which case happens often)" to deliver the whole crew on board British men of war; the crew have applied to Limozin for help, knowing they cannot secure justice once in England, but he has no legal authority to help them. Feels obliged, also, to report that by false rumors of high wages paid to seamen in England, many Americans are persuaded to desert and are in England before the masters of the ships can obtain assistance from the admiralty; these "tricks" will ruin American navigation. It is to the interest of the French government to assist in stopping these practices because they help man the enemy's ships. If war breaks out many British ships will fly American colors and gain access to French ports. The only way to avoid these "frauds" is to appoint agents in each port to make thorough investigations of all vessels on their arrival, requiring an oath from the master of the ship to be confirmed by the crew that all is in order; this must be done until the United States passes a law requiring certification at the port of departure. If this method is not approved, application should be made to the French minister to issue an order to the intendant of the marine or the first commissary of the marine to go through such an examination. As long as all such matters must go through the admiralty court, "where nothing is done without fees and heavy expences," trade will languish. Asks forgiveness for the length of his letter if his advice is not approved.

RC (DLC); 8 p.; addressed. Recorded in SJL as received 16 Oct. 1787.

From André Limozin

Most Honorable Sir   [14 October 1787]

I return your Excellency thousand and thousand thanks for the Kind informations mentioned in your Letter of the 9th of [this] Month. I shall never forget so much Kindnesses your Excellency is pleasd to shew me. Gratitude orders me to increase daily my attention for the Welfare and prosperity of America.

We receive just now intelligence from England by a Packet arrived this night from Portsmouth which she left the 12th instant in the Evening that the very same day an order was received from London for the Fleet which layd at Spithead to Sail the 14th instant without any further delay. The General opinion is that the Said Fleet is bound for the Mediterranean. I have the honor to be Your Excellency's Most obedient & very Humble & devoted Servant

ANDR LIMOZIN

I have agreable to your orders drawn this day on your Excellency Lvers 160.^{lt} 7 unto the order of Sartorious & Cie. at Sight.

RC (MHi); endorsed; without date, which has been assigned from internal evidence; and an entry in SJL which records the receipt on 16 Oct. of Limozin's letter of 14 Oct. (preceding) and one of "no date." The sight draft is in MHi and is endorsed by TJ: "Limozin 160^{lt}-7 for plants and bones paid Nov. 1. 1787."

From William Carmichael

MY DEAR SIR   Madrid 15. Octr. 1787

I received the Letter you did me the honor to write me the 25th Ulto. one post later than from its date it ought to have reached me. I am afraid there is some mistake with respect to the *manner* you imploy to express yourself *confidentially* to me. Please to examine whether you have made use of the same *characters* as those which you intrusted to Mr. Barclay. With all my endeavours your meaning is unintelligible. I am not pressed for the reimbursement of the Ct. D Expilly, but that may soon be the case. From your Answer to my letter on this Subject I continued the allowance to our Captives which other Nations allow theirs and I consulted you and Mr. Adams on this Subject because the whole of our African business was committed to your mutual direction. I conform entirely in your opinion with respect to the Ideas we ought to hold out of not redeeming our Captives, but I must avow, that my conviction arises from Political considerations, for I never think of their situation but my heart revolts at the Idea of Letting them remain the unhappy victims sacrificed to the future security of others. While I am on this Subject, I must mention to you that Mr. Lamb left in the hands of Mr. Montgomery of Alicant a power of Attorney to recover the Amount of an account which he produced before his Departure against the Ct. D Expilly. Mr. Montgomery has applied to me on the Subject and I have told him that as he was authorized by Mr. Lamb to recover the Debt He must have recourse to the Debtor, That Mr. Lamb being accountable himself to Congress He would naturally produce the account of his disbursements. On this Subject several Letters have been written by Mr. Montgomery to the Ct. D Expilly. The Latter appeals to me and I have given him the same answer that I gave to the house of Montgomery. I must observe however that the Count pressed me and I pressed Mr. Lamb to settle his accounts with the Ct. D Expilly in Spain. The Latter told me that he had received a gold Watch and gold Snuff Box from Mr. Lamb, who would never tell him the price which he wished to know in order to repay him. He also mentioned that Mr. Lamb had lent him the Vessel which he bought to transport himself and Mr. Randall to Algiers to be employed in the King of Spains Service to go to Tunis, which Conduct of Mr. Lamb I approved then and still it has my approbation. The Count Alledges that he recompensed handsomely the Captain and Crew and in Mr. Lambs account he is charged with the Wages expenditures &c. &c. These are little vexatious affairs that give me more Trouble than those of more Importance, and all this Trouble might have been avoided if Mr. Lamb had accepted the Counts offer to take the Vessel on his Catholic Majestys account at the price of its first cost and outfits. Captn. Obryan informs me that he writes you by the same opportunity by which he sends his last Letters to me. I am much afraid that Instead of Logies being his Dupe He is the Dupe of Logie whom I know personally. The Latter is given to Liquor, but even in his Cups is artful indeed. I know that above one half of what our well Intentioned Captain writes me the 27th. Ulto. is not well founded. I transmit thro' the hands of the Commis or undersecretary of State for the Department of Africa the Letter Your Excellency sent me for Mr. Chiappi. I had received from Mr. Jay the Ratification of the Treaty for my own Government with an Intimation that it was expected that I should correspond with the Agents of Congress in that quarter. I immediately Informed them of their appointment by Mr. Barclay being confirmed by Congress and sent to Dr. Francesco a copy of the Ratification, at the same time Assuring him that he would soon receive it in form. You will find or I am much mistaken, that these Agents will produce accounts of Disbursements against Congress. They will have Turkish and African Ideas. I am much afraid that these will not correspond with our œconomical plans. I have had the pleasure to put into the hands of the Ct. de F. Blanca a letter from Congress to his Catholic Majesty expressive of their Satisfaction of the good Offices imployed by his Majesty to facilitate our Treaty with Morrocco &c. &c. As soon as I have received the official answer which the Minister promised me on this Subject I shall Communicate it to you. Our Country is as grateful for services as it is sensible to Injuries. It will not forget the one or the Other. How much it is to be lamented that a scrupulous adherence to ancient systems should for a moment interrupt or prevent a universal and mutual good understanding between two Countries that Nature renders essentially useful to one and the other. The Enemies of Both take Advantage of this Circumstance and in their plans of revenge and Ambition ground their Hopes of Success in the Animosities which they themselves endeavour to excite between us. I trust that the wisdom of this Ministry and our earnest desire to Cultivate the friendship of their Sovereign will ultimately Render Abortive their Projects. The turn which the Affairs of Holland have taken excite the Attention of all our Politicans here. At present it is unecessary to repeat to you the Substance of all that has been said or done previous to the Day on which I had the honor to write you, except that this Court appeared decidedly disposed to support France in case of a war with G.B. Of this Determination the Minister made no Secret and orders have been sent to the Different Sea Ports to arm with all Expedition. Last week however the British Minister received a courier from Mr. Eden which brought pacific tidings; from their purport it would appear that the Affairs of Holland will be terminated without a war. Perhaps I may be wrong in having a different opinion. We may also perhaps know the British Character better than other Nations do. As I have been from *various circumstances* on a good footing with the British Minister here (one of the most artful men I ever knew in Politics) I provoked from him the Letter which I now inclose and which I beg you to return me immediately. You will see whether it conforms with Mr. Edens Language at Versailles. That man will not succeed here. The Ct. de Florida can never have any confidence in a person who has uniformly thro' life (to advance his fortune) been a Traitor to every Friend and every principle of Moral honesty. I have received with great pleasure your Notes on Virginia and as yet have given them but a Cursory perusal. I think you have victoriously combatted Buffon, Monsr. de P. and the Abbé Raynal. I do not know whether Dr. Franklin ever mentioned to you what passed at a Dinner at Paris at which I was present, on that contested point. I think the Company consisted of 14 or 15 persons. At Table some one of the Company asked the Doctor what were his Sentiments on the remarks made by the Author of the Recherches sur L'Amerique. We were five Americans at Table. The Venerable Doctor regarded the Company and then desired the Gentleman who put the question to remark and to Judge whether the human race had degenerated by being transplanted to another section of the Globe. In fact there was not one American present who could not have tost out of the Windows any one or perhaps two of the rest of the Company, if this Effort depended merely on muscular force. We heard nothing more of Mr. P's work and after yours I think we shall hear nothing more of the opinions of Monsr. Buffon or the Abbé Raynal on this subject. I have surveyed with a kind of remorse your map. I passed so near Monticello, I was so hospitably treated by so many Virginia Gentlemen it pains me now that I lost the only occasion that perhaps I shall ever have to be personally known to you. At a Colonel Lewis' house on the Cow or Calfpasture River I saw one of the Indian Sepultures you mention. The Feild where it was placed was then sewn with Rye. But I have seen Human Bones, points of arrows &c. dug out of Oyster shell Banks in Chester River at Many feet from the surface of the Earth. Have you ever made conjectures by what occasion these beds of shells of 12, 15, twenty and even thirty feet Depth have been formed not only to fence If I may use the Expression in some places our rivers but which extend themselves from the Banks to several acres inland? I have seen also in what we call our Forests, that on Lands placed near the Sources of our rivers on the Eastern shore of Maryland bodies of oak Trees &c. Dug out of the Earth at 12 and 15 feet and perhaps more (for I cannot trust my memory). How come they to be buried there? How long can wood thus buried resist the distroying effects of time. We know from Experience that our fence Stakes, that our Post and rail cannot but for a few years remain in the Situation in which we fix them. I beg your pardon for suggesting such trivial discussions to your Attention, and I have no excuse to plead, but my hope that they will soon become matter of reflection to myself when I become again an American Planter. Not to Intrude longer on your time and patience which I have already too much Abused, I have the honor to be with the greatest respect & Esteem Your Excys. Most Obliged & Hble. Servt.,   WM. CARMICHAEL

RC (DLC); endorsed. Recorded in SJL as received 31 Oct. 1787. The enclosed letter from Liston to Carmichael has not been found; it was returned in TJ to Carmichael, 15 Dec. 1787.

MONSR. DE P.: Cornelius de Pauw, whose *Recherches philosophiques sur les Américains* was published in Berlin and London, 1768, ff. Robert Liston (1742-1836), whom TJ came to know later in Washington, was THE BRITISH MINISTER at Madrid from May 1783 to August 1788.

From Fernan-Nunez

Paris, 15 Oct. 1787. Announces that he had his official audience with the king and royal family as ambassador from the court of Spain.

RC (DLC); 2 p.; addressed. Not recorded in SJL.

From Robert Montgomery

Alicante, 15 Oct. 1787. Acknowledges TJ's letter of 10 Sep. and will follow his advice concerning the consulate. Has just received a letter from Algiers, dated 29 Sep., which states that the plague has subsided and that the people go about their ordinary business; has also been informed that the crew of a Russian ship, captured by the Algerines, has been ransomed through the mediation of the Dutch consul: the captain for 3,000 Spanish dollars, 2 mates for $2,000 each; a carpenter and boatswain for $1,500 each; 10 men at $1,000 each; plus "Regency Duty" of 16 per cent; totalling $23,200. If this report is correct, this is so much greater than "anything ever paid before the Spanish Peace, that I fear our Poor Country men will be Obliged to look up to the universal Redamer for their first relief." Lamb arrived in Boston about the beginning of August.

RC (DLC); 2 p.; endorsed. Tr (DLC); in Short's hand. Recorded in SJL as received 31 Oct. 1787; copy enclosed in TJ to Jay, 3 Nov. 1787. In DLC: TJ Papers, 17: 2897 there is a memorandum in TJ's hand summarizing the figures given here by Montgomery for the ransoming of "the Russian crew taken last year" and converting the dollars to livres, showing that the average cost was 8,117 livres per man; in this memorandum there is also the following: "See Memoires secretes vol.29.pa.298. that 313 captives cost the two orders de la Merci et Les Mathurins 630,052^{tt} exclusive of the expenses of quarantine, clothing, transportation. This is 2012^{tt} = 383 Dollars each. Article Sep. 11. 1785" (undated, but evidently written early in 1788, perhaps in calculating the amount necessary to be included in the loan negotiated with Adams at Amsterdam in Mch.; see note 3 to Enclosure I, TJ to Jay, 16 Mch. 1788). There is also in DLC: TJ Papers, 33: 5719 an "Extract of a letter dated Napoli pmo 8bro. 1787," in Short's hand with a note by TJ, showing that the Court of Naples had redeemed 297 slaves at a cost of 299,539 ducats; the note by TJ stated that "the Ducat of Naples is nearly 4 livres" and calculated the cost of the slaves at "4032. livres each."

From William Stephens Smith

Dr. Sir   London October 15—1787.

Permit me to introduce the Bearer Dr. Walker a young Gentleman from Virginia.—Nothing new has transpired since my last of the 8th. inst.—Amsterdam I have no doubt has surrendered, as letters from there of the 9th. say, that 2 deputies were sent to the Princess, to know what terms she finally required, and authorized to give assurances of the disposition in the people to comply with her wishes in every respect. *Sic transit Gloria mundi.* From the stern brow of the British Bull and the continuance of warlike preparations, I am lead to suppose, *they do*[1] not think, france will quietly submit to sink beneath the horizon of political notice; that she is fallen from a respectable station, is true, and that nothing but the development of some great project, or immediate active exertions can reinstate her, must, even by her friends be acknowledged.

We are in daily expectation of hearing further from our Country, relative to the establishment of the fœderal Government, and I shall loose no time, in making communications to you, of what I may obtain on that head.

I am Dr. Sir, with great regard your most Obliged Humble Servant,   **W. S. Smith**

RC (MHi); endorsed. Recorded in sJL as received 23 Oct. 1787.

[1] Smith interlined "he does" over "*they do*" without deleting the latter.

To Madame Townsend

Paris Oct. 15. 1787.

I had the honor of receiving yesterday, Madam, from Commodore Jones, the inclosed letter for you, which he desired me to deliver to you with my own hand. I was accordingly setting out from home in expectation of your being at Paris, and of complying with his desire by waiting on you with the letter, when Mr. Short informed me you were in the country, and that a messenger from you was now with him. Supposing that I may safely confide the letter to this messenger, I have now the honor of inclosing it to you. The Commodore desired me also to shew you the letter which he had written to myself. I will ask your permission to perform this part of his injunctions to me whenever you return to Paris if you

[243]

will be so good as to apprise me when you return, and where I may have the honor of waiting on you. I have that of being with sentiments of much esteem & respect Madam Your most obedient & most humble servant, TH: JEFFERSON

PrC (CSmH). Enclosure: John Paul Jones to Mme. Townsend, enclosed in Jones to TJ, 4 Sep. 1787. In SJL TJ spelled the name "Townshend."

From André Limozin

Le Havre, 16 Oct. 1787. Since his letter of 14 Oct. he has learned that only six of the crew of the ship *Elephant* are Americans; has taken them under his protection and advanced their legal expences; the admiralty court has awarded them their wages and the customary allowance for their return to America and has ordered the English master of the vessel to pay the legal expences; is happy "to have procured justice to these poor fellows."

RC (MHi); 2 p.; endorsed. Recorded in SJL as received 19 Oct. 1787.

To André Limozin

SIR   Paris Octob. 17. 1787.

Congress alone has the power of appointing Consuls for the United states of America. No convention being as yet finally settled with this government for regulating the Consular functions, Congress have made no appointment for France, except of Mr. Barclay to be their Consul general. He found it necessary to name agents in the several ports to protect the citizens of the United states till Consuls should be named. Having appointed you Agent for the port of Havre, I should conceive you authorised to guard the interests of all the citizens of the United states coming to your port, and to claim for them the protection of the laws and magistrates of France. If any additional authority can be given by me for that purpose, I hereby fully give it to you as Agent for the United states. In the present case particularly I would recommend it to you to inform yourself with the most scrupulous care of the individuals of captain Crawford's crew who are citizens of the United states, and whether by their contract they can be carried to England. If they cannot, you best know to what tribunal or authority you must apply to protect them against being carried against their will to England, where they will certainly be impressed to serve against France, and, if taken prisoners by the latter, may perhaps be hung

[244]

as pyrates. I have the honour to be with much esteem, Sir, Your most obedient humble servt, TH: JEFFERSON

PrC (DLC).

To Philip Mazzei

Paris. Oct. 17. 1787.

'Si trova [Amerigo Vespucci][1] parimente dipinto nella real Galleria, tra' quadri del primo Corridore, e similmente nella Volta XXI. della medesima, tragli uomeni illustri in arme.' Vita di Amerigo Vespucci. dal Bandini pa. lxviii.

Nella 'tavola de' ritratti del Museo dell' illustriss. e eccellentiss. Sig. Cosimo Duca di Firenza e Siena' al fine del libro Delle vita da' pittori di Giorgio Vaseri, si trova queste parola. 'Seconda fila della banda di Mezzo dè Huomini harvi. Amerigo Vespucci. Colombo Genovese. Ferdinando Magellanes. Ferdinando Cortese.'

By these passages it would seem that the pictures of Americus Vespucius, of Columbus, of Magellan and Cortez exist at Florence. I should wish extremely to obtain copies of the two first, and even of the two last also, if not too expensive. Painters of high reputation are either above copying, or ask extravagant prices. But there are always men of good talents, who being kept in obscurity by untoward circumstances, work cheap, and work well. Copies by such hands as these might probably be obtained at such prices as I would be willing to give. But how to find out those good hands, covered by the veil of obscurity? Can Mr. Mazzei put me on a method of knowing 1. whether these portraits still exist? 2. Whether permission can be obtained to copy them? 3. If a painter, such as above described, can be found? 4. What he would ask for half length copies, of the size of the life? TH: JEFFERSON

PrC (DLC).

[1] Brackets in MS.

To Madame de Tessé

Paris Octob. 17. 1787.

The last parcel of seeds which I had the honor of sending you, Madam, overburthened you in quantity, and stinted you in variety. I now enclose you a list which has exactly the contrary faults. The variety is great, the quantities small. In some instances there is not more than one, two, or three grains. Your goodness will pardon this, as you know the difficulties which attend the obtaining supplies of seeds from America. These have been very long detained on their passage. I now send them to your hotel at Paris. The packages are all numbered in correspondence with the list inclosed. The second order of numbers from 1. to 29. are distinguished on the packages by the letter H. meaning the Herbaceous plants. On your return to Chaville I will do myself the honour of paying my respects to yourself, Madame de Tott, and Monsieur de Tessé. Permit me to express here my attachment to them, and to yourself those sentiments of esteem and regard with which I have the honour to be, Madam, your most obedient & most humble servant,

TH: JEFFERSON

PrC (MoSHi). Enclosure missing.

To André Thouin

[Paris, 17 Oct. 1787. Recorded in SJL under this date. Not found. André Thouin (1747-1824) was the French botanist with whom TJ was in correspondence again in 1807 and later. He was at this time head gardener at the Jardin du Roi; his papers, preserved in the library of the Muséum National d'Histoire Naturelle in Paris, include a register of letters received by him in which there are entries for five letters from TJ for the years 1787-1788, but the letters themselves are missing.]

To Madame de Corny

Paris Oct. 18. 1787.

I have now the honor, Madam, to send you the Memoire of M. de Calonne. Do not injure yourself by hurrying it's perusal. Only, when you shall have read it at your ease, be so good as to send it back, that it may be returned to the Duke of Dorset. You will read it with pleasure. It has carried comfort to my heart, because it must do the same to the king and the nation. Tho' it does not prove M. de Calonne to be more innocent than his predecessors, it shews him not to have been that exaggerated scoundrel which the calculations and the clamours of the public have supposed. It shews that the public treasures have not been so inconceivably squandered as the parliaments of Grenoble Thoulouse &c. had affirmed. In fine, it shews him less wicked, and France less badly governed, than I had feared. —In examining my little collection of books to see what it could furnish you on the subject of Poland, I find a small peice which may serve as a supplement to the history I had sent you. It contains a mixture of history and politics which I think you will like.

How do you do this morning? I have feared you exerted and exposed yourself too much yesterday. I ask you the question, tho I shall not await it's answer. The sky is clearing, and I shall away to my hermitage. God bless you, my dear Madam, now and always. Adieu. TH: J.

PrC (DLC). For a note on TJ's HERMITAGE (Mont Calvaire), see Cathalan to TJ under 3 Oct. 1787. THE MEMOIRE OF M. DE CALONNE was presumably his *Rêquete au Roi. Adressée à Sa Majesté, par M. de Calonne, Ministre d'État*, Londres, 1787.

From Madame de Tessé

a St. germain ce 18 octobre

Me. de Tessé a Reçu hier avec un nouveau témoignage des bontés de Monsieur Jefferson l'annonce des plus grandes Richesses. Elle a lu trois fois avant de se coucher l'état de ses biens, et l'a encore parcouru ce matin à son Réveïl. Elle y trouve avec une grande satisfaction des especes dont le nom ne lui est pas inconnu, mais dont les plans ne sont jamais arrivés en France et même en Angleterre. Elle va prendre des mesures pour que son trésor arrive demain a Châville en même tems qu'elle. Elle se flatte que son bienfaiteur voudra bien ne pas tarder a y recevoir l'hommage de sa Reconnoissance et de tous les sentimens dont elle est penetrée, ainsi que Me. de Tott.

RC (DLC); endorsed. The year has been supplied from internal evidence and an entry in SJL of the receipt of a letter of 18 Oct. from Mme. de Tessé, from "St. Germaine," on 19 Oct. 1787.

From Moustier

à Paris[1] le 19. Octobre 1787.

J'ai reçu ici, Monsieur, le troisieme paquet que vous m'avez fait l'honneur de m'adresser pour Mr. Jay. J'aurois fort desiré pouvoir prolonger mon séjour à Paris, mais je sentois qu'il me falloit un peu de marge ici pour les preparatifs de mon voyage. Le vent contraire qui continue ici allonge malgré moi cette marge que je voulois prendre. Ce qui m'en console c'est que je me flatte que je serai dedomagé des delais que j'eprouve et des inconveniens qui pourront en resulter, par l'agrement d'etre porteur d'une decision favorable sur le commerce de nos deux Nations. Je vous avouerai même, Monsieur, que je m'etois flatté, que le parti que j'ai pris de ne pas prolonger mon Sejour à Paris, auroit pû influer sur plus de promptitude dans cette decision. Si je pouvois reussir à persuader aux deux Nations les idées que je conçois sur leur avantage reciproque, dans une union et une bonne intelligence bien cimentées, je jouirois de la plus grande satisfaction que je puisse desirer. J'y ferai du moins tout ce que je pourrai et je preparerai, si je ne puis achever seul, le succès de cette tache interessante. Je sens combien de facilités j'aurois pû acquerir à profiter de vos lumieres et j'espere qu'à votre retour en Amerique, Monsieur, vous voudrez bien m'en accorder la communication.

Je ne prevois encore rien de certain sur le moment de mon depart. Je mettrai autant que je pourrai le tems à profit pour examiner avec attention cet interessant etablissement où l'activité qui y regne, les ressources qui s'y trouvent fournissent des motifs de satisfaction aux amis de la France et un frein aux mauvais desseins de ses ennemis cac[hés] ou declarés.

Le courage de Mde. de Brehan dans son entreprise se soutient tres bien. J'espere qu'elle en sera recompensée par le succès de son voyage. Elle me charge, Monsieur, de la rapeller à votre souvenir et de vous faire parvenir les assurances de son attachement pour vous.

Agreez je vous prie celles des sentimens d'estime et d'affection bien sinceres avec lesquelles j'ai l'honneur d'etre, Monsieur, Votre très humble et très obeissant Serviteur,

LE CTE. DE MOUSTIER

RC (DLC); endorsed. Recorded in SJL as received 23 Oct. 1787.

1 Entry in SJL reads: "Paris (for Brest)."

From John Bondfield

SIR   Bordeaux 20. 8bre. 1787.

I have the honor to transmit you the State of Imports of Tobacco from the United States to this Port from 1 January 1786 to 24 Sept 1787, since which are arrived four or five Vessels principally for account of the Contractors. I have divided the State in two parts the one containing the Imports on private Account the other from Mr. Morris, on Account of his Contract.

We have arrivals that left America 1 and 4 Sept. but being the same date of the Packet arrived at Havre you have consiquently all and more that our Informations contain. Every exertion on the part of the Marine department in this port to hasten the Equiptments of the fleets—a change must take place in the department of the finances. Confidence in the present Directors is wanting which occations negotiations very disadvantageous, a circumstance very prejudicial in the present mom[ent.]

I have the honor to be most respectfully Sir Your most Obedient Humble Servant, JOHN BONDFIELD

RC (DLC); endorsed. Recorded in SJL as received 24 Oct. 1787. Enclosure (DLC): List of imports of tobacco at Bordeaux, giving the date of arrival, port of departure, name of ship, captain, owner, and quantity of tobacco carried; there were 37 ships that entered with a total of 18,133 hhds. for the Morris contract during these twenty-one months, and 88 ships with 6,967 hhds. (plus a few fractional or broken lots of small but uncertain quantity) on private account.

To Guiraud & Portas

GENTLEMEN   Paris Oct. 20. 1787.

I have duly received your letter on the subject of the barratry committed by the Captain of your vessel, which you suppose to be left at Norfolk in Virginia. The best possible method for you to pursue is to address yourself to Mr. Oster, Consul of France living at Norfolk. It is perfectly within his line to take care of the property of the subjects of France, in such a situation, and being on the spot, he will be able to apply to the civil power, and to accomodate the remedy to the circumstances of the case. In the mean time I will write to him also, inclosing a copy of your letter, and will send it by the first conveiance, so that he may receive as early notice as possible. You will advise him what you would have done in every event. I have the honour to be, Gentlemen Your most obedient humble servant, TH: JEFFERSON

PrC (DLC).

From Ralph Izard

DEAR SIR   Charleston 20th. Octr. 1787.

I am favoured with your Letter of 1st. August, enclosing Messrs.

[249]

Berard's Proposals on the subject of Rice, which I have shewn to several Merchants, and am happy to find a general disposition among them to enter into Commercial Connexions with France. You know how they have been hitherto hampered by their engagements with the British Merchants, and their Trammels are not yet broken. Messieurs Brailsford, & Morris will make a Consignment of a Cargo of Rice to Messieurs Berard, & Co. This will be a beginning of what I wish to see carried to a considerable extent; and I think much will depend upon the success of this Adventure. Messieurs Brailsford & Morris are Men of Character, and Honour, and their House is as good, and solid as any in this State. I have the honour to be with great regard Dear Sir Your most obt. Servt.,

RA. IZARD

RC (DLC); endorsed. Recorded in SJL Index; received 24 Apr. 1788 (see TJ to Izard, 17 July 1788).

From André Limozin

MOST HONORED SIR   Havre de Grace 20th october 1787.

Since my former of the 16th. instant, I have received the Letter your Excellency hath honored me with the 17th of this Month. Altho Cap. Crawford was condemned to pay the wages of the 6 American Sailors amongst his crew and likewise their discharge, Mr. Rueland Correspondent of Captn. Crawford hath refused to comply with the admiraltys verdict under the pretext that Captn. Crawford is no more Master of the Said Ship that he is gone over to England to be imployed in the British Navy, in consequence of which departure Mr. Ruelan pretends that these men have no more reason to fear to be impressed, that more over the action of these Sailors being layd against a Man who at present has no more concern in the matter it must be lookd upon as void. Mr. Ruelan thinks I suppose that these Sailors being poor will not be able to advance money to obtain Justice, but I shall advance it, and do every thing which is necessary to make them free. I shall not suffer any american individualls molested as long as your Excellency will be pleased to grant me his Confidence. Nevertheless I think your Excellency should do very well to advise Congress to take it in Consideration that it is absolutely necessary for the American Nation, and its interest to have either Agents or Consuls legally appointed in France, and as long as things will remain as they are now, your Excellency will find at last how often your

[250]

Nation will be molested by that neglect. I beg of your Excellency to consider that there are but very few who would disburse their money in advance to the Lawyers (nay even take the troubles I was at) to procure Justice, and prevent molestation. Mr. Ruelan's Lawyer said at Court, I am indeed Surprised that Such a Noted Merchant as Mr. Andre Limozin will act as an Agent for the United States, altho he hath no apointment, for I defy him to shew any at least a legal one; therefore he should not meddle into business which dont concern him: and it is as clear as the day that these disobedient sailors are Supported by that Merchant in their awker behavior.

I have the honor to be with the highest regard Your Excellency's Most obedient & very Humble Servant, ANDRE LIMOZIN

RC (MHi); addressed and endorsed. Recorded in SJL as received 22 Oct. 1787.

To Martin Oster

SIR   Paris Oct. 20. 1787.

The inclosed letter from Messieurs Guiraud & Portas, merchants of France established at Cette, will explain to you it's object. Not acquainted with the organisation of our government, they propose to me to sollicit the interference of Congress. You and I know, Sir, that that body is too distant, too slow, and too much otherwise occupied. I hope I have not acted improperly in advising them rather to apply to yourself, and undertaking also to forward you a letter from hence to double the chance of your receiving it speedily. Being on the spot, you will be able to apply to the government and to accomodate the remedy to the circumstances of the case. I have the honour to be with sentiments of perfect esteem & respect Sir Your most obedient & most humble servant,

TH: JEFFERSON

PrC (DLC). Enclosure: Copy of Guiraud & Portas to TJ, 11 Oct. 1787.

From Madame de Bréhan

Brest the 22 8bre 1787.

The moment shall come very soon, Sir, which must take and carry us in your happy Country. I have but a regret—'tis that we cannot take you with us, but perhaps you will come soon. It is an hope that I will keep preciously. You have given me, Sir, a promise to write to me. Don't forget it I pray you and receive the adieux of one who knows how to value your merite and your friendship.

Will you be so good as to give this letter to Mr Short? Speak together of the travellers.

RC (DLC); unsigned; endorsed by TJ: "Brehan Mde. de." Recorded in SJL as received 25 Oct. 1787. The enclosed letter to Short is also dated at Brest, 22 Oct. 1787, and reads: "I must give you, Sir, many thanks for your kind wishes for my passage; I fear extremely, I shall be very sick, since only for going to the road yesterday, to see our frigate, I came back with a great disease: but I must suffer that with patience as also the too little cabbin which is destined to me. I believe I will be very glad to arrive at new York; you tell me, Sir, that I must keep my maners, it is better I think, to take those of the country, and I will do so. I will, Sir, write to you and shall tell you, with freedom, how I find myself with the country and with my health . . . (DLC: Short Papers; endorsed as received 26 Oct. 1787). The long, arduous voyage ahead of Madame de Bréhan, lasting almost three months and causing a rumor that the vessel had been lost, may understandably have had its influence in her failure to adopt (or even to approve) the manners of the country to which she was going. There can be little doubt, however, that she was glad to arrive in New York, though she had endured the voyage better than Moustier did (see Mme. de Bréhan to TJ, 1 Mch. 1788; Moustier to TJ, 13 Feb. 1788).

From Edward Carrington

New York, 23 Oct. 1787. Introduces Mr. Jarvis, a "Gentleman of New England" who brings this letter and a copy of the proposed plan of government; refers TJ to Jarvis for news on that subject. Is sending a full account of the convention in another letter of this day which is being carried by "the Chevalier Jones" who intended sailing on the packet but changed his passage to another ship because of the critical state of affairs in Europe; Jones should arrive soon.

RC (DLC); 2 p.; endorsed. Recorded in SJL as received 19 Dec. 1787.

From Edward Carrington

DEAR SIR   New York Octo 23. 1787

I have been honoured with your favor of the 4th. of August. Inclosed you will receive a Copy of the report of our late federal Convention, which presents, not amendments to the old Confederation, but an entire new Constitution. This work is short of the ideas I had the honor to communicate to you in June, in no other instance than an absolute negative upon the State laws.

When the report was before Congress, it was not without its direct opponents, but a great majority were for giving it a warm

[252]

approbation. It was thought best, however, by its friends, barely to recommend to the several Legislatures the holding of Conventions for its consideration, rather than send it forth with, even, a single negative to an approbatory act. The people do not scrutinize terms; the unanimity of Congress in recommending a measure to their consideration, naturally implies approbation: but any negative to a direct approbation would have discovered a dissention, which would have been used to favor divisions in the States. It certainly behoved Congress to give a measure of such importance, and respectable birth, a fair chance in the deliberations of the people, and I think the step taken in that body well adapted to that idea.

The project is warmly received in the Eastern States, and has become pretty generally a subject of consideration in Town-meetings and other Assemblies of the people, the usual result whereof are declarations for its adoption. In the Middle States appearances are generally for it, but not being in habits of assembling for public objects, as is the case to the Eastward, the people have given but few instances of collective declarations. Some symptoms of opposition have appeared in New York and Pensylvania; in the former, only in individual publications, which are attended with no circumstances evidencing the popular regard; the Governor holds himself in perfect silence, wishing, it is suspected, for a miscarriage, but is not confident enough to commit himself in an open opposition: in the latter the opposition has assumed a form somewhat more serious, but under circumstances which leave it doubtful whether it is founded in objection to the project or the intemperance of its more zealous friends. The Legislature was in session in Philada. when the Convention adjourned. 42 Members were for immediately calling a Convention before the measure had received the consideration of Congress, and were about to prepare a vote for that purpose. 19 Seceded and broke up the House, and although they, afterwards, added to their protest against the intemperance of the majority, some objections against the report, yet it is to be doubted whether they would have set themselves in opposition to it, had more moderation been used. The next morning the resolution of Congress arrived, upon which the 42, wanting 2 to compleat a House for business, sent their Sergeant for so many of the Seceders, who were brought by force, whereupon an Act was passed for calling a Convention in November. The Seceders are from the upper Counties,[1] have carried their discontents home with them, and some of them being men of influence, will occasion an inconvenience, but Gentlemen well acquainted with the Country are of opinion, that their opposition will have no extensive effect, as there is, in general, a Coalescence of the two parties which have divided that State ever since the birth of her own Constitution, in support of the new Government. From the Southern States we are but imperfectly informed. Every member from the Carolina's and Georgia, as well in Convention, as Congress, are warm for the new Constitution; and when we consider the ascendency possessed by Men of this description over the people in those States, it may well be concluded, that the reception will be favorable. In Virginia there may be some difficulty. Two of her members in Convention whose characters entitle them to the public confidence, refused to sign the report. These were Colo. Mason and Governor Randolph, nor was that State without its dissentients, of the same description, in Congress. These were Mr. R. H. Lee and Mr. Grayson, but upon very opposite principles—the former because it is too strong, the latter because it is too weak.[2] The Governor has declared that his refusal to sign, shall not be followed by hostility against the measure, that his wish is to get the exceptional parts altered if practicable, but if not then he will join in its support from the necessity of the Case.

Mr. Madison writes you fully upon the objections from Virginia, and therefore I will not impose on your patience by repeating them; one, however, being merely local, and an old source of jealousy I will present to your consideration my opinion upon. This is the ability of a bare majority in the federal Government, to regulate Commerce. It is supposed that a Majority of the Union are carriers, and that it will be for the interest, and in the power, of that majority to form regulations oppressing, by high freights, the agricultural States. It does not appear to me that this objection is well founded. In the first place it is not true that the Majority are carriers, for Jersey and Connecticut who fall into the division are by means such and New York and Pensylvania, who also are within that division, are as much agricultural as Carrying States: but, admitting the first position to be true, I do not see that the supposed consequences would follow. No regulation could be made on other than general and uniform principles. In that case every created evil would effect its own cure. The Southern States possess more materials for shipping than the Eastern, and if they do not follow the carrying business, it is because they are occupied in more lucrative pursuits. A rate of freight would make that an object, and they would readily turn to it; but the Competition amongst the eastern States themselves, would be sufficient to correct every abuse. A Navigation Act ought doubtless to be passed for giving exclusive benefits to American ships. This would of course serve the eastern States, and such, in justice ought to be the case, as it may perhaps be shown, that no other advantage can result to them from the Revolution. Indeed, it is important to the interests of the Southern states that the growth of a Navy be promoted, for the security of that wealth which is to be derived from their agriculture.

My determination to join in the adoption results from a Compound consideration of the measure itself, the probable issue of another attempt, and the critical state of our affairs. It has in my mind great faults, but the formers of it met under powers and dispositions which promised greater accommodation in their deliberations than can be expected to attend any future convention. The particular interests of States are exposed and future deputations, would be clogged with instructions and biassed by the presentiments of their constituents. Hence, it is fairly to be concluded that this is a better scheme than can be looked for from another experiment; on these considerations, I would clearly be for closing with it, and relying upon the correction of its faults, as experience may dictate the necessary alterations. But when I extend my view to that approaching anarchy which nothing but the timely interposition of a new government can avert, I am doubly urged in my wishes for the adoption.

Some[3] Gentlemen apprehend that this project is the foundation of a Monarchy, or at least an oppressive Aristocracy; but my apprehensions are rather from the inroads of the democracy. It is true there is a preposterous combination of powers in the President and Senate, which may be used improperly, but time is to discover whether the tendency of abuse, will be to strengthen or relax. At all events this part of the constitution must be exceptionable. But when we consider the degree of democracy of which the scheme itself partakes, with the addition of that which will be constantly operating upon it, it clearly appears to my mind, that the prevailing infractions are to be expected from thence. As State acts can go into effect without the direct controul of the General Government, having clearly defined the objects of their legislation, will not secure the federal ground against their encroachments. A disposition to encroach must, in the nature of the thing exist, and the democratic branch in the federal legislature, will be more likely to cover their approches, than resist them.

The Western Territory belonging to the United States has more effectually received the attention of Congress during this session than it ever did before. Inclosed you will receive the ordinance for establishing a Temporary Government there, and providing for its more easy passage into permanent State Governments. Under the old arrangement the country might upon the whole have become very populous, and yet be inadmissable to the rights of State government, which would have been disgusting to them and ultimately inconvenient for the Empire. The new arrangement depends on the accession of Virginia which there can be no doubt of obtaining. The Offices of the T. Government are filled up as follows. Genl. St. Clair Govr. Winthrop Sargent Secretary, Genl. Parsons, Genl. Armstrong junr. and Genl. Varnum, Judges.

Seven Ranges of Townships are Surveyed. They extend nearly to Muskingum and contain about 12 or 15 Millions of Acres. About 130,000 Acres have been sold according to the ordinance. The surveys will probably go no further in strict pursuance of the ordinance, but still the System will be preserved in the conditions of contracts for large Tracts of the Country, to companies of adventurers. The first instance of this mode presents itself in an authority to the Treasury Board in August last, to contract with a large Company of New Englanders, for all the Country from the seventh Range, to Sioto, within a due west line to be continued from the Northern boundary of the tenth Township. The whole of this Tract is supposed to contain about 5 Millions of Acres. The terms are, that the U.S. shall survey and demark the external boundaries, and ascertain the contents of the Tract, the Company to lay it out at their own expence, into Townships and sections agreably to the ordinance, subject to the reserves therein described except that one of the sections for future sale shall be granted for the purposes of religion, and there are also two compleat Townships granted for an University in or near the Middle of the Tract. All other lands good, bad, and indifferent, to be paid for at $\frac{2}{3}$rds. of a dollar per Acre in Securities, excluding the interest. Half a Million of dollars to be paid down upon closing the contract, and possession taken so far as such payment will cover. Afterwards payment and occupancy are to go on, pari passu at certain periods, under certain stipulations of reciprocal ensurance. This contract is now actually closed. Another offer is made by judge Symes and his associates from Jersey for about 2 Millions between the Miami upon the same terms, and sundry other propositions are forming, whereupon Congress have authorised the Treasury Board, to sell by Contract any quantity not less than a Million, making the terms of the Eastern Company the ground, with deviations from the grant for an University, and that for Religion, unless the Tract be equally large. This mode of sale will relieve the U.S. of much expence, and the progress of the sales promise to be sufficiently rapid to give our people early relief from the pressure of the domestic debt.

I am inclined to believe that some successfull experiment might be made for the sale [of] a part of the territory in Europe, and have suggested a trial with a few Ranges of the surveyed Townships. It did not strike Congress as eligible and of course no step was taken in it. I do not suppose it would be worth while to try the project on any but lands actually surveyed and well described.

We have received no accounts from Europe since your August dispatches. Of course the state of things there are in considerable obscurity as to us.

Your remarks upon the French loan have occasioned some discussion in Congress, but many reasons operate to prevent an assent to your proposition. By some it is supposed it would be found inconvenient to shift from Creditors that will not complain of our delinquency, to those that will, by others that we have reason to rely upon the indulgence of France in the case of a debt which was contracted for the common benefit of the two nations. My own opinion is that the transfer ought to be made if practicable.

I have the Honor to be with sincere regard dr. Sir Your Most Obt. Servt.,   ED. CARRINGTON

RC (DLC). Recorded in SJL as received 13 Dec. 1787. Enclosures: (1) Probably an official copy of the Constitution (see note to Washington to TJ, 18 Sep. 1787). (2) Copy of *An Ordinance for the Government of the Territory of the United States, North-West of the River Ohio* (JCC, XXXIII, 757, No. 584).

[1] At this point the words "are popular" are deleted.

[2] At this point the words "and Colo. H. Lee is by no means an advocate" are deleted.

[3] Carrington first began this paragraph: "My determination results from a" and then substituted the text as printed.

From C. W. F. Dumas

The Hague, 23 Oct. 1787. Thanks TJ for his intercession with the ministers of The Netherlands and Prussia; hopes they will keep their promises and that his situation will be improved out of respect for the government he represents. His only crime is his support of the principles of civil liberty, having for twelve years furthered the friendship between The Netherlands and the United States; these principles have been defeated by a government which is directly opposed to the interests of the United States and the real interest of The Netherlands. Wishes to obtain TJ's response to a suggestion he has already made to Jay, time not permitting a reply from the latter; that is that TJ and Adams send him to Brussels for a few months with credentials and secret instructions to negotiate a treaty of amity and commerce with that government; believes the time is favorable; that the expenses would be negligible; and that he could thereafter return to The Hague with added prestige.

RC (DLC); 4 p.; in French; endorsed. FC (Rijksarchief, The Hague: Dumas Letter Books; photostats in DLC); with numerous deletions of names, &c. Recorded in SJL as received 29 Oct. 1787.

From Fremyn de Fontenille

MONSIEUR   a paris le 23 8bre 1787.

J'ay remis hier le matin de votre part, a Mr. LeBegue Les memoires de Mr. de Calonne, qui Luy a fait un sensible plaisir, il m'a prié de vous temoignés sa reconnoissance. En revanche il y sera vendredy prochain vous mettre en possession de sa chambre, avec mon paravant que je vous ait offert par ma lettre il y a deux jours. Vous seres a L'abry du vent. Mr. LeBegue sera tres charmé de votre Connoissance, parce qu'il a eut Mr. Le chevalier de portail son neveu que le Roy avoit envoyé a l'amerique qui a ete tres connut et estimé de Mr. votre general Wasingston. Il vous remettra les memoires de Mr. de Calonne. Il m'a prie d'aller avec Luy. Come il est fort occupé d'affaires, il ne peut pas aller ni demain ni apres demain. Je Luy ait dit que vous venies ordinairement le vendredy, que Si vous ne pouvez y aller Ce jour la, Le Samedy. Si vous voules bien me faire la grace de me Le marquer, nous irons a votre hotel en passant, Scavoir si vous etes party.

J'ay L'honneur d'etre avec Les Sentimens Les plus distinguées et avec Respect Monsieur Votre tres humble et tres Obeissant Serviteur,   FREMYN DE FONTENILLE

Si vous alles monsieur demain ches freres hermite je vous prie de vouloir bien faire mes Compliments a tous nos messieurs de notre table et a M. Pellet si vous le voyes. Je vous prie de dire au bon frere joseph qui disent au Cuisinier qu'il est quelque chose de bon pour vous et pour Mr. Le Begue; quand ils ne sont pas avertis, La Cuisine est asses mal fournie et tres maigre.

Si vous me fait L'honneur de me repondre pour le jour que vous ires au mon valerien, mon adresse a paris, rüe des massons, proche la place de Sorbonne, no. 26.

[258]

RC (DLC); endorsed: "Fontenille le Chevalr. de." Recorded in SJL as received 24 Oct. 1787.

MA LETTRE IL Y A DEUX JOURS: Not found and not recorded in SJL, but see TJ to Fontenille, 24 Oct. 1787. For a note on the hermitage at MON VALERIEN, where TJ presumably met Fontenille and was expected on his next visit to share the apartment of MR. LEBEGUE, see Cathalan to TJ, 3 Oct. 1787.

From Lambert to La Boullaye

Paris 23. 8bre. 1787

M. Jefferson, Monsieur, m'a representé que d'après le relevé que la Ferme-générale a donné de ses achats de tabac et que vous avez communiqué à ce Ministre conformément à mes intentions, il n'y a eu depuis le 1er. Juin 1786 jusqu'au 3. 7bre. 1787 que *treize mille trente trois boucauds* au plus de tabac achetés aux prix et conditions fixés par la decision de Berni, au lieu de *quinze mille sept cent cinquante boucauds* qui devaient être achetés pendant ce tems sur le même pied que ceux de Mr. Morris selon cette decision.

Il ajoute que dans le nombre d'achats que l'on présente comme faits en conformité de la décision de Berni on comprend des tabacs qui ne sont point venus directement d'Amérique dans les ports de France sur Vaisseaux Français ou Américains mais qui ont été apportés tant d'Angleterre que d'Amérique sur des batiments Anglais, ce qui serait totalement contraire à l'objèt qu'on s'etait proposé.

Il représente que plusieurs negocians Français et Américains se sont plaints d'avoir eu à supporter la tarre légale de *quinze pour cent* au lieu de la tarre réele de *dix pour cent* à laquelle seulement les tabacs de M. Morris etaient assujettis.

Il observe encore que les *trois mille six cent cinquante boucauds* achetés dans la Mediterrannée ne doivent pas être imputés sur la quantité de ceux que la decision de Berni a eus en vüe, puisqu'il s'agissait de l'assimilation avec le traité de M. Morris qui n'a jamais du envoyer de tabacs dans la Mediterrannée ou le commerce est resté libre. Et cette observation me paroit fondée.

J'ai objecté a M. Jefferson: Que la possibilité des achats à des prix inferieurs à ceux fixés par la decision de Berni avait été prévue par l'article cinq de cette décision, qui ouvre un recours au Conseil en cas de contestation sur les qualités, et qui à plus forte raison a donc permis que dans le cas où l'on pourrait employer ce recours on traitât de gré à gré.

Il est vraisemblable que la différence des tarres n'a eu lieu que pour les parties ainsi acquises à prix défendu, et alors cette difference entrerait dans le prix defendu même.

Il importe cependant de verifier si dans le nombre des achats qui sont présentés comme faits conformément à la decision de Berni, il y en a eu quelques uns qui aient éprouvé de la différence sur les tarres. Cela importe ou pour reparer le mal s'il a eu lieu, ou pour montrer à M. Jefferson que les plaintes qu'il m'a déferées étaient à cet egard destituées de fondement.

Il est encore plus nécessaire de vérifier les faits relatifs aux tabacs venants d'Angleterre ou apportés d'Amérique sur Vaisseaux Anglais qui auraient été achetés aux mêmes conditions que ceux de M. Morris, car il est clair non seulement qu'on ne pourrait pas les employer à l'acquit de la décision de Berni mais qu'ils seraient aussi contraires à ses expressions qu'à son esprit.

On a parlé à M. Jefferson d'une partie de mille à onze cent boucauds de tabacs Anglais ainsi achetés au prix de M. Morris depuis la décision de Berni. Je suis porté à croire qu'elle n'entre point dans les tableaux qui nous ont été presentés; mais il faudrait toujours scavoir si le fait a de la realité, car il serait facheux que dans le tems ou le marché de M. Morris et la decision de Berni obligeaient de forcer les approvisionnements à un prix d'un sixième au dessus du prix courant, on eut encore étendu cette maniere facheuse de s'approvisionner.

Je vous serai donc obligé de vous faire rendre un compte très detaillé de tous les achats qui ont été faits en y joignant exactement les noms et les pavillons des Vaisseaux et le lieu de leur expédition soit d'Amérique soit d'Europe, comme aussi de ce qui s'est passé rélativement aux tarres.

En tout il est nécessaire que les engagemens que le Roi a sanctionnés et fait annoncer officiellement à ses alliés soient exactement remplis.

Le marché de M. Morris et l'effét correspondant de la decision de Berni s'etendant jusqu'à la fin de l'année, il faut donc au moins provisoirement, que les achats de tabacs venant directement d'Amérique sur Vaisseaux Francais ou Américains continuent sur le pied de *onze cent boucauds* par mois tant pour le mois de 7bre. ecoulé, que pour ceux d'octobre, novembre et decembre. Je crois que la ferme générale y est disposée, mais je dois pouvoir l'assurer à M. Jefferson. Je dois lui assurer aussi qu'après la verification des faits on aura égard a ce que cette verification montrera de juste dans ses reclamations.

Il y a un autre point très important à considerer.

Je vois d'après les connaissances que vous avez prises sur l'etat des approvisionnemens de tabac que le traité de M. Morris d'une part et la decision de Berni de l'autre, ont conduit à forcer ces approvisionnemens quoiqu'à prix onéreux pour le Roi et pour la Ferme générale au point que ses magasins renferment a peu près de quoi suffire à la consommation de deux années.

Il en resulte que la ferme générale pourrait lorsqu'elle sera délivrée du traité de M. Morris et de l'engagement pris d'après la decision de Berni suspendre tout achat pendant six mois et conserver encore l'approvisionnement d'une année et demie auquel elle est obligée.

On doit même convenir que cette conduite de sa part serait très naturelle et paraîtrait raisonnable à n'envisager que l'interêt du revenu que le Roi tire de sa Ferme du tabac.

Cependant si cette suspension avait lieu il en resulterait un événement extrémement funeste pour le commerce de deux nations, pour leurs relations politiques et pour le debouché des marchandises Françaises.

Les Américains privés pendant six mois en France de tout debit pour la principale production de leur territoire prendraient naturellement et exclusivement la route de l'Angleterre; et il pourrait ne plus dépendre de nous de les rappeller. Nul commerce ne scaurait soutenir une suspension absolue de six mois, et lorsqu'on lui a laissé former de nouvelles habitudes il ne les rompt pas aisément.

Il est donc de la plus grande consequence que le Roi et la ferme générale associés pour les benefices de la vente exclusive du tabac, ne se conduisent pas d'après le seul interêt de ce privilege exclusif, mais le combinent avec l'interêt politique et commercial qui prescrit de ne pas interrompre le commerce des Etats-unis en France.

Le seul moyen que j'envisage pour arriver à ce but est de repartir sur les cinq années du bail qui restent à courir, et autant qu'il se pourra sur chaque mois de ces cinq années, l'approvisionnement qui sera nécessaire pour fournir à leur consommation; de maniere que l'éxcédent actuel trouve son emploi, et qu'il ne reste à la fin du bail qu'environ *trente mille boucauds* en magasin.

Cette disposition supposerait un achat de *seize mille boucauds* au moins par année; et pour que les Américains puissent y compter et ne derangent pas la marche de leurs spéculations, il faudrait que je pusse notifier à M. Jefferson une soumission de la ferme générale portant engagement de continuer à compter du mois de Janvier 1788. jusqu'à la fin de son bail, d'acheter par mois et dans les ports de France environ *treize cent boucauds* de tabac apportés directement d'Amérique par Vaisseaux Français ou Américains, et de justifier tous les trois mois que ces achats se sont montés au moins à *quatre mille boucauds*; l'obligation ne portant que sur la quantité; et les prix devant demeurer libres, comme les Américains eux-mêmes l'ont desiré lors de leur reclamation contre le traité de M. Morris.

Je ne doute point que la ferme générale ne conçoive toute l'importance de cet arrangement et ne s'empresse à y concourir. Son patriotisme m'en est un sûr garant.

Je vous serai donc obligé de provoquer de sa part cette délibération afin que je puisse la notifier le plutôt possible à M. Jefferson et qu'elle puisse recevoir en Amérique une publicité qui previenne toute interruption de Commerce.

J'ai l'honneur d'etre avec un sincere attachement, &c.

(signé) LAMBERT

Tr (DLC); in the hand of William Short; at head of text: "(Copie)"; at foot of text: "(Test: W. Short Secy.)." PrC of preceding (DLC).

The text of Lambert's letter was actually enclosed in Dupont to TJ, 5 Nov. 1787, in response to the latter's request. TJ was scheduled to have a discussion with Lambert on the ensuing Friday, 26 Oct. 1787, concerning the tobacco trade (see TJ to Fontenille, 24 Oct. 1787).

From Abbé Morellet

MONSIEUR   mardi. 23 octob.

Un homme de mes amis qui a servi les etats unis avec zèle et à qui vous aves montré de l'estime me prie de m'interesser auprès de vous pour lui faire payer des arrerages qui lui sont dûs sur les engagemens que les etats ont pris avec les officiers comme lui. Sa lettre explique ses demandes mieux que je ne pourrois faire, la petite note qui y est jointe les presente encore d'une maniere plus precise. Ayes la bonté d'examiner l'une et l'autre et de me faire savoir ce que je dois lui répondre. Je suis bien malheureux de ne pouvoir aller chercher la réponse moi même. Beaucoup d'occupations m'empechent de profiter de cette occasion d'aller vous voir et vous renouveller les assurances du respect avec lequel je suis Monsieur Votre très humble et très obeissant Serviteur

L'ABBÉ MORELLET

RC (DLC); endorsed; year supplied from internal evidence and TJ to Morellet, 24 Oct. 1787. Recorded in SJL as received 23 Oct. 1787. Enclosures missing.

From Edward Rutledge

My dear Sir   Octr. 23. 1787

Your favor of the 14th: of July, afforded me a great deal of Pleasure. It was a new proof of your Esteem for the individual, and it was replete with Information, highly interesting to my Countrymen. I have endeavour'd, and not without Success, to convince several of our Mercantile people, as well as some of our Planters, how highly beneficial it will be to change the consignment of their Rice, from Great Britain to France; and that I might have some Share, in accomplishing a Measure which, I have much at Heart, I have determined to ship on my own Account, One Hundred and fifty or two Hundred Barrels. My wishes for advantageous Sales, are founded in public Considerations alone; and I am persuaded I shall not be disappointed. I have many Reasons for desiring to deprive the British Market of the Benefits of this branch of our Commerce. I will say nothing of the injuries which we have received from her; or, of the unworthy discrimination, which she daily makes between us, and other powers. But, it is a shameful, and an unnatural Relic of our former dependance, to transmit nearly the whole of our most valuable Staple, to a Country, in which it is not consumed, and which before it can be consumed must be subjected to a double freight, a double insurance, a variety of port charges, and many incidental Expences. That the connection between France and this Country might be drawn closer, and that she might not only rival but supplant Great Britain in this Branch of Commerce, two things should be attended to: the establishment of some safe free port, and the obtaining an accurate Knowledge of the Manner in which Rice is cleansed at Cowes, in the Isle of White. It is necessary that it should undergo some sifting after it has been eight or ten weeks in the Hole of a Vessel; and at the Isle of White it is landed, unpacked, and screen'd, which purifies it very much, and fits it for a more distant Market. The Method, and the Machine with which this is done, are both very simple, and consequently may be acquired in little time, and at a moderate expence. The advantages are not confined to the Rice which may be consumed in France; others will result to both nations from making the French port a Depot for what shall be intended for foreign Markets. Altho' I am sanguine in my Expectations, I foresee an impediment to this intercourse being as immediately extensive as I desire; which is, the immense debt that is due from this Country to our old Friends. Some mercantile Men think it a point of Honor to consign their Cargoes to the Persons who are their Creditors; and this inclination, well, or ill founded, I am not about to enquire, must be counterpoised by extra incouragements. All our Merchants however, are not under this embarrassment: in the Exception is the House of Brailsford & Morris; as they are unknown to you, they have desired me to say of them what I think they deserve: and I do not exceed their request when I tell you that, they are a House of punctuality, Judgment, and good Capital; and that in my Opinion they may be considered as truly trust worthy.

I thank you my good Friend for an offer of a Copy of the original impression of your Notes on Virginia. I beg you will send them, I shall accept them with a great deal of Pleasure. You seem to consider the quarter of the Globe from whence America was peopled, and the Manner, as now reduced to a certainty. But, it is not so absolutely determined, as to preclude conjecture. A Gentleman with a great deal more learning, and a great deal more Sense than I have, is convinced that America was peopled from Carthage. He maintains that when Hanno their famous Admiral was sent out to settle Colonies, some of their Vessels mist their port of Destination, and were never able afterwards to regain it; that the Trade-Winds blew them to the Coast of America, thro' the Gulph of Mexico. In this opinion he is confirmed from the exact resemblance which he observed between the People who inhabit that Country, and the Creek Indians, the first time he saw an Indian, and from words of both, sounding alike, and conveying the same meaning. Diodorus Siculus is the Author who particularly mentions Hanno's Voyage. You have him at Hand, we have him not, and you can refer to him. Think of it; and when I next write you, I will give you at Large the Conjectures of my Philosopher: at present I am too much engaged in the Squabbles of the Bar, (for we are in the midst of our term) to extend this Letter. Adieu my dear Sir. Keep me in your Esteem and believe me to be with great Truth Yours very sincerely, EDWARD RUTLEDGE

RC (MHi); endorsed. Not recorded in SJL Index. The sheets of SJL for 1788 are missing, so that, beginning with autumn of 1787 for letters from America and with December 1787 for letters from different parts of Europe, there is no available record showing when such letters were received; most of these, however, and most of the letters written and received during 1788, are recorded in SJL Index; in cases where there is no such record, mention will be made of the fact. The present letter, however, was evidently received with Bérard's letter of 17 Feb. 1788; see also Brailsford & Morris to TJ, 31 Oct. 1787 and 10 Jan. 1788. For the CONJECTURES OF MY PHILOSOPHER see Edward Rutledge to TJ, [ca. 1 Apr. 1789].

To Fremyn de Fontenille

MONSIEUR   à Paris ce 24. Octobre

Ayant eté obligé d'etre a Versailles tout[e la journée] d'hier, je n'ai pu repondre à la premiere lettre que v[ous m'avez] fait l'honneur de m'ecrire, et je viens de recevoir la [seconde] ce matin. Je vous fais mille remerciments de vos attentions. Je me trouve tellement occupé que je ne pourrai pas aller au Mont Valerien cette semaine, et pour le Vendredi particulierement j'ai un rendezvous d'affaires avec Monsieur le Comptroleur general. Mais j'oserai vous proposer, au lieu de notre diné au mont Valerien, un diné chez moi le Vendredi, avec Monsieur le Begue, dont je serai charmé de faire la connoissance. Si vous me ferez la grace de le prier de me faire cette honneur là, je vous en serai bien obligé. Nous dinerons en petit comité, à trois heures, et je prierai Monsieur le chevalier du Portail d'etre de la partie. J'ai l'honneur de le connoitre beaucoup, de l'estimer autant, et de temoigner le cas qu'on a fait de lui, de ses talens, et de ses services en Amerique. Je vous fais bien des remerciments Monsieur de l'obligeante offre de votre paravent; c'est une preuve de votre bonté, et un sacrifice de votre part dont je ne peux pas me permettre de profiter, et d'autant moins que j'irai très rarement à Mont valerien pendant l'hyver. J'oserai me flatter de la permission de Monsieur le Begue de l'attendre à diner içi, le Vendredi, et de vous le meme, Monsieur, et j'ai l'honneur d'etre

PrC (DLC); MS torn at upper right corner; lacks part of complimentary close and signature (see Vol. 9: 217, note 1).

Fontenille's PREMIERE LETTRE is missing; LA SECONDE is that of 23 Oct. 1787.

From John Jay

DR SR.   Office for foreign Affairs 24th. October 1787

Since the 8 Ult. when I last wrote to you, I have been favored with your Letters of the 6 and 15 Augt. last, which together with the Papers mentioned in the first of them, were immediately laid before Congress. Altho the Opinion of the most judicious and well informed seems to be that France and Britain will avoid War, and unite their Councils and their Efforts to preserve Peace, yet as great Events are often produced by latent and little Circumstances, especially between Courts who distrust each other, I should not be surprized if notwithstanding their Wishes to the contrary, something should happen to frustrate their pacific Designs.

[265]

You will receive herewith enclosed, two Letters from me dated the 27 July concerning the consular convention, with a Commission to you to form one; and also a certified copy of an act of Congress of the 23 July on the Subject of the Morocco Treaty and Papers. The want of a safe and private Conveyance has until now delayed the Transmission of these Letters and this Act. I also enclose the following Papers, vizt.

1. A certified Copy of an Act of Congress of 28th. Septr. respecting Duties on goods imported by foreign consuls.

2. A certified Copy of an act of 2d. Octr. Instant, instructing you not to promote any Negociation for transferring the Debt due to France from the U. States.

3. A certified Copy of an act of 11 Octr. Instant, approving the Manner in which the prize Money due to the Crews of the bon homme Richard and Alliance has been quotaed by France, and directing the board of Treasury to distribute it accordingly.

4. A certified Copy of an act of 12 Octr. Inst., reappointing you Minister plenipotentiary at the Court of Versailles, together with a Commission and Letter of Credence, and a copy of the latter for your Information.

5. A certified Copy of an act of 12 Octr. Inst. constituting the Residue of the Money appropriated the 14 Feby. 1785 for Treaties with Morocco &ca., a Fund for redeeming the american Captives at Algiers, and a Duplicate of the act of 18 July instructing you to redeem them.

6. A certified Copy of an act of the 16 Octr. Inst: directing you to have a Medal struck in honor of Chevalier Jones, and a copy of a Letter to his most Christian Majesty of the same Date on the same Subject. Congress were pleased to order that he should be the Bearer of this Letter; but I nevertheless think it proper that you should have a Copy of it.

7. Copy of a Letter of the 26 Ult. which I this Day received from the Governor of Rhode Island, requesting me to transmit to you the Papers which accompanied it, and which I now transmit accordingly.

8. A Copy of the fœderal Government proposed by the late Convention.

9. The Requisition of Congress passed the 11 Inst., and their printed Journals from the 10 May to 25 Septr. last, which with those heretofore sent will compleat your Set from the 6 Novr. 1786. I also send the newspapers from 8 Septr. to this Day.

As to the claims of certain Individuals against the State of So. Carolina, I have by order of Congress sent an Extract from your Letter on that Subject, together with a Copy of the papers relative to it, to the Governor of that State, in order that they may thereupon take such Measures as the Good Faith of the State and the Justice due to the Individuals in Question may appear to dictate.

The number of States represented in Congress almost daily diminishes, and I much fear will soon be so reduced as not to leave them in Capacity to dispatch any Business requiring nine.

Congress has been pleased to comply with the Request of Mr. Adams to return, and I enclose a Copy of their act on that Head.

As yet I am not authorized to say any thing relative to the proposed post office Convention. A Report on that Subject has lain for many Months before Congress, and still remains undecided.

What will be the fate of the new Constitution, as it is called, cannot easily be conjectured. At present the Majority seems to be in favor of it, but there will probably be a strong opposition in some of the States, particularly in this and Pensylvania.

I have the honor to be with great Esteem & Regard, Dr Sr your most obt. & hble. Servt.,   JOHN JAY

Dft (NK-Iselin). FC (DNA: PCC, No. 121); with minor variations in spelling and punctuation. Recorded in SJL as received 19 Dec. 1787. The unnumbered enclosures were: Jay to TJ, 27 July 1787 (two letters and enclosure), qq.v.; resolution of Congress ratifying the treaty with Morocco (see Jay to TJ, 24 July 1787, note); resolution of Congress, 5 Oct. 1787, authorizing John Adams to return to America "at any time after the 24th. of February . . . 1788" (printed in JCC, XXXIII, 612-3). The enclosures as numbered by Jay were: (1) Resolution of Congress, 28 Sep. 1787, agreeing with Jay's report concerning Sir John Temple's request to be informed whether it was proper for him to pay the duties demanded on "a small Box of Tea, and a piece of Silk for Lady Temple's use" under New York law, inasmuch as "there was no Treaty of Commerce subsisting between his Britannic Majesty and these States," wherein Jay set forth the opinion that "consuls are not by the Laws or Usage of Nations considered or treated as public Ministers, and therefore they are not entitled to the exemptions in question either here or elsewhere"

(same, p. 549-52). (2) Resolution of Congress, 2 Oct. 1787, agreeing to a report of the Commissioners of the Treasury, to whom had been referred TJ's letter of 26 Sep. 1786, recommending that for a number of reasons "it would be proper without delay to instruct the Minister of the United States at the Court of France not to give any sanction to any negociation which may be proposed for transferring the debt due from the United States, to any State or company of Individuals who may be disposed to purchase the same" (same, p. 589-93). (3) Resolution of Congress, 11 Oct. 1787, confirming the quotas assigned by the Court of Versailles to the ships under Jones' command and directing the Commissioners of the Treasury to distribute as soon as may be the funds paid by Jones "into the hands of the honorable Thos. Jefferson" (same, p. 663). (4) Resolution of Congress, 12 Oct. 1787, reappointing TJ as minister for three additional years (MHi, in clerk's hand, attested by Thomson; printed in JCC, XXXIII, 665); Commission to TJ, 12 Oct. 1787, to take effect on 10 Mch. 1788 (MHi, engrossed, signed by Arthur St. Clair and John Jay, attested by Charles

Thomson, with U.S. seal impressed on serrated paper over wax; FC in DNA: PCC, No. 80, III; printed in JCC, XXXIII, 688); and Letter of Credence, 12 Oct. 1787 (MHi, clerk's copy, signed by Arthur St. Clair and John Jay, but without attest or seal—this being the copy sent for TJ's information, the original, signed, sealed, and attested copy being enclosed for presentation to the King—and endorsed by TJ "Letter of credence"; FC in DNA: PCC, No. 80, III; printed in JCC, XXXIII, 689). In MHi there is a memorandum in TJ's hand reading as follows: "Letter of Credence for my commission from 1788 —1791. I think my former letter of credence was indefinite, and therefore that it is unnecessary to deliver this and improper." At the time he wrote this memo, TJ clearly intended it to explain the presence of the official Letter of Credence among his papers, but that copy has not been found; whether its absence is to be explained by some subsequent disappearance or by an actual presentation is not known, but the former is more probable. (5) Resolution of Congress, 12 Oct. 1787, stipulating that "the Balance of the appropriation for the Barbary Treaties" not hitherto used for that object be applied for the redemption of American captives in Algiers "subject to the direction of the Minister of the United States at the Court of Versailles"; and that the resolution of 14 Feb. 1785 and such of that of 18 July 1787 as directs provision to be made for this object, be repealed (DLC: TJ Papers, 34:5775, attested by Charles Thomson, and marked in margin: "secret"; another copy, also attested by Thomson, endorsed by TJ "Barbary captives," in DLC: TJ Papers, 34:5293; printed in JCC, XXXIII, 664). (6) Resolution of Congress, 16 Oct. 1787, unanimously agreed to, "That a medal of gold be struck and presented to the Chevalier John Paul Jones in commemoration of the valour and bril-

liant services of that Officer . . . And that the Honorable Mr. Jefferson . . . have the same executed with the proper devices"; together with a resolution that a letter be written to the king of France informing him that this medal has been bestowed (the original resolution read at this point that Jones had been promoted "to the rank of Rear Admiral") as much in consideration of the king's marks of approbation to him as from a sense of his merit, and stating that, "as it is his earnest desire to acquire greater knowledge in his profession, it would be acceptable to Congress that his Majesty would be pleased to permit him to embark with his fleets of evolution" (JCC, XXXIII, 689-90; the copies sent to TJ evidently have not survived in his papers, but there is a text in French in DLC: John Paul Jones Papers). (7) The copy of the letter from the Governor of Rhode Island to Jay, 26 Sep. has not been found, but see TJ to Jay, 5 Feb. 1788. (8) The copy of the Constitution was probably one of the official edition (see Washington to TJ, 18 Sep. 1787, note). (9) The report of the Commissioners of the Treasury stating the requisition of Congress for 1787 (the copy sent by Jay was evidently one of the printed broadsides distributed to the states; see JCC, XXXIII, 761, No. 596; text printed in same, p. 650-5).

Although Jay waited almost a month to send a copy of the proposed Federal Constitution to TJ and then did so without comment, he had sent a copy as early as 3 Oct. 1787 to Adams, saying: "I enclose a copy of the federal government recommended by the Convention, and which has already passed from Congress to the states. What will be its Fate in some of them is a little uncertain; for although generally approved, an Opposition is to be expected, and in some places will certainly be made to its Adoption" (DNA: PCC, No. 121).

From John Jay

DR SIR   Of. for for. A. 24th. Octr 1787

The Dispatches alluded to in my late Letters together with others of some importance are ready, and were intended to be conveyed to you by this Packet; but the Gentleman to whose care they were

[268]

committed declining to go in her, they must pass to you by some other Route. An opinion prevails that hostilities have probably commenced between France and Britain, and such is its Impression that some Gentlemen who purposed to sail in the french Packet, think it most adviseable to take passage in an american vessel. For my own part I think their apprehensions are premature; for as yet I am not informed of any Events from which I can infer a Probability that War has taken place.

A new Commission to commence at the Expiration of your present one has been ordered and is ready. You will receive it with the abovementioned Dispatches.

With Sentiments of great and sincere Esteem & Regard I have the Honor to be Dr Sr yr most ob & hble Servt.

Dft (NK-Iselin); unsigned. FC (DNA: PCC, No. 121). Recorded in SJL as received 13 Dec. 1787.

From John Paul Jones

SIR   New-York Octr. 24th. 1787.

I had the honor to address you a *confidential* Letter the 4th. Ult. enclosing one for Madame T. I here enclose another Letter for that worthy Lady, of which I request your particular care. I should have embarked in the Packet that will sail for Havre to morrow morning. But an account having arrived here, that the English Fleet is out and was seen steering to the Westward, and that a British Squadron is cruising in the North-Sea has induced me, with the advice of my Friends, to postpone my embarkation till the next opportunity, an American Ship, about the beginning of next Month. Mr. Jarvis will embark with me, and will bring you some Public Dispatches. I reserve the detail of the doings of Congress on my Subject till I come to Europe. At present I have the pleasure to transmit you this Packet containing 6 Letters, large and small, for you, 2 for Mr. Short, and 1 for the Marquis de la Fayette. I have confided the whole to Captain Lattin of Dillons Irish Regiment, who has promised to go directly to Paris and put the Packet into your hands.

I say nothing to you on public Affairs, convinced that any thing on that Subject from me would be Superfluous, after the information you receive from your Friends Mr. Maddison and Colo. Carrington. I congratulate you sincerely on your highly merited re-appointment to the Court of France, and am, with affectionate esteem and respect Sir, Your most obedient and most humble Servant, J PAUL JONES

RC (DLC: John Paul Jones Papers); endorsed. Recorded in SJL as received 13 Dec. 1787. The enclosed letter to "Madame T" has not been found; the "6 Letters . . . for you" must have been the following: Madison to TJ, 19 Aug. (missing); Tench Coxe to TJ, 3 Sep. (missing); Jay to TJ, 24 Oct. (2d let- ter); Monroe to TJ, 27 July; Madison to TJ, 6 Sep.; Carrington to TJ, 23 Oct. (2d letter); all of these are re- corded in SJL as received with Jones' letter on 13 Dec. 1787. The letters to Short and Lafayette have not been identified.

From James Madison

DEAR SIR New York Octr. 24. 1787.

My two last, though written for the two last Packets, have un- luckily been delayed till this conveyance. The first of them was sent from Philada. to Commodore Jones in consequence of informa- tion that he was certainly to go by the packet then about to sail. Being detained here by his business with Congress, and being un- willing to put the letter into the mail without my approbation, which could not be obtained in time, he detained the letter also. The second was sent from Philada. to Col. Carrington, with a view that it might go by the last packet at all events in case Commodore Jones should meet with further detention here. By ill luck he was out of Town, and did not return till it was too late to make use of the opportunity. Neither of the letters were indeed of much consequence at the time and are still less so now. I let them go forward nevertheless as they may mention some circumstances not at present in my recollection, and as they will prevent a chasm on my part of our correspondence which I have so many motives to cherish by an exact punctuality.

Your favor of June 20. has been already acknowledged. The last packet from France brought me that of August 2d. I have re- ceived also by the Mary Capt. Howland the three Boxes for W. H. B. F. and myself. The two first have been duly forwarded. The contents of the last are a valuable addition to former literary remit- tances and lay me under additional obligations, which I shall always feel more strongly than I express. The articles included for Con- gress have been delivered and those for the two Universities and for General Washington have been forwarded, as have been the various letters for your friends in Virginia and elsewhere. The parcel of rice referred to in your letter to the Delegates of S. Caro- lina has met with some accident. No account whatever can be gathered concerning it. It probably was not shipped from France. Ubbo's book I find was not omitted as you seem to have apprehended. The charge for it however is, which I must beg you to supply. The duplicate volume of the Encyclopedie, I left in Virginia, and it is uncertain when I shall have an opportunity of returning it. Your Spanish duplicates will I fear be hardly vendible. I shall make a trial wherever a chance presents itself. A few days ago I received your favor of the 15 of Augst. via L'Orient and Boston. The letters inclosed along with it were immediately sent on to Virga.

You will herewith receive the result of the Convention, which continued its session till the 17th of September. I take the liberty of making some observations on the subject which will help to make up a letter, if they should answer no other purpose.

It appeared to be the sincere and unanimous wish of the Convention to cherish and preserve the Union of the States. No proposition was made, no suggestion was thrown out in favor of a partition of the Empire into two or more Confederacies.

It was generally agreed that the objects of the Union could not be secured by any system founded on the principle of a confederation of sovereign States. A voluntary observance of the federal law by all the members could never be hoped for. A compulsive one could evidently never be reduced to practice, and if it could, involved equal calamities to the innocent and the guilty, the necessity of a military force both obnoxious and dangerous, and in general, a scene resembling much more a civil war, than the administration of a regular Government.

Hence was embraced the alternative of a government which instead of operating, on the States, should operate without their intervention on the individuals composing them: and hence the change in the principle and proportion of representation.

This ground-work being laid, the great objects which presented themselves were 1. to unite a proper energy in the Executive and a proper stability in the Legislative departments, with the essential characters of Republican Government. 2. To draw a line of demarkation which would give to the General Government every power requisite for general purposes, and leave to the States every power which might be most beneficially administered by them. 3. To provide for the different interests of different parts of the Union. 4. To adjust the clashing pretensions of the large and small States. Each of these objects was pregnant with difficulties. The whole of them together formed a task more difficult than can be well conceived by those who were not concerned in the execution of it. Adding to these considerations the natural diversity of human opinions on all new[1] and complicated subjects, it is impossible to consider the degree of concord which ultimately prevailed as less than a miracle.

The first of these objects as it respects the Executive, was peculiarly embarrassing. On the question whether it should consist of a single person, or a plurality of co-ordinate members, on the mode of appointment, on the duration in office, on the degree of power, on the re-eligibility, tedious and reiterated discussions took place. The plurality of co-ordinate members had finally but few advocates. Governour Randolph was at the head of them. The modes of appointment proposed were various, as by the people at large—by electors chosen by the people—by the Executives of the States—by the Congress, some preferring a joint ballot of the two Houses—some a separate concurrent ballot allowing to each a negative on the other house—some a nomination of several canditates by one House, out of whom a choice should be made by the other. Several other modifications were started. The expedient at length adopted seemed to give pretty general satisfaction to the members. As to the duration in office, a few would have preferred a tenure during good behaviour—a considerable number would have done so in case an easy and effectual removal by impeachment could be settled. It was much agitated whether a long term, seven years for example, with a subsequent and perpetual ineligibility, or a short term with a capacity to be re-elected, should be fixed. In favor of the first opinion were urged the danger of a gradual degeneracy of re-elections from time to time, into first a life and then a hereditary tenure, and the favorable effect of an incapacity to be reappointed, on the independent exercise of the Executive authority. On the other side it was contended that the prospect of necessary degradation would discourage the most dignified characters from aspiring to the office, would take away the principal motive to the faithful discharge of its duties. The hope of being rewarded with a reappointment, would stimulate ambition to violent efforts for holding over the constitutional term, and instead of producing an independent administration, and a firmer defence of the constitutional rights of the department, would render the officer more indifferent to the importance of a place which he would soon be obliged to quit for ever, and more ready to yield to the incroachments of the Legislature of which he might again be a member.—The questions concerning the degree of power turned chiefly on the appointment to offices, and the controul on the Legislature. An *absolute* appointment to all offices—to some offices—to no offices, formed the scale of opinions on the first point. On the second, some contended for an absolute negative, as the only possible mean of reducing to practice, the theory of a free government which forbids[2] a mixture of the Legislative and Executive powers. Others would be content with a revisionary power to be overruled by three fourths of both Houses.[3] It was warmly urged that the judiciary department should be associated in the revision. The idea of some was that a separate revision should be given to the two departments—that if either objected two thirds; if both three fourths,[4] should be necessary to overrule.

In forming the Senate, the great anchor of the Government, the questions as they came within the first object turned mostly on the mode of appointment, and the duration of it. The different modes proposed were, 1. by the House of Representatives, 2. by the Executive, 3 by electors chosen by the people for the purpose, 4. by the State Legislatures. On the point of duration, the propositions descended from good behavior to four years, through the intermediate terms of nine, seven, six and five years. The election of the other branch was first determined to be triennial, and afterwards reduced to biennial.

The second object, the due partition of power, between the General and local Governments, was perhaps of all, the most nice and difficult. A few contended for an entire abolition of the States; Some for indefinite power of Legislation in the Congress, with a negative on the laws of the States, some for such a power without a negative,[5] some for a limited power of legislation, with such a negative: the majority finally for a limited power without the negative. The question with regard to the Negative underwent repeated discussions, and was finally rejected by a bare majority. As I formerly intimated to you my opinion in favor of this ingredient, I will take this occasion of explaining myself on the subject. [Such a check on the States appears to me necessary 1. to prevent encroachments on the General authority, 2. to prevent instability and injustice in the legislation[6] of the States.

1. Without such a check in the whole over the parts, our system involves the evil of imperia in imperio. If a compleat supremacy some where is not necessary in every Society, a controuling power

at least is so, by which the general authority may be defended against encroachments of the subordinate authorities, and by which the latter may be restrained from encroachments on each other.[7] If the supremacy of the British Parliament is not necessary as has been contended,[8] for the harmony of that Empire, it is evident I think that without the royal negative[9] or some equivalent controul, the unity of the system would be[10] destroyed. The want of some such provision seems to have been mortal to the antient Confederacies, and to be the disease of the modern. Of the Lycian Confederacy little is known.[11] That of the Amphyctions is well known to have been rendered of little use whilst it lasted, and in the end to have been destroyed by the predominance of the local over the federal authority.[12] The same observation may be made, on the authority of Polybius, with regard to the Achæan League. The Helvetic System scarcely amounts to a confederacy and is distinguished by too many peculiarities to be a ground of comparison. The case of the United Netherlands is in point. The authority of a Statholder, the influence of a standing army, the common interest in the conquered possessions, the pressure of surrounding danger, the guarantee of foreign powers, are not sufficient to secure the authority and interests of the generality, against the antifederal tendency of the provincial sovereignties.[13] The German Empire is another example. A Hereditary chief with vast independent resources of wealth and power, a federal Diet, with ample parchment authority, a regular Judiciary establishment, the influence of the neighbourhood of great and formidable Nations, have been found unable either to maintain the subordination of the members, or to prevent their mutual contests and encroachments. Still more to the purpose is our own experience both during the war and since the peace. Encroachments of the States on the general authority, sacrifices of national to local interests, interferences of the measures of different States, form a great part of the history of our political system. It may be said that the new Constitution is founded on different principles, and will have a different operation. I admit the difference to be material. It presents the aspect rather of a feudal system of republics, if such a phrase may be used,[14] than of a Confederacy of independent States. And what has been the progress and event of the feudal Constitutions? In all of them a continual struggle between the head and the inferior[15] members, until a final victory has been gained in some instances by one, in others, by the other of them. In one respect indeed there is a remarkable variance between the two cases. In the feudal system the sovereign, though limited, was independent; and having no particular sympathy of interests with the great Barons, his ambition had as full play as theirs in the mutual projects of usurpation. In the American Constitution The general authority will be derived entirely from the subordinate authorities.[16] The Senate will represent the States in their political capacity, the other House will represent the people of the States in their individual capacity. The former will be accountable to their constituents at moderate, the latter at short periods. The President also derives his appointment from the States, and is periodically accountable to them. This dependence of the General, on the local authorities seems effectually to guard the latter against any dangerous encroachments of the former: Whilst the latter within their respective limits, will be continually sensible of the abridgment of their power, and be stimulated by ambition to resume the surrendered portion of it. We find the representatives of counties and corporations in the Legislatures of the States, much more disposed to sacrifice the aggregate interest, and even authority, to the local views of their Constituents, than the latter to the former. I mean not by these remarks to insinuate that an esprit de corps will not exist in the national Government, that opportunities may[17] not occur of extending its jurisdiction in some points. I mean only that the danger of encroachments is much greater from the other side, and that the impossibility[18] of dividing powers of legislation, in such a manner, as to be free from different constructions by different interests, or even from ambiguity in the judgment of the impartial, requires some such expedient as I contend for. Many illustrations might be given of this impossibility. How long has it taken to fix, and how imperfectly is yet fixed the legislative power of corporations, though that power is subordinate in the most compleat manner? The line of distinction between the power of regulating trade and that of drawing revenue from it, which was once considered as the barrier of our liberties, was found on fair discussion, to be absolutely undefinable. No distinction seems to be more obvious than that between spiritual and temporal matters. Yet wherever they have been made objects of Legislation, they have clashed and contended with each other, till one or the other has gained the supremacy. Even the boundaries between the Executive, Legislative and Judiciary powers, though in general so strongly marked in themselves, consist in many instances of mere shades of difference. It may be said that the Judicial authority under our new system will[19] keep the States within their proper limits, and supply the place of a negative on their laws. The answer is that it is more convenient to prevent the passage of a law, than to declare it void after it is passed; that this will be particularly the case where the law aggrieves individuals, who may be unable to support an appeal against a State to the supreme Judiciary, that a State which would violate the Legislative rights of the Union, would not be very ready to obey a Judicial decree in support of them, and that a recurrence to force, which in the event of disobedience would be necessary, is[20] an evil which the new Constitution meant to exclude as far as possible.

2. A Constitutional negative on the laws of the States seems equally necessary to secure individuals against encroachments on their rights. The mutability of the laws of the States is found to be a serious evil. The injustice of them has been so frequent and so flagrant as to alarm the most stedfast friends of Republicanism. I am persuaded I do not err in saying that the evils issuing from these sources[21] contributed more to that uneasiness which produced the Convention, and prepared the public mind for a general reform, than those which accrued to our national character and interest from the inadequacy of the Confederation to its immediate objects. A reform therefore which does not make provision for private rights, must be materially defective. The restraints against paper emissions, and violations of contracts are not sufficient. Supposing them to be effectual as far as they go, they are short of the mark. Injustice may be effected by such an infinitude of legislative expedients, that where the disposition exists it can only be controuled by some provision which reaches all cases whatsoever. The partial provision made, supposes the disposition which will evade it. It may be asked how private rights[22] will be more secure under the Guardianship of the General Government than under the State Governments, since they are both founded on the republican principle which refers the ultimate decision to the will of the majority, and are distinguished rather[23] by the extent within which they will operate, than by any material difference in their structure. A full discussion of this question would, if I mistake not, unfold the true principles of Republican Government, and prove in contradiction to the concurrent opinions of theoretical writers, that this form of Government, in order to effect its purposes must operate not within a small but an extensive sphere. I will state some of the ideas which have occurred to me on this subject. Those who contend for a simple Democracy, or a pure republic, actuated by the sense

of the majority, and operating within narrow limits, assume or suppose a case which is altogether fictitious. They found their reasoning on the idea, that the people composing the Society enjoy not only an equality of political rights; but that they have all precisely the same interests and the same feelings in every respect.[24] Were this in reality the case, their reasoning would be conclusive. The interest of the majority would be that of the minority also; the decisions could only turn on mere opinion concerning the good of the whole of which the major voice would be the safest criterion; and within a small sphere, this voice could be most easily collected and the public affairs most accurately managed. We know however that no Society[25] ever did or can consist of so homogeneous a mass of Citizens. In the savage State indeed, an approach is made towards it; but in that state little or no Government is necessary. In all civilized Societies, distinctions are various and unavoidable. A distinction of property results from that very protection which a free Government gives to unequal faculties of acquiring it.[26] There will be rich and poor; creditors and debtors; a landed interest, a monied interest, a mercantile interest, a manufacturing interest. These classes may again be subdivided according[27] to the different productions of different situations and soils, and according to different branches of commerce and of manufactures. In addition to these natural distinctions, artificial ones[28] will be founded on accidental differences in political, religious and other opinions, or an attachment to the persons of leading individuals. However erroneous or ridiculous these grounds of dissention and faction may appear to the enlightened Statesman, or the benevolent philosopher, the bulk of mankind who are neither Statesmen nor Philosophers, will continue to view[29] them in a different light. It remains then to be enquired whether a majority having any common interest, or feeling any common passion, will find sufficient motives to restrain them from oppressing the minority. An individual is never allowed to be a judge or even a witness in his own cause. If two individuals are under the biass of interest[30] or enmity against a third, the rights of the latter could never be safely referred to the majority of the three. Will two thousand individuals be less apt to oppress one thousand, or two hundred thousand, one hundred thousand? Three motives only can restrain in such cases. 1. A prudent regard to private or partial good, as essentially involved in the general and permanent good of the whole.[31] This ought no doubt to be sufficient of itself. Experience however shews that it has little effect on individuals, and perhaps still less on a collection of individuals, and least of all on a majority with the public authority in their hands. If the former are ready to forget that honesty is the best policy; the last do more. They often proceed on the converse of the maxim: that whatever is politic is honest. 2. Respect for character. This motive is not found sufficient to restrain individuals from injustice, and loses its efficacy in proportion to the number which is to divide the praise or the blame. Besides as it has reference to public opinion, which is that of the majority, the standard is fixed by those whose conduct is to be measured by it. 3. Religion. The inefficacy of this restraint on individuals is well known. The conduct of every popular assembly, acting on oath, the strongest of religious ties, shews that individuals join without remorse in acts against which their consciences would revolt, if proposed to them separately in their closets. When Indeed Religion is kindled into enthusiasm, its force like that of other passions is increased by the sympathy of a multitude. But enthusiasm is only a temporary state of Religion, and whilst it lasts will hardly be seen with pleasure at the helm. Even in its coolest state, it has been much oftener a motive to oppression than a restraint from it. If then there must be different interests and parties in Society; and a majority[32] when united by a common interest or passion can not be restrained from oppressing[33] the minority, what remedy can be found in a republican Government, where the majority must ultimately decide, but that of giving such an extent to its sphere, that no common interest or passion will be likely to unite a majority of the whole number in an unjust pursuit.[34] In a large Society, the people are broken into so many interests and parties, that a common sentiment is less likely to be felt, and the requisite concert[35] less likely to be formed, by a majority of the whole. The same security seems requisite for the civil as for the religious rights of individuals. If the same sect form a majority and have the power, other sects will be sure to be depressed. Divide et impera, the reprobated axiom of tyranny, is under certain qualifications, the only policy, by which a republic can be administered on just principles. It must be observed however that this doctrine can only hold within a sphere of a mean extent. As in too small a sphere oppressive combinations may be too easily formed against the weaker party; so in too extensive a one a defensive concert may be rendered too difficult against the oppression of those entrusted with the administration. The great desideratum in Government is, so to modify the sovereignty as that it may be sufficiently neutral between different parts of the Society to controul one part from invading the rights of another, and at the same time sufficiently controuled itself, from setting up an interest adverse to that of the entire Society. In absolute monarchies, the Prince may be tolerably neutral towards different classes of his subjects, but may sacrifice the[36] happiness of all to his personal ambition or avarice. In small republics, the sovereign will is controuled from such a sacrifice of the entire Society, but it is not sufficiently neutral towards the parts composing it. In the extended Republic of the United States, the General Government[37] would hold a pretty even balance between the parties of particular States, and be at the same time sufficiently restrained by its dependence on the community, from betraying its general interests.][38]

Begging pardon for this immoderate digression, I return to the third object abovementioned, the adjustment of the different interests of different parts of the Continent. Some contended for an unlimited power over trade including exports as well as imports, and over slaves as well as other imports; some for such a power, provided the concurrence of two thirds of both Houses were required; some for such a qualification of the power, with an exemption of exports and slaves, others for an exemption of exports only. The result is seen in the Constitution. S. Carolina and Georgia were inflexible on the point of the slaves.

The remaining object, created more embarrassment, and a greater alarm for the issue of the Convention than all the rest put together. The little States insisted on retaining their equality in both branches, unless a compleat abolition of the State Governments should take place; and made an equality in the Senate a sine qua non. The large States on the other hand urged that as the new Government was to be drawn principally from the people immediately and was to operate directly on them, not on the States; and consequently as the States would lose that importance which is now proportioned to the importance of their voluntary compliances with the requisitions of Congress, it was necessary that the representation in both Houses should be in proportion to their size. It ended in the compromise which you will see, but very much to the dissatisfaction of several members from the large States.

It will not escape you that three names only from Virginia are subscribed to the Act. Mr. Wythe did not return after the death of his lady. Docr. MClurg left the Convention some time before the adjournment. The Governour and Col. Mason refused to be parties to it. Mr. Gerry was the only other member who refused. The objections of the Govr. turn principally on the latitude of the general powers, and on the connection established between the President and the Senate. He wished that the plan should be proposed to the States with liberty to them to suggest alterations which should all be referred to another general Convention to be[39] incorporated into the plan as far as might be judged expedient. He was not inveterate in his opposition, and grounded his refusal to subscribe pretty much on his unwillingness to commit himself so as not to be at liberty to be governed by further lights on the subject. Col. Mason left Philada. in an exceeding ill humour indeed. A number of little circumstances arising in part from the impatience which prevailed towards the close of the business, conspired to whet his acrimony. He returned to Virginia with a fixed disposition to prevent the adoption of the plan if possible. He considers the want of a Bill of Rights as a fatal objection. His other objections are to the substitution of the Senate in place of an Executive Council and to the powers vested in that body—to the powers of the Judiciary—to the vice President being made President of the Senate—to the smallness of the number of Representatives—to the restriction on the States with regard to ex post facto laws—and most of all probably to the power of regulating trade, by a majority only of each House. He has some other lesser objections. Being now under the necessity of justifying his refusal to sign, he will of course, muster every possible one.[40] His conduct has given great umbrage to the County of Fairfax, and particularly to the Town of Alexandria. He is already instructed to promote in the Assembly the calling a Convention, and will probably be either not deputed to the Convention, or be tied up by express instructions. He did not object in general to the powers vested in the National Government, so much as to the modification. In some respects he admitted that some further powers could have improved the system. He acknowledged in particular that a negative on the State laws, and the appointment of the State Executives ought to be ingredients; but supposed that the public mind would not now bear them and that experience would hereafter produce these amendments.

The final reception which will be given by the people at large to this proposed System can not yet be decided. The Legislature of N. Hampshire was sitting when it reached that State and was well pleased with it. As far as the sense of the people there has been expressed, it is equally favorable. Boston is warm and almost unanimous in embracing[41] it. The impression on the country is not yet known. No symptoms of disapprobation have appeared.

The Legislature of that State is now sitting, through which the sense of the people at large will soon be promulged with tolerable certainty. The paper money faction in Rh. Island is hostile. The other party zealously attached to it. Its passage through Connecticut is likely to be very smooth and easy. There seems to be less agitation in this[42] state than any where. The discussion of the subject seems confined to the newspapers. The principal characters are known to be friendly. The Governour's party which has hitherto been the popular and most numerous one, is supposed to be on the opposite side; but considerable reserve is practiced, of which he sets the example. N. Jersey takes the affirmative side of course. Meetings of the people are declaring their approbation, and instructing their representatives. Penna. will be divided. The City of Philada., the Republican party, the Quakers, and most of the Germans espouse the Constitution. Some of the Constitutional leaders, backed by the western Country will oppose. An unlucky ferment on the subject in their assembly just before its late adjournment has irritated both sides, particularly the opposition, and by redoubling the exertions of that party may render the event doubtful. The voice of Maryland I understand from pretty good authority, is, as far as it has been declared, strongly in favor of the Constitution. Mr. Chase is an enemy, but the Town of Baltimore which he now represents, is warmly attached to it, and will shackle him as far as they can. Mr. Paca will probably be, as usually, in the politics of Chase. My information from Virginia is as yet extremely imperfect. I have a letter from Genl. Washington which speaks favorably of the impression within a circle of some extent, and another from Chancellor Pendleton which expresses his full acceptance of the plan, and the popularity of it in his district. I am told also that Innis and Marshall are patrons of it. In the opposite scale are Mr. James Mercer, Mr. R. H. Lee, Docr. Lee and their connections of course, Mr. M. Page according to Report, and most of the Judges and Bar of the general Court. The part which Mr. Henry will take is unknown here. Much will depend on it. I had taken it for granted from a variety of circumstances that he would be in the opposition, and still think that will be the case. There are reports however which favor a contrary supposition. From the States South of Virginia nothing has been heard. As the deputation from S. Carolina consisted of some of its weightiest characters, who have returned unanimously zealous in favor of the Constitution, it is probable that State will readily embrace it. It is not less probable, that N. Carolina will follow the example unless that of Virginia should counterbalance it. Upon the whole, although, the public mind will not be fully[43] known, nor finally settled for a considerable time, appearances at present augur a more prompt, and general adoption of the plan than could have been well expected.[44]

When the plan came before Congress for their sanction, a very serious report was made by R. H. Lee and Mr. Dane from Masts. to embarrass it. It was first contended that Congress could not properly give any positive countenance to a measure which had for its object the subversion of the Constitution under which they acted. This ground of attack failing, the former gentleman urged the expediency of sending out the plan with amendments, and proposed a number of them corresponding with the objections of Col. Mason. This experiment had still less effect. In order however to obtain unanimity it was necessary to couch the resolution in very moderate terms.

Mr. Adams has received permission to return with thanks for his services. No provision is made for supplying his place, or keeping up any representation there. Your reappointment for three years will be notified from the office of F. Affairs. It was *made*[45] *without a negative, eight states* being *present. Connecticut however*[46] *put in a blank ticket*, the *sense of* that *state having been declared against embassies. Massachusetts betrayed some scruple* on *like ground.* Every *personal consideration* was *avowed* and *I believe with sincerity* to have *militated against these scruples.* It seems to be understood that letters to and from the foreign Ministers of the U.S. are not free of postage: but that the charge is to be allowed in their accounts.

The exchange of our French for Dutch Creditors has not been countenanced either by Congress or the Treasury Board. The paragraph in your last letter to Mr. Jay, on the subject of applying a loan in Holland to the discharge of the pay due to the foreign officers has been referred to the Board since my arrival here. No report has yet been made. But I have little idea that the proposition will be adopted. Such is the state and prospect of our fiscal department that any new loan however small that should now be made, would probably subject us to the reproach of premeditated deception. The balance of Mr. Adams' last loan will be wanted for the interest due in Holland, and with all the income here, will, it is feared, not save our credit in Europe from further wounds. It may well be doubted whether the present Government can be kept alive thro' the ensuing year, or untill the new one may take its place.

Upwards of 100,000 Acres of the surveyed lands of the U.S. have been disposed of in open market. Five million of unsurveyed have been sold by private contract to a N. England Company, at ⅔ of a dollar per acre, payment to be made in the principal of the public securities. A negociation is nearly closed with a N. Jersey Company for two million more on like terms, and another commenced with a Company of this City for four million. Col. Carrington writes more fully on this subject.

You will receive herewith the desired information from Alderman Broome in the case of Mr. Burke. Also the Virga. Bill on crimes and punishments. Sundry alterations having been made in conformity to the sense of the House in its latter stages, it is less accurate and methodical than it ought to have been. To these papers I add a speech of Mr. C. P. on the Mississippi business. It is printed under precautions of secrecy, but surely could not have been properly exposed to so much risk of publication. You will find also among the pamplets and papers I send by Commodore Jones, another printed speech of the same Gentleman. The Musæum Magazine, and Philada. Gazettes, will give you a tolerable idea of the objects of present attention.

The summer crops in the Eastern and Middle States have been extremely plentiful. Southward of Virga. They differ in different places. On the whole I do not know that they are bad in that region. In Virginia the drought has been unprecedented, particularly between the falls of the Rivers and the Mountains. The Crops of Corn are in general alarmingly short. In Orange I find there will be scarcely subsistence for the inhabitants. I have not heard from Albemarle. The crops of Tobacco are every where said to be pretty good in point of quantity, and the quality unusually fine. The crops of wheat were also in general excellent in quality and tolerable in quantity.

Novr. 1. Commodore[47] Jones having preferred another vessel to the packet, has remained here till this time. The interval has produced little necessary to be added to the above. The Legislature of Massts. has it seems taken up the Act of the Convention and have appointed or probably will appoint an early day for its State Convention. There are letters also from Georgia which denote a favorable disposition. I am informed from Richmond that the new Election-law from the Revised Code produced a pretty full House of Delegates, as well as a Senate, on the first day. It had previously had equal effect in producing full meetings of the freeholders for the County elections. A very decided majority of the Assembly is said to be zealous in favor of the New Constitution. The same is said of the Country at large. It appears however that individuals of great weight both within and without the Legislature are opposed to it. A letter I just have from Mr. A. Stuart names Mr. Henry, Genl. Nelson, W. Nelson, the family of Cabels, St. George Tucker, John Taylor and the Judges of the General Court except P. Carrington. The other opponents he described as of too little note to be mentioned, which gives a negative information of the Characters on the other side. All are agreed that the plan must be submitted to a Convention.

We hear from Georgia that that State is threatened with a dangerous war with the Creek Indians. The alarm is of so serious a nature, that law-martial has been proclaimed, and they are proceeding to fortify even the Town of Savannah. The idea there is that the Indians derive their motives as well as their means from their Spanish neighbours. Individuals complain also that their fugitive slaves are encouraged by East Florida. The policy of this is explained by supposing that it is considered as a discouragement to the Georgians to form settlements near the Spanish boundaries.

There are but few States on the spot here which will survive the expiration of the federal year; and it is extremely uncertain when a Congress will again be formed. We have not yet heard who are to be in the appointment of Virginia for the next year.

With the most affectionate attachment I remain Dear Sr. Your obed friend & servant, Js. MADISON Jr.

RC (DLC: TJ Papers); partly in code; with a number of deletions and corrections, most of which were not interlinear and which were evidently made contemporaneously, but two of which, as indicated in notes 42 and 47 below, were clearly made by Madison late in life; endorsed. Tr of an Extract (DLC: Madison Papers); in Madison's hand, in highly abbreviated form (see note 38, below). Tr of an Extract (ViU); at foot of text, in the hand of Nicholas P. Trist: "Copied from the original at Montpellier (V. J. T. & C. J. R. & M. J. R. assisting) by N. P. T. Oct. 1. '34"; endorsed by Trist on verso of last leaf: "Madison James —Oct. 24. 1787 To Thomas Jefferson. Copied from the original at Montpellier, Oct. 1. 1834. N. P. Trist." (See note 44 below). Recorded in SJL as received 19 Dec. 1787. Enclosures: (1) The "information from Alderman Broome"

has not been found (see TJ to Madison, 20 Dec. 1787). (2) The "Virga. Bill on crimes and punishments" must have been a printed text showing the alterations that the bill underwent in the legislative session of Oct. 1786, but no such printed text is known to have been made and none is known to be in existence; it is also puzzling that Madison waited until this late date to send any text when the Bill was defeated early in the year (see Madison to TJ, 15 Feb. 1787; see also, Vol. 2: 506, note). (3) The "speech of Mr. C. P. [Charles Pinckney] on the Mississippi business" was that delivered on 16 Aug. 1786 in answer to Jay's speech on 3 Aug. 1786 on the negotiations with Spain; it was printed in broadside form by Congress and it was one of these printed texts that Madison sent to TJ (text of Pinckney's speech is printed in JCC, XXXI, 935-48). (4) The other "printed speech by the same gentleman," not actually enclosed but sent by Jones, was Pinckney's *Observations on the Plan of Government submitted to the Federal Convention, in Philadelphia, on the 28th of May, 1787,* New York, 1787 (Sowerby, No. 3016).

It is not known when or for what purpose Madison made the extract from this letter that is described above and referred to below as the Madison Extract, but it was probably made during TJ's lifetime. Certainly the handwriting is much firmer and less crabbed by age than the alterations made by Madison in the text of the letter that are known to have been added late in life (see notes 42 and 47, below). It is possible, even, that he obtained leave from TJ to make the extract not long after the latter returned from France. The fact that he had made such an extract and retained it may also explain why this letter of his was not kept by him among his own papers along with others that he received after TJ's death.

1 Preceding seven words interlined in substitution for "disagreement of opinion on serious," an alteration probably made contemporaneously.

2 This word written lineally in preference to "requires," deleted, evidently contemporaneously.

3 At this point Madison deleted lineally: "Others would have preferred," an alteration evidently made contemporaneously.

4 Preceding six words interlined and "to the other two" deleted, an alteration evidently made contemporaneously.

5 Preceding eight words interlined, probably contemporaneously.

6 This word written lineally in preference to "laws of," deleted.

7 Preceding three words interlined, perhaps contemporaneously.

8 At this point Madison deleted, evidently contemporaneously, the word "certainly."

9 The Madison Extract reads "prerogative."

10 At this point Madison deleted the word "necessarily," evidently contemporaneously.

11 At this point Madison deleted, evidently contemporaneously: "From that to every new instance it may be [premised?] that."

12 This word written over an erasure,

perhaps "jurisdiction," and presumably done contemporaneously.

13 This word interlined in substitution for "legislatures," an alteration perhaps made contemporaneously.

14 The Madison Extract reads "allowed."

15 This word, divided, lies in the right and left margins and may have been added later.

16 This word altered by overwriting, evidently contemporaneously, from "authority."

17 This word altered by overwriting, probably later, from "will."

18 This word interlined, evidently contemporaneously, in substitution for "impossibility and difficulty," deleted.

19 At this point Madison deleted lineally, evidently contemporaneously, the word "preserve."

20 This word altered by overwriting, perhaps contemporaneously, from what appears to read "was."

21 At this point Madison deleted lineally, evidently contemporaneously, "had a greater share in."

22 These two words interlined, perhaps contemporaneously, in substitution for "the public and private faith," deleted.

23 This word interlined, probably contemporaneously, in substitution for "principally," deleted.

24 The Madison Extract reads: ". . . but that they have precisely and in all respects the same interests and the same feelings."

25 This word interlined, probably contemporaneously, in substitution for "Government," deleted.

26 Preceding five words interlined, perhaps later, in substitution for "private rights," deleted.

27 This passage originally read: "These classes will again be subdivided by," and then was altered by overwriting, evidently contemporaneously, to read as above.

28 These two words interlined, evidently contemporaneously, in substitution for "others," deleted.

29 This word written lineally in preference to "act," deleted, evidently contemporaneously.

30 Preceding seven words interlined, evidently contemporaneously, in substitution for "men have a same interest," deleted.

31 This word written over another that may be "sovereignty" or "major-

ity," an alteration made contemporaneously.

[32] These two words interlined, evidently contemporaneously, in substitution for "the predominant party," deleted.

[33] This word altered by overwriting, perhaps contemporaneously, from "suppressing."

[34] Preceding four words interlined, perhaps contemporaneously.

[35] The Madison Extract reads: "combination."

[36] At this point Madison deleted "general," evidently contemporaneously.

[37] These two words interlined, evidently contemporaneously, in substitution for "authority of the whole."

[38] The text within brackets (supplied) constitutes the whole of the Extract in Madison's hand, which, however, varies in the following caption and opening sentence: "Extract of a letter to Mr. J—son dated Ocr. 24. 1787.—A negative in the General Government on laws of the States necessary 1. to prevent encroachments on General Government. 2. instability and injustice in state legislation."

[39] At this point the word "adopted"

is deleted, evidently contemporaneously.

[40] This word interlined, perhaps later, in substitution for "objection," deleted.

[41] This word written over "adopting," an alteration possibly contemporaneous.

[42] Late in life Madison placed an asterisk at this point and interlined "N.York."

[43] This word written over "officially," an alteration that was probably contemporaneous.

[44] The text of the Trist Extract, which begins with the third paragraph of the letter ("You will herewith receive the result of the Convention . . ." &c), ends at this point.

[45] This and subsequent words in italics are written in code and were decoded interlineally by TJ. The Editors have verified his decoding, employing Code No. 9.

[46] Madison wrote "74," the code symbol for "however," but TJ decoded this as "notwithstanding," the code symbol for which was "73."

[47] Late in life Madison put an asterisk at this point and wrote "Paul" in the margin opposite.

To Abbé Morellet

SIR   Paris Oct. 24. 1787.

I wish it were in my power to announce to the Count de Cambrai that the Treasury board of the United states had ennabled their banker here to answer the demands of the foreign officers. But it is not. As soon as I knew that there was a deficiency of money to pay the interest of this demand, I informed the Treasury board of it. They answered me they would supply the necessary sum as soon as it should be in their power; and I am persuaded they have not failed in inclination to do it. Of this I had the honour to notify the Count de Cambray the last year. It is not unknown to you that the part of our new machine of government which works the worst is that which respects the raising money; and it is that which has occasioned the late attempts to amend our confederation. Foreseeing that our Treasury board might not be able to remit money from America, I suggested to Congress the expediency of borrowing money in Holland to pay off the foreign officers. And in the month of July last, being assured they could command the money in Holland, I pressed a more particular proposition for this purpose. As I do not foresee any possible objection to the proposition I made them, I think myself sure of their acceding to it, and that I may receive notice of it in the month of December. I may be disappointed as to the time of receiving their answer, because the course of their business is slow: but I do not apprehend it will be much retarded, and still less that they will refuse it altogether. The moment I receive an answer, the Count de Cambrai may be assured it shall be communicated to him. In doing this I shall gratify not only my personal friendship for him, but also those sentiments of particular esteem and attachment with which I have the honour to be Dear Sir Your most obedient & most humble servant, TH: JEFFERSON

PrC (DLC).

From John Rutledge

Charleston, 24 Oct. 1787. Messrs. Brailsford & Morris, of that city, will ship some rice to France early in the winter and, being strangers, may wish to refer to TJ for information concerning French merchants; they are an honorable firm and their punctuality may be relied on. Hopes this venture may "open, and, in a short time, establish, an extensive and valuable Market for our great Staple."

RC (DLC); 2 p.; endorsed. Recorded in SJL Index; evidently received with Bérard's letter of 17 Feb. 1788, having been enclosed in Brailsford & Morris to TJ, 31 Oct. 1787, q.v., note.

From Lacépède

MONSIEUR   au jardin du roi le 25 oct. 1787.

M. le Cte. de buffon, étant privé par le mauvais état de sa santé, de l'avantage de répondre à votre excellence, me charge d'avoir l'honneur de la remercier du beau présent qu'elle vient de nous faire. Ce sera pour nous une bien agréable occupation, Monsieur, que de comparer d'après vos vues, les divers bois d'animaux de l'amérique septentrionale qui étoient joints à la dépouille de l'orignal, avec ceux des rennes, des cerfs, des chevreuils &c. de notre continent. Nous vous aurons l'obligation, Monsieur, de voir le domaine de l'histoire naturelle s'étendre, et plusieurs de ses parties s'éclaircir: c'est avoir bien des droits à l'estime publique, que de réunir comme vous les connoissances du naturaliste, à la science de l'homme d'état. Je suis avec respect Monsieur de Votre Excellence le très humble et très obéissant serviteur,

LE CTE. DE LACEPEDE
garde au jardin du roi

RC (MoSHi); endorsed. Recorded in SJL as received 3 Nov. 1787.

From James Maury

Liverpool, 25 Oct. 1787. Acknowledges TJ's letter of 8 July [i.e., 2 July]; "the prospect of war having materially altered the Business of Insurance in favor of American property in British Bottoms," he may need proofs that he is a citizen of the United States; asks TJ to provide him with such documents. Is concerned that the French are not inclined to continue their former prices for tobacco; they have "so much engrossed the article last year in Virginia" that few vessels have returned to Liverpool "more than half loaded"; this, of course, increases the value in England and those who shipped to that market will profit. Affairs in Holland are apparently to be settled as TJ intimated, but Holland will "pay the King of Prussia for it." Holds a great deal of American produce; will appreciate information on the prospects of war; will not use the information improperly, but it will help him protect Virginia interests lodged with him; "for your own Sake I wish your last years Crop was in the Same Situation."

RC (MHi); 3 p.; endorsed. An entry in SJL for the receipt on 11 Nov. 1787 of a letter from Maury of 26 Oct. 1787 undoubtedly refers to the present letter.

From Richard O'Bryen

[[*Algiers*] *25 Oct. 1787.* Recorded in SJL Index but not in SJL and, therefore, probably received sometime in 1788 (see Rutledge to TJ, 23 Oct. 1787, note. Not found.]]

From Zaccheus Coffin

Algiers, 26 Oct. 1787. Asks that TJ forward the enclosed letter and that it be sent to Boston, if convenient.

RC (MHi); 2 p.; at foot of text, in Coffin's hand: "American Slave in algier"; endorsed. Recorded in SJL as received 20 Nov. 1787. The enclosed letter has not been identified.

[288]

From C. W. F. Dumas

The Hague, 26 Oct. 1787. The enclosed gazette, specifically published to plague him, shows that his condition, instead of being mitigated, as TJ and Adams intended, has been aggravated and his existence rendered insupportable. Jacob van Staphorst, who is on his way to Paris, can relate many things concerning Dumas' distress which his own diminishing strength does not permit him to write. [*Postscript:*] This letter is not being sent until 30 Oct.

RC (DLC); 1 p.; in French. FC (Rijksarchief, The Hague: Dumas Letter Book; photostats in DLC). Recorded in SJL as received 4 Nov. 1787. Enclosures: (1) A copy of The Hague *Gazette* for 24 Oct. 1787, containing an extract from resolutions of the States General of 18 Oct. stating that they had received a letter of 4 Oct. from their ambassadors at Versailles (L'Estevenon de Berkenroode and Brantzen) informing them of TJ's "private visit" on the preceding day to each of them in which he asked that Dumas "be protected from all insult and danger to himself, his family, and property"; that the ambassadors could not refuse this request and therefore solicited such protection; that Fagel, secretary to the States General, had also received a letter from John Adams of 1 Oct. 1787, making a similar request; that Fagel was authorized to reply to Adams that the states of Holland and West Friesland had been asked at once to give Dumas proper protection on Dumas' own request of 28 Sep.; that the States General "would not willingly suffer Mr. Dumas to be disturbed any more than one of their own citizens; but are obliged to declare to Mr. Adams that the said Dumas deserved their protection but little, as he had behaved most indecorously in every respect; for which reason, they request Mr. Adams not to employ him any longer, but to appoint some one else to perform his duties during his absence"; and that a copy

of this resolution be sent to the ambassadors at Versailles for their information and in order that they might communicate it to TJ (translation printed in *Dipl. Corr., 1783-89*, III, 596-7). (2) Though not mentioned by Dumas, he also enclosed a letter of the same date to Jay, which in turn enclosed a copy of the extract from The Hague *Gazette*, explaining that in consequence of this attempt to injure him by vague expressions, he had been "threatened openly and loudly; insulted by persons employed for the purpose; followed by crowds, as a *Kees*, a name signifying dog, given to the Patriots in derision, as that of *Yankee* was applied to the Americans"; that the "whole political system of this country, with regard to Europe and America, is changed" and the "government . . . in fact military, the executive power . . . everything, the legislative nothing"; and that every attempt is made to depreciate the United States" (same, III, 595-6; FC in Dumas Letter Book, Rijksarchief, The Hague; photostats in DLC).

On this same date Dumas wrote to VAN STAPHORST giving an account of his intolerable situation and concluding: "Je vous conjure de voir Mr. Jefferson, rue neuve de Berry, près la Grille de Chaillot. Il est instruit de [mon] affreux état et peut vous mon[trer] la Gazette virulente de la Haie que je lui envoie aujourdhui, qui m'expose toujours plus" (same).

From William Stephens Smith

DR. SIR   London October 26th. 1787.

By introducing the bearer Mr. Daniel Parker (who I think you encountered once at my lodgings in Leicester fields) I have the

[289]

satisfaction of doing him a favour, and presenting to you a fund of Commercial and political knowledge, which you may draw freely upon during his stay at Paris, without being in the least apprehensive of failure or protest. I have been guilty of this, so frequently, lately, that I am apprehensive I may trespass upon your time, but I will in future only do it, upon occasions like the present, where the Gentleman may be served and you pleased.

I have nothing new to Communicate. Mr. P. will be able to give you full and satisfactory accounts, of the State of Politics here, and the determination to pursue with vigor the hostile measures of the Cabinet, should *they*, think proper to continue them. He is also perfectly well acquainted with the present situation of Affairs in Holland—but perhaps they are not spoken of in France— *Quis talia fando, abstinet a Lacrymis*

Tell me, whether we shall continue in peace or whether war is inevitable, I mean as it relates to Europe, and you will oblige Your most humble Servant, W. S. SMITH

RC (MHi); endorsed. Recorded in SJL as received 9 Nov. 1787.

From Le Mau de L'Eupay

A Arnas prèz villefranche En Beaujolois

MONSIEUR Le 27 8bre. *1787*

J'ai Reçü par M. de Laye Les trois volumes du cultivateur americain que vous avéz Eü La bonté de m'Envoyér, j'ai Resté si Longtems à vous en faire mes Remerciments, parceque j'étois bien aise de connoitre L'ouvrage pretieux que je tiens de vos liberalités; que d'obligations je vous ai, Monsieur, je ne connoissois qu'un Homme aimable et instruis de votre pais aulieu qu'aujourdhuy j'en connois mille. Vous etes faits pour nous donner des Loix puisque vous nous Retracés Les hommes du Siecle D'or, c'est ches vous aujourd'huy qu'il faut aller s'instruire de L'agriculture. Pourquoy etes vous si éloignés de moy, je me ferois un devoir de prendre de vos Leçons, vous avés un sol qui vaut Les mines de votre continent meridional. Comment, votre grain vous Rend trente pour un et Les meilleurs de nos fonds que L'on couvre d'angrais ne nous Rendent au plus que vingt. Ah, Monsieur, votre terre est La terre promise, c'est à votre humanité, à La douceur de vos mœurs et à La bonté de votre gouvernement que vous devés cette faveur; est il possible que dans un pais que nous Regardions comme un desert, L'on y trouve des hommes faits pour donnér des Loix à L'univers après luy avoir appris à pensér; que je m'estimerois heureux d'existér dans un aussi bon pais, je serois un homme au lieu que je ne suis qu'un Esclave.

J'étois tres flatté que Madame de Laye m'eut procuré L'avantage de faire votre connoissance, mais aujourdhuy que je connois votre Respectable famille (je puis parler ainsi d'après La Lecture de votre ouvrage), je m'en orgueillis et vous demande votre protection pour un neveu que j'envoye bientot dans vos isles ou sa malheureuse famille à cherchée un asile; puissent ils un jour vous Retrouver dans votre paradis terestre et Reclamér pour Eux Les bontés que vous avés aujourdhuy pour leur oncle.

J'ai L'honneur D'etre avec Les sentiments de La plus vive Reconnoissance et de La Respectueuse consideration avec Lesquels je serai toute ma vie Monsieur Votre tres humble Et tres obeissant serviteur,   LE MAU DE L'EUPAY
                                           Prieur Darnas

Monsieur et Madame de Laye me chargent de vous presenter leurs hommages. Monsieur nous a flatté d'avoir Le Bonheur de vous voir cet hiver.

RC (ViWC); endorsed. Recorded in SJL as received 1 Nov. 1787.

From John Adams

DEAR SIR   London Oct. 28. 1787

Mr. Daniel Parker will have the Honour to deliver you this. He is an intelligent American, and well informed as any Man you will see from hence. I beg leave to introduce him to you.

Let me thank you for your late Letter and the important State Papers inclosed with it.

I have ordered to your Address, a dozen Copies of my Boudoir for the Marquis, who desired Mr. Appleton and Mr. Paine to have them sent. I have called it a Defence of the American Constitutions, because it is a Resistance to an Attack of Turgot. The two volumes are confined to one Point, and if a City is defended from an Attack made on the North Gate, it may be called a Defence of the City, although the other three Gates, the East West and South Gates were so weak, as to have been defenceless, if they had been attacked.—If a Warriour should arise to attack our Constitutions where they are not defencible, I'l not undertake to defend them. Two thirds of our States have made Constitutions, in no respect better than those of the Italian Republicks, and as sure as there is an Heaven and an Earth, if they are not altered they will produce Disorders and Confusion.

I can tell you nothing of Politicks. All the world is astonished at the Secrecy of Mr. Pitt. Great Preparations for War, yet the World can find no Ennemy nor Object. Carmarthen "hopes the Scudd will blow over, and even that the Quarrell between the Port and Russia will be made up. While a Fire is burning in any quarter of Europe, no one can tell when or where it may Spread." The General Understanding is that the U.S. are to be let alone, and they have given general orders to the Navy, to let American Vessells and Seamen alone. They will have their hands full, I believe, and there is little Plunder to be made of Americans, so that we may be quiet,—as long as they will let us.—But our Countrymen will do well to think of the Possibility of Danger and of the means of Defence. A war would cost us more than we have of Cash or Credit, but if we should be attacked we must defend, Money or no Money, Credit or no Credit. Whether John Bull has Command enough of his Passions to see us punctually fulfill our Treaties, as we must do, without being transported with rage, you who know him can tell as well as I.—We know this Gentlemans hasty temper so well that I think we may very safely wish for the Continuance of Peace, between France and him, even upon Selfish Principles, tho' our Commerce and Navigation would be greatly promoted by a War, if we can keep out of it.

I tremble and agonize for the suffering Patriots in Holland. You may judge to what Lengths the spirit extends against them, by a formal Complaint of their High Mightinesses against Dumas, and a Requisition to me, to employ him no longer but to appoint some other Person in my absence. It is not I am well persuaded as Agent for the United States, but as a Friend of France or of the Patriotic Party against the Statholder, that he has unfortunately incurred this Censure and Displeasure. Yet as Mr. Dumas holds not his Character or Authority from me, I can do nothing, but transmit the Papers to Congress.

With great Esteem, I have the honour to be dear Sir, your most obedient Servant,   JOHN ADAMS

RC (DLC); addressed and endorsed. FC (MHi: AMT); in the hand of W. S. Smith. Recorded in SJL as received 9 Nov. 1787.

TJ's LATE LETTER was presumably that of 28 Sep. which Adams had acknowledged on 9 Oct. 1787 but in doing

so had not referred to any IMPORTANT STATE PAPERS INCLOSED therein; the letter itself does not mention any such enclosures. There is no record in SJL of another letter to Adams between 28 Sep. and 28 Oct., but it is possible that TJ sent a note by John B. Cutting cov-

ering some documents of a public nature (see TJ to Trumbull, 11 Oct.
1787). But it is more likely that
Adams' allusion to IMPORTANT STATE
PAPERS was only a light reference to
some such letter as that from Theresa
Murphy that TJ may have asked Adams
to forward to America (see TJ to
Murphy, 2 Oct. 1787). Adams may
have employed BOUDOIR in its literal
sense of a place in which to sulk, in-

tending it as a playful reference to his
DEFENCE OF THE AMERICAN CONSTITU-
TIONS; he may also have employed it as
a variant meaning of *study* (see OED,
citing Adams' reference to Brand Hol-
lis' calling his study a boudoir in Adams'
diary, *Works*, III, 405). For a note on
the FORMAL COMPLAINT OF THEIR
HIGH MIGHTINESSES AGAINST DUMAS,
see Dumas to TJ, 26 Oct. 1787, note;
also TJ to Jay, 3 Nov. 1787, first letter.

To John Jay

SIR   Paris Oct. 27. [i.e., 28][1] 1787.

When I had the honor of addressing you on the 8th. instant,
the appearances of war were such, that no one would have been
surprised to hear that hostilities were actually commenced at sea.
The preparatives were pushed with such a vivacity on the part of
England that it was believed she had other objects in view than
those she spoke out. However, having protected by her countenance
the establishment of the Stadtholder by the Prussian troops, and
compleatly detached the court of Berlin from that of Versailles,
she made a proposition to the latter to disarm, which was agreed
to. Mutual declarations for this purpose were signed last night at
Versailles, of which I have now the honour to inclose you copies.
Commissaries are to be appointed on each side to see that the disarming takes place. The count de Moustier having been detained
at Brest a fortnight by contrary wind, and this continuing obstinately in the same point, admits a possibility that this letter may
yet reach Brest before his departure. It passes through the post
office and will be opened and read of course. I shall have the honour
of addressing you more fully a week hence by a private hand. I
have now that of assuring you of the sincerity of that esteem and
respect with which I have the honour to be, Sir, your most obedient
& most humble servant,   TH: JEFFERSON

PrC (DLC). Enclosures (PrC in
DLC; Tr of a translation of the "Declaration" in MHi): Tr, in French, in the
hand of William Short, of the "Declaration" signed at Versailles, 27 Oct. 1787,
by Dorset and William Eden, requesting the king of France to explain his
position in regard to affairs in the
United Netherlands and suggesting that
all armaments and preparations for war

be mutually discontinued by France and
Great Britain; and the "Contre Declaration" of the French government, signed
at Versailles the same day, affirming
that it is not the intention of the king
of France to interpose by force in the
affairs of the United Netherlands, and
consenting to the proposition of Great
Britain to discontinue armaments. In
making the Tr of the "Contre Declara-

tion," Short erroneously put the signature of Dorset and Eden instead of that of Montmorin, who signed for the French government. Translations of both of the above documents are printed in *Dipl. Corr., 1783-89*, II, 107-8. TJ

sent another copy of the enclosures in TJ to Jay, 3 Nov. 1787, q.v.

1 This letter is recorded in SJL under 27 Oct. but has the following notation: "(shd have been 28)."

To André Limozin and Others

SIR   Paris Octob. 28. 1787

I have the honor to inform you that declarations on the part of France and England for the continuance of peace were signed last night at Versailles, of which be so good as to notify the citizens of the U.S. concerned in commerce at your port, for their future government.

I have the honor to be sir your most obedt. & most hble. Servt.,

TH: JEFFERSON

PrC (DLC); in the hand of William Short, signed by TJ; at foot of text in TJ's hand: "Limozin Loreilhe Cairnes Bondfeild Cathalan." Recorded in SJL under 28 Oct. as follows: "Agents. circular. notifying peace."

To Moustier

SIR   Paris Oct. 27. [i.e., 28] 1787.

The wind, which has so long detained you at Brest, continuing obstinately in the same point, admits a possibility that the present letter, may yet find you at Brest. It covers one to Mr. Jay announcing the signature of declarations at Versailles last night for the disarming, on the part of France and England: so that we may consider the peace as re-established for the present moment. These matters being doubtless communicated to you officially, I need not enter into details. I am to acknolege the receipt of your favor of the 19th. and of Madame de Brehan's of the 22d. and beg of you both to accept assurances of the sincere attachment and respect with which I have the honor to be her and your Most obedient & most humble servant,   TH: JEFFERSON

PrC (DLC). Recorded in SJL under 27 Oct. with a notation that the date should have been 28 Oct.   Enclosure: TJ to Jay, this date.

From Christopher Gadsden

DR. SIR   Charleston 29th. Octor. 1787

My Friend Mr. Izzard favor'd me with a Sight of Yours to him of the 18th Novr. and first of Augt. last together with Mr. De Calonne's and Les Srs. Jean Jaques Berard & Cie. Letters to you, the first dated 22d Octr. 1786 encouraging from authority the Opening and fixing a General Trade with the United States, the other proposing a Plan of Mutual Commerce between this place and France, particularly respecting Rice, which I have read with great pleasure and Attention, wishing it to be carried into Execution. From this Opening and the Honor I had to labor with you formerly in the political Vineyard, I take the Freedom to congratulate you on the noble Constitution agreed upon by our late Convention, and farther, on its seeming to give general Satisfaction, from whence tis hardly doubted it will be adopted; if so, and it is firmly and efficiently carried into Execution, a new and important Epocha must arise in our Affairs; The Apprehensions Strangers were under for some Time past, discouraging them from dealing with us so largely as many wish'd, will then diminish greatly and in a short Time cease altogether, as our Trade wou'd soon be on a safe, proper and respectable Footing, unsubjected in future to Frauds from Paper Tenders, and other too common unjustifyable Practices from unprincipled Debtors very prejudicial to their Creditors. Besides this Advantage a Diminution of that pernissious partiality to the British Trade will in my Opinion follow of Course. The Number of Foreigners that will from other than interested Mercantile Views frequent us, will soon tend to open the Eyes of our Countrymen thoroughly to their own Interest, and to see with astonishment to what a paltry Customer we have been so long and losingly attached, and that maugre all their Sophistry, that the Trade of France and Germany are of ten Times the Consequence to this State than theirs, and therefore ought by prudent Traders to have ten Times more attention. All the States may be said to be Shopkeepers, and what Folly for any, to give the Preference to that Nation that is of the least Importance to them, that consumes the smallest Quantity of their Produce, which with regard to our chief Staple Rice, is the Case of Gt. Britn. who tho' they have made Peace, are manifestly far from being cordial Friends with us. If France at this Crisis, continued her Encouragements, fix and support proper shifting Ports similar to that at Cowes attentively dispatching our Rice Ships, she will in no long Time, from the advantage of her being so almost infinitely a greater Consumer of that article than Gt. Bn., thin the Business to that Harbor, and in a few years dwindle it to nothing. But Attention and Patience in Commencement is every Thing. From what I have learn'd, the French Merchants we have had here, have been as impolitic in their method of introducing a Trade with us, as most of our People in trying the like with the new markets open'd to us since the Peace. We, besides the Infatuation of giving the British the Preference of our direct Consignments to their Island, have as stupidly, or more so, even in our few Essays to other markets suffer'd them to be conducted under their Auspices. Tis natural and commendable for all Powers to give a preference to their own Subjects, but on new Trials, of Trade especially, quaery whether the End wou'd not be sooner, more effectually and generally come at and fixed, by employing Men of the Place of establish'd Character and experience unsuspected of any improper Bias to the British Interest, well acquainted with the Nature and Quality of the Articles most suitable and wanted, for a few Years than for a new Adventurer, speaking a different Language to conduct it himself through the Medium of such an Interpreting Clerk as he can pick up, but this has been the method generally used here by the French Merchants and tis thought the Cause of many of the Losses and Disgusts they have experienced. Few People, ours particularly, like to close their Bargains but with the Principals; This City does not want for many Houses of this Character, mentioned among others Messrs. Brailsford & Morris are well establish'd here, both Natives of the united States the first of this City the other of Philada. Mr. Morris I am nearly connected with as having married my Daughter and shou'd be happy to be the Means of recommending that House to any unengaged Friends.

I make no doubt the Phylosophic part of Europe will admire the Constitution recommended by our Convention, the Trading part of Gt. Bn. perhaps, many of them, may be jealous of it consider'd in a commercial View in its probable Consequences to them by increasing the means of opening the Eyes of America and exposing many rooted prejudices to them particularly. I have little doubt* that part of the Island who so generally and pointedly hung upon our Skirts during the whole War will not be less busy on this Occasion. For my Part I bless God to have lived to see this important Point in so fair a Way to be accomplish'd, and if I live to see it compleatly so, I shall be apt to cry out with old Simeon: Now may thy Servant depart in Peace for mine Eyes have seen thy Salvation.

[296]

I beg your pardon, my dear Sir, and the Publics for trespassing so much on that Time which I am sure you wish to devote to the common Interest of the united States, and am with Sincere Esteem Yr. most Obedt. Hble. Servt., CHRIST. GADSDEN

* These subtil, dextrous, long-train'd, Systematical opponents well knowing the Constitution recommended must be approv'd of in toto, or not at all, therefore wou'd seem to approve of it as highly as any the most Zealous for it, only with an *All But*, which *But* alter'd wou'd gain they wou'd pretend universal Satisfaction, that it may be defer'd for that mighty reasonable *But* to another Convention hoping that will never happen and so the Bubble burst of Course.

RC (DLC); endorsed. Recorded in SJL Index, but not in SJL (see note to Rutledge to TJ, 23 Oct. 1787).

From John Trumbull

DR: SIR   London Octr. 30th. 1787

I have received your two letters of the 4th. by Mr. Cutting and the 11th. by post, and have made the enquiry you request with respect to the sailing of Capt. Dunn with your instruments. He certainly left this port at least four weeks ago, and I hope you will have news of his arrival at Rouen or Havre before this reaches you.

The Bill which you was so good as to enclose, was instantly honor'd.

There was no gaucherie in the commission to Mr. Brown. It is executed, and he promises to have the two pictures finished immediately.

I am told the Harmonica is never made to exceed three octaves. For one of that kind Longman & Brodsip ask me thirty guineas. I will enquire further on this subject.

We have just receiv'd account from America of the doings of the Convention. Mr. Cutting promises to inclose you by this post a paper containing the whole, least you should not have receiv'd them by any other opportunity.

I beg you to permit my Compliments to Mrs. Cosway and Mr. Short.

I am gratefully Your Friend & Servant,

JNO. TRUMBULL

RC (DLC); endorsed. Recorded in SJL as received 3 Nov. 1787.

[297]

From Wernecke

Phalsbourg, in Lorraine, 30 Oct. 1787. Knowing the importance of TJ's occupations, but also trusting in the kindness of TJ's heart, ventures to address him again on the affairs of his brother who died in Virginia in 1783; TJ's response of 19 Nov. 1786 to his former letter gave reassurance on this subject and he is confident that a just petition will meet with success; the only reason for the present inquiry is that his co-heirs never cease pressing him for news.

RC (MoSHi); 2 p.; in French; endorsed. Recorded in SJL as received 6 Dec. 1787.

From Brailsford & Morris

SIR   Charleston So. Carolina 31st October 1787.

Our friend Mr. E. Rutledge, having been so obliging as to indulge us with the perusal of your Letter addressed to him on the subject of our Produce, and at the same time enclosing the Proposals of Messrs. Berard & Co. declaring the terms on which they are enclined to encourage a preference of our Consignments: we cannot but feel ourselves sensibly indebted to your Excellency for your persevering exertions in our favour, and for your decided endeavors to enlarge our Trade, now circumscribed by British Policy, and Restrictions. Our being totally destitute of Manufactures, and the Staples of this State being very valuable, and considerable, both as to quantity, and quality, it is extraordinary that Great Britain alone, has made the necessary exertions to reap the benefits of our Commerce, and by a spirited exertion, endeavor to annihilate all opposition to her ambitous Views. A concurrence of Circumstances, tended to give a temporary success to her Plans. Old Prejudices in favor of English Goods, their marked superiority in many instances, the Wealth of her Merchants, and the multitude of their Agents that settled here on the peace, all united in strengthening her Interests. On the other Hand, the Calamities of the War, with the baneful effects of the Paper Depreciation, have been hard on those Commercial Houses who enjoyed the first reputations prior to the Revolution. Unable to cancel their Old Obligations, the European Trader cautiously avoided, the increasing the magnitude of their Debts, and refused those Credits which were essential to their wants so that our number is now nearly dwindled to a Cypher. To see the whole Wealth of our Country centering in the Hands of our decided Enemies; to see nine tenths of our Produce carried

[298]

out of our Ports by British Vessels, and in walking our Streets, whether convinced by the Dialect, or the Names of those who supply our wants, that we should rather conceive ourselves in the Highlands of Scotland, than in an American State, is the source of painful Reflection to every Citizen, who values the Happiness, or wishes to extend the Consequence, and Prosperity of his Country. It is unnecessary to inform your Excellency, that thro these States, the Shop:keeper is blended with the Merchant, and we are sorry to add, that these Scotch Agents, having a well established Credit in Britain, and their supplies being punctual, seasonable, and of the first quality, they successfully destroy every opposition, and confine to themselves the immense retail Business of the State.

It is wonderful, that since the Peace, we have never had a single French House, that commanded Respect, or that has been intitled to it. At this moment, there is none at all, and it would have been a happy Circumstance for France if there never had been one, as we have been only troubled with a set of needy Adventurers, without Fortune or Character, who by importing the refuse of the French Manufactures, have effectually strengthened our prejudices in favor of the British. There are a few Dutch, and Germans, who are honest, industrious, and enjoy a pretty good Credit, but they are limited in their resources, and are too phlegmatic for adventure. Thus Imports are from their own Country, and their Exports are invariably directed to the same quarter. Great Britain thus peculiarly situated, will no doubt leave no means unessayed to Continue, and confirm our Bondage, and it is certainly our Duty and Interest, to destroy it. We are rejoiced in saying, that we think your Excellency has opend the Door for accomplishing so desirable an event, for the British Merchant, being ready to make larger advances on Consignments than we have hitherto been able to obtain from those of any other Country, necessity has compelld us to accept their offers, and against our wishes, establish a preference in their favor. The Conditions tendered by Messrs. Berard & Co. are as liberal, as we would have them, and such is our respect for that House, in consequence of your Excellencys Recommendation of them, that we shall give them early, and decided Marks of our Confidence. The priviledge of drawing for 12£ to 15 Livres the Quintal, for such Parcels of Merchantable Rice, as we may ship from hence to their address, is rather more than sufficient, and more than we shall ever avail ourselves of, as Rice will generally be obtained at, or under 10/6 and provided our Paper Medium supports its Currency, we are of Opinion it will be the case the insuing Year. When Rice is not to be obtained under 12/ to 13/ ℔ Ct., we must either have short Crops, have an unusual demand for the West Indies, or purchase with a depreciated Currency, as otherwise no prudent Man would *willingly* speculate on it, Experience having shewn it an unprofitable adventure at these prices. During the present Year it has ruled from 13/6 to 16/ ℔ Ct. When at the first, we sold our Bills on London at 60 Days sight at a Premium of 20 ℔ Ct., but it no sooner rose to the latter price, than our Drafts were eagerly bought up at a Premium of 25 ℔ Ct.; hard Money then selling at a Premium of 22½ ℔ Ct., and with difficulty produced. Had Specie been the circulating Medium of the State, Rice would not have been higher than 10/6 to 11/ ℔ Ct., at which, with good Conduct, it might have been rendered a saving Remittance. Such Cargoes of Rice as are sent to Cowes and there sold for a Market are landed, sifted, and reshipped, and marked, at the expence of 1/ each Barrel which very moderate expence, is one very great inducement for sending our Vessels there. The charge for Light, &c. however in some measure make up for that reasonable compensation for so much trouble, but at the same time gives a necessary hint to the Merchants at L'Orient &c. &c. to be [as] limited in their Charges as possible; as otherwise, Cowes will maintain her superiority against all their exertions to rival her. Messrs. Berard & Co. notwithstanding their resources, are still very unequal to the supporting that proportion of our Trade, as may be directed to the French Coast, as we esteem it the best Market for our Tobacco, and nearly equal to any European Market for our Rice. It is generally supposed, that we have this Year made 100,000 Tunes of Rice of 550 ℔ Net, near 1,000,000 of Pounds of Indico, and several thousand Hogsheads of Tobacco, a very small part of which, would be more than sufficient to employ the funds of any House in Europe. Mr. Barrett, under the protection of Messrs. Le Couteulx & Co. of Paris, has made us a tender of his Services, and offered to accept Drafts for the half amount of Invoice, the remaining half to be paid on the arrival of the Vessel. These Conditions are inadmissible, as we will never draw without being certain of our Bills being honord, provided we confine ourselves within the limits agreed on, the distance between us rendering Communications too tedious for such a plan. We take the Liberty of enclosing your Excellency a Copy of our Letter to Mr. Barrett and an Extract of that We wrote to Messrs. Berard & Co. and that you may entertain a just Idea of the wretched situation of our Commerce, we transmit you a correct List of all Vessels that cleared out at our Custom House for the European Markets, from 20 November 1786 to the 12 June 1787, being the period in which the principal part of our Crop is shipped. This List declares in a few words the melancholy State of our Trade, and the happy effects of good Policy, and wholsome navigation Laws.

Very numerous are the Produce and Manufactures of France, that are suited to our Climate, and Wants, and we have no doubt, that with proper exertions on the part of the French Ministry, supported by a few of their Merchants of Opulence and Influence, that the Intercourse between the two Countries will soon become extensive, and mutually beneficial. Her Brandies, Wines, Fruits, Silks, Linens, Oil, Soap, and a multitude of other Articles, are lucrative returns for our Produce, and we are well convinced, that once the Communication is rendered frequent, that a multitude of objects would present themselves, of which, we have now no Idea, that would relieve our wants, and add to our Comfort. To any way, and in the smallest degree contribute to the effecting so happy a revolution, would be the height of our Pride and Ambition, and if there are any informations your Excellency may wish, and in our power to give, we beg that you will freely dispose of us. Our situation here is perfectly independent, free from the Clog of any Home, or Foreign Debt, and commanding resources that enable us to give every facility to our Commercial Operations. Relying on the Strength of our present Introductions and on your Excellencys anxiety to advance the Interest of our State, and of the Union in general, we take the Liberty of requesting your favorable mention of our firm where it can be useful in advancing the Interests of both Countries. We can only assure you, that we shall endeavor to support, and not disgrace your Recommendation. We have every reason to hope, that the Foederal System recommended by the Convention, will be acknowledged here, and adopted by our Sister States. Our Commerce will then experience the fruits of Order, and Energy, and those Nations, who now view us with Contempt, who ridicule our Folly and Disunion, and who are enriching themselves on our Spoils, will gladly court our rising Consequence and be happy in granting us liberal terms for the benefits we allow them from the participation of our Trade. We are with sincere Respect, Your Excellencys Most Obdt. Servants,

BRAILSFORD & MORRIS

RC (DLC); endorsed. Enclosures (DLC): (1) Tr of a letter from Brailsford & Morris to Nathaniel Barrett, Oct. 1787, acknowledging receipt through Rutledge of Barrett's proposals and the information that he had established himself at Honfleur, now a free port, and stating that its "situation is no doubt unexceptionable, and with proper encouragement may be rendered a successful Rival to Cowes"; that "Our Pride is every Day hurt at seeing our trade so fettered by British Policy, but till France shews equal wisdom, and her Merchants a generous and well regulated confidence, it will be difficult to divert our Commerce out of its present Channels"; that France is "indisputably a much better Market for our Rice, and Tobacco, than England, notwithstanding which, where France receives a 100 Barrels, England receives a 1000"; that "Two causes produce these strange effects, the first of which is, the heavy Debt due by this Country to Great Britain, and the greater part of our Shopkeepers being her Natives and Citizens, and the second, the more liberal advances, the British Merchant allows over the French in Consignements"; that Barrett's proposals "are every way inadmissible, for we should evince a strange infatuation, to consign our Property to any House, who only allows us to draw for 50 per Cent of the first cost, when our Friends in England, and several Ports of France permit us to value on them at 60 Days sight for the full amount of Invoice, or such proportion as we may think proper"; that they are fully satisfied with the responsibility of the house of Le Couteulx, since they had been for some time in correspondence with their firm at Cadiz and had also lately written them "concerning a Vessel we intend to address them at Rouen"; that they do not know whether on this occasion they will draw on Le Couteulx "for a shilling" or direct them to remit, "but as Circumstances are not always the same," they cannot always adopt the same conduct; that "Thro' the medium of Mr. Jefferson, who has transmitted here, some liberal offers from a respectable House at L'Orient, and which tended to confirm our Confidence in it, we shall direct some of our Vessels there the ensuing Winter, but without availing ourselves of the extension of limits"; that they would never consider subjecting themselves to one clause of his proposals—

that permitting them to draw for half of the original cost "upon inclosing Invoice Bills of Lading, and Orders for Insurance"—since the correspondent ought to have the privilege of drawing on transmittal of orders for insurance, for if it were necessary for invoice and bills of lading to be first in possession of the consignee, "by a concatination of circumstances, our Bill might appear first, and our signature be disgraced, an injury we would not submit to on any consideration whatever"; that they believe the "Trade of this Country, is well worth the attention of every European Power, as we are entirely destitute of Manufactures, and our produce will be this year full 100,000 Tierces Rice, near 1,000,000 ℔s. of Indigo, and some Thousand Hogsheads of Tobacco, independent of skins, Wax, &c."; that Rutledge "can give . . . every necessary intelligence" concerning themselves which they believe "Mr. Jefferson and the Marquis de la Fayette will be pleased to confirm"; that "We are anxious to emancipate our Country from those restraints imposed on her by the Policy of England, to expand her Commerce, and destroy every prejudice which now fetters and restrains her Operations"; and that they are engaged "entirely in the Whole-Sale on Commission, importing no Goods on our own Account, but confining our attention solely to the Interest of our Friends." (2) Tr of an extract of a letter from Brailsford & Morris to J. J. Bérard & Cie., Oct. 1787, stating that they had previously had from "Mr. Fitzsimons of Philadelphia" information of the "punctuality and solidity" of their house, which "prepossessions have since been confirmed, and increased by the recommendation of his Excellency Mr. Jefferson; that they had found the proposals of Messrs. Bérard, transmitted through TJ, liberal; that they were prepared, "without any farther and preparatory agreement between us, relying implicitly on your faithful adherance to the conditions you transmitted to our Ambassador," to ship "during the course of the shipping Season . . . one or more cargoes" of rice and tobacco; that they are "entirely in the Commission Line, importing no European Goods on our own Account but disposing of such Consignments as our European Friends are pleased to make us, we remitting for the Nett proceeds either by Bills, or Produce, as we think most for their advantage"; that this "plan of Business occasions our being large Exporters, and enables us to throw considerable Shipments into the Hands of our Correspondents"; that "the resources of France, her Manufactures, and Productions are but very partially known in this Country, and time can alone make us better acquainted with them"; that "Those prejudices respecting British Goods, which we imbibed with our Milk, are not easily eradicated, and will require continued and increasing attention, on your part, to destroy them on ours"; that hitherto it had been "your Misfortune, that none but the refuse of your Manufactures, the sweeping of your Shops, have been imported here, which has confirmed those mistaken opinions, that are generally entertained of your Fabricks"; that the British "pursue an opposite line of Conduct, sending out fresh Goods and of the first quality"; that "As we have successfully broken those fetters they [the British] had prepared for our Persons, we are very desirous of giving equal liberty to our Minds; to destroy every prejudice towards them, and instead of having our Commerce shackled by their Policy, to have it free of every restraint, and see it extend itself to every friendly power"; and that "Respecting our situation here, we refer you to Mr. Jefferson,

the Marquis de la Fayette, and Mr. Fitzsimons, to whom we have done ourselves the honor of writing by the present conveyance." (3) "A List of Exports from Charleston So. Carolina to Europe from the 20th. November 1786 to the 12th June 1787," giving the date of shipment, name of vessel, master's name, destination by country, and kind and quantity of articles shipped on each vessel—total shipments for the period amounting to 35,090 barrels and 4,395 half-barrels of rice; 2,609 hogsheads of tobacco; 2,232 casks of indigo; 136 hogsheads and 180 bales of skins; 1,814 barrels of turpentine; 710 barrels of tar; 1,028 barrels of pitch; 2,000 feet of lumber; 474,300 staves; and small quantities of miscellaneous items, including rosin, beeswax, horns, logwood, reeds, cedar, snakeroot, &c. (cf. with list of exports for 1782-1783, Vol. 8: 202-4). (4) Edward Rutledge to TJ, 23 Oct. 1787. (5) John Rutledge to TJ, 24 Oct. 1787. (The two last are mentioned as enclosures in Brailsford & Morris to TJ, 10 Jan. 1788; a third, Ralph Izard to TJ, 20 Oct. 1787, is also mentioned as having been enclosed, but evidently it was not, since the others arrived with Bérard's letter of 17 Feb. 1788 and Rutledge's arrived on 24 Apr. 1788.)

From David Bushnell

SIR Stamford, in Connecticut Octr. th.¹ 1787

In the latter part of the year, one thousand seven hundred and eighty five, I received a letter from Colonel David Humphreys, and soon after, another from Doctor Ezra Stiles, President of Yale College, in Connecticut, informing me, that your Excellency desired an account of my submarine vessel, and the experiments which I had made.

At the time I received those letters, I was seized with a severe illness, which disabled me from writing, and though I attempted it several times, obliged me to desist. Eversince I recovered my health, my situation has been such, that until this time, it has not been in my power to write to your Excellency, upon the subject.

I shall think myself happy if this, arriving, thus late, meets with your Excellency's acceptance, and give you the information you desired; and shall only regret, that I had it not in my power to write, as soon as I received the communications of those gentlemen.

Doctor Stiles in his letter to me transcribed from yours the following, "If he thought proper to communicate it, I would engage never to disclose it, unless I could find an opportunity of doing it for his benefit." In answer to this declaration, I shall submit the disclosure of it entirely to your Excellency, to do as you shall think proper, and beg leave to return you my sincere thanks for your generous intentions.

I have ever carefully concealed my principles and experiments, as much as the nature of the subject allowed, from all but my chosen friends, being persuaded that it was the most prudent course, whether the event should prove fortunate or otherwise, although by the concealment, I never fostered any great expectations of profit, or even of a compensation for my time and expenses, the loss of which has been exceedingly detrimental to me.

With this, your Excellency will receive a sketch of the general principles and construction of the submarine vessel, blended together, as they occur at this time, with many of the minutiæ. I should gladly exhibit every thing with the utmost minuteness; but apprehend I have not been sufficiently clear in what I have written, and have a doubt whether I could explain the whole intelligibly, without drawings, which I cannot easily execute or obtain. But should this not be sufficient, and you should wish to have a more minute description of the whole, or of any particular part not sufficiently explained here, I shall be happy to receive your Excellency's commands, and shall obey them, as soon as they come to hand, without any reserve.

As I am desirous this should not fall into improper hands, I could wish, if it were not too great a favour, to hear that this finds a safe conveyance to your Excellency.

In the mean time, with the most respectful sentiments, I am Your Excellency's Most Obedt. & most Hble Servt.,

D. BUSHNELL

P.S. Should your Excellency think proper to inform me of the safe arrival of this packet, I could wish such information might be directed to the care of Doctor Stiles.

RC (DLC); at foot of text Bushnell wrote: "His Excellency Thomas Jefferson Esquire," immediately after which TJ added: "M.P. of the US. at Paris," as if in correction, though he did not delete "Esquire." Recorded in SJL In-dex but not in SJL (see note to Rutledge to TJ, 23 Oct. 1787). Enclosure missing, but see below.

On TJ's inquiries concerning Bushnell's invention, see TJ to Hugh Williamson, 6 Feb. 1785; TJ to Washington, 17 July 1785; TJ to Stiles, 17 July 1785; and Washington to TJ, 26 Sep. 1785. The enclosed SKETCH OF . . . GENERAL PRINCIPLES AND CONSTRUCTION was published later in the *Transactions* of the American Philosophical Society, O.S., IV (1799), 303-13, under Bushnell's name.

[1] Date blank in MS.

From Salmour

[*Paris, Oct. 1787?*] Informs TJ that he has had his audience at Fontainebleau with the king and the royal family "en qualité de Ministre Plenipotentiaire de Son Altesse Serenissime Electorale de Saxe."

RC (DLC); 2 p.; in French; addressed; without date and not recorded in SJL. Salmour is listed for the first time in the *Almanach Royal* for 1788 as the minister from Saxony. He was, therefore, probably presented officially sometime during the autumn court at Fontainebleau.

From André Thouin

[*Paris, 1 Nov. 1787.* Recorded in SJL as received 3 Nov. 1787. Not found.]

From André Limozin

MOST HONORED SIR   Havre de Grace 2nd November 1787

I have received the Letter your Excellency hath honored me with the 28th ulto. which confirmed me the agreable news we had received here the 29th by an Express Sent by Court that all difficulties with Great Brittain were Settled. I have given hint of your Excellency's Letter to all the American Masters now in our Harbor.

I have been at great troubles about the Six American Sailors on board the Elephant. I have already lay'd out very near 300 Lyvers for the expences of the Law: and God only Knows when I shall be free from any more troubles relating that affair and when I shall see my money back, which does not puzzle me so much as the time I am obliged to loose to go to the Lawyers and to be at the Court every Courts day.

I have the Honor to be with the highest regard your Excellency's Most obedient & very Humble Servant,

ANDRE LIMOZIN

RC (MHi); endorsed. Recorded in SJL as received 4 Nov. 1787.

[305]

From Moustier

à Brest le 2. 9bre. 1787.

Vous avez très bien jugé, Monsieur, l'effet du vent qui me retient ici. Je suis dedomagé du delai que j'eprouve par la nouvelle que j'ai reçue. On ne me l'a point donnée directement et je ne l'ai sue que par le Commandant de la Marine qui a reçu avant hier ses ordres par un Courier. Je regarde comme un bien de s'assurer de la paix pour le moment, pourvû que l'on n'y compte pas trop. La secousse nous aura fait du bien et je suis à peu près sur que nous ne nous endormirons pas. Au reste à en juger par l'activité dont j'ai été temoin je doute que les Anglois eûssent eû l'avantage sur nous au printems. Le port est bien garni et la rade commençoit à l'etre. J'ai vû de mes yeux doubler 7. vaisseaux de ligne et quelques fregattes en cuivre, sans compter tous ceux qui l'etoient dejà. La célérité avec laquelle on fait des armemens ici, est surprenante. Nous avons aussi un grand avantage pour nous procurer des matelots qui etoient dejà ici en grand nombre lequel alloit augmenter chaque jour. Je crois, Monsieur, ces details satisfaisans pour les veritables amis de la France et c'est à ce titre que je vous les communique.

J'aurois bien desiré un mot dans votre lettre sur la decision de notre Cour relative au Commerce entre les deux Nations. Comme l'on me supose parti, je reste sans informations officielles. J'ai reçu par une autre voie le raport qui a dû etre fait sur cet objet avec toutes les pieces qui en forment la baze. Je me suis beaucoup occupé ici de recherches sur les bois de l'Amerique Septentrionale propres à la construction des Vaisseaux. Il y a eû la dessus des essais defavorables et l'exemple le plus frapant a été l'*America* qui est tombé en poussiere au point qu'il n'en est pas resté un morceau de bois sain. Cependant pour conserver le souvenir de la bonne volonté qu'ont eue les Americains-unis en le donnant au Roi, on construit actuellement un vaisseau neuf qui sera lancé dans peu de mois et portera le même nom. Si dans la realité le territoire des Etats Unis produit des bois de construction et autres munitions navales propres à notre marine militaire, il me paroit qu'il conviendroit pour leur reputation et par consequent pour les interets generaux que le Congrès fit l'entreprise de faire parvenir ici un assortiment bien fait de toutes les munitions navales qui pourroient y etre employées et devenir par la suite un grand objet de commerce fondé sur l'Agriculture et une navigation etendue. Si cette idée vous paroit utile vous pourrez, Monsieur, contribuer infiniment à son exécution en la presentant sous le jour qui vous paroitra le plus favorable. Je partirai muni de reponses à une infinité de questions et d'observations que j'ai faites à ce sujet.

Mde. de Brehan me charge de la rapeller à votre Souvenir. Elle est bien contrariée du retard qu'Elle eprouve. Je crains fort que nous n'ayons une navigation fort desagreable. Si j'etois seul, je n'y verrois que demi-mal.

J'ai l'honneur d'etre avec un très sincere et parfait attachement, Monsieur, Votre très humble et très obeissant Serviteur,

Le Cte. de Moustier

Votre lettre que j'ai reçue aujourdhui pour Mr. Jay a été jointe aux autres et je l'ai apostillée sur l'envelope *reçue le 2. 9bre.*

RC (DLC); endorsed. Recorded in SJL as received 6 Nov. 1787.

To John Sullivan

Sir   Paris Nov. 2. 1787.

In the letter which I had the honour of writing to your Excellency on the 5th. of October, I inclosed one from Vautelet by which you would see he did not intend to pay his son's bill. I now inclose you the bill regularly protested.

A pacification between France and England has taken place, by which the affairs of Holland are to remain as they are, the Stadtholder being restored. This country hopes to enjoy such a length of peace as may enable it to arrange it's finances. Some small affairs only have as yet taken place between the Russians and Turks. The preparations for war making by the Emperor give expectations that he has some great stroke in contemplation.

I have the honour to be with sentiments of the most perfect esteem & respect Your Excellency's most obedient & most humble servt,   Th: Jefferson

PrC (DLC). Enclosure not found.

From John Trumbull

London, 2 Nov. 1787. Sends letter by his friend [Daniel] Parker, whom he recommends to TJ; reports that the ship *James* left port the beginning of October; that he has executed his commission for TJ with Brown "respecting Mr. Payne's picture"; that the bill brought by Cutting was honored immediately; that his reward for his troubles in

[307]

connection with the shipment of the harpsichord will be rewarded "by hearing Miss Jefferson play a single lesson upon it"; that the harmonica is not made beyond three octaves and costs 30 guineas; and that he does not send a copy of the new constitution for the United States, "a work worthy the convention who fram'd it," because he has been assured that TJ will already have received a copy. "It remains for us to pray for its adoption by the several States; of which, at least so far as nine, I think there is little doubt."

RC (DLC); 2 p.; endorsed. Recorded in SJL as received 9 Nov. 1787.

To Mary Barclay

DEAR MADAM   Paris Nov. 3. 1787.

An intention which I have had for three weeks past to come and dine with Madame Bellanger at St. Germain's, and at the same time do myself the pleasure of seeing you, has prevented my writing to you. But the weather has hitherto obstinately defeated my purpose. I shall delay no longer therefore to beg of you to draw on me for the balance I mentioned to you whenever you have occasion. Your draught shall always be honoured on sight. Besides this I wish you to be assured that in every case of disappointment in receiving remittances, or other circumstance whatever, it will give me real pleasure to accomodate you with any sums you may have occasion for, and to render you every other service in my power. I beg of you therefore, Madam, to make use of me freely on every occasion which may arise, to count with confidence on every aid I can render you, and to assure yourself it will give me pleasure to have opportunities of being useful to you. I have the honour to be with very sincere esteem & respect, Dear Madam Your most obedient & most humble servt,

TH: JEFFERSON

PrC (MHi). Not recorded in SJL.

From Madame de Bréhan

Brest 3 9bre 1787.

I have read with great pleasure, Sir, the book that you have been so good as to lend to me. I take the first opportunity to send it back to you with many thanks, by the Vicount de Beaumont just return'd from North America. We are here without hope that the winds are disposed to change. I begin to lose all patience; it is a great contrariety to be so detain'd in this tedious town, when we should possibly be almost arrived at New-York. I wish ardently to see a Country of wich I have a so good an opinion as also of the inhabitants. Will you receive again, Sir, the new assurances of my true affection, and be so good as to make mention of me to Mr Short?

The 3. My Brother sends to you his bests compliments. Farewell, Sir, the winds come good and we set sail to morrow morning. Think at Friends who are very attach'd to you.

RC (MHi); endorsed. Not recorded in SJL; an entry in SJL Index for a letter from Mme. de Bréhan of 9 Nov. 1787 is, doubtless, an erroneous reference to this letter.

To John Jay

SIR   Paris Nov. 3. 1787.

My last letters to you were of the 8th. and 27th. of October. In the former I mentioned to you the declaration of this country that they would interpose with force if the Prussian troops entered Holland, the entry of those troops into Holland, the declaration of England that if France did oppose force they would consider it as an act of war, the naval armaments on both sides, nomination of the Bailli de Suffrein as generalissime on the Ocean, and the cold reception of Mr. Grenville here with his conciliatory propositions, as so many symptoms which seemed to indicate a certain and immediate rupture. It was indeed universally and hourly expected. But the King of Prussia, a little before these last events, got wind of the alliance on the carpet between France and the two empires: he awaked to the situation in which that would place him: he made some applications to the court of St. Petersburgh to divert the empress from the proposed alliance, and supplicated the court of London not to abandon him. That court had also received a hint of the same project; both seemed to suspect, for the first time, that it would be possible for France to abandon the Turks, and that they were likely to get more than they had plaid for at Constantinople: for they had meant nothing more there than to divert the Empress and Emperor from the affairs of the West by employing them in the East, and at the same time to embroil them with France as the patroness of the Turks. The court of London engaged not to abandon Prussia: but both of them relaxed a little the tone of their proceedings. The King of Prussia sent a

Mr. Alvensleben here expressly to explain and soothe: the K. of England, notwithstanding the cold reception of his propositions by Grenville, renewed conferences here through Eden and the Duke of Dorset. The Minister, in the affection of his heart for peace, readily joined in conference, and a declaration and counterdeclaration were cooked up at Versailles, and sent to London for approbation. They were approved, arrived here at 1. o'clock the 27th. were signed that night at Versailles, and on the next day I had the honor of inclosing them to you, under cover to the count de Moustier, whom I supposed still at Brest, dating my letter as of the 27th. by mistake for the 28th. Lest however these papers should not have got to Brest before the departure of the count de Moustier, I now inclose you other copies. The English declaration states a notification of this court in September by Barthelemy their minister at London, 'that they would send succours into Holland,' as the first cause of England's arming; desires an explanation of the intentions of this court as to the affairs of Holland, and proposes to disarm; on condition however that the king of France shall not retain any hostile views in any quarter for what has been done in Holland. This last phrase was to secure Prussia, according to promise. The King of France acknoleges the notification by his minister at London, promises he will do nothing in consequence of it, declares he has no intention to intermeddle with force in the affairs of Holland, and that he will entertain hostile views in no quarter for what has been done there. He disavows having ever had any intention to interpose with force in the affairs of that republic. This disavowal begins the sentence which acknoleges he had notified the contrary to the court of London, and it includes no apology to soothe the feelings which may be excited in the breasts of the patriots of Holland at hearing the king declare he never did intend to aid them with force, when promises to do this were the basis of those very attempts to better their constitution, which have ended in it's ruin as well as their own. I have analysed these declarations because, being somewhat wrapped up in their expressions, their full import might escape, on a transient reading; and it is necessary it should not escape. It conveys to us the important lesson, that no circumstances of morality, honour, interest, or engagement are sufficient to authorize a secure reliance on any nation, at all times, and in all positions. A moment of difficulty, or a moment of error, may render for ever useless the most friendly dispositions in the king, in the major part of his ministers, and the whole of his nation.   The present pacification is considered by most as only a short truce. They calculate on the spirit of the nation, and not on the agued hand which guides it's movements. It is certain that from this moment the whole system of Europe changes. Instead of counting together England, Austria, and Russia, as heretofore, against France, Spain, Holland, Prussia and Turkey, the division will probably be England, Holland, and Prussia, against France, Austria, Russia and perhaps Spain. This last power is not sure, because the dispositions of it's heir apparent are not sure. But whether the present be truce or peace, it will allow time to mature the conditions of the alliance between France and the two empires, always supposed to be on the carpet. It is thought to be obstructed by the avidity of the emperor who would swallow a good part of Turkey, Silesia, Bavaria, and the rights of the Germanic body. To the two or three first articles France might consent, receiving in gratification a well rounded portion of the Austrian Netherlands, with the islands of Candia, Cyprus, Rhodes, and perhaps lower Egypt. But all this is in embryo, incertainly known, and counterworked by the machinations of the courts of London and Berlin.

The following solution of the British armaments is supposed in a letter of the 25th. Ult. from Colo. Blackden of Connecticut now at Dunkirk to the Marquis de la Fayette. I will cite it in his own words. 'A gentleman who left London two days ago, and came to this place today informs me that it is now generally supposed that Mr. Pitt's great secret, which has puzzled the whole nation so long, and to accomplish which design the whole force of the nation is armed, is to make a vigorous effort for the recovery of America. When I recollect the delay they have made in delivering the forts in America, and that little more than a year ago one of the British ministry wrote to the king a letter in which were these remarkeable words "if your Majesty pleases America may yet be yours" add to this, if it were possible for the present ministry in England to effect such a matter, they would secure their places and their power for a long time, and should they fail in the end, they would be certain of holding them during the attempt, which it is in their power to prolong as much as they please, and at all events they would boast of having endeavored the recovery of what a former ministry had abandoned, it is possible.' A similar surmise has come in a letter from a person in Rotterdam to one at this place. I am satisfied that the king of England beleives the mass of our people to be tired of their independance, and desirous of returning under his government: and that the same opinion prevails in the ministry and nation. They have hired their news-writers to repeat this lie in their gazettes so long that they have become the dupes of it themselves. But there is no occasion to recur to this in order to account for their arming. A more rational purpose avowed, that purpose executed, and, when executed, a solemn agreement to disarm, seem to leave no doubt that the re-establishment of the Stadtholder was their object. Yet it is possible that, having found that this court will not make war in this moment for any ally, new views may arise, and they may think the moment favorable for executing any purposes they may have in our quarter. Add to this that reason is of no aid in calculating their movements. We are therefore never safe till our magazines are filled with arms. The present season of truce or peace should in my opinion be improved without a moment's respite to effect this essential object, and no means be omitted by which money may be obtained for the purpose. I say this however with due deference to the opinion of Congress, who are better judges of the necessity and practicability of the measure.

I mentioned to you in a former letter the application I had made to the Dutch Ambassadors and Prussian envoy for the protection of Mr. Dumas. The latter soon after received an assurance that he was put under the protection of the states of Holland: and the Dutch Ambassador called on me a few days ago to inform me by instruction from his constituents 'that the States General had received a written application from Mr. Adams, praying their protection of Dumas: that they had instructed their greffier Fagel to assure Mr. Adams by letter that he was under the protection of the states of Holland, but to inform him at the same time that Mr. Dumas's conduct, out of the line of his office, had been so extraordinary, that they would expect de l'honnetete de M. Adams, that he would charge some other person with the affairs of the United states, during his absence.'

Your letter of Sep. 8. has been duly received. I shall pay due attention to the instructions relative to the medals, and give any aid I can in the case of Ross's vessel. As yet however my endeavors to find Monsieur Pauly, avocat au conseil d'etat, rue Coquilliere, have been ineffectual. There is no such person living in that street. I found a M. Pauly, avocat au parlement, in another part of the town: he opened the letter, but said it could not mean him. I shall advertize in the public papers. If that fails, there will be no other chance of finding him. Mr. Warnum will do well therefore to send some other description by which the person may be found. Indeed some friend of the party interested should be engaged to follow up this business, as it will require a constant attention, and probably a much larger sum of money than that named in the bill inclosed in Mr. Warnum's letter.

I have the honour to inclose you a letter from Obrian to me containing information from Algiers, and one from Mr. Montgomery at Alicant. The purpose of sending you this last is to shew you how much the difficulties of ransom are increased since the Spanish negotiations. The Russian captives have cost about 8000 livres a peice on an average. I certainly have no idea that we should give any such sum: and therefore if it would be the sense of Congress to give such a price, I would be glad to know it by instruction. My idea is that we should not ransom but on the footing of the nation which pays least, that it may be as little worth their while to go in pursuit of us as any nation. This is cruelty to the individuals now in captivity, but kindness to the hundreds that would soon be so, were we to make it worth the while of those pyrates to go out of the streights in quest of us. As soon as money is provided I shall put this business into train. I have taken measures to damp at Algiers all expectations of our proposing to ransom at any price. I feel the distress which this must occasion to our countrymen there, and their connections: but the object of it is their ultimate good, by bringing down their holders to such a price as we ought to pay: instead of letting them remain in such expectations as cannot be gratified. The gazettes of France and Leyden accompany this. I have the honour to be, with sentiments of the most

PrC (DLC); lacks complimentary close which, in RC, was carried over to a new page. Enclosures: (1) Copies of the British declaration and the French counter-declaration of 27 Oct. 1787, copies of which were also enclosed in TJ to Jay, 27 Oct., q.v. (2) Copy of O'Bryen to TJ, 25 Sep. 1787. (3) Copy of Montgomery to TJ, 15 Oct. 1787.

For a note on THE APPLICATION . . . MADE TO THE DUTCH AMBASSADORS, see Dumas to TJ, 26 Oct. 1787. There is also in DLC: TJ Papers, 232: 42030 a rough outline of some of the topics covered by the present letter and also the private letter to Jay of this date (following), including such headings as

  "Obrien's lre
  Montgomery's lre

Ross' vessel
Medals
Chevr Luzerne
Arret &c
Agents"
and also including the following, evidently an extract of a letter to the PRUSSIAN ENVOY in response to TJ's APPLICATION . . . FOR THE PROTECTION OF MR. DUMAS: "Vous m'avez parlé dernierement de l'interet que Monsieur Jefferson prenoit à Monsieur Dumas, et des inquietudes que ce ministre avoit à son sujet. Vous pouvez le rassurer parfaitement et lui dire que M. Dumas ayant presenté une Note à Monsr. le Greffier Fagel, sur sa situation, les EE. G. G. ont recommandé aux EE. d'Hollande de le proteger et de le mettre à l'abri de toute inquietude."

To John Jay

SIR   Paris Nov. 3. 1787. Private.

I shall take the liberty of confiding sometimes to a private letter such details of the small history of the court or cabinet as may be worthy of being known, and yet not proper to be publicly communicated. I doubt whether the administration is yet in a permanent form. The Count de Monmorin and Baron de Breteuil are I believe firm enough in their places. It was doubted whether they would wait for the count de la Luzerne, if the war had taken place; but at present I suppose they will. I wish it also; because M. de Hector, his only competitor, has on some occasions shewn little value for the connection with us. Lambert, the Comptroller general is thought to be very insecure. I should be sorry also to lose him. I have worked several days with him, the M. de la Fayette, and Monsr. duPont (father of the young gentleman gone to America with the Count de Moustier) to reduce into one arret whatever concerned our commerce. I have found him a man of great judgment and application, possessing good general principles on subjects of commerce, and friendly dispositions towards us. He passed the arret in a very favorable form, but it has been opposed in the council, and will I fear suffer some alteration in the article of whale oil. That of tobacco, which was put into a separate instrument, experiences difficulties also, which do not come from him. Mr. duPont has rendered us essential services on these occasions. I wish his son could be so well noticed as to make a favorable report to his father; he would I think be gratified by it, and his good dispositions be strengthened, and rendered further useful to us. Whether I shall be able to send you these regulations by the present packet, will depend on their getting thro' the council, in time. The Archbishop continues well with his patroness. Her object is a close connection with her brother. I suppose he[1] convinces her that peace will furnish the best occasions of cementing that connection. It may not be uninstructive to give you the origin and nature of his influence with the queen.—When the D. de Choiseul proposed the marriage of the dauphin with this lady, he thought it proper to send a person to Vienna to perfect her in the language. He asked his friend the Archbishop of Toulouse to recommend to him a proper person. He recommended a certain Abbé. The Abbé, from his first arrival at Vienna, either tutored by his patron, or prompted by gratitude, impressed on the queen's mind the exalted talents and merit of the Archbishop, and continually represented him as the only man fit to be placed at the helm of affairs. On his return to Paris, being retained near the person of the queen, he kept him constantly in her view. The Archbishop was named of the assembly des notables, had occasion enough there to prove his talents, and, count de Vergennes his great enemy, dying opportunely, the Queen got him into place. He uses the Abbé even yet, for instilling all his notions into her mind. That he has imposing talents, and patriotic dispositions I think is certain. Good judges think him a theorist only, little acquainted with the details of business, and spoiling all his plans by a bungled execution. He may perhaps undergo a severe trial. His best actions are exciting against him a host of enemies, particularly the reduction of the pensions and reforms in other branches of oeconomy. Some think the other ministers are willing he should stay in till he has effected this odious, yet necessary work, and that they will then make him the scape-goat of the transaction. The declarations too which I send you in my public letter, if they should become public, will probably raise an universal cry. It will all fall on him, because Monmorin and Breteuil say, without reserve, that the sacrifice of the Dutch has been against their advice. He[2] will perhaps not permit these declarations to appear in this country. They are absolutely unknown, they were communicated to me by the D. of Dorset, and I believe no other copy has been given here.[3] They will be published, doubtless, in England, as a proof of their triumph, and may from thence make their way into this country. If the premier can stem a few months, he may remain long in office and will never make war if he can help it. If he should be removed, the peace will probably be short. He is solely chargeable with the loss of Holland. True they could not have raised money by taxes to supply the necessities of war; but could they do it were their finances ever so well arranged? No nation makes war now-a-days but by the aid of loans: and it is probable that in a war for the liberties of Holland, all the treasures of that country would have been at their service. They have now lost the cow which furnishes the milk of war. She will be on the side of their enemies, whenever a rupture shall take place: and no arrangement of their finances can countervail this circumstance.

I have no doubt, you permit access to the letters of your foreign ministers by persons only of the most perfect trust. It is in the European system to bribe the clerks high in order to obtain copies of interesting papers.—I am sure you are equally attentive to the conveyance of your letters to us, as you know that all are opened that pass thro' any post office of Europe. Your letters which come by the packet, if put into the mail at New York, or into the post office at Havre, wear[4] proofs that they have been opened. The passenger to whom they are confided should be cautioned always to keep them in his own hands till he can deliver them personally in Paris.

I have the honour to be with very sincere esteem & respect, Dear Sir, your most obedient & most humble servant,

TH: JEFFERSON

RC (NK-Iselin); endorsed. PrC (DLC).

The Duke of DORSET gave TJ the secret declarations perhaps for the specific purpose of suggesting to him the "important lesson" that TJ had drawn from the conduct of France and set forth in his public letter of this date—that is, that "no circumstances of morality, honour, interest, or engagement are sufficient to authorize a secure reliance on any nation, at all times, and in all positions." It is to be noted that Lord Carmarthen in London also presented copies of the declaration and counter-declaration to John Adams on 30 Oct. 1787 (*Dipl. Corr., 1783-1789*, II, 817). TJ's putting in the present PRIVATE communication much public information of high importance; his pointed reference to European habits of bribing clerks; his remarks about use of the post office by intelligence agencies; and his expression of confidence in Jay's treatment of letters from foreign ministers—these could scarcely conceal the unexpressed fear that the real danger lay in a possible communication by Jay to Congress. The publication of TJ's

dispatch of 27 May 1786 after Jay had sent it to Congress and also to the governors of the states had made him exceedingly sensitive to the danger of publication and the consequent handicap placed upon him as an effective minister. This experience must in turn have affected the manner in which he made diplomatic reports to Jay, as in the present instance (see notes to TJ to Jay, 27 May 1786). This letter was not PUBLICLY COMMUNICATED to Congress when Jay transmitted three letters from TJ early in 1788, one of them being dated 3 Nov. 1787 but referring to the "public" letter of this date (JCC, XXXIV, 29).

[1] This word interlined in substitution for "the Principal Minister," deleted.
[2] This word substituted for "they," deleted.
[3] This passage originally read: ". . . and I believe to no other member of the diplomatic corps," and then was changed by deletion and interlining to read as above.
[4] This word substituted for "bring," deleted.

From John Jay

DR. SIR   Office for foreign Affairs 3d. November 1787

Since the Date of my last which was the 24th. Ult., Congress has been pleased to pass an Act of which the enclosed is a Copy. It contains Instructions to you relative to the Demands of the United States against the Court of Denmark. As they are express and particular, Remarks upon them would be unnecessary. I am persuaded that the Manner in which the Business will be conducted and concluded, will evince the Propriety of its being committed to your Direction.

[316]

Advices from Georgia represent that State as much distressed by the Indians. It is said that the Apprehensions of the People there are so greatly alarmed that they are even fortifying Savannah. There doubtless is Reason to fear that their frontier Settlements will be ravaged. The Indians are numerous and they are exasperated,[1] and will probably be put to no Difficulties on Account of military Stores. These Embarrassments result from want of a proper Government, to guard good Faith and punish Violations of it.

With very sincere Esteem and Regard I have the Honor to be &ca:, JOHN JAY

FC (DNA: PCC, No. 121). Dft (NK-Iselin). Recorded in SJL as received 19 Dec. 1787. Enclosure (DLC): Tr of the resolution of Congress of 25 Oct. 1787, signed by Charles Thomson, authorizing TJ to settle with the king of Denmark for compensation equivalent to the value of the prizes of the United States which were delivered to Great Britain by Denmark, and to appoint John Paul Jones or any other person to act as agent for the negotiations, provided the final settlement "be not made by the Agent without the previous approbation of the said Min-

ister," and that the person so employed shall receive "five per Cent for all expences and demands whatever on that account" (printed in full in JCC, XXXIII, 705-6; an incomplete Tr of the above resolution, in the hand of William Short, is in DLC: John Paul Jones Papers).

[1] Following this, Jay first wrote in Dft: "and I fear not without Reason nor is it probable that they will be put to any Difficulties," then altered the sentence to read as above.

From La Blancherie

MONSIEUR   Paris ce 3. 9bre 1787.

Sur l'avis que Votre Excellence a eu la bonté de me faire donner de la demande de M. Adams, je viens d'examiner ce qu'il doit à l'Etablissement de la Correspondance. En 1782, Son Excellence prit l'engagement d'associé de la premiere Classe dont la contribution est de 96^{tt} par an, et elle fit le payement d'une année qui expira en 1783. Quelques parties de l'Etablissement ayant été suspendues en 1784, cette année est regardée comme non avenue. Il reste donc à acquitter les années, 1785, 1786, et 1787. Je me suis présenté à sa porte, pendant un court sejour que je viens de faire à Londres; mais il étoit à la Campagne. J'espere être plus heureux, cet hiver.

J'aurois bien de l'obligation à Votre Excellence, si elle avoit la bonté de m'accorder une audience pour [lui] faire ma Cour et lui rendre compte d'un établissement qui a pour but de lier les hommes de toutes les nations par la réciprocité des bons offices et qui s'honnore de l'approbation et de la protection de son Illustre Prédecesseur.

Je Suis avec Respect, Monsieur, Votre très humble et très obeissant serviteur,   LA BLANCHERIE
Agent général de Correspondance
pour les Sciences et les Arts

RC (DLC); endorsed. Recorded in SJL as received 4 Nov. 1787.

La Blancherie (1752-1811) operated his "Agence générale de Correspondance pour les Sciences et les Arts" from 1778 to 1788. His establishment had the aim of becoming a center of relations among learned men of all nations but which, as his experience with Adams that formed the subject of the present letter indicated, soon became a commercial enterprise.

To Lambert

Samedi. 3me. Novembre 1787.

Monsieur Jefferson est veritablement affligé d'avoir manqué hier de se rendre chez son excellence Monsieur le Comtrolleur general. Il reçut hier matin une lettre de Monsieur de la Fayette lui annonçant que Monsieur le Controleur general auroit la bonté de nous recevoir le *lendemain* à midi. Sans faire assez d'attention à la date, il croyoit que ce devoit etre le jour d'aujourdhui (Samedi) et il contoit d'avoir l'honneur de s'y rendre aujourdhui. Mais M. de la Fayette l'a fait revenir de son erreur. Il en fait mille excuses à Monsieur le Controleur general, et en est d'autant plus faché qu'il a manqué le moment de lui faire ses remerciments de toutes ses attentions aux affaires dont il a eté question, et de la bonté avec laquelle il s'est preté aux sacrifices de ses moments très precieux que ces discussions ont exigé, et dont il le prie d'agreer ici l'hommage de sa reconnoissance sincere, et de ses respects.

PrC (DLC). Not recorded in SJL.
UNE LETTRE DE MONSIEUR DE LA FAYETTE: Not found and not recorded in SJL.

From John Lowell

Boston, 3 Nov. 1787. Introduces Andrew Hall, of Medford, who "visits France with the joint View of establishing his Health and furnishing himself with usefull Knowledge." Has given a state of the local political affairs and the "Situation of the Petition of Monsieur and Madame De.Gregoire" in his letter of 10 June, "since which a Compromise has taken Place between the Government and the Lady"; intended to give a further account in this letter but is prevented from doing so by the sudden departure of the vessel; will soon introduce his nephew, Thomas Russell, of Boston, and will send further news by him. Mrs. Lowell and Miss Lowell join him "in a pleasing Recollection of Miss Jefferson."

RC (MHi); endorsed.
Lowell's letter of 10 June 1787 has not been found and is not recorded in SJL.

From Moustier

à Brest le 3. 9bre. 1787.

Au moment de partir, Monsieur, puisque tout est disposé pour mettre à la voile demain matin, il me vient un scrupule sur la negligence que j'aurois eûe de profiter de votre complaisance pour obtenir du vin de Frontignan. Comme je le destine aux Dames Americaines à qui je desire, en tout honneur, de plaire ainsi qu'à Messieurs les Americains, je voudrois bien n'en etre pas depourvu. J'ai l'honneur de vous prier en consequence, Monsieur, de vouloir bien, au cas que je n'eusse pas déjà fait la même demande, me procurer 100. bouteilles de bon vin de Frontignan par la voie que le fournisseur trouvera la plus sûre, ou que vous auriez eû la bonté de lui indiquer. J'en ferai le payement de la maniere qui lui conviendra le mieux et qu'il me fera connoitre. Le mauvais tems semble ne n'avoir contrarié precisement qu'autant qu'il fallait pour paroitre en Amerique en vrai Ministre de paix.

J'ai l'honneur d'etre avec un bien sincere et parfait attachement, Monsieur, Votre très humble et très obeissant serviteur,

LE CTE. DE MOUSTIER

RC (DLC). Recorded in SJL as received 9 Nov. 1787.

Although no enclosure is mentioned, Moustier must have sent with this letter the following unsigned note, addressed to "Madame la Presidente de Pichard en son hotel à Bordeaux," dated at Brest ce 3 9bre 1787": "Mr. Jefferson, Ministre des Etats unis de l'Amerique Septentrionale, desirant, chere cousine, avoir de votre bon vin, je vous demande de le traiter comme vous nous traiteriez nous même. C'est du Soterne principalement qu'il veut avoir; j'ignore encore le moment ou il en aura besoin, mais comme nous devons mettre à la voile demain, je lui envoye ce petit mot pour vous, et profite de cette occasion pour vous rennouveller l'assurance de ma bien tendre et bien constante amitié" (DLC: TJ Papers, 43: 7421).

From Anne Randolph

[3 Nov. 1787. Recorded in SJL Index but not in SJL and, therefore, probably received in 1788, for which year the pages of SJL are lacking. Not found.]

From Beaufort

Paris, 4 Nov. 1787. Is preparing a political work under the sponsor ship of the Archbishop of Toulouse which will be published within the next month. The work will consist of a statistical table, in four parts comparing the political and economic aspects of the constitutions of all of the European powers. Asks TJ to subscribe for the work.

RC (DLC); 2 p.; in French; signed: "De Beaufort ancien Secretaire de Legation de France, hotel de flandres, rue Dauphine"; endorsed. Recorded in SJL as received 4 Nov. 1787.

From Stephen Cathalan, Sr.

SIR   Marseilles the 4th. novber. 1787

I arived in Marseilles the 22th. ulto. after the meeting of our Ladies at Nismes, but my son with my daughter in Law, went to Cette to see the delivery of our Tobacco; from whence they re turned here the 1st. Inst. That has prevented me to have sooner the honour of addressing you, and making you our best thanks for all kind of services, and Civilities you have shewed to us during our stay at Paris; I beg you to receive my excuses if I can't well express in the English Idiom all my sentiments of gratude, but the best choised word would always be very short of the due sense I will ever retain.

I am now honoured with your agreable Letter of the 28th. ulto which brings me the Ministerial advice of the continuation of Peace between France and England. It is a pity a Capn. Darrel of the Vessel commerce (an English ship) has sailed from this harbour for New York before yesterday, I would have followed your orders, and perhaps it would have been the first new[s] in the continent. In this moment there is no vessel ready; here they are anxious to know how the affairs of Holland have been ranged as well as those of Russia and Turkey, which are the most inter esting for this Place; but I must tell you that here the general sprit was very Pattriotic, and wished for revenge, whatever loss they would have suffered in their trade by the war, for the national glory. When this happy declaration will be known, they will see I dare say, that every thing has been preserved and praise our good government.

I was very fortunate to sell my tobacco, tho a very heavy loss will arise, but if you can't obtain reddress on the etat des achapts and a total suspension of shippments in america, for more then

[320]

one year is not effectuated, I don't know what will become this article in this Port as well as in other Ports.

At Cette six Vessels have been dispatched this spring and summer with wines, Brandy, other articles, but specialy with silver money, to buy tobacco in america: this is calculating

200 hogshd. one in the other, makes about	1200 hoghd.
unsold here in sundry hands	480
my vessel returning, which will carry about	250
which I expect before the 15th. of the next Month (she carries about 50 Casks *fish oil*)	
expected by three other houses before next January about	900
in all	2830 hoghds.

I must acknowlegde that the Manufactory of Cette is very much provided, they have rented very extensive stores which are quitte full. They expect via Bordeaux 2000 hogshd. Maryland, which can't be contained at Louviers or at Toulouse for pipe, and 2000 more in January. There is the state of that commodity, which is very allarming.

Your Packet for Milan will be conveyed by the first opportunity.

Yesterday I have received a Couffe of rice from alexandria unshelled, the other will be sent by the first opportunity. Must I send them to you by land or via rouen?

Our Ladies and Eulalie begs you to accept their Best thanks for your kind remembrance and their respectfull compliments. I and my son ask from you the continuation of your honourable and worthy friendship, being always at your service, in whatever you may command us.

I have the honour to be very respectfully Sir of your Excellency the most obedient humble & Devoted Servant,

ESTIENNE CATHALAN, Pr.

RC (DLC); in the hand of Stephen Cathalan, Jr., signed by Stephen Cathalan, Sr.; endorsed. Recorded in SJL as received 10 Nov. 1787.

From John Brown Cutting

SIR   London 4 Novr. 1787

Notwithstanding Mr. Parker, who is soon to profit from the honor of a personal acquaintance with you in Paris, will smooth his passage to that intercourse by introductory letters both of Mr.

Adams and Colonel Smith, the weight of those characters with Your Excellency compar'd with the levity of my claims to Your confidence must make every post-recommendation of him from me unrequisite as it is unessential, yet I can no more desist from writing my testimony in his favour with theirs than I can omit such an occasion to repeat my grateful sense of that condescention on the part of your Excellency towards me, which so recently converted disappointments into instruction and vexation into delight.

In several wide conversations with Your Excellency, in which I was always debtor for much valuable knowledge and just observation, I recollect already to have mention'd Mr. Parker to You in terms of high estimation and regard. Instead therefore of again repeating them on paper, permit me rather barely to remind You that in speaking of American commerce, I not only ventur'd to insinuate the propriety of attempting to extend the India traffic and improve a new domestic channel for the fur-trade, (and likewise the facilities in both the one and the other, that the Government of France, or at any rate, some of her subjects cou'd give us;) but also to state to you my conception of the fitness of Mr. Parker in point of integrity, genius, property and mercantile knowledge to assist in planing, pursuing or sustaining such rational and comprehensive schemes of bussiness in both branches as might eventually alike promote the emolument of Individu[als] and the national wealth and prosperity.

If the opinions I then had the honor of dilating to you whether my own or those of others continue to impress you as they appear'd to do at that time; and if Your Excellency also after conversing with Mr. Parker shou'd concur with me in thinking him well qualified to agitate, capable to ripen and skilful to methodise and compleat extensive plans of commercial business in France I flatter myself You will not consider it too obtrusive or importunate in me thus to solicit in behalf of a man of merit and fortune, and an American merchant of real ability, a share of that countinance and confidence with which I thought Your Excellency lately both hon[ored] and obligd. Your most respectful And Obedt: Servt.,

JOHN BROWN CUTTING

RC (DLC); endorsed. Recorded in SJL as received 13 Nov. 1787.

To R. & A. Garvey

GENTLEMEN   Paris Nov. 4. 1787.

In my letter of Sep. 3. I had the honour to inclose you a bill of lading for a harpsichord shipped at London on board the ship James, whereof James Dunn was master, and which I had taken the liberty of having addressed to you. Hearing nothing of it's arrival I wrote to my friend in London to know if the vessel was actually sailed. He informs me by a letter of Oct. 30. that the vessel had left that port 4. weeks before that day, say about the beginning of October. Will you be so good as to inform me whether any such vessel has arrived at your port, and whether the instrument is delivered, because if it is not, it will be necessary for me to make enquiry at Havre. I presume you know that mutual declarations for the continuance of peace, and for disarming were signed at Versailles on the 27th. Ultimo, on the part of England and France.

I have the honour to be with much esteem Gentlemen your most obedient humble servant,   TH: JEFFERSON

PrC (MHi).

From William Carmichael

MY DEAR SIR   Escurial 5th Novr. 1787

Since my last I have found it necessary to follow the court hither, altho' the present State of my finances can ill support the Enormous Expence of Lodgings &c. in this Little place, in which there is not a garret unoccupied. Two or three days ago I had a conference with the Minister whom I found in the same friendly disposition with regard to the United States which he has ever professed to me and which his conduct has evinced. The present Situation of affairs in Europe excites an anxious curiosity in all thinking people here and I beleive that no couriers arrival was expected with more impatience, than that of one from Versailles in the present moment. The conjectures formed on this occasion are so various and contradictory, that it would be trespassing on your patience to Repeat them. I have kept a kind of diary for more than two months of the feigned or real opinions of Men respecting the Issue of an Affair which agitates their minds at this crisis. The versatility in their manner of speaking is really become an Amusement to me. The present Idea is peace. How this can be they have

[323]

not yet told me. The inclosed paper which is the Substance of the dispatch mentioned will show you the Nature of the Language held by one of the Parties here. I am told that the *Person* to whom it was addressed, was instructed to sound the Minister upon a garantee by this court of the Dutch constitution as it is at present.

The Language held by the Minister is said to be Moderate, but *firm* and *decisive*. Preparations are making to put the Marine on a respectable and formidable footing. Some say not with the requisite dispatch and vigor. The Person of whose Letter I sent a copy in my last is indefatigable in his endeavors to prevent this court from making a common cause with France in this business as well as in exciting the Principal Individuals of this Nation and of others against what he Styles the intermeddling and ambitious policy of that Court. He is a vigilant and artful Minister full of Statagem and Artifice. But not without his weak side when *intimately* known. I have transmitted to Morocco the Ratification you sent me with the Dispatches of this court, as the Safest and speediest manner of its reaching its destination. I have no letters from thence, but I have seen a Letter from Mogadore mentioning the Arrival of an American vessel in five weeks from Boston to purchase Mules. Yesterday the Infanta Wife of Dn. Gabriel was delivered of a Daughter, to whom 17. names have been given of which the Principal is Carlota. This Event occasions three days of Gala and Illumination. I have no direct news from America, the Ct. de F.B. told me that he had received a Letter advising that the Convention had broke up and that the measures adopted by that Body were announced. With very great respect & Esteem I have the honor to be Your Excellencys Obliged & Most Obedt. Sevt,

WM. CARMICHAEL

RC (DLC); endorsed. Recorded in SJL as received 22 Nov. 1787. Enclosure (DLC): Tr, in Carmichael's hand, of an extract, in French, of a dispatch from the court at Berlin to its chargé d'affaires in Spain, stating that the sole object of the King of Prussia in entering Holland was to seek amends due the Princess of Orange and reestablish her dignity; that, having subdued most of the province, he only wants peace in Holland and will withdraw his troops as soon as possible; that he wishes Floridablanca to be informed of this in the hope that Spain will encourage sentiments of peace in France and disperse "toutes ces nuages qui peuvent conduire à une incendie generale."

THE PERSON OF WHOSE LETTER I SENT A COPY IN MY LAST: This was the British minister at Madrid, Sir Robert Liston, whose letter (not found) was enclosed in Carmichael to TJ, 15 Oct. 1787. The arrival at Mogador of an American vessel from Boston TO PURCHASE MULES was perhaps a tribute to George Washington's enthusiasm for those animals. "Royal Gift," the ass presented to Washington by the king of Spain, had arrived in Boston late in 1785 and his progress through New England under the care of Washington's agent, John Fairfax, and a Spanish muleteer who could not speak English, had aroused great public excitement over the possibility of establishing mules in America. Washington had planned the trip of "Royal Gift" from Boston to Mount Vernon with all of the care and forethought that he gave to a military campaign, and had solicited the aid of such prominent individuals as Tench Tilghman, Robert Morris, Elias Boudinot, George Clinton, Jeremiah Wadsworth, and Thomas Cushing (*Writings*, ed. Fitzpatrick, XXVIII, 296-302). TJ himself had become interested as a result of Washington's enthusiasm (see TJ to Washington, 10 Dec. 1784).

To Pierre Samuel Dupont

[Before 5 Nov. 1787]

Monsieur Jefferson a l'honneur de souhaiter le bon jour à Monsieur du Pont, et de le prier d'accepter une exemplaire du livre de M. Adams. Il lui sera bien obligé pour son projet de la lettre de M. Lambert à M. de la Boullaye, il la renverra tout de suite. Pourroit Monsieur du Pont, sans s'incommoder, procurer pour M. Jefferson copie de la memoire de la ferme? Il lui en seroit infiniment obligé.

RC (Pierre S. duPont, Wilmington, Del., 1950); addressed: "A Monsieur Monsieur du Pont Conseiller d'etat cul-de-sac de la Corderie"; without date and not recorded in SJL, but probably written shortly before Dupont's reply of 5

Nov. 1787, following.

UNE EXEMPLAIRE DU LIVRE DE M. ADAMS: Adams' *Defence of the Constitutions* (see Adams to TJ, 25 Aug. 1787).

From Pierre Samuel Dupont

Paris 5 9bre 1787

J'ai l'honneur, Monsieur, de vous envoyer une minute de la lettre que vous désirez, et que je vous serai obligé de me faire repasser lorsque vous en aurez fait tirer copie.

Je tâcherai de me procurer et à vous aussi le Mémoire des Fermiers généraux que je n'ai pas encore.

Je vous remercie bien de l'ouvrage de Mr. adams qui me parait avoir une terrible érudition et chercher dans les opinions et les exemples des hommes ce que les Philosophes et les Législateurs doivent trouver dans la nature des choses et dans celle du coeur humain, dans le droit, dans la justice qui ne dependent ni des tems, ni des lieux.

Nous convenons assez généralement que les hommes n'ont encore été que très faiblement éclairés, que nos ancêtres etaient des ignorans et des Barbares, et nous allons ployer le genou devant eux pour leur demander comment nous pourrons nous y prendre pour cesser de l'être.

[325]

J'ai toujours eu peine à comprendre que l'on imaginât pouvoir tirer de bons principes de constitution des Républiques antiques où l'esclavage etait etabli, et où tous ceux qui exerçaient les travaux utiles, l'agriculture, les arts, n'étaient pas membres de l'etat.

Et des Républiques modernes fondées par le fanatisme et l'épée dans des siecles d'une générale férocité.

La vôtre est la seule sur laquelle la raison aît sensiblement influé.

Comment peut-elle arriver à sa perfection? Par une recherche encore plus approfondie de ce qui est raisonnable et juste.

On peut constituer de très bons gouvernemens sous différentes formes, pourvû que les droits des hommes y soient très connus et très respectés. Aucun de vos treize gouvernemens n'est *mauvais*. Celui de l'angleterre, moins parfait, n'est pas *mauvais*. Celui de la France, lorsqu'il y aura des assemblées provinciales bien constituées, ne sera pas *mauvais*.

Mais il peut cependant y avoir un Gouvernement parfait, qui serait le *Beau idéal* en matiere de gouvernement, qui n'est aucun de ceux-là, et auquel les nations doivent arriver un jour par le fait de la perfectibilité de l'esprit humain.

Le point sur lequel les américains me paraissent le plus loin de la vérité, c'est les principes de l'impôt. Je ne les crois même pas assez avancés pour entendre encore ce qu'on pourrait leur dire de raisonnable à ce sujet; et si je hasardais de l'écrire, je m'imposerais la loi d'être quinze ans sans publier mon ouvrage afin de laisser mûrir les opinions des Juges.

Je joins ici une petite brochure où je m'applaudis d'avoir mis quelques principes que j'ai retrouvés dans vos observations sur la Virginie.

La matiere semblait fort claire. J'ai obtenu quelques Eloges, et l'academie, composée de juges aussi instruits qu'honnêtes et sensibles, n'a adopté en résultat aucune de mes opinions.

Le mal des hopitaux n'est diminué que dans la proportion de quatre à un.

Nous aurons quatre hopitaux de douze cent malades chacun, dont les bâtimens couteront seize millions.

Et les secours aux domiciliés, les hospices, les maisons de santé à pension, n'auront lieu que vers le milieu du siecle prochain.

Les bonnes institutions sont comme les chênes; ceux qui sement le gland ne peuvent habiter dans les maisons auxquelles les Arbres serviront de Poutres.

Vos treize etats ont été vite parce qu'ils êtaient fondés sur la constitution anglaise déja bonne, et qu'ils ont ete hâtés dans leur developpement par la *serre chaude* de la guerre civile.

J'ai l'honneur d'etre avec le plus respectueux attachement Monsieur, Votre très humble et tres obeïssant Serviteur,

Du Pont

RC (MoSHi). Recorded in sjl as received 5 Nov. 1787. Enclosures: (1) Lambert's letter to La Boullaye, 23 Oct. 1787, q.v. under that date. (2) Copy of Dupont's pamphlet, *Idées sur les secours a donner aux pauvres malades dans une grande ville* . . . (Philadelphia and Paris; Sowerby, No. 2386).

From R. & A. Garvey

Rouen, 5 Nov. 1787. Have received TJ's letter of 4 Nov. and wish to inform him that the ship *James* arrived two days ago and is now being unloaded; will unload the harpsichord as soon as it can be reached. "Its lucky that Matters are made up, but I fear it won't be of a long Standing, the troubles in the East may Sooner or later kick up a Dust its not the Interest of Either France or England that the ottomans should be Ecrasés, and I dare say they will not look on calmly."

RC (MHi); 2 p.; in a clerk's hand, signed "Robt. & Anth. Garvey" in the hand of Anthony Garvey, with a postscript in the same hand which has been quoted in full above; endorsed. Recorded in sjl as received 6 Nov. 1787.

From Lafayette

[*Nemours [5?] Nov. 1787*. Recorded in sjl as dated "tuesday (Nov. 5)" and received on 9 Nov. 1787; however, Tuesday fell on 6 Nov. in 1787, so TJ was in error either in the day of the week or the date. Not found.]

From Madame Townsend

le 5 9bre. 1787.

D'apres la lettre que vous m'avés remise, Monsieur je vois avec plaisir la Confiance que le Commodore a si bien Placée, depuis longtems j'avois eu l'honneur d'entendre parler de votre Caractere, et j'aurois desirée plutot être a même d'avoir celui de vous connoitre. Je ne sais Monsieur a quel titre je reclamerois votre assistance dans ce moment, si ce n'est par la bonté naturelle de votre coeur. Les circonstances m'obligent de vivre tres ignorée, jusqu'a ce que je sois a même de jouir de ce qui m'est promis. J'ai un projet dont je desire vous faire part Monsieur, mais je me flates

[327]

que vous voudré bien me dire par un mot de votre main, Si vous desiré m'être utile. Ce sera joindre infiniment a votre honneteté pour moi de me dire avec franchise si je ne vous importunes pas.

J'ai L'honneur d'être tres parfaitement Monsieur votre tres humble et tres obeissante servante,   TOWNSEND

RC (MoSHi); endorsed: "Townsend Madme." Recorded in SJL as received 6 Nov. 1787.

From Pierre Samuel Dupont

Paris 6 9bre 1787

Je pense, Monsieur, qu'il serait très nécessaire que vous vissiez Mr. Lambert aujourd'hui sur les deux heures afin de faire signer la lettre provisoire, l'arrêt du conseil n'etant point encore expedié, et ne pouvant vraisemblablement l'etre assez tôt pour que vous puissiez l'envoyer par le Paquebot du havre.

La lettre suffira pour donner connoissance au Congrès et aux assemblées des dispositions générales, et il y a toute apparence que dans la semaine suivante l'arrêt sera expedié comme nous le desirons.

J'ai fait lire à Mr. le Cte. de Montmorin et remis à Mr. Lambert une note au sujet des amirautés pour les determiner à laisser l'article qui les concerne tel qu'il est proposé.

Et je ne crois pas qu'ils puissent resister à ce que leur a écrit Mr. le Mis. de la Fayette au sujet de la pêche de la Baleine. Mon confrere Mr. Boyetet a appuyé ses reflexions par une lettre à Mr. le Cte. de Montmorin dont il est ami particulier.

J'ai l'honneur d'etre avec le plus respectueux attachement Monsieur de votre Excellence Le très humble et tres obeissant serviteur,

DU PONT

RC (MoSHi); endorsed. Recorded in SJL as received 6 Nov. 1787.

To Pierre Samuel Dupont

[6 Nov. 1787]

Je vous renvoye, Monsieur votre Lettre et vous en remercie, et continue d'esperer que vous pourrez me procurer le Memoire des Fermiers Generaux. A ces Sentiments de reconnaissance de vos bontés j'en joins d'autres pour le pamphlet que vous m'avez envoyé au sujet des hopitaux, dans lequel je trouve cette exactitude geometrique d'idée qui caracterise tout ce qui sort de votre plume. Lorsque la Theorie se trouve confirmée par des Faits dont l'ecrivain n'avait point de connaissance, cela donne à l'esprit humain plus de confiance dans ses propres opérations. Notre Methode en Amerique fournit une preuve de la saineté de votre theorie. À l'egard du livre de M. Adams Je conviens que les détails historiques dans lesquels il entre, ne sont point nécessaires pour des personnes qui comme vous ont étudié la Nature de L'homme en comparant le tems présent au tems passé; mais il ecrit pour procurer au corps de notre Nation ce qu'il n'a pas encore eu l'occasion de connaitre autrement. Notre Constitution les presentait comme une balance des pouvoirs du gouvernement. Il pense qu'ils ne sont pas suffisamment convaincus de la Necessité de cette balance qu'ils sont trop disposés à confier à un seul de ses membres. Pour cela il leur rassemble les preuves des autres nations pour montrer les maux qui ont toujours suivi le manque de cette balance. Peut-etre pourrait-on dire que son livre est trop profond pour le Commun du Peuple; mais Leurs Chefs en profiteront.

J'étais malheureusement dehors quand votre lettre est parvenue chez moi, en sorte que je n'ai pu faire au Controleur général la visite que Vous me proposiez. Je la ferai demain. Je suis &c.

Tr (Pierre S. duPont, Wilmington, Del., 1950); in a clerk's hand; at head of text: "Copie de la Lettre de M. de jefferson á M. DuPont." This letter, without date and not recorded in SJL, is a reply to Dupont's letters of 5 and 6 Nov. 1787, qq.v. Enclosure: Dupont's copy of Lambert to La Boullaye, 23 Oct. 1787, q.v.

To Madame Townsend

Paris November. 6. 1787.

My esteem, Madam, for Commodore Jones, as well as your personal merit, make it my wish to be useful to you; and will ensure any aid which my situation permits in the execution of the plan you do me the honour to tell me you have formed. That you may not however over-value my opportunities of serving you, it is my duty to observe, that as sollicitations at court are probably what are most necessary for you, there is no person living who is less in the way of making or procuring them for you than I am. My business lying with the minister, and giving me immediate access to him, I have never cultivated any other acquaintance at court, but on the contrary have studiously avoided it. When you shall do me the honour however to develope the particular of your plan, I will tell you freely if there is any part of it in which I can aid you, and execute sincerely whatever I shall tell you. I have the honour to be with sentiments of perfect respect, Madam, your most obedient & most humble servant, TH: JEFFERSON

PrC (CSmH).

To John Jay

SIR   Paris Nov. 7. 1787.

By a letter of the 2d. inst. from the Count de Moustier I perceive he is still at Brest. The wind has now been near a month in the South-Western quarter, and if it remains there a few days longer, my dispatches by the packet may reach you as soon as those by Monsr. de Moustier. This being the last post which can reach the packet, should she sail on the 10th. I avail myself of it to inform you of the only circumstance, since the date of my letters delivered to Mr. Stuart, worth your knowlege; that is the appointment of the Chevalier de la Luzerne Ambassador to the court of London. This fortunate issue of those expectations which made him unwilling to return to America, together with the character of his successor, will I hope render it pleasing to Congress that his return was not too much pressed. He would have gone back with dispositions towards us very different from those he will carry for us to the court of London. He has been constantly sensible that we wished his return, and that we could have procured it, but that we did not wish to stand in the way of his promotion. He will view this as in some measure the effect of our indulgence, and I think we may count on his patronage and assistance wherever they may be useful to us. I have the honour to be with sentiments of the most perfect esteem & respect Sir, your most obedient & most humble servant,   TH: JEFFERSON

PrC (DLC).
MY LETTERS DELIVERED TO MR. STUART: TJ's last letters, before those delivered to Moustier, were dated 22 and 24 Sep.; the present letter was sent by Stuart (see Limozin to TJ, 9 Nov. 1787).

From Madame Townsend

le 7 9bre 1787.

Je ne sais Monsieur comment je pourrois reconnoitre toutes vos honnetetés. D'après l'exposé que vous avés eu en mains de ma situation, et le desir que vous avés de m'obliger, je ne vous cacherai rien. J'ai la perspective d'obtenir encore de la faveur, mais je ne puis l'esperer avant le mois de janvier prochain. J'ai toujours attendu, et la perte que j'ai faite de ma chere Protectrice m'a ôté les moyens de solliciter ce qui m'etois promis en juillet.

Je n'ai pu, n'y osés me confier a Personne dans toutes mes perplexités, et ne l'aurois jamais fait vis a vis de vous, Monsieur, si le Commodore Jones ne m'avoit prevenue. Depuis pres d'un mois j'ai le projet d'aller a Londres pour m'y procurer des fonds qui sont au Stock, je ne puis le faire par pouvoir D'atorney, il faut que j'y aille moi même. Les dernieres lettres que j'ai reçue D'Angleterre m'y oblige. Je vous confesse Monsieur qu'ayant trop attendu, je me trouve dans l'impossibilité de faire mon voyage. Si je vous ai inspiré assés de confiance Monsieur pour me rendre le Service de me faire le prêt (pour un mois) d'une somme de 25 ou 30 Louis vous me mettrai dans le cas de lever toutes les dificultés dont je suis accablée. Ne voulant me confier a personne pour un objet de cette nature soyés assuré Monsieur que me rendant ce service (si peu essentiel qu'il puisse vous paroitre) vous donnera a jamais des droits sur ma reconnoissance. J'aurai l'honneur de vous faire passer une notte que je vous prierai de garder jusqu'au premiers jours de decembre. Soyés assuré Monsieur de toute ma reconnoissance ainsi que de la sincere Estime avec la quelle j'ai L'honneur d'être tres parfaitement Monsieur votre tres humble servante, T. TOWNSEND

RC (CSmH); endorsed. Recorded in SJL as received 7 Nov. 1787.

To Madame Townsend

Paris Nov. 7. 1787

I am infinitely distressed, Madam, that your letter of to-day finds me in a situation incapable of furnishing the sum of money for which you have occasion. The difficulties of our Treasury which have detained Commodore Jones in America, have made themselves felt here for two or three months past. A failure to remit money here, has for so long left me without supplies, and besides being absolutely unprovided with money, I am daily contracting debts. Thus placed under the physical impossibility of supplying you with the money necessary for your journey, I hope you will do justice to the dispositions I entertain towards you, as well as to the sentiments of esteem & respect with which I have the honour to be, Madam, Your most obedient & most humble servant, TH: JEFFERSON

PrC (DLC).

[331]

From St. John de Crèvecoeur

SIR   New York 9th. Novr. 1787

I am much obliged to you for your Last Letter, as well as for the various and Interesting details it contained concerning the State of our national affairs. Great Indeed is the Change Lately brought about in the disposition of that Country; but who Cou'd have foreseen that the Parliaments Shou'd have Shew'd such a spirit of opposition to the Establishment of Provincial assemblies. It wou'd seem as if they were Jealous of that new Institution. Dont you think that the Time is now come to break those antiquated bodys and with the fragments to Establish Supreme Courts, solely for the Tryal of Causes; we see something similar here.—The new Constitution now in everybody's hands seem also to meet with Considerable opposition, particularly in this State and in Pensilvania. Some people seem considerably alarmed, but yet I trust to the good sense of the Inhabitants. I Trust that every man who attached to the Glorey and happiness of his country, as well as to his property will be for it.—Old as I am I cou'd even fight for the admission of this new federal government—now or never.

If this new Constitution fails I will do every thing in my Power to Leave this country which will become the scene of anarchy and confusion.—What an Interesting Journey your Last must have been! I'd give a good deal to see the Sketch of your observations. I Learnt the other day from Mr. Maddisson with great pleasure, that Congres had reappointed you their Plenipotentiary. May you soon be that of a strongly united nation. Accept the sentiments of Respect and most sincere Esteem with which I am Sir Your Very Humble Servt,   ST. JOHN

Mille Compliments a Mr. Short S'il vous Plait. J'ay soigneusement fait passer Touttes ses Lettres et Packets.

RC (DLC); endorsed. Recorded in SJL as received 21 Dec. 1787.

TJ's LAST LETTER was that of 6 Aug. 1787. Shortly after his arrival in Boston, Crèvecoeur had written William Short a pessimistic account of affairs in America. This letter was received in Paris just as the Count de Moustier and Madame de Brehan were about to depart, and the reply that Short gave Moustier for Crèvecoeur is almost an echo of what TJ could have been expected to say if his letter of 6 Aug. had been answered in time for him to

have expressed the sentiments himself. For this reason, and also because of the 18th-century habit of sharing among intimates such private letters on public affairs as conveyed news and observations, this letter written at the Hôtel de Langeac by the secretary of the minister cannot be disregarded. Its pertinent passages read as follows: "What you say of affairs in America gives me real uneasiness; and yet I think there is too much good sense among my countrymen to let them lose the advantages of the most happy revolution that has ever been effected. If they could but for a moment Sir have an idea of the sufferings of wretched humanity under despotic governments—if they could consider that the step from anarchy to despotism is but small, they would certainly use all their powers for the permanent establishment of order. If the cause of liberty should fail in America, which may bountiful avert! mankind must set themselves down contented under the domination of Kings and Nobles. But is it possible Sir, that in a country as much enlightened as America—is it possible that where the dignity of man is felt, and where his rights are understood, there should be danger of the one or the other being sacrificed? I think not; and I console myself on that consideration, amidst all the alarms which the letters from that country give rise to. The divisions and party quarrels of the United Provinces ought to be a lesson to the United States—these divisions have opened the door as it were to the Prussian troops—they have entered almost without opposition and are at the moment in possession of the whole country except Amsterdam, and it is expected every day that we shall hear of its surrendering also. A pretty piece of work, is it not Sir, for a whole nation to be thus chastised, plundered, and devoured by a foreign army—for what? because they have thought it their duty to stop on the road and prevent entering their country a woman whom they thought dangerous. Unfortunately this woman was a *Princess* and the sister of a King, who has an hundred thousand men at his orders. Let the Americans be well aware of admitting among them people whose persons are thus sacred and privileged —it is no matter whether they are called princes, Kings, nobles—under whatever name they may be they are equally dangerous."

To La Blancherie

à Paris ce 9me. Novembre 1787.

J'ai reçu, Monsieur, la lettre que vous m'avez fait l'honneur de m'ecrire sur le sujet de l'etablissement de la Correspondance. Quoique l'ami des sciences et des arts autant que personne, et disposé de leur etre utile autant qu'il m'est possible, il faut que l'on s'arrange à ses moyens, et que l'on se contente des limites que ces moyens imposent. Les sciences et les arts chez nous demandent toutes nos sacrifices, et l'Europe est trop riche d'en avoir besoin, et trop interessé à nos poursuites pour souhaiter de nous en detourner. Je m'occupe particulierement à faire venir de l'Amerique les objets les moins connus de son histoire naturelle. Les sommes que ce me coute, Monsieur, sont si considerables, que je vous avoue que je me trouve obligé de m'y borner. Quoique donc que je sois très sensible au merite de votre Etablissement, et que je lui souhaite toute sorte de succès, je ne me trouve pas dans la position d'y etre utile.

Monsieur Adams m'a ecrit sur le sujet de son abonnement, qui etoit pour le premier etablissement. Cet etablissement a eté discontinué dès la premiere année. Si le seconde, qui a eté fait après une année d'intervalle, etoit sur le meme plan, ou sur un plan different, il ne croyait pas que son abonnement pourroit etre renouvellé sans le consulter, et il ne contoit pas de le renouveller. Il a reçu, à d'assez longues intervalles, des masses des gazettes de la Correspondance dont le port lui a eté assez onereux. Il m'a prié d'en demander des eclaircissements, et m'a expliqué ses idées là-dessus. J'aurai l'honneur, Monsieur, de passer chez vous un de ces jours, pour demander des idées plus exactes, et pour me mettre à meme de remplir les vues de Monsieur Adams qui se conforment à ce qui est juste et honnete. En attendant, il vous prie, Monsieur, de ne le regarder comme tenant à l'Etablissement de la Correspondance. J'ai l'honneur d'etre avec la consideration la plus distinguée, Monsieur, votre très humble et tres obeissant serviteur,

TH: JEFFERSON

PrC (DLC).

From André Limozin

Havre de Grace, 9 Nov. 1787. Acknowledges TJ's letter of 7 Nov., transmitting a letter to John Jay to be delivered to "Mr. Stuart American Passenger who is to take his Passage on board the Packet for Newyork"; has sent his clerk to locate that gentleman, but, after two hours searching, he has not been found. Has succeeded in making "Mr. Ruellan" pay the expenses for the lawsuit of the six American sailors who were on board the ship *Elephant*; the sailors are "very happy that they have found with me such a warm protection"; asks opinion on the continuance of peace.

RC (MHi); 4 p.; addressed and endorsed. Recorded in SJL as received 11 Nov. 1787.
TJ's letter to Limozin of 7 Nov. has not been found and is not recorded in SJL; it was evidently only a covering note for TJ to Jay, 7 Nov. 1787, q.v.

From Lewis Littlepage

[Paris] 9 Nov. 1787. Being obliged to set out for London on Monday [12 Nov.], cannot immediately leave with TJ the amount of money still due Carmichael; expects to return before even a reply can be received from Madrid; if he is delayed, asks that the account be held until his return, when it will be immediately discharged.

RC (DLC); 2 p.; endorsed. Not recorded in SJL.

From John Adams

MY DEAR SIR   London. Nov. 10. 1787

Mr. Boylston is going to Paris, with a Cargo of Sperma Cæti

[334]

oil, and will be obliged to you for any assistance or advice you can give him.

I forwarded a few days ago, from Mr. Gerry, a Copy as I suppose of the Result of Convention.—It seems to be admirably calculated to preserve the Union, to increase Affection, and to bring us all to the same mode of thinking. They have adopted the Idea of the Congress at Albany in 1754 of a President to nominate officers and a Council to Consent: but thank heaven they have adopted a third Branch, which that Congress did not. I think that Senates and Assemblies should have nothing to do with executive Power. But still I hope the Constitution will be adopted, and Amendments be made at a more convenient opportunity.

What think you of a Declaration of Rights? Should not such a Thing have preceded the Model?

People here are Solacing themselves in the Prospect of the Continuance of Peace: and the tryumphant Party in Holland carry a high hand.—I suspect that both are rather too sanguine.—They have very insufficient Grounds for so much Exultation. My worthy old Friends the Patriots in Holland are extreamly to be pittied: and so are their deluded Persecutors. That Country I fear is to be ruined, past all Remedy. I wish that all the good Men had Sense and Spirit enough to go to America. With the usual Sentiments Yours,   JOHN ADAMS

RC (DLC); endorsed. Recorded in SJL as received 26 Nov. 1787.

From Edward Carrington

DEAR SIR   New York Nov. 10. 1787

Mr. Madison and myself have done ourselves the honor to write you very fully as late as the 23d. Ult., but as the Chevalier Jones is but now about to sail in a Merchant Man for Holland, from whence he means to go directly to Paris, I just use this additional opportunity to inclose you the papers from the period of our former letters to this date. They contain sundry peices upon the subject of the new Constitution and will serve to shew you the sentiments of its opponents, but you are not to conclude from the number of them that they shew the general sense of the people. We have learned from Virginia that several men of considerable influence are in the opposition, amongst whom Mr. Henry is numbered. It appears however, by the papers, that the new project is getting much into fashion in that state. Amongst the papers inclosed you will see the issue of several formal assemblies of the people. The legislature have directed that a convention be held in May, for the purpose of, "adopting, amending or rejecting" the proposed Government. The long postponement was occasioned by unfriendly intentions toward it, but I apprehend the rapidity of the movements of the other States in the business, will, by that time, have brought so many into the adoption, that even its enemies will see the *necessity* of joining.

The Chevalier Jones has been detained much longer in America than he expected at his arrival, owing to a deal of perplexities he has met with in the adjustment of his negotiations in France. The Treasury Board had his papers upwards of two months before they reported. They then proposed that the division which had been made of the prize money, by the Court of France, should be reversed as it respects the Commanders of the Bon homme Richard, and the Alliance, and that they should share upon the common mass of the two ships, instead of each taking upon the mass of his own. This was however disagreed to by Congress, and the division by the court of France confirmed. They also proposed that he should be ordered immediately, to pay up the balance retained by him when he made a payment to you, only deducting 5 ℔ Cent for Commission. This was also disagreed to, and he is allowed still to retain that balance until some future decision shall be made. Some propositions were made which he will shew you with the yeas and nays, from which there results a decided sense of Congress that he ought to retain so much money on some principle, but it could not be agreed whether it should be paid out of the public treasury or deducted from the property recovered. I own that, to me, it appeared probable that the money was necessarily expended, and that it ought to be taken from the property of those in whose service the expence was incurred. Whatever might have been the obligations of the court of France to pay the money, a long and expensive[1] of attendance was nevertheless necessary to obtain it, and since it had before been tried by Mr. Barclay without success, it is likely that personal considerations, which applied to Jones alone ensured the success he has met with.

You will receive some Resolutions upon the Denmark business which reverse those which formerly established the Chevalier Jones as the Agent. This was occasioned by several considerations. By some Gentlemen it was thought that the application to the Court involved a complaint of a breach of the Law of Nations which required an immediate diplomatic commission, and it having been suggested by the Board of Treasury that the security formerly given by Mr. Jones was somewhat impaired by a reduction of the property of those who were bound with him, it was thought by others that in justice to the people concerned, he ought to be called upon for additional security. Upon the whole it was unanimously thought best to shift the ground upon which the business stood leaving the eventual further employment of the Chevalier to you, who must be the best acquainted with his conduct. I find that this brave, and in my mind honest, Man has his enemies. These may represent him to you in an injurious light, and the statement I make is just intended to shew you how he really stands with Congress. It is expected that you will employ him if *you* do not think him unworthy of being trusted in the business which is to be done. In candor however I must tell you that you will be held accountable for whatever money may be received, but send who you will, I suppose you may draw the money through whatever channel you please so as to keep it out of the hands of the agent, should you not chuse entirely to hazard it in his hands.

We have just received notice from Kentucky that, at a Convention held for the purpose, the people of that district have determined upon their separation from Virga. in conformity to the Act of Fall 1785, and a request is made to Congress for their admission as a new state into the confederation. You have no doubt seen the Act of Virga. The period fixed for the commencement of the separate government is the beginning of 1789.

I have the Honor to be with great sincerity Yr. affectionate Humble Servt., ED. CARRINGTON

RC (DLC); endorsed. Recorded in SJL as received 19 Dec. 1787. The newspapers sent with this letter have not been identified.

1 A word was omitted here; perhaps Carrington intended to write "term" or "period."

From R. & A. Garvey

Rouen, 10 Nov. 1787. Have sent the harpsichord by cart and hope it arrives safely; ask that the "acquit à Caution No. 143" which goes by the "Cartman" be returned; attach their statement of disbursements, amounting to 87.^{lt} 15s. 6d., for which they have drawn a sight draft on TJ.

RC (MHi); 3 p.; with statement of account written on verso of address cover; addressed and endorsed. Noted in SJL as received 11 Nov. 1787. Sight draft in the amount stated above, drawn to the order of Perregaux & Co., endorsed "Paymt. Perregaux," is in MHi.

From Ralph Izard

DEAR SIR   South Bay Charleston 10th. Novr. 1787.

Your Letter of 1st. August came to my hands several weeks before Mr. Drayton received his on the subjects of Rice, Olives &c. to which I was referred. We are much obliged to you for the trouble you have taken, and for the information you have given. When I was in Italy, the Rice of that Country appeared inferiour to ours. I had been several years absent from America, and the difference did not then appear to me so great as it does now. The Seed which you have sent, and which you say is of the best kind, will bear no comparison with ours; and I am surprized to learn that the price is nearly equal. You say that our Rice dissolves when dressed with Meat. This must be owing to some mismanagement in dressing it. I have examined my Cook on the subject, and find that as Meat requires to be longer on the fire than Rice, they must be dressed seperately, until each is nearly done, and then the combination is to be made. The Water must boil before the Rice is put into it, or the grains will not be distinct from each other. The Rice you have sent will be planted. I hope great care will be taken to keep it at a distance from the other Rice Fields; for if the Farina should blow on them, it may be the means of propagating an inferiour species among us. For that reason I should be glad that you would not send any more of it. As the quality of our Rice is infinitely superiour to that of Italy, I am persuaded it will annually gain ground in France, and finally exclude the other entirely. This is a considerable object to us, and will likewise be of service to the Manufacturers of France. I believe Italy receives money from France in return for her Rice. We should want Negro Cloth, Blankets and implements of Husbandry as articles of absolute necessity; besides many others of convenience, and some of Luxury.—The loss of my Estate during the War and the distress to which I should have been exposed if it had not been recovered, have determined me to prevent my Sons, as much as may be in my power, from feeling a similar calamity to the extent that I should have felt it. My desire is to bring them up to some Business, or Profession, which I hope will secure them an Independence. The elder will be 17 years old next May. He is now at the College of New York, and has chosen the Profession of a Lawyer. He is a pretty good Classical Scholar and is now studying the Mathematics, which I think a necessary Foundation. My wish is that he should continue his studies in America till he is 21 years old, that he should be admited to the Bar in this Country, and then pass a year, or two in Europe. I have heard you speak of the University of Williamsburgh, and of the abilities of Mr. Wyth, which make me desirous of his being placed for two, or three years under the tuition of that Gentleman. My second son is between 11 and 12 years old. It is my desire that he should be an Engineer; and this is entirely conformable to his own wishes. He is now here under the direction of an excellent Tutor, and is much farther advanced than Boys of his age generally are. Brigadier General Du Plessis was here last Spring, and was very obliging in offering to take him with him to France, and to charge himself with the care of his education. I could not be induced to part with him so young, and to put him under the care of a Gentleman with whom I had so short an acquaintance. The Profession of an Engineer, when thoroughly understood, embraces a very considerable portion of human knowledge, and of the most useful kind. In War it will be improper for America to depend entirely upon Foreigners; and if my Son should become a Planter, it will be of great service to him to be well acquainted with Surveying, water courses, flood gates, machines, mills and Buildings of every kind. France is the proper school for him. If he should be sent thither, I should wish him to obtain Rank, when he should be found deserving of it, and that he should be at liberty to quit the service whenever he should be inclined to do so. I address myself to your Friendship upon this occasion, and request your advice in everything that relates to it. When would be the proper time to send him, where ought he to be placed, and what would be the annual expense? I am almost afraid of troubling you too much by requesting you to take the care of him. But when I consider of his being placed in a foreign Country, at such a distance from me, and entirely among strangers, I am alarmed, and detered from carrying my wishes into execution. To make my Sons useful and valuable Members of the Community in which they are to live, is the object nearest my Heart. Their dispositions, and capacities give me reason to hope that I shall not be disappointed.—It is thought here by many that the disputes in Holland will be terminated without a War. I wish that may be the case, but do not think it will be so. The conduct of the Statholder was, during the War, so hostile to the Interests of France, and Spain, that those Powers will not be satisfied to have him placed in a situation which will enable him to injure them again. The Printer of the Columbian Herald assures me that his Newspaper has been regularly sent for you to Mr. Jay. As you do not mention having received any of them, since those sent by Mr. Chateaufort, I fear they have miscarried. I applied to the Legislature for an order to have the Laws sent to you as often as they should be printed. This has been granted, and Mr. Dart, the Clerk of the Assembly, has promised me to take care that they shall be regularly transmited to Mr. Jay for you. I have the honour to be with great regard Dear Sir Your most obt. hble. Servt.,

RA. IZARD

Be pleased to present our respects to Miss Jefferson.

RC (DLC). Not recorded in SJL (see note to Rutledge to TJ, 23 Oct. 1787), but on 17 July 1788 TJ informed Izard that the present letter was received on 24 Apr. 1788.

From John Rutledge, Jr.

DR. SIR   Paris November 10th: 1787

The not having heard from my friends since I left America, renders my situation in this Country extremely disagreeable. When I embarked for Europe my Intention was to have continued in Paris untill the latter end of November, but, hearing that Parliament will meet in a few Days, determines me, if it is possible, to go over to England immediately. On coming to Europe I brought with me a hundred and fifty Guineas, with a Letter of Credit also on Messrs. le Coutulx for three thousand Livres, and thinking that this would be as much Money as I should want, whilst in france, desired my friends not to remit to me here; but to have funds lodged in London for me by the first of December. However, I find that I have calculated illy, that living in Paris is much more expensive than I expected and in short am under pecuniary Embarassments. That I shall hear from my friends by the next Packet, I regard as a thing certain—But convinced that I shall spend my time in England to much greater advantage, than I possibly can here, has determined me, rather than wait her arrival, to presume so much on our Acquaintance as to request that you will advance me untill the first of December, twenty or five and twenty Guineas? Thinking that I might have Letters in London, I the last week wrote to Mr. Rucker, requesting that he would enquire for me? I have just received his Answer in which he says, "if the non-receiving any letters puts you to an Inconvenience with regard to Money Matters draw on me immediately for forty or fifty Guineas, which are very much at your Service." But as my Acquaintance with this

[340]

Gentleman has been rather of the hot-bed kind, made during his short stay at Paris I regarded his offer as more meriting my thanks, than my acceptance: and determined not to avail myself of his friendship unless reduced to the most poinant distress. I have the honor to be with Sentiments of great Regard and esteem Your Excellency's most Obedt. J: Rutledge Junior

RC (DLC); endorsed. Recorded in SJL as received 10 Nov. 1787.

From the Commissioners of the Treasury

Sir Board of Treasury November 10. 1787.

We have the honor of transmitting to your Excellency two Acts of the United States in Congress of the 12th. and 25th. of October last: the one, relative to the Americans who are Captives at Algiers, the other to the Prize Money due to Captain Jones' Squadron from the Court of Denmark. Mr. Jarvis (who is so obliging as to take charge of our dispatches) will deliver to you the documents relative to this claim, which on Captain Jones' arrival were transmitted by him to Congress and referred to this Board.

We have no doubt but every exertion will be made use of on your part to obtain satisfaction from the Court of Denmark, and that such arrangements will be taken by you that the Monies recovered may remain (as the Act directs) in your hands till the further order of Congress.

In your Letter of the 17. June last you state the propriety of such measures being adopted for paying the Salaries due to the Foreign Ministers and public Servants in Europe, so that one may not in this respect be dependant on the other. This opinion is perfectly consonant to our Ideas; and we shall therefore transmit to Mr. Carmichael a Letter of Credit on Messrs. Wilhem and Jan Willink, and Nicholas & Jacob Van Staphorst of Amsterdam; authorising him to draw quarterly on that house for the Salary assigned to him; enclosed you will receive a Letter to the same effect.

We are sorry to find that Mr. Grand is so much in advance as your Letter States; such is the present state of the Treasury here that we have little or no prospect of being able to make any remittances to him from this Country, and by the last accounts we received from the Commissioners of Loans in Holland, the Loan which had been opened in that Country for a Million of Florins, filled so slowly that they were apprehensive of falling short of

Funds to face the February Interest. So soon as we receive Intelligence from Holland, that the subscription to the Loan will admit of a Reimbursement to Mr. Grand we shall give directions for that purpose. You will be pleased to make this communication to that Gentleman: for fear we should not be able to write to him by this opportunity.

It gives us pleasure to learn that you are likely to settle in a satisfactory manner the claims of Mr. Dobrie, upon which the disposition of the public Stores at Nantz depends. We shall be glad to be furnished with the result of this settlement as soon as possible together with a particular Abstract of the property subject to the Attachment, that we may give such directions about it as may be found necessary.

You will observe that the Act of the 12th of October last constitutes the Balance of the former Appropriation on Account of the Barbary Treaties a Fund for redeeming the American Captives at Algiers. At present we are not able to ascertain what this Balance is. We hope soon to be able to effect this when if the State of the Loans in Holland will admit of it (without hazarding the payment of the Interest) we shall transmit directions to the Commissioners to answer your drafts for the whole or such part of the balance as you shall find necessary for executing the intentions of Congress.

Whilst the fate of the Constitution proposed by the late General Convention at Philadelphia is in suspence there is every reason to apprehend that the several States will if possible be more remiss in the payment of their several Quotas than they have hitherto been. The completion of the Subscription to the late Loan in Holland is therefore an Object of great moment and as such we doubt not that whatever Influence you can use to promote this Object will be exerted.

We have the honor to be with the greatest respect Your Excellys. Most Obedt. Huml. Servts.,

SAMUEL OSGOOD
ARTHUR LEE

RC (DLC); in a clerk's hand, signed by Samuel Osgood and Arthur Lee. Recorded in SJL as received 19 Dec. 1787. Enclosures: (1) Tr of the resolution of Congress of 12 Oct. 1787 (same as enclosure No. 5 in John Jay to TJ, 24 Oct. 1787, q.v.). (2) Tr of resolution of Congress of 25 Oct. 1787, authorizing and instructing TJ to negotiate and settle, on the best terms possible, for the prize money due from Denmark, holding the money "till the further Order of Congress," with power to send John Paul Jones "or any other Agent" to conduct the negotiations, the agent to be allowed a commission of 5% for expenses (JCC, XXXIII, 705-6). (3) Tr of the Commissioners' letter to Willink & Van Staphorst, 10 Nov. 1787, instructing them to honor drafts made on them by TJ "on Account of his Salary, which is nine thousand Dollars

per Annum," which drafts will prob- plicate," in different clerks' hands, both
ably be made quarterly (Tr and "Du- signed by Osgood and Lee, in DLC).

From Mary Barclay

Sir [11 Nov. 1787]

I have had the honour of receiving your obliging favour of the
3d and shall be happy to see you whenever you make a visit to St.
Germains which I hope is not yet intirely given up. I propose
drawing on you in the course of this week for 724 livres which I
think was the sum you mentioned to me. I have had too many
instances of your desire to oblige and render me every service in
your power, to doubt of it on any occasion; and if I should be disappointed in receiving remittances which I expect next month will
with pleasure make use of the liberty you are so good as to allow
me, of applying to you. I have the honour to be with sincere esteem
and respect Sir your most obedient humble servant,

Mary Barclay

RC (MHi); endorsed; without date which has been supplied from internal evidence and an entry in SJL for the receipt of a letter of this date from Mrs. Barclay
on 13 Nov. 1787.
There is the following entry in TJ's Account Book under 24 Nov. 1787: "pd.
Mrs. Barclay's bill for 724.ᵗᵗ which balances my acct. with Mr. Barclay."

To Ferdinand Grand

Sir Paris Nov. 11. 1787.

Mr. Rutledge, who has the honor of being known to you, and
who is the son of my very particular friend, has occasion for 20 or
25 guineas. It would give me great pain to see him suffer, and it
is not in my power to assist him. The sums to which I limit my
draughts on Holland monthly, are generally pre-engaged by demands for the state of Virginia, or for the United states, in addition
to my own private occasions. Mr. Rutledge thinks himself sure of
replacing the money early in December, and if he does not, I will
do it in my draught at the close of that month, should not general
orders arrive earlier to set all our money-matters to rights here.
I will ask the favor of you therefore to accomodate Mr. Rutledge
with this sum, say 600.ᵗᵗ either in his name or my own as you
please. I believe he would wish to receive it tomorrow morning,
wherefore I would ask an order to your cashier by the return of

the bearer. I have the honour to be, with sentiments of the most perfect esteem, Sir Your most obedt. & most humble servt.,

TH: JEFFERSON

PrC (DLC).

TJ's prompt assistance to a young American in distress stands in marked contrast to his response to Madame Townsend's similar request a few days earlier (see TJ to Madame Townsend, 7 Nov. 1787).

From La Blancherie

MONSIEUR   Paris le 11 9bre 1787

J'ai reçu la lettre que vous m'avez fait l'honneur de m'écrire en date du 9 de ce mois. Je suis honteux de la peine que je vous ai causée, relativement aux détails dans lesquels vous entrez, sur ce qui vous empêche de prendre l'association. J'ai l'honneur de vous observer, que je ne vous l'avois point proposée. Si j'ai desiré d'avoir celui de vous voir à l'occasion de l'Etablissement, c'étoit pour vous entretenir de son objet, et des ressources gratuites, qu'il offre aux hommes, de tous les pays, pour la communication des connoissances, le progrès des sciences, et des arts, l'encouragement des gens à talents. Il faut si peu d'argent pour cet etablissement, que je vais auprès des personnages, tels que vous, Monsieur, beaucoup plus pour seconder les vues qui me paroissent vous animer que par d'autres motifs. Le principe de la réciprocité des bons offices, que j'ai établi, dirige, seul, mes démarches. Quand il sera bien senti, et beaucoup d'hommes ne sont [pas] assez murs pour cela, il n'y aura point de considerations capables d'en arrêter le developpement.

Quant à Mr. Adams, Je suis étonné, qu'il parle [d'un] premier et d'un second etablissement. Depuis qu'il a signé son engagement, il y a bien eu une interruption pendant une année, mais il n'y a point eu deux établissements, à moins qu'il n'appelle, ainsi, un changement, dans la forme d'administration, qui a eu lieu, l'année dernière; mais en regardant l'année d'interruption, comme non avenue, Il doit toutes celles, pour Lesquelles il n'a point renoncé à son association; d'autant mieux, que depuis le changement que j'ai fait à la forme d'Administration, j'ai annoncé dans la feuille, que tous les associés, à qui elle ne conviendroit pas, pouvoient renoncer à l'Etablissement, indépendemment de tout engagement. Je suis fâché que les feuilles que j'ai adressées, exactement, à M. Adams, lui aient couté du Port. J'avois pris des arrangements, pour que cela n'arrivat pas; c'étoit une raison de plus pour me faire

[344]

savoir qu'il n'en vouloit point. On me rend toujours service, en m'évitant des dépenses. Je continuerai encore, d'ici à la fin de l'année, l'envoi des feuilles, parce que cela ne m'occasionnera pas une grande dépense de plus et Je compte sur la justice de M. Adams. Au surplus je fais un réglement, pour qu'à partir de 1788, nul ne reçoive la feuille, et ne jouisse des autres avantages de l'Etablissement, à titre d'associé, sans avoir payé d'avance. Je vous demande pardon de tous ces détails, mais la bonté avec laquelle vous avez bien voulu m'annoncer, ce qui vous empêche de con-courir, par l'association, à la consistance de l'Etablissement, me justifiera à vos yeux.

Je suis avec respect, Monsieur, Votre très-humble et très-obéis-sant serviteur, LA BLANCHERIE

RC (DLC); endorsed. Recorded in SJL as received 12 Nov. 1787.

From Alexander Donald

DEAR SIR Richmond 12th. Novemr. 1787

Many thanks to you for your very Friendly and Polite letter of the 28th. July.

You will no doubt have seen before this time the result of the deliberations of the Convention, which was assembled at Philadel-phia last Summer, for revising, and amending the Federal Consti-tution. I am sorry to say it is like to meet with strong opposition in this state, at this moment I do believe that a great majority of the People approve of it, but I can easily conceive, that interested men will do every thing in their power, between this and the electing of our State Convention, to poison the minds of the People, and get them persuaded to give their votes for such Gentlemen as they know are decidedly against the adoption of the New Constitution. I will not presume to be competent to give an opinion on such a Complex subject, but I can see that there may be some objections made to it, but still it is my sincere opinion, that the Adoption of it will be the salvation of America, For at present there is hardly the semblance of Law or Government in any of the States, and for want of a Superintending Power over the whole, a dissolution seems to be impending. I staid two days with General Washington at Mount Vernon about Six weeks ago. He is in perfect good health, and looks almost as well as he did Twenty years ago. I never saw him so keen for any thing in my life, as he is for the adoption of the new Form of Government. As the eyes of all America are turned towards this truly Great and Good Man, for the First President, I took the liberty of sounding him upon it. He appears to be greatly against going into Publick Life again, Pleads in Excuse for himself, His Love of Retirement, and his advanced Age, but Notwithstanding of these, I am fully of opinion he may be induced to appear once more on the Publick Stage of Life. I form my opinion from what passed between us in a very long and serious conversation as well as from what I could gather from Mrs. Washington on same subject.

Our Assembly are now sitting. They have not yet done much business, but what has been done is highly commendable. They have in very strong and pointed language thrown out a proposal for emitting paper money, and they have repealed the Port Bill, which was attended with numberless inconveniencies to the Merchants. At the request of Colo. George Mason, I have drawn up a Plan for a new Bill, which will more effectually secure the Revenue than the former, and will remove the many objections that Merchantile People had to the Last. Till this Assembly an Idea seemed to prevail almost universally, that the Landed and Commercial Interests were opposed to each other. I have been at great pains to do away this erroneous opinion, and from the Laws that have been made for two years past, such unexpected consequences have followed, that the minds of the People are now disposed to hear reasoning upon the subject of Trade, from those who have been long engaged in it. Our installment bill for paying Debts engrosses much time and attention. This is a favourite Child of your Friend Colo. George Nicholas. I have only one objection to it upon the Principles they talk off, and that is the Precedent, I am satisfied that take the state altogether, it owes more money than the lands can produce for three years. Therefore the Debts cannot be paid in that time. I would be for giving four years, which surely would be much better for the Creditor, than going to Law, when he could not obtain a Judgement in less than seven, and if the sum is considerable, he must follow his Debtor into the Court of Appeals and from thence into Chancery, and after going through every Court when he has an Execution served upon the Estate of his Debtor thro a last Replyvin, (this is a new Trick) And in short every delay and Chicanery is made use of to stave off the payment of Just Debts and this Country which is blessed by Nature with many advantages is likely to go to Anarchy and Ruin, for want of a proper execution of the Laws, and of a Firm and Efficient Government.

In order to avoid the sickly season I left this place the latter end of June, and did not return till the 12th. Febr. I went as far as New York, where I staid a month. I was two weeks at Philada. in going, and returning. This gave me an opportunity of being frequently with Mr. Morris. He told me that he expected a renewal of his Contract with the Farmers General of France, and as the proceedings of the Counsil of Berni were forced upon them, and contrary to their wishes, he insinuated that individuals would find great difficulty in disposing of any Tobacco in that Kingdom. I hope Mr. Morris will be mistaken in both. Sure I am that it will be much against the Interest of this State in particular, For the inferior kinds of Tobacco are fit for the French market only. Therefore give any one man a monopoly of supplying that market, he of course sees a monopoly in the purchase of the inferiour qualities of Tobacco in this state and so fix the price as low as he pleases. I had intended to have shipt largely to France in future, in expectation of the Trade being thrown entirely open, but from what you have been so obliging as write me, and from what Mr. Morris has said to me, I am affraid to venture deep. I will however take my Chance of one Cargo from this River of 5. or 600. hhds. I will send it to Havre as you recommend, and I will take the liberty of writing my Friends there, that if they find any difficulty in selling the Cargo, to apply to you for advice, Being convinced that you will give them every assistance in your Power, for the good of this State, as well as for my particular Interest. You will oblige me exceedingly by writing me as early as possible your Sentiments on this subject, that I may regulate myself accordingly. If the Farmers are affraid that they may be disappointed in their quantity, were they to trust entirely to what might be sent to them in the way of Trade, I would willingly and gladly contract with them for Ten Thousand hhds. annually, at the same price they allow Mr. Morris, or even for a Livre per hundred less. I can afford to take less than Mr. Morris, As I can command a better Exchange for my bills, and will save the heavy Commission which he is obliged to pay to Old Mr. Alexander and others. And I may safely say, that being situated at this place; I could send better Tobacco than Mr. Morris can possibly collect to the Northward of this. In my last, I think I took the liberty of mentioning to you, that Mr. Robt. Burton and myself are connected in business, he is settled in London, where it is conducted under the Firm of Donald and Burton. You will probably recollect him as he lived several years at this place previous to the Revolution. If there is any prospect of obtaining a Contract for me, I beg you will inform him of it, and he will give any security that may be required for the performance of the same.

Your old school Companion W. Lewis, of Warner Hall was here staying with me when I had the pleasure of receiving your letter. It was so Friendly, and so very Flattering to my Pride, that I could not resist the vanity of showing it to him. He added to my Pride, by declaring (what I was pretty much convinced of before) that of all the Men he ever knew in his Life, he believed you to be the most sincere in your profession of Friendship. I am free to say, that when we used to pass some jovial days together at Hanover Town, I did not then imagine, that at this time you would be in Paris, Ambassador to the Court of Versailles. Some People in your High Caracter would be very apt to forget their old acquaintance, but you are not, and I must be allowed to do myself the justice to declare, I never entertained an Idea that you would.

I will do myself the pleasure of writing you again by the Bowman the Ship I intend sending to Havre. I hope she will sail in a month. I am with the highest Esteem and Respect Dear Sir Your mo: obt. Humb. St.,   ADONALD

RC (DLC); endorsed.

From Jean Antoine Houdon

Ce 12 9bre. 1787

Mr. Houdon a L'honneur de prevenir Monsieur de Jefferson que Le Buste de Mr. Le Mis. de La fayette sera emballé cette Semaine. Il a celuy de Luy envoyer aussi L'adresse de L'emballeur afin que Monsieur de Jefferson puisse Luy faire passer Les instructions pour L'adresse et la destination de ce Buste.

Mr. de Lorme, Emballeur, en Sa Maison, Rue de grenelle St. Honoré, vis à vis La Rue des deux Ecus.

RC (MHi); addressed. Not recorded in SJL.
There is in Vi the following receipt in Houdon's hand: "J'ai recu de la part de Monsr de jeferson La somme de mille Cinq Cent Livres concernant Le buste de Mr. Le Marquis de La fayet executé en Marbre a paris ce 1 Novembre 1787 Houdon"; endorsed by TJ: "Fayette's bust Houdon's rect. 1500.tt Nov. 1. 1787."

From La Boullaye

Paris le 12. 9bre. 1787

Vous m'aves fait l'honneur, Monsieur, de m'écrire, sur ce que les

Emploiés des fermes au Hâvre exigent les droits anciens sur une cargaison de potasse provenant du commerce américain.

Il n'est encore intervenu ni arrêt ni décision qui exempte de droits ces matieres. La Lettre que M. de Calonne vous ecrivit le 22 8bre. de l'année derniere annonçait seulement qu'il serait pris des informations à cet egard. Cependant comme la potasse est dans le nombre des objets venant d'amerique dont l'administration est disposée a favoriser l'importation en France, M. le Contrôleur Général s'est déterminé à accorder l'exemption de tous droits sur la cargaison dont il s'agit, et c'est avec plaisir que je vous transmets la décision de ce Ministre.

J'ai l'honneur d'être avec un respectueux attachement Monsieur, Votre très humble et très obeissant Serviteur,

DE LA BOULLAYE

RC (DLC); in a clerk's hand, with complimentary close and signature in La Boullaye's hand. Recorded in SJL as received 15 Nov. 1787.

To John Rutledge, Jr.

Monday Nov. 12. 1787.

Mr. Jefferson's compliments to Mr. Rutledge. If he will be so good as to go this morning to Mr. Grand's in Paris, they will furnish him the 600ᵗᵗ of which he has occasion. He will be so good as to ask for Mr. Grand the father, as having business with him particularly. The house being considerably in advance for the U.S. and the son less friendly than the father rendered it necessary for Mr. Jefferson to see the latter, and makes it best for Mr. Rutledge to do the same, that no difficulties or delays may be affected.

RC (NcD); addressed: "A Monsieur Monsieur Rutledge hotel d'Angleterre rue Traversiere St. Honoré." Not recorded in SJL.

To John Adams

DEAR SIR   Paris Nov. 13. 1787.

This will be delivered you by young Mr. Rutledge. Your knowledge of his father will introduce him to your notice. He merits it moreover on his own account.

I am now to acknolege your favors of Oct. 8 and 26. That of August 25. was duly received, nor can I recollect by what accident I was prevented from acknoleging it in mine of Sep. 28. It has been

[349]

the source of my subsistence hitherto, and must continue to be so till I receive letters on the affairs of money from America. Van Staphorsts & Willinks have answered my draughts.—Your books for M. de la Fayette are received here. I will notify it to him, who is at present with his provincial assembly in Auvergne.

Little is said lately of the progress of the negociations between the courts of Petersburg, Vienna, and Versailles. The distance of the former and the cautious, unassuming character of it's minister here is one cause of delays: a greater one is the greediness and instable character of the emperor. Nor do I think that the Principal here will be easily induced to lend himself to any connection which shall threaten a war within a considerable number of years. His own reign will be that of peace only, in all probability; and were any accident to tumble him down, this country would immediately gird on it's sword and buckler, and trust to occurrences for supplies of money. The wound their honour has sustained festers in their hearts, and it may be said with truth that the Archbishop and a few priests, determined to support his measures because proud to see their order come again into power, are the only advocates for the line of conduct which has been pursued. It is said and believed thro' Paris literally that the Count de Monmorin 'pleuroit comme un enfant' when obliged to sign the counter declaration. Considering the phrase as figurative, I believe it expresses the distress of his heart. Indeed he has made no secret of his individual opinion. In the mean time the Principal goes on with a firm and patriotic spirit, in reforming the cruel abuses of the government and preparing a new constitution which will give to this people as much liberty as they are capable of managing. This I think will be the glory of his administration, because, tho' a good theorist in finance, he is thought to execute badly. They are about to open a loan of 100. millions to supply present wants, and it is said the preface of the Arret will contain a promise of the Convocation of the States general during the ensuing year. 12. or 15. provincial assemblies are already in action, and are going on well; and I think that tho' the nation suffers in reputation, it will gain infinitely in happiness under the present administration. I inclose to Mr. Jay a pamphlet which I will beg of you to forward. I leave it open for your perusal. When you shall have read it, be so good as to stick a wafer in it. It is not yet published, nor will be for some days. This copy has been ceded to me as a favor.

How do you like our new constitution? I confess there are things in it which stagger all my dispositions to subscribe to what such an assembly has proposed. The house of federal representatives will not be adequate to the management of affairs either foreign or federal. Their President seems a bad edition of a Polish king. He may be reelected from 4. years to 4. years for life. Reason and experience prove to us that a chief magistrate, so continuable, is an officer for life. When one or two generations shall have proved that this is an office for life, it becomes on every succession worthy of intrigue, of bribery, of force, and even of foreign interference. It will be of great consequence to France and England to have America governed by a Galloman or Angloman. Once in office, and possessing the military force of the union, without either the aid or check of a council, he would not be easily dethroned, even if the people could be induced to withdraw their votes from him. I wish that at the end of the 4. years they had made him for ever ineligible a second time. Indeed I think all the good of this new constitution might have been couched in three or four new articles to be added to the good, old, and venerable fabrick, which should have been preserved even as a religious relique.—Present me and my daughters affectionately to Mrs. Adams. The younger one continues to speak of her warmly. Accept yourself assurances of the sincere esteem and respect with which I have the honour to be, Dear Sir, your friend & servant,   TH: JEFFERSON

P.S. I am in negociation with de la Blancherie. You shall hear from me when arranged.

RC (MHi: AMT); endorsed. PrC (DLC). The enclosed pamphlet for John Jay has not been identified.

YOUR FAVORS OF OCT. 8 AND 26: Adams' letters were dated 9 and 28 Oct.; TJ received letters from W. S. Smith which were dated 8 and 26 Oct. 1787 and which he also answered by this conveyance.

To John Bondfield

SIR   Paris Nov. 13. 1787.

It is sometime since I have done myself the honour of acknoleging regularly the receipt of your favors. Those of Oct. 6. 8.[1] 12. and 20. have been duly received. Had the war taken place, your apprehensions of the usurpation of our flag by British vessels would certainly have been verified. But even in peace it is very desireable to strip them of this advantage. I shall soon have the honor of communicating to you some regulations which will render it indispensably necessary: and I hope we shall not be much longer without putting our commerce in the ports of France under a regular superintendance.

I have taken the liberty of desiring Monsieur Lambert of Frontignan to send to your care 100 bottles of wine addressed to the Count de Moustier minister plenipotentiary for this court at New York. I will beg of you to receive it, pay the expences to and at Bordeaux and to forward it to Monsr. de Moustier at New York, notifying me what you shall have paid, which I will immediately replace in the hands of your banker here. I have the honour to be with much esteem Sir Your most obedient humble servant,

TH: JEFFERSON

P.S. Would it be practicable to find what proportion of our productions coming to the ports of this country are paid for in productions and manufactures of France? Adding thereto the sums expended here by the ships and crews?

PrC (DLC).   1 Bondfield's letter was dated 10 Oct.

To Stephen Cathalan, Sr.

SIR   Paris Nov. 13. 1787.

I have been daily expecting to communicate to you a regulation on the subject of tobacco, and an arrêt concerning all other articles of our commerce. Still however they are unfinished, tho' I think they cannot be so many days. In the mean time I am favored with your letter of the 4th. inst. and congratulate you on your happy meeting with the ladies of your family and your safe arrival at Marseilles. I will beg the favor of you to forward the Couffe of Egyptian rice by a Roulier or such other voiture as you think best. It will be quicker and more certain than to send it round by water: I will pray you at the same time to send me for my own use the articles below mentioned, as nearly in the quantities there stated as the usual packages will admit. A little more or less will make no odds.—The late pacification leaves little new to be communicated. It is believed that a new loan of 100 millions will be opened, and that the preamble to it will promise the Convocation des etats generaux for the next year. Present me in friendly terms to Madame Cathalan the elder and younger, and accept assurances of the esteem with which I have the honour to be Sir your most obedient humble servant,

TH: JEFFERSON

Anchois, une petite barrique
Sardines, une petite barrique
Thon, une petite quantité quelconque
Huile vierge d'Aix, veritable, [86.] livres
figues, veritables Marseillaises. 30. livres
raisins de Smyrne, sans pepin. [12.] livres
Brignons (espece de prune) [30.] livres
Olives, deux petites barriques.

P.S. Be so good as to send me the note of your disbursements and I will replace them in the hands of your banker here.

PrC (MHi). The figures in brackets (supplied) are from the invoice enclosed in Cathalan to TJ, 24 Jan. 1788, q.v.

To Dr. Lambert

à Paris ce 13me Novembre 1787.

J'aurois eté très charmé, Monsieur, de vous devenir utile en tachant de vous procurer le Brevet de Medecin de camp, que vous avez desiré. Si je n'aurois pû vous garantir le succès de mes efforts, j'aurois au moins repondu de leur sincerité. L'etablissement de la paix pourtant m'a epargné la peine de vous prouver combien peu vous auroient valu mes desirs de vous servir.

La personne dont Monsieur Cabanis vous a parlé au sujet de votre vin, etoit Monsieur le comte de Moustier qui est parti pour l'Amerique, ou il est nommé ministre plenipotentiaire de votre cour près le Congrès. Je lui avois proposé de tacher d'introduire le gout pour votre vin en Amerique. Il m'a chargé de vous demander une centaine de bouteilles de la même recolte de la mienne, dont je lui ai fourni un echantillon. Ayez la bonté donc, Monsieur, de lui envoyer cette quantité, en l'adressant 'à son Excellence Monsieur le Comte de Moustier, ministre plenipotentiaire de sa majesté très chretienne à la Nouvelle York.' Monsieur Bondfield, Consul Americain à Bordeaux, le recevra, et le fera passer à la Nouvelle York. Je lui ecrirai pour l'en prevenir. Envoyez le, s'il vous plait, par le canal de Languedoc, et la Garonne et ayez la bonté de m'annoncer le montant du prix et des fraix que j'aurai l'honneur de remettre à votre banquier ici. J'ai celui d'etre avec beaucoup de consideration, Monsieur, votre très humble et tres obeissant serviteur,

TH: JEFFERSON

PrC (MHi) endorsed.

[353]

To André Limozin

Sir   Paris Nov. 13. 1787.

It is some time since I have had the honour of acknowleging regularly the receipt of your favors. Those of Oct. 11. and 20. and Nov. 2. and [9.] have come duly to hand. I am very glad the American sailors have found the protection of so good a friend. I have been for some time in daily expectation of communicating to you some interesting regulations on our commerce. But as yet the minister has not finished them. These will render it necessary that our commerce in the ports of France be put under a regular superintendance, which I hope we shall be enabled to do ere long. It would be of great service to us could we by any means know what proportion of the American productions brought in[to] the several ports of France are paid for in productions and manufactures of this country, adding thereto the monies expended in the country by the ships and crews. Will you be so good as to tell me whether such a thing will be practicable.—I have taken the liberty of sending to your address by water a package containing the bust of the Marquis de la Fayette to be forwarded to the Governor of Virginia by any vessel going into James or York rivers, of which I will beg your care. I have the honor to be with much esteem Sir Your most obedient humble servant,   TH: JEFFERSON

PrC (DLC).

To James Maury

Dear Sir   Paris Nov. 13. 1787.

I received your favor of Oct. 25. the day before yesterday only. It would be needless for me therefore to add to what you already know on the subject of peace and war. The principal minister here is so intent on domestic improvements, and on peace as necessary to give leisure for them, that it will not be his fault if it be disturbed again. It will be equally unnecessary for me to give you a formal attestation of your being a citizen of the United states. Should any occasion for it arise hereafter I shall be always ready to certify it.—With respect to tobacco the contract with Mr. Morris and the order of Berni cease with this year. I am obtaining an arrangement for the five years which yet remain of the present lease to the farmers general, by which they will be obliged to take all the tobacco for which they shall have occasion from America, except about one fifth Northern, which they represent as necessary. They will be obliged to take such only as comes directly from America, without having touched at any European port, in *French* or *American* bottoms, and to make the purchase *in France*. It will be particularly watched that they purchase not a single hogshead in England. By this I hope to have completely effected the diverting so much of the tobacco trade as amounts to their own consumption from England to France. I am glad to find also by your letter that this operation will have the effect to raise the price of this commodity at the English market. 24000 hhds. of tobacco a year, less at that market than heretofore, must produce some change, and it could not be for the worse. The order to the farmers will name only 14,000 hhds. a year, but it is certain they must extend it themselves nearly or quite to 24,000, as their consumption is near 30,000. I am endeavoring to bring hither also, directly, the rice of America, consumed in this country. At present they buy it from London. I am of opinion they could consume the whole of what is made in America, especially if the rice states will introduce the culture of the Piedmont and Egyptian rices also, both of which qualities are demanded here in concurrence with that of Carolina. I have procured for them the seed from Egypt and Piedmont. The indulgences given to American whale oil will ensure it's coming here directly. In general I am in hopes to ensure here the transportation of all our commodities which come to this country, in American and French bottoms exclusively, which will countervail the effect of the British navigation act on our carrying business. The returns in French instead of English manufactures will take place by degrees. Supposing that these details cannot but be agreeable to you as a merchant and as an American, I trouble you with them; being with much sincerity and on all occasions, Dear Sir Your friend & servant,

Th: Jefferson

PrC (DLC).

To William Stephens Smith

Dear Sir   Paris Nov. 13. 1787.

I am now to acknolege the receipt of your favors of October the 4th. 8th. and 26th. In the last you apologize for your letters of introduction to Americans coming here. It is so far from needing apology on your part, that it calls for thanks on mine. I endeavor

[355]

to shew civilities to all the Americans who come here, and who will give me opportunities of doing it: and it is a matter of comfort to know from a good quarter what they are, and how far I may go in my attentions to them.—Can you send me Woodmason's bills for the two copying presses for the M. de la fayette, and the M. de Chastellux? The latter makes one article in a considerable account, of old standing, and which I cannot present for want of this article.—I do not know whether it is to yourself or Mr. Adams I am to give my thanks for the copy of the new constitution. I beg leave through you to place them where due. It will be yet three weeks before I shall receive them from America. There are very good articles in it: and very bad. I do not know which preponderate. What we have lately read in the history of Holland, in the chapter on the Stadtholder, would have sufficed to set me against a Chief magistrate eligible for a long duration, if I had ever been disposed towards one: and what we have always read of the elections of Polish kings should have forever excluded the idea of one continuable for life. Wonderful is the effect of impudent and persevering lying. The British ministry have so long hired their gazetteers to repeat and model into every form lies about our being in anarchy, that the world has at length believed them, the English nation has believed them, the ministers themselves have come to believe them, and what is more wonderful, we have believed them ourselves. Yet where does this anarchy exist? Where did it ever exist, except in the single instance of Massachusets? And can history produce an instance of a rebellion so honourably conducted? I say nothing of it's motives. They were founded in ignorance, not wickedness. God forbid we should ever be 20. years without such a rebellion. The people can not be all, and always, well informed. The part which is wrong will be discontented in proportion to the importance of the facts they misconceive. If they remain quiet under such misconceptions it is a lethargy, the forerunner of death to the public liberty. We have had 13. states independant 11. years. There has been one rebellion. That comes to one rebellion in a century and a half for each state. What country before ever existed a century and half without a rebellion? And what country can preserve it's liberties if their rulers are not warned from time to time that their people preserve the spirit of resistance? Let them take arms. The remedy is to set them right as to facts, pardon and pacify them. What signify a few lives lost in a century or two? The tree of liberty must be refreshed from time to time with the blood of patriots and tyrants. It is it's natural manure. Our Convention

[356]

has been too much impressed by the insurrection of Massachusets: and in the spur of the moment they are setting up a kite to keep the hen yard in order. I hope in god this article will be rectified before the new constitution is accepted.—You ask me if any thing transpires here on the subject of S. America? Not a word. I know that there are combustible materials there, and that they wait the torch only. But this country probably will join the extinguishers.— The want of facts worth communicating to you has occasioned me to give a little loose to dissertation. We must be contented to amuse, when we cannot inform. Present my respects to Mrs. Smith, and be assured of the sincere esteem of Dear Sir Your friend & servant,   TH: JEFFERSON

PrC (DLC).
It was to Adams that TJ owed the COPY OF THE NEW CONSTITUTION (see Adams to TJ, 10 Nov. 1787), and, thanks to the French chargé d'affaires in New York, TJ was wrong in think-

ing that it would be THREE WEEKS before he would receive other copies from America: Otto's copies arrived two days after the present letter was written (see Otto to TJ, 25 Sep. 1787).

From Madame Townsend

le 13 9bre. 1787

J'ai reçu l'honneur de votre lettre Monsieur, et depuis ce tems n'ai pas quittée, la Campagne. Je ne saurois vous exprimer combien je suis fachée de vous avoir importuné par une demande sur la quelle vous voulés bien prendre la peine d'entrer dans des details. Je sais que l'on a beaucoup de peine dans ce moment a réaliser des fonds, c'est ce qui fait que j'avois pris le parti d'aller a Londres pour vendre a la Banck. Je vous prie Monsieur de recevoir mes regrets de vous avoir importuné dans cette circonstance et de me croire tres sincerement votre tres humble et obeissante s.,

TOWNSEND

Voulés vous avoir la bonté de me dire le plus sure moyen d'envoyer une lettre en Dánmark?

RC (MoSHi); endorsed. Recorded in SJL as received 13 Nov. 1787.
There is no evidence that TJ replied to the present letter, though he may have done so in response to the query in

the postscript, which would seem to be a none-too-subtle hint that the fruitless outcome of her appeals to TJ was about to be communicated to John Paul Jones.

From the Commissioners of the Treasury

Board of Treasury, 13 Nov. 1787. Omitted mentioning in their letter of 10 Nov. "that in a late Report made by this Board to Congress, on the subject of the Prize Monies due to the late Squadron under the Command of Captain John Paul Jones, from the Court of Denmark, we gave it as our opinion that the Bonds heretofore given by Captain Jones for the discharge of the Trust reposed in him as Agent for the Captors, were not (from circumstances which had since arisen) sufficient."

RC (DLC); 2 p.; in a clerk's hand, signed by Samuel Osgood and Arthur Lee; at head of text: "(Duplicate)"; endorsed.

To John Trumbull

DEAR SIR   Paris Nov. 13. 1787.

Both your favors of Oct. 30. and Nov. 2. came safely to hand, and I have the pleasure to know that my harpsichord is safely arrived at Rouen and is now on the road to Paris. I thank you also for your attention to the commission to Mr. Brown, and shall be contented to receive the pictures when you come yourself. If you could do me the favor also to bring me one of the copies taken without the pencil (I forget the hard name by which they call it; it is greek however) I should be glad of it. You can combine quality and price, as, like the rest of the world, I like to have good things at a small price. I would prefer one of the historical kind, if there be any, as I think I saw some. The time when you will find most of the officers here, whose portraits you wish to take, will be a little before Christmas, say the 10th. of December.—Mrs. Cosway is well. But her friends are not so. They are in continual agitation between the hopes of her stay, and the fear of her recall. A fatality has attended my wishes, and her and my endeavors to see one another more since she has been here. From the meer effect of chance, she has happened to be from home several times when I have called on her, and I, when she has called on me. I hope for better luck hereafter. I am with much esteem Dear Sir Your friend & servant,   TH: JEFFERSON

PrC (DLC).

THE HARD NAME BY WHICH THEY CALL IT evidently proved an obstacle to others besides TJ: "The multiplying or copying pictures in oil colours by a mechanical and chymical process, as invented by Mr. [Joseph] Booth, was at first stiled POLYPLASIOSMOS, a Greek word, signifying multiplication. But the Gentlemen who have united themselves, with the inventor, into a Society, for the purpose of protecting and patronizing this ingenious art, have determined to design it, in future, by the title of POLYGRAPHIC: a term equally calculated to distinguish it from other attempts of copying Pictures; and, at the same time, more analogous, and more expressive of the invention in question, the grand object, and distinguishing property, or characteristic of which, is, to produce many pictures" (*An Address to the Public, on the Polygraphic Art, or the Copying or Multiplying Pictures, in Oil Colours, by a Chymical and Mechanical Process, the Invention of Mr. Joseph Booth, Portrait Painter,* London, the "Logographic Press," [1788], p. 2).

From Jacob Vernes

[*Paris*] *13 Nov. 1787*. Asks for the papers reporting on the manner in which the farmers-general have executed the resolves of Berni, which papers are necessary for the work in which he is engaged.

RC (DLC); 2 p.; in French; endorsed; at foot of text: "hôtel de Dannemark rüe Neuve St. Augustin." Not recorded in SJL. For the work on which Vernes was engaged, see note to his letter to TJ, 10 Apr. 1788.

From American Captains and Masters of Vessels at L'Orient

L'Orient, 14 Nov. 1787. Request that TJ use his influence and authority to obtain the appointment of David Divoux as interpreter and broker for foreign vessels in that port; Divoux possesses "sufficiently the necessary Languages and Capacitys" and has a good character; the present, sole interpreter and broker is "too much occupied to be able to full fill the Duty of his Place as it ought to be."

RC (DLC); 2 p.; signed by eleven masters of ships from Massachusetts, Pennsylvania, and Rhode Island. Not recorded in SJL but enclosed in J. David Divoux to TJ, 23 Nov., which TJ recorded as received 27 Nov. 1787.

To C. W. F. Dumas

SIR   Paris Nov. 14. 1787.

I have duly received your favors of Oct. 23. and 26. With respect to the mission you suggest in the former, no powers are lodged in the hands of Mr. Adams and myself. Congress commissioned Mr. Adams, Doctr. Franklin and myself to treat with the emperor on the subjects of amity and commerce, at the same time they gave us the commission to Prussia with which you are acquainted. We proposed treating through the Imperial Ambassador here. It was declined on their part, and our powers expired, having been given but for two years. Afterwards the same Ambassador here was instructed to offer to treat with us. I informed him our powers were expired, but that I would write to Congress on the subject. I did so, but have never yet received an answer. Whether this proceeds from a change of opinion in them, or[1] from the multiplicity of their occupations I am unable to say: but this state of facts will enable you to see that we have no powers in this instance to take the measure you had thought of.[2] I sincerely sympathize with you in your sufferings. Though forbidden by my

[359]

character to meddle in the internal affairs of an allied state, it is the wish of my heart that their troubles may have such an issue as will secure the greatest degree of happiness to the body of the people: for it is with the mass of the nation we are allied, and not merely with their governors. To inform the minds of the people, and to follow their will, is the chief duty of those placed at their head. What party in your late struggles was most likely to do this, you are more competent to judge than I am. Under every event, that you may be safe and happy is the sincere wish of him who has the honour to be with sentiments of great esteem, Sir, Your most obedient & most hble. servt., TH: JEFFERSON

PrC (DLC). PrC of a Tr (DLC); in the hand of William Short.

Dumas quoted a portion of this letter in his letter to the chargé d'affaires of the Austrian Netherlands at Brussels of 3 Dec. 1787, and enclosed a copy of that letter in his to John Jay, 4 Dec. 1787 (see notes below and Dumas to

TJ, 4 Dec. 1787).

1 The preceding eight words were omitted by Dumas in the extract sent to the chargé d'affaires at Brussels.

2 The extract sent by Dumas to the chargé d'affaires at Brussels includes only that part of the letter up to this point.

From C. W. F. Dumas

The Hague, 14 Nov. 1787. Avails himself of a French courier to transmit the enclosed, which shows that his situation, with that of a mass of good citizens, is like that of the lamb in the fable. [*Postscript:*] Having missed the courier, is obliged to send the letter by regular post.

RC (DLC); 2 p.; in French; endorsed. FC (Dumas Papers, Rijksarchief, The Hague). Recorded in SJL as received 20 Nov. 1787. Enclosure: Dumas to John Jay, same date, stating that the reigning system will ruin the province because of its inability to re-

strain the disorders which occur everywhere; rests his cause, his honor, and his interests with God and Congress (FC in Dumas Papers, Rijksarchief, The Hague; translation printed in *Dipl. Corr., 1783-89,* III, 597-9).

From Honnoré

[*Marseilles, 14 Nov. 1787.* An entry in SJL under 20 Nov. 1787 records the receipt of a letter from "Honnoré Lieut. and Neveu." Not found.]

To Wernecke

SIR   Paris Nov. 14. 1787.

On the 19th. of November 1786. I inclosed to Mr. Oster, consul of France in Virginia, your letter of the 9th. of that month, and recommended to him the procuring the documents you desired

[360]

relative to the death and possessions of your brother in that state. I supposed, and still suppose he was the most likely person to fulfill that commission well. I have received no answer. I would therefore advise you to write to him yourself on the subject, and if you could get a line from the minister in whose department he is, to recommend your case to him, it will ensure your object: and it is the only effectual method of doing it which I am able to advise. However, should I receive any answer to the letter I wrote, you may be assured I will communicate it immediately. I have the honour to be, Sir, your most obedient humble servant,

TH: JEFFERSON

PrC (DLC).

From William Carmichael

MY DEAR SIR   Sn. Lorenzo 15 Novr. 1787

The day after I had last the honor to write you, the Courier so impatiently expected from Versailles, arrived here with the Intelligence of the pacific arrangements which took place the 27 Ulto. This court seemed much pleased with the news and the Minister has received (as I have been told) the compliments of his Friends as having principally contributed to the Restablishment of Harmony. I have had an opportunity of seeing a letter written by Mr. Eden to the British Minister here, breathing the most pacific Sentiments and Insinuating that G.B. was *Sincerely* disposed to contribute its Efforts with those of France and this court to pacify the Dispute in the North. Many Handsome things were said of the Ct. de Montmorin in this Letter, which were *Intended* to be conveyed to him thro me. You see that *I take the hint.* At the same time, altho' I feel the truth of the handsome things written on this Subject, I somewhat doubt the Sincerity of the writer, as well on this point, as on the Intentions of his nation to cooperate with France in arranging the differences between the Russians and Turks. I know Mr. Listons manner of thinking and mode of acting tolerably well. Indeed I beleive no one here knows him so well. This knowledge has been acquired by a particular coincidence of Circumstances of a Nature not to be committed to paper, but which gave me an opportunity of seeing him under the various agitations of passions which developped his heart, the weaknesses of which put him of his guard. Late Conversations which I have had with him to which he gave the

[361]

Lead and which he has renewed without appearing to intend it, had excited suspicions which may appear groundless to those to whom it is impossible to convey the many little circumstances which contribute to excite them. But last night He was more clear and explicit than I expected from his character. I had dined with the Sardinian Ambassador and played after Dinner. Of course I staid much longer than I usually do. In the Afternoon he had been twice at my lodgings to look for me and left with my servant an Invitation to sup with him, which on returning I declined, as I had some writing to occupy my time. At Eleven he came to me, And told me that as I would not sup with him, he had come to eat his bread and cheese with me and hoped that we should be alone. In a very short time with many professions of personal Friendship for me, He began on the present situation of Affairs, the probability and improbability of the duration of the Late Established Harmony, the designs of France by gaining over Holland to tye up the hands of that Country, which were rendered evident by their attempts to engage this Country to acceed to their Treaty with the States and what think you, added he suddenly, of the article of their Treaty with you which excludes us from your ports in case of our being at war with France? To his remarks and his questions I gave such replies as I thought would contribute to a continuance of them. He then proceeded and said He knew the Ct. de Montmorin was an Able Minister, that Mr. Eden perhaps had been deceived by him, that he knew that the Former had very adroitly availed himself of circumstances to conciliate still more the Confidence of the King and Ministry here, that His C. M. had received a Letter from the King of France expressive of his acknowledgements of his great services which the prudent counsels given by the Latter had rendered him, that this Language was held by the Ct. de Montmorin in the direct correspondence which he had with the Ct. de F. B. and added that I must be too well acquainted with the Ct. de Montmorins character and with what passed here not to know that this was the Line of his conduct. In my answers I continued to guard the same rule that I had laid down to myself, with as little deviation as possible, but by assenting or contradicting, provoking further explanations. You will please to observe that what I have mentioned is the Substance of what I collected from his conversation, for it was carried on with much art on his part and very little on mine, for having no secrets to betray, I had nothing to apprehend. It became however more interesting. He has often mentioned to me how and where he would be probably employed when another replaces him here. His last object was Russia.—He now told me that as Mr. Eden would not arrive here until the month of March and as of course he could not leave this court until the others arrival, it was probable, that in the present critical Situation of Affairs at the Court of Petersburgh another would be sent thither, that he had received hints that he might probably be sent to N. America, cited Mr. Eden and shewed me a Letter from Mr. Fraser which indicated Mr. Pits intentions on this Subject. Some weeks ago he mentioned to me Mr. Pits intentions of sending a Minister to America. He expressed his fears of not being well received on account of his being a Scotsman. These apprehensions I removed as I could easily do, for tho' Born in America, My Countrymen well knew that I was educated at Edinburgh, that his personal reception would depend on his own conduct, and that his public would not certainly be influenced by any narrow or illiberal prejudices. I added that he knew that he might depend on all that I could do to render his period of residence agreable, but at the same time I told him in a good humored manner that I should put Mr. Jay on his guard, if I supposed that his instructions corresponded with the disposition which his Cabinet seemed to have manifested since the peace, which disposition I attributed to bad counsels and mistaken data. He turned to the subject of the Article in our treaty with France before mentioned and said that while that subsisted he did not know how it was possible G. Britain could be on cordial terms and I replyed that as by the Letter he had shewn me, it appeared that G.B. had the most pacific Intentions and as France by relinquishing what he supposed their designs upon Holland, manifested the same views, the Article ought to give no alarm, that England enjoyed the greatest share of our Commerce actually and that its own interests well considered, they ought to give an extention to our commerce instead of cramping it for such Conduct on their part would facilitate our payments for the produce which we received from them and in proportion as that Commerce increased our Demands for the Manufactures and even Luxuries of England would augment. I made use of these observations, because on many occasions he himself had broached them. From France the Transition was not difficult to Spain. Our Treaty with this country was brought in question. He endeavoured to know whether Spain wished to obtain an article in their Treaty with us of the same Nature as that in ours with France. On this Subject he could gain nothing from me. For altho' I am paid by the United States to serve them here I have never had any official Information since I have been their Chargé Des Affaires of the propositions made on part of the other, except what I have gathered by my own application or if you please address. I therefore entered into the history of Mr. Gardoquis nomination to America, of his being authorised to treat on the spot, that of course his propositions were made to Congress thro' Mr. Jay, that he had seen himself how long the Treaty had been in agitation, without being concluded, and of course might draw his own consequences from this delay, one of which would surely meet his reflections, that the late menacing aspect of affairs would rather accelerate than retard its conclusion. He seemed or appeared to seem startled at this remark, but consoled himself with the Lenteurs of this court and the little share of capacity possessed as he insinuated by Gardoqui. He spoke in a different style of the Minister named by France to replace the Chevalier de la Luzerne. In the course of this Conversation, which lasted till near three in the morning, He inquired about the principal Characters in America, the mode of Living, &c. &c. and more than once seemed apprehensive that unless speedy measures were taken by G.B. to cultivate a good understanding between the two Countries, the Rising generation in America would be so prejudiced by their mode of Education and the remembrance of the recent horrors of the war, that an effort for this purpose would become every day more difficult, if not Impracticable. I have judged it necessary to submit to your consideration this Conversation which appears to me singular and which perhaps would equally strike you, if I could as well convey the Manner as the Substance of it. Some things may have escaped my recollection but I think you have the most material. There is an object which however it may be necessary to add. Speaking of our former trade in the Mediterranean, the profits of which I asserted, were ultimately vested in G.B. I could not refrain from reminding him of the conduct of a person Employed by the Court of G.B. who endeavoured by an Information given to the Dey, to have Messrs. Lamb and Randall seized as well as the property they carried with them to Algiers. He with great warmth denied that the British Government had ever countenanced such procedure and to convince me of his own Manner of thinking offered to shew me a copy of a Letter which he had written in the year 1785 endeavoring to persuade the Ministry to favor our peace with the Emperor of Morrocco and thus to prevent the merit which Spain might claim from the conduct he foresaw it would take in procuring us a treaty with that Country. I also discovered that the *Foreign Minister* whom you saw at Versailles and whom you recommended to me, has been artfully employed, without adverting to the consequences, to repeat to the C. de F.B. as an *impartial* Person, what Mr. L——n suggested in favor of his Court and its conduct on the late Occasion. He has been listened to with apparent Attention and marks of satisfaction and Approbation. As I am on Intimate terms with him, I have this night been informed by him of the Nature of his late Conferences with the Minister which perfectly coincide with what I had learned from Mr. L——n.

I am told that orders are given to disarm. In fact the preparations made have occasioned little Expence to this government. The Minister wisely foresaw what has happened and acted accordingly. I have since I wrote you had an opportunity of knowing what passed between the M——r and the P——n Chargé des Affairs in two Conferences which the Latter had with him.

My Confrere is a very young Man and will always be so altho he has a good tutor in the British Minister. The Ct. Campomanes yesterday reiterated his thanks for your obliging mark of Attention in sending him your Notes on Virginia and Intimated a return on his part, which I suppose to be a copy of his own works now in the Press. The Cts. de Laccy and Oreilly to whom I lent the Copy you had the goodness to send me, have written for the work for themselves. Pray is there no French edition? for few read English here.

The Ratification has been sent on to Morrocco with the Dispatches of Court, as I believe I mentioned. I have no news from that quarter. The Ct. D'Expilly kissed his Majesty's and the hands of the Royal Family yesterday. This comes by a Spanish Courier, any news papers or Letters that you may chuse to address under cover to Dr. Miguel de Otamendi in the Secretary of States office by the Ct. de Fernan Nunez Courier or those of the Marquis Del Campo will be safely delivered me, as I have obtained permission for that purpose.

With great esteem & Respect I have the honor to be Your Excellency's Obliged & Humble Servt.,   WM CARMICHAEL

RC (DLC); endorsed. Recorded in SJL as received 25 Nov. 1787.

To R. & A. Garvey

GENTLEMEN   Paris Nov. 15. 1787.

I have received your favor of the 10th. instant and yesterday your bill for 87^{tt}-15-6 was presented and paid. As I know that the carts are sometimes later in setting out with their charge than what they give reason to expect, I wish it may be the case in this instance, as I would rather that my harpsichord should be withdrawn from the cart if it is still at Rouen, and sent by water. I am apprehensive the jolting of a cart on the paved roads may do injury to the instrument, and I had rather sacrifice the indemnification which the carter may claim, even if it should amount to the whole price. If it be not set out therefore I will desire you still to take this trouble for me of sending it by water, in addition to the trouble you have been so good as to take on all occasions for me. I have the honor to be with much esteem, Gentlemen, Your most obedt. humble servt.,   TH: JEFFERSON

PrC (MHi).

To Lambert

à Paris ce 15me. 9bre. 1787.

Monsieur Jefferson a l'honneur de faire part à son excellence, Monsieur le Comtrolleur General, qu'il y aura une personne qui partira pour l'Amerique à deux ou trois jours d'ici, et que ce seroit une occasion prompte et sure d'y envoyer les reglemens de commerce, dont Monsieur le Comtrolleur General a eu la bonté de s'occuper, si ces reglemens sont fixés. Le moment est d'autant plus interessant qu'à l'arrivée de cette personne en Amerique, touts les corps legislatifs seront probablement en seance. Monsieur Jefferson espere qu'il n'y a point d'indiscretion à donner cette information à Monsieur le Comtrolleur general. Il le prie d'agreer l'hommage de ses respects très humbles.

PrC (DLC).

From R. & A. Garvey

SIR   Roüen 17 November 1787.

In reply to your Excellencys letter, our reason for sending the Harpsicord by Land was because that it would have cost more by

[366]

water, and the river being out, the delay might have prouved too long; we send Musical instruments to Paris every day by Land, as yet we have had no complaint of their meeting with any accident. As it was well packed and in Good order when it left Roüen, we are confident it will have reached you all well. Allways at your and Friends commands, we remain Respectfully sir Your Excellencys most obedient & very humble Servants,

ROBT. & ANTH. GARVEY

RC (MHi). Recorded in SJL as received 18 Nov. 1787.

From André Limozin

MOST HONORED SIR   Havre de Grace 18th Novemb 1787

I have received yesterday the Letter your Excellency hath honored me with the 13th instant. I am extreamely happy to hear that my four Letters came safely and that your Excellency is well pleased with my proceeding towards the American Sailors. It gives me a great pleasure to learn likewise that your Excellency hath the Strongest hopes that good regulations are to take place in the behalf of the American trade, and that your Commerce shall be put under a regular Super Intendance. If every thing is layd in a proper manner, I hope that the American trade will Find a very great advantage by it, but I take the Freedom to own with Sincerity that I am afraid that there will be a great deficiency in what shall be done, because the trade, the Commerce is not perfectly well Known at our Court. It would have been very proper to have taken advices of Merchants of a long experience in Business. I suppose that our Ministers have the best intention, but having been never brought up in the Commercial Line, they are apt to make very great blunders. At Versailles they think that there is no Condition in Life where there is less Knowledge wanted than in Commerce, but they are very much mistaken. A Skillfull experienced Merchant would make an exceeding good minister, and on the Contrary if a Minister should turn out a Merchant he would find him self very much at a loss, and would own directly that there is no condition whatsoever which requires more abilities more Study more knowledge a Sounder Judgement more Skill more prudence more learning and more dexterity, all qualities which a long experience almost alone can procure.

The exportation from France since Peace hath been nothing important, and I dont advise your Excellency to make much inquiries about it because if the trifling value of that exportation was compared with the importance of the importation made here under the title of American Produces, our French Ministers would be directly terrifyd with the enormous difference. Your Excellency must consider that the Goods exported from this Port for America since 1763[1] dont amount to 800,000 Lvers. that the exportation from Lorient hath been trifling since America hath opend a trade with the East Indias that from Bordeaux and Nantes cant be considerable, and one would be at a very great loss to know exactly and to distinguish the Lawfull American importations, from those made by the British under the Cloak and protection of American Colours, for as I have mentionned it before, it is amazing the quantity of Scotch, London and Whitehaven ships come into France with American Colours. I have observed it in time and had I been properly intitled, the British should have payd dear for such Fraud, which I look upon as a detriment to the U S Commerce. As long as the U S will have no body lawfully appointed in the French Port, to Keep a watchfull Eye, and a Severe inspection, these frauds will continue because when a British Master is in that Case, he enters no protest against bad weather for fear that the crew should refuse to swear to the protest on the reason that it mentions that they are Americans. There is no call made after the Ships voucher and more over the Brokers who are imployed for the British are the Same used by the Americans, and these Brokers are intirely attached to the British interest. It would be very proper for the interest of the Commerce of the U. S. that they should be intitled to have a particular Broker for their ships who would not be intitled to transact the business of the British Masters. For as long as these brokers will act for the two Nations the Americans will be always Sufferers because the british temper is so hot and so obstinate that they will be masters wherever they are, and shew themselves.

I cant recommend too much the observations I have made that the Americans must enjoy the liberty to export from France for foreign as they do for Tobacco, free from duties, all their produces they bring and for which they cant find in France a ready sale. No. 1 { It is likewise proper to Sollicit a Law to pass, that the Americans will have liberty to ship in any French Port, in their own or French Vessells, all French Produces, which are in Entrepot, and these Goods must be lyable to no heavyer duties whatsoever than they would have been at the French Port from whence they were imported, if they had been exported thither direct for foreign.

The Same Law must likewise grant the Freedom to the Americans to ship in the French Ports Goods imported from foreign, paying only a single duty of about 2 or 3 ℔ ct. It is understood by the word of single duty, that these 2 or 3 ℔ ct. will be instead of duty coming in and duty going out. It will be *in lieu* of both and in consequence thereof these goods when imported from foreign and declared for exportation for the U S Country will be lodged in the Farmers Generals Storehouse under the Keys of their officers, in order to prevent fraud and the Shippers will be obliged to bring Certificates from the French Consul that the Said Goods have been landed in a Port of the U.S. under the fine of 3000 Lvers. in case of fraud. ⟩ No. 2

I am sory to be so troublesome to your Excellency in sending such Long Letters to read.

Your Excellency may depend on my very best Care, for the bust of the young Hero Marquis La Fayette for whom I have such a high regard, and to whom I am so much attachd.

I am most respectfully Your Excellency's Most obedient & very Humble Servant,   ANDRE LIMOZIN

No. 1. This Law would be of a very great advantage both for the French as for the Americans. I say for the French because it would inlarge the Sale of their products, and imploy good men and more French Ships, for not a Single American Ship would leave this Port, without buying a certain Stock or venture of Wines and Brandy, if these articles were not overloaden with heavy duties on the exportation from Bordeaux, on coming here, and on the exportation again from this Port, which duties prevent them to buy even what would be necessary to them for their own Consumption during their passage.

No. 2. If that Law should take place, it would be likewise very beneficiall for the French, because it would assure them a profitable barter with great many Foreign Nations for the Coffee Sugar, &c. which they are in want of, and it would likewise inlarge the Connexion of the French with America, in such manner that the ballance of the trade between the two Nations would not fall so much to the disadvantage of this Kingdom.

RC (DLC); endorsed. Recorded in SJL as received 20 Nov. 1787.
[1] An error for 1783; see Limozin to TJ, 19 Nov. 1787.

From Lauzier

MONSIEUR   Ce Lundy 19 9bre.

J'ai Eû l'honneur il y á deux jours de me présenter chez Vous pour vous prier de Me dire si vous Connoissés M. Joseph harisson qu'on dit Etre Beaufrere de M. Morris de philadelphie. La personne qui m'a chargé de prendre Ces renseignemens auprez de vous dezirerait savoir si M. Joseph harrisson a une maison de Commerce avec Crédit a philadelphie, et S'il Jouit de la reputation d'un honnête Négociant, et qui a de la fortune.

S'il Est en votre pouvoir, Monsieur, de me Satisfaire, Je vous auray une vraye obligation. Vous avés Eû la bonté de me faire dire que Je pouvois vous Ecrire, Et que vous voudriés bien prendre la peine de me repondre.

J'ai L'honneur d'etre avec une Consideration respectueuse Monsieur Votre très humble et très obt. ser.,   LAUZIER

avocat rüe vivienne a Lhôtel
de la Cour de france No. 16

RC (MHi); endorsed. The year has been supplied from an entry in SJL for the receipt of a letter of this date from Lauzier on 20 Nov. and TJ's reply on 22 Nov. 1787.

From André Limozin

Havre de Grace, 19 Nov. 1787. Did not have time to read the letter he wrote on 18 Nov. before it was sent; on reading the copy, notices that he or his clerk made some mistakes, including the mention of the year "1763" which should be "1783"; reminds TJ that he did not answer that part of his letter which asked an "opinion if that agreement with the British Court will last 6 or 7 months longer."

RC (DLC); 2 p.; endorsed. Recorded in SJL as received 21 Nov. 1787.

From Thomas Mann Randolph, Sr.

MY DEAR SIR   Virginia Novr. 19. 1787

I received your obliging, and esteemed Favour a few days since, and have communicated to Ammonett, what you mentioned. The poor Fellow makes his grateful acknowledgements to you, and I am now called on to follow him. Your proposed System of education for my Son Tom enlivens every spark of gratitude that my breast possesses. It will (I am sure) never be in my power to make you any returns for your kindness but no exertions on my part shall be wanted to compensate for your trouble. I have written to him a few days ago to Repair immediately to Paris, and when there to follow implicitly your Advice. I am told he is a Boy of good disposition and very studious. Pray do as you please with him.

My dear Friend I am respectfully Your Friend & Servt.,

THO. M. RANDOLPH

RC (MHi); endorsed.

From William Frederick Ast

SIR   L'Orient 20. Novr. 1787.

The American Captains in this Port labour under some Circumstances which are injurious to their business and of the Trade of America in general. I think it therefore my duty to acquaint Your Excellency of the same.

There is only one Broker here for all Foreign Nations who has either too much business or is too neglectfull to attend to his duty. The Dispatch and Business of the American Captains is therefore almost always hindered and neglected which is certainly a detriment to the American Trade. I have often been an eye witness that the Captains wanted, as few or hardly any of them know the Language of this Country, an Interpreter to get the Articles they want on board of their Ships. They often send all over the Town and cannot find the present Broker who is perhaps occupied about some other business or it may be on some party of pleasure &c. and must therefore put off their business till some other time.

There are now several American Captains here who are all desirous to have Mr. David Divoux appointed as Broker and Interpreter. I beg therefore leave to inclose and recommend the annexed Certificate or Petition of the Captains and Mr. Divouxs Letter to your Excellency's Consideration.

I know Mr. Divoux very well and think him fit to occupy the place as Interpreter and Broker, knowing the English and some Northern Languages and lives besides upon the Key, where the Captains almost can call him from on board of their Ships. I think he has render'd now, by what I have seen, more Service to the American Captains then the Broker who is paid for it. The Custom of this Town obliges the Captains to pay the Broker if they employ him or not, and so I think it is better to employ a Man that doth

[371]

do his duty, then to pay a Man that doth perhaps nothing else then to enter and clear the Ships out. I know several of them whom the present Broker has not seen except once when they came in and an other time when he clear'd them out. And some times, I am told, he doth not even do that.

Mr. Dumas has just now sent in his Accounts which I shall examine and transmit either to Mr. Barclay or Mr. Jay. Mr. Dumas makes sad complaints of the cruel usage of the Hollanders, that is of the Antigallican party as the Stadholder has got the upperhand. Now I suppose they will do all the Mischief to him they can.

O Vanity thy guilt is great! How can a people that call themselves *free* promote Dispotism!!! Should not once Billy or Mac Mac's Billy help Georgy or Mac Mac's Georgy to get a little more Power. Perhaps the posterity will read in the Journals of the [time:] and it came to pass—there were a people in a Land called Albion that became what they called in those times a great people—they did wonders, which they called in those times great wonders—but they became so fond of the[ir] Vanity that they would do things quite contrary to their own happyness—and they degenerated into dizzy heads. They involved themselves, by and with the Counsels of the Scribes Pharisees and their dizzy Highpriest whom they surnamed the Chief Ruler, into debts, as Experience has proved it, that have ruined them selves and their posterity.

I hope that soon some favourable News may arrive from America, for I am in a sore Situation.

With perfect Esteem and Regard have the honor to remain Sir Your Excellency's most obedient most humble Servt.,

WM. AST

RC (DLC). Not recorded in SJL; probably not sent until 23 Nov., the date of Divoux's letter, enclosed herewith, and received 27 Nov., the date TJ recorded the receipt of Divoux's letter. Enclosures: (1) American captains at L'Orient to TJ, 14 Nov. 1787. (2) Divoux to TJ, 23 Nov. 1787.

From Aaron Stephenson

Cambrai, 20 Nov. 1787. His former letter was written from the hospital at "Durlong" [Doullens] in Picardy; on the 8th. of the next month he "Departted from thence for the Redgment where I Arived in three Days"; has been informed by the major of the regiment that Col. Serrant received a letter from "Derek Levall" demanding Stephenson's discharge, but the colonel left without mentioning the letter; appeals to TJ, as a representative of his native land, for help; if he can reach Paris he will present himself to give an account of his past conduct.

RC (MHi); endorsed. Recorded in SJL as received 22 Nov. 1787.

Stephenson's former letter, dated 15 Sep. 1787, has not been found but is recorded in SJL as received 17 Sep. 1787, from "Doullens en Picardie." TJ may have referred this missing letter to Lafayette, or Stephenson may have written directly to Lafayette, for there is in MHi the following letter to Lafayette from Walsh-Serrant, Colonel of the Régiment de Dillon, dated 21 Nov. 1787: "Je n'ai receu qu'hier, Monsieur le Marquis, la lettre par laquelle vous me temoignez l'interest que vous prenez au nommé Aaron Stephenson, soldat du regiment de Dillon. Quelqu'attaché que je sois aux hommes de cette espece, je n'en suis pas moins empressé à faire quelque chose qui puisse vous plaire, et vous serez le Maitre, Monsieur le Marquis, du Congé de cette homme pour dix louis. Si vous trouvez que cent ecus soient un prix trop cher, j'auray l'honneur de Vous observer seulement que Stephenson a dit franchement que sa famille est aisée, et que nous ne le sommes pas au Regiment. . . ."

From Stephen Cathalan, Sr.

Marseilles, 21 Nov. 1787. Is glad to learn from TJ's letter of 13 Nov. that a regulation concerning tobacco has been obtained; is confident that this will be advantageous for the tobacco unsold in France and will "give a kind of Certitude for the future." A French vessel arrived from Baltimore with 360 hhds. of tobacco; one of his own vessels is expected in fifteen days which will bring 200 hhds. of tobacco and "185 Casks fish oil for Lamps"; expects the latter article will be covered in the new regulation concerning other items of American commerce. Fish oil pays no duty at Marseilles but when sent to other parts of France the duty is very heavy. Asks TJ to inform Sangrain, who "lights the Towns of Marseilles, Aix, and some others in the South of France," that this shipment is expected and to learn from him on what terms he would buy; has not yet learned what the oil cost in Philadelphia. A firm at Le Havre, not being able to sell tobacco to the farmers-general, have recently sold their holdings in Holland at prices from 28.^{tt}15 to 30.^{tt} per quintal. Some of the merchants in Marseilles who had small parcels of tobacco on hand asked the farmers-general what they would pay for it; the farmers-general, knowing of the new regulation, offered "20^{tt} for the virginia, tare 15$^{⅌}$ ct., deliverable at Cette," which offer was accepted. This gives warning of the difficulties ahead. Will send the articles TJ ordered. Has seen in the newspapers that the "convention to impower congress . . . was very much advanced, and approved by almost all the american nation; the regulation for Consuls will soon take place," and if TJ would honor his "Son with the appointment of Consul in the department of Marseilles . . . he will behave to the Satisfaction of the united States," and Cathalan will be further in TJ's debt. Has no news from Barclay. Hopes TJ will "become acquainted with abbé de Lomenie nephew of M. de Toulouse who had spocke to M. de Montmorin about tobacco." Has learned by a letter from Baltimore of 12 Sep. that the tobacco crop will be mediocre and that the price has risen there; he expects it to cost 32 to 35 shillings at Philadelphia. American wheat would bring 28^{tt} to 30^{tt} for 240 lbs., Paris weight, as Marseilles. His family ask to be remembered to TJ.

[373]

RC (DLC); 4 p.; in the hand of Stephen Cathalan, Jr., signed by Cathalan, Sr.; endorsed. At the foot of the text, TJ made calculations concerning the price of wheat, converting 240 French pounds into 262 American pounds, then using 29^{lt} as price for French measure, arrived at a figure of 6.^{lt} 13 per bushel. Recorded in SJL as received 27 Nov. 1787.

To R. & A. Garvey

GENTLEMEN   Paris Nov. 21. 1787.

I had the pleasure yesterday to receive my harpsichord in good order, and to withdraw from the Douane your acquit á caution No. 143. which I now inclose you with many thanks for your attentions. I have the honour to be with much esteem and regard Gentlemen Your most obedient & most humble servant,

TH: JEFFERSON

PrC (MHi). Enclosure missing.

From John Churchman

DEAR FRIEND   [Philadelphia] 11mo Novr. 22nd. 1787.

I received a favour dated the 8th of August last, mentioning the receipt of my last of June 6th. as well as that of my first memorial which I sent through another Channel. I hold myself under many obligations for the care taken herein and shall beg that a Copy of the Memorial already received from me may be sent the first opportunity to each of the Governments or Learned Societies in Europe, especially where there is any prospect of reward, in hopes they will also make entries as at Paris to secure the claim. As there are but few Opportunities from here to those foreign parts, I had early requested a Gentleman in London to forward a few Copies of memorials, but as I have never yet got a line from him, I am inclined to suppose miscarriage has prevented the compliance with my request. I shall at another Opportunity add something further in addition to my former by way of explanation of my Ideas. I shall likewise be glad that the necessary Steps may be taken particularly at Paris to endeavour to secure an exclusive priviledge of vending, Variation Globes, Charts or Tables constructed upon those principles, having understood something of this nature had been already granted in France to a Gentleman in America for his discovery of dying cloth a certain colour with the Bark of the Oak Tree. I have lately received a very polite Letter from Sir Joseph Banks president of the Royal Society in London, containing his opinion of the Scheme. I shall be happy to receive from time to time, a line directed to Philadelphia containing any information as to the success for which trouble I hope to have it in my power to make satisfaction in the manner heretofore proposed, and remain with the greatest sentiments of respect &c. &c., JOHN CHURCHMAN

P.S. I could not expect that any person who perhaps has not had leisure fully to investigate the matter to run the risk of loosing their reputation as a Philosopher in giving an hasty opinion on the Subject, but would be glad the general Principles may by all means be sent forward to as many places as may be convenient, for the reasons heretofore mentioned, and I shall from time to time send forward the further explanation or Illustration of my ideas. To save expence of postage from hence, I would hope the substance of the first Memorial may be copied and sent forward in the name of
J. C.

RC (MiU-C). Although no enclosure is mentioned, Churchman probably enclosed a "second" Memorial "To the Royal Acadamy of Sciences at Paris" stating that he had found "at the Royal Societys House in London by two weeks observations of the Variation of the Compass at different times of the day in the year 1779 the mean of the observations is 22° 11' West (Philosophical Transactions vol LXIX page 321)"; that he "hopes there is as great reason to suppose by the same rule the variation may be taken with as great certainty at Sea provided the Instrument is constructed in a proper manner, and expects it will be found easy to take the Latitude as well as the variation of the compass by a mean of the observations from the North Star, to avoid the inconveniency of Diurnal variation, refraction &ca. which he hopes may be repeated all Night at Pleasure"; and that, to meet some doubts that have been expressed, he would "be glad that observations might be made in different parts of the world when an opportunity may offer: for a further confirmation of a System which he hopes may be useful to the Navigator" (MS in MiU-C, signed by Churchman, dated 22 Nov. 1787).

TJ wrote Churchman on 18 Sep. 1789 that he had never received this letter. The explanation for this may be found in a letter (MHi) from an official of the British "Genl Post Office Lombard Street Jany 25th 1787 [1788?]" to an unknown person, bearing TJ's endorsement "Churchman John" and reading in part: "The enclosed Letter has been opened to be returned for payment of Postage, but as the length of time which must necessarily elapse in its progress to, and from the Continent of America, might be attended with disagreeable Consequences, I have ventured to recommend it to your immediate care, presuming you may have lived in Habits of Intimacy and Friendship with Mr. Jefferson. As a Friend to Science I would have paid the Postage of it myself, but I am so situated that I am incapable of paying so trifling a Sum."

From Dubosq

Paris, 22 Nov. 1787. Has been told TJ needs an accurate copyist; offers his services.

RC (DLC); 2 p.; endorsed; at foot of text: "Chés Duhamel, Epicier au Coin De la Rüe des Bourdonnais au 4e." Recorded in SJL as received 23 Nov. 1787.

[375]

From C. W. F. Dumas

The Hague, 22 Nov. 1787. Reminds TJ of the suggestion he made in his letter of 23 Oct. that he be sent to Brussels to negotiate a treaty of amity and commerce with the emperor; has just received information from a reliable source which leaves no doubt of the success of the mission; suggests that he be given a letter to the governor affirming that it is TJ's wish, "fondé sur la connoissance qu'Elle a des sentimens des Etats-Unis pour Sa Majesté Impériale et pour les Nations sous son obeissance," that Dumas negotiate a treaty, based on the terms of the treaties already existing between the United States and other powers; this treaty, when agreed upon, could be concluded by TJ and the emperor's minister, either at Paris or Brussels; is not certain whether TJ's authority to negotiate a treaty is still in force; but, if not, TJ could start proceedings to secure the necessary powers to conclude the treaty while the negotiations are in progress. The cost of such a mission would be moderate; his sojourn in Brussels would be approximately six weeks; he would be introduced without formality and the negotiations would be secret; when the treaty was agreed upon it would take two or three days to convey it to TJ, unless he prefers to receive it through the imperial ambassador in Paris. The importance and utility of such a treaty is obvious—"Ostende, &c. Fiume et Trieste, la protection de l'Empereur et son Pavillion par la Méditerranée surtout, specialement contre Alger et dans les Ports Ottomans, les Traités que celui-ci occasionnera avec les autres Puissances Italiennes." Hopes TJ will not wait to consult Congress before he replies because time is precious. A brief absence from The Hague, where he can now be of no service, would greatly alleviate his miserable state; but he would not suggest the mission if he were not convinced of its utility. The situation in Holland has not changed since his last letter.

RC (DLC); 4 p.; in French; endorsed. FC (Dumas Papers, Rijksarchief, The Hague; photostats in DLC); with numerous deletions. Recorded in SJL as received 27 Nov. 1787.

To Lauzier

à Paris ce 22me. Novembre 1787.

Je ne connois pas, Monsieur, le nommé Joseph Harrison dont vous me faites l'honneur de m'ecrire. Mais je crois etre un peu sur qu'il ne peut pas etre le beaufrere de Monsr. Robert Morris. Monsr. Morris n'a point de parens en Amerique; et si Monsr. Harrison fut son beaufrere du coté de Madame Morris il auroit porté le nom de White, et non pas de Harrison. Je vous aurois repondu plutot, mais je souhaitait de voir premierement un Americain qui est à Paris, et que je croyois devoir connoître ce Monsr. Harrison s'il etoit lié avec Monsr. Morris. Je l'ai vu aujourdhui. Il ne le connoit pas, et il doute,

[376]

comme moi, que Monsr. Morris ne peut pas avoir un beaufrere de ce nom-là. Il y a encore à Paris les fils de Monsieur Morris, qui, quoiqu'ils aient parti de l'Amerique bien jeuns, doivent encore me pouvoir dire s'ils ayent un oncle nommé Harrison. Je les verrai, et m'en informerai; et si je trouve que je me suis trompé en croyant que ce Monsieur n'est pas de leur famille, j'aurai l'honneur de vous la communiquer. J'ai celui d'etre avec beaucoup de consideration Monsieur votre tres humble et très obeissant serv.,

TH: JEFFERSON

PrC (MHi).

From Lucy Ludwell Paradise

DEAR SIR   Williamsburg Virginia Novr. the 22d. 1787

I take the liberty to trouble your Excellency with a few lines to acquaint you of our Arrival in Dear Virginia and at the same time to thank you for all the attentions you have been pleased to shew Mr. Paradise myself and family. The Passage we had was long and very disagreeable, as we had the great misfortune to have a Brute of a Captain to Command the Ship Juno, owing to the very unfortunate accident of Capt. Jn. Allanbys breaking his leg on the very day we were to have set sail. I had the happiness of meeting all my dear Relations, and friends, in perfect health, except my Brother, who has had the misfortune to be blined a year, and half. He bears it remarkably well, and enjoys good health and spirits. I beg you will make my best Compliments to your amiable daughters. And believe me to be Your Excellences most Obt. and much Obliged Humb. Servant and Friend,   LUCY PARADISE

RC (DLC); endorsed.

From J. David Divoux

L'Orient, 23 Nov. 1787. Is prompted by "the Encourragment of the Americans" to ask TJ's assistance in securing the position of broker and interpreter for the foreign nations at that port; the American captains have urged this step for several years; about ten months ago he presented a petition, supported by certificates, "to the Duke of Penthievre Grand Admiral of france," requesting the addition of another interpreter and stating his qualifications for the position, but the present interpreter petitioned against it and is favored by the duke's secretary, who possibly never showed the duke the documents accompanying his petition, and

[377]

who informed Divoux that the new appointment was unnecessary. The present broker maintains that there are already two persons holding that position because he and his father act jointly; the facts are that the father, who is old, lives in Port Louis and has as much as he can do there; the son lives "at ease" and does very little for the Americans. There is enough work to provide a livelihood for both. He has rendered more service to the Americans than the person paid to serve them. Barclay was aware of this and promised his assistance but "his going to Marocco and America prevented it."

RC (DLC); 4 p.; endorsed. Recorded in SJL as received 27 Nov. 1787. Enclosure: American Captains and Masters of Vessels at L'Orient, 14 Nov. 1787; this letter, in turn, appears to have been enclosed in Ast to TJ, 20 Nov. 1787, which was probably not sent until the present letter was written.

From Lanchon Frères & Cie.

L'Orient, 23 Nov. 1787. Acknowledge TJ's letter of 9 July; are sorry they did not see him when he was in L'Orient; are always glad to supply information on commerce. This port handles most of the American trade with France; nearly forty American vessels have entered L'Orient this year, many of them "on their Ballast from Spain and Ireland, coming chiefly for Salt here for the New England Fisheries." L'Orient is a preferred port because it is a free port and has a particularly safe harbor, "even to Ships of the greatest burthen"; its situation renders it most advantageous for American products, especially tobacco, "4 a 5000 Hogsheads of it being Carried annually from hence to Ireland by Smugglers." Are eager to promote American trade and, therefore, present "a General Complaint of the American Captains" who wish to employ "English Brokers only when they Want them, their fees being the heaviest of our port Charges"; the brokers do nothing but clear the ships in and out of port "which they could do without them"; hope this abuse to trade can be stopped. "Motives of personal Consideration prevented this letter from being Signed, and would have been suppressed was not the writer prompted by a Wish to Serve the Interest of America to send it without a signature." Further information may be obtained from "Mr. Ast the young man lately in the Employ of Mr. Barclay and now Clerk of Messrs. Lanchon Brothers & Co. here."

RC (DLC); 4 p.; unsigned; addressed. Recorded in SJL as "Anonymous. Lorient. Nov. 23.," received 3 Dec. 1787.
Although the letter was not signed and was endorsed by TJ as "Anonymous," the reference to his letter of 9 July 1787 makes it clear that the authors wished to identify themselves.

From Zachariah Loreilhe

Bordeaux, 23 Nov. 1787. Has received "Indirect but Certain account" that Thomas Barclay arrived in New York on 2 Oct. Acknowledges TJ's letter of 28 Oct.; has communicated the information therein to U.S. citizens interested in commerce.

RC (MHi); 2 p.; endorsed. Recorded in SJL as received 28 Nov. 1787.

To Mary Barclay

Nov. 24. 1787.

Mr. Jefferson's compliments to Mrs. Barclay. He has been expecting her draught for 724^{tt}-7s-6d since she did him the honour to write to him; but not receiving it he fears she may have waited an answer from him. He is ready to pay it at any moment, as he shall be to answer any further calls she may have occasion to make. He wishes health and happiness to herself, the young ladies and family.

RC (Mrs. Darrell T. Lane, Washington, D.C., 1946). Not recorded in SJL.

From Joseph Barrell

Boston Nov. 24th. 1787

Mr. Barrell (in behalf of the Owners of the Adventure to the Pacific) presents his most respectfull Compliments to His Excellency Mr. Jefferson, and Requests the honor of his acceptance of a medal struck upon the Occasion.

RC (MHi).

This letter was not received until 2 Feb. 1789 when it arrived as an enclosure in Colborn Barrell to TJ, 22 Sep. 1788. Joseph Barrell was one of the fourteen adventurers and original shareholders, principally of Boston and Salem, who underwrote THE ADVENTURE TO THE PACIFIC—that is, the epochal voyage of the *Columbia* that inaugurated the Northwest fur trade as an essential element in the Canton trade. The MEDAL STRUCK UPON THE OCCASION was made for distribution among the natives in the course of the voyage (see S. E. Morison, *Maritime History of Massachusetts*, Boston, 1941, p. 46-51).

From Anthony Garvey

Rouen, 24 Nov. 1787. Acknowledges TJ's letter of 21 Nov. "with the acquit a Caution for the Harpsicord." In July 1782 he "bought on Joint account with the House of Ridley & Pringle of Baltimore Goods to the Amount of 32,000,^{tt}" which goods were sent to them and arrived safely the following October; Ridley paid for half the purchase and the firm reported that "they sold to advantage" and would "send a remittance forthwith"; has "written them several letters since all to no purpose"; asks TJ's advice on how to proceed.

RC (MHi); 2 p.; endorsed. Recorded in SJL as received 25 Nov. 1787.

From William Drayton

SIR   Charleston, South Carolina Novr. 25. 1787.

I am directed by our agricultural Society to return their warmest Thanks to your Excellency for your obliging Attention and Communications on the Subject of their Institution; and particularly for the Trouble, which you took to obtain Information concerning the Culture and Cleaning of Rice in Italy. About two months ago I receiv'd a Tea-Canister full of the Lombardy Rice unhusk'd, which was brought to me from London, and which I knew only from the Hand-writing of the direction to come from you; and a Fortnight since, your Letter of the 30th. of July was forwarded to me by one of our delegates in the general Convention at Philadelphia. But I am sorry to add, that all his Inquiries concerning the Articles, which you intended to accompany it were fruitless. However the Contents of your Excellency's Letter alone prov'd a very valuable and acceptable Present to the Society, which they will endeavour to deserve by extending to the rest of the States, as well as our own, the happy Effects of which it may be productive.

The Introduction of the olive into this State, which your Excellency so warmly recommends, we will immediately attend to; and shall therefore gratefully accept your Offer to procure and forward a Number of the Plants to us. As a small Attempt towards opening a commercial Intercourse directly with France in the Article of Rice, and in order to supply your Excellency with a Sum necessary to execute our Commission, we purpose sending a few Barrels to Les Sieurs Jean Jaques Berard & Compe. de L'Orient (mention'd in your Letter to Mr. Rutledge) who are to hold the Amount Sales subject to your Order. You will be pleas'd to apply it, as far as it will go, in procuring and shipping the Olive Plants, which may be consign'd to the Care of Messrs. Brailsford & Morris, Merchants here, who will pay the Freight. I shall give your Excellency notice, when this Rice is shipp'd.

We shall be very careful in the Experiments, we intend in the Culture of the Lombardy Seed Rice, which you sent. The Grain in its natural state is different from ours, which is much larger, not so flat, and without a Beard. This last Circumstance may perhaps give it the Preference to ours in another Particular, besides those you mention'd, as it may prevent the Rice Birds from destroying so much of it, as they now do here. But I don't think the Quality of it varies in anything else, except the Colour after cleaning, which I conceive to be chiefly owing to the Grain not having undergone so much Friction (in what we call Beating) as ours does, to remove a Coat of very fine brownish Dust, or Flour, which adheres under the Husk to the interior Grain. With Regard to the Quality, you mention, of our Rice dissolving when dress'd au gras; perhaps the Lombardy Rice is not so liable to it, by having this Coat left on it, and being thereby better enabled to resist the Effect of boiling. But we remedy this Inconvenience by a very simple Process in the dressing. It is by suffering the Water, or the Soup, to boil before the Rice is added. If the Rice alone is intended for the Table, after putting it into the boiling kettle, the Scum which rises must be repeatedly taken off, and the Rice stirr'd to the Bottom two or three times. When neither Scum, nor water appears, and the Rice has swell'd as high as the water did at first, the kettle is to be taken off of the Fire, and suffer'd to remain by it about ten minutes, to soak, as our Cooks say. The Grain then appears, not only whole, but much disunited. I have taken the Liberty to inclose a Receipt in the Hand-writing of one of our most notable Ladies, the present Governor's Sister, for a Rice Pudding, which for it's goodness I think excellent, and from it's Cheapness has acquired the Name among us of "The poor Man's Pudding."

We could easily accomodate our Rice to a Frenchmans Eye by separating the broken from the whole grains, if we were certain of being able to dispose of all the former at a proportionably inferior Price; otherwise it would be attended with a considerable Loss to us, and realy it is only the Eye, that would be gratified by this Separation; for the broken Grains are equaly well tasted; and it is to please the Eye (and perhaps the Taste a little), that it is so much broken, by using a great deal more Friction and Labour to remove the brownish Coat of Flour, which is left on the Italian Rice, as I saw by some small Specimens you sent to Dr. Ramsay. We shall be very glad to receive a little of the Levant Rice unhusked, which you flatter us with the Hope of procuring.

The Seeds of the Sulla and Malta were so much injur'd, as I fear'd, by the Accident of their being unopen'd so long before Mr. Macqueen deliver'd them, that I have heard of only one or two grains, that vegetated. Of the Cork-Oak Acorns not one has succeeded. But we are not the less obliged to your Excellency's kind Intention in transmitting them to us. I believe it is very difficult to preserve seeds of any kind from the Effects of a Sea-Voyage. If we could be certain of the Master's, or other Person's care on board,

Plants would be much the best State, in which the Experiment of introducing the Productions of one Country into another by Sea should be made.

Your Excellency's merit, as an honorary member of our Society, induces us to request the Continuance of future Favours from you, as well as to thank you for the past.

I have the Honour to be, with the greatest Respect, Your Excellency's most obedt. & most humble Servant,

WM: DRAYTON

RC (DLC). Enclosure missing.

From Brizard

MONSIEUR   Paris le 26. 9bre. 1787.

Voici L'Eloge d'un ami de la Liberté, d'un Deffenseur des Moeurs et de la Vertu, d'un Excellent Citoyen qui n'est point inconnu dans le Nouveau Monde, dont Vous êtes le digne representant; c'est à ce Titre que J'ose vous en offrir L'Hommage. J'espere que dans ce que J'ai dit de L'ouvrage de Mabli sur Les *Etats Unis* vous ne verrez que mon admiration pour ceux qui ont fondé La Liberté de L'Amérique, mon respect pour les Hommes qui L'ont eclairée et mon amour pour La Verité, qui peut se faire Illusion, mais qui ne peut jamais deplaire au Sage Ministre D'un Peuple Libre.

Je suis avec respect Monsieur Votre très humble et très Obéissant serviteur,   BRIZARD

Messieurs les Abbés de Chalut et Arnoux me chargent de vous faire leurs Complimens.

RC (DLC); endorsed. Not recorded in SJL. Enclosure: Brizard's *Eloge historique de l'abbé de Mably, discours qui a partagé le prix au jugement de l'Academie royale des Inscriptions et belles-lettres en 1787*, Paris, 1787 (Sowerby, No. 226).

From C. W. F. Dumas

MONSIEUR   La Haie 27e. Nov. *1787*

En confirmant à Votre Excellence ma derniere du 22 de ce mois par La poste, et la priant instamment de vouloir m'en accuser la réception, ainsi que de celles des 23, 26 Oct. (sous couvert de MM. Van den Nyver fils & Compagnie, banquiers à Paris) et 14 Nov. par la poste, dont je suis inquiet, je prends le parti de faire passer la présente sous couvert d'ami à Amsterdam, pour l'acheminer de là après-demain.

Je brûle d'avoir la réponse favorable de Votre Excellence à ma dite derniere du 22e. de ce mois, pouvant l'assurer de n'y avoir rien avancé dont je ne sois moralement sûr, et que je ne partirai d'ici pour Bruxelles, après l'autorisation même de Votre Excellence, sans avoir fait confirmer les assurances de réussite par la même personne qui me les a déjà données, et qui préviendra alors, *officiellement*, de ce dont il s'agit, celui qu'il faut, et qui probablement est déjà prévenu de nos Entretiens *personnels* là-dessus.

Si Votre Excellence se faisoit scrupule de m'envoyer ici la Lettre de sa part pour le Gouvernement Général dans le goût environ indiqué dans ma précédente, il suffira qu'Elle m'en écrive une ici ostensible à mon homme, où approuvant mon voyage et m'y autorisant en termes généraux, Elle me marque que je trouverai ou recevrai à Bruxelles ses Lettres et Instructions ultérieures là-dessus.

Quant aux frais de Voyage et séjour, outre que je ne les hazarderai pas, comme j'ai dit, sans assurance suffisante, je les ménagerai scrupuleusement, en tiendrai et fournirai le compte détaillé et exact en son temps, et reviendrai ici lorsque la besogne sera finie et que Votre Excellence n'aura plus besoin de moi, attendre comme je pourrai, dans ma triste position, les ordres ultérieurs du Congrès. Il me paroît donc que cet objet ne doit nullement arrêter une affaire de cette conséquence,[1] dont le projet peut être porté à la connoissance du Congrès, avec toute la diligence que la distance admet, dès le commencement, à mesure, et immédiatement après sa rédaction finale, et dont les fruits seront, l'avantage manifeste des Etats-Unis, de leur Commerce et Navigation, et l'accroissement externe de leur dignité parmi les souverains du monde, avec l'honneur qui en résultera, premierement pour Votre Excellence, et puis, par subordination à ses auspices, pour moi-même, qui ne cherche ce relief que pour avoir de quoi opposer à l'intention sinistre qu'on a eue, par la réponse au Mémoire de Mr. Adams, et par la publication de cette réponse, de me perdre obliquement chez mes maîtres, directement aux yeux du Public, et de me mettre à la gueule du loup, de ce qu'il y a de plus désordonné dans l'humaine société. Heureux si mon motif louable peut procurer le plutôt le mieux quelques semaines de relâche au moins aux cruelles Epreuves que j'endure ici, et au milieu desquelles je suis, avec grand respect, De Votre Excellence le très-humble et très-obéissant serviteur,   C W F Dumas

RC (DLC). FC (Dumas Papers, Rijk-sarchief, The Hague; photostats in DLC). Recorded in SJL as received 5 Dec. 1787.

1 At this point in FC there is the following paragraph which Dumas omitted from RC: "Je viens d'apprendre de bonne part, que probablement la paix sera faite cet hiver en Orient. J'apprends aussi l'agréable et grande nouvelle de l'Edit du Roi, porté au Parlement, pour assurer en France un Etat civil aux Protestants; et celle pareillement d'une Légion Batave prise service du Roi."

From Joseph Fenwick

Paris, 27 Nov. 1787. If Col. Forrest sends him a letter, asks that it be forwarded to Brussels, "to the care of Messrs. F. Rombourg & Sons."

RC (MHi); 2 p.; without name of addressee; endorsed in TJ's hand. Not recorded in SJL.

To Anthony Garvey

SIR   Paris Nov. 29. 1787.

I have received your favor of Novemb. 24. and shall be very happy to give you any information I can which may enable you to obtain justice in your demands against Ridley & Pringle. It will be necessary for you to authorize some person in that country to act for you as your attorney. You will of course instruct that person what arrangements you would admit amicably; and if your debtors will not agree to them, they must be forced by law. You need not fear going to law in that country. It is administered with the most rigorous impartiality, costs but little, and you recover all lawful costs. I believe also that the delays are not considerable. I inclose you the form of a power of attorney used in America. I imagine you have correspondents at Baltimore or Philadelphia in whom you have sufficient confidence to appoint them your attornies. If you have not, it is not in my power to recommend any person in Baltimore, because I have little acquaintance there. I know a person not far from there in whom all faith might be placed, and who was an attorney by profession. But perhaps he may have quitted that profession. However if you cannot do better, and will let me know I will write to him for you; and do any thing further herein which may serve you. I am with great esteem Sir your most obedient humble servant,   TH: JEFFERSON

PrC (DLC). Enclosure (probably a MS rather than a printed power of attorney) missing.

The PERSON NOT FAR FROM Baltimore may have been Daniel Dulany (see Vol. 6: 556).

From Thomas Barclay

[*New York, 30 Nov. 1787.* A letter from Barclay of this date is recorded in SJL Index, which letter was enclosed in the Commissioners of the Treasury to TJ, 5 Dec. 1787, received 26 Jan. 1788, and enclosed in TJ to William F. Ast, 9 Feb. 1788, q.v.; see also TJ to Ast, 19 June 1788. Not found.]

From John Bondfield

SIR   Bordeaux 30th Novr. 1787

I receivd in due course your favor of the 13 Instant, the Vin de frontignan for Monsr. le Comte de Moustier shall be carefully forwarded to New York by the first vessel after its arrival here.

The American Ships to this have not been subjected to report the contents of their Cargoes inwards nor to take out specified clearances of their outward Cargoes, that no registres have preserved any Notes of the Imports or Exports other than the Custom house Books for Duties received, which being confounded in the accompts of their general recetts becomes impracticable to draw an Estimate of the general state.

The Exports from this Port to the United States have been confined to two or three small Cargoes of Wines and Brandys objects of small value.

The Ships that arrive from the United States with Tobacco on freight bring Staves to fill up the broken stowage which with 6.8 or 10 hhds. Tobacco on board for the Owners account serve to defray the Ships charges in Port which may be averaged at from 2400^{tt} to 3000^{tt} $\bar{P}$ Ship. The entire Sums the proceeds of the Sales of the Cargoes deductions of charges and commissions are remitted to other nations to pay their Exports and advances, france is not in any considerable advance to America on private Account.

In solution to your proscription the amount of the Exports and Imports hold no proportion or as $\frac{2}{100}$ths.

This inequality springs from different Sources principally the great debt contracted by America to England and Holland from the immoderate Import of 83 and 84, which involved America in Anticipation. Private Debts like National Ones must be paid off, the debtors are forced to give every Sixpence of their Savings to pay their engagements and are further obliged to take from their Creditors their necessaries who thereby become sole proprietors of the Crops. It requires great Capitals and long advances to succeed

[385]

in these pursuits. Also failures frequently happen but in that case the Debtors only change masters. The Nations are General Creditors. France dont carry her Views in the Commercial line to an equal extent. Time will bring about the revolution but not rapidly. If in twenty years the Manufactures of france improve in proportion to their Navigation they will command more commissions than they can Execute.

We have had a few Cargoes of Carolina produce which have arrived to a good Market. That province will be the first with which this Kingdom will form reciprocal Exchanges.

The Treaties subsisting betwixt france and the Ansiatic Cities and Portugal for oil Lumber &c. will confine them branches to the same regulations. The New England States can undersell the other nations her Competitors if the Navigation was conducted with equal Economy but tho' our Eastern Men are in some cases saving, they forget that Virtu in france and launch out into Expenses that destroy their Voyages.

All we have to ask of france is protection and equal privaledges. Trade is of a Nature that will always work its own Channel. America as a Commercial Nation is a Non Substantif.

I have the honor to be with due Respect Sir Your most Obedient Humble servant, JOHN BONDFIELD

RC (DLC); addressed and endorsed. Recorded in SJL as received 9 Dec. 1787.

From C. W. F. Dumas

The Hague, 30 Nov. 1787. Since the departure of his letter of 27 Nov. he has received the following address: "S. E. M. le Cte. du St. Empire Romn. de Trautmansdorf, Chambellan, Cons. d'Etat intime de S.M. l'Empr. et Roi, et son Ministre Plenipe. pour le Gouvernemt. Genl. des Pays-Bas à *Bruxelles*," which he forwards to TJ, "dans la supposition et espérance qu'Elle pourra et voudra concourir au projet important proposé."

RC (DLC); 1 p.; in French. Recorded in SJL as received 8 Dec. 1787.

From Jarnac

[*Versailles, 30 Nov. 1787.* An entry in SJL for 4 Dec. 1787 records receipt of a letter from "Jarnac Comte de." Not found.]

From Maria Cosway

MY DEAR SIR   Saturday Evening [1 Dec. ? 1787]

Why will you Make such a great dinner? I had told the Princess of the pleasure I intended My self tomorrow and she seemd very glad to go with me, but had not thought of any body else; to begin by Mr: d'Hancarville he is very sorry not to be able to wait on you as he has been particularly engaged for some time past. Mr: St: Andre I shall see this Evening. Monr: Nimscevik accepts with pleasure your kind invitation, Count Btorki is not here, but I shall deliver to him also your invitation. If my inclination had been your law I should have had the pleasure of seeing you More then I have. I have felt the *loss* with displeasure, but on My return to England when I calculate the time I have been in Paris, I shall not beleave it possible. At least if that could soften My regret, I shall encourage My immagination to favor Me. Addieu My dear friend, let me beg of you to preserve Me that name, I shall endeavour to deserve it: & all the Gods will bless us.

I hope Mr. Short will not be out as his usual when I have the pleasure to come to you.

RC (ViU); undated and unsigned; endorsed by TJ: "Cosway Maria." This letter, written toward the end of Maria Cosway's stay in Paris in 1787, has been assigned to this date because 1 Dec. was the Saturday preceding her departure for London (see Mrs. Cosway to TJ, 7, 10 Dec. 1787). It may be noted in this connection that the expenses recorded in TJ's Account Book under the heading "cuisine" for the week ending 24 Nov. and the week ending 1 Dec. totalled respectively 542^{lt}-17 and 382^{lt}-10, amounts which were greatly in excess of those for any other week during Mrs. Cosway's stay in Paris in 1787 and which would seem to confirm the supposition that it was around this date that TJ gave a GREAT DINNER. THE PRINCESS: Princess Lubomirska, mentioned by TJ in his letters to Mrs. Cosway, 24 Apr. 1788 and 14 Jan. 1789. MONR. NIMSCEVIK: Julian Niemcewicz, Polish patriot and writer who later emigrated to the United States. COUNT BTORKI: Count Potocki.

To Willink & Van Staphorst

GENTLEMEN   Paris December 1. 1787.

This serves to advise you that I have this day drawn on you in favor of Mr. Grand for two thousand seven hundred and thirty one florins five sols Banco, at four days sight, which be pleased to honour and charge to the United states of America. I have the honour to be Gentlemen Your most obedient humble servt.,

TH: JEFFERSON

PrC (DLC); at foot of text: "Messrs. Wilhelm & Jean Willinck, Nicholas & Jacob Van-Staphorsts, Bankers at Amsterdam."

[387]

To Stephen Cathalan, Sr.

SIR   Paris Dec. 2. 1787.

I could not, till yesterday, obtain the details you desired in your letter of Nov. 21 on the subject of whale oil. They are as follows, and are furnished me by Mr. Barrett, a Boston merchant established at Paris for the sole purpose of receiving consignments of whale oil, and selling them.

Black whale oil, or common whale oil costs in America £21 the ton lawful. Spermaceti oil costs £38 lawful money the ton.

The ton as measured in America, will yeild when delivered in France, only fifteen French quintals and a half, after allowing for difference of weight, waste &c. Mr. Barrett sells black whale oil at Paris for 40^{tt} the Quintal. Spermaceti whale oil should fetch 55^{tt} the quintal to yeild as good a profit here as it does when carried to England.

From these details I am in hopes you will be able to make such propositions as may suit you to M. de Sangrain, or to his agent at Marseilles. I do not make any to him, lest my ignorance in the details of commerce should do you more harm than good. I will endeavor, on your recommendation, to obtain the acquaintance of M. l'Abbe Lomenie. His talents and good dispositions may be useful in cementing our two countries. We have no foreign news of consequence, and you have correspondents here more *au fait* of domestic occurrences. My respects to the ladies and family and am with great esteem, Sir, your most obedient humble servant,

TH: JEFFERSON

PrC (DLC).

From C. W. F. Dumas

MONSIEUR   Lahaie 2e. Décembre *1787*

Ma derniere, où je communique une Adresse à Votre Excellence, étoit envoyée à Amsterdam pour être acheminée demain, lorsque celle de Votre Excellence du 14e. Nov. me fut remise. Je vois et sens, quoiqu'à mon grand regret, qu'Elle ne peut concourir au moyen honnête de me tirer pendant une couple de mois au moins de la situation vraiment pénible et cruelle où je me trouve ici, surtout pendant cet hiver. Il faudra donc l'endurer comme et tant que je pourrai. Mais oserois-je vous supplier, Monsieur, de vouloir bien porter à la connoissance du Congrès, par le Paquebot qui part ce

[388]

mois du Havre, les Points essentiels de ma Proposition, d'y ajouter votre opinion sur la convenance de l'affaire-même, et sur celle de m'y employer pour sa projection: comme aussi de vouloir bien m'informer en gros, si Votre Excellence a pu le faire, afin que j'aie au moins la seule consolation des malheureux, l'*espoir* quelconque. Ce que Votre Excellence m'apprend de l'offre faite par l'Ambassadeur Impérial de traiter, avec ce qu'on m'a dit depuis à moi, fait voir que la chose leur tient à coeur, et la propriété complete de ce qu'on m'a ajouté, que c'est aux Ministres des Etats-Unis à parler, comme aussi, l'influence sous laquelle l'affaire avoit été *déclinée* précédemment; ce qu'on ne demande pas mieux que de réparer maintenant.

Rien n'est plus vrai, Monsieur, que votre maxime (qui étoit *réellement* celle du défunt Gouvernement), que c'est avec la masse de la Nation que nous sommes alliés. Mais rien n'est plus vrai d'un autre côté que ceci: que cette masse, présentement = 0, et que de fait le Gouvernement Militaire est Législateur, Exécuteur, Juge; par conséquent, qu'il est *tout*. D'après ces deux prémisses, vous pouvez juger, Monsieur, du *Degré de bonheur* dont jouit et jouira une *Masse*, à qui il n'est permis de manifester d'autre volonté que celle de l'*obéissance passive*.

Je suis avec le plus respectueux dévouement, De Votre Excellence Le très-humble & très-obéissant serviteur,

C. W. F. DUMAS

RC (DLC). FC (Dumas Papers, Rijksarchief, The Hague; photostats in DLC). Recorded in SJL as received 8 Dec. 1787.

From James Maury

Liverpool, 2 Dec. 1787. Thanks TJ for his letter of 13 Nov.; is pleased that so much progress has been made in the commercial negotiations with France; hopes he will receive further details on this subject. Has observed with satisfaction "that the Diffusion of American produce directly to the various Markets of Europe has, contrary to the predictions of a Sett of malicious prophets, increased its value"; is concerned that the Americans take so few products from France, their best customer for tobacco; many French manufactures are as good as those of England but Americans are partial to English goods. Congratulates TJ on the prospect of soon "seeing the new plan of Government take effect in the Thirteen States"; this will make them "happy at home and respected abroad."

RC (MHi); 3 p.; endorsed. Recorded in SJL as received 10 Dec. 1787.

From Martha Jefferson Carr

[*3 Dec. 1787*. Recorded in SJL Index. Not found.]

From William Stephens Smith

DEAR SIR   London Decr. 3d. 1787

I have been honoured by the receipt of your Letter of the 13th. ulto. and notice the alarm of your patriotic spirit, on the subject of the newly proposed project, of a fœdral Constitution. I have read it frequently and with great attention, and tho' I am a great friend to fœdral Men and fœdral measures, and am decidedly of opinion, that some alterations were necessary, still on the plan proposed, I look with an anxious mind, and "trembling can't enjoy." Perhaps a three years absence from my Country has disqualified me, from being competent to decide on the question. I have a great Confidence in the Members of the Convention both as it relates to their Patriotism and abilities, and am willing to believe, that considering the stage of Society, the General Manners of our people, and the deranged state of our foreign and domestic affairs, it was necessary to fix a greater coercive power somewhere, and even to entrust it to the hands of an Individual, giving at the same time deliberative assemblies proper powers to check and even to controul, by the withholding supplies of Cash &c. But tho' I think it essential to the welfare and tranquility of a state, that Government should Correspond with the existing manners of the people, still for myself, I feel a great diffidence in deciding whether in the present case, there may not be an attempt to make too rapid advances on the theatre of Government; for I ever hold it a duty due to the Governed, to check as much as possible the advances and pressure which they are constantly making, and that the address and ingenuity of Government attached to the happiness of the people, should be exercised, to keep them (as long as their manners will in any degree admit of it,) within those pales where *pomp*, *luxury*, and *dissipation* are not countenanced and nourished. These I believe to be generally nourished, where Government is committed to the Hands of a few; the human Mind under those Circumstances, is apt to be inflated with pride, disposed to keep up what they call the dignity of their Station and instead of nourishing a superior degree of benevolence and attention to those who placed them there, they feel themselves on the high Horse of power and expect every knee to bend to their station. I should grieve for my Country, if in any degree, the engines of power should be permitted to move to the injury of the rights and Liberties of the people, properly defined and well founded.

I should have been much better pleased if the President was furnished with a Constitutional Council; as he is not, I am rather apprehensive he will seldom return bills to the two Legislative branches with his objections and reasons, and I agree with you, that in time our Country may experience inconvenience, from too successful a Court being paid by a foreign power to that Individual and a Stadtholderian Scene be exhibited in America. But with respect to our experiencing inconvenience in his election, similar to those of Poland, with submission, I would observe the meeting will not be general, nor on the plains of Monmouth,[1] but in 13 different places on the same day and there by ballot and not "viva voce," so that, it may be perfectly a silent transaction as it relates to the respective states. But when those votes are transmitted to the senate and house of Representatives, if there should not be a decided majority in favor of some one, disagreement and inconveniences may arise, and they may quarrel and fight for the fœdral Chair. But the point which to my mind is charged with the most hazard and inconvenience for the present day is the 8th. section of the first article particularizing the powers of Congress. God knows where it will end. If it was not for the fifth article I should dread it's establishment. And considering the situation of our Country and Government I shudder at its rejection, for if a great deal of pains is not taken to preserve the temper of the people, in case of giving existance to public objections, tumult and Confusion will ensue. I hope the subject will have a fair and candid investigation, and that the men of sense and Influence in our Country will take pains to instruct the public mind, and lead them to give their voices for those establishments, which are necessary for the dignity of their Governments but not inconsistant with their own dignity as a free and enlightened people. It is to this reserve in our leading men, that I lay a very large proportion of the real and immaginary inconveniences we have hitherto experienced. I believe that the people at large only wish to be informed and taught what is right and most likely to promote their happiness and they will pursue it. But when the best informed men in a Country will be totally silent and give the people up to guidance of their passions, headed by disorderly and vicious characters, and not even attempt to inform them of their errors—what in the name of Heaven can be expected—nothing Short of Shouting justice out of Countenance, giving a currency to injury and oppression, and treating with derision the most solemn national Compacts. These horrid scenes have been acted since the war in several parts of our Country. I speak decidedly, relative to my Native State, and entirely owing to that shamefull, nay criminal silence in those men who ought to put themselves forward, to instruct some and awe others by the wisdom of their observations, the weight and integrity of their Conduct. But they did not chuse to risk their popularity, or wished the people to force them into such establishments as would make the distance greater between them. But I will not despair. I will hope for the best and if necessary dare fight against the establishment of the worst.—Inclosed is the account Current between us submitted to your perusal and correction. Paine will tell you how he has scalded himself here by a Pamphlet. Johnne Bull is very wrath. I send it enclosed. And wishing you health and happiness and annexing Mrs. Smith's Compliments, remain your obliged friend &c.,

W. S. SMITH

RC (DLC). This letter was conveyed by Lewis Littlepage but not delivered until just before 2 Feb. 1788 (see TJ to Smith of that date). Enclosures: (1) Statement of account with TJ (missing, see TJ to Smith, 2 Feb. 1788). (2) Thomas Paine, *Prospects on the Rubicon*, London, 1787 (Sowerby, No. 2779; *The Complete Writings of Thomas Paine*, ed. P. S. Foner, N.Y., 1945, II, 621-51), a pamphlet written in opposition to Pitt's proposal that England unite with Prussia in support of the Stadtholder in Holland.

1 Below "Monmouth," Smith wrote "Warsaw."

To Brizard

4me. Decembre 1787.

Monsieur Jefferson a l'honneur de remercier Monsieur de Brizard de l'excellente ouvrage sur feu l'Abbé Mably, qu'il a eu la bonté de lui envoyer. L'eloge est vraiment digne de cet auteur celebre, et estimable autant que celebre. Ses ouvrages y sont analysés et characterisés de sorte à faire voir que l'analyste en feroit d'excellentes dans la meme genre s'il le voudroit. M. Jefferson prie très ardemment que sa patrie pourroit remplir toutes les esperances que Monsieur Brizard a la bonté d'en former. Il a l'honneur de l'assurer de sa consideration tres distinguée.

PrC (DLC).

From Clérisseau

MONSIEUR   a paris ce 4 Dec. 1787

J'ai l'honneur de vous faire part de la note que vous m'aves demandé. Je me serois fait un honneur de vous la porter et vous aurois expliqué ma note. Je suis de retour a paris, j'attend vos ordres pour me transporter auprès de vous, n'aiant rien tant a coeur que de vous manifester l'empressement que j'ai d'obliger un amateur zelé de ma cher Antiquité.

J'ai l'honneur d'estre tres respectueusement Monsieur Votre tres obeissant serviteur,   CLERISSEAU

RC (DLC); endorsed. Not recorded in SJL. Neither the NOTE that TJ requested nor the letter in which the request was made (if by letter) has been found.

From Du Bois

Paris, 4 Dec. 1787. Inquires concerning the present whereabouts of John Paul Jones and when he is expected to return to Paris; also wishes to know whether there is any means of obtaining payment of a note for 4,400^{lt} which has been due from Jones for some time; accepted the note because he knows that Jones has an excellent reputation.

RC (DLC); 2 p.; in French; without name of addressee and with the salutation, "Monsieur Le Comte," but endorsed by TJ and recorded in SJL as received 4 Dec. 1787 (see TJ's reply, following); signed: "Du Bois Commissaire gnl. du regt. des gardes francoises rue neuve des petits champs, en face de la compagnie des Indes."

To Du Bois

à Paris ce 4me Decembre 1787.

Je crois, Monsieur, que Monsieur Paul Jones doit etre actuellement à Copenhague, ou sur son passage de la Nouvelle York à Copenhague; et qu'il recevra très surement des lettres addressées à luimeme à Copenhague poste restante, ou chez Monsieur le Baron de Houze à Copenhague. Il doit faire un séjour assez considerable dans cette ville pour solliciter des remboursements de la cour du Dannemarc de la part du Congrès. J'ai l'honneur d'etre avec beaucoup de consideration Monsieur votre très humble et très obeissant serviteur,   TH: JEFFERSON

PrC (DLC). It is possible that Du Bois' inquiry was inspired by TJ's failure to answer Madame Townsend's letter of 13 Nov. 1787, which asked how a letter might be sent to Jones in Denmark, whereas Du Bois' inquiry of 4 Dec. did not specifically ask for that information, though TJ here supplied it. This is conjectural, and it is not certainly known that TJ did *not* answer Madame Townsend's letter.

From C. W. F. Dumas

MONSIEUR   Lahaie 4e. Dec. *1787*

Votre Excellence verra par la note jointe à l'incluse, que j'ai cru bien faire d'omettre ces mots, dans l'Extrait *from a change of opinion in them, or.*

Mr. De Linde est rappellé de sa Mission de Londres.

Ce soir et demain, fête de St. Nicolas, fait trembler ici tous les honnetes, bonnes et paisibles gens. Mr. v. Staphorst, qui est à Paris, vous dira pourquoi.

La poste part. Je suis avec le plus grand respect, de Votre Excellence, Le très-humble et très-obéissant serviteur,

C. W. F. DUMAS

RC (DLC). Recorded in SJL as received 9 Dec. 1787. Enclosures (FC in Dumas Papers, Rijksarchief, The Hague; photostats in DLC; translations printed in *Dipl. Corr., 1783-89,* III, 601-3, incorrectly dated 4 Oct. and 3 Oct. 1787, respectively): (1) Dumas to Jay, 4 Dec. 1787, reporting on his correspondence with TJ concerning his proposal of going to Brussels to carry on preliminary negotiations for a treaty of amity and commerce between the United States and the Austrian Netherlands; urging the importance of such a treaty and the certainty of successful negotiation; and stating that he has transmitted TJ's letter of 14 Nov. 1787 both verbally and in writing to the emperor's chargé d'affaires at Brussels. (2) Copy of Dumas' letter to the emperor's chargé d'affaires at Brussels, 3 Dec. 1787 ("la note jointe à l'incluse") quoting a portion of TJ's letter to Dumas of 14 Nov. 1787, q.v., and stating that he is writing directly to the U.S. secretary for foreign affairs for authorization, to be given either directly to him or through TJ, to carry on the preliminary negotiations for a treaty to be concluded by the ministers of the two countries either at Paris or Brussels.

From Abigail Adams

London Grosvenour Square December 5th 1787.

Mrs. Adams presents her respectfull compliments to Mr. Jefferson and asks the favour of him to permit petit to purchase for her ten Ells of double Florence of any fashionable coulour, orange excepted which is in high vogue here. Mrs. A. excepts green also of which she has enough. Mr. Muchier if in paris will be so kind as to take charge of it, and Mrs. Adams will send the money by Mr. Trumble who will be in paris some time next week.

By Letters this day received from Boston it appears that a convention was agred too by both Houses, and that it is to meet, the second wednesday in Jan'ry.

Mr. King writes that Mr. Jeffersons commission is renewed at the court of France, and Mr. Adams's resignation accepted, so that we shall quit this country as soon in the spring as we can go with safety.

Love to the Young Ladies & thank my dear polly for her pretty Letter.

RC (DLC). Recorded in SJL as received 13 Dec. 1787. Mary Jefferson's PRETTY LETTER has not been found.

From William Shippen

Philadelphia, 5 Dec. 1787. Introduces his son and asks TJ's "protection and friendship," knowing that TJ "will receive him affectionately" and that "no person in France can be of so much use to him"; has "directed him to continue in France four months," and to take TJ's "advice on the mode of his spending his time there to the greatest advantage and with the most Œconomy. Improvement more than pleasure is his object. He will necessarily blend them. I am misinformed if he has not spent eighteen months in England to great advantage. When you become acquainted with him, a Letter from your Excellency will be esteemed a great honor and the highest gratification." Refers TJ to his son for "news and politics of this country."

RC (DLC); 4 p.; endorsed.

From the Commissioners of the Treasury

SIR   Board of Treasury December 5. 1787.

We have the honor of enclosing to you a Letter from Thomas Barclay Esqr. late Commissioner for settling the Public Accounts in Europe relative to the Books and Papers of his Office. You will oblige us in removing them to your own house, and in taking charge of them till it is determined in what manner it will be best to dispose of them. It may be proper to observe that we consider the safe Custody of these papers to be of the greatest importance. You will likewise receive enclosed a Triplicate of our letter of the 10th: of last month, and a Duplicate of what we had the honor of writing on the 13th: of the same month. We have only to add that from the present state of Affairs in this Quarter, it will be absolutely impracticable to make any remittance from this Country, for the purpose of enabling you to carry into execution the Act of Congress of the 12th. of October; or to discharge the balance of Mr. Grands Account. Our only resource is the completion of the Loan in Holland, to forward which, your influence will, we are assured, not be wanting.

We have the Honor to be with Esteem Sir, Your most obedient & most Humble Servts., SAMUEL OSGOOD
ARTHUR LEE

RC (DLC); in the hand of Samuel Osgood and signed by him and Arthur Lee; endorsed as received 26 Jan. 1788. Enclosures: (1) Barclay to TJ, 30 Nov. 1787 (missing). (2) Tripl of Commissioners of Treasury to TJ, 10 Nov. and (3) Dupl of same to same, 13 Nov. 1787.

From John Adams

DEAR SIR London Decr. 6. 1787

The Project of a new Constitution, has Objections against it, to which I find it difficult to reconcile my self, but I am so unfortunate as to differ somewhat from you in the Articles, according to your last kind Letter.

You are afraid of the one—I, of the few. We agree perfectly that the many should have a full fair and perfect Representation.— You are Apprehensive of Monarchy; I, of Aristocracy. I would therefore have given more Power to the President and less to the Senate. The Nomination and Appointment to all offices I would have given to the President, assisted only by a Privy Council of his own[1] Creation, but not a Vote or Voice would I have given to the Senate or any Senator, unless he were of the Privy Council. Faction and Distraction are the sure and certain Consequence of giving to a Senate a vote in the distribution of offices.

You are apprehensive the President when once chosen, will be chosen again and again as long as he lives. So much the better as it appears to me.—You are apprehensive of foreign Interference, Intrigue, Influence. So am I.—But, as often as Elections happen, the danger of foreign Influence recurs. The less frequently they happen the less danger.—And if the Same Man may be chosen again, it is probable he will be, and the danger of foreign Influence will be less. Foreigners, seeing little Prospect will have less Courage for Enterprise.

Elections, my dear sir, Elections to offices which are great objects of Ambition, I look at with terror. Experiments of this kind have been so often tryed, and so universally found productive of Horrors, that there is great Reason to dread them.[2]

Mr. Littlepage who will have the Honour to deliver this will tell you all the News. I am, my dear Sir, with great Regard,

JOHN ADAMS

RC (DLC). FC (MHi: AMT); in the hand of William Stephens Smith. Recorded in SJL as received 13 Dec. 1787.

¹ Adams deleted at this point: "Ap-

pointment."

² Following this, one full sentence is heavily scored out in RC and does not appear in FC.

From John Adams

[London, 6 Dec. 1787. Recorded in SJL as received 17 Dec. 1787, "recommending of Cerisier." Not found. Antoine-Marie Cerisier, French historian and diplomat, was attached to the French embassy in Holland, where Adams met him in 1780 (Didot, Nouvelle biographie générale; Adams, Works, I, 330; VII, 492).]

From H. Fizeaux & Cie.

MONSIEUR   Amsterdam le 6. 9bre. [Dec.] 1787

Nous avons observé par la reponse dont vous nous avez honoré le 23. juillet que vous avez eu la complaisance d'envoyer nos lettres du 1er. Janvier et 16. Juillet derniers au trésorier des Etats-Unis, reclamant les fonds nécessaires au remboursement de la levée de ƒ 51,000. que nous fimes pour l'Amérique, et qui echeoit le 1er. du mois prochain.

Le silence que l'on a gardé de toute part sur cet engagement nous penètre de regret, parcequ'il nous menace de voir la confiance du public lesée par notre ministère, tandis que le respect que nous lui devons et à nous-mêmes nous rend également jaloux de l'exactitude des emprunts que nous lui offrons.

Cependant, Monsieur, l'usage veut qu'on publie les remboursements quinze jours avant leur terme, mais il faut toutefois être prealablement muni de l'objet annoncé. C'est pourquoi nous vous suplions de nous faire remettre immediatement ces fonds, si vous souhaitez que cette convention soit respectée, ou de nous dicter la reponse à faire aux intéressés, si elle ne doit pas l'être. Nous avons l'honneur d'être, &c.   (signed) H. FIZEAUX & Co.

Tr (MHi: AMT); in the hand of William Short and attested by him; this Tr is dated "9bre." but TJ recorded the (missing) RC in SJL as dated 6 Dec. and received 12 Dec. 1787. TJ immediately sent this Tr to Adams in his letter of 12 Dec., q.v.; the haste in copying may account for Short's error.

[397]

To Montmorin, with Enclosure

SIR   Paris Dec. 6. 1787.

I take the liberty of asking your Excellency's perusal of the inclosed case of an American hostage confined in the prisons of Dunkirk. His continuance there seems to be useless, and yet endless. Not knowing how far the government can interfere for his relief, as it is a case wherein private property is concerned, I do not presume to ask his liberation absolutely: but I will sollicit from your Excellency such measures in his behalf as the laws and usages of the country may permit.

The Comptroller general having been so good as to explain to me in a conversation that he wished to know what duties were levied in England on American whale oil, I have had the honor of informing him by letter that the antient duties on that article are £17-6s-6d sterling the ton, and that some late additional duties make them amount to about 18.£ sterling. That the common whale oil sells there but for about 20£ sterling the ton, and of course the duty amounts to a prohibition. This duty was originally laid on all foreign fish oil, with a view to favor the British and American fisheries. When we became independant, and of course foreign to Great Britain, we became subject to the foreign duty. No duty therefore which France may think proper to lay on this article can drive it to the English market. It could only oblige the inhabitants of Nantucket to abandon their fishery. But the poverty of their soil offering them no other resource, they must quit their country, and either establish themselves in Nova Scotia, where, as British fishermen, they may participate of the British premium, in addition to the ordinary price of their whale oil, or they must accept the conditions which this government offers for the establishment they have proposed at Dunkirk. Your Excellency will judge what conditions may counterbalance in their minds the circumstances of the vicinity of Nova Scotia, sameness of language, laws, religion, customs, and kindred. Remaining in their native country to which they are most singularly attached, excluded from commerce with England, taught to look to France as the only country from which they can derive sustenance, they will, in a case of war, become useful Rovers against it's enemies: their position, their poverty, their courage, their address, and their hatred will render them formidable scourges on the British commerce. It is to be considered then on the one hand that the duty which M. de Calonnes had proposed to retain on their oil may endanger the shifting this useful body of seamen out of our joint scale into that of the British; and also may suppress a considerable subject of exchange for the productions of France: on the other hand that it may produce an addition to his majesty's revenue. What I have thus far said, is on the supposition that the duty may operate a diminution of the price received by the fisherman. If it act in the contrary direction, and produce an augmentation of price to the consumer, it immediately brings into competition a variety of other oils vegetable and animal, a good part of which France receives from abroad; and the fisherman thus losing his market, is compelled equally to change either his calling or country. When M. de Calonne first agreed to reduce the duties to what he has declared, I had great hopes the commodity could bear them, and that it would become a medium of commerce between France and the United States. I must confess however that my expectations have not been fulfilled, and that but little has come here as yet. This induces me to fear that it is so poor an article, that any duty whatever will suppress it. Should this take place, and the spirit of emigration once seize those people, perhaps an abolition of all duty might then come too late to stop what it would now easily prevent. I fear there is danger in the experiment; and it remains for the wisdom of his majesty and his ministers to decide whether the prospect of gain to the revenue, or of establishing a national fishery may compensate this danger. If the government should decide to retain the duty, I shall acquiesce in it chearfully, and do every thing in my power to encourage my countrymen still to continue their occupation.

The actual session of our several legislatures would render it interesting to forward immediately the regulations proposed on our commerce; and the expiration of the order of Berny at the close of this month, endangers a suspension and derangement in the commerce of tobacco, very embarrassing to the merchants of the two countries. Pardon me therefore, Sir, if I appear sollicitous to obtain the ultimate decision of his majesty's council on these subjects, and to ask as early a communication of that decision as shall be convenient.

I have the honour to be with sentiments of the most profound esteem and respect, Your Excellency's most obedient and most humble servant, TH: JEFFERSON

ENCLOSURE

Jefferson's Memorandum Concerning Alexander Gross

Alexander Gross, a sailor from Cape Cod in Massachusetts was taken prisoner in 1778, by an English privateer, carried to Liverpool and emprisoned there four months. He was thence sent on board the Duke Man of war of 38. guns where he was obliged to do duty according to the English law made on that occasion. After three years he found means to escape and got on board a sloop called the Charlotte belonging to one McGregor and commanded by him, bound from Southampton to Cork, loaded with bark. His object was to get a passage from Ireland to America as there was a trade constantly going on between those countries. They had been out but four days, when on the 21st Feb. 1782, they were taken by the Countess D'Avaux a privateer from Dunkirk commanded by Capt. Carry. McGregor ransomed his vessel for £200 Stg. and prevailed on Gross to become hostage for the payment. This he agreed to the more readily because while on board an English Vessel or in English Dominions he was constantly liable to be taken and hung as a deserter, and because he relied that McGregor would soon pay the ransom and thus place him at liberty in France where he would be safe and from whence he could get a passage back to America. The ransomed vessel got into port but going out again on another voyage to Cork, perished at sea with every person on board her. Among these was McGregor her owner and master. Gross the hostage was put into prison at Dunkirk and in 1784 the captors became bankrupt. He is still kept in close jail. He has already cost 3052^{tt} a good part of it to the king at whose expence he now remains there. 1. Gross is a poor sailor without property and without connexions able to do anything for his redemption. 2. The vessel and her owner being lost, there is neither person nor thing in existence against which he can bring an action to compel that redemption. 3. The obligation to the captors is dissolved, because there can be no obligation where there is only one party in existence. 4. There seems to be no person to whom application can be made for the release of the hostage, because the captors having failed, their interest in his person is transferred to their creditors, and these dispersed over the earth cannot be collected to give their consent. 5. The King's expences are daily encreasing without the smallest probability of their ever being repaid.

The confinement of an hostage under such circumstances is an useless severity, and the doing it at the expence of the King, where there does not remain the least prospect of its being ever recovered, seems to authorize him in reason to discharge the hostage, unless any person will appear to sollicit his continuance in prison and to pay the expences. If he were placed at the expence of those who may think themselves interested in his confinement, they would soon take the trouble to satisfy themselves how impossible it is they should ever be repaid and they would release him. In pity to the hostage and in justice to the King, it is wished that he might be discharged or placed at the expence of the individuals, if any there are, who may wish him to remain in prison.

RC (Arch. Aff. Etr., Paris, Corr. Pol., Angleterre, vol. 562); at head of text, in a clerk's hand: "M. De R"; French translation (same), in a clerk's hand. PrC (DLC). Recorded in SJL under 7 Dec. 1787, with TJ to Lambert of that date, q.v. Enclosure: RC (Arch. Aff. Etr., Paris, Corr. Pol., E.-U., XXXIII); without caption or date, in the hand of William Short, with one addition in TJ's hand; "7 janr. 1788" written at head of text in a clerk's hand—possibly the date that the memo-randum concerning Gross was referred to Luzerne (see Montmorin to TJ, 6 Mch. 1788). PrC (DLC).

From William Stephens Smith

Dr. Sir London Decr. 6th. 1787.

I wrote you by Mr. Littlepage on the 4th.[1] inst. That Letter contains an account of Cash recieved and disposed of on your account. I do not know whether I have made a just calculation of the Livrs. expended in Paris on my account, but this and every other article is submitted to your alteration. I enclose the reviews of the last Month as both your and Mr. Adams's Names are mentioned, and have only time to say that by Letter from Mr. King at Boston octr. 27., that Congress have determined that the Commission at this Court shall expire and we return. They begin to feel an honest indignation towards those who are capable of insulting and unprovoked, discover a disposition to injure. This is fine and I doubt not will operate as you and I wish. Congress have also continued your Commission but made no other appointments as yet. In your Letters to your friends previous to my departure which will be in March next, I should wish to be remembered that I may on my arrival shake hands with them in honest Confidence. Yours sincerely, W. S. Smith

RC (MHi); endorsed. Recorded in SJL as received 13 Dec. 1787.

[1] That is, on 3 Dec.

From Nathaniel Barrett

Sir Paris Decr 7. 1787

The Cargo of Oil referd to in Messrs. Le Couteulx Letter has been deliverd By those Gentlemen to Mr. Sangrain's Agents at Rouen for the Illumination of Paris. The only Duties which ought to be demanded are 7.^{lt} 10s ⅌ 520^{lt} and 10s. ⅌ Livre, and on producing Certificates (which I have by me) of Exportation or purchase of Goods, this Duty to be returnd, or the Bonds discharged, this being the Case, there can be no possible Damage accrue, from the proposal of Messrs. Le Couteulx's for a delay of 8 mo. to procure the necessary Papers from America. It appears by the inclosed Extract of a Letter which I received a few days since, that no Idea is entertained in America of procuring a Certificate from the Consul, but that Certificates from the Government respecting the Cargo of the Sally Capt. Coffin were expedited to Boston for the public Seal, and that Capt. Hussey of the Brign. Fox would have obtained the same had he known that it was needful. The writer of the Letter (of which the inclosed is an Extract) is Peleg Coffin Esqr. of Nantucket, late Member of the Council of Massachusets and the person who gave Certificates to the owners of both Cargoes, to enable them to obtain a Bounty granted on Oils caught by the Inhabitants of Massachusets.

I have the honour to be very sincerely Sir Your most obedt & huml Servt,   NAT BARRETT

RC (MHi); endorsed. Recorded in SJL as received 9 Dec. 1787. Enclosures (MHi): (1) Le Couteulx & Cie. to Nathaniel Barrett, 5 Dec. 1787, stating that the person in charge of the sale of the three cases of whale oil had forgotten to weigh them properly and they are puzzled as to the amount for which to bill him; that if these cases have not yet been sold, they wish Barrett to have them weighed correctly; that they have presented to the collector the papers for the ship Fox as supplied by Captain Hussey, thus establishing that the oil was brought by an American ship; that the duty must be paid in full by the end of the month unless TJ can obtain six or eight months' respite while the French Consul in the United States sends on a certificate stating that the oil was produced from fish caught in American waters, unless the in-spector will waive the certificates for this time only because Captain Hussey did not know this was necessary; and requesting that Barrett beg TJ to save his friends from paying the large amount of duty and to tell them never again to make oil shipments unaccompanied by a certificate. (2) Extract of a letter from Peleg Coffin to Nathaniel Barrett, 1 Oct. 1787 (written at the foot of Barrett's letter), stating that Coffin has forwarded a certificate for his cargo to have the seal of the commonwealth attached, which certificate will then be forwarded to Paris; that Barrett's letter of 1 June did not arrive in time to obtain a certificate for the cargo on the Fox; and that, since the quantity shipped and the names of the shippers are not known, the certificates must wait for that information from Barrett or the ship's captain.

From Berenger de Beaufain

Erlangen, 7 Dec. 1787. Is a descendant of a French family exiled to Germany because of religion. His uncle, Hector de Berenger de Beaufain, went to America with General Oglethorpe in 1733, settled in South Carolina, became British collector of customs in 1747, received two grants of land from George II, and died in 1766, leaving all his property to the writer, his nephew, by will dated 1762. The will was probated in London soon after his uncle's death and permission was given to sell the lands. The executor, David Rhind, was unable to collect the debts due the estate. During the late war the estate was confiscated on the ground that the owner was British, although he is a German. Wrote on several occasions to John Rutledge, Henry Laurens, and J. Boomer Graves, British consul for the Carolinas and Georgia, but has had no answers to his letters. Asks TJ's protection in collecting the money due him for the sake of his family which is destitute. Visited his uncle in Charleston in 1763.

RC (DLC); 5 p.; in French. Recorded in SJL as received 18 Dec. 1787. Enclosure (DLC): Copy of inscription reading: "In the Cœmetary of this Church | lie the Remains | of | Hector Berenger de Beaufaïn, Esqr. | born in France in the Year of our Lord 1697: he came | from London to South Carolina in 1733 where he resided | the Remainder of his Life; in 1742 he was appointed | Collector of his Majesty's Customs, and in 1747 Member of | his Majesty's Council, for this Province. | He died Octob: 13. 1766 | deservedly regretted | A Man | of unshaken Integrity in the Discharge of his publick Trust | never relaxed to the Prejudice of the Crown Revenue | never rigorously enforced to the Oppression of the Innocent | of most benevolent Humanity | always ready to relieve the distressed | without Ostentation | of humblest Manners, tho possessed of eminent Talents | Master of the learned Languages | And [th]o a foreigner a profound Critic in the english Tongue | tho humble, inflexibly adhering to the Rules | of Justice, Honor and Politeness | complaisant in his Behaviour to all | thus meriting, He acquired | universal Esteem. | his fellow Citizens of this Province | so many Years the Witnesses and Admirers | of his virtue uniformly practised thro Life | have erected this Monument | sacred to the Memory | of his Merit and their Love | MDCCLXVII."

From Maria Cosway

Friday night [7 December 1787]

I cannot breakfast with you to morrow; to bid you adieu once is sufficiently painful, for I leave you with very melancholy ideas. You have given my dear Sir all your commissions to Mr. Trumbull, and I have the reflection that I cannot be useful to you; who have rendered me so many civilities.

RC (DLC); unsigned, unaddressed, undated, and unrecorded in SJL; dated from internal evidence and Maria Cosway's letter to TJ of 10 Dec. 1787, q.v.

To Lambert

MONSIEUR   à Paris ce 7me. Decembre 1787.

Depuis que j'eus l'honneur de parler à Votre Excellence au sujet des huiles de baleines, j'ai examiné le livre des impots Anglois, et je trouve effectivement que l'impot ancien sur ces huiles y etoit de £17.-6sh.-6d. sterling le tonneau; et je crois etre sur qu'on y a mis dernierement un impot additionel qui fait y monter le tout à environ 18. livres sterling le tonneau. L'huile de baleine *ordinaire* se vende à Londres de 19. à 21. livres sterling le tonneau. Cet impot donc est une veritable defence pour cette espece d'huile. Mais celle du *baleine spermaceti* y est payée de 50. à 60. Livres sterling le tonneau. Elle peut payer donc l'impot de 18. livres sterling, et laisser au pêcheur de 32. à 42 £ sterling le tonneau. Et c'est seulement cette espece d'huile que les Americains portent en Angleterre actuellement, et qu'ils continueront d'y porter à cause du gros prix que les Anglois y mettent. La quantité en est peu. C'est de plus une huile sans odeur, et qu'on brule consequemment en Angleterre dans tous les corridors, les antichambres, les escaliers, meme des maisons les plus riches, aux spectacles, &c. C'est encore une huile dont la limpidité resiste au froid le plus fort de l'hyver; et que melée, meme en petite dose, avec de l'huile de *baleine ordinaire*, lui donne la meme qualité de résistance au froid. Ce sont les qualités qui assurent, chez les Anglois qui les connoissent, le gros prix à l'huile du *baleine spermaceti*. Mais l'huile du *baleine ordinaire*, n'ayant point ces superiorités, si les impots qu'on y mettra vont en en augmentant le prix au consommateur, il peut preferer d'acheter des huiles vegetales qui entrent en concurrence: si ces impots vont en diminuant au pêcheur le produit de son travail, il peut n'y trouver plus de quoi vivre. Il lui faudra donc de quitter ou sa pêche ou sa patrie. S'il quitte sa pêche, les rochers et les sables de Nantucket ne lui offrent d'autres ressources. S'il quitte sa patrie, comme le seul parti qui lui reste, sera ce pour un pays voisin, où il retrouvera sa langue, sa religion, ses loix, ses habitudes, et peutetre ses parens, et d'où on lui tend les bras avec des grosses primes pour l'y inviter? Ou sera ce pour s'etablir où, en echange de toutes ces avantages, il aura pour toute consolation d'etre chez une nation estimable, amicale, et bienfaictrice? Je suis sur, Monsieur, que le gros de mes concitoyens prefereroit le dernier parti. Mais ce leur supposeroit toujours une certaine aisance que je crains qu'on ne trouve pas chez les Nantuckois. Si des motifs si purs et si moraux pourroient agir sur ces pauvres gens avec autant de force que les considerations seduisantes qui les invitent à la Nouvelle Ecosse, la France pourroit les partager egalement avec l'Angleterre. Ce ne changeroit pas le niveau des forces des deux nations. Mais en les laissant chez eux, en opposant, à leur egard, au regime rebutant d'Angleterre, une reception amicale, une marché sure pour le produit de leurs travaux et de leurs dangers, je dirois avec une certitude que je ne craindrois pas de voir dementie par l'evenement, que dans le cas d'une guerre, ils deviendroient presque tous des corsaires sur les ennemis de la France, et des corsaires redoutables par leur position, leur pauvreté leur adresse, leur hardiesse, et leur haine.

Mais c'est à vos lumieres, Monsieur, c'est à la sagesse de sa Majesté et de ses ministres de peser ces considerations, et de decider

de leur valeur. Si la reste d'impot que M. de Calonne avoit proposé de garder ne peut empecher les huiles de baleines de venir
s'echanger contre les productions nationales, s'il n'y a point de
risque de faire la double perte de transferer ce corps hardi de
matelots de notre coté à celle d'une nation qui nous en veut à tous
les deux, on peut faire l'essai de cet impot. Cet essai nous mettra à
meme de savoir surement si, sans diminution ulterieure d'impot,
les huiles de baleine *ordinaires* peuvent supporter la concurrence
des autres huiles. Dans ce cas, ce sera autant de gagné pour les
revenues de sa Majesté, et je ne me permets pas de regarder ce qui
est gagné pour lui comme perdu pour nous. Si je ne craignois pas
de devenir importun, j'oserois demander une decision aussitot
qu'elle pourroit etre convenablement faite; àfin que je pourrois la
faire passer à nos corps legislatifs, qui doivent etre, ou actuellement, ou bientot, en seance, et qui ne le sont qu'un fois l'année. Je
vous prie, Monsieur, d'agreer l'hommage de mes respects, et les
sentiments sinceres avec lesquelles j'ai l'honneur d'etre, de Votre
Excellence, le serviteur très humble et très obeissant,

TH: JEFFERSON

RC (Arch. Aff. Etr., Paris, Corr. Pol., Angleterre, vol. 562). PrC (DLC).

From John Trumbull

DR. SIR   London Decr. 7th. 1787.

I have your letter of Novr. 13th. by which I am happy to learn
that your Harpsichord is safe. It must be long since in your possession and I hope answers in every respect your wishes.

I fear Mr. Brown will not have compleated your commission in
time for me to bring: one of the Polyplasiosmos pictures I will
bring you ('tis such a ridiculous long word, that I don't believe
I have spelt it right).—I hope now to have the happiness to be
with you in a few days. Thursday next is the day at present fix'd for
me to leave London in company with Mrs. Church. I do not know
whether I may not be under a necessity of praying a delay of 2 or
3 days more to give me time for finishing my sketch of York Town,
in which my Conduct has been that of a true sinner who delays
his preparations to the latest moment and then has too little time.

I have found more difficulty in reconciling the formality of the
Parade, to the Variety necessary in a picture, than in anything of
the kind I ever attempted before: and have therefore untill this

[405]

hour found it impossible to satisfy my own wishes. I flatter myself with the Idea that I am now in the road to success and hope to have compleated the work by the day fix'd. At any rate I shall not over-run it more than 2 or 3.

Mrs. Cosway to my great mortification is expected in London every day. She was not arrivd this morning. If she had remain'd in Paris untill our arrival, you would have found a powerfull ally in Mrs. Church, who I am sure would have us'd every influence in conjunction with her other friends to have detain'd her a little longer.

I Beg my Compliments to Mr. Short, & am with the highest respect Dear Sir Your oblig'd friend & servant,

JNO. TRUMBULL

The Conventions of Massachusetts and Connecticut meet in January to consider the new Constitution. The approbation it meets in America seems very unanimous.

RC (DLC); endorsed. Recorded in SJL as received 13 Dec. 1787.
Trumbull did spell the RIDICULOUS LONG WORD correctly; see note to TJ to Trumbull, 13 Nov. 1787.

From Carra

Paris, 8 Dec. 1787. Has been charged with a memorial concerning Cazeau, a Canadian, in relation to a debt which Congress acknowledged by resolutions of 6 Feb. 1783 and 18 Mch. 1784; asks for an appoint-ment to present them to TJ.

RC (DLC); 1 p.; in French; signed: "Carra de la Bibliotheque du Roi, rue de la michodiere, à coté de la rue projettée." Recorded in SJL as received 9 Dec. 1787.
For the report and resolution on Cazeau's debt, see JCC, XXIV, 117; XXVI, 147-50.

To C. W. F. Dumas

SIR   Paris Dec. 9. 1787.

Your letter of Nov. 27. shewing that mine of Nov. 14. had not then got to hand, had given me alarm for it's fate, and I had sat down to write you a second acknolegement of the receipt of your two favors of Octob. 23. and 26. and to add the receipt also of those of Nov. 14. 22. and 27. A copy of my answer of Nov. 14. was prepared to be inclosed to you, but in that moment came your favors of Nov. 30. Dec. 2. and 4th. by which I perceived that the original had at length got safe to hand. By that you have seen that all interference, direct or indirect, on the part of Mr. Adams and myself in the business you had done me the honor to suggest, would be improper. Your dispatches for Mr. Jay shall go with mine in the packet of this month. These will bring the matter into the view of Congress. In the mean time I think it would be well to avoid exciting, at Brussels or any where else, the least expectation thereon, because it is impossible for us to know what that body may in it's wisdom, and with all circumstances under it's eye, decide should be done. They had in the year 1784. made up their minds as to the system of commercial principles they wished to pursue. These were very free. They proposed them to all the powers of Europe. All declined except Prussia. To this general opposition they may now find it necessary to present a very different general system, to which their treaties will form cases of exception, and they may wish to lessen rather than multiply those cases of exception. Add to this, that it is in contemplation to change the organization of the federal government, and they may think it better to leave the system of foreign connection to be formed by those who are to pursue it. I only mention these as possible considerations, without pretending to know the sentiments of that honourable body, or any one of it's members, on the subject: and to shew that no expectations should be raised which might embarrass them or embroil ourselves. The proposed change of government seems to be the proper topic to urge as the reason why Congress may not at this moment chuse to be forming new treaties. Should they chuse it, on the other hand, the reserve of those who act for them, while uninstructed, cannot do injury.

I find the expectation very general that the present peace will be [of sho]rt duration. There are circumstances in favour of this opinion; there are other against it. Certain it is that this country is in a state so unprepared as to excite astonishment. After the last war, she seems to have reposed on her laurels, in confidence that no power would venture to disturb that repose. It is presumable her present ministry will propose to vindicate their nation and their friends. The late events have kindled a fire which, tho smothered of necessity for the present moment, will probably never be quenched but by signal revenge. Individuals will in the mean time [have] incurred sufferings which that may not repair. That yours may be lessened for the present, and relieved in future is the sincere wish of him who has the honor to be with sentiments of great esteem and regard, Sir, your most obedient and most humble servant,

TH: JEFFERSON

PrC (DLC).

From John Lowell

Boston, 9 Dec. 1787. Introduces Thomas Russell Greaves, son of Thomas Russell, a well-to-do merchant of Boston, who is interrupting his studies in law to go to France to seek relief from "some alarming pulmonary Complaints" and to "acquire a competent Knowledge of the french Language"; asks TJ to befriend him, advise him "how to avoid the Inconveniences and Dangers to which his Youth may expose him, and to point out to him the best Method of obtaining usefull Knowledge while in that Country."

RC (MHi); 2 p.; endorsed.

From James Madison

DEAR SIR   New York. Decr. 9th. 1787.

Your favour of the 17th. of Sepr. with sundry other letters and packets, came duly by the last packet. Such of them as were addressed to others, were duly forwarded. The three Boxes, marked I M, G.W. and A D, it appears were never shipped from Havre. Whenever they arrive your commands with regard to the two last shall be attended to, as well as those relating to some of the contents of the first. I have not been able to get any satisfactory account of Willm. S. Browne. Alderman Broom tells me that he professed to receive the money from him, for the use of Mr. Burke. I shall not lose sight of the subject, and will give you the earliest information of the result of my enquiries. The annexed list of trees will shew you that I have ventured to substitute half a dozen sorts of apples in place of the pippins alone, and to add 8 other sorts of American trees, including 20 of the Sugar Maple. They were obtained from a Mr. Prince in the neighbourhood of this City, who deals largely in this way, and is considered as a man of worth. I learn from him that he has executed various commissions from Europe and the West Indies, as well as places less distant; and that he has been generally very successful in preserving the trees from perishing by such distant transplantations. He does not use moss as you prescribe but incloses the roots in a bag of earth. As moss is not be got, as he says, it is uncertain whether necessity or choice gives the preference to the latter. I inclose a Catalogue of his nursery and annex the price of the sample I send you, that you may, if you incline, give orders for any other supply. I doubt whether the Virga. Red Birds are found in this part of America. Opossums are not rare in the milder parts of New Jersey, but are very rare thus far Northward. I shall nevertheless avail myself of any opportunities which may happen for procuring and forwarding both. Along with the Box of trees, I send by the Packet to the care of Mr. Limozin 2 Barrels of New Town pippins, and 2 of Cranberrys. In one of the latter the Cranberries are put up dry, in the other in water; the opinions and accounts differing as to the best mode. You will note the event of the experiment.

The Constitution proposed by the late Convention engrosses almost the whole political attention of America. All the Legislatures except that of R. Island, which have been assembled, have agreed in submitting it to State Conventions. Virginia has set the example of opening a door for amendments, if the Convention there should chuse to propose them. Maryland has copied it. The States which preceded, referred the Constitution as recommended by the General Convention, to be ratified or rejected as it stands. The Convention of Pennsylvania, is now sitting. There are about 44 or 45, on the affirmative and about half that number on the opposite side; A considerable number of the Constitutional party as it was called, having joined the other party in espousing the federal Constitution. The returns of deputies for the Convention of Connecticut are known, and prove, as is said by those who know the men that a very great majority will adopt it in that State. The event in Massachusetts lies in greater uncertainty. The friends of the New Government continue to be sanguine. N. Hampshire from every account, as well as from some general inducements felt there, will pretty certainly be on the affirmative side. So will New Jersey and Delaware. N. York is much divided. She will hardly dissent from N. England, particularly if the conduct of the latter should coincide with that of N. Jersey and Pennsylva. A more formidable opposition is likely to be made in Maryland than was at first conjectured. Mr. Mercer, it seems, who was a member of the Convention, though his attendance was but for a short time, is become an auxiliary to Chace. Johnson the Carrolls, Govr. Lee, and most of the other characters of weight are on the other side. Mr. T. Stone died a little before the Government was promulged. The body of the people in Virgina. particularly in the upper and lower Country, and in the Northern Neck, are as far as I can gather, much disposed to adopt the new Constitution. The middle Country, and the South side of James River are principally in the opposition to it. As yet a large majority of the people are under the first description. As yet also are a majority of the Assembly. What change may be produced by the united influence of exertions of Mr. Henry, Mr. Mason, and the Governor with some pretty able auxiliaries, is uncertain. My information leads me to suppose there must be three parties in Virginia. The first for adopting without attempting amendments. This includes Genl. W and the other deputies who signed the Constitution, Mr. Pendleton (Mr. Marshal I believe), Mr. Nicholas, Mr. Corbin, Mr. Zachy. Johnson, Col. Innis, (Mr. B. Randolph as I understand) Mr. Harvey, Mr. Gabl. Jones, Docr. Jones, &c. &c. At the head of the 2d. party which urges amendments are the Governor and Mr. Mason. These do not object to the substance of the Government but contend for a few additional guards in favor of the Rights of the States and of the people. I am not able to enumerate the characters which fall in with their ideas, as distinguished from those of a third Class, at the head of which is Mr. Henry. This class concurs at present with the patrons of amendments, but will probably contend for such as strike at the essence of the System, and must lead to an adherence to the principle of the existing Confederation, which most thinking men are convinced is a visionary one, or to a partition of the Union into several Confederacies. Mr. Harrison the late Governor is with Mr. Henry. So are a number of others. The General and Admiralty Courts with most of the Bar, oppose the Constitution, but on what particular grounds I am unable to say. Genl. Nelson, Mr. Jno. Page, Col. Bland, &c. are also opponents, but on what principle and to what extent, I am equally at a loss to say. In general I must note, that I speak with respect to many of these names, from information that may not be accurate, and merely as I should do in a free and confidential conversation with you. I have not yet heard Mr. Wythe's sentiments on the subject. Docr. McClurg the other absent deputy, is a very strenuous defender of the new Government. Mr. Henry is the great adversary who will render the event precarious. He is I find with his usual address, working up every possible interest, into a spirit of opposition. It is worthy of remark that whilst in Virga. and some of the other States in the middle and Southern Districts of the Union, the men of intelligence, patriotism, property, and independent circumstances, are thus divided; all of this description, with a few exceptions, in the Eastern States, and most of the middle States, are zealously attached to the proposed Constitution. In N. England, the men of letters, the principal officers of Government, the Judges and Lawyers, the Clergy, and men of property, furnish only here and there an adversary. It is not less worthy of remark that in Virginia where the mass of the people have been so much accustomed to be guided by their rulers on all new and intricate questions, they should on the present which certainly surpasses the judgment of the greater part of them, not only go before, but contrary to, their most popular leaders. And the phenomenon is the more wonderful, as a popular ground is taken by all the adversaries to the new Constitution. Perhaps the solution in both these cases, would not be very difficult; but it would lead to observations too diffusive; and to you unnecessary. I will barely observe that the case in Virga. seems to prove that the body of sober and steady people, even of the lower order, are tired of the vicisitudes, injustice and follies which have so much characterised public measures, and are impatient for some change which promises stability and repose. The proceedings of the present assembly are more likely to cherish than remove this disposition. I find Mr. Henry has carried a Resolution for *prohibiting* the importation of Rum, brandy, and other ardent spirits; and if I am not misinformed all manufactured leather, hats and sundry other articles are included in the *prohibition*. Enormous duties at least are likely to take place on the last and many other articles. A project of this sort without the concurrence of the other States, is little short of madness. With such concurrence, it is not practicable without resorting to expedients equally noxious to liberty and œconomy. The consequences of the experiment in a single State, as unprepared for manufactures as Virginia may easily be preconceived. The Revised Code will not be resumed. Mr. Henry is an inveterate adversary to it. Col. Mason made a regular and powerful attack on the port Bill; but was left in a very small minority. I found at the last Session that that regulation was not to be shaken; though it certainly owes its success less to its principal merits, than to collateral and casual considerations. The popular ideas are that by favoring the collection of duties on imports it saves the solid property from direct taxes; and that it injures G. Britain by lessening the advantage she has over other Nations, in the trade of Virginia.

We have no certain information from the three Southern States concerning the temper relative to the New Government. It is in general favorable according to the vague accounts we have. Opposition however will be made in each. Mr. Wiley Jones, and Governour Caswell have been named as opponents in N. Carolina.

So few particulars have come to hand concerning the State of things in Georgia that I have nothing to add on that subject, to the contents of my last by Commodore Jones.

We have two or three States only yet met for Congress. As many more can be called in when their attendance will make a quorum. It continues to be problematical, whether the interregnum will not be spun out through the winter.

We remain in great uncertainty here with regard to a war in Europe. Reports and suspicions are strongly on the side of one. Such an event may be considered in various relations to this Country. It is pretty certain I think that if the present lax State of our General Government should continue, we shall not only lose certain capital advantages which might be drawn from it; but be in danger of being plunged into difficulties which may have a very serious effect on our future fortunes. I remain Dear Sir with the most sincere esteem & affection, Your Obedt. Servt.

P.S. I have delivered your message to Mr. Thomson and settled the pecuniary matter with him.

The letters which you put under the same cover, with the seals of one joining the superscription of the contiguous letter, come when the weather has been warm, in such a State that it is often difficult to separate them without tearing out the superscription. A bit of paper between the adjoining letters over the seal would prevent this inconveniency.

No.	1	—6.	New Town Spitzenburg apples			
	2	—20.	New Town pippins	do.		
	3	—6.	Esopus Spitzenburg	do.	50 trees at 2/	£5. 0. 0
	4	—6.	Jersey Greening	do.		
	5	—6.	R. Island Greening	do.		
	6	—6.	Everlasting	do.		
	7	—10.	American Plumbs	1/6		15.
	8	—8.	live oaks	9d.		6.
	9	—20.	Sugar Maples	2/		2.
	10	—10.	Candle berry Myrtles	9d.		7. 6
	11	—6.	Standing American Honey-Suckles	1/6		9.
	12	—6.	Three thorned Accacia	1/6		9
	13	—6.	Rhododendrons	2/		12
	14	—6.	Dogwood Trees	1/6		9
			Box & Matts			5. 6

Dollar at 8 Shillgs. = £10.13. –

RC (DLC: Madison Papers); unsigned; endorsed. Madison omitted the copy of the catalogue of Prince's nursery which he mentioned as enclosed (see TJ to Madison, 6 Feb. 1788).

From John Adams

DEAR SIR   Grosvenor Square Decr 10. 1787

I last night received, the Ratification of my last Loan and the inclosed Resolution of Congress of 18 July last, for the Redemption of Prisoners of Algiers. It is probable You have received it before, but as it is, in your Department to execute it, and possible that you may not have received it, I thought it Safest to transmit it to you, as I have now the honour to do, here inclosed. Mr. Vanberckel, Son of the Minister, is arrived at Falmouth by the Packet, but not yet in London. By him, I expect my Dismission. The American Newspapers, already arrived both from New York and Boston, announce it to have passed in Congress, the 5. of October, and now as we say at Sea, huzza for the new world and farewell to the Old One.

All Europe resounds with Projects for reviving, States and Assemblies, I think: and France is taking the lead.—How such assemblies will mix, with Simple Monarchies, is the question. The Fermentation must terminate in Improvements of various kinds. Superstition, Bigotry, Ignorance, Imposture, Tyranny and Misery must be lessened somewhat.—But I fancy it will be found somewhat difficult, to conduct and regulate these debates. Ex quovis ligno non fit Mercurius. The world will be entertained with noble sentiments and enchanting Eloquence, but will not essential Ideas be sometimes forgotten, in the anxious study of brilliant Phrases? Will the Duke of orleans make a Sterling Patriot and a determined son of Liberty? Will he rank with Posterity among the Brutus's and Catos?—Corrections and Reformations and Improvements are much wanted in all the Institutions of Europe Ecclesiastical and civil: but how or when they will be made is not easy to guess.— It would be folly I think to do no more than try over again Experiments, that have been already a million times tryed. Attempts to reconcile Contradictions will not succeed, and to think of Reinstituting Republicks, as absurdly constituted as were the most which the world has seen, would be to revive Confusion and Carnage, which must again End in despotism.—I shall soon be out of the Noise of all these Speculations in Europe leaving behind me however the most fervent good Wishes for the Safety and Prosperity

[413]

of all who have the Cause of Humanity, Equity, Equality and Liberty at heart. With the tenderest Affection of Friendship, I am and ever shall be my dear Sir Yours, JOHN ADAMS

RC (DLC); endorsed. FC (MHi: AMT); in the hand of William Stephens Smith. Recorded in SJL as received 19 Dec. 1787. Enclosure (DLC): Tr of the resolutions of Congress of 18 July and 12 Oct. 1787, signed by Charles Thomson (see enclosure 4 in Jay to TJ, 24 July; enclosure 5 in Jay to TJ, 24 Oct. 1787).

From Peter Carr

DEAR UNCLE   Spring forest 10th. Decem. 1787

When I last had the pleasure of writeing to you, I was at Wm. & Mary attending the different masters of that university; I remained there untill the first of August; since which time I have been here, waiting for money to enable me to return; but have never yet been able to procure it. So soon as I do I shall go down. I mentioned to you in my last, that the want of a Spanish dictionary had prevented any progress in that language. That want still subsists, and will I fear, for some time; as no such book is to be had, in any of the shops here. My progress in the other branches of literature, I doubt not you have heard from Messrs. Wythe and Madison.

Mr. Elder inform'd me some time ago, that you had put a small box of books for me, under his care, when he was about to embark for Virginia which through his negligence are lost.

My mother receiv'd your letter of the 25th of July in which you enumerate the particular letters you have receiv'd from her from which enumeration I judge you must have receiv'd my letter dated some time in April in which I beged your advice on several subjects of importance in life. If you have answered it, the letter has never come to hand; and therefore must request you to solve the questions contained in *that* whenever you shall write.

My brother Sam will be here from Maryland some time this month, and will proceed hence to Wm. & Mary, according to the directions of my Uncle Carr. I fear he is much too young yet. Add to that the natural volatility of his disposition; and his being unrestrained there will give him an opportunity of indulging it. Dabney is here oweing to a long indisposition; he is however better, and will be sent to Prince Edward as soon as he is able to ride as far. With love to Patsy and Polly Believe me to be Dr. Sir, what I really am—Your dutiful & affectionate nephew,

PETER CARR

RC (ViU); endorsed.

From Maria Cosway

MY DEAR FRIEND   London 10 December [1787]

You promised to come to breakfast with Me the Morning of My departure, and to Accompany me part of the way, did you go? I left Paris with Much regret indeed, I could not bear to take leave any More. I was Confus'd and distracted, you Must have thought me so when you saw me in the Evening; why is it My fortune to find Amiable people where I go, and why am I to be obliged to part with them! T'is very Cruel: I hope our Correspondance will be More frequent and punctual then our Meetings were while I was in Paris. I suspected the reason, and would not reproach you since I know your Objection to Company. You are happy you can follow so Much your inclinations. I wish I could do the same. I do all I can, but with little success, perhaps I dont know how to go about it.

We have had a very good journey, except the two last days I was very ill. It has been a pleasure to Me to find My relations and friends, but it does not lessen the pain of finding My self so far from those of Paris. Accept this short letter this time. I Mean to send a Much longer one soon, but Mean while answer Me this by a long one. I hope your lovely daughters are well. Remember Me to Mr. Short, & believe me ever Yours Most affly.,

M. COSWAY

Mr. Cosway desires his Compliments.

RC (MHi); year supplied in date from internal evidence and an entry in SJL of the receipt of a letter of 10 Dec. on 17 Dec. 1787.

From James Jarvis

London, 10 Dec. 1787. On 10 Nov. he received from Jay, the Commissioners of the Treasury, and others, sundry dispatches and letters for TJ; sailed the following day on a vessel bound for Amsterdam; landed at Dover on 9 Dec.; his business will detain him in London for a few days and he is therefore turning the dispatches over to Trumbull; hopes TJ approves; asks him to acknowledge the receipt of the letters at once.

RC (DLC); 3 p. Recorded in SJL as received 19 Dec. 1787. The letters and dispatches recorded as received with this letter on 19 Dec. are those from Jay of 27 July (two letters), 24 Oct., and 3 Nov. 1787; from Edward Carrington of 23 Oct. and 10 Nov. 1787; from Nicholas Lewis, 20 Aug. 1787 (missing); from James Madison, 18 July and 24 Oct. 1787; from Commissioners of the Treasury, 10 Nov. 1787; and from George Washington,

[415]

18 Sep. 1787. Trumbull probably brought only a part of these letters and John Paul Jones the remainder. In his letter to TJ of 18 Dec. Adams reported that Trumbull left "last Thursday" (13 Dec.) and that Jones "went off a day or two ago" (ca. 16 or 17 Dec.). It is probable, therefore, that both Jones and Trumbull arrived about the time that TJ entered all of the letters in SJL (see Jones to TJ, under 20 Dec. 1787).

From Uriah Forrest

DEAR SIR   London 11th. Decr. 1787.

For some time passed it was my intention to pay my respects to your Excellency in Paris, that pleasure I can no longer promise myself, having fixed the 10th. of next month for my departure to America; and not having yet quite adjusted my arrangements for future business. I go direct to Patowmack and hope to be honor'd by your commands; any thing you may wish forwarded either South or North of that River shall have my attention. I do not know how you can any way make me useful either here or in America, if however an opportunity should present itself, I shall not suffer it to escape.

I am afraid the proposed constitution will serve to increase the disorders that it's framers wished to extinguish. It contains many good articles, but I am free to own there appears to me some so very bad, as to throw the weight in that scale. I cannot reconcile myself to the Idea of a Chief Magistrate being eligible a second Time, much less continuable for Life. Were not the Members too strongly impressed with the late commotion in Massachusetts? We surely have sufferd the people of this Country and those who are disaffected in Our own, to influence our opinion respecting the true state and situation of our people and Government. The most trifling events have been Magnified into Monstrious outrages. Will the next generation Credit Us that, in the first twelve Years of the Independence of thirteen free powerful and separate States, only one rebellion happend, and that that one terminated so speedily and honourably towards Government? The peoples judgments were no sooner inform'd than they return'd to allegiance, and were convinced that their grievances were immaginary, and that they were not oppressed in the manner a few desperate Characters had attempted to teach them.

I am obliged to own myself one of those who do not wish to see the people more obedient to their rulers in the next twelve, or any other twelve years, than they have been in the last. A proper spirit of resistance is the best security for their liberties, and they shou'd now and then warn their rulers of it. As I am in the legislature and shall be in the convention for the consideration of this proposed Constitution and it is surely a question of the utmost consequence, I wish to acquire every possible information. If your Excellency will indulge me with such observations on it as hath occurd to you, it will indeed oblige me. Rest assured that no other use shall be made of them, than the correcting of my judgment and opinion on the subject.

With every degree of consideration & respect I have the honor to be Sir, Your most Obedt huml Sevt,   URIAH FORREST

RC (DLC); endorsed. Recorded in SJL as received 17 Dec. 1787.

From Abigail Adams

Grosvenour Square december 12th 1787

Mrs. Adams's compliments to Mr. Jefferson and in addition to her former memorandum she requests half a dozen pr. of mens silk stockings. Mr. Trumble will deliver to Mr. Jefferson four Louis and one Guiney. Mr. parker will be so good as to take charge of them, if no opportunity offers before his return.

RC (DLC). Not recorded in SJL, but certainly received on 19 Dec. when Trumbull arrived with other letters.

To John Adams

DEAR SIR   Paris Dec. 12. 1787.

In the month of July I received from Fiseaux & co. of Amsterdam a letter notifying me that the principal of their loan to the United states would become due the first day of January. I answered them that I had neither powers nor information on the subject, but would transmit their letter to the Board of treasury. I did so by the packet which sailed from Havre Aug. 10. The earliest answer possible would have been by the packet which arrived at Havre three or four days ago. But by her I do not receive the scrip of a pen from any body. This makes me suppose that my letters are committed to Paul Jones who was to sail a week after the departure of the packet: and that possibly he may be the bearer of orders from the treasury to repay Fiseaux' loan with the money you borrowed. But it is also possible he may bring no order on the subject. The slowness with which measures are adopted on our side the water does not permit us to count on punctual answers: but on the contrary renders it necessary for us to suppose in the present case that no orders will arrive in time, and to consider whether any thing, and what should be done? As it may be found expedient to transfer all our foreign debts to Holland by borrowing there, and as it may always be prudent to preserve a good credit in that country because we may [be] forced into wars whether we will or no, I should suppose it very imprudent to suffer our credit to be annihilated by so small a sum as 51,000 guelders. The injury will be greater too in proportion to the smallness of the sum: for they will ask 'How can a people be trusted for large sums who break their faith for such small ones?' You know best what effect it will have on the minds of the money lenders of that country should we fail in this payment. You know best also whether it is practicable and prudent for us to have this debt paid without orders. I refer the matter therefore wholly to your consideration, willing to participate with you in any risk, and any responsability which may arise. I think it one of those cases where it is a duty to risk one's self. You will perceive, by the inclosed, the necessity of an immediate answer, and that if you think any thing can and should be done all the necessary authorities from you should accompany your letter. In the mean time should I receive any orders from the Treasury by P. Jones, I will pursue them, and consider whatever you shall have proposed or done, as *non avenue*. I am with much affection Dear Sir Your most obedient & most humble servt.,

TH: JEFFERSON

RC (MHi: AMT); endorsed, in part: "Decr. 12. Ansd. 18 1787." PrC (DLC). Enclosure: Tr of H. Fizeaux & Co. to TJ, 6 Dec. 1787, q.v.

From Henry Remsen, Jr.

[*12 Dec. 1787*. Recorded in SJL Index. Not found.]

To La Boullaye

SIR   Paris December 13. 1787.

I take the liberty of troubling you again on the subject of Mr. Barrett's claim of duties paid on whale oil, and which ought to be refunded according to the letter of M. de Calonne. I find that the Receveur de Romaine at Rouen has received satisfactory proof that the ship Fox, commanded by captain Hussey, and wherein these oils came, was an *American vessel*: but that he requires the certificate of the Consul of France at Boston that the oils were *de la pêche Americaine*. I have the honour to inclose you a letter from Captain Hussey declaring expressly that they were of the American fishery. If this letter shall satisfy you of the fact, I wish it could be received as evidence, in order to put an end to this matter. There exists no claim of reimbursement under M. de Calonne's letter, but Mr. Barrett's. Of course no indulgence or relaxation of the rigid rules of evidence which can be extended to him, can be drawn into example. It will be the more just too in his case, as the letter of M. de Calonne did not say that the certificate of the Consul of France would be required: consequently the shippers of oil from America did not suppose it necessary. They concluded that the declaration of the master of the vessel would suffice in this, as in other cases.

Should you consider the Captain's letter, Sir, as insufficient to establish the fact that the oils he brought were of the American fishery, I will then ask of you a delay of eight months that Mr. Barrett may send to America for the papers necessary to prove this fact regularly. This might be expressed, if necessary to be sans tirer en consequence.

When the Arret shall be published, Sir, for the general regulation of the commerce between France and the United states, it will become important that the proofs required here of American property be as *complete*, yet as *convenient*, as possible. It is as much our interest, as it is that of France, to exclude the British from a participation of the benefits of that Arrêt, and my wishes and endeavours will go pointedly in that direction. I do not know within whose office it will fall to decide on the nature of the proofs which shall be asked for. If it should be within yours, I will ask a conversation with you on the subject before you form the rules; because I think I can give information on the subject which may tend to guard the government against abuses, whilst it facilitates the proceedings of the honest trader. If these rules are to be formed by any other person, I will be obliged to you to inform me who it is, that I may address myself to him. I must beg your pardon for the trouble I give you, Sir, and assure you of the sentiments of perfect esteem and respect with which I have the honour to be your most obedt. & most humble servt.,　　　Th: Jefferson

PrC (DLC). Enclosure missing, but it was clearly a letter from Hussey written in accordance with the instructions given in Coffin to Barrett, 1 Oct. 1787 (see second enclosure to Barrett to TJ, 7 Dec. 1787).

To Carra

MONSIEUR   à Paris ce 13me. Decembre 1787.

Si le dimanche matin de 9. à 10. heures pourroit vous convenir je serois charmé de vous recevoir chez moi au sujet de la dette des etats unis à Monsieur Cazeau. Ce n'est pas que je suis aucunement autorisé de m'y meler. C'est une affaire qui appartient au departement de la tresorerie à la Nouvelle York, et qu'il faudra traiter à la Nouvelle York, à moins qu'il n'ait eté une convention particuliere de le traiter à Paris ou ailleurs. Mais peutetre que je pourrois vous donner la-dessus des renseignements, ou des conseils, ce que je ferai avec plaisir, ayant l'honneur d'etre avec bien de consideration Monsieur votre tres humble et tres obeissant serviteur,

TH: JEFFERSON

PrC (DLC).

To H. Fizeaux & Cie.

SIR   Paris December 13. 1787.

Having forwarded your letter of July 16. to the Board of Treasury of the United states, I had presumed that the arrangements for the paiment of the loan negotiated by you, were going on between them and you. Your favor of the 6th. inst. is the first information to the contrary, and allows me little time to take measures to effect this paiment in time. It was necessary for me to write to Mr. Adams in London, and obtain his concurrence for the calling for the requisite[1] sum from the produce of a loan opened by the mediation of Messieurs Willincks and Van Staphorsts. Ten days will be necessary to receive his answer, and five more to convey to you orders for the paiment. You see then the impossibility of my conveying to you those orders fifteen days before paiment as you mention to be the custom. But as the effect of the measures I am taking will depend ultimately on the state of the loan conducting by Willincks and Staphorsts I have written to know of them whether it will admit our drawing on them for the amount of your debt. I have also mentioned to them that I would take

[420]

the liberty of desiring you to confer with them on the subject. If you find on that conference that they will pay the demand on our order, you will be able to tranquilize the creditors,[2] as I presume I may count on receiving Mr. Adams's concurrence in this measure, and no moment shall be lost in forwarding to you the necessary draughts. I will only add a request that you will be so good as to accomodate the interests of the creditors[2] as much as you can to the situation of our loan and the wishes of our commissioners to arrange this matter in the best manner practicable. You may be assured of hearing from me finally the moment I receive Mr. Adams's answer.

I have the honor to be with great regard and esteem gentlemen your most obedient & most humble servt.,

Th: Jefferson

PrC (DLC).

[1] This word interlined, in substitution for "necessary," deleted.
[2] This word interlined, in substitution for "lenders," deleted.

From H. Fizeaux & Cie.

[*Amsterdam*, *13 Dec. 1787*. Recorded in SJL as received 19 Dec. 1787. Not found. Probably enclosed, with other letters from the same, in TJ to the Commissioners of the Treasury, 30 Dec. 1787, q.v.]

To Nicolas van Staphorst

Sir   Paris Decemb. 13. 1787.

In consequence of a letter from Messrs. Fizeaux & co. containing a demand of ƒ51,000 due from the United states the 1st. day of next month, I have proposed to Mr. Adams the answering that demand from the produce of the loan going on in your hands and those of Messrs. Willincks. Having had the honor of a conference with your brother on that subject, I have addressed the inclosed letter to the joint commissioners of the loan, to know whether, with the approbation of Mr. Adams, we may count on them to effect this paiment. I will take the liberty of asking your personal and particular exertions in this case, as a failure to make this paiment might not only stop the progress of the loan now open in your hands, but defeat further views of the same nature which I have submitted to Congress, and of which I hope their approbation. If you conclude that this paiment can be made, it is essential that

[421]

Messieurs Fizeaux & co. be satisfied of it as early as possible. I have therefore desired them to confer with you.

I thank you for your particular attention to the demands I had made for the current expences of the legation of the U.S. here, which your brother has done me the favor to communicate to me. I have the honor to be with great esteem Sir your most obedient and most humble servant, TH: JEFFERSON

PrC (DLC).

YOUR BROTHER: Jacob van Staphorst was in Paris at this time (see Dumas to TJ, 4 Dec. 1787). For the FURTHER VIEWS which TJ had submitted to Congress (and which, as the present letter shows, Jacob and Nicolas van Staphorst were privy to), see TJ to Jay, 26 Sep. 1786).

To Willink & Van Staphorst

GENTLEMEN   Paris Dec. 13. 1787.

I have just received from Messrs. H. Fizeaux & co. a notification that a loan of 51,000f obtained for the United states by the mediation of their house will become due the first day of the next month. I immediately communicated the same to Mr. Adams, and proposed to him the authorizing you to pay that sum out of the monies obtained by you on the loan lately opened by him in Amsterdam, if you should have as much. I expect his answer in ten days. It remains for me to ask of you whether the state of that loan will enable you to do this. I must add that I think the object very interesting to the honor and credit of the United states, and that you will render them the most acceptable and essential service in exerting yourselves to accomplish this paiment. As the term is close at hand, I have taken the liberty to desire Messieurs Fizeaux & co. to confer with you on this subject, hoping you will be able to give them such information as that they may tranquillise the lenders. Be so good as to give me immediate answer whether you will be able to satisfy this demand, because it will be on your answer, as well as Mr. Adams's, that I shall take the final measures in this business. I have the honor to be with great esteem, Gentlemen, your most obedient & most humble servant,

TH: JEFFERSON

PrC (DLC).

From Francis Hopkinson

MY DEAR SIR   Philada. Decr. 14th. 1787

I have only Time to scribble a Line or two. You have no Doubt received from some of your Friends the new System of Government for our Country. This has been the Subject of great Debate in our Convention for three weeks past and perhaps the true Principles of Government were never upon any Occasion more fully and ably develop'd. Mr. Wilson exerted himself to the astonishment of all Hearers. The Powers of Demosthenes and Cicero seem'd to be united in this able Orator. The principal Speeches have been taken in short hand and will soon be published. I shall take Care to secure you a Copy. The Result will appear by the enclosed. Delaware had before adopted the new Constitution by the unanimous vote of Representatives. It is much feared that Virginia will not come in. The Interest of the Lee's, of Mr. George Mason, and Govr. Randolph are against it. Chace is also opposing it in Maryland.

We have received a further supply of the Encyclopedia. Your last Letter to me contained your account. Mr. Rittenhouse has long since received a Letter from you mentioning some Books you have sent him address'd to the Care of Mr. Maddison, but I believe directed for me. These have not come to Hand. I can only add that I am as ever Your truly affectionate,   Fs. HOPKINSON

Capt. Robinson sailed from this Port at the Time mentioned and was never more heard of or any of his Crew. I have little Doubt but that James Lillie was lost with him. The owners recollect the name, but the muster Roll of that Crew cannot be found. I have taken a good deal of Pain to get it.

RC (DLC); endorsed. Enclosure missing; it may have been a broadside or a MS copy of the resolution adopted by the Pennsylvania ratifying convention on 12 Dec. 1787 (text in Elliot's *Debates*, I, 319-20). A statement about this action was printed in *Penna. Packet*, 13 Dec. 1787, and on the following day the same paper had an account of the procession to the court-house, "where the Ratification of the Constitution of the United States was read" on 13 Dec. Hopkinson may have sent a copy of either paper.

To William Carmichael

DEAR SIR   Paris Dec. 15. 1787.

I am later in acknoleging the receipt of your favors of Oct. 15. Nov. 5. and 15. because we have been long expecting a packet which I hoped would bring communications worth detailing to you, and she arrived only a few days ago, after a very long passage indeed. I am very sorry you have not been able to make out the cypher of my letter of Sep. 25. because it contained things which I wished you to know at that time. They have lost now a part of their merit, but still I wish you could decypher them, because there remains a part which might still be agreeable to you to understand. I have examined the cypher, from which it was written. It is precisely a copy of those given to Messieurs Barclay and Lamb. In order that you may examine whether yours corresponds I will now translate into cypher the three first lines of my letter of June 14. '1420. 1250. 1194. 1307. 1531. 458. 48. 1200. 134. 1140. 1469. 515. 563. 1129. 1057. 1201. 1199. 1531. 1571. 1040+. 870. 423. 1001. 855. 521. 1173. 917. 1559. 505. 1196. 51. 1152. 698. 141. 1569. 996. 861. 804. 1337^x. 1199.' This will serve to shew whether your cypher corresponds with mine, as well as my manner of using it. But I shall not use it in future till I know from you the result of your re-examination of it. I have the honor now to return you the letter you had been so good as to inclose to me. About the same time of Liston's conversation with you, similar ones were held with me by Mr. Eden. He particularly questioned me on the effect of our treaty with France in the case of a war, and what might be our dispositions. I told him without hesitation that our treaty obliged us to receive the armed vessels of France with their prizes into our ports, and to refuse admission to the prizes made on her by her enemies: that there was a clause by which we guarantied to France her American possessions, and which might perhaps force us into the war if these were attacked. 'And it is certain, said he, that they would have been attacked.' I added that our dispositions would have been to be neutral, and that I thought it the interest of both those powers that we should be so, because it would relieve both from all anxiety as to the feeding their West Indian islands, and England would moreover avoid a heavy land war on our continent which would cripple all her proceedings elsewhere. He expected these sentiments from me personally, and he knew them to be analogous to those of our country. We had often before had occasions of knowing each other: his peculiar bitterness towards us had sufficiently appeared, and I had never concealed from him that I considered the British as our natural enemies, and as the only nation on earth who wished us ill from the bottom of their souls. And I am satisfied that were our continent to be swallowed up by the ocean, Great Britain would be in a bonfire from one end to the other. Mr. Adams, as you know, has asked his recall. This has been granted, and Colo. Smith is to return too; Congress having determined to put an end to their commission at that court. I suspect, and I hope they will make no new appointment.

Our new constitution is powerfully attacked in the American newspapers. The objections are that it's effect would be to form the 13. states into one: that proposing to melt all down into one general government they have fenced the people by no declaration of rights, they have not renounced the power of keeping a standing army, they have not secured the liberty of the press, they have reserved a power of abolishing trials by jury in civil cases, they have proposed that the laws of the federal legislature shall be paramount the laws and constitutions of the states, they have abandoned rotation in office: and particularly their president may be re-elected from 4. years to 4. years for life, so as to render him a king for life, like a king of Poland, and have not given him either the check or aid of a council. To these they add calculations of expence &c. &c. to frighten the people. You will perceive that these objections are serious, and some of them not without foundation. The constitution however has been received with a very general enthusiasm, and as far as can be judged from external demonstrations the bulk of the people are eager to adopt it. In the Eastern states the printers will print nothing against it unless the writer subscribes his name. Massachusets and Connecticut have called conventions in January to consider of it. In New York there is a division. The Governor (Clinton) is known to be hostile to it. Jersey it is thought will certainly accept it. Pennsylvania is divided, and all the bitterness of her factions has been kindled anew on it. But the party in favor of it is strongest both in and out of the legislature. This is the party antiently of Morris, Wilson &c. Delaware will do what Pennsylvania shall do. Maryland is thought favourable to it: yet it is supposed Chase and Paca will oppose it. As to Virginia two of her delegates in the first place refused to sign it. These were Randolph the governor, and George Mason. Besides these Henry, Harrison, Nelson, and the Lees are against it. Genl. Washington will be for it, but it is not in his character to exert himself much in the case. Madison will be it's main pillar: but tho an immensely powerful one, it is questionable whether he can bear the weight of such a host. So that the presumption is that Virginia will reject it. We know nothing of the disposition of the states South of this. Should it fall thro', as is possible notwithstanding the enthusiasm with which it was received in the first moment, it is probable that Congress will propose that the objections which the people shall make to it being once known, another Convention shall be assembled to adopt the improvements generally acceptable, and omit those found disagreeable. In this way union may be produced under a happy constitution, and one which shall not be too energetic, as are the constitutions of Europe. I give you these details, because possibly you may not have received them all. The sale of our Western lands is immensely succesful. 5. millions of acres had been sold at private sale for a dollar an acre in certificates, and at the public sales some of them had sold as high as 2 4/10 dollars the acre. The sale had not been begun two months by these means, taxes &c. our domestic debt, originally 28. millions of dollars was reduced by the 1st. day of last October to 12. millions and they were then in treaty for 2. millions of acres more at a dollar private sale. Our domestic debt will thus be soon paid off, and that done, the sales will go on for money, at a cheaper rate no doubt, for the paiment of our foreign debt. The petite guerre always waged by the Indians seems not to abate the ardor of purchase or emigration. Kentucky is now counted at 60,000. Frankland is also growing fast.

I inclose you a letter from Mr. Littlepage on the subject of money he owes you. The best thing you can do, I think, will be to desire your banker at Madrid to give orders to his correspondent here to receive the money and remit it to you. I shall chearfully lend my instrumentality as far as it can be useful to you. If any sum of money is delivered me for you before you write on the subject I shall place it in Mr. Grand's hands subject to your order, and give you notice of it. No money-news yet from our board of treasury.

You ask me if there is any French translation of my Notes. There is one by the Abbé Morellet: but the whole order is changed and other differences made, which, with numerous typographical errors, render it a different book, in some respects perhaps a better one, but not mine. I am flattered by the Count de Campomanes's acceptance of the original. I wish I had thought to have sent one to Don Ulloa (for I suppose him to be living, tho' I have not heard of him lately). A person so well acquainted with the Southern part of our world, and who has given such excellent information on it, would perhaps be willing to know something of the Northern part. I have been told that the cutting thro' the isthmus of Panama, which the world has so often wished and supposed practicable, has at times been thought of by the government of Spain, and that they once proceeded so far as to have a survey and examination made of the ground; but that the result was either impracticability, or too great difficulty. Probably the Count de Campomanes or Don Ulloa can give you information on this head. I should be exceedingly pleased to get as minute details as possible on it, and even copies of the survey, report &c. if they could be obtained at a moderate expence. I take the liberty of asking your assistance in this.

I have the honor to be with very great respect and esteem, Sir, your most obedient and most humble servant,

TH: JEFFERSON

PrC (DLC). Not recorded in SJL (see note to Rutledge to TJ, 23 Sep. 1787). Enclosures: (1) Robert Liston to Carmichael, date unknown, enclosed in Carmichael to TJ, 15 Oct. 1787. (2) Lewis Littlepage to TJ, 9 Nov. 1787.

From Alexander Donald

DEAR SIR   Richmond 15th. Decemr. 1787

Since my last respects to you, I have the Honor of receiving your favour of the 17th. Septr., forwarded from New York, by our Friend Mr. Maddison. I thank you for the Political information contained in your letter. As a Citizen of the West, I deprecate all Wars, But as a Citizen of America, I can have no objection to the Powers of Europe going to Logger Heads. The advantages we will reap from it, must be great indeed; Without we can find some marcut for our Flour, we shall be obliged to give [up] our growing any for the future. I am not under any apprehensions of the English harrassing our Trade, in case a war does take place. I am more affraid of our Sister States to the Eastward going to the Old Trade of Privateering. They found the advantages of it so sensibly in the last War, That I can hardly think they will be idle in the next.

The Books and Maps are not yet come forward. Mr. Maddison has promised to send them by the first opportunity. I have seen several of the Gentlemen for whom the former are intended, and I have informed them that they will be delivered as soon as they come to hand. I happened to be writing to your old acquaintance Warner Lewis a day or two after your last letter came to hand, and I wrote him that you had sent him a Copy of the book as a token of your remembrance of him. I know this will please him, and if I know you, I am confident that I will not incur your displeasure by taking this Liberty with you. On the whole, I fear that I will not be able to acquit myself with Credit in this consignment. You may remember that your Countrymen in General are not much given to Books, (except the history of the four Kings, which they are in general very perfect in). But Besides, you will see by the inclosed advertisement, that there is an eddition of the Book Just going to be Published in Philadelphia the price of which is to be only a dollar to subscribers. One part of your Instructions I shall most religiously adhere to, not to part with a single Copy without the money is paid me for it.

The day after I received your letter, I had an opportunity to write Colo. N. Lewis. I advised him that I had a ship that would sail to France about this time, and that if he had any shrubs which he wanted to send you, I desired him to forward them to me as soon as possible; and that they would be taken care of. I have not heard from him, but as I shall have another opportunity to Havre de Grace in two or three weeks, I hope they will be here before that Time. The Hams will not be fit to ship before March or April, when they also will be sent you. I beg you will believe that I was sincere in my proffered Services, and that the frequenter you give me an opportunity of convincing you of this, the more you will oblige me. If Mr. Eppes sends any Cyder to my care, it shall be forwarded as you desired.

If you can procure for me one groce of the best Claret in France, in time to send by return of my ship Bowman, I will be very thankful to you for it. I want it of the first grade and high flavour. I don't limit you to any price. Order it to be delivered to Messrs. Callow, Carmichael & Co. of Havre, who will also pay for it. If this wine pleases me; I may become troublesome to you. I tasted some that you sent Mr. Eppes. It was good, but I have drank better.

I intend to send you by this Ship some of our later News Papers that you may see what is going on here. I am grieved to inform you that the Constitution lately proposed by the Convention at Phila. is daily loosing ground. And I am now pretty much convinced that it will not be adopted in this State.

I am with every sentiment of esteem & respect Dear Sir Your mo: obt. huml. Servt.,   ADONALD

RC (DLC); endorsed. Enclosure (DLC): Clipping from *The Virginia Independent Chronicle* (Richmond, Augustine Davis), for 12 Dec. 1787: "Now in the Press, and shortly will be published, by Prichard & Hall, Printers, Philadelphia, *Notes on the State of Virginia*; Written by his Excellency Thomas Jefferson, Minister Plenipotentiary from the United States of America to the court of France. . . . The work will be comprised in a handsome octavo volume, with an elegant type, and good paper, and delivered to the subscribers neatly bound and lettered at the moderate rate of one dollar. The price to non-subscribers will be seven shillings and six pence Virginia currency.—The encouragement the undertakers of this work have already met with in their applications to the public, induces them to believe that few copies of their edition will remain unsubscribed for; it is therefore the interest of Gentlemen to give in their names as subscribers as soon as possible to those authorised to receive them.—Subscriptions are taken in at Mr. Davis's Printing-Office in Richmond where a specimen of the work is left for inspection." The list of contents in the advertisement included Appendixes "No.1.No.2.No.3."

To John Adams

DEAR SIR   Paris Dec. 16. 1787.

I wrote you on the 12th instant, that is to say, by the last post. But as that channel of conveiance is sometimes unfaithful I now inclose you a copy of my letter of that date, and of the one of Fiseaux & co. inclosed in that. I have since received my letters by the packet, but, among them, nothing from the Board of Treasury. Still their orders may be among the dispatches with which Paul Jones is charged for me, who was to sail a week after the packet. If he brings any orders, what you shall have done as I observed in my former letter shall be considered as if not done. On further consideration and consultation the object of my letter seems to increase in importance and to render it indispensible in us to do what we can, even without orders, to save the credit of the U.S. I have conferred with Mr. Jacob Van Staphorst, who is here, on this subject. He thinks the failure would have so ill an effect that it should certainly be prevented, he supposes the progress of your late loan may by this time furnish money in the hands of Willincks and Van Staphorsts to face this demand, and at any rate that these gentlemen will exert themselves to do it. By his advice I wrote to ask of them if I might count on their doing it, provided I forwarded your orders, and I wrote to Fizeaux & Co. what steps I was taking, desired them to confer with Willincks and Van Staphorsts, and to regulate the expectations of our creditors accordingly. The answer of Willincks and Van Staphorsts which I shall receive the 22d. inst. and yours which I hope to receive about the same time will decide what is to be done. Still it will be about the 28th. before Fizeaux can receive it through me, and he sais notice should have been given by the middle of the month.

I see by the American papers that your commission to the United Netherlands continues till the spring. Will you have to go there to take leave? If you do, and will give me notice in time, I will meet you there. In so doing I shall gratify my wish to see you before you leave Europe, to confer with you on some subjects, and become acquainted with our money affairs at Amsterdam, and that ground in general on which it may be rendered necessary, by our various debts, for me sometimes to undertake to act. I am very ignorant of it at present. I am with great and sincere esteem Dr. Sir Your most obedient & mo. humble servt.,

TH: JEFFERSON

RC (MHi: AMT); endorsed, in part: "Ans. 25." PrC (DLC). Not recorded in SJL. Enclosures: Tr of TJ to Adams, 12 Dec. 1787 and its enclosure.

From Eugène MacCarthy

L'Ile d'Oléron, 16 Dec. 1787. Sends a certificate from the Commissioner at L'Orient attesting that he served during the year 1779 under John Paul Jones; family affairs forced him to be absent when the prize money for those serving on the *Bonhomme Richard* was divided; learns with regret that he was omitted in the division; asks aid in recovering the share due him; would not trouble TJ with this matter if money were the only consideration; considers the prize money as evidence that he supported the cause of liberty with zeal and devotion—a cause very dear to him.

RC (ViWC); 2 p.; in French; signed: "MacCarthy Lieutenant au regt. de Walsh"; endorsed. Recorded in SJL as received 24 Dec. 1787. Enclosure not identified.

There is a brief biography of MacCarthy in Contenson, *La Société des Cincinnati de France*, Paris, 1934, p. 217; see TJ's reply to MacCarthy, 3 Jan. 1788.

To De Corny

SIR   Paris Dec. 17. 1787.

It is time to give you an account of your copying machine, which, after repeated trial, I find very inadequate to it's offices. Instead of having two rollers only, thus placed, ⊖ where the pressure of the upper roller is resisted in the same ⊖ points by the lower one, and so forces the copy extremely, it is made with one roller above and two below, thus ◯ so that at the point where the upper roller presses, there is ∞ a void below, which permits the sliding board to bend and withdraw itself from the pressure. The lower rollers are also very small and of wood, so that they bend. The springs are of wire rolled spirally like a bell wire, and do not perform their office as well as steel springs by any means.

I have shewn it to a very excellent mechanic who has made several for persons here by my order. He agrees that the good materials of this will save half the expence of the machine, and he will ask 5. Louis for making those which must be changed. The machine would then be perfect and worth nine or ten guineas. I told him I would communicate to you the result of our consultation, and you will decide for yourself. I have the honour to be with sentiments of great esteem and respect Sir Your most obedient & most humble servt., TH: JEFFERSON

PrC (DLC).

To Parent

à Paris ce 17me Decembre 1787.

Votre lettre, Monsieur, du 20me. Juin m'apprit que M. Bachey avoit encore dans ce moment là quatre feuillettes de vin de Meursault goutte d'or, de la meme crue et qualité de celui que vous m'avez envoyé. Je l'ai trouvé si bon que j'en prendrai trois feuillettes, s'il lui en reste autant actuellement. S'il n'en a plus, faites moi la grace de me procurer une seule feuillette de la meme qualité de la goutte d'or, où vous en trouverez au mieux, et envoyez me le en bouteilles aussitot que possible. Je vous prierai aussi de m'envoyer une feuillette de vin rouge de Vollenaye en bouteilles aussi. Ayez la bonté de m'avertir au plutot par quelle porte de Paris le voiturier entrera, à quel jour, et quelle quantité de vin il aura pour ma compte, àfin que je pourrois placer d'avance les ordres necessaires à la Douane pour qu'il ne soit pas obligé de les y deposer, mais au contraire de les mener chez moi en droiture. Tirez sur moi pour le montant qui sera duement payé. Ayez la bonté de me dire s'il reste encore à M. de la Tour aucunes de ces 4. feuillettes de vin de Monrachet de 1784. que j'ai vu dans sa cave, et dont j'ai acheté une. Je suis avec beaucoup d'estime et d'amitié Monsieur votre très humble et très obeissant serviteur, TH: JEFFERSON

PrC (DLC).

From John Adams

DEAR SIR London Decr. 18 1787

Last night I received your Letter of the 12. Mr. Jarvis and

Commodore Jones are arrived here from New york both charged with large Dispatches for you. Mr. Jarvis Sent his Packet on by Col. Trumbul who departed from hence for Paris last Thursday. Comr. Jones went off a day or two ago, but both will arrive to you before this Letter. The Papers they carry, with a Renovation of your Commission at the Court of Versailles contain I presume orders and Instructions about every Thing in Holland.

As my Dismission from the Service arrived at the Same time, not a word has been said to me. Nevertheless Nil Americanum Alienum, and I have the honour to agree with you in Your opinion of the Propriety of keeping good our Credit in Holland. I should advise therefore that the Interest on Mr. Fizeaux's Loan at least should be paid, and the Creditors requested to wait for their Capitals till further orders can be obtained from Congress. If they will not consent to that, I would pay them Principal and Interest provided there is Money enough in the hands of our Bankers and neither you nor they have received contrary orders. No Authorities from me will be necessary. Your own Letter to Messrs. Willinks and Vanstapherst will be sufficient. But if they make any difficulty, which I cannot conceive for want of any orders from me, I will send them.

You have received Authority to negotiate the Redemption of our unfortunate Countrymen in Algiers. To you therefore I send a Petition which I received from them a few days ago. With the highest Regard, I am Dear Sir your most obedient and most humble Servant,   JOHN ADAMS

N.B. The Letter which Colo. Trumbull will deliver addressed to Count Sarsfield, may be sent to his hotel as the Count is on the point of departure for Paris. On referring to a resolve of Congress of the 11th. of october 1787. I find the interest of the foreign debt and that part of the principal due in 1788. has commanded their attention and I suppose put in proper train for operation. Yours,

J. ADAMS

RC (DLC); postscript in hand of William Stephens Smith; endorsed. FC (MHi: AMT); in Smith's hand. Recorded in SJL as received 24 Dec. 1787. Enclosure missing.

From François Baudin

St. Martin, Ile de Ré, 18 Dec. 1787. Thanks TJ for the information in his letter of 20 Sep., for transmitting his letter to Congress, and for

[432]

giving him reason to hope that a consul will be appointed for the island. A consul there is essential because of the number of American ships which are forced to come into port by contrary winds. Thomas Fitz-Simons of Philadelphia, to whom he wrote about being appointed consul, tells him that probably an American will be appointed; however, since it would not be worthwhile to set up an establishment for that purpose only, he has written FitzSimons and Robert Morris to support his appointment and asks TJ to support him also. If, in the meantime, he can be of service to any Americans or can supply TJ with any information about the number of American ships in that port, he will be glad to be of service.

RC (DLC); 4 p.; in French; signed: "Baudin & Cie."; endorsed by TJ: "Baudin deliver letters for him to"—and in another hand, "Paul Turot Negt. Rue Git le coeur pour M. Baudin."

To Berenger de Beaufain

MONSIEUR   à Paris ce 18me. Decembre 1787.

Je viens de recevoir l'honneur de votre lettre du 7me courant, et j'ai celui de vous informer que pour expulser la personne qui a usurpé vos possessions en Caroline ou dans la Georgie il faudra ou envoyer quelqu'un la bas, muni de pleins pouvoirs de votre part pour intenter les procès necessaires pour cet effet, ou d'en munir quelqu'un sur le lieu. Mais dans le dernier cas il faudra etre sur que la personne a laquelle vous vous adressez consentira de se charger de vos affaires. Il n'est pas probable que Monsr. Laurens ou Monsieur John Rutledge consentiront de s'en charger, parce que le premier n'a pas eté jamais de la robe et il y a longtems que le dernier a cessé de l'etre: et ce n'est pas qu'aux gens de la robe qu'appartiennent ces affaires là. Si M. Boomer Graves est le Consul de votre nation en Caroline et la Georgie, en le munissant de vos pleins pouvoirs, et en priant votre gouvernement de le charger de la poursuite de vos affaires, il pourroit bien les faire. Mais toutefois il me paroit meilleur d'y envoyer un de vos fils ou quelque autre personne fidele. Vous n'oublierez pas de le munir de vos titres. Si je pourrois vous etre utile en faisant passer vos lettres là bas je le ferai avec plaisir, ayant l'honneur d'etre avec beaucoup de consideration Monsieur votre très humble et très obeissant serviteur,

TH: JEFFERSON

PrC (DLC).

To John Bondfield

SIR Paris Dec. 18. 1787.

I have deferred acknoleging the receipt of your favor of Nov. 30. in daily hope of accompaying it with the ultimate decision on our commerce. But it seems to walk before us like our shadows, always appearing in reach, yet never overtaken. I am disappointed in the proportion of returns of country produce from your port to America. I had received a statement from l'Orient by which I found they had made two fifths of their returns in commodities. And I expected the proportion was greater from Bordeaux on account of the article of wine. I see then we must have patience till our countrymen can clear away their debts and their prejudices.

Having in the course of my journey the last spring examined into the details relative to the most celebrated wines of France, and decided within my own mind which of them I would wish to have always for my own use, I have established correspondences directly with the owners of the best vineyards. It remains for me to do this at Sauterne. I have therefore written the inclosed letter to M. Diquem who makes the best of that name, to begin a correspondence on this object, and to ask of him for the present 250. bottles of Sauterne of the vintage of 1784. I have taken the liberty to tell him you would receive the package and forward them to me by a waggon: and I have assured him that his draught on me shall be paid at sight. But he does not know either my name or character public or private, and may have doubt. Will you be so good as to remove them both for the present and future, and even for the supply now asked for to offer to pay him, assured that your draught on me for reimbursement shall be honoured at sight. I must ask you also to add on the letter the address of M. Diquem with which I am unacquainted, and to inform me of it for my future government. Perhaps I should have addressed myself to Monsr. Salus his son in law, as I am not certain whether he is not either jointly or solely interested at present in the vineyards. I am with very great esteem and respect Sir Your most obedient and most humble servant, TH: JEFFERSON

PrC (DLC). Tr (MHi). Enclosure: TJ to D'Yquem, 18 Dec. 1787. MONSR. SALUS: See Lur-Saluces to TJ, 7 Jan. 1788.

To D'Yquem

MONSIEUR   à Paris ce 18me. Decembre 1787.

N'ayant pas l'honneur de vous etre connu, c'est à votre bonté qu'il me faut avoir recours pour excuser la liberté que je prenne de m'adresser à vous directement. J'aurai besoin des petits approvisionnements de vin blanc de Sauterne pour ma consommation annuelle pendant ma residence en France, et meme après ma retour en Amerique, quand cet evenement aura lieu. Je sçai que la votre est des meilleures crues de Sauterne, et c'est de votre main que je prefererois de le recevoir directement, parce que je serai sur de le recevoir naturel, bon et sain. Permettez moi donc Monsieur de vous demander s'il vous reste encore de vos vins de Sauterne, premiere qualité, de l'année 1784. et si vous aurez la bonté de m'accomoder de deux cent cinquante bouteilles. Dans le cas que vous voulez bien me faire cette grace, j'oserois vous supplier de les faire emballer sous l'inspection de votre propre homme d'affaires. Votre traite sur moi à Paris pour le montant sera payée à vue: et Monsr. John Bondfeild, Consul de l'Amerique à Bordeaux recevra les caisses ou paniers, et me les fera passer. Accordez moi encore, s'il vous plait, la grace de votre permission de m'adresser à vous directement toutes les fois que j'aurai besoin d'un approvisionnement de vin blanc de Sauterne pour ma propre consommation, et d'agreer les assurances des sentiments de consideration avec lesquels j'ai l'honneur d'etre, Monsieur, votre très humble et tres obeissant serviteur,

TH: JEFFERSON

PrC (DLC).

From C. W. F. Dumas

The Hague, 18 Dec. 1787. Acknowledges TJ's letter of 9 Dec. and respects his reasons for taking no further steps in the matter of the proposed treaty; hopes his previous letters for America have been sent by this month's packet and that the enclosed will go by that conveyance also. Has no more belief in the continuance of peace than is generally held elsewhere; considers TJ's remarks perceptive and true. TJ's sympathy for him in his misfortunes and his hopes for their termination soften the pain occasioned by them; would be happy to endure his state for the honor of being associated with TJ if he were the only one concerned.

RC (DLC); 2 p.; in French; endorsed. FC (Dumas Papers, Rijksar- chief, The Hague; photostats in DLC); dated 16 Dec. 1787. Recorded in SJL as received 23 Dec. 1787. Enclosure: Dumas to Jay, 18 Dec. 1787 (FC, same, dated Dec. 1787; translation printed in *Dipl. Corr., 1783-89*, III, 603-4), concerning affairs in Holland and his own situation.

From Uriah Forrest

[*London, 18 Dec. 1787*. Recorded in SJL as received 24 Dec. 1787. Not found.]

From Harrison

[*18 Dec. 1787*. Recorded in SJL Index without further identification. Not found.]

From André Limozin

Le Havre, 18 Dec. 1787. Not having a reply to his letters of 18 and 19 Nov., fears that the observations in his letter of 18 Nov. were not approved; if such is the case, he wishes to be informed. Observes, nevertheless, that if the duties on yellow beeswax imported from America into France were lessened, its importation would be greatly increased; the present duty is 5.^{lt} 10s. per 100 "neat." France should encourage its importation because not enough is imported to meet the demands for bleached wax and wax candles; "Mans is the place of the greatest repute in France for bleaching the wax, and for manufacturing the best wax candles." He desires "nothing so much as the prosperity of the Commerce of the U.S." The ship *Juno*, Capt. Jenkins, will sail for New York about 3 Jan.; will accept any commissions TJ may wish to send.

RC (DLC); 4 p.; endorsed. Recorded in SJL as received 21 Dec. 1787.

From André Limozin

Le Havre, 18 Dec. 1787. Transmits "copies of vouchers belonging to Willie Thomas Master of the Scooner of Polly and Sally of Salem." Capt. Thomas has appealed for help; his ship was chartered by the agent of the company which has the exclusive privilege of the Senegal trade with France to carry a cargo from thence to Le Havre. Under these circumstances he anticipated no difficulty and "expected that he could believe himself in the greatest Security by the approbation or leave granted by the Kings Commissary to give passage to 5 Men sent by the agents of the Said Company." On his arrival at Le Havre the customs officers notified him that "if he should enter his Vessel and

[436]

Cargoes for this Place, both would be lyable to Seizure, because the Laws of this Kingdom forbid Severely to all foreigners to import in French Harbors from our Islands any of their produces whatsoever." The administrators of the Senegal Company have made only verbal promises to apply for permission to land his cargo, "will not Sign any writings on that matter and even decline to promise to indemnify the Said Master in the least manner for his lying days, or for his demeurage." Limozin asks TJ to intercede in behalf of his countryman and to apply to the proper officer promptly for the necessary permission to land his cargo "without being lyable to any duty of Tonnage which if it be required by the Custom house must be to the charge of the Said Senegal Company who by their chartering the Said American vessell must be Supposed to have granted her for this voyage the benefit and immunities of her priviledges." He has "not the least concern in that transaction"; has gone to considerable trouble to aid an unfortunate American, in accordance with his practice ever since the Revolution of doing all he can to further American trade; has received no compensation for his services and wants only gratitude.

RC (DLC); 6 p. Recorded in SJL as received 21 Dec. 1787. Enclosures not found, but see note to Limozin to TJ, 28 Dec. 1787.

From Stephen Cathalan, Sr.

Marseilles, 19 Dec. 1787. Thanks TJ for the useful information in his letter of 2 Dec.; will report what settlement he makes for the whale oil which he expects in the near future. Has received letters from Philadelphia which inform him that the price of tobacco there is high because of scarcity; that his friends were able to procure only 132 hhds. of tobacco for his ship which sailed for Philadelphia on 16 Oct. and is expected back the first of January; they are, therefore, sending rice and flour "for lading." His friends in Philadelphia had received news of "the bad Situation of Tobacco in France" and were confident that TJ "would obtain reddress." The American brig *Nancy* arrived ten days ago from Charleston with tobacco, turpentine, indigo, beeswax, and staves; she will return to Charleston in about twenty days and would be a good opportunity for sending the "other Couffe of Rice unshelled from egypt" if it is to go to Carolina and TJ will send instructions for sending it; otherwise he will send it to TJ as he did the first parcel, which went off on 7 Dec. with the other articles TJ ordered—except the oil which will be sent directly from Aix. All the fruits this year are of a "bad quality"; and are "scarce and dear"; he has not, therefore, sent the full quantity TJ ordered and did not send many raisins because the new crop has not been received. Has had a number of letters from Paris "but not one mentions a word about public affairs"; hopes matters may be settled to mutual satisfaction. His family join him in wishing TJ health and happiness. Has had no letters from Barclay, but his friends tell him that Barclay has arrived in Philadelphia and has very little to pay what he owes; when TJ has "good news" of Barclay, hopes he will forward it.

RC (DLC); 4 p.; in the hand of Stephen Cathalan, Jr., signed by Cathalan, Sr.; endorsed. Recorded in SJL as received 28 Dec. 1787.

From John Paul Jones

SIR   [ca. 19 Dec. 1787]

I am just arrived here from England. I left New York the 11th. Novr. and have brought public dispatches and a number of private Letters for you. I would have waited on you immediately instead of writing, but I have several *strong reasons* for desiring that no person should know of my being here till I have seen you and been favored with your advice on the steps I ought to pursue. I have a Letter from Congress for the King, and perhaps you will think it advisable not to present it at this moment. I shall not go out till I hear from or see you. And as the People in this Hôtel do not know my Name, you will please to ask for the Gentleman just arrived, who is lodged in No. 1.

I am with great esteem & respect Sir Your most Obedient and most humble Servant,

JPAUL JONES
Hotel de Beauvais ruë des vieux Augustines

RC (DLC: John Paul Jones Papers); at head of text: "*Private*." Undated and not recorded in SJL but probably written ca. 19 Dec. because on that day TJ recorded in SJL a number of letters brought from America by Jones and James Jarvis; the latter transmitted his letters by John Trumbull and it is impossible to tell from the record in SJL which letters were delivered by Jones and which by Trumbull (see Jarvis to TJ, 10 Dec. 1787; Adams to TJ, 18 Dec. 1787).

From Ferdinand Grand

[*Paris, 20 Dec. 1787*. Recorded in SJL as received 20 Dec. 1787. Not found.]

From John Langdon

[*20 Dec. 1787*. Recorded in SJL Index. Not found; this letter is probably an answer to TJ to Langdon, 18 Sep. 1787, q.v.]

To James Madison

DEAR SIR   Paris Dec. 20. 1787.

My last to you was of Oct. 8 by the Count de Moustier. Yours

[438]

of July 18. Sep. 6. and Oct. 24. have been successively received, yesterday, the day before and three or four days before that. I have only had time to read the letters, the printed papers communicated with them, however interesting, being obliged to lie over till I finish my dispatches for the packet, which dispatches must go from hence the day after tomorrow. I have much to thank you for. First and most for the cyphered paragraph respecting myself. These little informations are very material towards forming my own decisions. I would be glad even to know when any individual member thinks I have gone wrong in any instance. If I know myself it would not excite ill blood in me, while it would assist to guide my conduct, perhaps to justify it, and to keep me to my duty, alert. I must thank you too for the information in Thos. Burke's case, tho' you will have found by a subsequent letter that I have asked of you a further investigation of that matter. It is to gratify the lady who is at the head of the Convent wherein my daughters are, and who, by her attachment and attention to them, lays me under great obligations. I shall hope therefore still to receive from you the result of the further enquiries my second letter had asked.—The parcel of rice which you informed me had miscarried accompanied my letter to the Delegates of S. Carolina. Mr. Bourgoin was to be the bearer of both and both were delivered together into the hands of his relation here who introduced him to me, and who at a subsequent moment undertook to convey them to Mr. Bourgoin. This person was an engraver particularly recommended to Dr. Franklin and Mr. Hopkinson. Perhaps he may have mislaid the little parcel of rice among his baggage.—I am much pleased that the sale of Western lands is so successful. I hope they will absorb all the Certificates of our Domestic debt speedily in the first place, and that then offered for cash they will do the same by our foreign one.

The season admitting only of operations in the Cabinet, and these being in a great measure secret, I have little to fill a letter. I will therefore make up the deficiency by adding a few words on the Constitution proposed by our Convention. I like much the general idea of framing a government which should go on of itself peaceably, without needing continual recurrence to the state legislatures. I like the organization of the government into Legislative, Judiciary and Executive. I like the power given the Legislature to levy taxes; and for that reason solely approve of the greater house being chosen by the people directly. For tho' I think a house chosen by them will be very illy qualified to legislate for the Union, for foreign nations &c. yet this evil does not weigh against the good of preserving inviolate the fundamental principle that the people are not to be taxed but by representatives chosen immediately by themselves. I am captivated by the compromise of the opposite claims of the great and little states, of the latter to equal, and the former to proportional influence. I am much pleased too with the substitution of the method of voting by persons, instead of that of voting by states: and I like the negative given to the Executive with a third of either house, though I should have liked it better had the Judiciary been associated for that purpose, or invested with a similar and separate power. There are other good things of less moment. I will now add what I do not like. First the omission of a bill of rights providing clearly and without the aid of sophisms for freedom of religion, freedom of the press, protection against standing armies, restriction against monopolies, the eternal and unremitting force of the habeas corpus laws, and trials by jury in all matters of fact triable by the laws of the land and not by the law of Nations. To say, as Mr. Wilson does that a bill of rights was not necessary because all is reserved in the case of the general government which is not given, while in the particular ones all is given which is not reserved might do for the Audience to whom it was addressed, but is surely gratis dictum, opposed by strong inferences from the body of the instrument, as well as from the omission of the clause of our present confederation which had declared that in express terms. It was a hard conclusion to say because there has been no uniformity among the states as to the cases triable by jury, because some have been so incautious as to abandon this mode of trial, therefore the more prudent states shall be reduced to the same level of calamity. It would have been much more just and wise to have concluded the other way that as most of the states had judiciously preserved this palladium, those who had wandered should be brought back to it, and to have established general right instead of general wrong. Let me add that a bill of rights is what the people are entitled to against every government on earth, general or particular, and what no just government should refuse, or rest on inference. The second feature I dislike, and greatly dislike, is the abandonment in every instance of the necessity of rotation in office, and most particularly in the case of the President. Experience concurs with reason in concluding that the first magistrate will always be re-elected if the constitution permits it. He is then an officer for life. This once observed it becomes of so much consequence to certain nations to have a friend or a foe at the head of our affairs that they will interfere with money and with arms. A Galloman or an Angloman will be supported by the nation he befriends. If once elected, and at a second or third election outvoted by one or two votes, he will pretend false votes, foul play, hold possession of the reins of government, be supported by the states voting for him, especially if they are the central ones lying in a compact body themselves and separating their opponents: and they will be aided by one nation of Europe, while the majority are aided by another. The election of a President of America some years hence will be much more interesting to certain nations of Europe than ever the election of a king of Poland was. Reflect on all the instances in history antient and modern, of elective monarchies, and say if they do not give foundation for my fears, the Roman emperors, the popes, while they were of any importance, the German emperors till they became hereditary in practice, the kings of Poland, the Deys of the Ottoman dependancies. It may be said that if elections are to be attended with these disorders, the seldomer they are renewed the better. But experience shews that the only way to prevent disorder is to render them uninteresting by frequent changes. An incapacity to be elected a second time would have been the only effectual preventative. The power of removing him every fourth year by the vote of the people is a power which will not be exercised. The king of Poland is removeable every day by the Diet, yet he is never removed.—Smaller objections are the Appeal in fact as well as law, and the binding all persons Legislative, Executive and Judiciary by oath to maintain that constitution. I do not pretend to decide what would be the best method of procuring the establishment of the manifold good things in this constitution, and of getting rid of the bad. Whether by adopting it in hopes of future amendment, or, after it has been duly weighed and canvassed by the people, after seeing the parts they generally dislike, and those they generally approve, to say to them 'We see now what you wish. Send together your deputies again, let them frame a constitution for you omitting what you have condemned, and establishing the powers you approve. Even these will be a great addition to the energy of your government.'—At all events I hope you will not be discouraged from other trials, if the present one should fail of it's full effect.—I have thus told you freely what I like and dislike: merely as a matter of curiosity for I know your own judgment has been formed on all these points after having heard every thing which could be urged on them. I own I am not a friend to a very energetic government. It is always oppressive. The late rebellion in Massachusets has given more alarm than I think it should have done. Calculate that one rebellion in 13 states in the course of 11 years, is but one for each state in a century and a half. No country should be so long without one. Nor will any degree of power in the hands of government prevent insurrections. France with all it's despotism, and two or three hundred thousand men always in arms has had three insurrections in the three years I have been here in every one of which greater numbers were engaged than in Massachusets and a great deal more blood was spilt. In Turkey, which Montesquieu supposes more despotic, insurrections are the events of every day. In England, where the hand of power is lighter than here, but heavier than with us they happen every half dozen years. Compare again the ferocious depredations of their insurgents with the order, the moderation and the almost self extinguishment of ours.—After all, it is my principle that the will of the Majority should always prevail. If they approve the proposed Convention in all it's parts, I shall concur in it chearfully, in hopes that they will amend it whenever they shall find it work wrong. I think our governments will remain virtuous for many centuries; as long as they are chiefly agricultural; and this will be as long as there shall be vacant lands in any part of America. When they get piled upon one another in large cities, as in Europe, they will become corrupt as in Europe. Above all things I hope the education of the common people will be attended to; convinced that on their good sense we may rely with the most security for the preservation of a due degree of liberty. I have tired you by this time with my disquisitions and will therefore only add assurances of the sincerity of those sentiments of esteem and attachment with which I am Dear Sir your affectionate friend & servant, TH: JEFFERSON

P.S. The instability of our laws is really an immense evil. I think it would be well to provide in our constitutions that there shall always be a twelvemonth between the ingrossing a bill and passing it: that it should then be offered to it's passage without changing a word: and that if circumstances should be thought to require a speedier passage, it should take two thirds of both houses instead of a bare majority.

RC (DLC: Madison Papers); endorsed. PrC (DLC). PrC of an Extract (DLC) made from Tr in TJ's hand, with numerous alterations and variations in phraseology. This Extract was enclosed in TJ to Uriah Forrest, 31

Dec. 1787, where, because of the importance of the variant expressions, it is printed as an enclosure.

This famous letter has been printed many times from 1826 to the present. Its two forms have caused confusion and have led at least one scholar to assume that liberties had been taken with the text (Ford, IV, 473, citing HAW as the offender). The Forrest version, along with its covering letter, appears to have been first printed in *The Port-Folio*, XXI (July, 1826), 8-12, and was copied in the *National Intelligencer* for 23 Sep. 1826 and perhaps in other papers also. It is very likely that TJ intended or hoped that Forrest would cause the Extract to be printed in America, though he clearly did not wish to be identified as its author: "Make what use you please of the contents of the paper," he wrote to Forrest, "but without quoting its author." The Madison version of TJ's comment on the constitution seems to have been printed first in TJR, II, 272-7, and was immediately reprinted in the *Working Man's Advocate*, I, No. 16 (13 Feb. 1830); it has appeared also in all previous editions of TJ's writings and in many other places.—The LADY . . . AT THE HEAD OF THE CONVENT was Madame de Béthisy de Mézières (see Vol. 7: 411, note).

From James Madison

DEAR SIR   New York Decr. 20 1787

The packet has been detained here since the date of the letter which you will receive along with this, by some preparations suggested by an apprehension of war. The delay is very unfavorable to the trees on board for you.

Mr. *De la Forest* the *Consul here called on me a* few days ago and *told me he had information* that the *farmers general and Mr. Morris* having found their *contract mutually advantageous* are *evading* the *resolutions of the committee* by *tacit arrangements for it's continuance.* He observed that the object of the *farmers was singly profit* that of the *government twofold revenue and commerce.* It was consequently the wish of the *latter* to render the *monopoly as little hurtful* to the *trade with America as possible.* He suggested as an *expedient that farmers should be* required *to divide* the *contract among six or seven houses French and American* who should be *required to ship annually* to *America a* reasonable proportion *of goods.* This he supposed would produce some *competition* in the *purchases here* and would introduce a *competition also* with *British goods here.* The latter *condition he said* could not be well required of, or executed by a *single contractor* and the *government could not abolish the farm.* These ideas were *meant for you.*[1]

Since the date of my other letter, The Convention of Delaware have unanimously adopted the new Constitution. That of Pennsylvania has adopted it by a Majority of 46 against 23. That of New Jersey is sitting and will adopt pretty unanimously. These are all the Conventions that have met. I hear from North Carolina that

[443]

the Assembly there is well disposed. Mr. Henry, Mr. Mason, R. H. Lee, and the Governour, continue by their influence to strengthen the opposition in Virginia. The Assembly there is engaged in several mad freaks. Among others a bill has been agreed to in the House of Delegates *prohibiting* the importation of Rum, *brandy*, and all other spirits not distilled from some American production. All brewed liquors under the same description, with Beef, Tallow-Candles, cheese &c. are included in the prohibition. In order to enforce this despotic measure the most despotic means are resorted to. If any person be found after the commencement of the Act, in the use or *possession* of any of the prohibited articles, tho' acquired previous to the law, he is to lose them, and pay a heavy fine. This is the form in which the bill was agreed to by a large majority in the House of Delegates. It is a child of Mr. Henry, and said to be his favorite one. They first voted by a *majority of 30.* that all legal obstruction to the Treaty of peace, should cease in Virginia as soon as laws complying with it should have passed in all the other States. This was the result of four days debate with the most violent opposition from Mr. Henry. A few days afterwards He renewed his efforts, and got a vote, *by a majority of 50*, that Virginia would not comply until G.B. shall have complied.

The States seem to be either wholly omitting to provide for the federal Treasury, or to be withdrawing the scanty appropriations made to it. The latter course has been taken by Massachusetts, Virginia and Delaware. The Treasury Board seem to be in despair of maintaining the shadow of Government much longer. Without money, the offices must be shut up, and the handful of troops on the frontier disbanded, which will probably bring on an Indian war, and make an impression to our disadvantage on the British Garrisons within our limits.

A letter from Mr. Archd. Stuart dated Richd. Decr. 2d. has the following paragraph "Yesterday a Boat with sixteen men, was brought down the Canal from Westham to its termination which is within one mile and an half of Richmond."

I subjoin an extract from a letter from Genl. Washington dated Decr. 7th. which contains the best information I can give you as to the progress of the works on the Potowmack.

"The survey of the Country between the Eastern and Western waters is not yet reported by the Commissioners, though promised to be made very shortly, the survey being compleated. No draught that can convey an adequate idea of the work on this river has been yet taken. Much of the labour, except at the great falls, has been bestowed in the bed of the river, in a removal of rocks, and deepening the water. At the great falls the labour has indeed been great. The water there (a sufficiency I mean) is taken into a Canal about two hundred yards above the Cateract, and conveyed by a level cut (through a solid rock in some places, and much stone every where) more than a mile to the lock Seats, five in number by means of which when compleated, the craft will be let into the River below the falls (which together amounts to seventy six feet). At the Seneca falls, six miles above the great falls, a channel which has been formed by the river when inundated is under improvement for navigation. The same, *in part*, at Shannandoah. At the lower falls, where nothing has yet been done, a level cut and locks are proposed. These constitute the principal difficulties and will be the great expence of this undertaking. The parts of the river between requiring loose stones only to be removed in order to deepen the water where it is too shallow in dry seasons."

The triennial purge administered to the Council in Virga. has removed from their seats Samson Matthews and Mr. Selden. Col. Wm. Heth and Majr. Jos: Egglestone supply their places. I remain Dr. Sir Yrs. Affectly.,   Js. MADISON Jr.

RC (DLC: Madison Papers); partly in code; endorsed.

1 All words in italics *preceding* this point are written in code and were decoded interlineally by TJ, who corrected Madison's occasional use of the symbol for "a" where "&" was intended; his decoding has been verified by the Editors, employing Code No. 9. All italicized words *following* this point are underscored in the MS.

To Edward Carrington

DEAR SIR   Paris Dec. 21. 1787.

I have just received your two favors of Octob. 23. and that of Nov. 10. I am much obliged to you for your hints in the Danish business. They are the only information I have on that subject except the resolution of Congress, and warn me of a rock on which I should most certainly have split. The vote plainly points out an Agent, only leaving it to my discretion to substitute another. My judgment concurs with that of Congress as to his fitness. But I shall enquire for the surest banker at Copenhagen to receive the money, not because I should have had any doubts, but because I am informed others would have had them. Against the failure of a banker were such an accident or any similar one to happen, I cannot be held accountable in a case where I act without particular interest. My principal idea in proposing the transfer of the French debt was to obtain in the new loans a much longer day for the reimbursement of the principal, hoping that the resources of the U.S. could have been equal to the article of interest alone. But I shall endeavor to quiet, as well as I can, those interested. A part of them will probably sell at any rate: and one great claimant may be expected to make a bitter attack on our honor. I am very much pleased to hear that our Western lands sell so succesfully. I turn to this precious resource as that which will in every event liberate us from our Domestic debt, and perhaps too from our foreign one: and this much sooner than I had expected. I do not think any thing could have been done with them in Europe. Individual speculators and sharpers had duped so many with their unlocated land warrants that every offer would have been suspected.—As to the new Constitution I find myself nearly a Neutral. There is a great mass of good in it, in a very desireable form: but there is also to me a bitter pill, or two. I have written somewhat lengthily to Mr. Madison on this subject and will take the liberty to refer you to that part of my letter to him. I will add one question to what I have said there. Would it not have been better to assign to Congress exclusively the article of imposts for federal purposes, and to have left direct taxation exclusively to the states? I should suppose the former fund sufficient for all probable events, aided by the land office.

The form which the affairs of Europe may assume is not yet decypherable by those out of the Cabinet. The Emperor gives himself at present the airs of a Mediator. This is necessary to justify a breach with the Porte. He has his eye at the same time on Germany, and particularly on Bavaria, the elector of which has for a long time been hanging over the grave. Probably France would now consent to the exchange of the Austrian Netherlands to be erected into a kingdom for the Duke de Deuxponts against the electorate of Bavaria. This will require a war. The empress longs for Turkey; and viewing France as her principal obstacle would gladly negotiate her acquiescence. To spur on this she is coquetting it with England. The king of Prussia too is playing a double game between France and England. But I suppose the former incapable of forgiving him or of ever reposing confidence in him. Perhaps the spring may unfold to us the final arrangement which will take place among the powers of this continent.

I often doubt whether I should trouble Congress or my friends with these details of European politicks. I know they do not excite that interest in America of which it is impossible for one to divest himself here. I know too that it is a maxim with us, and I think it a wise one, not to entangle ourselves with the affairs of Europe. Still, I think, we should know them. The Turks have practised the same maxim of not medling in the complicated wrangles of this continent. But they have unwisely chosen to be ignorant of them also, and it is this total ignorance of Europe, it's combinations and it's movements which exposes them to that annihilation possibly about to take place. While there are powers in Europe which fear our views, or have views on us, we should keep an eye on them, their connections and oppositions, that in a moment of need we may avail ourselves of their weakness with respect to others as well as ourselves, and calculate their designs and movements on all the circumstances under which they exist. Tho' I am persuaded therefore that these details are read by many with great indifference, yet I think it my duty to enter into them, and to run the risk of giving too much, rather than too little information. I have the honour to be with perfect esteem and respect, Dear Sir, your most obedient & most humble servant, TH: JEFFERSON

P.S. The resolution of Congress relative to the prize-money received here speaks of that money as paid to me. I hope this matter is properly understood. The treasury board desired me to receive it, and apply it to such and such federal purposes, and that they would pay the dividends of the claimants in America. This would save the expence of remittance. I declined however receiving the money, and ordered it into the hands of their banker, who paid it away for the purposes to which they had destined it. I should be sorry an idea should get abroad that I should have received the money of those poor fellows and applied it to other purposes. I shall in like manner order the Danish and Barbary money into the hands of bankers, carefully avoiding ever to touch a sou of it, or having any other account to make out than what the banker will furnish.

PrC (DLC).

To John Jay

SIR   Paris Dec. 21. 1787.

The last letters I had the honour of addressing you were of the 3d. and 7th. of November. Your several favors, to wit, two of

July 27. two of Oct. 24. and one of Nov. 3. have all been delivered within the course of a week past: and I embrace the earliest occasion of returning to Congress my sincere thanks for the new proofs I receive therein of their confidence in me, and of assuring them of my best endeavors to merit it. The several matters on which I receive instruction shall all be duly attended to. The Commissioners of the treasury inform me they will settle the balance appropriated to the Barbary business, apprise me of it, and place it under my power. The moment this is done I will take the measures necessary to effect the intentions of Congress. The letter to you from the Governor of Rhode island desires my 'attention to the application of the claimants of the brig Apollonia'; which shall surely be complied with. I trust that an application will be made by the claimants. It will be the more important, as the letter in this case, as in that of the sloop Sally formerly recommended to me, is directed to an Advocate whom all my endeavours have not enabled me to find. I fear therefore that the papers in both cases must remain in my hands till called for by the person whom the parties shall employ for the ordinary sollicitation and management of their appeals. I suppose they will engage some person to answer from time to time the pecuniary demands of lawyers, clerks, and other officers of the courts, to wait upon the judges and explain their cases to them which is the usage here, to instruct their lawyers and confer with them whenever necessary, and in general to give all those attentions which the sollicitation of private causes constantly require here. Their management indeed is very much a matter of intrigue, and of money.

The public affairs of Europe are quiet at present, except as between the Turks and Russians: and even these some people suppose may be quieted. It is thought that Russia would accomodate easily. The peace between France and England is very generally considered as insecure. It is said the latter is not honestly disarming: she is certainly augmenting her land forces; and the speech of the king and debates of the court members prove their diffidence in the late accomodation. Yet it is believed their premier is a friend of peace, and there can be no doubt of the same dispositions in the chief minister here. The divisions continue between the king and his parliament. A promise has been obtained for convoking the States general, as early as 1791. at farthest. The embarrassments in the department of finance are not yet so cleared up as that the public can see their way thro' them. The arrival of the Count de la Luzerne, just now announced, will probably put their marine preparations into new activity.

I have the honor to inclose you three letters from Mr. Dumas. By one of the 23d. of October he proposed to me that Mr. Adams and myself should authorize him to go to Brussels on the subject he explains to you. I wrote him the answer of Nov. 14. by which I expected he would see that nothing could be done, and think no more of it. His subsequent letters however giving me reason to apprehend that, making too sure of the expediency of the treaty he proposed, he might excite expectations from that government, I wrote him the letter of Dec. 9. to suggest to him that his proposition might not be so certainly eligible as he seemed to expect, and to advise him to avoid doing any thing which might commit or embarrass Congress. The uneasiness of his present situation, and the desire of a refuge from it had probably suggested to him this idea, and occasioned him to view it with partiality.

This will be accompanied by the Gazettes of France and Leyden. There being no passenger to go by the packet, within my knowlege, my letter will go thro' the post office. I shall therefore only add assurances of the esteem and respect with which I have the honour to be, Sir, your most obedient and most humble servant,

Th: Jefferson

PrC (DLC). Enclosures: It is not clear which three of Dumas' letters TJ enclosed, but see Dumas to TJ, 23 Oct.; 22, 27, 30 Nov.; and 2 and 4 Dec. 1787, and their notes.

LETTER . . . FROM THE GOVERNOR OF RHODE ISLAND: See Jay to TJ, 24 Oct. 1787, enclosure No. 7.

From La Boullaye

Monsieur   Paris le 22. Xbre. 1787

J'ai reçu, avec la Lettre que vous m'aves fait l'honneur de m'écrire, copie de celle par laqu'elle le Capitaine Hussey déclare que les huiles de Baleine importées par le Vaisseau le Renard sont de produit de la pêche américaine: cette déclaration ne remplit pas entierement le voeu des réglemens en cette matière; il faudrait le temoignage du Consul de France: mais puisque vous voules bien le suppléer, il ne tiendra pas à moi que cette déclaration ne soit jugée suffisante. Je pense, comme vous, qu'il est essentiel que dans le réglement projeté la preuve et la proprieté Americaine soit aussi complette et aussi facile que faire se pourra. Je ne suis point chargé, du moins quant à présent, d'indiquer à cet egard les formalités nécessaires; cependant je recevrai avec plaisir les instructions que vous étes à même de donner à ce sujet.

Agrées, je vous prie, les assurances de l'estime et du respect avec lequel J'ai l'honneur d'être Monsieur, Votre très humble et très obeissant serviteur, DE LA BOULLAYE

RC (DLC); in a clerk's hand, dated and signed by La Boullaye. Recorded in SJL as received 23 Dec. 1787.

From La Platière

MONSIEUR Paris rue Meslé no. 58. Le 22 Xbre 1787.

Une Des plus Nobles fonctions d'un historien est de pouvoir transmettre a La posterité Les noms des Grands hommes qui ont Bien merité De Leur patrie. J'aurai souvent occasion De parler Dans Mon ouvrage Des heros qui ont Coôperés a La révolution Des etats de L'amerique septentrionale, c'est a ce titre que j'ai l'honneur de Demander a votre Excellence, La permission De lui dédier un procès historique De ce quil y a de plus interessant dans cette Grande révolution. Si les manes des Guerriers qui ont sacrifiés Leur vie pour L'amour De La liberté sont sensibles aux hommages qu'on Leur Rend, elles ne pourront qu'applaudir au Choix que j'ai fait. Le roi mon maitre, a bien voulu m'accorder cette Grace pour Le *Cardinal D'amboise*, Le roi de prusse pour *frederic Deux*, votre Excellence aura sans doute La meme Bonté.

Je suis avec un sincere Respect De votre Excellence Le Tres humble et tres obeissant serviteur,

LE COMTE DE LA PLATIERE
Colonel de Troupes Legeres.

RC (DLC); endorsed. Recorded in SJL as received 24 Dec. 1787.
MON OUVRAGE: *Galerie universelle des hommes qui se sont illustres dans l'empire des lettres depuis le siècle de Léon X. jusqu'à nos jours*, Paris, 1787-88 (Sowerby, No. 149; see also TJ's reply of 27 Dec. 1787).

To André Limozin

SIR Paris Dec. 22. 1787

I have the honor now to acknolege the receipt of your favors of the 18th. and 19th. of November and two of the 18th. of the present month. I did not write to you immediately on receipt of the two first, because the observations they contained were to be acted on here. I was much obliged to you for them, as I have been frequently before for others, and you will find that I have profited by them in the arret which is to come out for the regulation of our commerce, wherein most of the things are provided for which you have from time to time recommended. With respect to the article of yellow wax, I think there is a general clause in the arret which will take it in; but I am not sure of it. If there be not it is now too late to get any alteration made. You shall receive the Arret the moment it is communicated to me.

I have examined the case of Captn. Thomas, with all the dispositions possible to interpose for him. But on mature reflection, I find it is one of those cases wherein my sollicitation would be ill received. The government of France, to secure to it's own subjects the carrying trade between her colonies and the mother country, have made a law, forbidding any foreign vessels to undertake to carry between them. Notwithstanding this, an American vessel has undertaken, and has brought a cargo. For me to ask that this vessel shall be received, would be to ask a repeal of the law, because there is no more reason for recieving her, than there will be for recieving the 2d. 3d. &c. which shall act against the same law, nor for receiving an American vessel more than the vessels of other nations. Capt. Thomas has probably engaged in this business, not knowing the law: but ignorance of the law is no excuse in any country. If it were, the laws would lose their effect, because it can be always pretended. Were I to make this application to the Comptroller general, he might possibly ask me whether in a like case of a French vessel in America acting through ignorance against law, we would suspend the law as to her. I should be obliged honestly to answer that with us there is no power which can suspend the law for a moment; and Capt. Thomas knows that this answer would be the truth. The Senegal company seems to be as much engaged in it as he is. I should suppose his most probable means of extrication would be with their assistance, and availing himself of their privileges and the apparent authority he has received from the officers of government there. I am sorry his case is such a one as I cannot present to the Minister. A jealousy of our taking away their carrying trade is the principal reason which obstructs our admission into their West Indian islands. It would not be right for me to strengthen that jealousy. I have the honour to be with much esteem Sir your most obedient humble servt.,

TH: JEFFERSON

PrC (DLC).

[451]

To Quesnay de Beaurepaire

SIR   Paris Dec. 22. 1787.

The hour of the departure of the post permitting me to continue to write to America till one oclock, and your departure for Versailles rendering it necessary you should receive by three oclock the Plan for an Academy, which you had been pleased to send me, it has been impracticable for me to give it but a cursory and partial reading, and now leaves me but a moment to return you my thanks for th[at] communication, and my sense of the disinterestedness and zeal you shew in it. A friend to science and the arts, I cannot but be pleased with every rational proposal for extending them. I am fearful however from the accounts which we receive thence of poverty, debts, distress and the want of money, that my countrymen may not be in a situation to support effectually so extensive an institution, and to reward it's professors and promoters as they may merit: in fine that neither the population nor wealth of Richmond and it's vicinities may fulfill their expectations. Permit me at the same time to assure you that no one would rejoice more than myself to see those fears dissipated, and your undertaking prove successful. I have the honor to be with much esteem Sir your most obed. humble servt.,   TH: JEFFERSON

PrC (DLC). Enclosure (missing): Doubtless a manuscript version of Quesnay's plan for an academy at Richmond which was later printed as *Mémoire Statuts et Prospectus, concernant l'Académie des Sciences et Beaux Arts des Etats-Unis de l'Amérique, établie à Richemond*, Paris, 1788 (see Sowerby, No. 1119).

On Quesnay's academy at Richmond, see Quesnay to TJ, 6 Jan. 1788, 2 and 8 Mch. 1789; TJ to Quesnay, 6 Jan. 1788; TJ to Limozin, 22 Jan. 1788; also R. H. Gaines, "Richmond's First Academy, Projected by M. Quesnay de Beaurepaire in 1786," *Virginia Historical Collections*, XI (1891), 167-75; "Laying the Corner Stone of Quesnay's Academy," VMHB, XI (1904), 253-5; Mrs. Suzanne K. Sherman, "Post-Revolutionary Theatre in Virginia, 1784-1810," Ch. ii, unpublished thesis, Library of the College of William and Mary; John G. Roberts, "An Exchange of Letters between Jefferson and Quesnay de Beaurepaire," VMHB (1942), 134-42, and "Francois Quesnay's Heir," same, 143-50. Part of Quesnay's *Mémoire* has been translated in Samuel Mordecai's *Richmond in By-Gone Days*, Richmond, 1946, p. 200-10. For a discussion of the various states of the text of the *Mémoire*, see John C. Wylie, *Papers of the Bibliographical Society of America*, XXXV (1941), 73-4.

From George Gilmer

DEAR SIR   23 Decr 1787 Pen Park

It hurts me to intrude on you, with nothing new or interesting, but what you must receive from those who shed ink more im-

[452]

portantly than I possibly can, but your earnest friendship must be my apology.

Your kind opinion which coincided with several here I flattered myself would settle the point clearly as to Marrow-bone but behold these adepts in the law have abandoned their former opinion, and consider the whole as a life estate the being introduced in lieu of my Estate in the last will, and advise me to treat with those that are to inherit when capable from the trust will which has not been recorded. Mr. John Harmer has relinquished all his claim this side the water to his nephew John Lambert, who says it would be absurd and a nullity for him to relinquish a claim when by the laws of this country he can not inherit being an alien. He wishes to perpetuate his claim to the Confiscated property and the lands not devised by the last will. The Gentlemen here are in doubt if the term property does not comprehend lands. If so all property is directed to be sold, or does it escheat to the commonwealth? Others think the Antinati [ante nati] to this revolution are capable of inheriting, however Dear Sir I will not tresspass too much on your goodness, and conclude this business with beging you to inform me If I should venture the matter with our Assembly. Its a dangerous ground, and Mr. Henry advised against it some time past when the Farfaxes confiscation was recent. As it is now situated this estate is unproductive and keeps me in an anxious situation. Your opinion shall be my guide. Only the last will recorded.

The Politics vibrating at present you'l hear from such able hands that I may as well be silent. Though never an enthusiast in religion, Politics some times animate me. The new constitution is maltreated by its adversaries, and though perhaps as perfect as to be expected, when erected by thirteen people, and condenced into one aggregate form. It is shaken to the foundation by Henry, who appears to wish more federal plans than one, my political optics discover by such a plan there will be formed a pabulum for eternal contention.

It afforded me pleasure to hear from Mr. Wythe while in Richmond that he supposed you had got over the inconvenience of your luxation. If not let me advise you to abandon cataplasms poultices and Goulards extract, and rely on a flesh brush, Electricy, and friction with powdered bark, what presumption you'l say, when you have had the skill of the ablest Parisians. I sincerely hope the complaint is removed.

Your reappointment affords me pleasure knowing the essential services you will effect, pain that we are to be deprived the pleasure of seeing you here, for you'l be reappointed still, may you be happy.

Is your edition out with map? I only had a Glymps of the first, write on Dear Sir that we may improve, and be induced to read.

Your Sister Nancy was lately married to Mr. Hastings Marks of Charlottesville where they at present reside.

Some time past sent you some Ginzeng and Georgia Bryar seed. You'd afford me real pleasure by giving me liberty to collect for you any thing you wish. My son Walker is intended for Scotland in the spring and Mr. C. Meriwether. Mr. Epps paid a visit to the hills for a night or two, with his usual impatience, with more propriety at present, as he was anxious to return to nurse his twins, two little Girls. He out does us at Pen Park. Mrs. Gilmer presented me two months past with her eleventh child a fine boy named Harmer in hopes of sequestering from the Church which the old Gentleman talked of building.

Mrs. Gilmer unites in most affectionate compliments to you and the sweet Girls with Dear Sir Your Obt. humble Servant,

GEORGE GILMER

RC (MHi); without name of addressee; endorsed.

From John Paul Jones

[*Paris, 24 Dec. 1787*. Recorded in SJL as received 24 Dec. 1787. Not found.]

From André Limozin

MOST HONORABLE SIR   Havre de Grace Decembr 24th 1787.

I am very glad to Learn by the Letters your Excellency hath favord me with the 22nd. Instant that an arrest in the behalf of the Commerce of the US is soon to take place; and that you have not slept away the informations I have taken the freedom to send to your Excellency.

Give me leave to say that we are not of the Same opinion about Capt. Thomas's Circumstance.

Your Excellency is beseech'd to take in Consideration, that the liberty of the whole Trade in Senegal is in the possession of a Company. Nobody else whatsoever can without the consent and approbation of that Company neither import in that port nor export from thence any good. It is for the Service of that Company, it is for the proprietors of that great priviledge that Thomas charterd his vessel, and even he did it by the authorisation and consent of the Kings Commissary at Senegal, for when one acts against the laws of a Kingdom, it is either with force or in a Clandestine manner that frauds are performed. But Thomas is not in that Case. The Company, the proprietors of the trade of Senegal find Thomas's Vessell suitable for their Service. They are in want to send dispatches to france, on account of the Politick affairs being afraid of a war, they are very glad to find under their hand an American Vessell. The Kings Commissary gives his Sanction to the agreement, because he is him self wishing to forward dispatches to France, and he thinks that Conveyance much Safer than to send them by a french ship, because there was a very great apprehension of War. The obligation deliverd by Mr. Chevremous one of the Directors of the Senegal's Company in this Place to Captn. Thomas must be considered as an approbation of the behavior of the agents of the Said Company at Senegal. Thus one Cant Say that Thomas hath committed any fraud, and that his Ship ought to be lyable to Seizure.

The Senegal Company injoys for the Senegal's trade the Same priviledges as the East Indias Company which surely would have the liberty to charter a Foreign Ship for their Service.

I beg of your Excellency to take the troubles to cast your Eyes upon the vouchers I have sent, and I hope that your Excellency will not refuse his assistance to an unfortunate Countryman in distress, and who Knows no other Protector but your excellency. I have the honor to be with the highest regard Your Excellency's Most obedient & very Humble Servant,

ANDRE LIMOZIN

RC (MHi); endorsed. Recorded in SJL as received 27 Dec. 1787.

From Parent

MONSIEUR   a Beaune ce 24 Decembre 1787

En Reponse a l'honneur de la votre du 17 du Courant par laquelle vous me marque de vous achetté troit feuillette de vin blan de la goute d'or, je suis eté chez Mr. Bachey qui en a Encorre trois feuillette, mais il ne veut vendre que deux dans ce moment icy et il veut en avoir Cent livres de la feuillette et pas a moins; et je suis esté Chez Mr. Latour, il n'a plus de Montrachet de 84 mais il en a de 85, et il veut en avoir 300^{tt} de la feuillette pas a moins. Il y a le fermier Dents de Clermont de Chagny qui en a Six feuillette de 84, mais il veut en avoir 300^{tt} de la feuillette, mais je le crois meilleur que celuy de Mr. Latour. Je n'ait point voulü vous en achetté sans vous en donné avis, ainsy Monsieur vous voudré bien me faire sçavoir si vous le voulez Prendre a ce prix-la ou non par le premier Courie, parce que il m'a dit hier qu'il en avoit vendue une feuillette il y a quinze [jours] 120^{tt}, et que l'on attendoit les Reponce pour les trois autre; ainsy je luy ait fait vendre vingt deux pieces de vollenay à trois cent quarante livres il y [a] huit jours et il m'a promis qu'il laissera ses deux feuillette-la a 100^{tt} la feuïllette jusqua votre Reponse; ou si vous voulé, je vous enverre une feuillette de vin blanc de Meursault qui vous Couterai toujours 84 ou 86 la feuillette en premiere qualité, et qui ne seroit pas si bon parceque depuis deux mois les vins vieux ont beaucoup augmenté Dans Nos Cantons. Et a l'egard des Seps de vignes de Clos de vougeot et Romané et Chambertin et montrachet je vous en Enverré si vous en Soüété. Si je n'estoit pas este malade depuis le mois D'octobre jusqua la fin de Novembre je vous en auroit fait passé Comme je Vous l'avois promis. Je Suis tres Sïncerement Monsieur Votre tres humble et tres obeissant Serviteur, PARENT

RC (MHi); endorsed. Recorded in SJL as received 28 Dec. 1787.

From Nicolas & Jacob van Staphorst

Amsterdam 24 December 1787

We are honored with Your Excellency's most esteemed favor of 13 Inst. to our N.V.S. who is highly flattered to have served you by his particular Exertions in securing the regular payment of your current demands for the Legation of the U.S. Exclusive of our personal Respect for Your Excellency, which will always urge us to do all in our power to oblige you, We are so firmly persuaded of our Duty, and have so strong an inclination to guard the Interests and Credit of the United States from any disgrace or Reflexions we can avert, that we experienced great pleasure at our Success in this matter; Which would be considerably augmented were we able to announce at present, a similar Fate to your Application to the Commissioners of the Loans here, to pay the ƒ51,000. that the United-States are engaged to reimburse the 1r. proximo. To their Answer We refer you; Notwithstanding which, We trust Your Excellency may be quiet on the Subject, as we will strain every Nerve to have your Wishes gratified, having, to further them, already offered to bear our Half of the Advance that may be incurred by so doing. Thus we can flatter ourselves, Your Excellency will shortly be relieved from your Apprehensions of the Shock the Credit of the United-States would sustain, from a Want of punctuality in this Instance.

Your Excellency may depend upon the proper Steps being taken towards Messrs. Fizeaux, With whom We have already conversed on the Business. We are very respectfully Your Excellency's Most obedient and very humble Servants,

NIC. & JACOB VAN STAPHORST

RC (DLC); in a clerk's hand, signed; endorsed. Recorded in SJL as received 31 Dec. 1787.

From Willink & Van Staphorst

Amsterdam 24 Decbr. 1787

We are honored with Your Excellency's very esteemed favor of 13 Inst. informing us Messrs. H. Fizeaux & Co. of this City had notified to you that a Loan of ƒ51,000. cr., negotiated by them for the United States, becomes reimbursable the First Proximo, And that as you judged the punctual discharge of it, to be highly interesting to the Honor and essential to the Credit of the United States, You had wrote his Excelly. John Adams Esq. to join you, in pressing us to provide Messrs. Fizeaux & Co. with the necessary Funds.

We have not yet heard from Mr. Adams on the Subject, and sincerely regret the Application should have been so late, that We are called to conclude upon the matter without the necessary time to weigh its consequences with the requisite attention. Besides we are deprived of any communication respecting it from the Board of Treasury, the official Persons to give direction for Payments of such a Nature, and who ought to have apprized us of same. This Oversight on the part of the Commissioners, even had we plenty of Money belonging to the United States, places us in the ever disagreeable Predicament of assuming unnecessary Responsibility; Wherefore we request Your Excellency to second the strong Repre-

[457]

sentation we shall now reiterate to the Treasury-Board, to have greater punctuality shewn us in future on similar occasions.

The Funds we have in hands of the U.S. will suffice to face the Interest that will be payable by them the 1 February next, And leave a Surplus Provision for your and Mr. Adams' Drafts during a short time. Thus the Payment of the ƒ51,000. would be an actual Advance from us, there being little or no probability the Bonds of the last Loan will sell, while there are so many Calls for Money by different Countries, whose Governments are firmly established and Punctuality has been long experienced. You may depend our Zeal and Wish to serve the United-States will prompt us to do all that can be expected on the occasion, and we shall not fail giving you the earliest Intelligence of our determination. However as you mention that you wait Mr. Adams and our Answer, to take the final Measures in the Business, We presume you have other means to raise Monies for discharge of the Loan obtained by Messrs. Fizeaux & Co. If so, We earnestly entreat you to avail yourselves of them; Which will much oblige us and promote the Interests of the United-States. We are very respectfully Your Excellency's Most obedient and very humble Servants,

WILLEM & JAN WILLINK
NIC. & JACOB VAN STAPHORST

RC (DLC); in the same clerk's hand as the preceding letter from N. & J. van Staphorst, signed by a member of each firm; endorsed. Recorded in SJL as received 30 Dec. 1787, a day before the preceding letter.

From John Adams

DEAR SIR   London Decr. 25. 1787

By the last Post I answered your Letter of the 12, and Yesterday received yours of the 16. Com. Jones has before now delivered you dispatches that will serve no doubt for your direction. Mr. Van staphorst, will have no Objection to an handsome Commission, for paying off, the Debt Mr. Fizeaux mentions: and Mr. Fizeau, will be glad to have it paid off, that the Money Lenders not knowing what to do with their Money may be tempted to put it into his French loan. But I am persuaded the Money Lenders on receiving their Interest would very willingly let the Principal remain, till the arrangements of Congress can discharge it. It will cost the United States Eight Per Cent, to transfer this debt, and four or five thousand Guilders are worth saving.

It would rejoice me in my soul to meet you, before I embark for America. But I am so ill, of an uncommon Cold, the present weather is so formidable and a Journey to Holland in the winter is so cruel, that I am obliged to excuse myself from taking leave in Person of the States general, and shall send a Memorial. The Time for me is short and there are many Things to do, so that I must confine myself to London, but if you could venture over here and see the August Spectacle of Mr. Hastings's Impeachment, you would make us all very happy.

I should advise you, by all means to make a Journey to Holland; but not before the Month of May. A Letter to some of the Corps Diplomatique, will introduce You to them and to Court, and Messrs. Willinks and Vanstaphorsts will shew you Amsterdam, and explain to you Money matters.

With Sincere Esteem and affection, I am Dear Sir your most obedient and most humble Servant,   JOHN ADAMS

RC (DLC); endorsed. FC (MHi: AMT); in the hand of William Stephens Smith. Recorded in SJL as received 30 Dec. 1787.

From Maria Cosway

London decembr Christmas day [1787]

How do you do My dear friend? You came to the invitation of my breakfast the Morning of my departure! and what did you think of Me? I did it to avoid the last taking leave, I went too early for any body to see Me. I cannot express how Miserable I was in leaving Paris. How I regreted not having seen More of you, and I cannot have even the Satisfaction to unburden My displeasure of [it] by loading you with reproches. Your reasons Must be Sufficient, and My forcing you would have [been] unkind and unfriendly as it woud be cruel to pretend on what is totaly disagreable to you. Another reason keeps ever since I am perfectly sure t'was[1] My fault but my Misfortune, and then we can bear to be Contradicted in our wishes with More resignation.

Have you seen yet the lovely Mrs. Church? You Must have seen her by this time: what do you think of her? She Colls' me her Sister. I coll' her My dearest Sister. If I did not love her so Much I should fear her rivalship, but no I give you free permission to love her with all your heart, and I shall feel happy if I think you keep me in a little corner of it, when you admit her even to reing Queen.—I have not receivd any letter from you. I feel the loss of

[459]

it. Make it up by sending Me very long ones and tell Me all you do how you pass your time. When you are at your Hermitage, all that regards you will be interesting to me. Have you seen Any of the Gentlemen who I had the honor to introduce to you and who received so politly. The Abbè Piatolli is a wor[thy Man?][2] Mr. Niemicewiz a very Amiable gen[tleman . . .] the Prince Charteressi worthy of [. . .] Manners Custums and principles you [. . .] improve him in all he has so far [. . .] Natural disposition and talent!

Again I request write to Me [. . .] My best Compliments to Mr. Short and believe dear sir Yours Most Affly,

MARIA COSWAY

RC (MHi); about one-third of last leaf torn away; addressed; the year in date has been supplied from internal evidence (see Maria Cosway to TJ, 7 and 10 Dec. 1787).

[1] Thus in MS; Mrs. Cosway may have intended to say: "t'was not My fault but My Misfortune."

[2] Several words missing here and at the places indicated by other brackets.

From Lafayette

Nemours tuesday [25? Dec. 1787]

Inclosed, My dear friend, I send You the Proposed Constitution which I Have Received on My Way. What do You think of the powers of the president? I am affraid that our friends are gone a little too far on the other side. But suppose it is the Case, and General Washington is the president, I know him too well not to think He will find the danger, and lessen the authority Before He Goes over. Adieu, my dear sir.—Pray write me Your opinion on this Constitution; I Confess those presidential powers seem to me too Great. Let me Have a printed Copy of the tobacco letter and the arrêt du Conseil as soon as You Can. What is your opinion about a form of election divided in two electionnering Houses, the Upper one Making a list of ten Clergyman or Nobles, the lower one Making a list of ten Commoners. Then Both House to Unite and one of the Number to choose One clergy man, one Noble, and two Commoners to Represent the district.—Adieu, My dear sir.

RC (DLC); without name of addressee, signature, or date, except the day of the week; in Lafayette's hand and endorsed by TJ: "Fayette. M. de"; date assigned from internal evidence and the following facts. Washington sent TJ a copy of the proposed Constitution of the United States in his letter of 18 Sep. 1787, q.v., which arrived, with the other letters sent from

America by John Paul Jones and James Jarvis, on 19 Dec. 1787. Washington probably used the same conveyance to send a copy to Lafayette; the first Tuesday after 19 Dec. was 25 Dec. in 1787. The two items which Lafayette requested in this letter—the arrêt of 29 Dec. 1787 (printed as an enclosure to Lambert to TJ, 29 Dec.), for which Lafayette had helped prepare the way and which he knew was in the process of being drawn up, and the printed copy of Calonne's letter to TJ of 22 Oct. 1786 (Vol. 10: 474-8)—were enclosed in Lafayette's letter to George Washington on 1 Jan. 1788, the following Tuesday (*The Letters of Lafayette to Washington*, ed. Gottschalk, N.Y., 1944, p. 334-6; Gottschalk, *Lafayette, 1783-89*, p. 334-5).

From John Rutledge

DR. SIR   Charleston Decr. 25. 1787

I have had the pleasure of receiving your Letter, of the 6th. of August, and should have acknowledged the receipt of it, long ago, but, have been very much in the Country, and engaged, since my Return from Philadelphia. You will have the Goodness to excuse the delay.

I am extremely obliged to you, for the great Politeness and Attention with which my son informs me you have honoured him, and thank you, for your friendly Hints, respecting his European Tour about which I will write to you.

If he has gone to England, be pleased to forward the inclosed to him, as soon as it gets to Hand. I presume you have his Address. If not, pray commit the dispatches to the Care of, and send 'em under Cover to Mr. Adams.

My Brother Edward, I, and some of our friends, propose making a Trial of the French Market, for Rice; and will ship about 1000 Barrels, in a Vessell for L'orient, in about 12 days: I hope she will arrive before Lent, and give Us a Chance for a good Price.

By the declarations received Yesterday from London, of oct. 27, from the Duke of Dorset and Mr. Eden, on the part of G. Britain and the Count de Montmorin, on that of France, it seems as if the late Appearance of war has vanished.

I have before me your Letter to the Agricultural Society. We are greatly obliged to you, for your Attention to the Objects mentioned in it. The Governor proposes to cultivate the olive, immediately, on an extensive plan, and, it is probable that other Gentlemen will follow his Example: I proposed writing to you on the subject of Rice, but the short Notice of the present opportunity obliges me to postpone the doing so till another.

I am with sincere Esteem & Regard Dr. Sir Yr. obliged & very hble Servt.,   J: RUTLEDGE

[461]

RC (DLC); addressed and endorsed. The enclosed dispatches have not been identified.

To John Paul Jones

Wednesday Dec. 26. 1787.

Mr. Jefferson's compliments to Commodore Jones and returns him the book he was so good as to give him the perusal of. He incloses him a letter he has just received, and asks his information as to the justice of the claim. He will be obliged now to occupy himself some two or three days about commercial arrangements just now made at Versailles and which he must translate, have printed, and accompany with observations letters &c. to America by a ship to sail tomorrow sennight for New York. He will endeavor not withstanding to get on in the Danish business as soon as possible.

RC (The Rosenbach Co., New York, 1946). Not recorded in SJL. Enclosure: Eugène MacCarthy to TJ, 16 Dec. 1787.

From Giuseppe Chiappe

Mogador, 27 Dec. 1787. Has received through his brother in Morocco TJ's letter of 15 Sept. 1787, informing him that the appointments made by Barclay of himself and his brothers as consuls have been confirmed by Congress; assumes that official papers will be received from Congress in due time; promises to correspond with TJ and the minister at London concerning all matters of interest to the United States and promises at all times to uphold the dignity of his office. "Le Capn. Wm: Cowell de Son Asconner Machias, venu de Boston avec un Chargement de Planches et autres moindres Denrées, est parti dernierement pour Surinam avec 61. Mules; Je l'ay assisté au possible; et actuellement J'en use de même envers le Capn: Joseph West de l'Asconner l'Adventure, qui pour le même objet se trouve encore dans son Emplette; les Deux m'ont étes adressés par Mr: Codman Junior de Boston. L'arrivée de ces deux Batiments qui ont parus pour la premiere fois dans nos Contrées pour en essayer le Comerce, fait esperer une lucrative continuation de part et d'autre." Encloses a list of presents recently presented at that court by the Turkish minister which were well received; also encloses a translation of the "Diplome par le quel il a plû a Sa Majesté Impériale de me honorer a l'occasion que Je l'ay notitiée de l'arrivée des deux Susdits Batiments Americains." Has noted TJ's directions for sending mail through Cathalan and gives directions for forwarding mail which TJ will send him; the present letter goes by the French consul general at Salé.

[462]

RC (MoSHi); 4 p.; in French; endorsed. Enclosures: (1) The list of presents made by the Turkish minister has not been found. (2) The translation into Italian of "las Patente que S.M.I. diò al Senor Josephi Chiappe," dated 9 Nov. 1787, is in MoSHi.

To H. Fizeaux & Cie.

GENTLEMEN   Paris Dec. 27th. 1787.

I have duly received your favor of the 20th. instant, and have learnt thro' another channel that my letter to Messrs. Willincks and Van Staphorsts, of the same date with that I wrote to you, did not get to their hands by the same post: so that I shall receive their answer one post late, that is to say, on Saturday next. Of course I shall not be able to answer you definitively till Monday the 31st., the earliest post day after Saturday. I am possessed of Mr. Adams' approbation of the resource for paiment which I had proposed: so that it rests now solely with Messieurs Willincks and Van Staphorsts. And as you will have known their decision, I hope the delay will have been less inconvenient. It should not have taken place at all, had I known a little sooner that it would be necessary for me to interfere in this business. The sole object of the present letter is to inform you of the circumstances beforementioned which disable me from answering you finally by the present post. I have the honour to be with much esteem Gentlemen Your most obedient & most humble servant,   TH: JEFFERSON

PrC (DLC).
YOUR FAVOR OF THE 20TH INSTANT: Not found, but recorded in SJL as received 26 Dec. 1787.

To La Platière

MONSIEUR LE COMTE   à Paris ce. 27me Decembre 1787

Je vous suis infiniment obligé de m'avoir procuré l'occasion de connoitre la merite de votre excellente galerie des hommes illustres, et je demande votre permission de m'abonner pour un exemplaire, et de garder [. . .] ce livre celui que vous avez eu la bonté de m'envoyer. C'est à vous Monsieur, à considerer combien l'honneur que vous [me] proposez fera de tort à votre ouvrage. Son merite ne pourra pas manquer de lui assurer l'accueil le plus flatteur chez les caracteres les plus illustres, et d'aller de pair avec l'eclat de leurs noms. A moi inconnu du monde, et ne meritant pas d'en etre

[463]

connu, l'honneur sera plus convenable de vous lire et de vous louer, de feliciter mes compatriotes de la bonheur de trouver leurs efforts pour la liberté consacrés à la renommée par votre plume, et de vous rendre l'[homm]age des sentiments respectueux avec lesquels j'ai l'honneur d'etre Monsieur le Comte Votre tres humble et tres obeissant serviteur, TH: JEFFERSON

PrC (DLC).
On the same date as the above letter TJ made the following entry in his Account Book: "pd 17 livraisons of Galeries des hommes &c. 68f" (see also La Platière to TJ, 22 Dec. 1787).

To Stephen Cathalan, Jr.

SIR   Paris Dec. 28. 1787.

I have this day received your favor of the 19th instant and avail myself of the first post to pray you to send the second Couffe of rice of Egypt by the American brig Nancy, Capt. Shewell, consigned to Mr. William Drayton chairman of the society for agriculture at Charlestown in South Carolina, writing a line to him at the same time to inform him of it, and that it comes from me. I will write by a vessel about to sail from Havre for New York.

I thank you for your attention to the little articles I had troubled you to get for me, and which, I doubt not will arrive in good time. —I think I shall with certainty be able in three or four days to forward you our new commercial regulations. As to tobacco, the farmers will be ordered to buy 14,000 hhds. a year, in France, brought in French or American vessels, and to make returns every 4. months to prove they have purchased within that time 4666 hhds. The price is left free. The right of entrepot will be given in all the ports which may receive vessels from America, for tobacco as well as other articles.—Most people think there will be war. Yet the great alliance now on the carpet may perhaps suffice to re-settle the affairs of Holland without a war. It is believed the Emperor has taken Belgrade. I think that war will go on. Present me in the most friendly terms to your father and the ladies and accept assurances of the esteem with which I have the honor to be Sir your most obedt. and most humble servt., TH: JEFFERSON

PrC (DLC).

[464]

From Lanchon Frères & Cie.

L'Orient, 28 Dec. 1787. TJ's attention "to the interests of America" persuades them that much will be done for the tobacco trade; are eager to know what can be expected from the farmers-general during the next year; although they have information that the farmers' agents "will have orders to receive in February next on the lowest terms they can purchase," they are keeping up the prices on the tobacco they have in store until they have TJ's opinion. "Since the last Spring the Farms have received no Tobaccos that were not contracted for, except, when it could be obtained under the regulated prices." Believe that fixed prices, if proper ones are allowed, favor the seller "who has also the liberty of holding in reserve such Tobaccos as will command a higher price with another purchaser"; the farmers-general receive much inferior tobacco, the price allowed bears no relation to the quality. Have been informed that no further contracts will be allowed; suppose this will prevent a renewal of Mr. Morris' contract; nothing further need be said "on the advantage of leaving the Supplies of the Farm open to everyone."

RC (ViWC); 3 p.

From André Limozin

Le Havre, 28 Dec. 1787. Writes again on the case of William Thomas, who is honest and will be certainly ruined if TJ does not "take his defense in hand"; encloses an additional document that Thomas has just found among his papers which shows clearly that he acted with the full knowledge and permission of the governor of Senegal. The agents of the Senegal Company "refuse to promise him the least indemnity for his demeurage, if it continues any longer his freight will not be Sufficient to pay his expences." Limozin has spoken to the agents who have promised to write the same day to the director of the company in Paris asking him to take the matter up with TJ and to prepare with TJ the necessary application "to the Ministers" to permit Thomas to discharge his cargo.

RC (MHi); 4 p.; endorsed. Recorded in SJL as received 31 Dec. 1787. Enclosure (MHi): Tr of a certificate of clearance for Capt. William Thomas, master of the schooner *Polly & Sally*, dated Salem, 6 Aug. 1787, and of a certificate of clearance, in French, dated Senegal, 20 Oct. 1787.

To Parent

MONSIEUR   à Paris ce 28me. Decembre 1787.

Je viens de recevoir la lettre que vous m'avez fait l'honneur de m'ecrire le 24me. du courant, et je me profite du premier courier pour vous prier d'acheter pour moi les deux feuillettes de vin de

Meursault de Monsr. Bachey, de l'année 84. à 100 francs s'il ne les vendra moins. Et de me procurer en meme tems une feuillette de vin de Vollenaye, premiere qualité, et de l'année 84. Vous aurez la bonté de les faire mettre en bouteilles &c. comme je vous ai marqué dans ma lettre du 17me. courant.

Quant au vin de Monrachet, je n'en prendrai pas dans ce moment. Peut-être que ci-après je pourrais avoir l'honneur de vous en demander. Je vous prie d'expedier les vins de Meursault et de Vollenay au plutot. Je serai bien aise de recevoir aussi les seps de vignes que vous avez eu la bonté de vous charger de me procurer, quand ce sera convenable. Je suis avec beaucoup d'attachement Monsieur votre trés humble et trés obeissant serviteur,

TH: JEFFERSON

PrC (MHi).

From Robert Shewell

Marseilles, 28 Dec. 1787. Learned a few days ago "at the table of Mr. Cathalan" that TJ wishes to send "(by way of experiment) to America, some seed Rice, Indian Corn, or Maize"; offers his services; is going to sail for Charleston within twenty days and will proceed from there to his "native City of Philada."; from either of these places he can forward by water any articles TJ wishes to send by him; is "perfectly secure from Algerine Cruizers, tho' at the same time, shou'd be better satisfy'd" if TJ could tell him whether the United States will have peace with that country.

RC (DLC); 2 p.; endorsed.

From Lambert, with Enclosure

Versailles, December 29. 1787.

I have the honour, Sir, to send you a copy of an Arret passed in Council, for encouraging the Commerce of the United States of America in France. I shall furnish you with a number of others as soon as they shall be printed.

You will therein see that several considerable favors, not before promised to the American Commerce, have been added to those which the king announced to you, in the letter addressed to you on the 22d. of october of the last year.

If in the mean time any duties have been levied, contrary to the intentions of that letter, they shall be repaid on sight of the vouchers.

I have also ordered a verification of the facts whereon it was represented to you, that the decision of the 24 of may 1786, relative to the Commerce of tobacco, had not been fully executed. Be assured that if it shall appear that engagements have been evaded, which were taken under the sanction of the king, effectual provision shall be made for their scrupulous fulfillment.

You will learn also with pleasure that the measures I have taken to prevent the interruption of the Commerce of tobacco, have had full success.

This commodity shall not be excepted from among those to which the right of entrepot is given. The farmers general shall have no preference in the purchases, the proprietors shall be perfectly masters of their speculations, and free to export their tobaccoes by sea to foreign countries.

Measures only must be taken to prevent those frauds to which the entrepot might serve as a pretext; and the chambers of commerce for the ports shall be consulted, in order that the precautions necessary for this purpose, may not be in a form incompatible with that liberty which Commerce ought to enjoy in its operations.

Although the present stock of the farmers general amounts to about three years consumption I have engaged that company to continue to purchase yearly from the 1st day of january 1788. to the end of their lease fourteen thousand hogsheads of tobacco brought directly into the ports of France in French or American bottoms, and to shew at the end of every four months that their purchases amount to four thousand six hundred and sixty six hogsheads.

As to the prices, you have been sensible yourself of the necessity of leaving them free; and this freedom of price was the principal object of the applications of the American and French merchants when they complained of the contract of M. Morris.

The determination then taken to force the purchases of tobacco, tho at high prices, insomuch that the farmers general now find themselves possessed of three years provision, shews that the interests of the planters and merchants of the United States of America have ever been precious to the King.

The arret of Council herein inclosed, and the other regulations which I have the honour of communicating to you, are a further confirmation of a truth tending somuch to strengthen the bands which unite the two nations.

I have the honour to be with a very sincere and inviolable attachment, Sir, your most humble and most obedient servant.

Signed LAMBERT.

ENCLOSURE

AN ACT OF THE KING'S COUNCIL OF STATE, For the encouragement of the Commerce of France with the United States of America.

December 29, 1787.

Extract from the records of the Council of State.

The KING desirous of encouraging the commerce of his subjects with the United-States of America and of facilitating between the two Nations connections reciprocally useful: Having heard the report of the sieur Lambert, Counsellor of State and of the Royal Council of finance and commerce, Comptroller general of finance, HIS MAJESTY BEING IN HIS COUNCIL, has ordained and does ordain as follows:

ARTICLE FIRST.

WHALE-OILS and Spermaceti, the produce of the fisheries of the citizens and inhabitants of the United States of America, which shall be brought into France directly in French vessels or in those of the United-States shall continue to be subjected to a duty only of seven livres ten sols the barrel of five hundred and twenty pounds weight, and whale fins shall be subject to a duty of only six livres thirteen sols four deniers the quintal with the ten sols per livre on each of the said duties; which ten sols per livre shall cease on the last day of December one thousand seven hundred and ninety; His Majesty reserving to himself to grant further favors to the produce of the whale fisheries carried on by the fishermen of the United States of America which shall be brought into France in French vessels or in those of the United States, if on the information which His Majesty shall cause to be taken thereon, he shall judge it expedient for the interest of the two Nations.

II.

THE other fish-oils and dry or salted fish, the produce in like manner of the fisheries of the citizens and inhabitants of the United States, and brought also directly into France, in their, or in French vessels, shall not pay any other nor greater duties than those to which the oils and fish of the same kind, the produce of the fisheries of the Hanseatic towns, or of other the most favored Nations, are or shall be subject in the same case.

III.

THE manufacture of candles and tapers of spermaceti shall be permitted in France, as that of other candles and tapers.

[468]

IV.

CORN, wheat, rye, rice, peas, beans, lentils, flax-seed and other seeds, flour, trees and shrubs, potash and pearl-ash, skins and fur of beaver, raw hides, furs and peltry, and timber brought from the United States directly into France, in French vessels or in those of the United States, shall not be subject but to a duty of one eighth per cent on their value.

V.

VESSELS built in the United States and sold in France, or purchased by Frenchmen shall be exempt from all duties on proof that they were built in the United States.

VI.

TURPENTINE, tar and pitch the produce of the United States of America and brought directly into France in French vessels or in those of the United States shall pay only a duty of two and a half per cent on their value, and as well the duties mentioned in this as in the further article shall be exempt from all addition of sous per livre.

VII.

THE exportation of arms of all sorts, and of gun powder for the United States of America, shall be always permitted in French vessels or in those of the United States, paying for the arms a duty of one eighth per cent on their value: and gunpowder in that case shall be exempt from all duty on giving a cautionary bond.

VIII.

PAPERS of all sorts, even paper hangings and coloured papers, pasteboard and books shall be exempt from all duties on their embarcation for the United States of America, in French vessels or in those of the United States, and shall be entitled in that case to a restitution of the fabrication duties on paper and pasteboard.

IX.

THE Admiralty duties on the vessels of the United-States entering into, or going out of the ports of France, shall not be levied but conformably with the Edict of the month of june last in the cases therein provided for, and with the Letters-patent of the tenth of january one thousand seven hundred and seventy for the objects for which no provision shall have been made by the said Edict: his Majesty reserving to himself moreover to make known his intentions as to the manner in which the said duties shall be levied, whether in proportion to the tonnage of the vessels or otherwise, as also to simplify the said duties of the Admiralty and to regulate them as far as shall be possible on the principle of reciprocity, as soon as the orders shall be completed which were given by his Majesty according to the twenty-sixth article of the said Edict of the month of june last.

X.

THE entrepot (or storing) of all the productions and merchandize of the United States shall be permitted for six months in all the ports of France open to the Commerce of her Colonies; and the said entrepot shall be subject only to a duty of one eighth per cent.

XI.

To favour the exportation of arms, hardware, jewellery bonnetery (*), of wool and of cotton, coarse woolens, small draperies and stuffs of cotton of all sorts, and other merchandizes of French fabric, which shall be sent to the United States of America, in French vessels or in those of the United States, His Majesty reserves to himself to grant encouragements which shall be immediately regulated in his Council, according to the nature of each of the said merchandizes.

XII.

As to other merchandizes not mentioned in this act, brought directly into France from the United States in their or in French vessels, or carried from France to the said United States in French vessels or in those of the United States, and with respect to all commercial conventions whatsoever His Majesty wills and ordains that the citizens of the United States enjoy in France the same rights, privileges and exemptions with the subjects of His Majesty: saving the execution of what is provided in the ninth article hereof.

XIII.

His Majesty grants to the citizens and inhabitants of the United States all the advantages which are enjoyed or which may be here after enjoyed by the most favored nations in his Colonies of America and moreover His Majesty assures to the said citizens and inhabitants of the United States all the privileges and advantages which his own subjects of France enjoy or shall enjoy in Asia and in the scales leading thereto: provided always that their vessels shall have been fitted out and dispatched in some port of the United States.

His Majesty commands and orders M. le duc de Penthievre, Admiral of France, the Intendants and commissaries de parti in the provinces, The commissaries de parti for the observation of the ordinances in the admiralties, the officers of the admiralties masters of the ports, judges des traites, and all others to whom it shall belong to be aiding in the execution of the present regulation which shall be registered in the offices of the said admiralties read published and posted wherever shall be necessary.

Done in the King's council of State, His Majesty present, held at Versailles the twenty ninth of december one thousand seven hundred and eighty seven.

Signed LE CTE. DE LA LUZERNE

(*) *This term includes: bonnets stockings, socks underwaist coats, drawer gloves and mitaines as sold by the bonnetiers.*[1]

English text of the printed version, being a leaflet of four numbered pages with the French and English texts in parallel columns (the latter in italics), having at the head of the text of the English translation the following:

"LETTER from M. LAMBERT, Councellor of State & of the Council royal of Finance and Commerce, Comptroller general of finance to M. Jefferson, Minister plenipotentiary for the United States of America at the Court of Versailles"; and at the foot of text: "A PARIS, DE L'IMPRIMERIE ROYALE. 1787"; measuring 16.5 by 14.6 cm. (DNA: PCC, No. 87, II; another copy RPA, Letters to the Governor, XX, 94). RC (DLC: TJ Papers, 35: 6076-7); in French, in a clerk's hand, signed by Lambert.

Enclosure: Text here printed is from the printed copy in its final, corrected form, filed with RC of Lambert's letter (DLC: TJ Papers, 35: 6078-81); a pamphlet of eight numbered pages in the usual form in which arrêts were printed; with French and English texts in parallel columns (the latter in italics); measuring 17.5 by 12.5 cm., and bearing the following imprint: "A

PARIS, DE L'IMPRIMERIE ROYALE. 1787." In DNA: PCC, No. 87, II there is a proof of the arrêt with a number of corrections of typographical errors in both the French and English texts, and having at its head the following in a clerk's hand: "2e. Epreuve non encore Collationne ni confrontée avec l'original" (see Short to Jay, 1 Jan. 1788, in which this copy was enclosed).

SCALES LEADING THERETO: TJ himself suggested this phrase for a particular reason (see TJ to Jay, 31 Dec. 1787); the word was used perhaps as in the phrase "Échelles du Levant," referring to "certaines villes de commerce qui sont sur la Méditerranée, vers le Levant, telles que Smyrne, Alep, &c." (Littré, *Dictionnaire Abrégé*, Paris, 1886, 361; see also OED under *scales*, sb.7,b.).

[1] This footnote explanation is not in the French text.

From Brissot de Warville

Paris, 30 Dec. 1787. Sends a letter to be forwarded to Crèvecoeur with the mail TJ is sending by the next packet to America. Has been busy since he returned from London and has, therefore, been unable to see TJ; will see him as soon as he is free. After the following Tuesday his address will be "No. 11. rue St. Nicaise."

RC (DLC); 2 p.; in French; endorsed. Not recorded in SJL. The enclosed letter to Crèvecoeur has not been found.

To H. Fizeaux & Cie.

GENTLEMEN   Paris Dec. 30. 1787.

I have this day received the answer of Messieurs Willinck & Van Staphorsts, by which it appears necessary that the board of treasury should be applied to for the reimbursement of the capital of your loan. I shall immediately therefore write to the board of treasury to press this matter. In the mean time I have desired Messieurs Willincks & Van Staphorsts to pay you the interest of this present year becoming due the day after tomorrow, for which you need only apply to them, no other order being necessary than the letter abovementioned which I forward to them by this post. The lenders receiving this will I am in hopes be contented to wait for the capital till the board of treasury can give final orders for it's reimbursement. I trust you will be willing to serve us by quieting them on this subject. I have the honor to be with much esteem, gentlemen, Your most obedient & most humble servt.,

TH: JEFFERSON

PrC (DLC).

To the Commissioners of the Treasury

GENTLEMEN   Paris Dec. 30. 1787.

In my letter of Aug. 5. I had the honour of inclosing to you a letter written me by Messrs. Fiseaux & co. reminding us that the principal of the loan of 51,000 florins obtained by them would become due on the first day of the ensuing year. A few days ago I received another from them calling for the money. At first I was disposed to answer them that I was in no wise authorised to do any thing in it, and that it rested with you altogether. But on consulting with some persons better acquainted with the delicacy of credit in Holland, I found there was reason to fear that a failure to pay this money might not only do essential injury to our credit in general, but even hinder the progress of the loan going on in the hands of Willincks & Van Staphorsts: and that it would be for the interest of that loan itself, to pay this demand out of it if possible. I wrote therefore to Mr. Adams to consult him about it, and to know, if he was of the same opinion, whether he would venture to join me in directing such an application of the money. I wrote at the same time to Willincks & Van Staphorsts to know whether they would have as much money in their hands to spare, and whether they would venture to pay it on our order. Mr. Adams approved of the proposition and was willing to join in ordering the paiment. Willincks & Van Staphorsts answered that they had in their hands money enough to pay the February interest of the former loan, and to answer for some time yet Mr. Adams's and my draughts for our subsistence: but that if they should pay the principal of Fiseaux' loan, it would be an advance of their own: they likewise observed that to pay such a sum without your orders, placed them under an unnecessary responsibility. Upon this I concluded to ask them only to pay this year's interest now becoming due, to desire Fiseaux to receive this and with it to endeavor to quiet the creditors till your orders could be received. I have this day written to Fiseaux and to

Willincks & Van Staphorsts to this purpose, and avail myself of a vessel about to sail from Havre to communicate the whole transaction to you, and to express my wish that you will be pleased to give an answer to Fiseaux. I inclose you his letters to me on the subject. From what I can learn, I suspect that if there were a cordial understanding between the Willincks & Van Staphorsts, if the former had been as well disposed as the latter, the matter would have been settled with Fiseaux. I have the honour to be with much respect Gentlemen your most obedient & most humble servant,

TH: JEFFERSON

PrC (DLC). Enclosures: Fizeaux & Cie. to TJ, 6 and 13 Dec. 1787 (the latter missing).

SOME PERSONS BETTER ACQUAINTED WITH THE DELICACY OF CREDIT IN HOLLAND: These probably included Etienne Clavière and almost certainly included Jacob van Staphorst.

To Willink & Van Staphorst

GENTLEMEN   Paris Dec. 30. 1787.

I receive this day your favor of the 24th. instant. I had before received from Mr. Adams a letter approving of the application of so much of the money in your hands to the paiment of Fizeaux' debt, if there were so much. He presumed my draught on you would suffice, but offered to join if you required it. However from what you say in your last letter I have concluded to refer it to the board of treasury to take such measures for the reimbursement of Fizeaux' loan as they shall think proper and shall accordingly write to them. But in the mean time I must ask you to pay to Mr. Fiseaux the interest of this year, becoming due the day after tomorrow, in order to keep the lenders quiet till I can receive the orders of the board of treasury. On the presumption that you will do this, I will desire Mr. Fizeaux to call on you for the interest and press him to tranquillize the creditors with that. I shall not draw any bill on you for the purpose, supposing that this letter will answer the same end. Mr. Adams being about to leave Europe rather avoids further meddling. I shewed his letter to Mr. Jacob Van Staphorst, approving of what I had proposed: and if you shall desire it I will obtain his express approbation for your paiment of the interest abovementioned. I have the honour to be gentlemen, your most obedient & most humble servant,   TH: JEFFERSON

PrC (DLC).

To John Adams

DEAR SIR   Paris Dec. 31. 1787.

Mr. Parker furnishes me an opportunity of acknoleging the receipt of your favors of Nov. 10. Dec. 6. 10. 18. and 25. which I avoid doing thro post. The orders on the subject of our captives at Algiers have come to me by the last packet. They are to be kept secret even from the captives themselves, lest a knolege of the interference of government should excite too extravagant demands. The settlement of the prices, in the first instance, is important as a precedent.—Willincks & Van Staphorsts answered that they had money enough to pay the February interest, and our draughts for salary for some time, but that the paiment of Fiseaux' capital would oblige them to advance of their own money: they observed too that the paiment of such a sum without the orders of the treasury would lay them under an unnecessary responsibility. I therefore concluded the business by desiring them to pay the year's interest becoming due tomorrow, and praying Mr. Fiseaux to quiet the lenders with that till I could procure the orders of the Treasury to whom I wrote immediately an account of the whole transaction. I was the better satisfied with this on receiving your letter of the 25th. by which I find it your opinion that our credit may not suffer so materially. The declining the paiment came from the Willincks, the Van Staphorsts having offered to advance their moiety. I inclose you a letter I have received from the Comptroller general and an arret on the subject of our commerce. They are the proof sheets, as, at the moment of writing my letter, I have not yet received the fair ones. But the French column is correct enough to be understood. I would wish them not to be public till they are made so on the other side of the water.—I think the alliance of this court with the two imperial ones is going on well. You will have heard of the Emperor's having attempted to surprise Belgrade and failed in the attempt. This necessarily engages him in the war, and so tends to continue it. I think it settled that this country abandons the Turks.

Mr. Parker takes charge of the 10. aunes of double Florence for Mrs. Adams. The silk stockings are not yet ready. I had ordered them to be made by the hermits of Mont Calvaire who are famous for the excellence and honesty of their work, and prices. They will come by the first good opportunity. Be so good as to present my respects to her, and to be assured of the sincere attachment and respect of Dear Sir your most obedient & most humble servant,

TH: JEFFERSON

[474]

RC (MHi: AMT); endorsed. PrC (DLC). Enclosure: Printed copy of Lambert to TJ, 29 Dec. 1787, and proof sheets of the enclosure to that letter, q.v. See also TJ to Jay, 31 Dec. 1787.

To the Agents for the United States in France

[*Paris, 31 Dec. 1787.* An entry in SJL under this date reads: "Agents circular." No copy of such a letter has been found but it evidently was a brief letter enclosing the printed copies of Lambert to TJ, 29 Dec. 1787, and the annexed arrêt, being no doubt similar to the circulars of 31 May and 29 Oct. 1786, qq.v. Although the letters may have actually been written on this day, they were probably not sent out until 2 Jan. 1788 (see Short to Jay, 1 Jan. 1788; TJ to Limozin, 2 Jan. 1788).]

From Burrill Carnes

[*Nantes, before 31 Dec. 1787.*] Has a vessel bound for Alexandria in a few days; offers to execute any commissions entrusted to him.

RC (MHi); 1 p.; endorsed; undated but evidently one of two undated letters recorded in SJL Index as received in 1787.

From Burrill Carnes

[*Nantes, ca. 31 Dec. 1787*] Asks for instructions for forwarding the continental accounts and those of Schweighauser & Dobrée, which he had intended to send by "Mr. Prentiss of Boston," the bearer of this letter, but recollects that Mr. William Ast, at L'Orient, informed him that they should first be sent to him to be entered "in the Continental Books in his possession."

RC (MHi); 2 p.; endorsed; without place or date; assigned to this date because TJ's letter to Carnes, 6 Jan. 1788, is a reply to the present letter and there are entries for two undated letters from Carnes recorded in SJL Index at the end of 1787.

To Uriah Forrest, with Enclosure

DEAR SIR   Paris Dec. 31. 1787.

Just before I received your favour asking my opinion on our new proposed constitution, I had written my sentiments on the subject fully to my friend Mr. Madison. They concurred so exactly with yours that the communication of them could answer no end but that of shewing my readiness to obey you. I therefore extracted that

[475]

part from my letter to him, and have reserved it for a good private conveiance which has never offered till now by Mr. Parker. Tho I pretend to make no mystery of my opinion, yet my distance from the scene gives me too much diffidence in my views of it to detail them lengthily and publicly. This diffidence is increased by my high opinion of the abilities and honesty of the framers of the constitution. Yet we cannot help thinking for ourselves. I suppose I see much precious improvement in it, but some seeds of danger which might have been kept out of sight of the framers by a consciousness of their own honesty, and a presumption that all succeeding rulers would be as honest as themselves. Make what use you please of the contents of the paper, but without quoting it's author, who has no pretension to see what is hidden from others. I have the honour to be with great esteem & respect Dr. Sir Your most obedt. humble servt, TH: JEFFERSON

ENCLOSURE

'I like much the general idea of framing a government, which should go on of itself peaceably, without needing continual recurrence to the state legislatures. I like the organization of the government into Legislative, Judiciary, and Executive. I like the power given the Legislature to levy taxes, and, for that reason solely, I approve of the greater house being chosen by the people directly. For though I think a house so chosen, will be very far inferior to the present Congress, will be very illy qualified to legislate for the Union, for foreign nations &c. yet this evil does not weigh against the good of preserving inviolate the fundamental principle that the people are not to be taxed but by representatives chosen immediately by themselves. I am captivated by the compromise of the opposite claims of the great and little states, of the latter to equal, and the former to proportional influence. I am much pleased too with the substitution of the method of voting by persons, instead of that of voting by states: and I like the negative given to the Executive conjointly with a third of either house; though I should have liked it better had the Judiciary been associated for that purpose, or invested separately with a similar power. There are other good things of less moment. I will now tell you what I do not like.—First, the Omission of a Bill of rights, providing clearly, and without the aid of sophisms, for freedom of religion, freedom of the press, protection against standing armies, restriction of monopolies, the eternal and unremitting force of the habeas corpus laws, and trials by jury in all matters of fact triable by the laws of the land, and not by the law of Nations. To say, as Mr. Wilson does, that a bill of rights was not necessary, because all is reserved in the case of the general government which is not given, while in the particular ones all is given which is not reserved, might do for the audience to which it was addressed: but it is surely a gratis dictum, the reverse of which might just as well be said; and it is opposed by strong inferences from the body of the instrument, as well as from the omission of the clause of our present confederation which had made the reservation in express terms. It was hard to conclude because there has been a want of uniformity among the states as to the cases triable by jury, because some have been so incautious as to dispense with this mode of trial in certain cases, therefore the more prudent states shall be reduced to the same level of calamity. It would have been much more just and wise to have concluded the other way, that as most of the states had preserved with jealousy this sacred palladium of liberty, those who had wandered should be brought back to it: and to have established general right rather than general wrong, for I consider all the ill as established, which may be established. I have a right to nothing which another has a right to take away; and Congress will have a right to take away trials by jury in all civil cases. Let me add that a bill of rights is what the people are entitled to against every government on earth, general or particular; and what no just government should refuse, or rest on inferences.

The second feature I dislike, and strongly dislike, is the abandonment in every instance of the principle of rotation in office, and most particularly in the case of the President. Reason and Experience tell us that the First magistrate will always be re-elected if he may be re-elected. He is then an officer for life. This once observed, it becomes of so much consequence to certain nations to have a friend or a foe at the head of our affairs that they will interfere with money and with arms. A Galloman or an Angloman will be supported by the nation he befriends. If once elected, and at a 2d. or 3d election outvoted by one or two votes, he will pretend false votes, foul play, hold possession of the reins of government, be supported by the states voting for him, especially if they be the central ones, lying in a compact body themselves, and separating their opponents; and they will be aided by one nation in Europe, while the majority are aided by another. The election of a President of America some years hence will be much more interesting to certain nations of Europe than ever the election of a king of Poland was. Reflect on all the instances in history, antient and modern, of elective monarchies, and say if they do not give foundation for my fears. The Roman emperors, the Popes while they were of any importance, the German emperors till they became hereditary in practice, the kings of Poland, the Deys of the Ottoman dependancies. It may be said that if elections are to be attended with these disorders, the seldomer they are repeated the better. But experience says that to free them from disorder they must be rendered less interesting by a necessity of change. No foreign power, nor domestic party, will waste their blood and money to elect a person who must go out at the end of a short period. The power of removing every fourth year by the vote of the people is a power which they will not exercise, and if they were disposed to exercise it they would not be permitted. The king of Poland is removeable every day by the diet. But they never remove him. Nor would Russia, the emperor &c. permit them to do it. —Smaller objections are the Appeal on matters of fact as well as law; and the binding all persons, Legislative, Executive, and Judiciary by oath to maintain that constitution. I do not pretend to decide what would be the best method of procuring the establishment of the manifold good things in this constitution, and of getting rid of the bad, whether by adopting it in hopes of future amendment; or, after it shall have been duly weighed and canvassed by the people, after seeing the parts they generally dislike, and those they generally approve, to say to them, 'We see now what you wish. You are willing to give to your federal government such and such powers: but you wish at the same time to have such and such fundamental rights secured to you, and certain sources of convulsion taken away. Be it so. Send together your deputies again. Let them establish your fundamental rights by a sacrosanct declaration, and let them pass the parts of the constitution you have approved. These will give powers to your federal government sufficient for your happiness.' This is what might be said, and would probably produce a speedy, more perfect and more permanent form of government. At all events, I hope you will not be discouraged from making other trials, if the present one should fail. We are never permitted to despair of the commonwealth.—I have thus told you freely what I like, and what I dislike merely as matter of curiosity, for I know it is not in my power to offer matter of information to your judgment, which has been formed after hearing and weighing every thing which the wisdom of man could offer on these subjects. I own I am not a friend to a very energetic government. It is always oppressive. It places the governors indeed more at their ease, at the expence of the people. The late rebellion in Massachusets has given more alarm than I think it should have done. Calculate that one rebellion in 13. states in the course of 11. years, is but one for each state in a century and a half. No country should be so long without one nor will any degree of power in the hands of government prevent insurrections. In England, where the hand of power is heavier than with us, there are seldom half a dozen years without an insurrection. In France, where it is still heavier, but less despotic, as Montesquieu supposes, than in some other countries, and where there are always 2. or 300,000 men ready to crush insurrections, there have been three in the course of the three years I have been here, in every one of which greater numbers were engaged than in Massachusets, and a great deal more blood was spilt. In Turkey, where the sole nod of the Despot is death, insurrections are the events of every day. Compare again the ferocious depredations of their insurgents with the order, the moderation and the almost self extinguishment of ours, and say finally whether peace is best preserved by giving energy to the government, or information to the people. This last is the most certain and the most legitimate engine of government. Educate and inform the whole mass of the people, enable them to see that it is their interest to preserve peace and order, and they will preserve it, and it requires no very high degree of education to convince them of this. They are the only sure reliance for the preservation of our liberty.—After all, it is my principle that the will of the majority should prevail. If they approve the proposed constitution in all it's parts, I shall concur in it chearfully, in hopes they will amend it whenever they shall find it works wrong. This reliance cannot deceive us, as long as we remain virtuous; and I think we shall be that, as long as agriculture is our principal object, which will be the case while there remain vacant lands in any part of America. When we get piled upon one another in large cities, as in Europe, we shall become corrupt as in Europe, and go to eating one another as they do there. —I have tired you by this time with disquisitions which you have already heard repeated by others a thousand and a thousand times, and therefore shall only add assurances of the esteem & attachment, with which I have the honor to be, Dear Sir.[']

RC (Andre deCoppet, New York, 1949). PrC (DLC). Tr (DLC); in a later hand. Enclosure (PrC in DLC): Tr of an Extract from TJ's letter to Madison of 20 Dec. 1787, with numerous variations in phraseology (see note to TJ to Madison, 20 Dec. 1787).

TJ was not correct in saying that he had written Madison JUST BEFORE I RECEIVED YOUR FAVOUR: Forrest's letter of 11 Dec. arrived on 17 Dec. and his letter to Madison was written three days later. MY SENTIMENTS . . . CONCURRED SO EXACTLY WITH YOURS: Actually Forrest's sentiments may have been expressed in his letter of 11 Dec. 1787 in the certain knowledge that they concurred with TJ's, for it is very likely that he had read or had heard discussions of TJ's views as set forth in his letters of 13 Nov. 1787 to Adams and Smith, both of whom he was seeing at this time in London.

To John Jay

SIR   Paris Dec. 31. 1787.

Since the receipt of the letter of Monsieur de Calonne of Octob. 22. 1786. I have several times had the honour of mentioning to you that I was endeavouring to get the substance of that letter reduced into an arrêt, which, instead of being revocable by a simple letter of a comptroller general, would require an arrêt to repeal or alter it, and of course must be discussed in full council and so give time to prevent it. This has been pressed as much as it could be with prudence. One cause of delay has been the frequent changes of the Comptroller general; as we had always our whole work to begin again with every new one. Monsieur Lambert's continuance in office for some months has enabled us at length to get through the business; and I have just received from him a letter and arrêt duly authenticated; of which I have the honour to send you a number of printed copies. You will find that the several alterations and additions are made, which on my visit to the seaports I had found to be necessary, and which my letters of June 21. and Aug. 6. particularly mentioned to you. Besides these we have obtained some new articles of value, for which openings arose in the course of the negociation. I say *we* have done it; because the Marquis de la Fayette has gone hand in hand with me through the business, and has been a most invaluable aid. I take the liberty of making some observations on the articles of the arrêt severally, for their explanation as well as for the information of Congress.

Article 1. In the course of our conferences with the Comptroller general we had prevailed on him to pass this article with a suppression of all duty. When he reported the arrêt however to the council, this suppression was objected to, and it was insisted to reestablish the duties of 7^{tt}-10s and of 10s the livre reserved in the letter of Monsr. de Calonne. The passage of the arrêt was stopped, and the difficulty communicated to me. I urged every thing I could, in letters, and in conferences to convince them that whale oil was an article which could bear no duty at all. That if the duty fell on the consumer, he would chuse to buy vegetable oils; if on the fisherman, he could no longer live by his calling, remaining in his own country; and that if he quitted his own country, the circumstances of vicinity, sameness of language, laws, religion, and manners, and perhaps the ties of kindred would draw him to Nova Scotia, in spite of every encouragement which could be given at Dunkirk: and that thus those fishermen would be shifted out of a scale friendly to France, into one always hostile. Nothing however could prevail. It hung on this article alone for two months, during which we risked the total loss of the arret on the stability in office of M. Lambert: for if he had gone out, his successor might be less favorable; and if Mr. Neckar were the successor, we might lose the whole, as he never set any store by us, or the connection with us. About ten days ago it became universally believed that Mr. Lambert was to go out immediately. I therefore declined further insisting on the total suppression, and desired the arret might pass leaving the duties on whale oil as M. de Calonne had promised them; but with a reservation which may countenance our bringing on this matter again at a more favourable moment.

Article 2. The other fish oils are placed in a separate article; because whatever encouragements we may hereafter obtain for whale oils, they will not be extended to those which their own fisheries produce.

Article 3. A company had silently and by unfair means obtained a monopoly for the making and selling spermaceti candles: as soon as we discovered it, we sollicited it's suppression, which is effected by this clause.

Article 4. The duty of an eighth per cent is merely to oblige the masters of vessels to enter their cargoes for the information of government; without inducing them to attempt to smuggle.

Article 6. Tar, pitch, and turpentine of America coming in competition with the same articles produced in the Southwestern parts of France we could obtain no greater reduction than to 2½ per cent. The duties before were from 4. to 6. times that amount.

Article. 10. The right of Entrepot given by this article is almost the same thing as the making all their ports, free ports for us. The ships are indeed subject to be visited, and the cargoes must be reported in ports of Entrepot, which need not be done in the Freeports. But the communication between the entrepot and the country is not interrupted by continual search of all persons passing into the country, which has proved so troublesome to the inhabitants of our freeports as that a considerable proportion of them have wished to give back the privilege of their freedom.

Article 13. This article gives us the privileges and advantages of native subjects in all their possessions in Asia, and in the *scales leading thereto.* This expression means at present the isles of France and Bourbon, and will include the Cape of good hope should any future event put it into the hands of France. It was with a view to this that I proposed the expression, because we were then in hourly expectation of a war, and it was suspected that France would take possession of that place. It will in no case be considered as including any thing Westward of the Cape of good hope. I must observe further on this article, that it will only become valuable on the suppression of their East India company; because as long as their monopoly continues, even native subjects cannot enter their Asiatic ports for the purposes of commerce. It is considered however as certain that this company will be immediately suppressed.

The article of tobacco could not be introduced into the Arrêt, because it was necessary to consider the Farmers general as parties to that arrangement. It rests therefore of necessity on the basis of a letter only. You will perceive that this is nothing more than a continuation of the order of Berni, only leaving the prices unfixed; and like that it will require a constant and vexatious attention to have it's execution enforced.

The states who have much to carry, and few carriers, will observe perhaps that the benefits of these regulations are somewhat narrowed by confining them to articles brought hither in French or American bottoms. But they will consider that nothing in these instruments moves from us. The advantages they hold out, are all given by this country to us, and the givers will modify their gifts as they please. I suppose it to be a determined principle of this court not to suffer our carrying business, so far as their consumption of our commodities extends, to become a nursery for British seamen. Nor would this perhaps be advantageous to us, considering the dispositions of the two nations towards us. The preference which our shipping will obtain on this account may counterpoise the discouragements it experiences from the aggravated dangers from the Barbary states. Nor is the idea unpleasing which shews itself in various parts of these papers, of naturalising American bottoms, and American citizens in France, and in it's foreign possessions. Once established here, and in their Eastern settlements, they may revolt less at the proposition to extend it to those Westward. They are not yet however at that point; we must be contented to go towards it [a] step at a time, and trust to future events for hastening our progress.

With respect to the alliance between this and the two Imperial courts nothing certain transpires. We are enabled to conjecture it's progress only from facts which now and then shew themselves. The following may be considered as indications of it. 1. The Emperor has made an attempt to surprise Belgrade. The attempt failed, but will serve to plunge him into the war, and to shew that he had assumed the character of mediator only to enable himself to gain some advantage by surprise. 2. The mediation of France is probably at an end, and their abandonment of the Turks agreed on; because they have secretly ordered their officers to quit the Turkish service. This fact is known but to few, and not intended to be known: but I think it certain. 3. To the offer of mediation lately made by England and Prussia, the court of Petersburgh answered that having declined the mediation of a friendly power (France) she could not accept that of two courts with whose dispositions she had reason to be dissatisfied. 4. The States General are said to have instructed their Ambassador here lately to ask of M. de Montmorin whether the enquiry had been made which they had formerly desired, 'By what authority the French engineers had been placed in the service of Holland?' and that he answered that the enquiry had not been made, nor should be made. Tho' I do not consider the channel thro' which I get this fact as absolutely sure; yet it is so respectable that I give credit to it myself. 5. The King of Prussia is withdrawing his troops from Holland. Should this alliance shew itself, it would seem that France, thus strengthened, might dictate the reestablishment of the affairs of Holland in her own form, for it is not conceivable that Prussia would dare to move, nor that England would alone undertake such a war, and for such a purpose. She appears indeed triumphant at present; but the question is who will triumph last?

The hermitage on Mont Calvaire, or Mont Valérien. (See p. xxxv.)

ARRÊT AN ACT

DU CONSEIL D'ÉTAT DU ROI, OF THE KING'S COUNCIL OF STATE.

Pour l'encouragement du Commerce de France avec les États-Unis de l'Amérique. For the encouragement of the Commerce of France with the United States of America.

Du 29 Décembre 1787. December 29. 1787.

Extrait des Registres du Conseil d'État. Extracted from the records of the Council of State.

LE ROI voulant encourager le Commerce de ses Sujets avec les États-Unis de l'Amérique, & faciliter entre les deux Nations des relations réciproquement utiles: Oui le rapport du sieur Lambert, Conseiller d'État, & ordinaire au Conseil royal des finances & du commerce, Contrôleur général des finances, SA MAJESTÉ ÉTANT EN SON CONSEIL, a ordonné & ordonné ce qui suit: THE KING desirous of encouraging the commerce of his subjects with the United States of America, and of facilitating between the two Nations connections reciprocally useful: Having heard the report of the sieur Lambert, Counsellor of State and of the Royal-Council of finance and commerce, Comptroller general of finance, HIS MAJESTY BEING IN HIS COUNCIL, has ordained and does ordain as follows:

ARTICLE PREMIER. ARTICLE FIRST.

Les huiles de baleine, & le WHALE-OILS and spermaceti

First page of an Act to encourage commerce (See

I inclose you a letter from Mr. Dumas. I have received one from him myself wherein he assures me that no difficulties shall be produced by what he had suggested relative to his mission to Brussels. The gazettes of France and Leyden to this date accompany this letter, which, with the several papers put under your cover I shall send to Mr. Limozin, our agent at Havre, to be forwarded by the Juno, Capt. Jenkins, which sails from that port for New York on the 3d. of January. I have the honour to be with sentiments of the most perfect esteem and respect, Sir, your most obedient & most humble servant, TH: JEFFERSON

PrC (DLC). Enclosures: (1) Printed copy of Lambert to TJ, 29 Dec. 1787. (2) Dumas to Jay, 18 Dec. 1787, enclosed in Dumas to TJ, same date. TJ actually did not enclose *any* of the printed copies of the arrêt; instead, a proof was enclosed in Short to Jay, 1 Jan. 1788, for reasons there given. TJ sent "a very large bundle" of printed copies to Jay by post (see TJ to Limozin, 2 Jan. 1788).

For an explanation of the phrase SCALES LEADING THERETO, see Lambert to TJ, 29 Dec. 1787, note. THE ISLES OF FRANCE AND BOURBON: Mauritius and Reunion, respectively, in the Indian ocean. THIS COMPANY WILL BE IMMEDIATELY SUPPRESSED: See note to Bérard to TJ, 6 May 1786.

To André Limozin

SIR   Paris Dec. 31. 1787.

In your favor of the 18th. instant you were so kind as to inform me that the American ship Juno, Capt. Jenkins, would sail from your port for New York about the 3d. of January. I avail myself therefore of that opportunity for the conveyance of dispatches to Mr. Jay, which are of great consequence. As it is improper they should go thro' the post office, I send a servant with them express and take the liberty to direct him to put them into your hands, in hopes you will be so good as to get Capt. Jenkins to take charge of them and to deliver them carefully and immediately on his arrival at New York to Mr. Jay. The trunk directed to Colo. Hamilton is from his sister in law, Mrs. Church, who is here at present. It probably contains caps, or something of that kind. The smaller package in waxed cloth is said to contain Newspapers for Mr. Crevecoeur French Consul at New York. I have received your favor of the 28th. on the subject of Capt. Thomas, and will confer with Mr. Fraise whenever he will do me the honor to call on me, and I will afterwards write to you.—The Emperor has failed in an attempt to surprise Belgrade. This engages him in that war, and is one among several proofs that it will continue. If the alliance should take place as expected between France, Spain, and the two Imperial courts, it would seem they might dictate the re-establishment of affairs in Holland without a disturbance of the peace in this quarter. I am with much esteem, Sir, your most obedient humble servant, TH: JEFFERSON

PrC (DLC).

From Abbé Morellet

le 31. decemb.

Monsieur jefferson a eu la bonté de me promettre de faire revenir de Londres la planche jointe aux observations sur la virginie lorsque le libraire anglois en auroit fait usage pour son edition. Je le prie de vouloir bien me procurer le retour de cette planche qui manque encore à 250 exemp. de l'édition francoise et lesquels demeureroient invendus sans cela. Je lui serai bien obligé de donner ses ordres en consequence. Je prens la liberté de lui envoyer en même tems la machine à tirer des copies dont je lui ai parlé et dont je me deferai volontiers si j'en trouve dix louis ou même moins si l'on juge qu'elle vaille moins. Elle peut faire plaisir à quelqu'un. Je prie monsieur jefferson d'agreer tous les respects de S.T.H. Serviteur, L'ABBÉ MORELLET

RC (DLC); endorsed; undated, and not recorded in SJL, but clearly written in 1787 (see TJ to Stockdale, 1 Jan. 1788).

To William Stephens Smith

DEAR SIR Paris Dec. 31. 1787.

I duly received your favor of the 6th. inst. but that of the 4th. therein mentioned to come by Mr. Littlepage, has never come to hand. He remembers nothing of it. It was the more material as you mention it to have contained my account of which I must therefore trouble you to send me another copy. I must remind you also of Mr. Adams's picture, as I should be much mortified should I not get it done before he leaves Europe: and ask you for the address of my shoemaker and taylor that I may know how to apply to them after your departure. Tho' I had rather have seen you sent to Lisbon than remaining at London, yet I am not contented with your liberation altogether. I hope work will be found for you on the other side the Atlantic, since it is thought there is so little to do on this. You know how little good, friends can do for us in our country. Mine however shall not be unadmonished of the pleasure it will give me that they become yours also. You are going to be happy, whether you have something to do or nothing. You have a wife who will make you happy in spite of your teeth, even were you disposed to run restive against your own felicity. You will be having children too every day which will be making you happier and happier every day. Your sun of joy is climbing towards it's zenith, whilst mine is descending from it. So good night: god bless you. Your's affectionately,

TH: JEFFERSON

PrC (DLC). THAT OF THE 4TH: Smith's letter was dated 3 Dec. 1787, q.v.

From Willink & Van Staphorst

Amsterdam, 31 Dec. 1787. Since their letter to TJ of 24 Dec. two mails have arrived from England but no letter has been received from Adams. Since the time has come to discharge the debt due to Fizeaux & Cie. they have "provisionally taken such Means as will secure the Credit of the United States from Disgrace" and have paid the interest on the loan; trust they will receive Adams' authorization because his relation to them "renders him the most proper Substitute to give us the directions the Board of Treasury has unaccountably omitted to forward."

RC (DLC); 2 p.; endorsed.

From Madame d'Aujouer

Paris, rue de Seine St. Victor "pres le jardin du Roy," [1787?] Introduces herself as a relative "de monsieur carroll de marilend" and requests an appointment on a Tuesday or Wednesday morning. She desires news of Carroll, having had none for some time and not having written herself since the loss of her husband.

RC (DLC); endorsed; undated and not recorded in SJL or SJL Index. See Charles Carroll of Carrollton to the "Countess of Auzouer," 20 Sep. 1771, as printed in *Maryland Historical Magazine*, XXXII (1937), 203-8.

From Jacques Finck

[*Paris, 1787?*] "Jacques Finck, ci-devant Maitre d'hôtel de Monsieur Franklin, alors Ambassadeur en France, implore, avec respect et confiance," TJ's "puissante intercession" for the recovery of the sum

[485]

of 3,035^{tt} claimed to be due to him by Franklin, "si justement révéré chez toutes les Nations," whom he had served for three years; Finck set forth the details of his dispute over the arrangement that produced this debt, and of the effort he had made to bring the matter to Franklin's attention; he enclosed a copy of the agreement that William Temple Franklin, who managed the household, caused him to sign.

RC (DLC); clerk's copy, undated but perhaps written in 1786 or 1787; endorsed by TJ: "Finck." Enclosure (DLC): "Copie de l'arrangement que M. Franklin petit fils a fait souscrire par Finck, pour la dépense de bouche de M. Franklin, Ambassadeur."

There is no evidence that TJ interceded in Finck's attempt to recover these housekeeping expenses.

From Alexander Donald

Richmond, 1 Jan. 1788. Has received a letter from Nicholas Lewis asking him to assist Derieux, who wished to sell some bills of exchange; he gladly assisted him after seeing the letter TJ had written Derieux, but he believes "it would have been as well, had you not mentioned to him the sum which his Aunt would probably leave him at her Death, for it appears to me that he reckons upon it, as much almost as if [it] was actually now in his possession, For in place of laying out the money received for his bills in a piece of good land and some Negroes &c. he has out of the first end of it, purchased a Phaeton and Horses." This is a "bad symptom of his Œconomy," and if his aunt lives a few years and refuses further assistance, he will be ruined. Had he known what Derieux was going to do he would have advised him. "Colo. Lewis has sent a specimen of Indian Corn and seeds, which will be forwarded by this opportunity"; hopes they arrive safely; some hams will be sent in the spring. Does not think England wants war or that France is in a condition to begin war; if he is right "they will each concede a little"; "But should there be a war in Europe, it gives me pleasure to find that the People . . . will take no part with either, but will avail themselves of the great advantages which must result from a state of perfect neutrality." This he believes will be their conduct for some time. Sends a letter he received from Warner Lewis. The box containing copies of TJ's "Book" for various persons has not yet arrived.

RC (DLC); 2 p.; endorsed. Enclosure (DLC): Warner Lewis to Alexander Donald, 22 Dec. 1787, which reads in part: ". . . I am exceedingly concerned at the probability of a war in Europe, and of such an one as will in all likelihood be general. If it should be general, the parts you have allotted to the different powers, I think, will be found to be perfectly just. I have no doubt myself that the Emperor of Germany will take that part which France espouses; and I hope America will have wisdom enough to take no part at all.—The more I contemplate the new constitution, as it is called, and the more I consider the situation of my country, the more I am persuaded of the necessity of making immediate trial of it. With this idea, that I may have an opportunity of giving a vote for it, I have offered my services to the county I live in. Whether I shall be elected or not, is a matter of some doubt. . . . The mortification of rejection will by no means be a sore one to me. I thank my friend Jefferson for his recollection of me amidst the business with which he is surrounded; and I shall receive the present of his book with that pleasure, which every testimony of his remem- brance and regard will always impress upon me."

William Short to John Jay

SIR   Paris Jan. 1. 1788

Mr. Jefferson charges me to explain to Your Excellency the reason of your not receiving the copies of the Arrêt of the King's Council as mentioned in his letter. After having written and sealed it with the certainty of receiving the printed copies this morning, he is in the instant informed by the printer that it is impossible for him to deliver them although printed, until he shall have received from Versailles the original on parchment, in order to compare with it the copies printed. This seems an unalterable law of the press and it is in vain that I have tried to prevail on the King's printer, at whose table I am writing at present, to deviate from it in this instance.

Mr. Jefferson was obliged to set off this morning for Versailles. He has desired me to come here, and if nothing better could be done, to obtain uncorrected proof-sheets which I have done, and have the honor of forwarding to your Excellency together with a copy of the Comptroller's letter to him. News of the diligence by which these copies will be sent, being arrived, and the person who carries them, fearing to be left, I have only time to add that if the Vessel should still be detained some days at Havre, Your Excellency will receive yet the number of copies of the Arrêt mentioned in Mr. Jefferson's letter.[1] I cannot help profiting of this circumstance to re-iterate to your Excellency assurances of the pleasure it would give me at all times to be charged with any of your commands, and to add how much I should consider myself honored by any communications you should please to make me.[2]

I have the honor to be with sentiments of the most profound respect Your Excellency's most obedient & most humble Servant,

W SHORT

RC (DNA: PCC, No. 87, II). Dft (DLC: Short Papers); with a number of variations in the text; only those which are concerned with content rather than form have been noted below. Enclosures: See note to Lambert to TJ, 29 Dec. 1787, and TJ to Jay, 31 Dec. 1787.

[1] Short wrote the following in Dft,

then drew a line through it: "Mr. Jefferson was obliged to set off this morning for Versailles. He desired I should, if nothing better could be done, send you a copy of the Comptroller's letter to him, together with either a manuscript or proof-sheet copy of the Arrêt. The Printer has not yet determined which he will allow me to send, his office being at some distance from this place and I have fears that the hour of the diligence will not allow the Messenger to wait untill I should be able to write after his determination. I therefore continue the letter without being certain what kind of a copy of the Arrêt will be sent to your Excellency. It will however be the best I can get. Should the vessel be detained some days longer at Havre you will still receive by it the number of copies as mentioned in Mr. Jefferson's letter." See illustration in this volume.

2 Dft ends at this point; following this Short wrote in Dft: "(à l'Imprimerie Royale)."

To John Stockdale

SIR   Paris Jan. 1. 1788.

I wrote you last on the 10th. of October, and having received no answer to my letter, I presume it must have miscarried and therefore send you a copy of it on the adjoining leaf. To this I take the liberty of referring you as to it's contents. I must press the immediate sending the plate of my map, as the bookseller here had not struck off his whole quantity, and apprehends he shall suffer if he is not supplied soon. As a matter of curiosity I am desirous of knowing how the Notes of Virginia have sold with you. Having not received any Reviews from you since those of August, I am uninformed how they have treated it. I suppose too there are more volumes of Bell's Shakespeare (fine paper) out now, and something more of Coke Littleton. Be so good as to send these articles with those desired in my letter of Octob. 10. and add from Lackington's catalogue the following

Ferguson's art of drawing. 8vo. 4/6
Art of drawing in Perspective. 12mo. 10d.
Art of drawing in water colours. 12mo. 10d.

Send me at the same time an account with the corrections in my former letter, and the new additions, and I will send you a bill of exchange for the balance by the first post after I receive it. I am Sir Your very humble servant,   TH: JEFFERSON

PrC (DLC). Enclosure: Copy of TJ to Stockdale, 10 Oct. 1787.

From George Washington

DEAR SIR   Mount Vernon January 1st. 1788

I have received your favor of the 15th.[1] of August, and am sorry that it is not in my power to give you any further information relative to the practicability of opening a communication between Lake Erie and the Ohio, than you are already possessed of. I have

[488]

made frequent enquiries since the time of your writing to me on that subject while Congress were sitting at Annapolis, but could never collect any thing that was decided or satisfactory. I have again renewed them, and flatter myself with better prospect of success.

The accounts generally agree as to its being a flat country between the Waters of Lake Erie and Big Beaver; but differ very much with respect to the distance between their sources, their navigation, and the inconveniencies which would attend the cutting a canal between them.

From the best information I have been able to obtain of that Country, the sources of the Muskingham and Cayohoga approach nearer to each other than any water of Lake Erie does to Big Beaver: But a communication by this River would be more circuitous and difficult, having the Ohio in a greater extent, to ascend; unless the latter could be avoided by opening a communication between James River and the Great Kanhawa, or between the little Kanhawa and the West branch of Monongahela, which is said to be very practicable by a short portage. As testimony thereof, the States of Virginia and Maryland have opened (for I believe it is compleated) a road from the No. branch of Potomack, commencing at, or near the mouth of Savage River, to the Cheat River, from whence the former are continuing it to the navigable Water of the little Kanhawa.

The distance between Lake Erie and the Ohio, through the Big Beaver, is, however, so much less than the rout through the Muskingham, that it would, in my opinion, operate very strongly in favor of opening a canal between the source of the nearest water of the Lake and Big Beaver, altho the distance between them should be much greater and the operation more difficult than to the Muskingham. I shall omit no opportunity of gaining every information relative to this important subject; and will, with pleasure, communicate to you whatever may be worthy of your attention.

I did myself the honor to forward to you the plan of Government formed by the Convention, the day after that body rose; but was not a little disappointed, and mortified indeed (as I wished to make the first offering of it to you) to find by a letter from Commode. Jones, dated in New York the 9th. of Novr. that it was, at that time, in his possession. You have, undoubtedly, received it, or some other 'ere now, and formed an opinion upon it. The public attention is, at present, wholly engrossed by this important subject. The Legislatures of those States (Rhode Island excepted) which have met since the Constitution has been formed, have readily assented to its being submitted to a Convention chosen by the People. Pensylvania, New Jersey and Delaware are the only States whose Conventions have as yet decided upon it. In the former it was adopted by 46 to 23 and in the two latter unanimously. Connecticut and Massachusetts are to hold their Conventions on the 1st. and 2d. tuesdays of this Month, Maryland in April, Virginia in June, and upon the whole, it appears, so far as I have had an opportunity of learning the opinions of the people in the several States, that it will be received. There will, undoubtedly, be more or less opposition to its adoption in most of the States; and in none a more formidable one than in this; as many influencial characters here have taken a decided part against it, among whom are Mr. Henry, Colo. Mason, Govr. Randolph and Colo. R. H. Lee; but from every information which I have been able to obtain, I think there will be a majority in its favor notwithstanding their dissention. In New York a considerable opposition will also be given.

I am much obliged to you, my dear Sir, for the account which you gave me of the general state of affairs in Europe. I am glad to hear that the Assembleé des Notables has been productive of good in France. The abuse of the finances being disclosed to the King, and the Nation, must open their eyes, and lead to the adoption of such measures as will prove beneficial to them in future. From the public papers it appears that the Parliaments of the several Provinces, and particularly that of Paris, have acted with great spirit and resolution. Indeed the rights of Mankind, the priviledges of the people, and the true principles of liberty seem to have been more generally discussed and better understood throughout Europe since the American revolution than they were at any former period.

Altho' the finances of France and England were such as led you to suppose, at the time you wrote to me, would prevent a rupture between those two powers, yet, if we credit the concurrent accounts from every quarter, there is little doubt but that they have commenced hostilities before this. Russia and the Porte have formally began the contest, and from appearances (as given to us) it is not improbable but that a pretty general war will be kindled in Europe. Should this be the case, we shall feel more than ever the want of an efficient general Government to regulate our Commercial concerns, to give us a national respectability, and to connect the political views and interests of the several States under one head in such a manner as will effectually prevent them from forming a seperate, improper, or indeed any connection, with the European powers which can involve them in their political disputes. For our situation is such as makes it not only unnecessary, but extremely imprudent for us to take a part in their quarrels; and whenever a contest happens among them, if we wisely and properly improve the advantages which nature has given us, we may be benefitted by their folly—provided we conduct ourselves with circumspection, and under proper restrictions, for I perfectly agree with you, that an extensive speculation, a spirit of gambling, or the introduction of any thing which will divert our attention from Agriculture, must be extremely prejudicial, if not ruinous to us. But I conceive under an energetic general Government such regulations might be made, and such measures taken, as would render this Country the asylum of pacific and industrious characters from all parts of Europe, would encourage the cultivation of the Earth by the high price which its products would command, and would draw the wealth, and wealthy men of other Nations, into our own bosom, by giving security to property, and liberty to its holders.

I have the honor to be With great esteem & regard Dear Sir Yr. most obed. & most Hble Servt,   Go. WASHINGTON

RC (DLC: TJ Papers); endorsed, in part, incorrectly: "May 30. 87"; MS torn at upper right-hand margin so that the date is missing (supplied from FC). FC (DLC: Washington Papers); with omissions and variations of phrasing not noted here.

¹ FC reads (correctly): "14th."

From Nathaniel Barrett

Boston, 2 Jan. 1788. Introduces his friend, J. C. Jones, and his wife; hopes the voyage will have restored Mrs. Jones' health. "Knowing your polite Attention to evry Lady from this Country, I need not ask Leave to introduce one, whose peculiar merits will render an acquaintance both pleasing to you and her. From Mr. Jones you will obtain evry Information of the political and commercial state of this Continent." Encloses newspapers for Appleton, at Rouen, after TJ and Lafayette have read them; also sends papers and letters to Brissot de Warville to whom he asks TJ to introduce Jones. "The arret which is said to be passed for prohibiting the Introduction of Oils gives much Alarm here", because it will affect himself and many others; hopes some concession will be made to the American fishery or all "our Exertions will be to no purpose"; however, having no official information, does not fully credit the report. Encloses a prospectus published by a "professor of the french Language at our University" who is "tho't equal to what he has undertaken, will have the best Assistants, and only needs some Encouragement abroad."

RC (DLC); 2 p.; endorsed. Enclosures missing; the professor who issued the prospectus (evidently the first in a long series) was Joseph Nancrède (communication of Clifford K. Shipton to the Editors, 28 Apr. 1955).

To André Limozin

Sir Paris Jan. 2d. 1788.

You will receive herewith a letter from me [enclosing] a letter from the Comptroller general on the subject of our tobacco and an Arret on our other articles of commerce. I send a very large bundle of them by post, addressed to Mr. Jay, which I beg you to forward by the Juno, Capt. Jenkins, who is probably not yet sailed. They were not yet printed when my courier set off yesterday. I have the honor to be with much esteem Sir Your most obedt. humble servt., TH: JEFFERSON

PrC (DLC). TJ intended to enclose a copy of his circular to American agents of 31 Dec. 1787, which in turn enclosed a copy of Lambert to TJ, 29 Dec. 1787 and its enclosed arrêt, but he sent it separately (see Limozin to TJ, 4 and 5 Jan. 1788).

From John Rutledge, Jr.

London, 2 Jan. 1788. Acknowledges letters forwarded by TJ, reports that his father was to sail for Carolina on 3 Oct. 1787 and that he will write TJ from that place. Momentarily expects remittances from his father; does not lack money for current needs; this has been advanced by a gentleman in London, but is anxious to repay TJ money borrowed when he left Paris; expects to remain in London about six weeks longer and would deem it a privilege to fulfill any commissions TJ may have for him; sends compliments to Short and thanks TJ for his friendly attentions in Paris.

RC (DLC); 2 p.; endorsed.

To G. Boutelier, Père & Fils

Gentlemen Paris Jan. 3. 1788.

I have received from Thomas Newell a letter stating a cont[rac]t he has at Nantes for the insurance of a ship and cargo wherein he was interested. He desires me to write on the subject, to you in whom I find he has a great, and I dare say a well-merited confidence. If you find I can be useful in the matter, without going out of the line of propriety, I shall be glad to be informed of it from you. In the mean time I have charged Mr. Carnes, agent for the United States at Nantes, to have the honour of conferring with you on the subject, as it naturally falls within his province rather than mine to attend to the interests of individuals of the United States in his port, and to do from time to time what may be necessary for them. I will beg the favor of you therefore to confer with him whenever it may be material for the interests of Mr. Newell, and have the honour to be Gentlemen your most obedient & most humble servt., TH: JEFFERSON

PrC (DLC). The letter from THOMAS NEWELL is missing (see TJ to Newell, 3 Jan. 1788).

To Burrill Carnes

SIR   Paris Jan. 3. 1788.

The inclosed letter from Thomas Newell of Georgia, with the protest and affidavits accompanying it will make you acquainted with all I know of his case. As it is one of those arising in your port, and more at hand to be superintended by you, I take the liberty of recommending it to your care, as far as you find you can be useful to him, leaving the particular trouble and management with Messieurs Bouteiller pere and fils in whose hands he has entrusted them himself. I send you the protest and affidavits, as they may be wanting. They are the only papers he sent me. I am with much esteem Sir your most obedt. humble servt.,

TH: JEFFERSON

P.S. Be so good as to deliver the inclosed letter to Messrs. Bouteiller, having first read and sealed it.

PrC (DLC). Enclosures: (1) Newell to TJ, 27 Dec. 1787 (see TJ to Newell, 3 Jan. 1788) and the papers accompanying it. (2) TJ to Boutelier, 3 Jan. 1787.

To Lambert

SIR   Paris January 3. 1788.

I am honoured with your Excellency's letter of the 29th. of December, inclosing the arrêt on the commerce between France and the United states. I availed myself of the occasion of a vessel sailing this day from Havre for New York to forward it to Congress. They will receive with singular satisfaction this new testimony of his majesty's friendship for the United states, of his dispositions to promote their interest, and to strengthen the bands which connect the two nations. Permit me, Sir, to return you personally my sincere thanks for the great attention you have paid to this subject, for the sacrifices you have kindly made of a time so precious as yours, every moment of which is demanded, and is occupied by objects interesting to the happiness of millions; and to proffer you the homage of those sincere sentiments of attachment and respect with which I have the honor to be your Excellency's most obedient and most humble servant,

TH: JEFFERSON

PrC (DLC).

From André Limozin

Le Havre, 3 Jan. 1788. Acknowledges TJ's letter of 31 Dec.; will take care of all the articles delivered him and will recommend the same care to "Captn. Jenkins who is a very worthy good Quaker, born in Boston, and very much attached to the good of his Country"; Jenkins has delayed sailing until 11 Jan. Hopes Fraize has called on TJ on behalf of Capt. Thomas; otherwise Thomas "would be very unhappy to have given his Confidence to the agents of the Senegal Company and to the Governor of that place." Hopes the alliance between France, Spain and the two imperial powers has been effected; without it, fears war between France and England joined with Holland.

RC (MHi); 2 p.; endorsed.

To Eugène MacCarthy

SIR   Paris Jan. 3. 1788.

I have been later in acknoleging the receipt of your letter of the 16th. December, because Commodore Paul Jones being here it was proper to submit the claim to his information. I have now the honour to inform you that you may draw on me for the sum of seven hundred and thirty one livres three sous one denier expressing in your draught that it is for your share of prize money of the Bonhomme Richard, and at 30 days sight, because the funds are in Holland which are to answer it. Your draught in that form shall be honoured. I am with much respect Sir Your most obedient & most humble servant,   TH: JEFFERSON

PrC (DLC); at foot of text: "Monsr. MacCarthy Lt. au regiment de Walsh. l'isle d'Oleron."

To Thomas Newell

Sir   Paris Jan. 3. 1788.

I have duly received your letter of Dec. 27. inclosing the protest and two affidavits respecting the loss of your vessel. I have written to Messieurs Bouteiller, letting them know I shall be ready to render any service in the case I can with propriety, but recommending them to confer from time to time thereon with Mr. Carnes the American agent at Nantes, to whom I have also written desiring his assistance and attention to your case. It falls properly within his province and not mine, he is very worthy of your confidence, and it will be well for you that he confer with Messieurs Bouteiller, as they are interested as insurers. It will be best for you to correspond with Mr. Carnes on this subject. I have inclosed to him your letter, Protest, and Affidavits. I am Sir your very humble servant,   Th: Jefferson

PrC (DLC); at foot of text: "Mr. Thomas Newell at Savannah." YOUR LETTER OF DEC. 27 and its enclosures were sent to Carnes in a letter of this date, q.v., and have not been found. Newell's letter of the 27th must have been written when he was in England or France, perhaps as he was sailing for Savannah; this would explain both TJ's early response and the address given at the foot of the text.

To Nicolas & Jacob van Staphorst

Gentlemen   Paris Jan. 3. 1788

I received your favor of the 24th. of December after I had wr[itten] and sent off my letter of the 30th. to the houses of Willincks & Van Stap[horst] jointly. I return you my sincere thanks for your attention to [the] application for the current demands of the legation of the U.S. as well as for your generous offer to advance one moiety of that due to Fizeaux. You will perceive by my letter of the 30th. that I [wrote] finally to ask of the Commissioners of the loans to pay the interest of that loan only, for the last year, and to await further orders from the board of Treasury. In the mean time I hope Mr. Fizeaux and the persons interested in his loan will have no uneasiness on account of the delay of the orders for their reimbursement. Be pleased to accept assurances of the attachment and esteem with which I have the honour to be Gentlemen, Your most obedient & most humble servt.,   Th: Jefferson

PrC (DLC).

From André Limozin

Le Havre, 4 Jan. 1788. Received TJ's letter of the 2d covering a large parcel for Jay, but TJ forgot to enclose for Limozin the letter from Lambert and the arrêt. Bundle for Jay will be forwarded on the *Juno,* Captain Jenkins.

RC (MHi); endorsed.

From Hogguer, Grand & Cie.

MONSIEUR   Amsterdam le 5 Janvier 1788.

Nous avons l'honneur de vous prévenir que, malgré l'espoir dont vous nous avéz favorisés par vôtre lettre du 27. Xe., Messrs. Willinck & Van Staphorst se refusent encore à nous remettre les fonds des ƒ51,000, que nous avons à rembourser pour le congrés; déjà plusieurs Porteurs se sont presentés, et nous avons calmé leur mécontentement en les invitant à revenir sous une 15ne. de jours. Souffrés, Monsieur, que nous offrions encore une fois à vôtre considération la modicité de l'objet, et le préjudice qu'il va porter au crédit de l'Amérique, en lui otant pour jamais la confiance du Public, si le Congrés ne remplit pas aujourdhui les conditions que Ses Ministres ont contractés avec Lui. Veuillés donc encore Renouveler, Monsieur, vos Instances auprès de Messrs. Willinck & Van Staphorst pour prévenir une pareille Catastrophe.

Ces Messieurs nous ont cependant remis les ƒ2500, relatifs aux interets échus le 1er. de ce mois, et nous avons en consequence annullé le remboursement dont nous vous prevîmmes le 13. Xbre. sur M. Grand.

Permettés nous, Monsieur, de vous faire part du changement de notre Société par les Circulaires ci jointes.

Nous avons l'honneur d'être avec une parfaite Considération, Monsieur Vos trés humbles & trés Obeissans Serviteurs,

HOGGUER GRAND & CO.

RC (DLC); endorsed. Enclosures (DLC): Two printed circular letters, dated 1 Jan. 1788; the first signed by Hogguer, Grand & Cie. stating that the firm has been reorganized to include the firm of Fizeaux & Cie.; the second, signed by Fizeaux & Cie. stating that Fizeaux, the elder, wishing to retire, the firm will be dissolved and its interests transferred to Hogguer, Grand & Cie.

From André Limozin

Le Havre, 5 Jan. 1788. Acknowledges TJ's letter of 31 Dec. 1787 covering the "arret and the Letter from the Comptroller General. . . . I expected good many more favors than those granted."

RC (MHi); 2 p.; endorsed. See TJ to American agents, 31 Dec. 1787.

To Burrill Carnes

SIR   Paris Jan. 6. 1788.

The Continental book of accounts in possession of Mr. Ast contains I presume only the accounts settled by Mr. Barclay. That of Schweighauser & Dobreé is put into a separate channel, and moreover is not yet a settled account. I think therefore it need not incur the delay of going to Lorient, but should come on to me directly by the first proper conveiance. You will be so good as to inform me how to repay some small disbursements you have incurred relative to these arms. I am with much esteem Sir your most obedt. humble servt.,   TH: JEFFERSON

PrC (DLC).
This letter is apparently an answer to a letter from Carnes to TJ, 5 Jan. 1788, which is recorded in SJL Index but has not been found.

From Elizabeth Wayles Eppes

DEAR SIR   Eppington January. 6. 1788.

Your favor of July 28. gave me inexpressible joy, for my heart ached for the safety of my sweet Polly. Your encomiums on her manners, &c. delight me not a little, as I now hope I saw her with an impartial eye, tho clame not the least merit, for her natural disposition is truly amiable.

Your account of dear Patsy adds much to my happiness. The day is far distant I fear for the finishing you are so polite as to flatter me with. You have almost made me vain, tho' I recollect the part of the world you are in, a little flattery is fashionable, however be assured it will afford me very great pleasure to render the dear girls every service in my power. I have the pleasure to inform you your Sister Carr and her family are quite well. She informed me the other day of your Sister Nansy's marriage with Mr. Marks. We

[497]

all join in wishing you a perpetual round of health and happiness. Your affectionate friend,   E EPPES

RC (ViU); endorsed.

To William Macarty

SIR   Paris Jan. 6. 1788.

I took the liberty of writing to you in the month of June last to endeavor to get me a supply of china, like, or nearly like a sample you were so kind as to carry from here for me. You informed me afterwards there were no dishes of near that pattern to be had, and for plates they asked 36^{tt} the dozen. As there have been some arrivals from India since that time, perhaps those articles can now be had. If they can, and at prices which you think tolerably reasonable, I will beg the favor of you to procure them for me immediately and send them by the Diligence or other quick and safe conveiance, well packed. Your draught for the amount shall be duly honored. I state below the articles I have occasion for. As Mr. Loreilhé is generally absent from Lorient, I took the liberty the other day to inclose to you a copy of the new regulations for our commerce, wishing it to be made known in substance without being permitted to get into the public papers. I am with much esteem, Sir, your most obedt. humble servt.,   TH: JEFFERSON

PrC (DLC). Attached to this letter is a list of the china that corresponds in all details with that printed with TJ to Macarty, 20 June 1787.

From Quesnay de Beaurepaire

EXCELLENCE   paris le 6 janvier 1788

J'ai eu l'honneur de voir ce matin M. le Mis. de la Fayette et de raisonner avec lui de mon projet, de l'établissement de mon académie. J'ai vu que les Spectacles incérés dans le projet ne vous plaisoient pas; en conséquence Je ne balance pas a les Suprimer entièrement, et je n'en ferai plus mention sur mon plan. Je parlerai seulement de l'ostentation de la lotterie pour laquelle je me flatte que vous voudrez bien me donner votre aprobation (S'il étoit nécessaire de s'en servir pour quelques années pour assurer un heureux début aux artistes et profésseurs).

Avant tout je vais travailler avec le plus grand soin à la rédaction du plan et des règlemens à faire pour la police intérieure; je

[498]

sens que le succès de mon affaire, ainsi que le suffrage de Votre Excellence, tient à cela; et ce ne sera qu'avec ce plan et les règlemens bien rédigés avec le plus grand soin, que je me présenterai à Votre Excellence et à Messieurs de la Fayette et de la Luzerne, dont les Suffrages sont après le Vôtre les plus précieux et les plus faciles pour déterminer le public.

Je prie Votre Excellence de me continuer l'honneur de Sa protection et de me croire, avec le plus profond respect de Votre Excellence le très humble et très obeissant Serviteur,

QUESNAY DE BEAUREPAIRE

RC (ViWC); endorsed. Recorded in SJL Index as dated 5 Jan. 1788.

To Quesnay de Beaurepaire

SIR   Paris Jan. 6. 1788.

I have never expressed an objection to the part of your plan relative to the theatre. The utility of this in America is a great question on which I may be allowed to have an opinion, but it is not for me to decide on it, nor to object to the proposal of establishing one at Richmond. The only objection to your plan which I have ever made, is that contained in my letter to you. I feared it was too extensive for the poverty of the country. You remove the objection by observing it is to extend to several states. Whether professors itinerant from one state to another may succeed, I am unable to say, having never known an experiment of it. The fear that these professors may be disappointed in their expectations has determined me not to meddle in the business at all. Knowing how much people going to America over-rate the resources of living there, I have made a point never to encourage any person to go there, that I may not partake of the censure which may follow their disappointment. I beg you therefore not to alter your plan in any part of it on my account, but to permit me to pursue mine of being absolutely neutral. Monsieur de la Luzerne and the Marquis de la Fayette know too much of the country themselves to need any information from me, or any reference to my opinion; and the friendly dispositions which they have towards you will ensure you their good offices. Convinced of the honesty of your intentions and of your zeal, I wish you every possible success, and shall be really happy to see your plan answer your expectations. You have more courage than I have, to take upon yourself the risk of transplanting and contenting so many persons. I beg you to be assured of the sincerity of the esteem with which I have the honour to be Sir your most obedient & most humble servt.,

TH: JEFFERSON

PrC (DLC).

To Robert Shewell

SIR   Paris Jan. 6. 1788.

I have received your favor of Dec. 28. and had before desired Mr. Cathalan to get the favor of you to take the couffe of rough rice for Mr. Drayton at Charleston, and will beg your particular attention to have it kept in the coolest and dryest part of your ship, as it is sent for from Egypt on purpose to introduce the seed into Carolina. I hope you will arrive before the season for sowing comes on. I have nothing further to trouble you with, but the inclosed letter to be put into the post office in Charleston. With respect to the Algerines, I see no probability of peace with them. We have not money either to bribe or to fight them. Wishing you a safe and happy voiage, I am Sir Your very humble servt.,

TH: JEFFERSON

PrC (DLC). Enclosure: Evidently TJ to Thomas Newell, 3 Jan. 1788.

From Francis Coffyn

Dunkerque, 7 Jan. 1788. Acknowledges TJ's [circular] letter of 31 Dec. and its enclosure; has communicated information therein to merchants concerned with American trade and has taken precautions to prevent its being published.

RC (DLC); 2 p.; endorsed.

From Lur-Saluces

a Yquem ce 7 Janvier 1788

Gendre de M. D'Yquem, Monsieur, et possesseur de tous ses biens, J'ai l'honneur de repondre à la lettre que vous lui aviés adressée.

J'ai fait tirer et mettre en bouteilles, avec le plus grand soin, le vin que vous desirés. J'espere que vous en Seres Content. Toutes

[500]

les fois que vous pourés en avoir besoin, Je serai enchanté de recevoir directement vos demandes et Je ferai porter la plus grande attention pour que vous Soyes Servi avec toute la perfection possible. J'envoie à Mr. John Bondfeild ma lettre pour qu'elle vous soit adressée plus Surement.

Je vous prie de vouloir bien agreer l'assurance des Sentiments avec lesquels J'ai l'honneur d'etre tres parfaitement, Monsieur, Votre tres humble et très obeissant Serviteur,

LE CTE. DE LUR-SALUCES

RC (MHi); endorsed.

From William Stephens Smith

DEAR SIR   London Jany. 9th. 1788.

After sincerely wishing you many happy returns of the season, I take the liberty of introducing Mr. Thomas L. Shippen of Philadelphia. He has many interesting and not a few amiable lines of Character, and promises fair to make a shining and respectable Character. He has sometimes appeared to me rather exposed to step on slippery and dangerous ground and risk his usefulness in future life to the gratification of a little Vanity in the cultivation of the acquaintance of titled men and Ladies of birth; their names he soon gets and I am apprehensive will never forget, unless his friends check or disregard the conversations when leading to those points. However he pursues this line by the particular advice of his uncle Arthur. If he does not run wild after the tinsel of life, it will be fortunate for his Country and very pleasing to his friends. He now commences his Continental tour and I expect to see him on his return either a remarkable amiable improved Gentleman, or a sensible Coxcomb who has seen the world. Do my dear Sir, if you discover any points in which your advice and friendly observations may serve him, compliment him with them. I think he is capable of taking them as he ought. We begin to bustle and prepare for departure, which will be on the 25th. of February. I have been very sick, which will account for my silence. I sent by Mr. Littlepage your account. I hope he *delivered* the Letters. Remember me to Mr. Short and tell him that I really blush at being so much behind hand with him in our Correspondence. I send by Mr. S. his handkerchiefs and am with the greatest regard & respect Dr. Sir Your obliged Humble servt.,   W. S. SMITH

RC (MHi); endorsed. There is a letter from John Adams of this date recorded in SJL Index, no copy of which has been found; the above letter from Smith is not entered in SJL Index; TJ may, therefore, have mistakenly entered Smith's letter under the name of Adams.

THOMAS L. SHIPPEN, son of Dr. William Shippen, Jr., of Philadelphia and nephew of Arthur Lee (HIS UNCLE ARTHUR), spent some weeks in Paris where he seems to have cultivated THE ACQUAINTANCE OF TITLED MEN AND LADIES OF BIRTH but where he also came under TJ's influence. In a long, discursive, affectionate letter to his father written at various intervals in Feb. and March 1788 (and carried to America by Smith), young Shippen provided a graphic account of TJ as a host and counsellor to young Americans travelling on the continent. "That best of men Mr. Jefferson," he wrote on 14 Feb., "told me this Evening at Made. de Corny's where Mrs. Church lives, that he was very happy to serve his Countrymen here in the article of their letters, and that he charges always the postage to Congress &c so that I shall hope a parcel from you directed to him at least by every French Packet. . . . A great many people are kind to me here. Mr. Jefferson invites me to dine twice a week and I amuse myself vastly well in every way. Chastellux has treated me with the same neglect that he has shewn invariably to every American of my acquaintance." A week later (20 Feb.) Shippen drew a picture of a typical "Versailles day" for the American minister and of the manner in which TJ presented his young friend at Court: "Yesterday was the finest day I ever saw, the brightest sun, the clearest air, the most delightful temperature. I improved it by going with my best friend Mr. Jefferson to Versailles. He had made choice of that day to present me to the Court, and he introduced me as nephew to the President of Congress. The etiquette of Versailles requires that all persons who are presented at Court shall have some pretensions to that honor from rank, and it has established, that in the case of Republics where there are no *hereditary distinctions*, those of *office* shall be substituted. Those therefore who have held high offices in Republics, or they who are nearly related to them, and those only are allowed to make

their bow to the French Court. It seems to me a most unnecessary and absurd regulation, as a man who possesses the confidence of his Country in a sufficient degree to be entrusted with her affairs abroad, must be supposed adequate to the task of making choice of persons fit to be presented at the Court where he resides. It would not I think be leaving a great deal too much to his discretion.   The ceremony is rather tedious, but carries through the whole of it so much of novelty to a stranger, and so much of Oriental splendor and magnificence, that it is certainly well worth seeing once. We arrived at Versailles at ½ past ten and were not done bowing until near 2. The carriage drove up to the Count de Montmorin's (successor to Count de Vergennes in the department of *foreign affairs*,) where in a large saloon ornamented with pictures larger than life of the Royal family, stood the introductor and his secretary and several members of the Diplomatic Corps. To them I was first introduced, and some of them (particularly the Pope's Nuncio) asked me some questions about my Country which however served to shew rather a desire to be attentive to me, than to be informed of what they did not know already. The Russian Ambassador was also very polite, and the Envoy of the Duke of Wirtemberg quite oppressive in his civilities. We had been there an hour when the Count de M. having ended a conference with the Imperial Ambassador came into our Hall and Mr. Jefferson introduced me to him. He invited me to dinner and took Monseigneux le Nonce with him into his audience chamber. He would have preceded the Imperial Ambassador had he been there at the same time. At 12 we left the Count M.'s and crossed the Court to the Salle des Ambassadeurs where coffee, chocolate and wine were offered to our acceptance. After waiting there long enough to read the papers of the day, we were taken successively into the apartments of the King Queen the Princess Victoire and Adelaide (the King's Aunts,) Monsieur, the Count d'Artois, Madame and the Countess d'Artois and the Princess Elizabeth the King's sister and the Arch Bishop or Ministre Principal of France. These personages have all separate households and distinct portions of the Palace allotted to them, and you may form some judgment of the manner in which they support their rank when you know that between them they expend 36,000,000 of livres a year without including any of the contingent expences of Ministers, their tables &c. All the *departments of State* have each of them a suite of rooms in the Palace. The situation of this superb building is worthy of its grandeur, and both well suited to the Court of a great Nation. Lewis the 14th. seems in this as in all his other works to have consulted nothing but the grandeur and glory which ought to shroud his person and adorn his reign. He did not once consider when he expended here 50,000,000 of Louis d'Or, how many thousands of his subjects were doomed to want and wretchedness, nor did he discover until exhausted nature had left him on his death bed, that the greatest glory of a Monarch consists in the happiness of his people. In his last moments he is said to have enjoined the dauphin to protect and comfort his people, and to do what he had never been able to do himself, in making them happy. The fact was that he had never made that his object, until it was in his power no longer to pursue it. The business of bowing being over, which any but a Scotchman would have been tired of, I left Mr. Jefferson at the C. de M. and went in search of your old pupil Walker who has retired to Versailles to study the French. I found him in decent apartments and in a kind family. We walked out together chapeau à la main and visited the unrivalled gardens of this enchanting paradise—What walks! What groves! What water works! But you have seen them all— and I must leave it to your memory to recal them to your imagination. Walker was pleased with my attention but mortified that we were to part so soon; I promised him to make a longer visit soon, and returned to Count M.'s at 3 oclock. Here I found about 30 long and hungry faces venting their malignity and ill nature in sour looks at each other, and with this agreable pastime we amused ourselves a quarter of an hour while the cloth was laying above stairs, and they were preparing the dinner. At the end of that time we went up stairs and passed thro the dinner room into that where Made. de Montmorin receives her company and only waited there long enough for the ambassadors to pay their respects to the ladies before dinner was announced. Such a general relaxation of muscles

I had never seen—for besides the long time they had been in waiting and the late hour of the day there is something in the air of Versailles which begets ungovernable appetites. They were all hungry and appeared equally rejoiced at the very splendid and *plentiful* repast which the Count's hospitality had provided. It was indeed a superb feast. After dinner I was introduced very formally with all my titles (which were by 3 out of 4 supposed hereditary) to Mde. La Comtesse and her 2 daughters both of whom are Comtesses also. We drank coffee and a very amiable and distinguished Chevalier who has a place at Court but whose name I do not know, made up to me and held me in an interesting conversation great part of which was in the hearing of the ladies until Mr. Jefferson beckoned to me that it was time to part. Upon the whole, I was well pleased with the day, and considering that I had not an acquaintance but Mr. J. when I went received very uncommon marks of politeness and attention.   The night was as fine as the day and we enjoyed our ride thro' it to Paris most amazingly. Mr. J. was communicative confidential and instructive beyond any thing I had ever experienced and left me at my Hotel impressed with every sentiment of respect admiration and gratitude. It has not been with less pleasure than that which I enjoyed in the transactions of this day that I have in this unreserved manner recounted them to you and I cannot close my relation without making the observations which have since as well as at the time occurred to me. When we were introduced to the King, it was after waiting 5 minutes in his antichamber into which we were brought by his direction being told that he was ready to receive us. How did he do it? He was just pulling on his coat, a servant was tying his hair in which there was no powder, while one of his attendants was arranging his sword belt, and when the file of ambassadors Envoys Ministers &c. in full dress, representatives of monarchs mighty as himself and of Republics more great because more virtuous, were prostrating themselves before him emulous of each other in demonstrating their obsequious adulation, he hitched on his sword and hobbled from one side of the room to the other, spoke 3 words to a few of the ambassadors and 2 to a German Prince who was presented with me, and left the room. I revolted at the insufferable

[503]

arrogance of the King but I was more mortified at the suppleness and base complaisance of his attendants. I rejoiced that I was not a citizen of such a government, but that I belonged to a Country, and that she would always have a right to my services, where the people respect sincerity, and acknowledge no other tyranny than that of Honor.

I observed that although Mr. Jefferson was the plainest man in the room, and the most destitute of ribbands crosses and other insignia of rank that he was most courted and most attended to (even by the Courtiers themselves) of the whole Diplomatic corps—The king is bound up by etiquette to distribute his monosyllables among those of *Ambassadorial* rank—consequently he was an exception. This proved to me that substantial sense, extensive acquirements and unimpeached integrity command even among those who cannot boast of their possession, respect veneration and applause, and that they are preferred by all to empty ornament and unmeaning grandeur, when they give themselves time to weigh the intrinsic properties of each, and coolly to form the result. I observed too in the midst of all their splendor an uneasiness and ennui in their faces which did not bespeak content or happines: and this conspired with every thing I had seen before to convince me that *a certain degree of equality* is essential to human bliss. Happy above all Countries is our Country where *that equality* is found, without destroying the necessary subordination."—TJ and Lafayette apparently cooperated in their attentions to young Americans as they did in their efforts in behalf of Franco-American trade relations, and in consequence young Shippen had the good fortune to receive from Lafayette "a ticket for the French Academy which was holding a séance publique for the reception of a new member." The new member was Henri Cardin d'Aguesseau, councillor of state, descendant of Louis XV's famous Chancellor, and relative of Madame de Lafayette, and he placed young Shippen in his *tribune* between his wife and sister. Shippen thought the spectacle a brilliant display of fashion, cultivated society, and eloquence; and

he said that when Beauzée responded to the address of the *récipiendaire* and "in summing up his virtues called him worthy of the delightful spouse whose charms would be more than a sufficient reward for the most transcendant merit," that "dear creature put 3 of her fingers into her mouth and bit them to conceal her confusion and leaned upon her father who sat behind her. How inimitable was the scene!" There followed the feast of Longchamp, which Shippen enjoyed from the carriage of "A young Nabob from the East who came here from London some weeks ago with the recommendations of Dr. Price and whose acquaintance I made at Mr. Jefferson's." Shippen concluded his long letter with a tribute to TJ that evidently proceeded from more than mere gratitude: "Mr. Jefferson is in my opinion without exception the wisest and most amiable man I have seen in Europe. He has had the goodness to favor me upon many occasions with his advice. He wishes me very much to travel thro' Italy, and insists upon it that I must travel alone, and with my own horses. From the first, he says I shall have the best opportunity of making remarks and acquiring information which will be useful to me hereafter, that I shall be entirely free from interruption distraction &c and that the desagrement of travelling without a companion will become in 3 days habitual and agreable. From the second he promises me the most œconomical mode of travelling. He thinks that by purchasing 2 horses and a carriage here, I may travel by short days journeys thro' Europe with very little additional expence and that at the end of my journey I may sell them again for nearly their original cost. . . . It is my design to go to Holland in May, and Rutledge proposes to accompany me. . . ." He concluded: "If you will write a letter of thanks to Mr. Jefferson I will thank you. He has supplied to me the want of you better than I thought it could have been supplied, and if any one but yourself were the father, the son could not lose by the substitution" (Thomas Lee Shippen to William Shippen, 14. Feb.—26 Mch. 1788; DLC: Shippen Family Papers).

From Brailsford & Morris

Charleston, 10 Jan. 1788. Hope TJ has received their letter of 31 Oct. 1787 and its enclosures from John and Edward Rutledge and Ralph Izard; in accordance with that letter, have shipped "1000 Tierces" of rice to L'Orient on the *Henrietta*, Capt. Wickes, addressed to Bérard & Cie., of which 250 bbls. were shipped for a friend in Philadelphia and not under their direction. As Bérard & Cie. are under no obligation to accept the shipper's drafts, and as it "would be a cruel Mortification" to have their signature "disgraced by the return of a Bill," they have desired the holders of their drafts to apply to Le Couteulx & Cie. "*in case of need*" and have asked Messrs. Bérard to deliver to that house the whole cargo to indemnify them, if Bérard & Cie. will not accept the drafts. Since Bérard & Cie. have mentioned to TJ their readiness to accept up to 15 livres per hundred, Brailsford & Morris will draw for no more than 12 livres, although the rice cost them 13s. per hundred. Mr. Bee and Mr. Rutledge have made shipments on the same vessel. Should Le Couteulx & Cie. ask about them, hope TJ will furnish the information desired.

RC (DLC); 2 p.; endorsed.

From Le Roy

MONSIEUR   aux Galeries du Louvre ce 10 Janvier 1788

Permettez vous que J'aye L'honneur de vous faire remettre cette lettre pour vous prier de la faire passer à M. Franklin par la premiere Occasion favorable. Je vous en Serai très obligé. C'est une lettre de M. De Buffon et par laquelle ce grand Ecrivain remercie votre Illustre compatriote de La lettre pleine de Sentiment et d'intérêt qu'il lui a écrite il y a quelque tems Sur la maladie fâcheuse dont ils Sont attaqués l'un et L'autre. C'est une chose vraiment touchante que ce commerce de Sensibilité à travers les Mers entre deux Vieillards si célèbres, et d'un mérite aussi rare.

M. Paine, Monsieur, m'avoit fait espérer qu'il m'avertiroit Lorsque des Dames Virtuoses iroient chez vous pour Jouïr de L'instrument nouveau et curieux que vous avez, mais Je crains que son départ pour L'Angleterre ne s'y oppose. Quoiqu'il en Soit j'aurai au premier moment L'honneur de vous aller voir et de vous renouveller Les assurances des Sentimens de l'attachement distingué avec Lequel J'ai L'honneur d'être Monsieur Votre très humble et très obéïssant Serviteur,   LE ROY

RC (ViWC); endorsed. Enclosure: Buffon to Franklin, 1 Jan. [1788] (PPAP; dated 1 Jan. 1787 in *Cal. Franklin Papers*, III, 331).

[505]

From André Limozin

Le Havre, 10 Jan. 1788. Has had no letter from TJ since his two former letters; informs TJ that Captain Thomas has received permission from the Controller General to unload his cargo at Le Havre; that Captain Jenkins will sail the next day; encloses a copy of a letter just received and asks TJ's advice on the scheme proposed therein.

RC (MHi); 2 p.; endorsed, in part: "relative to Capt. Thomas's aff." Enclosure (MHi): Copy of a letter from Quesnay de Beaurepaire, dated "Paris le 7 Janvier 1787" [i.e., 1788], expressing his desire to charter "un batiment de 500 Tonneaux portant, ou etant susceptible de monter 12 Canons de 6. et de 12 pour faire voile vers le mois de may, pour la riviere de James en Virginie, afin d'y transporter toutes les choses necessaires a cet etablissement, et beaucoup d'autres marchandises appartenant a divers negocians de Paris; ainsi que quinze a vingt passagers"; and asking whether Limozin or some other merchant of Le Havre would be able to procure a vessel and, if so, what it would cost to charter her.

From Willink & Van Staphorst

Amsterdam, 10 Jan. 1788. Acknowledge TJ's letter of 30 and 31 Dec. 1787; advise that they have paid Fizeaux & Cie. the interest due on their loan to the United States and have asked them to assure the creditors that the principal of that loan is secure; have honored TJ's draft for 2750 florins "for the Current Expence of the Legation to the Court of France."

RC (DLC); 2 p.; endorsed. TJ letter of 31 Dec. 1787 not found.

From André Limozin

Le Havre, 11 Jan. 1788. Encloses two bills of lading signed by Charles Jenkins, master of the *Juno*, the first for three boxes of books and one small parcel, addressed to James Madison, the charges for which, 42.^{tt}3.3., have been annexed and also entered in TJ's account; the second bill of lading covered the "Case for Col. Hamilton."

RC (MHi); 2 p.; addressed by a clerk; postmarked; endorsed. Enclosures: (1) Bill of lading for books and parcel (MHi). (2) Same for trunk for Alexander Hamilton (not found; see TJ to Limozin, 31 Dec. 1787).

To John Adams

DEAR SIR   Paris Jan. 13. 1788.

I informed you in my letter of the 31st. of December of the measures I had taken relative to the reimbursement of the 51,000

[506]

gelders to Fizeaux & co. to wit, that I had asked the Willincks and Van Staphorsts to pay the interest, and written to the board of treasury for their orders as to the principal. I inclose you a letter just received from Fizeaux & Co. now Hugguer, Grand & Co. by which you will perceive that they have recieved the interest, but that the creditors will not consent to delay the reimbursement of their capital. I inclose you a copy also of what I now write to the Willincks & Van Staphorsts, and will beg of you to give or refuse your sanction, as you think best, but in a letter sent directly to them, because I find by their letters to Mr. Jac. Van Staphorst, they will not be contented with the indirect authorisation of your former letter to me. Perhaps in any other case, the creditors would have been quieted. But Fizeaux is retired from business and chuses to wind up all his affairs. Probably therefore he has not endeavoured to quiet the creditors; perhaps he may consider their clamours as an useful engine to hasten his extrication from this business. Be that as it may, their clamours, should they be raised, may do us great injury. But of this you are the best judge. I am with great and sincere esteem, Dear Sir, your most obedient & most humble servant, TH: JEFFERSON

RC (MHi: AMT); endorsed. PrC (DLC). Enclosures: Copies of (1) Hogguer, Grand & Cie. to TJ, 5 Jan. 1788. (2) TJ to Willink & Van Staphorst, 13 Jan. 1788. (3) TJ to Hogguer, Grand & Cie., 13 Jan. 1788.

From Mary Barclay

St. Germain-en-Laye, 13 Jan. 1788. Being disappointed in her expectation of remittances, does not hesitate to make use of the liberty TJ has offered of applying to him on such occasions; will draw on him in about 10 days for 1,200,^{lt} at sight, if agreeable; asks when the next packet will sail for America; wishes to send TJ a letter to be forwarded.

RC (MHi); 2 p.; endorsed.

To William Drayton

SIR   Paris Jan. 13. 1788.

By capt. Shewell, who is sailing about this time from Marseilles for Charleston I directed to be forwarded to you one of two couffes of rough rice which I had had brought from Egypt. The other came on to me here, and will be carried from Havre to New York addressed to you, to the care of the delegates of S. Carolina in Congress. I wish both may arrive in time for the approaching seed time, and that the trials with this, and the Piedmont rice may furnish new advantages to your agriculture. I have considerable hopes of receiving some dry rice from Cochin-china, the young prince of that country, lately gone from hence, having undertaken that it shall come to me. But it will be some time first. These are all but experiments; the precept however is wise which directs us to 'try all things, and hold fast that which is good.'

Your letter of May 22. 87. informs me that mine of May 6. 1786. had never got to hand. I now have the honour to inclose you a copy of it, of no other consequence than to shew you that I was incapable of so inexcusable an inattention, as the miscarriage of that letter exposed me to the charge of in your mind. I shall take opportunities of forwarding to you more of the seed of the Spanish St. foin, some of which I have received directly from Maltha. I have the honour to be with sentiments of the most perfect esteem and respect, Sir, your most obedt. & most humble servt.,

TH: JEFFERSON

PrC (DLC). Enclosure: Copy of TJ to Drayton, 6 May 1786, q.v.

To Hogguer, Grand & Cie.

GENTLEMEN   Paris Jan. 13. 1788.

In my letter of Dec. 30 to Messrs. H. Fizeaux & co. I informed them that I would write to the treasury board for orders relative to the reimbursement of the 51,000 gelders. I did so immediately. I now receive your favor of the 5th. instant informing me the creditors insist on immediate paiment. I have no means in my power but to refer it again to the discretion and situation of Messrs. Willincks & Van Staphorsts to know whether they will pay this sum. If they will, I write to them by this post to give them all the authority for this purpose which I can give. I write at the same time to Mr. Adams, praying him to say, in a letter addressed to them directly, what he shall think proper on the occasion. I wish they may find themselves in a situation to make the paiment: if they do not, I have no other resource but that of the Treasury board, to whom I have already written. You will be so good as to call on Messieurs Willincks & Van Staphorsts on this subject, after such an interval of time as may be requisite for the passage of my letter to Mr. Adams at London, and of his from thence to Amsterdam. I have the honor to be Gentlemen your most obedient & most humble servt., TH: JEFFERSON

PrC (DLC). Tr (MHi: AMT); in the hand of William Short.

To André Limozin

SIR   Paris Jan. 13. 1788.

By the Carrosse which goes from hence to Havre I have forwarded a package of rough rice addressed to you. I am in hopes it may arrive in time to go with the inclosed letter by the Juno, capt. Jenkins. I will beg the favour of you to put on it this address 'For Mr. William Drayton, Charleston: to the care of the Delegates of S. Carolina in Congress,' and to pay the freight for me. Should Capt. Jenkins be gone, be so good as to send it by any other vessel going to New York or Charleston, and to no other port whatever. I have had this rice brought from Egypt, to furnish S. Carolina with a species of that grain which it does not yet possess. I wish the captain of the vessel therefore would so place it as that it may not be exposed either to heat or moisture, which would destroy it's vegetative power. I have the honour to be with great esteem Sir your most obedient & most humble servant,

TH: JEFFERSON

PrC (DLC). Enclosure: TJ to South Carolina Delegates in Congress, same date, following.

To the South Carolina Delegates in Congress

GENTLEMEN   Paris Jan. 13. 1788.

In hopes that a Couffe of rough rice which I have just received from Egypt may reach Havre in time to go by the Juno, capt. Jenkins, I have sent it off for that port. It is addressed to Mr. Drayton at Charleston, and I take the liberty of recommending it to your care, to be forwarded so as that it may arrive in time for the season of sowing, if possible. I have the honor to be with sentiments of the most perfect respect, Gentlemen, Your most obedient & most humble servt.,   TH: JEFFERSON

PrC (DLC).

From Jacob van Staphorst

Paris, 13 Jan. 1788. A letter from his brother states that there is hope of settling shortly with Fizeaux & Cie. to TJ's satisfaction; no advice has been received from Mr. Adams; suggests that TJ write to both houses in accordance with conversation of yesterday. Mr. Ingraham's vessel, the *Amsterdam*, which sailed from Philadelphia in December, arrived in the Texel, but letters had not been brought up when his brother wrote.

RC (DLC); 1 p.

To Willink & Van Staphorst

GENTLEMEN   Paris Jan. 13. 1788.

In my letter of Dec. 30. I had the honour to inform you that in consequence of yours to me of the 24th. I would ask of you to pay the interest on the 51,000 gelders for the last year, and that I would write to the Treasury board to take their own measures for reimbursing the capital. I wrote to them accordingly. I at the same time desired Messrs. Fizeaux & Co. to call on you for the interest and to quiet the creditors with that till the orders of the treasury board can be received. They acknoleged the receipt of the interest from you: but add that the creditors will not be content to wait at all for their principal, and have allowed them fifteen days only for it's reimbursement. I can but refer the matter back to you, and say that if, on a view of their inquietude, as well as of all other circumstances, you should think it expedient to reimburse the principal to Fizeaux & Co., now Hugguer, Grand & Co., this present letter shall convey to you all the authority for so doing which may depend on me. I write this day to Mr. Adams to say to you on the same subject whatever he shall think proper. Tho' anxious that the credit of the U.S. may not suffer by this failure, nor the progress of your present loan be stopped by it, I can only venture to rest the reimbursement on your own discretion and your dispositions to serve the interests of the United states. I have the honour to be gentlemen your most obedient humble servant,   TH: JEFFERSON

PrC (DLC).

[510]

From William Macarty

SIR   Lorient 14 January 1788

I have communicated the Arret and Letter you did me the Honor to send me, to the Merchants Interested in the American Trade.

We fear they will not answer the Intention of Government. The experience we have had in the partial Execution of the Decision of the 24 May 86 will make Speculators very cautious in future.

The confidence that was placed in that regulation lead Numbers into the Shipping of Tobacco for France; Several have their Tobacco on hand here at present, to the great detriment of the Shippers in America and the Merchants here, The Farmers General having refused to purchase for Eight months past. I have none myself, but I feel for others who suffer.

The delays and Difficulties which I met with in 86 in the reception of my Tobacco, and the difference in the price, from what I thought I had a right to expect in consequence of the favour granted by Government, have ruin'd me, and will no doubt prevent my endeavours to encrease the Commercial Connections, having their usual effect.

The opposition every Commercial regulation meets with, from the Farmers General and their officers, will unavoidably distroy all confidence in them, so long as they have it in their power to Intrepret the Laws as their Interest may dictate, or subject the Merchant to a Litigeous contestation, which neither his time or inclination will permit him to pursue.

It is certain, you, and every person that were consulted on that subject, understood and expected that the Trade in General were to enjoy every advantage that Mr. Morris had by his contract. It is certain Mr. Morris's Tobacco has been paid at the rate of 36^{tt} ℔ Ct. and it is as certain that the Farmers General have not paid us here more than $32^{tt}10$ ℔ Ct. on an Average from the manner they Insisted on classing the quality of our Tobacco, notwithstanding the quality of our Cargo's were always far Superior to any deliver'd by Mr. Morris's Agents, by which we are deprived of at least $2.^{tt}$ ℔ Ct. besides the 30s ℔ Ct. allowed on the Tobacco not deliver'd in the Ports where there is manufactures. We have a right, in Justice to our friends to claim 2^{tt} on every 100 wt. of Tobacco that we have deliver'd to the Farmers General Since that decision, and if we do not obtain it, we are deprived of the advantages Intended, and we have been lead into an Error extremely detrimental to us and our friends.

I fear notwithstanding the Good Intention of the Minister, that, the Great Influence the Farmers General have, will prevent Justice being obtain'd. I know they pretend that they have paid the Tobacco agreable to its quality, at the prices fix'd by the Decision but I am convinced they will not have the candor to acknowledge that their officer here constantly refused to receive any as first quality, except a few hhds. in a cargo, for forms sake notwithstanding we have deliver'd them Several Cargos directly from James River.

These are facts, known to every one here which I take the Liberty to communicate to you and hope they may be of some service to others, if not to me. The conduct of the Farmers General or their officer here has been extriordinary and trifling from the begining, and of a nature to disgust the Americans from coming to this Port, if not to other's.

I am with great Respect Your most Humble and Obedient Servant, WM. MACARTY

RC (DLC); endorsed.

From William Macarty

SIR   Lorient 14 January 1788.

I am honor'd with your Letter of the 6. Inst. and in consequence have procured some of the china you desire which shall be sent on imediately. I dont find any that will answer among the new china, and it is impossible to procure the dishes or compotiers. There is Some dishes that would answer but the owner will not seperate the small dishes from the large ones. They are in Setts of five dishes at 21.^{tt} 3 Sizes would answer your dementions.

I wish it may be possible to recover some additional prize of the Farmers General. It would be of great Service to me, and enable me to extricate myself from the difficulties I Labour under for Some time past.

I am with great Respect Your most obedt Servt.,

WM. MACARTY

RC (DLC).

[512]

From Wilt, Delmestre & Cie.

MONSIEUR   L'Orient 14 Janvier 1788.

La Stagnation générale du Commerce de L'amerique septentrion-
nalle, plusieurs pertes essuyées consécutivement dans le cours de
l'an dernier, et principallement la détention continuelle de nos fonds
en cette partie du monde, depuis la paix, nous ont obligés à suspendre nos payments le 1er. Octobre dernier. Nous nous sommes
occupés depuis à prouver à nos créanciers d'Europe la vérité de
nos malheurs et lorsqu'ils ont été convaincus de leur cause, Ils se
sont réunis pour nous procurer les moyens de continuer nos traveaux, et en conséquence nous ont fait une remise de 68 pour cent
sur ce que nous devons en Europe, et n'exigent de ce que nous avons
en Amérique que ce qui poura nous revenir après avoir payé en
entier tous nos créanciers dans cette partie du monde; les ayant
assurés que la loi de l'américque portait que partout où nos créanciers de ce continent sauraient mettre des arrêts, Ils seraient payés
en entier, s'il y avait de quoi, indépendament des autres créanciers
d'Europe. Mais comme quelquns de nos créanciers d'amérique
peuvent ne pas savoir où mettre des arrêts dans leur pays, et pourai-
ent venir en Europe réclamer ce que nous leur devons, notre Conseil
et nos créanciers d'Europe sont d'avis que nous fassions homologuer
le traitté que nous avons fait avec ces derniers. En conséquence
nous en avons envoyé une copie à notre avocat à Rennes, qui nous
a répondu que, pour parvenir à obtenir cette homologation suivant
nos désirs, qu'il faudrait envoyer à la Cour La Loix d'Amérique
qui fonde le privilège des *créanciers amériquains sur les sommes
qu'ils arrêtent parcequ'ils seraient regardés comme privilegiers.*
C'est pourquoi, Monsieur, Nous prenons la liberté de vous faire
part de toutes ces choses, et vous suplions de nous envoyer un
certificat signé de vous (étant le seul en France qui puissiez nous
rendre ce service) qui constate cette loi.

Nous vous en aurons une parfaite reconnaissance, et avons L'honneur d'être, avec un profond respect, Monsieur. Vos trés Humbles
& obeissants Serviteurs,   WILT DELMESTRE & CO

P:S: En france, lorsqu'un Negociant failli a déposé, Aucun de
ses Créanciers n'a de privilège particulier sur les arrêts qu'il fait
mettre sur ce qui appartient à son Débiteur, La somme arrêté rentre
à la masse. Voudriez vous ajouter à votre complaisance, de nous
dire si en amerique la Loix est différente, c'est à dire si, en faisant

[513]

une masse de nos Créanciers en amérique, et déléguant au général tout ce que nous y avons, les fonds rentrants ne doivent pas être répartis à mesure, au prorata, ou si chacun doit s'y faire payer par ses propres arrêts.

Notre Intention, en tout ceci, serait de sattisfaire en même tems tous nos créanciers en amérique, et le plustot possible, pour remplir la 6e. close de notre traitté cy Joint, savoir de remettre à nos créanciers d'Europe, dans l'espace de 18 mois une acte de renonciation de la part de nos créanciers d'Amérique sur ce que nous leur devions avant notre faillitte, et surtout afin de pouvoir continuer nos traveaux sans interruption. LES DITS

RC (DLC); endorsed. Enclosure (DLC): Statement of bankruptcy and articles of agreement between Wilt, Delmestre & Cie. and their European creditors on a basis for settlement of their accounts, dated 1 Oct. 1787.

From John Bondfield

SIR   Bordeaux 15 Jany 1788

Since mine of the 28 nov. I am honor'd with your favors of the 18 and 31 Decr., the first covering a Letter to M. D'Yquem, that estate at present belongs to the Comte de Lur his son in Law to whom I inclosd your Letter, to which you have inclosed his answer.

I have receivd from him five Cases of his wine and have shipt them on board the Actif for Rouen. They goe addrest to the care of Mr. Elie Lefevre with orders to forward them to you so soon as at hand, it is preferable to send bottled wine by water Carriage which is equaly expeditious, less subject to breakage and considerable less charge. I shall pay the amount to Le Comte when he shall apply.

The Vin de frontignan which you Commissiond Mons. Lambert to forward is not yet come to hand.

By your favor of the 31 Xbre. I recevd the arret du Conseil of the 29 Xbre. and Monsr. Lambert's Letter both which I communicate as occasion offers to all interested in Trade with the United States.

The stocks of Tobacco imported by private Trade is bought up in quantitys of from 50 to 100 hhds. for Holland, Ireland, Hamburg and the Baltic. We shall be soon with little of that article on hand and the importers will be masters to obtain a good price for their remaining stock. This port has had a greater proportion than

John Adams. Portrait by Mather Brown, 1788. (See p. xxxvii.)

Birthday illuminations for the Prince of Orange. (See p. xxxvii.)

any other in Europe of Tobacco, and greater than the demand, which naturaly caused a momentary stagnation. If in Europe the quantity dont exceed the consumption, like to electrical matter the places in want will draw from them that have the abundant, and establish the Equilibre.

Ministry appears attentif to your representation and desireous to remove every difficulty that opposes the mutual intercourse. Time alone will bring about the exchange, long habits are difficult to remove by introduction of others unless very striking advantages result. The Language is an irremovable barier to a general Correspondence. The advantages will Center with a few, who will engross the Trade. With due respect I have the honor to be Sir Your most Obedient Humble Servant, JOHN BONDFIELD

RC (DLC); addressed and endorsed. Enclosure: Lur-Saluces to TJ, 7 Jan. 1788, q.v. Bondfield may also have enclosed the bill of lading signed by Captain A. Doudet of *L'Actif* for "Cinq Caisses de vin de Cinquante Bouteilles" consigned to TJ and an *acquit* from Doudet for duty and carriage costs; these are dated 16 and 18 Jan. 1788 and are in DLC: TJ Papers, 38: 6504-5.

From Burrill Carnes

SIR   Nantes 15th Jany. 1788

In answer to the honor of your Letters 31st. Ultimo 3d and 6th Insts., I immediately communicated to the Merchants of this City the Letter and arret relative to American Commerce which appears very favorable, and by some French Merchants, that part which respects the East Indies they think too much so for their Interest, supposing that what is meant by the same priviledges as are allow'd the subjects of France, are the same as are granted the East India Company, there being no freedom allowed any other subjects, except it be to the Islands of France and Bourbon. Mr. Adine, Directeur du Bureau de la ferme in this City, appears rather doubtful respecting the 8th pr. Cent duty, whether it is the eigth part of a Hundred or the eigth of one pr. Cent. Would therefore trouble you Sir to favor me with a line on this subject, and could wish at same time to Know whether by the right of storing for Six months is not meant six months from the arrival of the Goods. I have waited upon Messrs. Bouteiller respecting Captn. Newel's business. It is hoped the proofs given by him may yet prevent a law suit. At any rate Sir nothing shall be wanting on my part to promote his Interest.

Respecting the Accounts with Messrs. Schweighauser and

[515]

Dobrée, I am truely sorry Sir the examination has proved so tedious, but having the whole to look over Article by Article, I hope will be some apology for so great a delay. Not being able to find a private conveyance I have ventured to send them by the Dilligence that left town last Evening, and hope they will come safe to hand. I have only to observe to you Sir that in every particular respecting the exactitude of the charges, compared with the original Vouchers, it does not appear that any reproach can be made Messrs. Schweighauser and Dobrée in any one instance. I have the honor to be most respectfully Sir Your most Obedient & very Humble Servant,

BURRILL CARNES

P.S. It is impossible Sir at present to put you in the way of reimbursing the triffle I have expended for the Arms &c. but will do it whenever occasion offers.

RC (DLC); endorsed.

From De Grasse

MONSIEUR   Paris Le 15 Janvier 1788.

J'ai l'honneur de vous faire part de la perte que je viens de faire du Cte. de Grasse mon père, qui est mort la nuit dernière.

Les honneurs dont les etats-unis d'amérique l'ont Comblés me Seront aussi précieux qu'ils l'étoient à lui-même, et ce Sera pour moi une consolation, Si vous voulez bien prendre part à ma douleur extrême.

Je suis avec Respect Monsieur Votre trés humble et trés Obeissant Serviteur,   LE CTE DE GRASSE

RC (DLC); endorsed.

From Parent

Beaune, 16 Jan. 1788. Has purchased two quarter-casks of white wine and one of red Volnay; has bottled and packed them to send to TJ but fears they cannot be transported without breakage in the present cold weather; will send them as soon as it is warm enough.

RC (MHi); 2 p.; in French; endorsed.

[516]

From William Stephens Smith

DEAR SIR   London Jany. 16th. 1788

I have received yours of the 31st. of Decr. ulto. and cannot express my astonishment sufficiently strong at the perusal of the first sentence relative to Mr. Littlepage's not having delivered my Letter of the 3d. of Decr. I waited upon him with it, and when I gave it him, begged he would be particularly carefull of it as it contained our accounts. He promised, and put it into a small box of papers where he said it would be particularly safe and that immediately on his arrival he would present it to you. I was informed before I saw him that he was an inquisitive *curious promising* young Gentleman and I am now convinced of it. I wish however he would learn to perform.

I enclose you the impressed Copies of the letter and account. As I have not time to copy the former, I must beg you to return it by the first opportunity and in the latter permit me to correct an error viz. to charge the amount of the small Copying press £5.5.0 and to add two other small charges for Mr. Short viz. 2 pair of shoes sent by Trumbull £0.17.0 and 6 handkerchiefs by Shippen £1.1.0 total amount of additions £7.3.0. Of course the account as I have stated it, leaves a ballance in my favor of £3.4.5. I am apprehensive I have not calculated the two last articles with which I have credited you, right, as they were stated in livres. However, this and all others I submit to your correction and upon your own statement after adding the amount of my cloak, I should be happy to know the ballance due to you.

I have again attacked Mr. Adams on the subject of the picture and he has promised if Mr. Trumbull on his return will take it, he will send it to you and I will take charge of it when finished if necessary. I will also duly inform you of the address of your taylor and shoemaker previous to my departure, which will be from Falmouth in the April packett. I have the pleasure of transmitting to you 2 Letters received within the ½ hour from New York addressed to you. Should they contain any public intelligence, I should thank you for it as we have not a line. There is nothing particularly interesting here. Dr. Price informed me yesterday that Mr. Pitts revenue for the last quarter has fallen miserably short and that even his affairs in Holland were not likely to blow over with that tranquility which they hoped for, and concluded with a sigh, he was rather apprehensive his administration would

[517]

yet meet with a disgraceful period. I have not a doubt of it if the Quadruple alliance takes place.

I have the pleasure of informing you that our last accounts from Boston and Philadelphia state that the proposed confœderation, was undergoing a very accurate investigation, upon just liberal and patriotic principles. I have not the least objection nay I wish it may be altered, in some points, but I seriously would (notwithstanding its defects) rather it should be adopted as it is than be entirely laid aside, for I am not the least apprehensive that our Countrymen for the Century to come at least, will submit to tyrannical establishments. I am rather fearfull they are too generally advocates for an unbounded freedom of action and the liberty of putting such constructions upon public acts as pro:tem: are best suited to their particular views and interests.

Adieu. Yours most sincerely, W. S. SMITH

RC (DLC); endorsed. Enclosures: (1) Copy of Smith to TJ, 3 Dec. 1787, and enclosure. (2) Two letters from America (not identified).

To John Stockdale

SIR   Paris Jan. 16. 1788.

I wrote you on the first day of this month, and hope you will have received the letter. To the books I then desired, be pleased to add Volney's travels thro Egypt, Syria &c. printed by Robinson; The history of the internal affairs of Holland since 1783, printed also by Robinson if I recollect rightly. Send them in boards. I am with much esteem Sir Your most obedt. humble servt.,

TH: JEFFERSON

PrC (DLC).

From Robert Walker

Paris, 16 [Jan.?] 1788. Asks TJ to give him permission to draw on Grand for £30 sterling "in discount for Mr. W. draft on Messrs. Donald & Burton of London."

RC (DLC); 2 p.; endorsed by TJ: "Walker. (of Petersbg. Virga.)." This note, dated "Hotel de Chaulnes. Wednesday 16th 1788." is not recorded in SJL Index; since Wednesday fell on the 16th of the month in January, April, and July of 1788, it could

have been written only on those three dates; it has been arbitrarily assigned to the first date.

On the firm of DONALD & BURTON of London, who were engaged in the tobacco trade, see Donald to TJ, 12 Nov. 1787. Dr. Robert Walker, of

Petersburg, Va., studied in Philadelphia under Dr. William Shippen and was graduated from the University of Edinburgh in 1787; he died in 1816 (W. B.

Blanton, *Medicine in Virginia in the Eighteenth Century*, Richmond, 1931, p. 44, 83, 87; see W. S. Smith to TJ, 15 Oct. 1787 and 9 Jan. 1788, note).

From William Franklin

SIR   London Janry. 18, 1788. Norton Street, No. 43.

I received, some Time ago, a Letter from my Son, Wm. Temple Franklin, requesting me to make Enquiry after a Box which he had left, when here, with a Mr. Woodmason, to be ship'd for Havre, containing, besides some valuable Books for his Grandfather, a set of Blackstone's Commentaries for you. After making the most particular Enquiry in my Power, I learnt that the Box had been shipp'd on Board a foreign Vessel which had not been at this Port since, nor could any Intelligence be obtained of her, or the Master. On transmitting this Information to my Son, he wrote me, that, "as you had paid him for Blackstone's Commentaries, he thought he ought to replace them; that he would be much obliged to me if I would do it for him, and let him know the Amount, and that it was the last Edition in 8vo. neatly bound and lettered." I have omitted complying with his Request longer than I ought to have done, partly owing to my being much absent from London, and partly to my having some Expectation given me by the Ship's Broker, that he might probably have it in his Power to obtain some Intelligence of the Vessel, or the Master, from some of his foreign Correspondents. This Hope, however, having failed, I can no longer postpone informing you, that I am willing either to send you the Books, agreeably to my Son's Request, or, as you may perhaps have supplied yourself with another set, pay the Amount to your Order, in favour of any Person in London.

I have the Honor to be, Sir, Your most obedient Servant,

WM: FRANKLIN

RC (DLC: Franklin Papers); endorsed.

To De Grasse

à Paris ce 18me. Janvier 1788.

J'ai eté sensiblement touché, Monsieur, de la perte que vous venez de faire de Monsieur le comte de Grasse votre pere. C'est un nom cher et respecté à tous mes compatriotes, et dont la memoire

[519]

leur sera toujours precieuse. L'evenement glorieux de la prise de York-town, où il a eu tant de part, lui conservera dans l'histoire une place à toujours distinguée. Agreez, Monsieur, je vous en prie, mes vifs regrets, et les sentiments d'estime et d'attachement avec lesquels j'ai l'honneur d'etre, Monsieur le Comte votre tres humble et tres obeissant serviteur, TH: JEFFERSON

PrC (DLC).

From Eugène MacCarthy

Rochelle, 18 Jan. 1788. In accordance with TJ's letter of 3 Jan. 1788, has drawn on TJ at 30 days for 731 livres 3 sols "to the order of Mr. Missy Merchant of this town." Cannot sufficiently thank TJ for his "polite favour and Speedy Redress."

RC (ViWC); 2 p.; endorsed.

From Maupin

paris le 18 janvier 1788.
MONSIEUR   rue du pont aux choux, no. 43.

On peut faire réellement, quoique Scientifiquement, les plus grandes conquêtes au profit des Nations, et en general de toutes les Sociétés, et non Seulement n'en recevoir aucun prix ni aucune marque de reconnoissance, mais encore en être pour ses frais. J'en Suis un exemple.

Cependant, Monsieur, je voudrois, entre autres choses, perfectionner la vigne dans les lieux où elle est établie; et l'établir dans un grand nombre de pays où, jusqu'à présent, elle n'a pu l'être.

Ce double projet, Monsieur, n'intéresse pas moins, sans doute, les Etats unis de l'Amerique, que la plus grande partie des Etats de l'Europe, et c'est pourquoi j'ai l'honneur d'annoncer particulièrement à Votre Excellence la nouvelle découverte que j'ai faite à ce Sujet, et que je me suis engagé envers le public de notifier à tous les Ministres des Cours étrangères.

Au lieu de me borner, Monsieur, à vous donner avis de cette découverte, j'aurois pu vous en donner la démonstration puisqu'elle est imprimée, mais comme d'après les termes de mon avis, je n'aurois pu la communiquer à Votre Excellence que sous une condition, j'ai pensé qu'en invitant même Votre Excellence à se la procurer, ainsi que mon projet patriotique et universel, je devois me borner à les lui annoncer.

[520]

Je suis avec un profond respect Monsieur Votre tres humble et tres obeissant serviteur, MAUPIN

RC (DLC).

From De Grasse

MONSIEUR Paris ce 19 janvier 1788.

Je reçois au moment la Lettre dont vous M'avés honoré, et mon Empressement à y répondre doit vous prouver combien je suis flatté de ce qu'elle contient d'obligeante. Les Etats unis de L'amerique ont reconnu de la manière la plus noble les Services que mon Père a été assés heureux pour Leur rendre à york town. Quatre pièces de Canon qui lui ont été donné, et son association à L'ordre de Cincinnatus attesteront toujours qu'il a Le Bonheur de mériter L'estime des Etats. Je me suis fait un trophée de ces récompenses glorieuses. Les Cannons font aujourd'hui partie de mes armes et ma reconnoissance a dicté la Légende qui les unit (libertas americana). Qu'il me Soit permis, Monsieur, de vous témoigner tout le désir que j'aurois de joindre à ces Preuves de satisfaction L'aigle de Cincinnatus. Dans l'origine il étoit convenu qu'elle passeroit au premier Enfant Mâle de celui auquel Le Congrè avoit cru devoir L'Envoyer. Je suis Persuadé que Le roy ne s'opposeroit pas à ce que j'Eusse cette marque flatteuse de services rendûs à L'amérique, si vous aviés La Bonté d'En faire la demande au nom des Etats. Il est bien consolant Pour moy, Monsieur, de Penser que la Mémoire de mon Père Leur est chère, comme vous avés La Bonté de M'En assurer. C'est ce qui me persuade qu'ils ne désapprouveront pas la démarche que je réclame de L'intérêt dont Vous L'avés honoré.

Je suis avec respect, Monsieur Votre tres humble Et tres obeissant serviteur, LE CTE AUGUSTE DE GRASSE

RC (DLC); endorsed.

To De Grasse

MONSIEUR LE COMTE à Paris ce 19me. Janvier 1788.

Par les reglements de l'institution des Cincinnati, je crois que ce sont les Generaux François qui ont servi en Amerique qui peuvent seuls donner l'ordre, c'est à dire M. le Comte d'Estaing, M. le

[521]

Comte de Rochambeau et M. le Marquis de la Fayette. C'est aussi de mon devoir d'observer que le Congrès, ayant toujours gardé soigneusement le silence sur cette ordre, leurs ministres n'oseroient pas de s'y meler. J'aurois eté charmé, Monsieur, si j'aurois pu vous etre utile dans cette occasion, mais ce n'est pas le cas où on peut s'adresser au Congrès. Agreez donc, je vous en prie, mes regrets, et les assurances de l'estime et d'attachement avec lesquelles j'ai l'honneur d'etre Monsieur le Comte votre tres humble et tres obeissant serviteur,   TH: JEFFERSON

PrC (DLC).

From André Limozin

Le Havre, 19 Jan. 1788. Wrote to TJ on 11th and "took the Freedom to enclose a Copy of a Letter I had received with orders to charter a Large Ship for New york, and beg'd your Excellency's informations on that matter." Has since received TJ's letter of the 13th and its enclosure. Barrell of rice was only delivered this day, but since Captain Jenkins was obliged by contrary winds to put back into harbor, he has promised to take the greatest care of the rice. The packet is just arrived from New York.

RC (MHi); 2 p.; endorsed. On the enclosed COPY OF A LETTER, see note to Limozin to TJ, 10 Jan. (not 11th as stated) 1788.

To William Macarty

SIR   Paris Jan. 19. 1788.

I this moment receive your favour on the subject of the China. If I understand you rightly, dishes may be had taking them in lots or nests of five in each, of different sizes; and that a lot or nest of five dishes costs 21.^{tt} In this case I would take half a dozen lots or nests, if I have not misunderstood your description of them; and would beg the favor of you to send me an half a dozen nests. If I am mistaken you will be so good as to set me right. I am with great esteem Sir Your most obedt. humble servant,

TH: JEFFERSON

PrC (DLC).

To Wilt, Delmestre & Cie.

GENTLEMEN   Paris Jan. 19. 1788.

I am sincerely sorry for the circumstances which have rendered necessary the letter you have done me the honour to address me for the purpose of knowing what are the laws of America in the cases of mercantile failures. I am sorry also that it is not in my power to give any satisfactory answer to your enquiries. The laws are different in the different states. I have had the means of being acquainted with those of one state only, to wit, Virginia: and it is so long since these were familiar to my mind that I cannot answer for them with great certainty. The laws of Virginia, if I remember rightly, form the creditors into a mass, and entitle them to be paid pro ratâ as far as the effects within that state will go. But I am not able to say whether it is the American and foreign creditors together, or only the American creditors to which they give the effects. In some states they have adopted the English bankrupt laws with small changes. But to be on a sure ground it would be necessary for you to enquire of an able lawyer in each of the states in which you have effects.

I am with very great esteem Gentlemen Your most obedient & mo. humble servt.,   TH: JEFFERSON

PrC (DLC).

From Blome

ce dimanche 20 Janvier

M. de Blome a l'honneur de faire bien des compliments à Monsieur Jefferson et aura celui de l'attendre demain matin à onze heures puisqu'il veut bien prendre la peine de venir chez Lui; et il le recevra avec autant d'empressement que de plaisir.

RC (MHi); assigned to this year because it is the only time while TJ was in France that 20 Jan. fell on Sunday; also, see TJ to Bernstorff, 21 Jan. 1788.

From Johann Ludwig de Unger

MONSIEUR   Salzliebenhalle ce 20me. du Janvier 1788.

Les gracieuses bontés dont Votre Excellence a daigné m'honorer quand, durant le Séjour des Trouppes de Brunswic dans la Province de Virginie, j'eus le Bonheur de Vous aprocher, Monsieur, et

[523]

d'admirer de près les Qualités éminentes qui Vous distinguent, m'enhardissent d'oser rappeller au Souvenir de Votre Excellence un Homme qui à jamais Lui est respectueusement dévoué, et Lui demander en même tems une Grâce et un bienfait en faveur d'un Sujet natif du Pais de Brunswic qui vient de s'établir en Virginie. Ce Sujet, nommé Hartmann, a Servi dans nos Trouppes pendant la guerre en Amérique dans la Qualité de Port-Enseigne; Après la Paix faite il a réussi à trouver un Etablissement avantageux en Virginie au moien d'un Mariage qu'il y a contracté. Par le Décès d'un de ses proches Parens dans ce Païs-ci, il lui est echû un heritage asses considérable, et il est venu se rendre en Personne à Brunswic pour se mettre en possession de son héritage, qui lui sera d'un Secours infini pour améliorer son sort en Amérique, où il compte de retourner incessament. Selon les Loix de ce Païs-ci, tous les Biens hérités qui sortent dans l'Etranger sont sujets à des Droits de retenue très considérables, qui montent au delà de 30 pour Cent de leur Valeur, vis à vis des Païs avec lesquels il n'existe pas des Conventions particulières ou des Traittés d'Abolition. Je sais que dans les Provinces d'Amérique on vient d'établir de ces Loix humaines qui permettent la sortie des héritages dans L'Etranger, libre et sans aucune retenue, et je ne doutte pas que la Certitude de l'Existence d'une Loi de cette nature en Amérique, engageroit la Régence du Païs de Brunswic à réciproquer une Loi si généreuse et à exemter l'Eritage apartenant au Sr. Hartmann des Charges usitées. Oserois-je demander à Votre Excellence la grâce de vouloir bien pour cet effet faire expédier, et me faire parvenir, un Certificat portant: "qu'en Amérique, et particulièrement dans la Province de Virginie, les héritages, et en général les Biens sortant des Emigrans, sont entièrement libres de toute Retenue." Votre Excellence, en m'accordant cette Demande, feroit un Bienfait infini au Sr. Hartmann qui est un très honette Homme et qui sera sûrement un Propriétaire très utile dans la Province à laquelle il s'est attaché par des si doux Liens.

Elle ajouteroit en même tems aux bontés infinies dont Elle a comblé ci devant un homme qui se rappelle avec Entousiasme l'Avantage de jouir de sa Protection et de ses Lumières. C'est ce même souvenir, Monsieur, et la respectueuse Confiance, que Votre Caractère généreux m'inspire, qui m'impose le Devoir de marquer à Votre Excellence, que le Duc de Brunsswic, après notre retour dans le Païs, m'a comblé de bienfaits. En me nommant Capitaine de ses Trouppes et en me confiant en même tems l'Administration de ses Salines, ce Prince magnanime a daigné me faire un sort qui me rend des plus heureux. Je le suis infiniment dans ce moment, où il m'est permis de réitérer à Votre Excellence l'Hommage de mes Respects et de mon Admiration.

Daignés, Monsieur, me conserver quelque Part à Vos précieuses Bontés, et à l'Honneur de Votre bienveillance. J'ambitionnerai toujours de les mériter, par les sentimens respectueux avec lesquels j'ai l'Honneur d'être, Monsieur, de Votre Excellence, le très humble et le très obeissant Serviteur, JEAN LOUIS DE UNGER

RC (DLC).

To Bernstorff

Paris January 21. 1788.

SIR

I am instructed by the United States of America in Congress assembled to bring again under the consideration of His Majesty the King of Denmark, and of his Ministers, the case of the three prizes, taken from the English during the late war by an American squadron under the command of Commodore Paul Jones, put into Bergen in distress, there rescued from our possession by orders from the Court of Denmark, and delivered back to the English. Dr. Franklin, then Minister Plenipotentiary from the United States at the Court of Versailles, had the honour of making applications to the Court of Denmark for a just indemnification to the persons interested, and particularly by a letter of the 22d. of December 1779 a copy of which I have now the honor of inclosing to your Excellency. In consequence of this, the sum of 10,000£ sterling was proposed to him, as an indemnification through the Baron de Waltersdorff, then at Paris. The departure of both those gentlemen from this place soon after, occasioned an intermission in the correspondence on this subject. But the United States continue to be very sensibly affected by this delivery of their prizes to Great Britain, and the more so as no part of their conduct had forfeited their claim to those rights of hospitality which civilized nations extend to each other. Not only a sense of the justice due to the individuals interested in those prizes, but also an earnest desire that no subject of discontent may check the cultivation and progress of that friendship which they wish may subsist and increase between the two countries prompt them to remind his Majesty of the transaction in question, and they flatter themselves that His Majesty will concur with them in thinking that as restitution of the prizes is not practicable, it is reasonable and just that he should render and that they should accept a compensation equivalent to the value of them. And the same principles of justice towards the parties and of amity to the United States which influenced the breast of His Majesty to make through the Baron de Waltersdorff the proposition of a particular sum will surely lead him to restore their full value, if that were greater, as is believed, than the sum proposed.

In order to obtain therefore a final arrangement of this demand, Congress have authorized me to depute a special agent to Copenhagen to attend the pleasure of His Majesty. No agent could be so adequate to this business as the Commodore Paul Jones, who commanded the squadron which took the prizes. He will therefore have the honour of delivering this letter to Your Excellency in person, of giving such information as may be material relative to the whole transaction, of entering into conferences for its final adjustment, and being himself principally interested, not only in his own right, but as the natural patron of those who fought under him, whatever shall be satisfactory to him will have a great right to that ultimate approbation which Congress have been pleased to confide to me.

I beg your Excellency to accept the homage of that respect which your exalted station, talents and merit impress, as well as those sentiments of esteem and regard with which I have the honor to be Your Excellency's most obedient & most humble servant,

TH: JEFFERSON

PrC (DLC); in the hand of William Short, signed by TJ. Enclosure: Franklin to Bernstorff, 22 Dec. 1779 (PrC of a Tr, in the hand of William Short, in DLC; printed in Sherburne, *John Paul Jones*, p. 288-90).

From J. Louis Brethoux

MONSIEUR   Marseille Le 21. Janvier 1788.

C'est un peu tard reconnoitre à Votre Excellence Les bontés qu'Elle nous a témoigné pendant notre Séjour à Paris. Les mauvais tems que nous avons eu à L'époque de notre départ, et pendant notre route, découragèrent beaucoup La Santé de ma femme; elle fut obligée de s'arrêter à Lyon, où Elle se remit en Etat de continuer sa marche, elle arriva Icy fort faible; à peine fut elle remise Qu'Elle a eu un [. . .] considérable, qui s'est dissipée. La saison n'est pas bien propre pour son rétablissement parfait. Elle me charge de vous prier d'agréer ses hommages. Elle s'est rapelée que vous désiriez un ouvrage sur La culture des Oliviers que Votre Excellence n'avoit pas trouvé à Paris, nous L'avons envoyé à Mr. Grand avec prière de la faire passer à Votre Excellence. Il y a aussi des fruits de nos voisinages, qui seront envoyés à Votre Excellence. Nous la prions de recevoir ces bagatelles, ce qui nous flatera infiniment. Depuis Douze jours nous avons un hyver bien favorable aux Dieux de La terre, et à La Santé; nous n'avions eu que des Brouillards, et des vents d'Est, qui occasionnoient des incomodités et La végétation étoit très sensible, Les amandiers commencoient à fleurir, nous avions des Légumes comme dans Le mois de mars. Les tems qui règnent sont bien favorables, il gèle toutes les nuits, et le plus beau soleil dans Le courant de la Journée. Il paroit que La tranquilité des mers est assurée pour Quelques mois, La dernière guerre a été trop couteuse aux deux nations.

Je suis avec Respect, Monsieur, Votre très humble, et très obeissant serviteur, JN. LOUIS BRETHOUX

RC (DLC); endorsed. The OUVRAGE SUR LA CULTURE DES OLIVIERS that Brethoux sent to TJ through Ferdinand Grand was perhaps the 1762 Florence edition of *Trattato di Piero Vettori delle lodi e della coltivazione degli ulivi*, a work that TJ possessed (Sowerby, No. 789). There is in DLC: TJ Papers, 236: 42376-7, a three-page MS containing notes on the same subject in an unidentified hand in Italian, endorsed by TJ: "Olive, cultivation of."

From William Macarty

L'Orient, 21 Jan. 1788. Sent TJ a package of china by the diligence on 17 Jan. for which he drew for 228.ᵗᵗ 2, at one day's sight on TJ, payable to Dussault, from whom the china was bought.

RC (DLC); 1 p.; endorsed. Although not mentioned in the letter, there may have been enclosed in it a MS (DLC) entitled: "Note des Porcelaines expédiées le 17 Janvier 1788 en une Caisse pour partir par la messagerie du 21 à l'adresse de Monsieur Jefferson," dated 17 Jan. 1788 and listing the china ("2 Douzaines, d'Assiettes en Couleur . . . 2 Soupières, pre[miè]re grandeur . . . 8 Plats longs, 5me. grandeur . . . 4 Douzaines, d'Assiettes à Dessert . . .") and its total cost. The cancelled draft for 228.ᵗᵗ 2, endorsed by J. Dussault, is also in DLC. Another sight draft by Macarty on TJ for 202 livres 4 sols, dated 20 Jan. 1787, is also in DLC and bears this notation by TJ: "paid to Mr. McCarty himself June 20. 1787."

To André Limozin

SIR   Paris January 22. 1788.

Your favors of Jan. 10. 11. and 19th. have been duly received. With respect to the plan of an Academical institution to be transported to Virginia and there established, tho' you do not name the person who applies to you for a ship, yet I conjecture it to be the same who has communicated to me a slight view of such a plan here. So far as it may concern your interest I shall write to you freely, only begging you will not communicate it to any person living, nor use it for any other purpose but to keep yourself clear of what might be a losing speculation. The projector I take to be an honest man: but his project much too vast and too expensive for the present circumstances of the country for which he proposes it. Consequently it must fail, and with loss to somebody. He expects indeed subscriptions here for a great deal of money; but when I saw him last there was not one actual subscription. He is of so sanguine a temper that he cannot bear a doubt to be suggested of the failure of his plan. Perhaps he views it additionally with the fondness of a man possessing little, and having no other prospect of subsistence. I understand he is embarrassed to procure money for his daily subsistence. Still I think his views honest, and that he will draw others into loss without intending it. As to your furnishing him with a vessel, you best know how to act in it with security.

I am much obliged to you for your care of the rice, and hope it will arrive in time for the sowing season. I inclose you a letter from America which I suppose to be from the Mr. Madison to whom were addressed the three boxes of books which Capt. Jenkins has carried out. I did suppose they had gone by the September packet and wrote him accordingly.—By the packet lately arrived he has sent me

> a box of plants
> 2. barrels of apples
> 2. barrels of Cranberries.

Be so good as to send the box of plants by the Diligence or by a Roulier as you shall see best. I had rather by the Diligence unless it be very heavy indeed and of course too expensive for the object. The barrels of Apples and cranberries can come by water only, as the motion of land carriage would reduce them to mummy.

Nothing yet transpires which may indicate surely either peace or war. The ill humour between the cabinets of Versailles and London increases. Yet a war may not necessarily follow. I have hopes that this country may effect all her foreign purposes by negociation without war. There are however difficulties in the way of this. I am with much esteem Sir your most obedient humble servt.,

TH: JEFFERSON

[528]

PrC (DLC). The SAME WHO HAS COMMUNICATED TO ME . . . SUCH A PLAN: Quesnay de Beaurepaire (see Quesnay to TJ, 22 Dec. 1787; Limozin to TJ, 10 Jan. 1788). The enclosed letter from James Madison to Limozin has not been identified, but see Limozin to TJ, 24 Jan. 1788.

To Joseph-Léonard Poirey

ce 22me. Janvier. 1788.

Memoire d'argent payé pour M. le Marquis de la fayette.

			sterl.	
1786.	Presse a copier		£15 – 11 –	
	Transport &c.			48ᵗᵗ – 5
Aug.	3. Capper's Travels.			
	De Londres	5		
	Andrew's history	1 – 8		
			413ᵗᵗ	
2.	Moitié du Madeire		537ᵗᵗ – 15	
	Moitié du transport &c.		50 – 19	
Sep.	14. Petite presse a copier		145 – 10	
			1195 – 9	

Monsieur Jefferson a l'honneur de faire ses compliments à Monsieur Poyret. Il vient de recevoir de Londres la note de ce qui à couté la presse à copier qu'il y a acheté pour M. le Marquis de la fayette. Il y a ajouté le vin de Madeire qui leur est venu de l'Amerique, et quelques autres petits objets, montant à 1195ᵗᵗ–9. Il a estimé le Louis de 24ᵗᵗ à vingt shelings selon l'échange ordinaire.

PrC (DLC).

Poirey had served with Lafayette in the Virginia campaign of 1781 in the capacity of military secretary, and was also secretary to the Marquis at this time; Lafayette caused him to be admitted as an honorary member of the Society of the Cincinnati in 1791 (Contenson, La Société des Cincinnati de France, p. 245), an event which caused Lafayette to say to Washington: "You have made M. Poirey the happiest man in the world for which Mde de Lafayette and myself are very thankfull" (Gottschalk, ed., Letters of Lafayette to Washington, privately printed, 1944, p. 353).

From Jan Ingenhousz, with Note by Jefferson

DEAR SIR   Vienne en Autriche Jan. 23. 1788

I took the liberty to recommend to your protection a lettre to our common Friend Benjamin Franklin, which was of great importance for me. As scarce one letter of three which Dr. Franklin or other of my american Friends have dispatched to me have come to hands, and as the same fatality befell those letters I wrote to him and to others, I should be extremily happy to be informed as soon as possible, if you have recieved allready intelligence that your dispatches which accompanied the lettre I sent you in septembre last has reached Newyork or Philadelphia. This information will spare me a great deal of trouble, which in case of failure of that lettre, I must undergoe, by writing a duplicate and taking many arrangements. I only begg the favour of a line on this head as soon as you will be informed that your dispatches accompanying my letter mentioned has reached america.

I begg you pardon for the trouble I give you and I ame respectfully Dear Sir your most obedient humble servant,

JOHN INGEN HOUSZ

Note. I received the letter referred to on the 9th. of Oct. which was the day before the departure of the Ct. de Moustier. I do not know whether my packet had been before made up and sent to him, consequently whether it went by him or the November packet boat.

RC (DLC); addressed and endorsed. The memorandum at the foot of the text is in TJ's hand.

From Sarsfield

[Before 23 Jan. 1788]

J'ay instruit hier, Monsieur, Mr. Adams du depart de ses livres Et Je lui ai dit a qui Il devoit s'adresser a Londres pour les avoir a leur arrivée; Mais Je n'ay pu lui en mander les Prix parce que Je n'en avois pas encore la notte; Je la Joins icy.

Je rencontrai hier un jeune homme que J'ay vu a Londres Chez M. Adams, Je Scay qu'il Se nomme Skippen mais a cela pres, Je Ne Scay aucun detail sur ce qui le touche. Si Vous voulez avoir la bonté de M'en donner quelqu'un, Je vous En aurai beaucoup d'obligation.

J'ay lhonneur d'Etre avec un tres Sincere attachement, Monsieur Votre tres humble et tres obeissant Serviteur,

SARSFIELD

RC (MHi); without indication of addressee or date; endorsed. Enclosure missing.

The above letter was assigned to this date because it must have been written shortly before Sarsfield's letter of 23 Jan., following (TJ's reply to the present letter is missing); and under 23 Jan. 1788, TJ made the following entry in his Account Book: "pd Ct.

Sarsfield for Mr. Adams for books 79.^{lt}" SKIPPEN: Thomas Lee Shippen (see note to Smith to TJ, 9 Jan. 1788).

From Sarsfield

Paris 23 Jr 1788

J'ay recu, Monsieur, les 79^{lt} que vous m'avez Envoyée pour M. Adams, Je n'ay plus qu'à recevoir la nouvelle de l'arrivée des livres Et qu'il en soit content. Il lui en manque un qui lui fera bien faute, mais on ne peut le trouver.

J'ay l'honneur de vous faire bien des remerciemens de l'instruction que vous avez Eu la bonté de me donner sur M. Shippen. J'iray demain matin le Chercher. Il est Surprenant que M. son oncle ne Lui ait point donné de lettre pour moy.

J'ay L'honneur d'Etre avec un tres Sincere attachement, Monsieur, Votre très humble et tres obeisst Serviteur,

SARSFIELD

RC (MHi); endorsed. Recorded in SJL Index as dated 22 Jan.

L'INSTRUCTION ... SUR M. SHIPPEN: TJ obviously wrote to Sarsfield on 23 Jan. 1788 enclosing payment of LES 79^{lt} and also giving him information about Thomas Lee Shippen, but that letter has not been found.

To John Paul Jones

SIR

The United States of America in Congress assembled having thought proper by their resolve of the 25th of October 1787 to authorize and instruct me finally to settle and conclude all demands of the United States against His Majesty the King of Denmark, on account of their prizes delivered to Great Britain during the late war, and to dispatch yourself or any other agent to the court of Denmark with such power and instructions relative thereto as I might think proper, provided the ultimate conclusion of the business be not made by the said agent without my previous approbation, I hereby authorize you to proceed to the court of Denmark, for the purpose of making the necessary representations on the subject, and for conferring thereon with such persons as shall be appointed on that behalf by the said Court, or for agreeing provisionally on the arrangements to be taken, transmitting the

[531]

same to me at Paris for final approbation. Given under my hand and seal at Paris this 24th. day of January in the year of our Lord 1788, and of the independance of the United States of America the twelfth.   TH: JEFFERSON

PrC (DLC: John Paul Jones Papers); in the hand of William Short, signed by TJ. This PrC was probably lent by TJ to Sherburne, who printed it in his *John Paul Jones*, p. 291.

From André Limozin

MOST HONORED SIR   Havre de Grace 24th Janry. 1788.

I am very thankfull for the kind informations your Excellency is so obliging as to give me not only concerning the Skeme of an academical institution to be transported to Virginia, but about the Situation of Political business. I shall never forget the important Services I experience from your Excellency in that occasion.

I did not read the Copy I transmitted to your Excellency of the Letter I received about that academical Institution, other wise I should not have sent it without mentioning the name of the writer who is a M. Quesnay de Beaurepair, who is intirely a Stranger to me. Some american Gentlemen told me that he was of a good family but that he professed in America all sorts of Conditions, and that he was look'd upon there as rather Crazy. I have answerd him that no owners would charter their Ships unless all the undertakers or Subscribers to the Plan would give full Security for the performance of all the Conditions of the Charter party, because I shall never forget all the troubles I have met with the chartering of a Ship for one Dr. Bancrofft which was sent back with a Cargoe of oak Bark, which is still remaining as dung.

I am in the greatest perplexity for my mercantile undertakings about the political Circumstances. We are now in the very best season of the year to make profitable purchases, of Coarse Linnens for our West Indias. If I was certain that there will be no war, I should purchase during January and February, because after that season, the prices will get up, (if peace continues) and will rise at least of 8 or 9 ℔ Ct. which difference is very important. Should a War take place the prices would surely decline of 25 ℔ Ct. It is a dreadfull circumstance to be in Such Condition to not be able to Know what one can do with Safety. If a War should break out our Port is too near England, we must leave of our West India trade. All these considerations puts me under necessity to be so troublesome towards your Excellency, for informations about the Political business.

Your Excellency incloseth me a Bill of Lading for a Box of Plants which is forwarded by Roulier and plombd. Therefore you are beseechd to return me in time the acquit a Caution duely Certifyed.

Your Excellency will observe that the said acquit a Caution mentions likewise the 2 Barrles apples, 2 Barrles Cranberries, but when the Searchers of the Custom house came to plomb these four Barrles, they found that they leak'd very much and as much as if they were full of Liquor, that induced my Clarke to require that they should be opend in their presence, which was done, and all the apples and cranberries were found rotten, which the Chief officers have certify'd in the margin of the said acquit a Caution.

I am very much Surprised that they have sent such large apples, which could not keep, because they are too full of juice. They smell like our apples with which we make Syder in this Country. Upon these two Barrles, there were only eight apples which were not much rotten, nevertheless a part of them was touched. The loss would not be considerable if one was not obliged to pay the same freight for them as if they been deliverd in a good order.

Captn. Jenkins ever since he was obliged to put back for this harbor by contrary winds is still detained in this harbor for the same cause.

I have settled with the Senegals Company the accounts of Capt. Thomas who looks upon me as one of these Gods mentioned in the Fables. He had written by Capt. Jenkins a dozen of Letters where in he expresseth the Sincerest gratitude for what I have done in his behalf. It is a very great Satisfaction for me to meet with People of such feelings.

The Letter your Excellency was so obliging as to forward me is from M. Madison. I am certainly indebted to your Excellency for the most polite Contents of that Letter, for I have not the honor to be acquainted with the Said Mr. Madison. Therefore please to receive my most sincere thanks for it.

I have the honor to be with the highest regard, your Excellency's Most obedient & very Humble Servant, ANDRÉ LIMOZIN

Golden Pepins would keep much longer than these large Syder apples, because the Pepins are a sort of a dryer apple and have I think a thicker skin.

RC (DLC); addressed and endorsed. Limozin was not acquainted with MR. MADISON, but two days after writing the present letter he sent two letters on the *Juno* by CAPTN. JENKINS under the following cover: "The Honorable James Madison Esq in Congress New York"—an error of address that TJ surprisingly confirmed in his to Limozin of 6 Feb. 1788. The first of Limozin's enclosures was a long letter to Benjamin Franklin in which he said that TJ had applied to him for advice relating to the recent arrêt on American trade; that he "was sorry to find that only a small part of the favors I had required was granted"; that when the war ended "a very considerable Number of american Prisoners came from England . . . in the greatest distress," having neither shoes nor stockings and in many cases no trousers; that they had applied to him for assistance, but "when I showed to these unhappy fellows the orders I had from Mr. Barclay to not let them have a farthing because Congress had not provided for them, I heard at once 4 and 500 Tongues threatening me to pull down my house"; that he had been obliged to assist every one of them according to need; that when Franklin was at his house, he had promised to mention these circumstances to Congress in order to procure Limozin some recompense if not reimbursement; that "Mr. Thomas

Jefferson hath been informed with all my proceedings which have met with his approbation"; that an American ship, the *Polly and Sally*, Captain Thomas, was about to be seized for having taken on freight at Senegal; that when he had "applyd to Mr. Jefferson and claimed his protection," TJ "found that the Master having transgressed the law it would not be possible Considering his appointment for him to take the defense of that Master"; that Limozin had thereupon taken it on himself "and succeeded not only to get the master leave to unload but procured him justice for his freight and due demeurage" (see Limozin to TJ, 18 Nov.; 18, 24, and 31 Dec. 1787; 10, 11, and 24 Jan. 1788; and TJ to Limozin, 22 Dec. 1787 and 22 Jan. 1788). The second of Limozin's enclosures under cover to Madison was a letter to Jay enclosing a copy of that to Franklin and stating that Franklin had "promised me when he was here that if I should apply to any proper person about it he would not refuse me his assistance" (both letters to Franklin and Jay are dated 26 Jan. 1788 and both are in DNA: PCC, No. 82, III, p. 359, 363-74, accompanied by a letter from Madison to Franklin, 20 Apr. 1788, saying that the "external address to me was made on a supposition of my being an attending member of Congress").

From Stephen Cathalan, Jr.

Marseilles, 25 Jan. 1788. Acknowledges letters of 28 and 31 Dec.; has sent "Second Couffe Egyptian Rice on Captn's. Shewell Vessel" to "William Drayton Esq. Chairman of the Society of Agriculture of Charlestown Sh. Carolina"; encloses bill of lading; hopes TJ has received the articles he desired; the barrel of oil was sent from Aix some days ago; encloses bill, amounting to 272.^{tt} 5, for charges on the above commissions. Has received the arrêt of Council of State and Lambert's letter to TJ on American trade; has communicated its substance to the merchants concerned; wishes the regulation concerning tobacco mentioned in the letter had been included in the arrêt, thus giving it the force of law; fears the farmers will evade it; a letter from them to their agent in Marseilles on 4 Jan. does not mention the new regulation; they continue to say they will not purchase tobacco for a long while, being "so much provided," and when they do, they will not pay more than 30^{tt} for Virginia tobacco. Their agent has replied that the merchants know about the new regulation and will not be willing to lose that much

[534]

money. Although it would be difficult "to Conciliate all the interests of So many Merchants, of this Place, of the northern Ports of France, and of America," Cathalan has a plan which is "the only means to make an head against Farmers"; by the plan he, alone, would have charge of all sales of tobacco arriving in France. "The first tobacco arived will be the first Sold, according to the date of their arival in the respective places without any prefference"; thus the farmers-general would be required to purchase certain amounts from each port; the prices asked would not be "extravagant ones, but calculated on their cost on the genuine Invoices, and on the prices of holland and england." If the farmers refused the prices asked, there would be no sale, but advances would be made to the holders of the tobacco and a protest sent to government; sustained in this plan by TJ and all the merchants, redress could be obtained; his charge for acting in this capacity would be 2 per cent. The alternative to such a plan is sale by one merchant at the price offered by the farmers, to the detriment of all the others. Was unfortunate on his cargo; his friend in Philadelphia could get only 123 hhds. of tobacco there and filled the rest of the vessel with flour and rice for Cadiz; although the Spanish government buys tobacco only from its colonies, his cargo arrived when the tobacco stores were exhausted; the government administrator wrote Madrid for permission to buy the whole cargo at 22 piastres per quintal, taking 8 hhds. immediately; before permission was received ships arrived from the Spanish colonies; therefore the administrator refused the rest of Cathalan's cargo and paid only 20 piastres for the 8 hhds. taken; the whole transaction, including the loss in France on the remainder of the cargo, was 60,000^{lt} "difference for a day." His family presents their respects; thanks TJ for news which is always acceptable.

RC (DLC); 4 p.; endorsed. Enclosures: (1) Bill of lading for cask of rice (missing). (2) Invoice for shipping rice to Drayton, and shipping various articles to TJ, including figs, nuts, anchovies, sardines, oil, &c., amounting to 272.^{lt}5 and receipt to Cathalan for the charges of shipping the rice to Marseilles (DLC).

From William Macarty

L'Orient, 25 Jan. 1788. The dishes which are available are not the same pattern as those sent, but may answer the purpose; the "Nest, or *Jeu* consists of 5 Dishes, from the Smallest to the Largest Size" and costs 21^{lt} the set; there are two sorts, one "Oval Dishes Scollop'd Edge, with a red Border like the Bleu Border round your China"; the other "of the Same form with yours with a pale red, chass'd Border covering about half the Rim of the Dish, Both Sorts with detach'd flours"; if these will answer, they will be sent immediately.

RC (DLC); 2 p.; endorsed.

To Montmorin

[SIR]   Paris Jan. 26. 1788.

In the course of the last war His Majesty thought proper to equip a small squadron for an occasional cruize and to give the command of it to the Chevalier Paul Jones. The American frigate the Alliance was joined to it at the King's desire. Of the prizes which they took three put into Bergen in distress, and being reclaimed by the British Minister at the Court of Copenhagen, were taken out of possession of the captors and delivered up to him. These prizes have been estimated at 50,000 guineas. Dr. Franklin applied to the Court of Denmark for indemnification, and they, by the Baron de Waltersdorff then at Paris offered 10,000 guineas, which was not accepted. Both those gentlemen having left Paris soon after, the pursuit of this claim suffered an intermission. Congress have now instructed me to conclude it and for that purpose to send a special agent to Copenhagen. I have appointed the Chevalier Paul Jones for this purpose, who will set out on tuesday next. About one half of the sum to be obtained belonging to subjects of France, I have thought it my duty to state this matter to Your Excellency as you might be willing to take measures on your part also for supporting their interests. Whether Your Excellency should think it best to do this through your Minister at Copenhagen or through any other agent whatever, the Chevalier Paul Jones will conduct himself in concert with such agent. The interference of His Majesty cannot fail to have the most powerful effect towards obtaining that justice which is due to the brave officers and men who composed the squadron.

I have the honor to be with sentiments of the most perfect esteem and respect Your Excellency's Most obedient & most humble servant,   TH: JEFFERSON

PrC (DLC); in the hand of William Short, signed by TJ.

From J. P. P. Derieux

MONSIEUR   Colle ce 28th Janvier 1788.

J'ai reçu par le Colo. Nicholas Lewis, les deux Lettres obligeantes que vous m'avés fait L'honneur de m'écrire le 16. Sepbre. dernier. J'y ai lu avec la plus grande reconnaissance la démarche affectionée que vous avés eu la bonté de faire en ma faveur auprès

[536]

de ma cousinne Bellanger; elle est sans prix et du plus heureux présage pour moi, puisqu'après avoir déterminé cette chère parente à effectuer ses bonnes intentions, vous me promettés encore auprès d'elle, des bontés qui ne pourront que les accroître. Permettés moi donc, Monsieur, de vous regarder dès cet instant comme un Bienfaiteur direct, et de fonder sur un tel avantage L'espoir le plus Certain du bonheur et de la félicité.

Il ne dépendra pas de moi, Monsieur, de tirer tout L'avantage possible de votre recommandation auprès du Colo. Lewis. Je briguerai toujours ses conseils avec tout l'empressement que ses qualités essentielles inspirent naturellement. Il m'a des-ja beaucoup aidé à L'égard de la Négotiation de mes lettres de Change, en me procurant à Richmond la connaissance de Mr. A. Donald qui, comme votre ami et le sien, a paru se faire un vrai plaisir de L'occasion qui se présentoit de m'être util; il n'avoit pas de fonds pour lors à pouvoir disposer, mais il m'a adressé à Mr. de Letele, qui les a pris payable à Paris à L'ordre de Mr. Caron de Beaumarchais, dont il est ici L'agent. Elles sont à 45. Jours de vue, et au nombre de trois, L'une de 4000.^{tt} L'autre de 5000.^{tt} et la dernière de 6000,^{tt} touttes trois endossés de Mr. Nich. Lewis, ainsi que vous avés eu la bonté de voulloir bien l'y authoriser.

Je suis actuellement occupé avec M. Lewis des moyens d'employer mes fonds de la manière la plus avantageuse, il m'a promis de m'accompagner le mois prochain à une Vente de nègres et de Bestiaux qui doit avoir lieu pour lors, et de m'y donner les meilleurs renseignements qui lui seront possible.

Vous me promettés dans des termes si obligeants, Monsieur, les suittes de votre bienveillance, que je ne puis plus longtems me refuser et à Mde. de Rieux la liberté de vous en demander encore une nouvelle preuve. Nous avons toujours différé à faire baptiser notre dernier fils, dans l'espoir que nous serions peut être un jour assés heureux, pour avoir L'occasion de solliciter pour lui, un nom aussi Généralement chéri et respecté de la France et de L'Amérique. Vos bontés nous sont d'un si Grand encouragement, que nous ozons espérer que vous voudrés bien nous faire L'honneur d'en être le parain avec Mde. Bellanger, qui m'a des-ja écrit y être très disposée. Les amitiés que je reçois journellement de Mr. Lewis et son épouse ne me permettent pas de doutter qu'ils vous représentassent avec ma cousine dans cette cérémonie, lorsque vous aurés eu la bonté de leur envoyer les pouvoirs nécessaires et d'usage. Permettés moi, Monsieur, de me féliciter d'avance d'une faveur dont L'étendue ne peut être Comparée qu'aux sentiments de reconnaissance et de respect infini avec Lesquels je suis Monsieur Votre très humble et tres obeissant serviteur, P. DE RIEUX

Mde. de Rieux, qui est extrêmement sensible à L'honneur de votre souvenir, vous prie de voulloir bien agréer l'assurance de son respect, et assurer de ses plus tendres amitiés, Mademoiselle Jefferson.

Mde. Mazzei vient de mourir après six Jours de maladie; je prens la liberté de joindre ici une lettre pour son mari, et une autre pour madame Bellanger, qui m'écrit que vous voulés bien lui prêter votre Couvert.

Charlotteville ce 8. avril 1788.

Mr. Lewis n'ayant pas eu l'occasion de vous adresser ses Lettres dans le tems que je lui avois remis celle cy pour vous, je viens de la rouvrir pour vous apprendre, Monsieur, qu'après avoir quelque tems balancé sur le parti que je prendrois, je me suis enfin déterminé après plusieurs bons et sages conseils à m'établir à la ville, où je tiens store et fais en même tems valloir une assés bonne ferme qui tient à la maison, cy devant propriété de Thomas West; j'en ai la jouissance pour Cinq ans, au moyen du prêt d'une somme de 200 pièces, dont le remboursement doit avoir lieu à l'expiration de ce terme d'années. J'augure d'autant mieux de tous mes arrangements à ce sujet, qu'ils ont généralement reçus L'approbation de Mr. Lewis, qui a la bonté de me donner des marques journalières de la recommandation particulière dont vous avés bien voulu m'honorer auprès de lui.

Quant à des nègres, je n'en ay encore acheté que deux têtes, plusieurs personnes m'ayant fait craindre qu'on ne donnât bientôt dans cet Etat La Liberté aux Esclaves. J'ai acheté trois bons Cheveaux de Labour, un Waggon, tous les outils nécessaires à L'agriculture, et j'ai placé le reste de mes Capitaux dans un commerce intérieur, où je suis déterminé de ne faire ny Crédits ny Emprunts. Je l'ai des-ja commencé avec assés de succès, et si cela continue, j'ai lieu d'espérer assés favorablement de mes progrès ultérieurs.

Pardonnés, Monsieur, si je vous fais tous ces détails, mais j'ose espérer que vous en trouverés mon excuse dans les marques singulières que vous m'avés donné de vos bontés.

RC (DLC); endorsed.

From Pelegrino de Mamo

[*28 Jan. 1788*. Recorded in SJL Index. Not found.]

From William Carmichael

Madrid, *29 Jan. 1788*. Introduces Francesco de Molinedo, who will pass through Paris on his way to London, where he will act as chargé d'affaires for the court of Spain.

RC (DLC); 2 p.; endorsed.

From John Adams

DEAR SIR   Grosvenor Square Jan. 31. 1788

Permit me to introduce to you my young Friend Mr. Alexander Edwards of South Carolina, a modest and amiable young Gentleman who came particularly recommended to me, and whom I have found by Several Months Acquaintance to merit every Attention and Encouragement. I am, my dear Sir yours most affectionately,
                                                    JOHN ADAMS

RC (DLC).

From John Banister, Sr.

[*31 Jan. 1788*. Recorded in SJL Index. Not found.]

To Maria Cosway

Paris Jan. [31, 1788]

I went to breakfast with you according to promise, and you had gone off at 5. oclock in the morning. This spared me indeed the pain of parting, but it deprives me of the comfort of recollecting that pain. Your departure was the signal of distress to your friends. You know the accident which so long confined the Princess to her room. Madame de Corny too was immediately thrown into great alarm for the life of her husband. After being long at death's door he is reviving. Mrs. Church seemed to come to participate of the distress of her friend instead of the pleasures of Paris. I never saw her before: but I find in her all the good the world has given her credit for. I do not wonder at your fondness for each other. I have seen too little of her, as I did of you. But in your case it was not my fault, unless it be a fault to love my friends so dearly as to wish to enjoy their company in the only way it yeilds enjoiment, that is, en petite comité. You make every body love you. You are sought and surrounded therefore by all. Your mere domestic cortege was so numerous, et si imposante, that one could not approach you quite at their ease. Nor could you so unpremeditately mount into the Phaeton and hie away to the bois de Boulogne, St. Cloud, Marly, St. Germains &c. Add to this the distance at which you were placed from me. When you come again, you must be nearer, and move more extempore. You complain, my dear Madam, of my not writing to you, and you have the appearance of cause for complaint. But I have been above a month looking out for a private conveiance, without being able to find one, and you know the infidelity of the post office. Sometimes they mislay letters to pocket the frankmoney: and always they open those of people in office. As if your friendship and mine could be interesting to government! As if, instead of the effusions of a sincere esteem, we would fill our letters with the miserable trash called state secrets!—I am flattered by your attention to me in the affair of the tea vase. I like perfectly the form of the one Mrs. Church brought. But Mr. Trumbull and myself have seen one made for the count de Moustier, wherein the spout is suppressed, and the water made to issue at a pretty little ornament. When he returns he will explain this to you, and try to get me a vase of the size and form of Mrs. Church's, but with this improvement. In this business I shall beg leave to associate your taste with his. Present my compliments to Mr. Cosway. I am obliged to trust this letter through the post office, as I see no immediate chance of a private conveiance. Adieu, my dear Madam: think of me often and warmly, as I do of you.

PrC (ViU); unsigned; without day or year which have been supplied from internal evidence, together with an entry in SJL Index of a letter written on this date. There is also an entry in SJL Index for a letter from Maria Cosway of 6 Jan. 1788, but this appears to be another instance (of which there are several) of error in making the entry, for (1) TJ does not record the letter dated "Christmas day" (25 Dec. 1787) to which the present letter was a reply, and (2) no letter of 6 Jan. 1788 from Maria Cosway has been found. The evidence would seem to indicate that it was on that date that TJ received the "Christmas day" letter and that he entered it erroneously in SJL Index.

To Elie Lefebvre Frères

SIR   Paris Jan. 31. 1788.

Mr. Bondfeild of Bordeaux having informed me that he has sent to your address five boxes of wine for me, I take the liberty of inclosing you an order for it's free passage at the Douane, clear of duty. Any disbursements you will be so good as to make for freight, transportation &c. shall be paid on your draught. I suppose it will be best to send it on from Rouen to Paris by a roulier or waggon, which trouble I must ask you to take. I am with sentiments of perfect esteem, Sir your most obedient humble servt.,

TH: JEFFERSON

PrC (MHi).

From James Swan

Le Havre, 31 Jan. 1788. Apologizes for not sooner paying the "respect which I owe you as a Gentleman . . . as the Representative of the Sovereignty of my country"; arrived in last packet; his wife and children will follow him in May or June; until their arrival, will stay around Le Havre, Rouen, and Caen attending to business matters. Encloses some thoughts "put together in much haste at the commencement of the insurrection in Massachusetts"; as they have been of some use, is less concerned about their form.

RC (DLC); 2 p.; endorsed. Enclosure: A copy of *National Arithmetick: or, Observations on the finances of the Commonwealth of Massachusetts: with some hints respecting financiering and future taxation in this State: tending to render the Publick Contributions more easy to the People*, Boston, [1786]. TJ's copy (DLC) had a presentation inscription on the title-page, but most of this, including the author's name, was cut away by the binder. It also contains numerous corrections in ink in the text, a fact which probably explains Swan's remark about the hasty composition and the form of the piece. See Sowerby, No. 3620.

James Swan was a Scottish-born merchant from Boston who had been a zealous Son of Liberty and one of the "Mohawks" that staged the Boston Tea Party of 1773. He had risen prosperously during the Revolution, but had over-extended his commercial and land ventures after the war and had come to France to rebuild his fortune.

He wrote a memorial on Franco-American commerce at the suggestion of Lafayette during the latter's visit to America in 1784. This memorial was translated by the French consul at Boston, Létombe, who forwarded a copy in his dispatch of 1 Mch. 1787 (both in Arch. Aff. Etr., Paris, Mémoires et Documents, E.-U., xv; see Swan to TJ, 1 Mch. 1788). This memorial was concerned with the causes that had hindered the growth of trade between France and the United States and suggested means of promoting it. Swan enlarged his manuscript and published it in book form during his stay in France under the title *Causes qui se sont opposées aux progrès du commerce, entre la France, et les Etats-Unis de l'Amérique. Avec les moyens de l'accélérer, et la comparaison de la dette nationale de l'Angleterre, de la France, et des Etats-Unis; en six lettres adressées à Monsieur le Marquis de la Fayette* (Paris, 1790). He later became a purchasing agent in America

[541]

for the French Republic; his activities in this area and other phases of his colorful career are summed up in a graphic portrayal by Howard C. Rice, Jr., "James Swan: Agent of the French Republic, 1794-1796," *New England Quarterly*, X (1937), 464-86. Swan spent twenty-two years in a debtor's prison (1808-1830), presumably because he would not permit his wife, who lived in a handsome manner in a residence at Dorchester built in the style of a French chateau, to pay a small debt that he regarded as unjust. A few weeks after addressing the present letter to TJ, Swan wrote the following revealing lines to his friend Henry Knox: "Wherever I be, and in whatever situation, if I cannot be acquainted with the first in the place, I make it a rule not to be acquainted at all—as I have said before, I find it much more agreeable, and cheaper—and besides, is supporting a character of rank I maintained at home" (same, p. 466). TJ's copy of Swan's book, which he saw and commented on in MS form, is in DLC (Sowerby, No. 3608; see TJ to Swan, 23 Mch. 1789). See also TJ to Limozin, 30 July 1788.

From Nicolas & Jacob van Staphorst

Amsterdam 31 January 1788

We were honored in due time with your Excellency's respected favor of 3rd. Inst. and have postponed replying to it, in the hope We should be able to advise the Discharge of the Fifty One Thousand Guilders due by the United States the 1st. Instant at the House of Hry. Fizeaux & Co. which we should certainly have accomplished, had not our Colleagues' different Opinion on the Subject been fortified by your Excellency's Letter of 30. Ulto. confining your Wishes that the Interest only upon this Engagement might be paid, and the Redemption of the Capital await further Orders from the Board of Treasury. A Corroboration whereof by Mr. Adams, and his Requisition for Three Thousand Pounds Sterling indispensably necessary for himself and Colonel Smith previous to their Departure from Europe, defeated all the Progress We had made in bringing over Messrs. Willinks to our Sentiments upon this Business.

A Letter [is] since received from the Commissioners of the Treasury explaining the actual Situation of the Finances of the United States, and the utter impossibility of their remitting, prior to the Operation of the New Federal Government, for the Interests that will fall due in this Country, the Provision for which very important Object, they trust may be drawn from the Sale of the remaining Bonds of the last Loan raised here. Messrs. Willinks and ourselves will in consequence this day address your Excellency, with a Proposal on the Subject, Which being the only means to secure the Credit of the United States will we flatter ourselves be honored with your Approbation and Ratification.

[542]

Your Excellency's succeeding, by Mr. Adams's Retreat, to a more intimate and close Relation with the Commissioners of Loans raised in Holland for the United States, is highly pleasing to us. Your Excellency may be assured to experience every Proposition on our Part, to promote the public Good, and to evince the personal Esteem we entertain for you.

We are most respectfully Your Excellency's Most obedient and very Humble Servants,   NIC. & JACOB VAN STAPHORST

RC (DLC); addressed and endorsed.

From Willink & Van Staphorst, with Enclosures

Amsterdam 31 January 1788

We are honored with Your Excellency's respected favor of 13. Inst. urging us again to pay the f51,000 Guilders reimbursable by the United States the First Instant at the House of Henry Fizeaux & Co. which we should have effected, had you and Mr. Adams wrote us clearly and decidedly to do it; instead of which you both desired us to discharge only the Interest and wait the Orders of the Board of Treasury about the Principal. And now that We have your joint Approbation, the official Communication We have of the actual Situation and Prospect of the Finances of the United States would render such a partial Payment[1] of no avail towards the Support of the public Credit, unless effectual measures shall be adopted, to provide Funds for the f270 m. Interest that will be due the First of June next; A single day's Retard in which would ground a prejudice of long duration.

We inclose you a Copy signed by us, of a Letter We received from His Excelly. John Adams Esqr. under date of 22. Instant, with a dereliction to Your Excellency of his Relation towards us as Commissioners of Congress on Loans in this Country. In[2] consequence whereof you will likewise have herewith a Copy signed by us of the Letter addressed us under date of 5 December last by the Commissioners of the Treasury of the United States; Which we are certain will impress upon your Excellency's Mind, the Necessity of acceding to the Proposal agreed to by us in our Letter of 18 Instant to the Board of Treasury of the United States, of which we inclose a signed Copy, anticipating the Commissioners

[543]

Advice of the real State of the Federal Finances, and offering a Plan embracing the Object they so eagerly sollicit, and "to provide a Fund for answering the Interest which might become due 'till such time as a more efficacious System of General Revenue was provided." And it is peculiarly flattering to us, that the sole Objection possible to be started, if any should be deemed sufficiently weighty to enter into competition with the extreme advantages that will result to the United States from the Acceptance of this Proposal, would be the Payment of One Years Interest on the Two Loans of the Liquidated debt; Which exclusive of being obviated by being only an Advance of Payment, is removed by the disposition of the Board of Treasury to make a Sacrifice, should this Point be considered as One where the Commissioners say, "The last expedient we are sensible may subject you to Inconvenience, but the Sacrifice will we doubt not be considered by the Government of the United States when its more solid Establishment may induce them to call forth and compensate, in a proper Manner, your present Exertions to support their Credit."

It is highly pleasing to us that the Importance We attributed to the proposed Arrangement for Sale of the remaining Bonds of the last Loan, is fully corroborated by their Letter, and our Acceptance of it quite consonant to the Wishes of the Commissioners of the Treasury. But as we cannot flatter ourselves, to have the Answer of the Board, in season to conclude with the Subscribers, and receive the Monies from them, for which some Credit is always given, We submit our Acceptance of the Proposal for Sale of the remaining Bonds unto your Excellency's Approbation and Ratification; Which will not admit of a difficulty, should Your Excellency view the Business of the Magnitude and Importance We do, and be equally convinced as we are, that there exists no other means of preserving unsullied the Credit and Honor of the United States.

We request Your Excellency's speedy decision, in order that We may consolidate and execute the proposed Arrangement; Which is likewise requisite to enable us to carry into effect the other disposals of the United States.

We are respectfully Your Excellency's Most obedient and very Humble Servants, WILHEM & JAN WILLINK
NIC. & JACOB VAN STAPHORST

[544]

ENCLOSURE

Willink & Van Staphorst to
Commissioners of the Treasury

GENTLEMEN   Amsterdam 18 Janny. 1788.

We had the honour to address you our last respects the 25. Oct. Since are deprived of your favours.

Instead of the approbation of Mr. Adams to pay the 51m. ƒ reimbursable by the united States the 1r. Inst. at the House of Mes. Hy. Fizeaux Co. which we confidently expected in order to Discharge the Same in Support of the honour and Credit of Congress, this Minister has acquainted us with his recall, and that from the Public monies in our Hands, his and Colo. Smiths Expences for returning &c. must be Supplied, which he has informed our Correspondent in London will Amount to Three Thousand pound Sterling. Upon this unforeseen Intelligence we have Most Seriously reflected on the Accounts of the United States with us, and the probability of being able to keep up unsullied their Credit in this Country untill the federal System, now agitating, might be adopted, organized and Operate So as to enable you to make regular Provision for payments of the Interests and redemptions of the principals of your European Debt.

Your very unaccountable Silence and reserve to us, on these Objects, which it is however essentially necessary for us to have the most just and authentic Accounts of, have driven us to the necessity of depending on the Public Papers, and our private Connections, for the Information to direct our opinion and decision. The repeated non Compliance with requisitions made by the Honble. Congress to the respective States for Funds to face the federal Exigences, altho founded upon your reports recommended with peculiar Energy, deprive us of all hopes that you will be able to provide us with Monies that will fall due here before the Operation of the New Government; wherefore we judge it of the utmost importance to Secure if possible the Credit and Dignity of the United States untill this desirable Event Shall place it fully in your Power, as we are persuaded it has been your inclination, to Satisfy with punctuality all the Creditors of the United States, to which the resources of your Country, called forth by a judicious and efficient executive Government, are we doubt not abundantly Competent. The only Certain mode to Effect this being to procure a further Sale of the Bonds remaining in our hands, of the last Loan of One Million Guilders, we have used every persuasive Argument in our Power to induce the Subscrivers to make Another Engagement for part of them, but hitherto ineffectually. [The Most Capital[3] Broker in the money Line here who has been Very Instrumental in Creating and Supporting the Credit of Congress, by taking himself and vending large shares of their Loans from the first outset, and who thro Confidence in the Justice and Wisdom of the United States has undertaken to extend their Credit and augment their internal resources, by furnishing them large Sums of Money in purchase of Stock of your Liquidated Debt, has made us a proposal, which we believe if accepted, he wou'd Carry into Execution, and thus ease you of all Cares Anxieties and Sacrifices that might attend your

[545]

Remitting us before the time Necessary to provide us funds for the Interest that will fall due in 1789.][4] An object so highly Consequential and, we believe, convenient to the United States that we have promised to State and Urge its Acceptance with our Warmest recommendation, which we now do to you Gentlemen, in the belief it will not be declined seing the then possibility of maintaining the Public Credit unimpeach'd so long as the Situation of the United States will require. [We cou'd discharge the Sum due by Congress the 1 Inst. at the House of Henr. Fizeau & Co.

to which Sum	f 51000.
Add calls of Mr. Adams £3000 abt.	35000.
Interest in Feby. 1788[5]	80000.
Do. in June abt.	270000.
Do. in Feby. 1789	80000.
Make the fixed demands of these Objects	f516000.

Which might by the proposed Arrangements be Supplied to us provided you would authorize us to pay the Money Lenders in the Bonds of the Last Loan of One Million Guilders with a discount of 10 ℔ct. for benefice on the Exchange by remittances from America &c. One Years Interest Only On two Loans of your Liquidated Debt negotiated here being

$$\left.\begin{array}{r} 840000 \\ 500000 \end{array}\right\} \text{Dollars}$$

1340000 Doll: at 6 ℔ct.	80,400	
Off 10 ℔ct.	8,040	
Remains Doll:	72,360 abt.	180000
		f696000

Which we could face by Ballance in hand	f131000	
Sale of 677 Bonds remaining deducting 8 ℔ct. about	622840	753840
Leaving a ballance in favour of the United States		f 57840

to be applied to payments of the Sallary of Th. Jefferson Esqr. and other incidental Expences.][4]

In proposing this Matter to you, we are well aware it is of an Extraordinary nature and militating against established rules, but on the other hand the Circumstances and Object that would be accomplished are likewise out of the usual Line and Scarce to have been expected in the present floating State of your Government, and we trust the latter will intirely over balance and Triumph over any difficulties the former might occasion, when you will have considered that to your Evident great Conveniency at the most important Crisis your Credit will probably ever be Exposed to will be added the placing the honor Dignity and Credit of your Government upon a foundation that will Command such

[546]

reverence and Confidence as would insure you future Pecuniary Assistance from the Money Lenders of this Country, whenever the Moment may render Expedient for the United States to Attest or Vindicate their rights and respectability or undertake any great internal regulation or Improvement to which your Locality furnishes such ample Fields.

Hints have been given us, that it would be Extreemly Agreable and a Matter of Much Convenience to the french Court to transfer the debt due by the United States to it unto the Money Lenders here, even under Guaranty of the Court of Versailles, a fresh proof of its Confidence in your Government, which as well as the former Acts of friendship you have Experienced, we [are] certain it would be highly gratifying to the United States to retaliate, and we flatter ourselves this business might be Compleated here was the Credit of America placed upon the firm basis the present Arrangement would ground and Consolidated by the Introduction of the New federal System.

Against the allegation that may be made that Congress makes a difference between the payment of Interest to the foreign and Domestick Creditors of the United States, and therefore their Arrangements respecting their home Contracted debt should not influence the Credit of the Loans raised here may be truely opposed that our Money lenders would not Conceive or Admit the Justice of such a distinction, since the Solemn Faith of the same Government has been repeatedly pledged to both discriptions of Creditors. Therefore a demur of Interest upon the two aforementioned Loans of the Liquidated Debts would Certainly much distress the Credit of the United States here. The holders only make the demand for one year, since they are Assured by the plan of the new Government that in future all Continental Taxes will be Levied in Specie and Consequently the object they are destined to provide for will be discharged in the Same Manner, so that in fact Congress will pay no more here than it will Shortly afterwards be Obliged to pay in America for the Same Object and that in a property which would otherwise remain undisposed of. This People here are Convinced of from the Natural Idea they entertain that one of the first Measures of the New Government will be an efficient inforcement of all the former requisitions of Congress to the different States, a Measure equally pregnant with Justice to the Public Creditors and such States as have fully or in a great part Complied to such legal Claims, but as well merited retribution to the dilinquent, who by this means being obliged to supply in Money, what they may be deficient in their allotted faculty of paying in Indemts, will be Compelled to furnish Specie for the Interest upon Such part of the Liquidated Debt as is now asked by the proposed arrangement, and thus the United States will be rather gainers than Otherwise. It pained us Exceedingly to learn from Mr. Fizeaux & Co. that they had wrote you in Jany. and June 1787 upon the Subject of the reimbursement due at their house the 1. Inst. about which they or us have not received a Line. We most earnestly request the same fate may not attend this Letter, but that you will answer it by the first and Different Conveyances, the more so as it will be Expected in Course by the Brokers here, who have made the proposal now offered to your Consideration, and which its advantages we have accepted under the Condition of your approbation and ratification.

We must once more impress upon your mind that there being no probability of making Sale of the Bonds otherwise than by Closing with this proposal, should it be declined, we shall not be able to Discharge the next June Interest, unless furnished with timely remittances. We now Inclose you Abstract of the Account Current of the United States with us up to 31 Ulto. on which you will find included the Payment of a Jany. Interest due upon the ƒ51000, Negotiated for Congress by H. Fizeaux & Co. the ballance ƒ131230 holld. Currency We Carry to the Credit of the New Account of the United States. May we intreat your examination of Same, to honour with Attention our reiterated requests to have your approbation to such as we have furnished.

We are respectfully Gentlemen Your most obt. & Very Humble Serts.,

WILHELM & JAN WILLINK
NIC. & JACOB VAN STAPHORST

RC (DLC); endorsed. Tr of Extracts (MHi: AMT); in the hand of William Short; transmitted in TJ to Adams, 6 Feb. 1788, q.v. Enclosures (DLC; Tr of Extracts of Enclosures 2 and 3 in MHi: AMT): (1) Tr of Adams to Willink & Van Staphorst, 22 Jan. 1788, acknowledging their letter and stating that he had "since received another letter from Mr. Jefferson informing me that the creditors in Holland insist on immediate payment of the principal sum of 51,000 Guilders &c"; that Smith had transmitted them a sealed packet from the Commissioners of the Treasury "which may contain Orders to your Satisfaction"; that, "however this may be, considering the opinion of Mr. Jefferson who is to have in future the principal Direction of American affairs under Congress, and the board of treasury, and considering the convenience of having all our concerns in one System at Amsterdam, and the Injury that might arise to our credit if such as demand payment should be disappointed, I have concluded upon the whole to advise and direct the payment of these obligations to the house of Fizeaux, provided you have money enough in hand or are willing to advance it"; that, however, he would be obliged to draw soon for almost £3,000 sterling for his and Smith's services and disbursements; that "If the American minister in London and the Secretary of his legation should be obliged to leave Europe without paying their debts, there is malice enough in this Country to make all Europe resound

with it, and more to the injury of our credit than even a failure in the punctual payment of the 51,000 Guilders"; and that "You will have one Consolation Gentlemen that about Three thousand Pounds sterling will set you free from all future demands of Mr. Adams and Col. Smith, two very expensive articles. If you Gentlemen or the Money lenders in Holland will take the pains to enquire of anybody who is properly informed, of the thriving state of American affairs, the flourishing condition of their agriculture, Fisheries, Commerce and even Manufactures, you must see that only the difficulty of agreeing on the manner of raising the revenue has hitherto prevented their paying both principal and Interest whenever these became due. If there is a Man in Holland or in the World who will trust his money in English funds in preference to American, that man is a fool. He discerns nothing of the signs of the times. I doubt not gentlemen of your ability to pay the 51,000 Guilders and my demands and Coll. Smith's too. I presume that Mr. Morris's bills which I transmitted you, are honored, but shall be glad to be inform'd of it by you, if you please." (2) Tr from Commissioners of the Treasury to Willink & Van Staphorst, 5 Dec. 1787, expressing their regret that the prospect of completing the "one million loan is so very unfavorable"; that the great work of adopting "a more efficacious System of General Revenue" had been before a convention of the states and would in all probability be completed in the coming summer; that "In the meanwhile the prospect of its Establishment occasions an almost total Stagnation in the receipts of revenue arising from direct taxation which for some time has been the feeble source of supply to the General Treasury. It will therefore altogether be impossible for us at present to make any further remittance in order to provide for the June interest"; that for this as well as the expenses of the foreign ministers "during the course of the ensuing year we are constrained to rely on your exertions to complete subscriptions or to make advances to make up any deficiencies so that the credit of the United States may not suffer any further injury"; and that they confirm Adams' directions to Willink & Van Staphorst to pay Dumas $1,300 per annum. (3) Willink & Van Staphorst to Commissioners, 18 Jan. 1788 (printed above); in DLC there is a Tr of Extract entirely in TJ's hand, with the following caption: "Extract of a letter from Willincks & Staphorsts to the board of Treasury Jan. 11 [i.e., 18]. 1788," with two marginal notes which have been quoted below.

1 TJ wrote in RC at this point: "viz. that to Fizeaux & Co.," an addition that was incorporated in the text of the extract sent to Adams.

2 TJ inserted a bracket in RC before this sentence with the following instruction to Short for copying the extracts to be sent to Adams: "from here to the end"; Short's Tr includes the first paragraph of the letter and the full text from this point on.

3 In TJ's extract, he inserted an asterisk at this point and wrote the following in the margin: "Stadnitzki. There have been three particular brokers always concerned for the U.S. Stadnitzki is one; Supportus and Votater the other two. Supportus is Hope's brother and dare not meddle with anything he disapproves, and as he is lately become averse to France and every thing connected with her Supportus will not dare to act for us again."

4 The text in brackets (supplied) is the whole of that part included in TJ's extract.

5 In extract, TJ inserted a cross before the word "Interest" and wrote at foot of page: "see end of Journ. Congr. of 1787. all the contracts of European loans."

Memoranda Concerning Algiers

[ca. Jan. 1788]

Dr. Warner from Algiers.

He is surgeon in the British navy: has resided in Algiers 3 years on leave: is now called to England, but expects leave to return to Algiers.

American prisoners. Two are dead of the plague, one of the small pox, and Capt. Coffyn is lately dead of a consumption. The dey bought some of our captives, and beylick (the government) the rest. They are all employed in labour, except the two captains (Obrian and Stephens) and the 2. mates. These have been withdrawn by the Spanish consul. All captives may be withdrawn by any responsible person, paying the owner from half a chequin to a chequin (10 livres) a month. He must feed and clothe them moreover. Food is worth about a chequin and clothing half a chequin a month. If they run away, or die in his possession he is answerable for their value exorbitantly fixed. The custom is to send them to the hospital as soon as they are taken sick, and if they die there the person is not answerable. Our four have all died in the hospital. The captives of no nation have been ransomed since the Spanish treaty for less than 500, 550 to 600 chequins. The Neapolitans paid the Spanish price. The French captives redeemed by the religious order were malefactors sent by Spain to Oran, in punishment, and fugitives from France. Slaves from thence are valued but at half price because of their worthless character. The English have a right by treaty to demand their subjects without ransom, though taken in the vessel of another nation. Yet Logie, their consul at Algiers has never demanded the English taken in our two ships. There is no danger of our prisoners escaping, if taken out on the usual conditions.

Logie is a drunkard, and his wife a prostitute. None of the other consuls associate with him. The French consul is a respectable man. There is but one English and one French merchant there. The English merchant is Wolf, by birth an Irishman, 50 years old, sensible, honest, long resident there, well acquainted with the country, and it's politicks, and respected by the government and by all the Consuls. He has a wife and 2 children. He has been promised the English consulship, but disappointed. He was recommended by the Dey and Count d'Espilly to be Spanish consul, but they had before named another. All the foreign consuls receive from six to eight hundred guineas a year, salary, clear of deductions.

The method of doing business with that government is to go as a private man, to sound privately, to make a good friend by presents, before the business is declared. He thinks it would have cost us a million of dollars to obtain peace when Lamb was there. Lamb did not drink there, nor conduct himself otherwise amiss. He had little to do with Logie. He was misadvised by the French Consul. His watches &c would not have been accepted because not in the taste of those people. The moment too was unfavorable, because the Spaniards, Neapolitans, and Portuguese were then suing for peace.

The Dey is 80 years old with ulcers in his legs. When he dies all treaties must be renewed. The French and English do not pay an annual tribute: but they make presents from time to time. The English are most respected. The Americans considered as their descendants and on equal ground. The French well respected. The Spaniards despised and considered as a conquered nation. In general the Northern people are more respected than the Southern.

Their road is very dangerous: the harbour safe, and strongly defended. They have 9 vessels from 20. to 36. guns and 4. or 5. smaller. They are sharp built, and swift; but so lightly built that one good broadside of a frigate suffices for them. Their rigging is good, and their guns of the same caliber, all these things being furnished them by the Danes, Swedes, and Dutch. Besides this they have a Frenchman who casts very good cannon and mortars for them. Their cannon are badly pointed and worked in action, being served by ignorant natives. 4. or 5. of these vessels belong to the government, and they name the officers to all the rest and have a third of the prizes. But these vessels were never known to act together. Therefore 3. good frigates in constant cruize would suffice. Nor need they cruize in Nov. Dec. Jan. Feb. because the Algerines never go out in these months. Nor do they go out at all when they hear that there are vessels cruising off their port for them. They heard once that 3 American frigates were cruising for them off the streights of Gibraltar, and all their vessels were ordered not to go out of the streights. They go sometimes as far as the channel and the Western isles.

MS (DLC); entirely in TJ's hand; undated, but certainly written before 5 Feb. 1788 (see TJ to Jay of that date) and evidently during late Jan. 1788; endorsed: "Algiers."

From Madame de Corny

[ca. Jan. 1788?]

J'ay l'honneur d'offrir mille complimens a Monsieur de jefferson, je le prie de trouver bon que Mde. church me laisse sa voiture. J'ay toujours desirer l'achetter, mais ne voulant pas qu'elle me fit aucun sacrifice sur le prix, j'attendois qu'il luy fut fait des offres pour regler les miennes. J'attend une voiture d'angleterre, elle peut etre encor 2 mois a arriver, j'ay une voiture a repeindre, il ne m'en restera qu'une seule pour Mr. de corny et moi. Ainsi je n'aurois nul moyen d'aller voir Mr. de jefferson ni d'être util a Kitty. Je desire obtenir son consentement et surtout le persuader que la necessite seul me fait la loi, sans quoi je craindrois de luy causer la moindre contradiction. Mais j'espere qu'[il] voudra bien apprécier ma position. J'ay l'honneur de luy renouveller l'assurance de mon attachement.

RC (DLC); endorsed by TJ: "Corny Mde De"; unsigned and undated, but probably written shortly before Mrs. Church departed for London on 16 Feb. 1788.

To William Carmichael

Dear Sir   Paris Feb. 1. 1788.

I have a moment's warning only of the departure of Mr. Symonds for Madrid, which place however he will not reach till the month of April, which is another reason for my making this letter merely the vehicle for a cypher which I can answer for in point of correspondence with mine. I take the liberty at the same time of recommending the bearer hereof to your notice. I have the honour to be with much respect & esteem Dr. Sir Your most obedt. & most humble servt.,   Th: Jefferson

PrC (DLC). The enclosed cipher has not been found, but see note to TJ to Carmichael, 25 Sep. 1787.

From Anthony Garvey

Rouen, 1 Feb. 1788. Encloses vouchers [concerning John Jackson]; will do whatever TJ directs for "the Poor Man in question, and who appears to be an object of Great Commiseration"; thanks TJ for his letter of 29 Nov. but fears that the money is lost "as I have Got to do with Men that have lost all Shame and honour."

RC (MHi); 2 p.; endorsed. The enclosed papers were transmitted by TJ to Henry Knox, 6 Feb. 1788, q.v.

From André Limozin

Le Havre, 1 Feb. 1788. Two ships flying American colors arrived "yesterday" with 749 hhds. of tobacco shipped by Johnson & Muir in accordance with Morris' contract with the farmers-general; the ships, the *Sally* and *Potomac*, left Annapolis 26 Dec.; it would be "surprising" if the farmers received the tobacco in spite of the resolution and convention passed at Berni. Is informed by the masters of these ships that other ships are being loaded at Baltimore under Morris' contract. Capt. Jenkins sailed 27 Jan. 1788 taking the barrel of rice, for which the bill of lading and account of costs are enclosed.

RC (MHi); 4 p.; addressed and endorsed on the verso of the account of disbursements. Enclosures: (1) Bill of lading for rice (missing). (2) Statement of cost for shipping a barrel of rice on the *Juno*, Capt. Jenkins, to the care of James Madison, New York, amounting to 36.ᵗᵗ17.6 (MHi).

To Abigail Adams, with Enclosure

DEAR MADAM   Paris Feb. 2. 1788

The silk you desired was delivered to Mr. Parker a month ago, on the eve of his departure for England, as he supposed. He went however to Holland. Mr. Valnay is so kind as to take charge of that now, as also of the silk stockings. I doubt whether you may like the stockings on first appearance. But I will answer for their goodness, being woven expressly for me by the Hermits of Mont Calvaire with whom I go and stay sometimes, and am favoured by them. They have the reputation of doing the best work which comes to the Paris market. I inclose you their little note of the weight and price, for they sell by weight. I inclose also a state of our accounts subsequent to the paiment of the small sum by Colo. Smith which balanced our former transactions. You will make such additions and amendments to it as you shall find right. I have not yet been able to find M. de la Blancherie at home, so as to settle Mr. Adams's affair with him; but I will do it in time, and render you an account. There being no news here to communicate to you, be pleased to accept my thanks for the many kind services you have been so good as to render me and your friendly attentions on every occasion. I have considered you while in London as my neighbor, and look forward to the moment of your departure from thence as to an epoch of much regret and concern for me. Insulated and friendless on this side the globe, with such an ocean between me and every thing to which I am attached the days will seem long which are to be counted over before I too am to rejoin my native country. Young poets complain often that life is fleeting and transient. We find in it seasons and situations however which move heavily enough. It will lighten them to me if you will continue to honour me with your correspondence. You will have much to communicate to me, I little which can interest you. Perhaps you can make me useful in the execution of your European commissions. Be assured they will afford me sincere pleasure in the execution. My daughters join me in affectionate Adieus to you. Polly does not cease to speak of you with warmth and gratitude. Heaven send you, madam, a pleasant and safe passage, and a happy meeting with all your friends. But do not let them so entirely engross you as to forget that you have one here who is with the most sincere esteem and attachment Dear Madam your most obedient & most humble servant,   TH: JEFFERSON

[553]

ENCLOSURE

Mrs. Adams in acct. with Th:J

		Dr.	Cr.
		£	£ s
1787. Oct. 3. To paid for 5. aunes cambrick sent by Dr. Cutting	60^{tt}	2-10	
By cash to Colo. Smith			2-10
Dec. 19. By cash by Mr. Trumbull 120^{tt}			5
1788. Jan. 9. To pd. Hermits of M. Calvaire 12 pr. silk stockings	168^{tt}		
To pd. for 10. aunes double Florence @ 4^{tt}-15	47-10		
23. To pd. Ct. Sarsfeld for books for Mr. Adams	79		
	294-10	12- 5-5	
Balance in favor of Th:J			7- 5-5
		14-15-5	14-15-5

RC (MHi: AMT); endorsed. PrC (DLC). Enclosures: (1) Note of weight and price of stockings (missing). (2) TJ's account with Abigail Adams (RC in MHi: AMT; PrC in DLC); RC endorsed: "Sent this Balance due to Mr Jefferson by Mr Parker Febry 22 1788 Abigail Adams."

From Samuel Blackden

DEAR SIR   Brussells February 2d. 1788

I have to pray you to pardon the trouble I am about to give you, when I request answers to three or four questions relative to the American Flag, which some circumstances that have Occurr'd since I had the honour of seeing you Render it Necessary for me to Obtain, and as there is no one so well qualified to give them as yourself so I am persuaded from your former kindness no one will do it more kindly.

The Prospect held out to me is Very flattering provided the situation of affairs permit you to answer in the affirmative, but be that so or not I shall equally feel my obligations to you for the Many instances I have experienced of your politeness and friendship.

1st. If I purchase a Ship at Ostend, and produce to you the authenticated bill of sale which will prove her to be the property of an American can you grant me such certificate as will enable me to send her to Any port of the World where American Ships are admitted, as for instance the french Islands in the West and east indies and the other settlements in the last Mentioned Country.

2d. Will it be necessary for me to bring the returns of any such Voyage, under American colours, to any port in America, or shall I be at liberty to sell it where I find it most advantagious.

3d. Will the bill of sale be sufficient Evidence of her being American property, if not what further will be necessary.

4th. I beg you to inform me whether any American Ships coming from India will be admitted into any ports in france, and if they will be, which the Ports are.

I am now on a short tour through this delightful country of Flanders where on this first of February the Appearance of the fields is like the month of October, and so mild has been the Winter that a pair of skates has not been Used more than one day. I shall go from hence to Antwerp and then back to Dunkerque where I hope to be honored with your Answer. In the Meanwhile I beg you to Accept my sincere wishes for your health and happiness, and to present my respects to Miss Jefferson and Mr. Short, whom with yourself I hope to have the pleasure of Seeing in Paris in a few weeks.

I have the Honour to be with the highest respect and esteem Dear Sir Your Much Obliged and Most Obedient Servant,

SAM BLACKDEN

Address At No. 4. Rue St. Julien at Dunkerque.

RC (DLC); endorsed.

From Gaudenzio Clerici

HONBLE. SIR   Milan the 2d. February 1788.

I happened to be at the Comte del Verme's house the day after the arrival of the books mentioned in Your letter of the 15th August; and was immediately shewn the kind present You have been pleased to send me, for which I return, Honble Sir, my very humble thanks to You. Should we in compliance to some liberal readers have made such a desirable present to an Italian Public to what a mercyless castration under the hands of inexorable mutilators should the free Monticello-Production undergo! Ramsay's History of S. Ca. and Georgia was equally a thing that I very much wished to peruse again. And by Your present to the Comte del Verme, and thro' the friendly regards the Comte is pleased to honor me with, I get now the opportunity I desired. My personal acquaintance with the Doctor's abilities and integrity during my long stay at Charleston has inspired me a very high esteem for him. Altho' a warm friend to America, I know him to feel and to speak with his tho' unparaphrastical cascado eloquence much in favor of justice and unjustly distressed foreign people. We have no news, that I think worth the writing. If there is any however, I dare say you will receive them with the same ordinary by a better hand. Demolishing Churches; new thoughts about suppressing Convents and making money for war; restricting the number of parsons and parishes, reformation of Ecclesiastical education, I am sure are no news to You. *Opera fesse di ballo, Mascherare* is every thing we have and we wish at this present season di Carnovale. We want dancing and raree-shows and ramadans to forget miseries and wretchedness as much as the Africo-americans want the Banjar to digest with their Kuskus the hardships of their lives, and the unsafe treatments of their Overseers. And I presume, You don't want to be troubled with my long letters. So I finish, always with my earnest and sincere entreats for your remembrance of a person who wishes whilst he lives to have the honor to be Honble. Sir Your very Huml. & very obt. Servt.,

GAUDENZIO CLERICI

RC (DLC); addressed.
KUSKUS: A food made from cereal, originally from African millet (OED).

To John Rutledge, Jr.

DEAR SIR   Paris Feb. 2. 1788.

I should have sooner answered your favor of Jan. 2. but that we have expected for some time to see you here. I beg you not to think of the trifle I furnished you with, nor to propose to return it till you shall have that sum more than you know what to do with. And on every other occasion of difficulty I hope you will make use of me freely. I presume you will now remain at London to see the trial of Hastings. Without suffering yourself to be imposed on by the pomp in which it will be inveloped, I would recommend to you to consider and decide for yourself these questions. If his offence is to be decided by the law of the land, why is he not tried in that court in which his fellow citizens are tried, i.e. the King's bench? If he is cited before another court that he may be judged, not according to the law of the land, but by the discretion of his judges, is he not disfranchised of his most precious right, the benefit of the laws of his country in common with his other fellow citizens? I think you will find on investigating this subject that every solid argument is against the extraordinary court and that every one in it's favor is specious only. It is a transfer from a judicature of learning and integrity to one, the great mass of which is both illiterate and unprincipled. Yet such is the force of prejudice with some, and of the want of reflection in others, that many of our constitutions have copied this absurdity without suspecting it to be one. I am glad to hear that our new constitution is pretty sure of being accepted by states enough to secure the good it contains, and to meet such opposition in some others as to give us hopes it will be accomodated to them by the amendment of it's most glaring faults, particularly the want of a declaration of rights.—The long expected edict for the protestants at length appears here. It's analysis is this. It is an acknolegement (hitherto witheld by the laws) that protestants can beget children and that they can die and be offensive unless buried. It does not give them permission to think, to speak, nor to worship. It enumerates the humiliations to which they shall remain subject, and the burthens to which they shall continue to be unjustly exposed. What are we to think of the condition of the human mind in a country where such a wretched thing as this has thrown the state into convulsions, and how must we bless our own situation in a country the most illiterate peasant of which is a Solon compared with the authors of this law. There is a modesty often which does itself injury. Our countrymen possess this. They do not know their own superiority. You see it; you are young, you have time and talents to correct them. Study the subject while in Europe in all the instances which will present themselves to you, and profit your countrymen of them by making them to know and value themselves. Adieu, my dear Sir, and be assured of the esteem with which I am your friend & servt.,   TH: JEFFERSON

RC (ViU); addressed, in part: "chez S. E. Monsr. Adams." PrC (DLC).

To William Stephens Smith, with Enclosure

DEAR SIR   Paris Feb. 2. 1788.

Mr. Payne happened to be present when I received your favour of January 16. I read to him that part which stated the circumstances of your delivery of the letter of Dec. 3 to Mr. Littlepage and of the place where he put it for greater care. Payne conjectured what had happened, that it's separation from the common mass of letters had occasioned it to be overlooked. He repeated the circumstances to Littlepage on his return to his lodgings, and he immediately re-examined and found the letter, which I now have. I inclose you your press copies, with a supplement to our account, as far as my memorandum book or an examination of our letters enable me to make it out. You will be so good as to examine and correct the new articles where they need it, and whatever balance may remain, Mr. Trumbul will receive and employ it for me. With respect to Mr. Adams's picture, I must again press it to be done by Brown, because Trumbul does not paint of the size of the life, and could not be asked to hazard himself on it. I have sent to Florence for those of Columbus (if it exists) of Americus Vesputius, Magellan &c. and I must not be disappointed of Mr. Adams's. When done, Mr. Trumbul will receive and forward it to me. Be so good also as to let me know who undertook the map of S. America, and even to get from him some acknolegement in writing, of what he is to do.—I am glad to learn by letters which come down to the 20th. of December that the new constitution will undoubtedly be received by a sufficiency of the states to set it a going. Were I in America, I would advocate it warmly till nine should have adopted, and then as warmly take the other side to convince the remaining four that they ought not to come into it till the declaration of rights is annexed to it. By this means we should secure all the good of it, and procure so respectable an opposition as would induce the accepting states to offer a bill of rights. This would be the happiest turn the thing could take. I fear much the effects of the perpetual re-eligibility of the President. But it is not thought of in America, and have therefore no prospect of a change of that article. But I own it astonishes me to find such a change wrought in the opinions of our countrymen since I left them, as that threefourths of them should be contented to live under a system which leaves to their governors the power of taking from them the trial by jury in civil cases, freedom of religion, freedom of the press, freedom of commerce, the habeas corpus laws, and of yoking them with a standing army. This is a degeneracy in the principles of liberty to which I had given four centuries instead of four years. But I hope it will all come about. We are now vibrating between too much and too little government, and the pendulum will rest finally in the middle. Adieu, yours affectionately,

Th: Jefferson

[558]

ENCLOSURE

Colo. W. S. Smith in account with Th: J.
Dr.

To balance in my favor, as by your account
rendered Dec. 3. 1787. [£]3.18.7

1786. Oct. 2. To paid Petit for cambrick &c.
purchased for Mrs. Smith 164.^{tt}
I have no account of the particulars of this
last article, and suppose I must have sent
it to you. The list came in your letter of July
18. 1786. The things went by Mr. Bullfinch,
as said in my letter of Aug. 9. 1786. Your's
of Sep. 18. 1786. acknoleges receipt: but
none of them specify of articles.

20. To paid for Chastellux' travels
and Lattre's map of N. America 12.14

1787. Feb. 9. To paid for 2. pr. of Corsets for
Mrs. Smith. 48.^{tt} 48.
I suspect this article should not be charged,
as perhaps it may be included in the credit
you give me in these words 'By Corsets, cambrick and lace for Mrs. Smith as pr. account
188.^{tt} 15. This article is not dated in your
account; nor have I retained a note of it. I see
it stands posterior to all the articles of 1787.
Petit thinks it was for double Florence white
and coloured, linen batiste &c. You will be
able to set it to rights by the account to which
you refer and which I presume is in your
possession.
To paid for a cloak, the account of which is
now inclosed. 195.^{tt}12.6

420 . 6.6 17.10.3

£21. 8.10
To 2 pr. shoes sent you by Mr. Short 16.^{tt} 13. 4

22. 2. 2

Cr.

By pd. for small copying press for me (see your letter
July 5. 1786) £ 5.10.
By 2. pr. shoes for Mr. Short not charged in your account 17.
6. handkerchiefs for do. 1. 1.
By 2. waistcoats and 2 pr. breeches of cotton for me (see
my letter Sep. 13. 1786.)
By A waistcoat and pr. breeches of Casimer (see my
letter Oct. 22. 1786.) No account was sent me of the
above, but I presume the taylor has rendered it to you,
or can now do it.

PrC (DLC). Enclosure (DLC); also enclosed: PrC of Smith to TJ, 3 Dec.
1787, and its enclosure.

[559]

From Parent

MONSIEUR   a Beaune ce 3 feuvrier 1788

[Il vous] Plaira faire Recevoir Par le Sieur George Chauveaux, voiturier ordinaire de Noux près Chatillion, Les Six panier de vin, dont deux volleney, marqué PS Né. 1 et 2 et quatre panier vin blanc Goute D'or, aussy marqué de même, numéroté trois, quatre, Cinq, Six, donc il y en [a] soixante et deux en Chaque panier; et vous luy feré payé seize livres Dix Sols pour chaque panier et Rien autre. Et je luy ait Remis un petit pacquet de Seps de vignes, qui est de Douze Montrachet, dont Six de Monsieur de Clermont et Six de Monsieur de Charsenay, et Dix de Clos de Veougot, et Neuf de Chambertin, et huit de Romanée, que vous recevrés par le même voiturier, qui doit vous les menée Gratice. Et si il ne vous les Remette pas, vous luy en Retiendré vingt quatre livres sur la voiture. Les deux feuillette de blanc Coute 200^{tt} D'achat, et la feuillette de Vollenay, le meilleur que j'ay peu trouvé à Vollenay, 90^{tt} Pour les bouteille achetté, vingt-quatre livres le Cent, il y en a trois Cent trois quarterons. 90^{tt} pour les paniers, et l'enballage sept livres par panier, 42^{tt} Et pour avoir Soutiré et collé les trois feuillette et mis en bouteille, Douze livres; et pour les bouchons et la Cire et la paille et la fisselle, sept livres Dix sols. Il sont partie le trente de janvier, vous devé les Reçevoir le Douze ou le treize feuvrier au plus tard, et vous voudré bien, Monsieur, m'en faire accuser la Réception après que vous les auré Reçüe. Je Suis très Sincerement Monsieur Votre tres humble et tres obeissant Serviteur,

PARENT

RC (MHi); at foot of text the various charges, amounting to 441.^{tt} 10s, are recapitulated and 16.^{tt} 10, the cost of transportation per hamper, multiplied by 6; on verso, in the hand of TJ's servant, Petit, there is an un-signed acknowledgment of the receipt of 371 bottles of wine (one bottle was broken, see TJ to Parent, 20 Feb.); below Petit's receipt, in TJ's hand: "droits d'entree 75-3 Voiturage du vin 99 des ceps."

From Elie Lefebvre Frères

Rouen, 4 Feb. 1788. Acknowledge TJ's letter of 31 Jan.; have not yet received from Bondfield the bill of lading for the 5 cases of wine and do not know name of ship, or its captain, by which the wine was shipped; ask TJ to send the bill of lading if he has it; recommend sending the wine on by water.

RC (MHi); 1 p.; in French.

From Collow Frères, Carmichael & Co.

Sir   Havre, 5 Feby. 1788.

We have the honor of informing your Excellency that the Ship Bowman, Captn. D. Butler, arrived here this morning from Virginia and brought a Packet, apparently of News Papers with a letter from our friend A. Donald Esqr. of Richmond addressed to you. The former we have forwarded apart by this days Post, and the latter you will be pleased to receive enclosed.

We are informed by Mr. Donald that you have been kind enough to promise to procure for him a Groce of fine Claret and he has directed us to receive the same, and to pay for it, which we shall do with much pleasure when we know the Cost.

The Ship Bowman belongs to Mr. Donald and comes loaded with 490 Hogsheads of Tobacco for the Contract of Mr. Morris. We hope to get her dispatched back in ten days or a fortnight, when we shall be extremely happy if we can be serviceable in forwarding letters or any thing else which you may wish to send by that Conveyance. We expect hourly another Ship, called the Portsmouth from James River, loaded for the Private Account of Mr. Donald and his friends in Virginia, as indeed the Bowmans Cargo originally was, with an intention to consign it to us for Sale to the Farmers General, until they were deterred from attempting that Destination by Advices recently received from France. We fear we shall be obliged to send the Portsmouth to a Foreign Port, as the Farmers General refuse at present to take Tobacco from the General Trade, or if they did, we have reason to think it would be at Prices which cannot be accepted, being much below those at other Markets. She will not therefore in all probability return from this Port to America.

Will your Excellency permit us to observe to you (since we happen to have this opportunity of doing so) that the very great uncertainty in which our Friends in America remain with regard to the Chance of their Tobacco being received in France has been in many instances, highly detrimental to their Interests.

May we take the liberty to ask of your Excellency, if the Trade is likely soon to be established on any regular footing?

By the Resolutions at Bernis of the 12th May 1786 (which, we understand, the Trade of the United States was principally indebted for to you) we had good grounds to believe that after the Expiration of Mr. Morris's Contract, no more of the same

[561]

kind would be made, but that France would be entirely supplied from the General Trade. But we now hear, from some people, Reports of that Contract being renewed and even extended; and others again say, this is not the fact, but that the Trade will be kept open and the Farmers take annually a certain quantity, at least, from the General Trade.

Such a State of uncertainty confounds and embarrasses every operation with a view to the Tobacco Trade, between America and France, and therefore we hope we shall be excused the liberty we take in presuming to enter upon this Subject, more especially as we are convinced that the Communication of every Circumstance which affects the Trade and Interests of the Subjects of the United States of America so very essentially, as this does, will be favorably received by your Excellency.

We have the honor to be with Sentiments of the highest Respect, Sir, Your most obedient and most humble Servants,

COLLOW FRERES CARMICHAEL & CO.

RC (DLC); endorsed. Incorrectly entered in SJL Index as being dated 9 Feb. 1788, which was evidently the date of receipt. Enclosure: Donald to TJ, 15 Dec. 1787.

From C. W. F. Dumas

MONSIEUR   La Haie 5e. Fevr. 1788

En acheminant à votre Excellence la Dépeche ci-jointe, qui j'espère pourra encore partir par le Paquebot de ce mois du Havre, j'ai, au milieu de mes maux de corps et d'âme, besoin de demander à Votre Excellence de ses bonnes nouvelles, tant personnelles que publiques. Elle aura pu voir par les Supplémens de la Gazette de Leide depuis le commencement de cette année que je tâche de faire le meilleur usage de tout ce que j'apprends de certain et de positif, pour le crédit des Etats-Unis; et, j'ose dire, avec succès. Ceux qui cherchent à le déprécier, débitent que la plus forte opposition au nouveau Gouvernement fédéral viendra du côté de la Virginie. Je ne puis mieux m'adresser sur cela qu'à Votre Excellence; son autorité me mettra à même de contredire positivement ceux qui affectent de répandre cela. En attendant, l'on m'apprend d'Amst. que le Paquet de Janvier est arrivé de N. York (on ne me dit pas si c'est au Havre ou en Angleterre) avec la nouvelle que 4 Etats ont déjà accédé au nouveau Gouvernement fédéral; que 6 autres délibéroient encore, avec toute apparence d'une accession pareille; et que par conséquent ce salutaire ouvrage arrivera à la perfection plutôt-même que ses plus zélés partisans n'avoient osé l'espérer. On m'apprend aussi, que le Congrès fait une troisième Vente, de 3 millions d'acres; que cette nouvelle réduction de la Dette domestique de l'Union (qui, si je calcule bien, n'est donc plus que de 7 millions au plus en circulation) en devient plus rare au Marché, que le prix en a conséquemment augmenté, et probablement augmentera de plus en plus, &c. Puissent toutes ces bonnes choses m'être confirmées par Votre Excellence, de qui je suis avec le plus respectueux dévouement le très-humble & très-obéissant serviteur,   C W F Dumas

RC (DLC). FC (Rijksarchief, The Hague, Dumas Letter Books; photostats in DLC). Enclosure (FC, same): Dumas to Jay, 2 Feb. 1788, informing him (as he did TJ in the covering letter) that he has been looking after American interests by having published in "the Leyden Gazette, the best paper in this country, . . . the report of the Federal Convention . . . together with the ordinance of Congress respecting the government of the Northwest Territory, and the treaty with Morocco . . . besides all other certain accounts respecting the state of things in America, particularly the admirable arrangement by which the internal debt has been so much reduced. The three articles in the supplements to that Gazette of the middle of January, the 29th of the same month, and the 1st of February, are extracts of my letters to Mr. Luzac" (translation in *Dipl. Corr., 1783-89*, III, 608-9).

To John Jay

Sir   Paris Feb. 5. 1788.

The letter of Dec. 12. which Mr. Remsen did me the favor to write me during your indisposition has been duly received; and I shall be happy to hear that the cause is removed which deprived me at that moment of the pleasure of hearing from you. My last were of the 21st. and 31st. of December. I am afraid that my intelligence may have appeared sometimes to come late to hand. My letters by the Ct. de Moustier suffered his long delay in Brest by contrary winds. That too which he carried of Oct. 27. was particularly interesting, as it inclosed notice of the pacification between France and England. My letter of Dec. 31. by Capt. Jenkins, who was to have sailed Jan. 3. was detained with his vessel in Havre by contrary winds till Jan. 27. It conveyed the Arret and letter relative to our commerce, which were interesting also. On account of the multitude of falshoods always current here, under specious appearances, I am obliged to be slow of belief. But whenever a fact worth communicating, is so far authenticated as to be worthy belief, I never fail to avail myself of the first safe opportunity of communicating it to you.

The last letter on the subject of the brig Absolonia from Rhode island having re-established the orthography of the advocate's name (Dupeuty, instead of DePauly as the first letter had called him) I have found him and delivered him the letters and now inclose an answer from him to Messrs. Topham, Ross & Newman. No remarkeable circumstance has happened in the political affairs of Europe since my last. The season permits little activity between the Turks and Russians. The emperor, since the maneuvre to surprise Belgrade which failed, has been gathering strength towards that quarter, but no open act of hostility has yet taken place. [The principal minister here seems immoveably pacific. Their late loan is filled[1] up indeed, but with subscriptions only; not cash.[2] This comes in slowly, and the payments yet to be made are less sure than could be wished. I am assured they can obtain no money in Holland. The negociations with Russia and the Emperor proceed, but they proceed slowly. The hopes of the dutch patriots are just kept alive.[3] Their ambassador does not yet return to the Hague. The Prussians[4] are about to withdraw from Holland, and to be replaced by Hessians in the pay of the Republic. The health of the principal minister here is so low, that he does business with nobody but the King and Queen, and the ministers. Much is said and believed of his retiring from office, and being succeeded by the Duke de Chatelet; but I do not believe it, because facts seem to evince him master of the minds both of the King and Queen.][5] The bickerings with the parliament continue. The edict in favor of the non-catholics has at length passed. You will see a copy of it in the gazettes: and wonder that so small an effort of common sense could have excited so much contradiction. A violent opposition is raised against the Arret for the encouragement of our commerce inclosed in my last. All the chambers of commerce have remonstrated against it [and the ministers are alarmed. The Count de la Luzerne, on whose friendly dispositions it was supposed we might rely, does not manifest any[6] partialities for us.][5] The instability of the laws in this country is such that no merchant can venture to make any speculation on the faith of a law. I hope however that no material alteration will be permitted in the present instance. Therefore I should think it better not to alarm our merchants with any doubts about the continuance of it.—Commodore Jones set off this day for Copenhagen to settle the demands for prize money against that court.—I have lately seen a person just come from Algiers, who knew well all our captives there. Capt. Coffyn is dead of a consumption, two have died of the plague and one of the small pox. He thinks that since the price given by the Spaniards and Neapolitans for the redemption of captives, they will never sell another of any nation for less than from five to six hundred chequins. He supposes that exclusively of the redemption of our captives, it would have cost us a million of dollars to make peace when Mr. Lamb arrived there. The Spaniards, Neapolitans and Portuguese were then all suing for peace. This has increased excessively the pride of those pyrates. As soon as money is provided I shall set the business of redemption afoot. This letter goes by post. The gazettes to this day are inclosed. I have the honour to be with the most perfect esteem and respect, Sir, your most obedient & most humble servant, TH: JEFFERSON

RC (DNA: PCC, No. 87, II); partly in code. PrC (DLC); accompanied by the text *en clair* for the coded passages, in TJ's hand. The enclosed letter from Deputy to Topham, Ross & Newman has not been found (but see Jay to TJ, 24 Oct. 1787).

Remsen's letter of 12 Dec. 1787 has not been found. A PERSON JUST COME FROM ALGIERS: This was Dr. Warner, British naval surgeon, whom TJ must have seen a few days earlier (see memoranda on Algiers, printed at end of Jan. 1788). On the VIOLENT OPPOSITION . . . AGAINST THE ARRET, see note to TJ to Jay, 23 May 1788.

1 This word from TJ's text *en clair*; Jay decoded it as "filling."

2 In text *en clair*, TJ deleted at this point: "nor are the subscriptions thought to be solid."

3 In text *en clair* TJ first wrote "hindered from being extinguished," and then altered the phrase to read as above.

4 In text *en clair* TJ first wrote "Prussian troops" and then altered it to read as above.

5 The text in brackets (supplied) is written in code and in RC was decoded interlineally by Jay, employing Code No. 10. The text printed here follows Jay's decoding, with some minor corrections from TJ's text *en clair* and others indicated in notes, 1, 2, 3, 4, and 6.

6 In text *en clair* TJ first wrote "is certainly no" and then substituted the words "does not manifest any."

From Zachariah Loreilhe

Bordeaux, 5 Feb. 1788. Regrets the necessity of making an application to TJ which he is aware is improper; but since not only his but also Barclay's welfare is at stake, he ventures to ask TJ to procure a "Sauf Conduit"—which can be obtained without difficulty—to protect him from being thrown into jail by his and Barclay's "Mercyless Creditors." He remained in France, when Barclay sailed for America, to settle their accounts and would have been subject to criminal prosecution if he had left; since Barclay's departure his own "liberty has been very precarious"; expects within a month to be enabled by Barclay to make their creditors "Some proposals which very posibly may not be al-

[565]

together to their satissfaction" and expects, therefore, they may deprive him of his liberty; in which case it will be impossible to settle their affairs.

RC (MHi); 4 p.; endorsed.

To John Adams

Dear Sir   Paris Feb. 6. 1788.

The Commissioners of the treasury have given notice to Willincks and Van Staphorsts that they shall not be able to remit them one shilling till the new government gets into action; and that therefore the sole resource for the paiment of the Dutch interest till that period is in the progress of the last loan. Willincks & V.S. reply that there is not the least probability of raising as much on that loan as will pay the next June interest, and that if that paiment fails one day, it will do an injury to our credit which a very long time will not wipe off. A Mr. Stanitski, one of our brokers, who holds 1,340,000 dollars of our domestic debt offers, if we will pay him one year's interest of that debt, he will have the whole of the loan immediately filled up, that is to say he will procure the sum of 622,840 florins still unsubscribed. His year's interest (deducting from it 10 percent which he will allow for paiment in Europe instead of America) will require 180,000 florins of this money. Messrs. W. & V.S. say that, by this means, they can pay Fiseaux debt, and all the Dutch interest and our current expences here, till June 1789. by which time the new government may be in action. They have proposed this to the commissioners of the treasury, but it is possible that the delay of letters going and coming, with the time necessary between their receiving the answer and procuring the money, may force the decision of this proposition on me at the eleventh hour. I wish therefore to avail myself of your counsel before your departure on this proposition. Your knowlege of the subject enables you to give the best opinion, and your zeal for the public interest, and, I trust, your friendly dispositions towards me will prompt you to assist me with your advice on this question, to wit, if the answer of the Commissioners does not come in time, and there shall appear no other means of raising the June interest, will it be worst to fail in that paiment, or to accept of about 700,000 florins, on the condition of letting 180,000 be applied to the paiment of a year's interest of a part of our domestic debt? Do me the friendship to give me an answer to this as soon as possible and be assured of the sentiments of esteem and respect with which I have the honour to be Dear Sir Your most obedient & most humble servt., TH: JEFFERSON

RC (MHi: AMT). PrC (DLC). Enclosures (with RC): Extracts of Willink & Van Staphorst to TJ, 31 Jan. 1788, and of enclosures 2 and 3 in that letter, q.v.

To William Drayton

SIR   Paris Feb. 6. 1788.

The letter which I had the honor of addressing you on the 13th. of the last month informed you that I had forwarded to you a couffe of Egyptian rice by Capt. Shewell who was to sail from Marseilles directly to Charlestown, and another by the Juno, Capt. Jenkins sailing from Havre to New York. This last was addressed to the care of the S. Carolina delegates in Congress and bills of lading for both are now inclosed. To the same address I now send a small box containing cork acorns of the last year, a small paper of Sulla-seed from Maltha, and a larger one of the same species of seeds from plants growing in my own garden. I am persuaded from what I see and have heard of this plant that it will be precious for your climate. I wish all these articles may get safely to hand, and have the honour to be with sentiments of the most perfect esteem and respect Sir Your most obedient & most humble servant,
                                            TH: JEFFERSON

PrC (DLC). The enclosed bills of lading have not been found.

To Henry Knox

SIR   Paris Feb. 6. 1788.

The inclosed papers, stating the claims of John Jackson, an English pilot, on the justice and liberality of the United states, have been addressed to me. I can do nothing better than to forward them to you, as I suppose the claim to belong properly to your department. I formerly forwarded to the President of Congress an application from the same person, but never learnt whether any thing was done in it.

I have the honour to be with sentiments of the most perfect esteem and respect Sir your most obedient & most humble Servt.,
                                            TH: JEFFERSON

PrC (DLC). Tr (DNA: PCC, No. 150, III); endorsed and with a separate label which reads, in part: "to the Secretary at War (Copied for Congress)." Enclosures (same): (1) Tr of a letter from an unidentified source to R. & A. Garvey, dated Hull, 14 Jan. 1788, asking assistance for John Jackson, of Hull. (2) Tr of John Paul Jones' certificate concerning Jackson, 15 Nov. 1779. (3) Affidavit of two justices of the peace and the mayor of the "Town and County of Kingston upon Hull" testifying that the said Jackson is now living in that place and is the same person to whom Jones' certificate was issued. See TJ to Jay, 12 July 1785, and notes there; also Garvey to TJ, 1 Feb. 1788.

To André Limozin

Sir   Paris Feb. 6. 1788.

The box of plants you were so kind as to forward to me are arrived at the Douane. I shall send for them tomorrow morning, and have the Acquit à caution withdrawn. If it comes to me before the hour of the post it shall be inclosed in this letter. If not, it shall certainly come to you in my next.

The Mr. Madison who has written to you, is a member of Congress from the state of Virginia. He is a person of the first abilities in the United states, and of the greatest influence in our public affairs. He is the same for whom I often trouble you with boxes of books, letters &c.

I do not see that there are at present any strong symptoms of war. On the contrary the prevailing ministers both here and at the court of London, are known to be friends of peace. It is true that the distrust between the two courts is now extreme. But they are both shackled by the want of money, so that on the whole, peace seems the most probable at present.

I am with much esteem Sir your most obedient & most humble servt.,   TH: JEFFERSON
Feb. 6. The acquit à caution is inclosed.

PrC (DLC). Enclosure not found.

To James Madison

Dear Sir   Paris Feb. 6. 1788.

I wrote you last on the 20th. of December since which your's of the same day and of the 9th. have come to hand. The apples and cranberries you were so kind as to send at the same time were all spoiled when they arrived at Havre, so that probably those articles will not keep during the passage. The box of plants is arrived at the Custom house here, but I shall probably not receive them till after I shall have sealed my letter. They are well chosen, as to the species, for this country. I wish there had been some willow oaks (Quercus Phellos Linnaei) among them, either the plants or acorns, as that tree is much desired here, and absolutely unknown. As the red-birds and opossums are not to be had at New York, I will release you from the trouble of procuring them else-where. This trouble, with the incertainty of their coming safe, is more than the importance of the object will justify. You omitted to inclose Prince's catalogue of plants which your letter mentions to have been inclosed. I send herewith two small boxes, one ad-dressed to Mr. Drayton to the care of the S. Carola. delegates, with a letter. Will you be so good as to ask those gentlemen to forward the letter and box without delay. The box contains cork acorns, and Sulla, which should arrive at their destination as quick as possible. The other box is addressed to you, and contains, cork acorns, Sulla, and peas. The two first articles are to be forwarded to Monticello to Colo. Nicholas Lewis, taking thereout what propor-tion of them you please for yourself. The peas are brought me from the South of France and are said to be valuable. Considering the season of the year I think it would be best to sow them at New York, and to send the produce on next winter to such persons as you please in Virginia, in order to try whether they are any of them better than what we already have. The Sulla is a species of St. foin which comes from Malta, and is proof against any degree of drought. I have raised it in my garden here, and find it a luxuriant and precious plant. I inclose you the bills of lading for the three boxes of books which ought to have gone last fall, but are only lately gone by the Juno Capt. Jenkins. Your pedometer is done, and I now wait only for some trusty passenger to take charge of it. I hope there will be one in the March packet. It cost 300. livres. Your watch you will have received by the Ct. de Moustier. With respect to the Mercures de France always forwarded to you for Bannister, I must beg you never to let them go so as to subject him to postage for them.

I am glad to hear that the new constitution is received with favor. I sincerely wish that the 9 first conventions may receive, and the 4. last reject it. The former will secure it finally, while the latter will oblige them to offer a declaration of rights in order to complete the union. We shall thus have all it's good, and cure it's principal defect. You will of course be so good as to continue to mark to me it's progress. I will thank you also for as exact a state as you can procure me of the impression made on the sum of our domestic debt by the sale of lands, and by federal and state exertions in any other manner. I have not yet heard whether the law passed in Virginia for *prohibiting the importation of brandies. If it did, the late arret here for encouraging our commerce will be repealed. The minister will be glad of such a pretext to pacify the opposition.*[1] I do not see that there are at present any strong symptoms of rupture among the Western powers of Europe. Domestic effervescence and the want of money shackle all the movements of this court. Their prevailing sentiments are total distrust of England, disgust towards the k. of Prussia, jealousy of the two empires, and I presume I may add a willingness to restore the affairs of the Dutch patriots, if it can be done without war.

I will beg the favor of you to send me a copy of the American philosophical transactions, both the 1st. and 2d. volumes, by the first packet and to accept assurances of the sincere esteem with which I am dear Sir your affectionate friend & servant,

TH: JEFFERSON

P.S. Among the copies of my Notes to be sent to S. Carolina, be so good as to forward one for Mr. Kinlock whom I think I omitted to name in the list.

RC (DLC: Madison Papers); partly in code. PrC (DLC: TJ Papers); accompanied by text *en clair* of the coded passage. Enclosure: Bill of lading for three boxes and "a small Parcell" of books consigned to Madison, with directions in the margin for their distribution (the three boxes were for Wythe, Madison, and Donald, and the small parcel was for "Doctor Raintie Charleston South Carolina"), shipped on the *Juno*, Captain Charles Jenkins, from Le Havre on 20 Dec. 1787; the bill of lading bears on verso Jenkins' receipt, dated at New York, 11 Apr. 1788, and issued to Richard Phillips for "Thirty Three shilling & Nine Pence in full for the freight of the within Goods" (DLC: Madison Papers).

[1] This and preceding words in italics are written in code and have been decoded by the Editors, employing Code No. 9. TJ's text *en clair* agrees with the decoding save that it has the phrase "for pacifying" instead of "to pacify."

To Alexander Donald

DEAR SIR   Paris Feb. 7. 1788.

I received duly your friendly letter of Nov. 12. By this time you will have seen published by Congress the new regulation obtained from this court in favor of our commerce. I should have made them known to you at the same time but that there is a sort of decency which requires that first communications should be made to government. You will observe that the arrangement relative to tobacco is a continuation of the order of Berni for five years, only leaving the price to be settled between the buyer and seller. You will see too that all contracts for tobacco are forbidden till it arrives in France. Of course your proposition for a contract is precluded. I fear the prices here will be low, especially if the market be crowded. You should be particularly attentive to the article which requires that the tobacco should come in French or American bottoms, as this article will in no instance be departed from.

I wish with all my soul that the nine first Conventions may accept the new Constitution, because this will secure to us the good it contains, which I think great and important. But I equally wish that the four latest conventions, whichever they be, may refuse to accede to it till a declaration of rights be annexed. This would probably command the offer of such a declaration, and thus give to the whole fabric, perhaps as much perfection as any one of that kind ever had. By a declaration of rights I mean one which shall stipulate freedom of religion, freedom of the press, freedom of commerce against monopolies, trial by juries in all cases, no suspensions of the habeas corpus, no standing armies. These are fetters against doing evil which no honest government should decline. There is another strong feature in the new constitution which I as strongly dislike. That is the perpetual re-eligibility of the President. Of this I expect no amendment at present because I do not see that any body has objected to it on your side the water. But it will be productive of cruel distress to our country even in your day and mine. The importance to France and England to have our government in the hands of a Friend or a foe, will occasion their interference by money, and even by arms. Our President will be of much more consequence to them than a king of Poland. We must take care however that neither this nor any other objection to the new form produce a schism in our union. That would be an incurable evil, because near friends falling out never reunite cordially; whereas, all of us going together, we shall be sure to cure the evils of our new constitution, before they do great harm.[1]—The box of books I had taken the liberty to address to you is but just gone from Havre for New York. I do not see at present any symptoms strongly indicating war. It is true that the distrust existing between the two courts of Versailles and London is so great that they can scarcely do business together. How-

[571]

ever the difficulty and doubt of obtaining money makes both afraid to enter into war. The little preparations for war, which we see, are the effect of distrust rather than of a design to commence hostilities. However, in such a state of mind, you know small things may produce a rupture. So that tho peace is rather probable, war is very possible.

Your letter has kindled all the fond recollections of antient times, recollections much dearer to me than any thing I have known since. There are minds which can be pleased by honors and preferments, but I see nothing in them but envy and enmity. It is only necessary to possess them to know how little they contribute to happiness, or rather how hostile they are to it. No attachments soothe the mind so much as those contracted in early life: nor do I recollect any societies which have given me more pleasure than those of which you have partaken with me. I had rather be shut up in a very modest cottage, with my books, my family and a few old friends, dining on simple bacon, and letting the world roll on as it liked, than to occupy the most splendid post which any human power can give. I shall be glad to hear from you often. Give me the small news as well as the great. Tell Dr. Currie that I believe I am indebted to him a letter, but that, like the mass of my countrymen I am not at this moment able to pay all my debts: the post being to depart in an hour, and the last stroke of a pen I am able to send by it being that which assures you of the sentiments of esteem and attachment with which I am dear Sir your affectionate friend & servt.,　　　　　　Th: Jefferson

PrC (DLC). Tr of Extract (DLC: Monroe Papers); in TJ's hand, with the following caption: "Extract from the letter of Th: J. to A. Donald dated Paris Feb. 7. 1788. which was quoted to the Virginia convention." On the use of this extract, see Monroe to TJ, 12 July 1788, and Madison to TJ, 24 July 1788.

[1] Tr of Extract includes all of the text from the beginning of this paragraph to the end of this sentence.

To the Georgia Delegates in Congress

Gentlemen　　　　　　　　　　　　Paris Feb. 7. 1788.

I take the liberty of recommending to you the case of Mr. Fanning who addresses to you the inclosed letter. If, without engaging yourselves in too much trouble, you could procure for him exact information as to the predicament in which his rights stand, and what may be necessary for him to do to secure them finally, you will render service to a person who appears to have merit. He is settled in this country as a subject thereof: and he will furnish any money which may be necessary. Being without a single acquaintance in that country, he has been obliged to take the liberty of addressing himself to you in hopes that from a principle of benevolence you will obtain for him the information requisite, or advise him to some person in Georgia who may be willing to undertake to look after his rights, and whose integrity and diligence may be relied on.

I have the honour to be with sentiments of the most perfect esteem and respect Gentlemen Your most obedt. & most humble servant, TH: JEFFERSON

PrC (DLC). Enclosure not found.

To the Commissioners of the Treasury

GENTLEMEN   Paris Feb. 7. 1788.

Your favors of Nov. 10. and 13. and Dec. 5. have been duly received. Commodore Jones left this place for Copenhagen the 5th. instant to carry into execution the resolution of Congress of Oct. 25. Whatever monies that court shall be willing to allow, shall be remitted to your bankers either in Amsterdam or Paris as shall be found most beneficial, allowing previously to be withdrawn from it Commodore Jones' proportion which will be necessary for his subsistence. I desired him to endeavor to prevail on the Danish minister to have the money paid in Amsterdam or Paris by their banker in either of those cities if they have one.

Mr. Ast (secretary to the Consulate) is at Lorient. Whether he comes up with his papers or sends them, they shall be received, sealed up and taken care of. I will only ask the favor of you that I may never be desired to break the seals unless very important cause for it should arise.

I have just received from Messrs. Willincks & Van Staphorsts a letter of Jan. 31 in which are these words. ' The official communication we have of the actual situation and prospect of the finances of the U.S. would render such a partial paiment as that to Fizeaux' house of no avail towards the support of the public credit unless effectual measures shall be adopted to provide funds for the 270,000 florins interest that will be due the 1st. of June next, a single day's retard in which would ground a prejudice of long duration.' They inform me at the same time that they have made to you the following communication, that Mr. Stanitski, our principal broker and a holder of 1,340,000 dollars of certificates of our domestic debt, offers to have our loan of a million of gilders (of which 622,840 are still unfilled) immediately made up, on condition that he may retain thereout 180,000 gilders being one year's interest on his certificates, allowing a deduction of 10 percent from his said interest as a compensation for receiving it in Amsterdam instead of America, and not pretending that this shall give him any title to ask any paiment of future interest in Europe. They observe that this will enable them to face the demands of Dutch interest till the 1st. of June 1789, pay the principal of Fizeaux' debt, and supply the current expences of your legations in Europe. On these points it is for you to decide. I will only take the liberty to observe that if they shall receive your acceptance of the proposition, some days credit will still be to be given for producing the cash, and that this must be produced 15. days before it is wanting, because that much previous notice is always given to the creditors that their money is ready. It is therefore but three months from this day before your answer should be in Amsterdam. It might answer a useful purpose also could I receive a communication of that answer ten days earlier than they. The same stagnation attending our passage from the old to the new form of government which stops the feeble channels of money hitherto flowing towards our treasury, has suspended also what foreign credit we had. So that at this moment we may consider the progress of our loan as stopped. Tho' much an enemy to the system of borrowing, yet I feel strongly the necessity of preserving the power to borrow. Without this we might be overwhelmed by another nation merely by the forces of it's credit. However you can best judge whether the paiment of a single year's interest on Stanitski's certificates in Europe instead of America may be more injurious to us than the shock of our credit in Amsterdam which may be produced by a failure to pay our interest. I have only to offer any services which I can render in this business either here or by going to Holland at a moment's warning if that should be necessary.

I have the honour to be with sentiments of the most perfect esteem and respect, Gentlemen Your most obedient & most humble servt., TH: JEFFERSON

PrC (DLC). Recorded in SJL Index as being dated 1 Feb. 1788.

[574]

To André Limozin

Sir   Paris Feb. 8. 1788.

In my letter of yesterday I forgot to mention that I had sent off by the Diligence of the day before two small boxes addressed to you, and which I wished to have forwarded by the packet to New York. As each box had it's address, and one of them signed by me I am in hopes you will have conjectured what my forgetfulness prevented me from giving you notice of. I am with much esteem Sir Your most obedient humble servt.,   TH: JEFFERSON

PrC (MHi). TJ erred in thinking he wrote a LETTER OF YESTERDAY; he meant to refer to that of 6 Feb. (see TJ to Limozin 14 Feb. 1788).

To William Frederick Ast

Sir   Paris Feb. 9. 1788

You will perceive by the inclosed letter that it is the wish of Mr. Barclay that the books and papers of the Consular office be removed to this place, and deposited with me till further orders. The Commissioners of the Treasury have signified to me their concurrence in this measure. I should not chuse to receive them otherwise than in one or more trunks, sealed: as I do not purpose to open them while they remain in my possession. I must therefore desire you to deliver them in this form, with a list of the particulars contained in the boxes. From what I learn, the balance due to you cannot be paid till the month of June: but I beleive it may certainly be paid to you at that time. I am with much esteem Sir Your most obedient humble servant,   TH: JEFFERSON

PrC (DLC). Enclosure: Barclay to TJ, 30 Nov. 1787 (missing).

To William Franklin

Sir   Paris Feb. 9. 1788.

I am honoured with your favor of January the 18th. the delay of which needed no apology at all, the proposal it conveyed being the result of an excess of delicacy in your son. The office he was so kind as to undertake for me, that of purchasing sundry articles for me in England, was a friendly and not a commercial one. He was to receive no profit on it, he should therefore be liable to no loss. It is as honourable in him to propose the reimbursement for the miscarriage of Blackstone's commentaries, as it would be otherwise in me to accept it. Permit me therefore, Sir, through you to assure him it is impossible for me to accept it, to reiterate my thanks to him for his friendly office, and for the advantage it has procured me of an occasion of assuring you of the sentiments of esteem and respect with which I have the honour to be Sir Your most obedient & most humble servant, TH: JEFFERSON

PrC (DLC).

To Anthony Garvey

SIR   Paris Feb. 9. 1788.

No orders have ever been given to me relative to the disabled pilot on whose behalf you do me the honour to write. I have therefore done what I thought was best for him: that is I have inclosed his papers to our Secretary at war, and recommended to him a speedy decision, which I doubt not I shall receive. This may be retarded by the present crisis of a transition from the antient to a new form of government. As soon as I receive it however I will communicate it to you, and be happy in every occasion of serving those whom you befriend. I have the honour to be with much esteem, Sir, Your most obedient & most humble servt.,

TH: JEFFERSON

PrC (DLC).

To James Swan

SIR   Paris Feb. 9. 1788.

Your favor of Jan. 31. has come duly to my hands, together with the pamphlet, for which be pleased to accept my thanks, together with my congratulations on your safe arrival in France. I shall be happy to have an early occasion of renewing them on the arrival of Mrs. Swann and your family. I am in hopes Paris will have attractions enough to draw both you and her to it for a while at least, and to furnish me with an occasion of testifying to you both in person those sentiments of esteem and respect with which I have the honor to be Sir Your most obedient & most humble servant,

TH: JEFFERSON

PrC (MHi).

[576]

From André Limozin

Le Havre, 10 Feb. 1788. Acknowledges TJ's letters of 6 and 8 Feb.; the latter refers to a letter of "yesterday" and since no letter of 7 Feb. has been received and since two boxes which have arrived by the diligence are not addressed in TJ's hand, asks for further information concerning the boxes mentioned in the letter of 8 Feb. Thanks TJ for writing to Madison on his behalf; is always ready to render any services he can to TJ and his friends; thanks TJ for information on political affairs; will appreciate further news of this nature.

RC (MHi); 4 p.; addressed. See TJ to Limozin, 14 Feb. 1788.

From Brissot de Warville

MONSIEUR   Paris ce 10 fevrier 1788. No. 11. rue St. Nicaise.

Nous croirions Vous Manquer, Mr. Claviere et moi, et trahir la cause de L'humanité, si, formant ici une Société pour L'abolition de La traite des Nègres à L'Instar de celle de Londres, Nous ne Vous faisions pas part de cette entreprise, et si nous ne vous invitions pas à concourir à ce projet par Votre appui et Vos Lumières. Nous avons fixé à Mardi prochain La 1ère. assemblée dont L'objet est d'organiser cette société, et d'arrêter Les objets dont elle s'occupera. Vous nous ferés un vrai plaisir de L'honorer de votre présence et de vos conseils. Si vos affaires ne Vous le permettoient pas, Nous espérons que M. Short, que nous Invitons à y venir, Vous remplaceroit. Je vous prie de vouloir bien me prévenir de ce que Vous ferés. L'assemblée se tiendra *à 6. heures précises, Maison de M. Claviere, au Coin des rues Grange aux belles et des marais, au bout de la rue Lancry, derrière L'opéra.*

Je suis avec Respect Monsieur Votre très humble et très Obt. Serviteur   BRISSOT DE WARVILLE

Vous verrés dans le dernier No. de L'analise des papiers Anglois, Les détails relatifs à cette Société.

RC (DLC).

To Brissot de Warville

SIR   Paris Feb. 11. 1788.

I am very sensible of the honour you propose to me of becoming a member of the society for the abolition of the slave trade. You

[577]

know that nobody wishes more ardently to see an abolition not only of the trade but of the condition of slavery: and certainly nobody will be more willing to encounter every sacrifice for that object. But the influence and information of the friends to this proposition in France will be far above the need of my association. I am here as a public servant; and those whom I serve having never yet been able to give their voice against this practice, it is decent for me to avoid too public a demonstration of my wishes to see it abolished. Without serving the cause here, it might render me less able to serve it beyond the water. I trust you will be sensible of the prudence of those motives therefore which govern my conduct on this occasion, and be assured of my wishes for the success of your undertaking and the sentiments of esteem and respect with which I have the honour to be Sir your most obedt. humble servt., TH: JEFFERSON

P.S. I send you the journals of Congress of 1787.

PrC (DLC).

From Brissot de Warville

MONSIEUR   *Paris* ce Lundi 11 fevrier 1788.

Nous ne pouvons qu'applaudir aux Motifs qui Vous empêchent de Vous rendre à Notre invitation, et nos regrets diminuent un peu en pensant que Votre opinion est la même que La Nôtre, et que Vous La Seconderés par les moiens qui ne compromettront point Votre caractère public et ce que Vous devés au corps respectable dont vous êtes L'organe.

Je suis avec respect Monsieur Votre très humble et très Obeissant Serviteur,   BRISSOT DE WARVILLE

RC (DLC); endorsed.

From Jean Nicolas Démeunier

MONSIEUR   Rue Ste. Anne No. 87. Le 11 fevrier 1788.

M. Mazzei m'a traité d'une manière bien injuste et bien peu honnête. Il imprime qu'il est votre *ami* et il me reproche de n'avoir pas marqué dans *L'essai sur Les états unis* tout ce qui est de vous. Vous savés, Monsieur, si cela étoit possible. Les excellentes

notes que J'ai recueillies dans nos Conversations ont été souvent
La réponse Verbale à Mille questions que vous m'avés permis de
vous Faire. Vos remarques de vive voix, et vos remarques par
écrit ne pouvoient être employées Autrement, et nous étions convenus que je Les employerois de Cette manière. Les Foibles
éloges que je vous ai donné en plusieurs endroits annoncent assés
mon estime et mon respect pour votre personne et vos Talens,
et personne ne s'est mépris sur Les Services nombreux que J'ai
tiré de vous.

M. Mazzei ne s'est donc pas donné La peine de vérifier les
détails. Il veut ignorer qu'on n'a point vendu *L'essai sur Les etats
unis*, que c'est par zèle pour vos intéressantes républiques que
j'en ai Fait Tirer quelques exemplaires, que Je n'ai Jamais Songé
à mettre de L'importance à Ce Morceau, qu'il est dans L'encyclopédie Méthodique, et que L'encyclopédie n'en offrira pas un grand
nombre rédigé avec Le même soin.

Je pourrois Lui dire que j'ai réfuté moi même M. L'abbé Raynal
sur Le nombre des malfaiteurs qui ont peuplé les colonies, sur la
population et Les Cultures dont elles sont Susceptibles, et Sur
d'Autres objêts; que ce n'est pas un beau role de montrer de La
partialité et de retirer 10. Lignes où L'imprimeur a oublié de
mettre des guillemets, surtout Lorsqu'il s'agit d'un article de
L'encyclopédie; que Les petites erreurs qui s'y trouvent Sur
L'époque et Les détails sur La Fondation des Colonies ne sont pas
importantes; que Hutchinson, Belknap, &c., Se Sont eux mêmes
Trompé; qu'enfin, Je m'en Suis rapporté à vous, Monsieur, et que
vous avés pris La peine de Corriger Le Manuscrit de votre main;
que L'auteur des *recherches sur Les etats unis* sera peut-être
Critiqué à son Tour, sur Les mêmes points; qu'en parlant de nos
affaires il a bien aussi commis plusieurs erreurs; qu'il a dit par
exemple que *nos pauvres ne mangent pas un morceau de pain qui
n'aie payé rigoûreusement Les droits*; que dans une page il est
économiste et qu'ailleurs il prêche Les impôts indirects; qu'après
avoir inséré le Morceau de M. de Condorcet qui me regarde et
dont Je ne me plains pas, parcequ'il est décent (quoiqu'il soit très
inexact dans La phrase qu'il Cite de moi), il indique avec éloge
L'ouvrage de M. Adams qui pense aussi que Les critiques de M.
Turgot sur les Constitutions Américaines ne sont pas exactes.

Vous avés vu mon Zèle, Monsieur, vous Savés La peine que je
me suis donné pour le Morceau sur Les etats unis. Peu Satisfaits
des critiques exagérées que Se permettoient Sur vos Constitutions

Les hommes Les plus estimables de notre Littérature, Nous avons Senti L'un et L'autre qu'il seroit utile de répandre des Idées plus justes sur vos gouvernemens. Je me suis chargé de ce Soin, et grâces à vos Lumières et à vos Conseils, Monsieur, mon travail ne S'avère pas infructueux. Si L'impression de L'Encyclopédie n'eut pas exigé que Je devançasse Le Livre de M. Mazzei, si vous aviés paru disposé à L'attendre, Je Lui aurois Laissé très volontiers Le mérite de La nouveauté. Mes motifs étoient bien purs et désintéressés, puisqu'il m'en a Coûté de L'argent, et J'en appelle à votre Conscience, et à L'élévation de votre Caractère, Monsieur, N'est-il pas dur d'entendre Les reproches qui m'ont blessé [amèrement].

J'ai fait de ces misérables injustices de La Littérature Le Cas qu'elles méritoient. Mais vous avés Mille bontés pour moi; on ne peut rien ajouter au respectueux attachement que Je vous ai voué; et quoique je n'aie pas besoin de me Justifier Auprès de vous, Monsieur, Je n'ai pu contenir mes plaintes. Un homme comme vous, Monsieur, ne Les trouvera pas importunes, et Le bonheur de vous Connoître me Fait oublier Les indécentes Critiques.

Je vous prie d'agréer Le respectueux attachement, avec Lequel J'ai L'honneur d'être Monsieur Votre très humble et très obéissant Serviteur, DÉMEUNIER

P.S. Permettés moi, Monsieur, de vous demander si vous avés une traduction de La nouvelle Constitution que vous proposés à L'état de Virginie. J'en aurois besoin pour L'article Virginie et je voudrois n'être pas obligé de Le traduire.

RC (DLC); endorsed.
On the matter of Mazzei's relationship with TJ's criticism of Démeunier's essay on the United States, see Vol. 10: 3-65, especially 9-11.

From Lambert

Paris 11e. Février 1788.

Je vous serai obligé, Monsieur, de vouloir bien vous trouver chez moi, Mercredi prochain [13 Feb.], treize de ce mois, à sept heures du soir, pour conférer sur les observations qui ont été faites au sujet de l'arrêt du Conseil du 29 Décembre dernier.

J'ai l'honneur d'être avec un très sincere et inviolable attachement, Monsieur, Votre très humble et très obeissant Serviteur, LAMBERT

RC (DLC); in a clerk's hand, signed by Lambert.

From John Adams

DEAR SIR London Feb. 12. 1788

I have received your Letter of the 6th. and had before received the same Information from Amsterdam.

I know not how to express to you, the sense I have of the disingenuity of this Plott. The Difficulty of selling the obligations I believe to be mere Pretence, and indeed the whole appears to me to be a concerted Fiction, in consequence of some Contrivance or Suggestion of Mr. Parke, the great Speculator in American Paper, who, though I love him very well, is too ingenious for me. I feel myself obliged to write this in Confidence to you, and to put you on your Guard against the immeasurable avarice of Amsterdam as well as the ungovernable Rage of Speculation. I feel no Vanity in saying that this Project never would have been suggested, if it had not been known, that I was recalled. If I was to continue in Europe and in office I would go to Amsterdam and open a new Loan with John Hodshon before I would submit to it. The Undertakers are bound in Honour, as I understood it, to furnish the Money on the new Loan. They agreed to this upon Condition that I would go to Amsterdam to sign the Obligations. The Truth is that Messrs. Willinks and Vanstaphorst have been purchasing immense Quantities of American Paper, and they now want to have it acknowledged and paid in Europe. It appears to me totally impossible that you or I should ever agree to it, or approve it, and so far as I can comprehend it is equally impossible for the Board of Treasury or Congress to consent to it. You and I however cannot answer for them: but I think We cannot countenance any hopes that they will ever comply with it. The Continental Certificates and their Interest are to be paid in America at the Treasury of the United States. If a Precedent is set of paying them in Europe, I pretend not to Sufficient foresight to predict the Consequences. They appear however to me to be horrid. If the Interest of one Million Dollars is paid this Year in Europe, you will find the Interest of Ten Millions demanded next year. I am very sorry to be obliged at the moment of my Retirement to give opinions which may be misrepresented and imputed to Motives that my soul despizes: but I cannot advise you by any means to countenance this Project: but it is my Serious Opinion that the Judgment of Congress, or the Board of Treasury, ought to be waited for, at all hazards. If the Brokers, Undertakers and Money

[581]

lenders will take such Advantages of Us, it is high time to have done with them; pay what is due as fast as we can, but never contract another farthing of Debt with them. If a little Firmness is shewn in adhering to the Resolution of waiting the orders of Congress, it is my opinion, Care will be taken in Amsterdam that our Credit shall not suffer. The Interest of our Commissioners, of the Brokers, Undertakers and Money Lenders, all conspire to induce them to prevent a failure. But in my Judgment a failure had better take Place than this Project. I shall not write with the same frankness to Willinks, but I shall give them my opinion that the Judgment of Congress must be waited for.

My dear Friend farewell. I pity you, in your Situation, dunned and teazed as you will be, all your Philosophy will be wanting to support you. But be not discouraged, I have been constantly vexed with such terrible Complaints and frightened with such long Faces these ten years. Depend upon it, the Amsterdammers love Money too well, to execute their Threats. They expect to gain too much by American Credit to destroy it. I am with Sincere Affection and great Esteem, your Friend & Servant,

JOHN ADAMS

RC (DLC); endorsed. FC (MHi: AMT); in the hand of William Stephens Smith; with several minor omissions and variations in spelling which have not been noted here.

To Samuel Blackden

DEAR SIR   Paris Feb. 12. 1788.

I have duly received your favor of the 2d. instant: but am not able to inform you what kind of voucher is necessary in the dominions of France to prove a vessel to be an American bottom. If you will send me a copy of a bill of sale of any vessel I will annex to it a certificate that you are a citizen of the United states, on the principle of 'valeat quantum valere potest.' When you shall have received a cargo in any port of the French dominions, you will be free to carry it where you please, except that you cannot bring it into France if it come from either the East or the West Indies. It is expected they will suppress their East India company. In this case we cannot foresee what new regulations they will make. I would [inclose] a copy of a late arret for encouraging our trade but that it is bulky to go by post. If you go to Dunquerke you may see it in the hands of Mr. Coffin. Wishing you every success you can desire I am with much esteem Dear Sir Your most obedient humble servt., TH: JEFFERSON

PrC (DLC).

To C. W. F. Dumas

SIR   Paris Feb. 12. 1788.

I have duly received your favor of the 5th. inst. inclosing that for Mr. Jay. The packet was gone, as I presume: but I have another occasion of forwarding it securely. Your attentions to the Leyden gazette are in my opinion very useful. The paper is much read and respected. It is the only one I know in Europe which merits respect. Your publications in it will tend to reestablish that credit which the solidity of our affairs deserve. With respect to the sale of lands, we know that two sales of 5. millions and 2. millions of acres have been made. Another was begun for 4. millions, which in the course of the negociation may have been reduced to 3. millions as you mention. I have not heard that this sale is absolutely concluded, but there is reason to presume it. Stating these sales at two thirds of a dollar the acre and allowing for 3. or 400,000 acres sold at public sale and a very high price, we may say they have absorbed 7. millions of dollars of the domestic federal debt. The states by taxation and otherwise have absorbed 11. millions more: so that that debt stands now at about 10. millions of dollars and will probably be all absorbed in the course of the next year. There will remain then our foreign debt between 10 and 12. millions, including interest. The sale of lands will then go on for the paiment of this. But as this paiment must be in cash, not in public effects, the lands must be sold cheaper. The demand too will probably be less brisk. So we may suppose this will be longer paying off than the domestic debt.—With respect to the new government, 9. or 10. states will probably have accepted it by the end of this month. The others may oppose it. Virginia I think will be of this number. Besides other objections of less moment, she will insist on annexing a bill of rights to the new constitution, i.e. a bill wherein the government shall declare that 1. Religion shall be free. 2. Printing presses free. 3. Trials by jury preserved in all cases. 4. No monopolies in commerce. 5. No standing army. Upon receiving this bill of rights, she will probably depart from her other objections; and this bill is so much of the interest of all the states that I presume they will offer it, and thus our constitution be amended and our union closed by the end of the present year. In this way there will have been opposition enough to do good, and not enough to do harm. I have such reliance on the good sense of the body of the people and the honesty of their leaders, that I am not afraid of their letting things go wrong to any length in any case. Wishing you better health, and much happiness I have the honor to be with sentiments of the most perfect esteem and respect Sir your most obedient and most humble servt.,

TH: JEFFERSON

PrC (DLC).

In stating that the *Gazette de Leide* was the only paper he knew in Europe WHICH MERITS RESPECT, TJ was undoubtedly expressing an honest conviction, but he also knew that he was reflecting an opinion that Dumas himself had set forth in a letter to Jay that had recently passed through TJ's hands (Dumas to Jay, 2 Feb. 1788; see note to Dumas to TJ, 5 Feb. 1788). Moreover, he was evidently impressed by the fact that Dumas had caused the Constitution, the Northwest Ordinance, and other documents from America to be printed in that journal, and he must have intended that his present compliment on the paper and the contents of this letter would be passed along to Luzac, its editor. Dumas took the hint and saw to it that Luzac received the praise and the letter—after being edited. An extract of the letter, omitting that part devoted to the sales of land in the Northwest Territory, appeared in the *Gazette de Leide* of 29 Feb. 1788 under the following caption: "Extrait d'une Lettre de Philadelphie du 10. Janvier." TJ's comment on the insistence by Virginia of a Bill of Rights as it appeared in this extract will serve to show how Dumas rewrote that part of the present letter: "les Virginiens insisteront principalement sur ce qu'il soit ajouté à la nouvelle Forme de Gouvernement un Bil des Droits; c'est-a-dire, un Acte, par lequel le Gouvernement commun de toute la Confédération détermine et constate les principes fondamentaux de la Liberté des Citoyens dans une République, qui soit telle de fait et non simplement de nom. Ces principes sont notamment: I. *Que la Religion doit être libre:* II. *Que la Presse doit être libre et exempte de toute disposition arbitraire:* III. *Que*

dans tous les cas les Citoyens doivent être maintenus dans le droit d'etre jugés par Jurés: IV. *Que le Commerce ne soit restreint par aucuns Priviléges exclusifs ni Monopoles:* V. *Qu'il n'y ait point d'Armée permanente et soudoyée, dangereuse pour la Liberté des Citoyens.*—Si la Virginie obtient, que ce Bil des Droits soit accordé aux Citoyens de l'Amérique, elle se départira probablement de ses autres difficultés: Et il y a d'autant plus d'apparence, qu'elle y réussira, que les principes à y établir ne sont pas autres que ceux qui ont déjà été posés comme fondamentaux dans la Constitution de Massachusett's et dans celles de la plûpart des autres Etats. Ceux-ci d'ailleurs y ont un intérêt si évident qu'ils pourront prévenir la Virginie et lui offrir le Bil des Droits, qu'elle demande. Ainsi l'opposition à la Constitution projettée aura été assez forte pour faire du bien, mais non pour lui nuire: Et l'on peut se flatter avec raison d'après le bon-sens et la sagesse, que le Peuple Américain a montrés jusqu'ici dans toute sa conduite, ainsi que d'après la probité et le Patriotisme éclairé de ceux qui le gouvernent, que sa Constitution-Fédérative sera définitivement corrigée et les liens de son Union plus étroitement resserés avant la fin de l'année courante." Luzac may have made some of the alterations in TJ's letter in addition to those by Dumas; but the attempt to amplify and explain caused the editor or editors of it to mistake the precise nature of a bill of rights. It also caused the display of a natural lack of familiarity with the chain of influence that ran through the adoption of bills of rights by Massachusetts and other states in their constitutions—beginning, of course, with that of Virginia of 12 June 1776.

From C. W. F. Dumas

Monsieur   Lahaie 12e. Fevr. 1788

J'apprends avec le plus grand intérêt, que très probablement Votre Excellence fera dans peu un voyage dans ce pays. Au milieu de tous les ennuis et chagrins qui m'obsèdent et me tuent, ce sera depuis bien longtemps le premier plaisir que je serai capable, et qu'il me sera permis, grace à Dieu, de goûter, que d'avoir le bonheur de connoître personnellement Votre Excellence, et de l'accompagner partout pour pouvoir Lui être aussi utile qu'Elle le désirera et qu'il me sera possible, priant Votre Excellence d'être bien persuadée, qu'officiellement et personnellement Elle pourra disposer de ma main et de toute ma personne; et qu'ainsi Elle n'aura pas besoin de s'inquiéter d'un secrétaire, Lui offrant de Lui en tenir lieu en tout et partout avec la plus grande fidélité et assiduité. Je suppose que ce ne peut être qu'à Amsterdam où Votre Excellence a affaire. Tant mieux; ce n'est aussi que là où je crois que mes Services pourront être de quelque usage et poids. Cependant, n'excluons aucun autre endroit où Elle pourroit avoir besoin de moi. Permettez, Monsieur, que Mr. Short agrée ici mes meilleurs complimens, avec ceux de ma famille.

S'il y a quelque chose où je puisse être bon à Votre Excellence avant son départ de Paris, ou durant son trajet, n'épargnez pas, Monsieur, celui qui est avec le plus respectueux dévouement, De Votre Excellence Le très-humble et très-obéissant serviteur,

C W F Dumas

RC (DLC). FC (Rijksarchief, The Hague, Dumas Letter Books; photostats in DLC).

From La Vingtrie

De l'hôtel de L'empereur rue grénelle St. Honoré
Monsieur   [Before 12 Feb. 1788]

J'aurois eu L'honneur de me présenter à votre hôtel pour vous prier, et d'excuser ma démarche en m'adressant à vous pour une affaire qui m'est purement personelle, et de vouloir bien me Dire, si je pourois trouver ici quelqu'un qui me vendît des terres aux états unis de L'amérique, ma patrie adoptive. Mais, n'ayant point d'habit habillé, je me sers de La voie Epistolaire, qui vous évite peut-être une visite importune et à moi Le déplaisir de Le sentir.

[585]

La résidence de mes camarades dans votre patrie, La Lecture des ouvrages de Messrs. de crevecoeur et price me font attendre avec l'impatience la plus vive L'heureux moment où je me verrai parmi Des hommes qui se sont fait une forme de gouvernement où la Dignité de L'homme n'est point avilie par de frivoles et abusives distinctions, où Le total n'est point occupé à L'unité.

Étre Libre, être avec des égaux, voilà, Monsieur, Les deux grands motifs de mon émigration, je n'en ai point d'autre. Je vous prie, Monsieur, de vouloir bien pardonner mon importunité et mon ignorance en faite d'étiquette; comme envoyé des états de L'amérique vous avez un titre; mais je suis certain que Monsieur jefferson est trop au-dessus pour se facher d'une insience, bien pardonable d'ailleurs à un militaire.

J'ai L'honneur D'être avec un profond respect Monsieur Votre très humble et très obéissant serviteur,

DE LA VINGTRIE

off.r. au régiment d'auxonne artillerie

RC (MoSHi); endorsed; without date, which has been supplied from TJ's reply, following, q.v. Recorded in SJL Index as Feb. 1788.

To La Vingtrie

à Paris ce 12. Fevr. 1788.

Je ne connois personne ici, Monsieur, qui a des terres à vendre en Amérique, et meme s'il y en avoit, je ne vous conseillerois pas du tout d'en acheter ici. Si vous etes dans l'intention de vous établir en Amérique, il vaudroit mieux d'y passer, d'y voyager, et d'y rester quelque-tems avant de décider le centre de votre etablissement. Le climat, le sol, la société, influent beaucoup sur notre bonheur. [Allez] donc les voir, et les choisir à votre gré. Et peutêtre même que vous trouverez encore la difficulté de la langue, et la difference d'us[ages] plus [rebutantes] que vous ne le croyez. M. de crevecoeur vous fait voir notre [beau coté]. Je prends la liberté de vous envoyer une petite brochure de M. Franklin où vous verrez que tout n'est pas de [connoître ses egaux]. Enfin qu'aussi bien que les autres nous avons du bon et du mauvais. Il seroit sage de l'examiner de plus près avant de décider tout à fait. J'ai l'honneur d'être avec beaucoup de considération, Monsieur votre tres humble et tres obeissant serviteur,

TH: JEFFERSON

[586]

PrC (MoSHi). Enclosure: Benjamin Franklin's *Avis a ceux qui voudraient s'en aller en Amerique*, first printed, in French and English, at Passy in 1784 (Luther S. Livingston, *Franklin and His Press at Passy*, N.Y., 1914, p. 43-8); TJ later caused Franklin's famous tract to be reprinted, evidently to meet such needs as the present (entry in Account Book for 20 Sep. 1788 reads: "paid for reprinting Dr. Franklin's advice to emigrants 18 f 16 U.S."). Mazzei also included the text in his *Recherches Historiques et Politiques*, IV, 76-92. It is not clear which printing was enclosed.

To Zachariah Loreilhe

SIR   Paris Feb. 12. 1788.

Mr. Barclay's interest and the desire to serve you would always induce me to go as far as my duty would permit me. But I have been obliged always to decline asking for sauf-conduits, and arrets de surseance, because they may commit me disagreeably with the minister and the creditors, and because it is my duty to avoid asking private favours, and to reserve my applications for those which are public and important. I asked a sauf-conduit in the case of Mr. Barclay considering him as a minister: but the court viewed it in a different light. I am sincerely sorry therefore that I cannot be useful to you on this occasion without departing from the line which I suppose to be right. I trust however you have some acquaintance here who may make the application you desire, and cover you from the useless severities of your creditors. I am with very great respect Sir Your most obedient & most humble servant,   TH: JEFFERSON

PrC (DLC).

From Francis dal Verme

SIR   Milan the 12th. of Feby. *1788*.

How humiliating it is to me, Sir, to date this letter under this day, being an answer to your most Kind of the 15th. Aug. 87. Would I intend to make a proper apology for it to you, I am affraid I should be quite unsuccessful, so I shall tell you the plain truth, and give up entirely to your own Kindness the judgment of it. About the meddle of 7ber. I received yours, by which I was told you had send'd already the books, which you was so Kind to favour me with, to Marseilles, from where I expected to receive them every day. I thought then for to spare you the trouble of receiving two letters of mine in the space of eight, or ten days,

[587]

that I should defer a post or two before answering yours, and by that enable me to do it all at once with the intelligence of being myself in possession of them. The first step is the difficult one, to the next we are no more strangers; so it has been possible to me to delay from post to post till this very-day, which is the first after I have received Soule's History, Ramsay's history, and two of your Notes on the State of Virginia, one of these last I gave to Mr. Clerici, whom I see very often, whose letter is this inclosed one. Sincerity, it is commonly allowed, is a powerful mediator, and pleading now before an indulgent judge can't but obtain pardon, and forgetfulness; A Waranty to my hopes are the flattering expressions with which in your letter you are pleased to magnify the little I had the honour to do for you in your Apparition at Milan, which has been too short to let me enjoy your Company, and too long for not being I very-much concerned at your departure. However there may be a Kind of redress even to this, but it depends entirely from you, as it is to permit me to take now, and then the liberty of troubling you with a line. I hope by the first time I shall enjoy this pleasure, that I will be able to give you proper tanks for the Knowledge you have afforded to me by the perusual of the historys, and particularly of the Notes on Virginia you have sended me, for which I give you now the most sincerest thanks.—What has been till now settled by the Federal Convention, whose president is now G. Washington, I Know as far as it has been said in the Leyden news papers, But you Know how deficient are always such mercenary intelligences; so, excuse my liberty. I beg once for ever, you will favour me with all, relative to America, as that is a Country which will one day or other afford me Still more pleasure, than what I have already felt there; I am acquainted with a place called Monticello, how glad would I be to find there it's Master at home. A french officer had once the good luck to meet Him, I have read his description, very likely you remember him. Could I be transported now in a Baloon where I long very much to be again, I would very easily be told by my acquaintances and friends what power Congress has now got, and how his acts are to be no more opposed, what is the National debt, and what is the share of it to each State; the number of inhabitants, if Emigrations be great, and if they want great importation of Negroes, their treatys of commerce, and what trade do they carry to the west, and east Indias, if the navigation of Missisipi is not opposed by the Spaniards, if they have discover'd any mine of Gold, or Silver, or if Commerce supplies to the want of them, if the Indians are still troublesome to the back settlers, if the Bank notes of philadelphia are still in full credit through all the states, if they have render'd navigable some rivers, whose falls prevented the navigation. In short you see how investigative I would be should I find myself there upon the Spot. But as this won't be the case for some time so I beg you to be Kind enough as to answer me at least some of these questions, those which will take up less of your precious time, and for fear of being even now too troublesome to you I have the honour to be Sir your most obedient, and most humble Servent,

CT. FRANCIS DAL VERME

RC (DLC); endorsed. Incorrectly entered in SJL Index as dated 2 Feb. 1788. Enclosure: Clerici to TJ, 2 Feb. 1788.

The FRENCH OFFICER who had published an account of Monticello was Chastellux (see Vol. 6: 191, note).

From Moustier

à Newyork le 13. Fevrier 1788

J'ai payé un peu cher, Monsieur, mon empressement de me rendre dans votre patrie. A commencer de mon départ de Paris, j'ai fait un voyage à tous égards infiniment désagréable, et ma santé étoit sur la fin tellement dérangée qu'elle commençoit à me donner des inquiétudes. Heureusement elle s'est bien rétablie et avec une promptitude qui m'a surpris. Pour être pleinement dédomagé de ce que j'ai souffert et du sacrifice que j'ai fait de mes intérêts, qui ont surtout été lésés par la perte d'une partie de mon mobilier, il ne me reste à désirer que de savoir que vos compatriotes se sont aperçus, non seulement de l'empressement du Ministre du Roi, mais aussi de celui du Cte. de Moustier. J'ai lieu de me louer des témoignages d'affection et des égards de plusieurs d'entre eux, parmi lesquels il y en a qui méritent assurément d'être particulièrement distingués. Ce ne sont cependant en général que les Officiers du Congrès et un petit nombre d'habitans principaux de cette Ville qui m'ont fait des avances auxquelles je me suis montré très sensible. Il est fâcheux que l'étiquette, que j'ai trouvée à mon grand étonnement plus outrée et plus bizarre dans une république qui vise à la perfection, que dans les cours d'Allemagne et d'Italie, mette autant de gêne dans la fréquentation des personnes. Quant à la société, j'espère la modérer, mais quant au Congrès, comme

[589]

c'est un Corps Souverain, je n'aurai qu'à gémir des résolutions qui y seront prises pour élever une barrière entre ses membres et moi. Il faut convenir franchement que la prétention que le grand nombre a à la première visite de la part des Ministres Etrangers ne pourroit que diminuer la considération dûe à ceux-ci, et qu'il est de l'intérêt même du Congrès de maintenir. Comment prétendre que ceux-ci soient constamment à l'affut de l'arrivée de Députés, qui se succèdent sans cesse sans produire aucune sensation, et dont la plupart vont s'établir obscurément dans des chambres garnies, ce qui me paroît philosophiquement parlant fort raisonable, mais ce qui ne donne guères de cet éclat, qui doit accompagner à un certain degré des personnes qui se disent représentans d'un Souverain. Je crains qu'on ne se soit un peu mépris sur l'étendue de la représentation en voulant l'étendre jusqu'à chaque individu d'une délégation. Collectivement, je regarderai très volontiers une Délégation comme représentant un Etat Souverain, puisque chaque Etat veut l'être, même dans le sens le plus étendu. C'est sur ce principe que je règlerai la visite que prescrit le cérémonial fixé par le Congrès le lendemain de mon audience que j'ai demandée depuis longtems. Je me propose de la faire à *Messieurs les Députés de....* Un billet pour chaque délégation, au lieu d'un billet pour chaque délégué. Je ne crois pas qu'on puisse raisonnablement demander autre chose, que de voir un Délégué d'une grande Puissance traiter d'égal à égal Une Délégation d'une Puissance partielle; Ce n'est que dans la Délégation collective qu'il se trouve cette égalité, dans laquelle j'observe même que l'avantage est du côté de la Délégation qui reçoit la première visite. S'il en étoit autrement, la conséquence du raisonnement des délégués individuels seroit, que chaque d'eux pourroit prétendre à être regardé comme le Congrès qui représente le Souverain, de même que chacun d'eux prétend être traité comme Sa législature assemblée qui représente son Etat. Au reste, je ne mettrai aucune passion dans cette discussion qui est d'un genre qui m'est fort désagréable et que je suis fâché de voir dominer dans Un peuple, qui devroit aller plutôt au vrai but de la Souveraineté, que de s'occuper d'apareil et de minutieuses cérémonies. 4. Membres se sont mis à mon égard audessus de la formalité qui occupe leurs confrères, Mr. Maddison, Mr. Hamilton, Mr. Armstrong et Mr. Howard. J'ai surtout à vous remercier de m'avoir fait connoître le premier que je désire fréquenter encore de plus en plus. Mes premières occupations et ma correspondance me prennent actuellement beaucoup de tems. J'espère en employer ensuite beaucoup à prouver aux Américains que je suis Un Ministre ami d'une Nation faite pour être leur amie. Je regrette de n'avoir reçu aucune lettre par le dernier paquebot. J'espère qu'à l'avenir ceux qui viendront m'aporteront de vos nouvelles qui m'intéresseront toujours bien vivement. De mon côté je serai bien exact à vous donner des miennes et à vous renouveller les assurances du bien sincère attachement et de la considération distinguée avec lesquels j'ai l'honneur d'être, Monsieur, Votre très humble et très obeissant Serviteur,   LE CTE. DE MOUSTIER

Le 19. Je vous fais mon Compliment de l'accession de Massassuchett. Ma Soeur, qui se proposoit d'avoir l'honneur de vous écrire, en est empêchée par un violent catarre accompagnée de fièvre qui la retient au lit depuis hier. Elle me charge de vous exprimer particulièrement ses regrets.

RC (DLC); postscript written in upper right-hand corner of first page.

From Angenend

[14 Feb. 1788. Recorded in SJL Index. Not found, but probably presenting a bill. There is the following entry in TJ's Account Book under 15 Feb. 1788: "pd. Angenend (taylor) in full 400.^{lt}"]

To André Limozin

SIR   Paris Feb. 14. 1788.

I have received your favor of the 10th. When I wrote to you on the 8th. and referred you to a letter of the preceding day, it was a mistake. I should have referred you to a letter of the 6th. as I wrote on the 6th. and 8th. only, and not on the 7th. The packet meant in my letter of the 8th. went by the diligence. It was covered with linen addressed to you in the handwriting of my servant. On opening it, you would find in it two small wooden boxes of equal size, the one addressed to 'Mr. James Madison of the Virginia delegation in Congress,' the other 'to Mr. William Drayton. Charleston S. Carolina recommended to the care of the South Carolina delegates in Congress by their humble servt. Th: Jefferson.' I wished these to [go to New Yor]k by the packet and to be spec[ially re]commended to [. . . k]now nothing [. . . .] Mr. Short thinks [. . . Sm]ith's letters. We have noth[ing in the way of

[591]

news but there is a report?] which, if true, may in a few days [reveal what this co]untry means to do. If it prove true [I shall communicate with you? im]mediately. If you do not hear fr[om me you may suppose that? th]ere is nothing of importance. I am [. . . .] humble servt.,
TH: JEFFERSON

P.S. The bust of Monsr. de la Fayette will go off tomorrow for Havre addressed to you. I will beg of you to forward it to the Governor of Virginia either by the Bowman Capt. Butler now in your port destined for Richmond in Virginia, or by another packet which will arrive soon in Havre from the same owner and addressed to Messrs. Callow frere & Carmichael co. as is the Bowman. The freight will be paid in Virginia.

PrC (DLC); MS mutilated so that the first and last parts only of the lines affected at the bottom of the page are left; this mutilation involves from two or three to eight or ten words, which have in some instances been supplied conjecturally with the aid of TJ's similarly mutilated letter of 21 Feb. 1788, where, in turn, missing words have been supplied by utilizing what remains of the present letter. The fact that these two letters have mutilations whose configurations are the same would seem to indicate that, in this period at least, TJ filed his press copies alphabetically. Postscript in present letter is written in margin.

From Bertrand

MONSIEUR   Paris le 15 fevr. 1788.

J'ai l'honneur de vous envoyer la déclaration du Nommé Jean Schmit, matelot, natif de Baltimore en Virginie, détenu au Dépôt de mendicité de Rennes où il a été conduit par la Maréchaussée qui l'a arrêté près de Lorient faute de passeports. Vous verrés par cette pièce, Monsieur, que ce marin a dit que le Vaisseau Le Hambourg sur lequel il était, a échoué près de Bordeaux, et que son intention était d'aller s'embarquer au havre de grace. Mais je dois vous observer que lorsqu'il a été interrogé par le Lieutenant de Maréchaussée de Vannes qui l'a condamné au renfermement, il a déclaré, qu'ayant eû un différent avec le second Capitaine, propriétaire en partie du Bâtiment sur lequel il passa de Philadelphie à Bordeaux, il fut mis à terre et on ne voulut point le payer parcequ'il refusait de retourner à bord; que pour se rendre à Lorient, il prit à laRochelle un passeport qu'il a perdu en route, et que lorsqu'il a été rencontré par les Cavaliers, il allait à Brest où étaient deux Vaisseaux américains dont il voulait profiter pour retourner dans son pays. Je vous prie, Monsieur, de vouloir bien me marquer si vous êtes dans l'intention de réclamer cet Américain et de lui procurer les moyens de se rendre dans le lieu de sa naissance où il parait désirer de se retirer.

Je suis avec respect, Monsieur, Votre très humble et très obéissant Serviteur, DE BERTRAND

RC (DLC). Enclosure (DLC): Printed form of declaration of the workhouse at Rennes, concerning "Jean Schmit natif de Batimor," filled in and signed by "Petiet" and dated 22 Jan. 1788.

To Collow Frères, Carmichael & Co.

GENTLEMEN   Paris Feb. 15. 1788

I am honoured with your letter of the 5th. instant covering one from my friend Mr. Donald. The packet of newspapers came also safely to hand. Mr. Donald's order for wine not leaving me time to have it brought from Bordeaux, I send him two hampers from my own stock, containing 124. bottles, for which I shall charge him only what I paid in Bordeaux. This indeed is dear, being three livres a bottle, but it is Chateau Margau, of the year 1784, bought by myself on the spot and therefore genuine: and Mr. Donald observed to me he would not limit any price. These go off by water, and therefore will probably not be in time but for the Portsmouth. I send by the same boat a package for the Governor of Virginia containing the bust of the Marquis de la Fayette. It is addressed to Mr. Limozin and I have desired him to ask the favor of you to send it with the wine of Mr. Donald. I inclose to you the late regulations relative to our commerce, by which you will perceive that I am promised there shall be no more such contracts as that with Mr. Morris: nor indeed any purchases of tobacco made but in a port of France.

I have the honour to be with much esteem, Gentlemen, Your most obedient & most humble servant, TH: JEFFERSON

PrC (DLC). Enclosure: Printed copy of Lambert to TJ, 29 Dec. 1787, and its enclosure, qq.v.

To Jean Nicolas Démeunier

SIR   Paris Feb. 15. 1788.

Mr. Mazzei having asked of me information on the subject of the United States, I lent him the notes I had written for you. I

[593]

saw in his manuscript afterwards things respecting you which I could not approve, and expressed to him strongly my desire that he should change them. I thought he would do it; but have not had time to look into his work since it's publication. I beg you to be assured that I participate in no sentiments of his or any other person relative to you which are not full of respect and esteem. I shall be sorry to see either him or any other writer indulge themselves in expressions which your candour and talents should sheild you from. I shall have the pleasure of seeing you at your own house one of these days, and of giving you further assurances of the esteem and attachment with which I have the honour to be Sir Your most obedient & most humble servant, TH: JEFFERSON

PrC (DLC).

To Alexander Donald

DEAR SIR   Paris Feb. 15. 1788.

I received your favor of Dec. 15. two days after I had written my letter of the 7th. inst. and at the same time with one from Callow Carmichael & co. informing me that your vessel would sail from Havre about the 19th. instant. The shortness of warning not admitting time to order claret for you from Bordeaux early enough to go either by the Bowman or by your next ship, I send you two hampers from my own cellar, containing 124 bottles. I am afraid it will not get to Havre in time for the Bowman. You say you had tasted at Mr. Eppes's some wine I had sent him, which was good, but not equal to what you have seen. I have sent to him twice; and what you say would correspond to the first batch. The second was of Chateau Margau of the year 1784. bought by myself on the spot, and a part of the very purchase from which I now send you. It is of the best vintage which has happened in nine years, and is of one of the four vineyards which are admitted to possess exclusively the first reputation. I may safely assure you therefore that, according to the taste of this country and of England there cannot be a bottle of better Bordeaux produced in France. It cost me at Bordeaux three livres a bottle, ready bottled and packed. This is very dear; but you say you do not limit me in price. I send you a note of the principal wines of this country, their prices &c. and shall be happy to have you furnished with any of them which you may wish for your own use, only giving me notice enough before hand to have them provided and lodged at Havre or Bordeaux. Notice for the latter need be very short when you have a vessel coming to Bordeaux. Notice for Hermitage must be very long.

I thank you for supplying my omission as to Mr. Warner Lewis. You did what I would have done myself, if time had not hurried my recollections. The books and maps, by some inattention at Havre, sailed from that place for New York only the last month. Sell them for what you please. It will always be that much more than they are worth. The map may perhaps give to these copies a preference over the American edition, which will probably be without a map. Your attention to forward plants, hams, cyder &c. is very obliging. The last two articles being prohibited, must pass as the captain's sea-stores. Can you by any opportunity send me some of the Lima-bean, or Sugar bean, which is not to be had here or in England, and is asked from me by a friend. I thank you for the Newspapers. They are a great treat to me; and the advertisements are not the least interesting parts of them. Nothing new having transpired since my last, I have only to repeat assurances of the sincere esteem and respect with which I am Dear Sir your affectionate friend & servt., TH: JEFFERSON

PrC (DLC). The enclosed NOTE OF THE PRINCIPAL WINES has not been found, but it must have been based upon the notes compiled by TJ during his tour of Southern France and must have been similar to the more extended notes compiled after his journey through the vineyards of the Moselle and the Rhine in 1788—notes drawn from the travel journals of 1787-1788 and which formed the basic list from which TJ supplied information about European wines to many persons from 1788 on-ward (DLC: TJ Papers, 234:41990-6; to be printed in Second Series).

The first AMERICAN EDITION of *Notes on Virginia* was printed in Philadelphia in 1788 by Prichard and Hall; it was pirated from the Stockdale edition of 1787 (Coolie Verner, *A Further Checklist of the Separate Editions of Jefferson's Notes on the State of Virginia*, Charlottesville, 1950, p. 9; Sabin No. 35897). See note to Donald to TJ, 15 Dec. 1787.

To Pierre Samuel Dupont

15 Feb. [1788]

I am much obliged to you, Sir, for the communication of the draught of the Arret. I am sure there never would have come a single cod-fish to the entrepots: therefore I am curious to know what were the real motives which produced this opposition.

I shall so represent the matter in my letters as that nothing shall be thought of it. I have the honour to be with great thankfulness

[595]

for your favors, and with sincere esteem & respect Dr. Sir your most obedt. humble servt., TH: JEFFERSON

RC (Pierre S. duPont, Wilmington, Del., 1950); without name of addressee and year which have been assigned from internal evidence. Enclosure (missing): Doubtless a MS Dft of the arrêt of 22 Feb. 1788, excepting fish oils and other products derived from fish from the benefits allowed to the United States in the arrêt of 29 Dec. 1787 (printed copies are in DNA: PCC, No. 87, II, accompanied by a translation into English by John Pintard; another printed copy in DLC; see TJ to Jay, 23 May 1788, enclosure).

From Benjamin Franklin

DEAR SIR   Philada. Feb. 15. 1788

Mr. Frazer, who will have the honour of delivering this Line to your Excellency, is a Gentleman of respectable Character here, and as such I beg leave to recommend him to your Civilities.

He has in France a young Sister, who was left there some time since in a Convent for Improvement in her Education, and has it seems been seduc'd to resolve on remaining there; and on abandoning her Relations and Religion. Their Mother is a Citizen of these States, and reclaims her Child; and 'tis hoped that there is no Law in France, which may prevent her Succeeding in so just a Demand, founded on a Natural Right. I am persuaded that if you can be of Use to Mr. Frazer in this Business, you will chearfully afford him your Advice and Assistance, in which you will at the same time much oblige Your Excellency's most obedient & most humble Servt,   B. FRANKLIN

PrC (DLC: Franklin Papers). This letter evidently exists only in the PrC in the Franklin Papers; the RC is not recorded in SJL Index and was not, so far as is known, answered by TJ. From these facts it is plausible to infer that the letter that was supposed to have been delivered by MR. FRAZER was not sent, or at least not delivered.

To André Thouin

MONSIEUR   à Paris ce 15me. Fevr. 1788

Je suis tout honteux de n'avoir pas répondu plutôt à la lettre que vous m'avez fait l'honneur de m'écrire. La raison en a été que je me suis proposé tous les jours d'aller au jardin du roy pour vous parler du projet de M. du Quesnay, mais mes occupations m'ont empêché, et m'empêchent encore. Il n'y a personne qui souhaite au projet de M. du Quesnay un succès plus complet que moi. Vous dites bien, Monsieur, que c'est beau et très vaste. Et vous sentirez sans doute qu'un projet très vaste dans un pais très pauvre et peu-peuplé peut manquer. Je me suis fait un loi de ne persuader jamais à personne d'aller en Amérique sans une certitude immanquable qu'ils y trouveront de quoi subsister. Ne voyant pas cette certitude pour les professeurs et autres qui y iroient sur le plan de M. du Quesnay, je ne peux pas me compromettre près d'eux par des déclarations dont la base me seroit douteux. Si mes déclarations entreroient pour quelque chose dans leurs motifs d'y aller, et s'ils s'y trouveroient malheureux, ils pourroient m'en faire des justes reproches. Ceux aussi qui y mettroient de leur argent pourroient faire de même. M. du Quesnay donc sera assez juste pour approuver la retenue que je me propose d'observer. Il est trop raisonnable de me souhaiter de faire ce qu'en conscience je ne peux pas faire. Je me tiens neutre. Je ne parle à personne de son project à moins d'y être obligé. Et dans ce cas j'évite de dire rien qu'y pourroit nuire. J'espère, Monsieur, que vous approverez ma manière d'agir à son égard. J'aurois voulu me prêter à tout ce qu'il désire: et vos instances en auroient été un motif de plus, et des plus puissants. Agréez, je vous prie, les assurances de mon estime et de mon attachement sincère, avec les sentiments respectueux avec lesquels j'ai l'honneur d'être, Monsieur, votre tres humble et tres obeissant serviteur, TH: JEFFERSON

PrC (DLC).
LA LETTRE . . . M'ECRIRE: Thouin's letter to TJ, to which this is an answer, has not been found; it is recorded in SJL Index as dated 24 Jan. 1788. TJ also recorded in SJL Index a letter from Thouin of 15 Feb. (no doubt a reply to the above), which has not been found.

Memoranda for John Trumbull

[ca. 15 Feb. 1788]

Polyplasiasmos
Mr. Adams's picture by Brown
mine by do.
} to be sent by the Diligence. Mine is paid for

Tea vase.

Enquire if a triangular odometer is to be bought in London, and at what price. It is placed between the spokes of the wheel.

Might I not expect from Mr. Walker the machinery of the Celestini?

I have wrote to Mr. Stockdale, bookseller Piccadilly 3. letters, viz. Oct. 10. Jan. 1. and Jan. 16. desiring him to send the plate of my map immediately, and also some books, and his account. I have never received an answer. I must beg Mr. Trumbull to see him, to ask an explanation, and to send the map plate with the pictures.

Desire my taylor (Colo. Smith will give his name and address) to make me 2. pr. buff Casimir breeches of the colour sent herewith, and 2 pr. Cotton breeches of the same stuff and colour of those he has made for me heretofore.

Ask the cost of a chariot as neat &c. as Mrs. Church's coach.

Receive from Mrs. Adams and Colo. Smith the small balances of their accounts. To that of Mrs. Adams is still to be added 8. Louis paid to Monsr. Blancherie by order of Mr. Adams.

PrC (DLC); in TJ's hand, with caption: "Memms for Mr. Trumbull"; undated, but clearly written just prior to Trumbull's departure for London on 16 Feb. 1788; see Trumbull to TJ, 26 Feb. 1788.

To Schweighauser & Dobrée

GENTLEMEN   Paris Feb. 16. 1788.

I have duly received your favor of Jan. 29. Having sent a sample of the muskets to the commissioners of the treasury and asked their instructions relative thereto, and having reason to expect these very soon, it would be improper in me to consent to any previous disposal of them.

Mr. Carnes wrote me on the 15th. of January that he had sent off, the day before, the papers relative to your accounts. I have therefore been in daily expectation of receiving them, but they are not yet delivered to me. In truth I begin to be uneasy for fear of a miscarriage. Will you be so good as to consult with him, and to have me furnished with such indications as may enable me to search them out? And it would not be amiss to satisfy yourselves by examination that the person to whom Mr. Carnes delivered them has not left them at Lorient. Be assured that after I receive them, this affair shall experience no unnecessary delay from me. I am with sentiments of great esteem, gentlemen your most obedt. and most humble servt.,   TH: JEFFERSON

PrC (DLC). YOUR FAVOR OF JAN. 29: Not found.

To Johann Ludwig de Unger

SIR   Paris Feb. 16. 1788.

I receive with a great deal of pleasure your favor of January 20. and congratulate you sincerely on your present happy situation. The favours dealt out to you by your sovereign are a proof of his penetration and good administration. Inclosed is the certificate which you desire for Hartmann. Besides the duty to truth which would have called on me for this, and my desire to serve whomsoever you befriend, I found myself further biassed in his favor by observing his opinion to coincide with mine that nothing in Europe can counterbalance the freedom, the simplicity, the friendship and the domestic felicity we enjoy in America. I have been led to quit it by a domestic loss, but could not be induced to be long absent from it. I am here with two daughters, being all the family I have left. I retain a strong remembrance of the happy moments in which you participated, and to which you contributed so much at Monticello. That you may continue to be the object of the favors of your sovereign and the blessings of heaven is the sincere prayer of him who has the honour to be with sentiments of sincere affection Sir Your most obedient & most humble servant,

TH: JEFFERSON

PrC (DLC). Enclosure not found, but see Unger to TJ, 20 Jan. 1788, for the form of certificate desired.

From Simon Bérard

ce Dimanche 17 au Soir [Feb. 1788]

J'ai l'honneur d'envoyer à Son Excellence trois lettres qui ont été addressées à mon frère à L'orient par les Navires Américains et françois, Good Hope, Captn. forrester, Henrietta, Wicks et L'oiseau, Capne. Meno (à ma maison), tous trois Venants de Charlestown, chargés à sa Consignation de

1364. Tierces ⎫
100. Barl: ⎬ Ris
107. Boucauds de tabac
3. Bs. Indigo
9700. Merrain
17. tonneaux fer en Saumons
Et Pour Compte de divers
140. Tierces de Ris
220. Barls   Do.

[599]

Ces trois navires y sont arrivés le 13 courant. Mon frère se proposoit d'indiquer la Vente publique de deux chargements pour le 28. et de faire passer le troisième au Havre, où il aparoit, quoiqu'un peu tard pour le Carême, on en tireroit meilleur parti qu'en les vendant tous à L'orient; le dernier prix y avoit été 24^{tt}:10s, mais il ne se flattoit pas d'obtenir actuellement audelà de 20 à 21.^{tt}

Votre Excellence peut être assurée qu'il ne négligera aucun moyen pour les intérêts des Propriétaires, et pour répondre à ses Vües en Justifiant la bonne idée qu'elle a donné de la maison de mon frère, et encourageant ces Premiers essays Pour les décider à l'avantage des deux Nations.

J'ai l'honneur de Présenter mes Salutations et mon respect à Son Excellence,   S. BERARD

RC (DLC); endorsed; without month and year which have been supplied from internal evidence (see Brailsford & Morris to TJ, 10 Jan. 1788), and an entry for a letter from Bérard of this date in SJL Index. The TROIS LETTRES enclosed must have been those from Brailsford & Morris, 31 Oct. 1787 and its enclosures; Gadsden to TJ, 29 Oct. 1787; and another not identified.

To Angelica Schuyler Church

Paris Sunday. Feb. 17. 1788.

You speak, Madam, in your Note of Adieu, of civilities which I never rendered you. What you kindly call such were but the gratifications of my own heart: for indeed that was much gratified in seeing and serving you. The morning you left us, all was wrong. Even the sun shine was provoking, with which I never quarelled before. I took it into my head he shone only to throw light on our loss: to present a chearfulness not at all in unison with my mind. I mounted my horse earlier than common, and took by instinct the road you had taken. Some spirit whispered this to me: but he whispered by halves only: for, when I turned about at St. Denis, had he told me you were then broke down at Luzarches, I should certainly have spurred on to that place, and perhaps not have quitted you till I had seen the carriage perform it's office fully by depositing you at Boulogne. I went in the evening to Madame de Corny's, where we talked over our woes, and this morning I found some solace in going for Kitty and the girls. She is now here, just triste enough to shew her affection, and at the same time her discretion. I think I have discovered a method of preventing this dejection of mind on any future parting. It is this. When you come again, I will employ myself solely in finding or fancying that you have some faults, and I will draw a veil over all your good qualities, if I can find one large enough. I think I shall succeed in this. For, trying myself to-day, by way of exercise, I recollected immediately one fault in your composition. It is that you give all your attention to your friends, caring nothing about yourself. Now you must agree that I christian this very mildly when I call it a folly only. And I dare say I shall find many like it when I examine you with more sang froid.—I remember you told me, when we parted, you would come to see me at Monticello. Now tho' I believe this to be impossible, I have been planning what I would shew you: a flower here, a tree there; yonder a grove, near it a fountain; on this side a hill, on that a river. Indeed, madam, I know nothing so charming as our own country. The learned say it is a new creation; and I believe them; not for their reasons, but because it is made on an improved plan. Europe is a first idea, a crude production, before the maker knew his trade, or had made up his mind as to what he wanted. Let us go back to it together then. You intend it a visit; so do I. While you are indulging with your friends on the Hudson, I will go to see if Monticello remains in the same place. Or I will attend you to the falls of Niagara, if you will go on with me to the passage of the Patowmac, the Natural bridge &c. This done, we will come back together, you for a long, and I for a lesser time. Think of this plan, and when you come to pay your summer's visit to Kitty we will talk it over. In the mean time heavens bless you, Madam, fortify your health, and watch over your happiness. Your's affectionately,

TH: J.

RC (Peter B. Olney, Old Saybrook, Conn.). PrC (MoSHi).

YOUR NOTE OF ADIEU: Not found. This letter, which shows how far TJ had emerged from the infatuation that had led him on the road to ST. DENIS fifteen months earlier, bears comparison with that to Maria Cosway of 12 Oct. 1786. It was also clearly written after TJ had received Trumbull's letter of this date, dispatched from Chantilly at half "past 9 oC[lock] Sunday Morn."

From Richard Claiborne

SIR   London No. 15 Bartlets Buildings 17. February 1788.

I have received a letter from Mr. L'Ormerie, respecting the Tract or parcel of Land, sold to him by Colonel Saml. Blackden, on which subject, he informed me he had spoken to you, and I have answered him this day, which reply he will no doubt show you. I have to express to your Excellency that I will chearfully subscribe to any thing that may do justice, and give satisfaction to Mr. L'Ormerie, and am well convinced that Mr. Banks will do the same. Colonel Blackden I have not heard from some time; when he wrote me last he was at Dunkirk, Hotel D'Angleterre, and was about to leave it on a Tour to some other part of France; his address will however be easy to be obtained there, and I hope he will proceed to have every thing adjusted and concluded properly.

Yesterday I received letters from Virginia, informing me that the material subjects then in hand before the Legislature were, The Foederal Constitution, the payment of British Debts, a law exonerating the person of a Debtor from Confinement, a Bankrupt Law for the Merchants, and a Law making answerable every species of property a man has by sale and execution, on motion of a Jury, for all Debts contracted thereafter. It was apprehended that the new Constitution would not be agreed to under its present form; a special Convention was to be appointed to take it in hand, and to decide on its merits. Mr. Henry and Genl. Lawson were against the payment of British Debts, and Mr. Mason and Colonel Nicholas, in favor of them. Mr. Henry appears to have the most leading weight in the House, haveing spun out the session much longer than was expected, because things did not please him on the first view. It appears that the Kentuckie Country, will be a seperate Government, in about 12 months.

The greatest subjects on the Tapis here are, The Trial of Mr. Hastings, the proceedings against Sir Elijah Empey, and the Slave Trade. The latter appears to be engrossing the general attention of the people of England, and many petitions are already before Parliament upon the subject.

I am sorry to hear from Virginia, that the Production of Mr. Adams on the American Constitutions, has rendered him very unpopular in that Country generally.

Hoping you have health and happiness; I have the honor to be, with the greatest respect, Your Excellency's most obedient, and most humble Servant,   RD. CLAIBORNE

RC (CSmH).

From André Limozin

Le Havre, 17 Feb. 1788. Has not received an answer to his letter of

10 Feb. and is, therefore, concerned about the two boxes mentioned therein. The bust of Lafayette has not yet come to hand.

RC (MHi); 2 p.; endorsed.

From John Trumbull

DR. SIR   Chantilly h past 9 oC Sunday Morn [17 Feb. 1788]

I am afraid of having done a very foolish thing. We have been oblig'd to leave at Luzarches (where our Carriage broke yesterday) one of our trunks. It contains books and the Servants Clothes, and I have been foolish enough, as well as our servant, to take no receipt for it. I have address'd it to Mr. Short to be left at the Messagerie Royale at Paris, at which place the people promise to deliver it on Tuesday morning. What I beg is that you will be so good as to send Pitite to the Messagerie, Rue notre Dame de Victoires on Tuesday to inquire for it. If he does not find it that you will be so kind as to send him to Luzarches, where we have left it at the Poste Royale. The people who keep the Inn keep the Post and the Messagerie.

The trunk is a large English boot trunk which belong'd to Mrs. C. En Carriage.

We have arriv'd so far safe, and with the help of the Smiths we hope to get to Boulogne.

Many Respects from Mrs. Church. Your

JNO TRUMBULL

RC (DLC); endorsed; date supplied from internal evidence and an entry in SJL Index under this date (see TJ to Angelica Schuyler Church, same date; Trumbull to TJ, 18 Feb.; TJ to Trumbull, 20 Feb. 1788).

To Bertrand

MONSIEUR   à Paris ce 18me. Fevrier 1788

Je vous fais bien des remercimens pour votre bonté en me faisant part de la déclaration du nommé Jean Schmit. J'y trouve pourtant une preuve assez [sûre] que cette personne n'est pas des etats-unis. Il se dit natif de Baltimore *en Virginie*. C'est comme si on se [nommait] natif de Paris en Espagne. La ville de Baltimore est en Maryland, et je le crois impossible qu'un natif put ignorer le nom de son païs. J'ai eu occasion de voir plusieurs exemples de matelots Anglois et Irlandois, qui, s'ayant sauvé de leurs batiments,

[603]

se sont déclinés comme Américains [pensants] que sous ce nom là ils pourroient passer avec plus d'indulgence; et je soupçonne que le nommé Jean Schmit est ou Anglois ou Irlandois. Je ne propose pas donc, Monsieur, de faire des réclamations sur son compte. Répétant mes remercimens pour votre attention, j'ai l'honneur de vous assurer des sentiments de considération et d'attachement avec lesquels j'ai celui d'etre Monsieur votre tres humble et tres obeissant serviteur, TH: JEFFERSON

PrC (DLC).

To La Boullaye

SIR   Paris Feb. 18. 1788.

I have the honour to inclose you a letter from Mr. Barrett an American, on whose case I have before taken the liberty to trouble you. He reclaims the extra duties which he has been obliged to pay on whale oils brought hither under the encouragement of Monsieur de Calonne's letter, and which the letter which Monsieur de Lambert did me the honour to write me promises shall be refunded. That his claim is substantially just I have no doubt: and should you be disposed to receive substantial proofs, tho not rigorously formal, there will be no danger that the indulgence will ever be drawn into precedent, because it is the only claim which ever can be presented under that letter. Permit me to beg your favorable attention to this claim and as speedy a discussion of it as can be admitted, and at the same time to assure you of those sentiments of esteem and respect with which I have the honor to be Sir your most obedient & most humble servant,

TH: JEFFERSON

PrC (DLC). Enclosure: Probably Barrett to TJ, 7 Dec. 1787, q.v.

From William Macarty

L'Orient, 18 Feb. 1788. Has arranged with his creditors in France to settle his affairs; the loss of 15,000^{lt} since the peace, with what he expects to lose on outstanding debts, will put him considerably in arrears; could recover the loss if he were permitted to proceed to America with his ship under American or French colors, from thence to the West Indies, and return to France to sell his cargo; as he has been settled in France since 1781, and as the funds to be thus raised are for the payment of debts in France, hopes that an application for this permission, through TJ, to Messrs. La Luzerne and Lambert would be granted; hopes TJ will make such application and that Lafayette will lend his influence.

RC (DLC); endorsed.

From John Rutledge, Jr.

DR SIR   London feby: 18th: 1788

Two days ago, on my return from Bath, I had the pleasure to receive your letter of the second Instant. I shall not leave London as soon as I proposed, but will continue here until the Trial of Mr. Hastings shall be over. As to the first question which you desire I will consider and decide for myself, namely if the Offence of Hastings is to be decided by the law of the land? I answer in the affirmative. An impeachment before the Lords, by the Commons of Great Britain, is a prosecution of the known and established law, coeval, I think, with the Constitution itself being a present-ment to the most high Court of criminal jurisdiction by the most solemn grand Inquest of the whole Kingdom. You next ask why he is not tried in the Court of Kings bench? There are peculiar Circumstances which attach to Mr. Hastings case, in my Opinion, reasons against that subordinate mode of proceeding. How could he have a jury from any Vicinity in Asia, to try this cause in the Court of Kings Bench? Or would you summon from another hemisphere english Inhabitants, the bosom Associates of his Cor-ruption, to Convict this Captain General of delinquincy of those very Crimes upon which their fortunes have been founded—upon which they have fed, fatten'd and flourished in the East. As to the trying him by a jury from Middlesex for high Crimes committed on the Banks of the Ganges besides the incompetency of such a pannel to comprehend many of the Questions to be tried, I do not think any fiction, usage or analogy of english law would sustain the propriety of such proceedings. The Accusations against Mr. Hastings are for enormities of the deepest die, speculation, cor-ruption, breach of Orders, plunder, torture, murder, devastation, tyranny and violations of the Laws of the land, of nature and of Nations. He is possess'd of enormous wealth, great Influence and preponderating Power. These would probably deter the injured from a subordinate legal prosecution and therefore good reasons why he is not tried in the ordinary Mode before the court of Kings

bench. The third question is answered in the reply to the first—
he is not *"disfranchised of his most precious right"* but judged
according to the ancient and known law of the land by which he
is amenable for Offences against public justice and liable to be
impeached and tried before the Peers. As to this Court being
"illiterate and unprincip[led]" doubtless there are many among the
Individuals, who compose it, who are both "illiterate and unprincipled." But then it must be confess'd that there are many personages also, of great judicial learning, constitutional experience
and unblemished Integrity who have seats in this Court. Even all
the Bishops have never been quite without probity and talents.
The Lord Chancellor and the chief Justices give their Opinions
as they would in their respective Courts on any similar Subject,
and also the twelve Judges sit on the woolsacks continually and
furnish their sage Opinions on every doubtful point during the
whole trial. Upon the whole the usage of Impeachment appears to
me to be the only efficient, legal Check which the People at large,
through the Organ of their Delegates, have upon the Abuses of
the executive in its administration of great Public Affairs.

With respect to the fate of Hastings, People in general think
that the Kings great friendship for him secures him, but I myself
think his being acquitted very doubtful. In the event of any Accident
happening during the Trial, to the Kings life, it certainly will go
hard with him. But should he be even acquited, nay, made a Peer
of and loaded with honors, yet when the World come to be possess'd of the speeches of Burke, Fox and Sherridan and see the
proofs with which they do abound of his Cruelty and Villainy *they*
certainly will condemn him, and will be as much astonished at his
Acquital as they will be shock'd at his Infamy. I feel exceedingly
for the distresses of france. If her Embarrassments are half as
great as they, in this Country, are reported and believed to be,
her state must be lamentable indeed. The reports here of the french
King's folly, of the madness of his Ministers and the obstinacy of
his Parliaments have flattered and pamper'd John Bull beyond
expression. They have added to his natural insolence; he carries
his Brest higher now than ever, and is bellowing for War. I believe the trial of Mr. H. will not be over in less than six weeks.
It is not necessary for me to repeat what I mentioned in my last
that should your Excellency have any Commands I shall be happy
in being charged with them. Be pleased my dr. Sir to make my

Compliments to Mr. Short and believe me to be with the most invio[late] attachment Your sincere Friend & humble Servant,

J. RUTLEDGE Junior

RC (DLC).

From John Trumbull

DR. SIR   Boulogne Monday Evg. 9.oC. 18th. Feby. 1788

I wrote you yesterday morning from Chantilly of our adventure and my blunder of the trunk at Luzarches (which last I trust to your goodness to rectify). We reach'd Clermont two posts & ½ from thence at 12 oClock, where we found one of our hind wheels broke, the other and one fore one breaking. Happily we were nigh an excellent Smith, who with the help of some new tire nails and half a dozen of clamp bands put us in order to proceed; and we reach'd Amiens last night, without further misfortune, but in continual apprehensions of being let down in the mud. We now find ourselves safe by a warm fire, fortunately our Captain waiting for us and the wind fair; so we sail tomorrow morning.

Mrs. Church begs to be affectionately remember'd. I shall inform you of our further progress when we reach England, as I know your anxiety for the safety of your friends. Compliments to Mr. Short. I am Your Oblig'd friend,   JNO TRUMBULL

RC (DLC); endorsed.

From Jacob Vernes

[*18 Feb. 1788*. Recorded in SJL Index. Not found, but see Vernes to TJ, 10 Apr. 1788.]

From James Madison

DEAR SIR   New York Feby. 19. 1788

By the Count de Moustier I received your favour of the 8th. of October. I received by his hands also the watch which you have been so good as to provide for me, and for which I beg you to accept my particular thanks. During the short trial I have made she goes with great exactness. Since the arrival of the Count de

Moustier, I have received also by the Packet Mr. Calonne's publication for myself, and a number of the Mercure's for Mr. Banister. The Bearer was a Mr. Stuart. I had a conveyance to Mr. Banister a few days after the Mercure's came to hand.

The public here continues to be much agitated by the proposed fœderal Constitution and to be attentive to little else. At the date of my last Delaware Pennsylvania and New Jersey had adopted it. It has been since adopted by Connecticut, Georgia, and Massachusetts. In the first the minority consisted of 40 against 127. In Georgia the adoption was unanimous. In Massachusetts the conflict was tedious and the event extremely doubtful. On the final question the vote stood 187 against 168; a majority of 19 only being in favor of the Constitution. The prevailing party comprized however all the men of abilities, of property, and of influence. In the opposite multitude there was not a single character capable of uniting their wills or directing their measures. It was made up partly of deputies from the province of Maine who apprehended difficulties from the New Government to their scheme of separation, partly of men who had espoused the disaffection of Shay's; and partly of ignorant and jealous men, who had been taught or had fancied that the Convention at Philada. had entered into a conspiracy against the liberties of the people at large, in order to erect an aristocracy for the rich the *well-born*, and the men of Education. They had no plan whatever. They looked no farther than to put a negative on the Constitution and return home. The amendments as recommended by the Convention were as I am well informed not so much calculated for the minority in the Convention, on whom they had little effect, as for the people of the State. You will find the amendments in the Newspapers which are sent from the office of foreign affairs. It appears from a variety of circumstances that disappointment had produced no asperity in the minority, and that they will probably not only acquiesce in the event, but endeavour to reconcile their constituents to it. This was the public declaration of several who were called the leaders of the party. The minority of Connecticut behaved with equal moderation. That of Pennsylvania has been extremely intemperate and continues to use a very bold and menacing language. Had the decision in Massachusetts been adverse to the Constitution, it is not improbable that some very violent measures would have followed in that State. The cause of the inflamation however is much more in their State factions, than in the system proposed by the

Convention. New Hampshire is now deliberating on the Constitution. It is generally understood that an adoption is a matter of certainty. South Carolina and Maryland have fixed on April or May for their Conventions. The former it is currently said will be one of the ratifying States. Mr. Chace and a few others will raise a considerable opposition in the latter. But the weight of personal influence is on the side of the Constitution, and the present expectation is that the opposition will be outnumbered by a great majority. This State is much divided in its sentiment. Its Convention is to be held in June. The decision of Massts. will give the turn in favor of the Constitution unless an idea should prevail or the fact should appear, that the voice of the State is opposed to the result of its Convention. North Carolina has put off her Convention till July.[1] The State is much divided it is said. The temper of Virginia, as far as I can learn, has undergone but little change of late. At first there was an enthusiasm for the Constitution. The tide next took a sudden and strong turn in the opposite direction. The influence and exertions of Mr. Henry, and Col. Mason and some others will account for this. Subsequent information again represented the Constitution as regaining in some degree its lost ground. The people at large have been uniformly said to be more friendly to the Constitution than the Assembly. But it is probable that the dispersion of the latter will have a considerable influence on the opinions of the former. The previous adoption of nine States must have a very persuasive effect on the minds of the opposition, though I am told that a very bold language is held by Mr. H——y and some of his partisans. Great stress is laid on the self-sufficiency of that State, and the prospect of external props are alluded to.

Congress have done no business of consequence yet, nor is it probable that much more of any sort will precede the event of the great question before the public.

The Assembly of Virginia have passed the district Bill of which I formerly gave you an account. There are 18 districts, with 4 new Judges, Mr. Gabl. Jones, Richd. Parker, St. George Tucker and Jos. Prentis. They have reduced much the taxes, and provided some indulgences for debtors. The question of British debts underwent great vicicitudes. It was after long discussion resolved by a majority of 30 against the utmost exertions of Mr. Henry that they should be paid as soon as the other States should have complied with the treaty. A few days afterwards he carried his point by a majority of 50 that G. B. should first comply. Adieu Yrs. Affecty., Js. MADISON Jr.

P.S. Mr. St. John has given me a very interesting description of a System of Nature lately published at Paris. Will you add it for me. The Boxes which were to have come for myself G.W. and A. D. &c have not yet arrived.

RC (DLC: Madison Papers).

The DISTRICT BILL is to be found in Hening, XII, 532-58. Mr. H——Y: Patrick Henry.

[1] At this point Madison inserted a cross and wrote at the bottom of the page: "see letter from Col. Davie to J.M."; this note was evidently made when his letters were returned to him after TJ's death. Madison undoubtedly referred to a letter from William R. Davie to him discussing at some length North Carolina's attitude toward the Constitution—but the letter was dated 10 June 1789 (DLC: Madison Papers).

From Thomas Paine

SIR   Feby. 19th. 1788

I mentioned to you that I had some conversation with the Marquis de la fayette respecting the Bridge, and his opinion is that it would be best to make some direct proposition to which either yes or no should be given. My principal object is to get the Bridge erected because until then all conversation upon the subject amounts to but little. My chief expectation as to the money part was on Mr. Morris but his affairs appearing to be deranged lessens very considerably that dependence. I am casting about to find some way to accomplish this point, or at least assist towards it before I return to America and the enclosed is on that subject. I shall be glad you would peruse it and give me your opinion, after which I will send it to the Marquis. If he and you concur in opinion respecting the propriety of it I will have it translated and presented to some of the Ministry, tho perhaps it would be best to take some method to let it be first seen in order to know whether it will be agreeable that it should be presented. If you can return it to me tomorrow I will then send it to the Marquis. Your Obedient Humble Servant,   THOMAS PAINE

RC (DLC); endorsed. Enclosure missing.

For an account of Paine's effort to promote his patented iron BRIDGE in France, see Don C. Seitz, "Thomas Paine, Bridge Builder," *Va. Quar. Rev.*, III (1927), 571-94. Paine's presence in Paris enabled him not only to gain Lafayette's assistance in his project, but also to join the marquis and TJ in discussing the merits of the proposed Federal Constitution: Lafayette wrote to Knox that "Mr. Jefferson, Common Sense," and himself were debating the constitution "in a convention of our own as earnestly as if we were to decide upon it" (Lafayette to Knox, 4 Feb. 1788, quoted in Gottschalk, *Lafayette, 1783-89*, p. 374).

To John Adams

DEAR SIR   Paris Feb. 20. 1788

I am in hopes daily of receiving a letter from you in answer to my last. The delay of the letters which contained the proposition to the board of treasury takes away all probability of their answering in time, and I foresee that I shall be closely pressed by circumstances on that point. I have settled your matter with de la Blancherie, at the sum you fixed (8 Louis). He demanded 12. but without a shadow of reason I think.

This letter will probably find you near your departure. I am in hopes it will be only a change of service, from helping us here, to help us there. We have so few in our councils acquainted with foreign affairs, that your aid in that department, as well as others will be invaluable. The season of the year makes me fear a very disagreeable passage for Mrs. Adams and yourself, tho we have sometimes fine weather in these months. Nobody will pray more sincerely than myself for your passage, that it may be short, safe and agreeable, that you may have a happy meeting with all your friends, be received by them with the gratitude you have merited at their hands, and placed in such a station as may be honourable to you and useful to them. Adieu, my dear Sir, and accept assurances of the unchangeable esteem and respect with which I am Your friend & servant,   TH: JEFFERSON

RC (MHi: AMT); addressed and endorsed; postmarked 25 Feb. PrC (DLC).

From James Madison

DEAR SIR   New York Feby. 20. 1788

I have this moment received an answer to a letter written to Mr. W. S. Browne on the subject of Mr. Burke's affairs. The answer is written by direction of Mrs. Brown and informs me that her husband is absent on a voyage to the West Indies and is not expected back till April; that when "he arrives he no doubt will be ready to deliver the effects on proper application. The amount of effects I can say nothing to, but they have been stored ever since with care. The cash I believe is the same as you mention—as to tendering any thing but the hard cash you need be under no apprehension. His character is well established in this town (Providence R. Island) and he despises the man that would offer

[611]

paper when he had received cash." This is all the information I have to give on the subject.

By letters just received from Virginia I find that I shall be under the necessity of setting out in 8 or 10 days for Virginia. I mention this circumstance that it may explain the cause if I should not write by the next conveyance. Yrs. affty.,

Js. MADISON Jr.

RC (DLC: Madison Papers); endorsed by TJ.

To Parent

MONSIEUR à Paris ce 20me. Fevrier 1788.

Le vin que vous avez eu la bonté de m'envoyer est arrivé en bon état. Il n'y avoit qu'une bouteille de cassée. Votre traite sur moi pour le montant sera payée. Je vous prie d'y mettre trois ou quatre jours de vue, pour éviter l'effet d'une absence casuelle quand le porteur peut se présenter chez moi avec votre billet. Je vous fais bien de remerciments de votre attention et suis avec beaucoup de considération Monsieur votre très humble et très obeissant serviteur, TH: JEFFERSON

P.S. Les ceps m'ont eté remis aussi en bon état. J'ai donné 6.^{tt} au voiturier pour l'attention qu'il leur avoit porté.

PrC (MHi).

From Henry Remsen, Jr.

Office for foreign affairs [*New York*], 20 Feb. 1788. Acknowledges, in Jay's absence, TJ's letters of 19, 22, and 24 Sep., 8 and 27 Oct., 3 and 7 Nov. 1787, which "have been communicated to Congress, who have not until lately made a House." Sends packets of newspapers, one from Charleston, which was sent to office for foreign affairs for transmittal.

RC (DLC); 2 p.; endorsed.

To John Trumbull

DEAR SIR Paris Feb. 20. 1788.

Mrs. Church's trunk was safely delivered here last night by the waggoner. It had been opened of course at the Douane, but

I presume the same honesty, which brought it here, guarded it there and every where from pillage. It shall go off for London by tomorrow's diligence and will arrive I presume on the 25th. We have had great lamentations over your mishap, however hope it was the only one. It was fortunate that it happened in the day and not in the night. I rode that day to St. Denis and should certainly have gone on to Luzarches had I known you were there in distress. You had a fine day yesterday for crossing the channel, and would have had a disagreeable one had you arrived a day sooner. You will be so good as to write to me the moment you receive notice of the arrival in America either of the Count de Moustier (who sailed Nov. 14.) or of the French packet which sailed 4. days before him. You know how anxious we are for him here. I wrote Mrs. Church by the last post that her daughter was well, as she continues to be. I am with much esteem Dr. Sir Your friend & servant, TH: JEFFERSON

PrC (DLC).

From Abigail Adams

MY DEAR SIR   London Febry. 21 1788.

In the midst of the Bustle and fatigue of packing, the parade and ceremony of taking leave at Court, and else where, I am informed that Mr. Appleton and Mrs. Parker are to set out for Paris tomorrow morning. I Cannot permit them to go without a few lines to my much Esteemed Friend, to thank him for all his kindness and Friendship towards myself and Family, from the commencement of our acquaintance, and to assure him that the offer he has made of his correspondence, is much too flattering, not to be gratefully accepted.

The florence and stockings were perfectly to my mind, and I am greatly obliged to you sir, for your care and attention about them. I have sent by Mrs. Parker the balance due to you, agreable to your statement, which I believe quite right.

Be so good as to present my regards to the Marquiss de la Fayette and his Lady, and to the Abbés. Assure them that I entertain a gratefull remembrance of all their civilities and politeness during my residence in Paris. To Mr. Short and the young Ladies your daughters say every thing that is affectionate for me, and be assured my dear sir, that I am With the Greatest respect Esteem & regard Your Friend and Humble Servant,

ABIGAIL ADAMS

RC (DLC).

To J. Louis Brethoux

SIR   Paris Feb. 21. 1788.

I am now to acknolege the receipt of the letter you did me the honour to write me on the 21st. of January together with the book on the culture of the olive tree. This is a precious present to me, and I pray you to accept my thanks for it. I am just gratified by letters from South Carolina which inform me that in consequence of the information I had given them on the subject of the olive tree, and the probability of it's succeeding with them, several rich individuals propose to begin it's culture there. This will not interfere with the commerce of France because she imports much more oil than she exports, and because the consumption of oil in the United states at present is so inconsiderable that should their demand be totally withdrawn at the European market and supplied at home, it will produce no sensible effect in Europe. We can never produce that article in very great quantity because it happens that in our two Southernmost states, where only the climate is adapted to the olive, the soil is so generally rich as to be unfit for that tree and proper for other productions of more immediate profit. I am to thank you also for the raisins of Smyrna without seed which I received from you through Mr. Grand. Be so good as to present my friendly respects to Madame de

PrC (DLC); lacks part of complimentary close and signature (see Vol. 9: 217, note 1).

To C. W. F. Dumas

SIR   Paris Feb. 21. 1788.

I have received your very friendly letter of the 12th. instant. My journey to Amsterdam is among possible events only, and scarcely probable. Should I take it, one of it's gratifications will be the pleasure of seeing you at the Hague, and you only, because my business being at Amsterdam with private individuals only,

I should mean to slide on without being seen or known to any but those with whom my business would lie. The few moments of leisure which I might have, I would employ in seeing things rather than men, and the last abuse to which I would abandon them would be that of useless ceremony and etiquette. I thank you for your kind offers of service; but the purposes of my journey will require little writing. The only trouble I shall permit myself to give you will be that of consigning a few moments at the Hague to the information of which I shall stand in need, and to receive personally those assurances of attachment and respect which I feel sincerely for yourself and family and with which I have the honour to be Sir Your most obedient & most humble servt.,

TH: JEFFERSON

PrC (DLC).

To André Limozin

SIR   Paris Feb. 21. 1788

I have received your favor of the 17th. Mine of the 14th. which did not go from here till the 15th. got to your hands probably on the 17th. after you had written. It will have given you the necessary information relative to the boxes, and I shall be glad to know if they went by the packet. The bust of the Marquis de la Fayette went by the Diligence d'eau la bonne union a M. Gonard and left this the 16th instant. M. Pierre Vincent Lucat merchant at Rouen is the person whose duty it is to transfer it there to the Diligence d'eau for Havre and to have it delivered to you. In my letter of the 14th. I mentioned to you that there [was a re]port which if t[rue migh]t explain what this count[ry means to do and that if] I found it true I would commun[icate it to you immediately. I find it h]owever to be false, and I think that [this country has no] present intention of engaging itself shortly [in a war but that it has ever]y expectation of being forced into one. [Were I in your position I] should make my speculations on the supposition [that there will not be a war] for 6. or 12. months to come. I am with very great esteem Sir your most obedt & humble servvt.,

TH: JEFFERSON

PrC (DLC); MS mutilated; for note on this mutilation and on words supplied conjecturally, see TJ to Limozin, 14 Feb. 1788.

[615]

To John Bondfield

SIR   Paris Feb. 22. 1788.

Your favour of the 15th. January came safely to hand. I immediately sent a passport for the wines to Monsieur Elie la Fevre at Rouen. He had not then received the wine or any notification of it; but, I doubt not, it is on it's way. Your draught for the amount has not yet been presented, but shall be honoured whenever it is. I must ask of you a second favour of the same nature. The inclosed letter to the President Pichard is to ask of him 250. bottles of his wine de la Fite of 1784. and to begin a correspondence for receiving my supplies regularly from him. Will you be so good as to supply any defect in the address of the letter before you deliver it? I have taken the liberty therein to tell him you will be so good as to pay him the amount if he should prefer the receiving it there to the drawing on me for it in Paris. I must also trouble you with the forwarding the wine by water to Paris.

Some opposition has been excited here to the late arret. It is quieted by another arret declaring that the right of entrepot shall not be extended to our cod-fish. The Emperor has declared war against the Turks. There is every appearance however that this country will remain in peace. I am with much esteem, Sir, your most obedt. & most humble servt.,   TH: JEFFERSON

PrC (DLC). Enclosure: TJ to Pichard, same date, q.v.

From C. W. F. Dumas

MONSIEUR   La Haie 22e. fevr. 1788

Dans le même temps que j'avois l'honneur d'écrire à Votre Excellence la mienne du 12e., Elle me favorisoit de la précieuse sienne de même date, que j'ai bien reçue en son temps.

J'ai cru devoir en communiquer tout de suite le contenu vraiment important, consolant, encourageant, d'abord à mon digne ami Mr. van Staphorst à Amsterdam; et puis aussi à Mr. Luzac à Leide en le priant néanmoins de ne pas risquer, par trop de correctifs (par exemple pour un million de plus ou de moins que peuvent devoir encore en ce moment les Et. unis) d'énerver dans l'opinion publique l'impression favorable qu'y ont faite mes précédentes insertions. Quant à l'article du nouveau Gouvernement, la raison et nature de l'opposition de la Virginie y est si précisément

[616]

et si supérieurement déterminée et caractérisée, que je l'ai laissé le maître d'en tirer parti dans tout son entier pour un article dans sa feuille, persuadé qu'il fera le plus grand honneur au Peuple Américain et à ses Conducteurs, et qu'il anéantira pour toujours les mauvaises impressions que d'autres papiers ont cherché à donner de l'opinion, notamment de la Virginie.

Un brave homme d'ici vient de me remercier cordialement, de ce que les éclaircissemens qu'il m'avoit demandés, et que je lui ai donnés, l'ont déterminé à garder ses Effets Américains (d'environ 15 mille florins), contre l'avis de ses Courtiers, qui l'avoient allarmé sur le prétendu schisme des Etats-Unis.

Je me trouve, grâce à Dieu, convalescent d'une très-fâcheuse fièvre de nerfs, qui m'avoit presque réduit aux Abois.

L'on fait dès à présent de grands préparatifs ici pour le 8 de Mars prochain, jour de naissance du Prince. Toute la Ville sera illuminée, les hôtels des Ministres étrangers, et par conséquent aussi celui des Etats-unis comme les autres. Dieu nous fasse à tous la grâce, que cette fête se passe sans désordre et malheur!

Je suis avec le plus vrai respect, De Votre Excellence Le très-humble et très-obéissant serviteur, C W F DUMAS

Lorsque Votre Excellence en aura le loisir, une juste idée de l'opposition de Rhode-Island, de son origine, causes, et durée probable, me feroit grand plaisir de la part de Votre Excellence; comme aussi quelles deux autres Provinces nommément s'opposent encore et jusqu'à quel point.

Je n'ai pas laissé ignorer à Mr. Luzac l'idée distinguée qu'a Votre Excellence de son Papier.

RC (DLC); endorsed. FC (Rijksarchief, The Hague; Dumas Letter Books; photostats in DLC).

For the extract of TJ's letter as published in the *Gazette de Leide* on L'ARTICLE DU NOUVEAU GOUVERNEMENT, see TJ to Dumas, 12 Feb. 1788.

From Dr. Lambert

⟦*22 Feb. 1788.* Recorded in SJL Index. Not found.⟧

To Pichard

MONSIEUR LE PRESIDENT   à Paris ce 22me. Fevrier 1788

En passant par Bordeaux au mois de Mai de l'année passée, je me fis l'honneur de me présenter chez vous pour vous faire ma cour et pour vous remercier des bontés que vous aviez témoigné à Monsieur Barclay, notre Consul, dans l'affaire désagréable qui lui étoit arrivée à Bordeaux. En m'empressant de vous prier d'en agréer ici le renouvellement, je prends la liberté d'y ajouter la demande d'une grâce. Les vins excellents, nommés de la Fite, sont de votre crue. Si vous en avez de l'année 1784. et voulez bien m'accomoder à 250. bouteilles, je vous en serai infiniment obligé. Si c'est [possible] de les faire mettre en bouteilles, et de les faire emballer chez vous, ce seroit sans doute une garantie que le vin seroit naturel, et la soutirage &c. bien faite. Si non, Monsieur Bond-field [aura] la complaisance de le faire faire, et en tout cas de les recevoir et de me les faire passer à Paris. Il aura celle aussi de vous en payer le montant à Bordeaux, ou je le ferai à votre ordre à Paris, si cela vous seroit plus commode. Voulez vous bien me permettre aussi, Monsieur, pendant ma demeure ici, et même après ma retour en Amérique, de m'adresser à vous même directe-ment tous les fois que j'aurai besoin des vins de votre maison? Ce me seroit une obligation précieuse, et me fourniroit de tems à tems des occasions de vous renouveller les assurances des senti-ments de respect et d'attachement

PrC (MoSHi); lacks part of complimentary close and signature (see Vol. 9: 217, note 1). See note to Moustier to TJ, 3 Nov. 1787.

From William Stephens Smith

Calculation and Business only

DEAR SIR   London Feby. 22d. 1788. No. 3 Adams Street Adelphi

I have received your favour of the 2d. inst. and will attempt to explain the two articles with which I credited you in my account Current of the 3d. of Decr. ulto. The first article ammounting to Liv. 113.^{tt}5 is stated by Mr. Short in his letter of the 21. of Novr. 1787 and is composed as follows, viz.

8 ells of double florence	at 4.^{tt}15. =	38.^{tt}	0
6 ditto of White	at 4. 15	28.	10
2 ditto of lawn	at 6. 5	12.	10
3 ditto of black lace	at 5. 5	15.	15
12 pairs of Gloves		17.	10
	Liv.	112.	5

The second article amounting to 188.^{tt}15 arises from a statement

[618]

of two bills dated Paris the 13th. of August: 1786. added to the ammount of the Corsetts and is Indicated thus

12 ells of lace at 6^{it} livr.   72.^{it} 0

5½ ditto of Cambrick   12.10   68.^{it}15 ⌈not stated but

2 pr. of Stays at 24 each   48. 0 ⎱supposed to

              Lr. $\overline{188.\ 15}$ ⌊amount to 48

The lace and Cambrick in the last article were brought by Mr. Bulfinch and the Corsetts by Franks. The whole of the other were delivered by Mr. Short to Mr. Parker, but conveyed to London by Mr. Appleton.

The 164 livr. which you paid Petit on the 2d. of October 1786. must have arisen from the 2 articles which Mr. Bulfinch brought for Mrs. Smith the one of 72 and the other of 68.15 which being added to the ammount of 4 pair of Shoes for Mrs. Adams at 6 livr. pr. pair equals Liv. 24 (and which in the note which accompanied the articles was erased and marked thus—pd.) total amount of which is Liv. 164.^{it}15. This Statement being just, our accounts will stand thus—

Cr. with Cash on ballance   £ 3.18. 7

Chattellux travels and Lattre's

   Map   Livs.   12.14   11. 0 ⌈the livers calcu-

A Cloak   195.12. 6.   8.12.10 ⎱lated 24 to the

                 $\overline{£13.\ 2.\ 5}$ ⌊pound Sterg.

Dr. to Cash for Small copying press

   and Case   £ 5.10. 0

   to ditto Shoes not charged

   for W. Short   17. 0

to ½ doz. handkerchiefs, for ditto   1. 1. 0

to Waistcoats and breeches paid taylor

   as per enclosed acct.   7. 9. 0

                 $\overline{£14.17.\ 0}$

The Ballance due me if my statement and calculation is right is £1.10.7 but I must again submit the whole to your revission and correction, particularly the calculation of the Livers both in the Dr. and Cr. I shall write the circulating news on another sheet and by some other conveyance. Adieu my dear Sir. Yours sincerely,

W. S. SMITH

RC (MHi); endorsed.

Smith's CALCULATION of the balance at £1 10 7 was not right (he repeated the figure in his to TJ, 29 Feb. 1788); it should have been £1 14 7.

From William Stephens Smith

Dear Sir London Feby. 22d. 1788.

I wrote by this evenings post and attempted to explain in a satisfactory manner our account. I shall be pleased to be informed that I have succeded, and that every article appears clear to you. You have never yet informed me whether the picture I send you was the one you saw at Bermingham or Brumigum, and whether the price I gave, was anything near what you could have obtained it for, previous to its visit to the Capital.

Mr. Adams has taken leave of the King, and I suppose will soon put himself in motion towards America. There is a circumstance happened lately which it may be well for you to know. It is, that the resolve of Congress of the 5th. of October last which gave him permission to return, also put a period to his Commission to the United Netherlands, upon which Mr. Adams wrote memorials addressed to the Prince of Orange and their High Mightinesses the States General and enclosed them to their secretary requesting him to present them. This after consultation he declined to do, and has returned the letters, giving as a reason, that as Mr. Adams presented a Letter of Credence from Congress on his arrival, and there is no regular letter of recall accompanying the memorials, they can neither be presented nor received. This has produced a disagreable sensation and perhaps may lay the foundation of disrespectful observations, which thus knowing the case, you will be more collected to meet. Mr. Adams thinks he can do nothing to check this disagreable Impression and of course, home he will go. I have taken the liberty to hint that a visit *pro hac vici* to the Hague may do good, he at present thinks otherwise. He has not a Letter of recall here neither of Course, agreable to diplomatic etiquette his letter of Credence is not regularly counteracted but no objections have been started, relative to want of formality. Whether this arises from a general or particular scourse, I cannot say. But we go. I must refer you to my letter to Mr. Short for scandal and slander and have the pleasure to inform you that Connecticut has adopted the *national* Government by a majority of 135 to 40. Will you be so good as to tell Mr. Mazzei, that I cannot find nor have I heard from his Bookseller. He is an odd fish. He writes me that Mr. Morini in London has a sett of his Books for me. I should be much pleased if Mr. Mazzei in France will condescend to inform Mr. Smith in England in what part of the little City of London Mr. Morini is to be found. With great veneration for his Coolness and moderation I am Dear Sir, your obliged Humble Sert,   W. S. SMITH

RC (DLC); endorsed. Probably received on 1 Mch. 1788.

SCOURSE: Smith seems to have employed the obsolete word *scorse* in the sense of exchange (OED). His letter to SHORT was in reply to the latter's of 14 Feb. 1788 and commented upon La Luzerne's arrival in London: "As to your questions relative to the Marquis de la Luzerne, I answer—he exerted himself to arive here time enough to pay his respects to the Queen on her birth-day, and was invited to dine with the Minister of foreign Affairs, who gave an entertainment on the occasion and to enliven the feast Monsr. De Calonne was also a Guest. Some think it fortunate that the Ambassador is near sighted, as otherwise he might have supposed it an insult and lost his dinner,—but the former was not made nor the latter lost. With respect to the Eagle and blue Ribbon [*of the Cincinnati*] he does not appear in it, your opinion of him is just, indeed not one of them who have been here, have shewn it. This pleases you, I know. It has not a different effect upon me, and even Mr. Ternant tho' he left it behind him when he went to St. James, could not find favour in the Eye of Majesty. Notwithstanding the most pointed introduction from the Ambassador, both the King and Queen passed him with a glaring and apparently premeditated insult and so strongly marked as to produce a buz

of who is it? Do you know him? Does anybody know him?—insomuch that before night his name was writ in every private memorandum book with notes critical and explanatory, and when they found that he had been in service in America and in Holland, some were not backward in expressing their astonishment, that the Ambassador could introduce a person who had acted so pointedly against the views and interest of the King &c. &c. &c.—The opposition to the edict in favour of American Commerce which was passed in france in Decr. last, is trumpeted here pretty loud. I do not think it unlikely that John may frighten Louis out of it; I am clearly of opinion, he has more influence there, than he ought to have, and we ought to have a penetrating eye, to their intrigues and negotiations." Smith urged Short to visit London prior to their departure in the April packet, and added: "tell Shippen I think it is also worth his while to return here to see . . . the tryal of Mr. Hastings. He may travel for 20 years and not see a more dignified scene or a grander spectacle. It will furnish a page in the British history more glaring (if possible let the decision be what it may) than the decapitation of Charles, or the expulsion of the Stewarts" (Smith to Short, 22 Feb. 1788, DLC: Short Papers; endorsed in part "[received] March 1.").

From John Stockdale

SIR   Piccadilly 22nd. Febry. 1788.

I duly received your three Letters, but owing to the alterations I have been making in my house, by enlarging my Shop &c. has prevented me for this two Months past of paying that respect to you, and attention to my business that it required. But I have now got the Shop in excellent order and my business in a proper train, tho' I am a little discomposed by having been complained of by the House of Commons for having published what they deem a Lible, they have order'd me to be prosecuted. I have sent your Copper

Plate this day and next week I hope to send you all the Books order'd. I am with great respect Sir Your much obliged & very humble Servt.,   JOHN STOCKDALE

RC (MHi); TJ listed the following on the verso: "Grandison Bell's Shakesp. after 32. 46 49. Coke after 4th part 395. Priestl. biogr & pamphlet. Observer. by Cumberland. Nature displayed. Reviews." There is a check mark before each of these items, except "Grandison."

From John Trumbull

DEAR SIR   London 22d. Febry. 1788.

I wrote you from Boulogne to say that with all our accidents Mrs. Church was safe. We cross'd the channel in beautiful weather and in four or five hours, but our unpropitious Genius would not let us escape even on such a day without mishap. In going out of the harbor we ran foul of a post which marks the channel, damag'd the vessell and frighten'd us. After landing safe however at Dover we set off in two Chaise for Town and near Canterbury that with the servants broke down. Such a series of adventures was curious, but happily the more so, as no person was in the least hurt in any of them. We arriv'd in Town the 20th. at night.

Mrs. Cosway is angry that I brought no letter from you. I do not know any other method of compromising the affair than by your writing a very voluminous one.

Stockdale assures me that He will send your plate by the diligence which sets off tomorrow morning, and that the books, account, and letter shall follow very soon.

I have bought one of the Polyplasiosmos pictures for a guinea and a half. Tis small, but one of the best specimens. I will send it to you very soon. Have spoken to Brown who promises; but I am afraid will not perform as Mr. Adams has very little time to spare. (Of that little however He will give me a part.) Brown says you paid him ten pounds for your picture. Do you mean I should pay the same for the other???

The other commissions will make a subject for another letter.

I beg my Compliments to Mr. Short. To him I shall write by the next post. I am most gratefully Dr. Sir Your friend & Servant,

JNO: TRUMBULL

RC (DLC); endorsed.

[622]

From Jean-Armand Tronchin

Paris ce 23. fevrier 1788.

M. Tronchin, Ministre de la République de Genêve, comptant entièrement sur l'amitié dont l'honore Monsieur de Jefferson, Ministre plénipotentiare des Etats-Unis, prend la liberté de lui adresser le Mémoire des Intéressés de la manufacture de Bourges, créanciers des Etats-Unis, avec prière de vouloir bien l'appuier de tout son crédit. M. Tronchin joint à ce mémoire la copie d'une lettre de M. de Marbois, chargé des afaires de france près le Congrès, qui expose l'intérêt que le Ministère de france prend à cette manufacture; il espère en consequence que Monsieur De Jefferson voudra bien accueillir cette recommendation, et il a l'honneur de lui présenter ses hommages.

RC (MoSHi); endorsed. Enclosures missing.

From Segond

[*25 Feb. 1788*. Recorded in SJL Index. Not found.]

From Willink & Van Staphorst

Amsterdam 25 February 1788

We had the honor to address your Excellency the 31 Ulto. to which agreeable to your information thro' Mr. Jacob Van Staphorst, We expect your Answer after Mr. Adams shall have transmitted his Sentiments upon the Proposal we forwarded to the Board of Treasury. We flatter ourselves there will be no unnecessary Delay in this and that you will authorize us to carry into execution, the only feasible Plan to consolidate permanently the Credit of the United States, actually in a most critical Situation, and since the two principal Money Brokers complain very heavily that the ƒ51,000 Guilders due at H. Fizeaux & Co. are not reimbursed, urging us to it in the strongest manner. Equally impressed as they can be of the Importance of effecting it, We dare not comply, until We have Your Excellency's approbatory Reply to our last Letter; as such partial Payment would be of no Service, unless We can secure the discharge of the June Interest, and this depending solely upon Your Excellency, We shall wait Your De-

[623]

cision. Should the Proposal contrary to our sanguine expectation be rejected, It will be our Duty to reserve all the Money possible, to face the June Interest. Punctuality in the Loan raised by us being the main and most interesting Object; To which the Reimbursement of the ƒ51M due at Fizeaux & Co. and every other disposal of Congress except in favor of your Excellency must give way notwithstanding the Discredit that may attend, and even their Insufficiency to supply us wherewithal to pay the June interest of ƒ270,000.

We crave your Excellency's speedy Answer, for our Government and have the honor to be very respectfully Your Excellency's Most obedient and very humble Servants,

WILHEM & JAN WILLINK
NICS. & JACOB VAN STAPHORST

RC (DLC); endorsed.

From Abigail Adams

DEAR SIR   London Febry. 26. 1788

Mr. Adams being absent I replie to your Letter this day received, that Mr. Adams has written to you upon the subject you refer to. Our time here is short and pressing. Yet short as it is Mr. Adams is obliged to Set out on fryday for the Hague in order to take leave there. Owing wholy to the neglect of Congress in omitting to send him a Letter of recall, tho he particularly requested it of them, when he desired permission to return, and has several times since repeated the same request. A memorial would then have answered, but now it cannot be received, and he finds at this late hour that he must cross that most horrid passage twice, and make a rapid journey there and back again as it would be greatly injurious to our credit and affairs to give any reasonable cause of offence. He would be delighted to meet you there. But time is so pressing that he cannot flatter himself with that hope, nor be able to stay a day after he has compleated his buisness. Yet as this Letter may reach you about the day he will leave London you will consider whether there is a possibility of seeing each other at the Hague.

I had sent my arrears to you before Mr. Trumble thought of informing me that it was to be paid to him. The Eight Louis you have since been so kind as to pay for Mr. Adams shall be paid Mr. Trumble.

I thank you my dear sir for all your kind wishes and prayers. Heaven only knows how we are to be disposed of. You have resided long enough abroad to feel and experience how inadequate our allowance is to our decent expences, and that it is wholy impossible for any thing to be saved from it. This our countrymen in general will neither know or feel. I have lived long enough, and seen enough of the world, to check expectations, and to bring my mind to my circumstances, and retiring to our own little farm feeding my poultry and improveing my garden has more charms for my fancy, than residing at the court of Saint James's where I seldom meet with characters so innofensive as my Hens and chickings, or minds so well improved as my garden. Heaven forgive me if I think too hardly of them. I wish they had deserved better at my Hands.

Adieu my dear sir and believe me at all times and in all situations your Friend & Humble Servant, A A

RC (DLC); endorsed.
MR. ADAMS IS OBLIGED TO SET OUT ON FRYDAY: That is, on 29 Feb.; TJ must have received Mrs. Adams' letter on Saturday, 1 Mch., the day on which he and Short received their letters from Smith of 22 Feb. 1788.

To William Frederick Ast

SIR
Paris Feb. 26. 1788.

I think with you that it will be best for you to finish the public accounts of the United States as you propose in your letter of Feb. 18. before you pack them in trunks. I will only beg of you to finish them as expeditiously as you can. As soon as this is done, we will settle the whole balance which may be due to you from the United states and I will exert myself to have it paid you. I have a prospect of being able to get this paiment for you in the month of April: but I am not sufficiently sure of it, to accept your draught. Should I be disappointed in my expectations, my acceptance will have done you no good and would dishonor myself. The moment I can procure paiment for you, or such a certainty as I can rely on, you shall hear from me. I am with much esteem Sir Your most obedient & most humble servt.,

TH: JEFFERSON

PrC (DLC). YOUR LETTER OF FEB. 18: Not found.

To Simon Bérard

Sir   Paris Feb. 26. 1788.

I send you by the bearer a bill of exchange for two thousand four hundred livres drawn on you by Mr. Edward Rutledge, one of the persons who has lately sent rice to your consignment. It is now offered for your acceptance. The proceeds of it are for the nephew of the drawer now in London. Will you be so good as to inform me whether it would be equally convenient for you at the end of the thirty days sight to have it paid in London, according to the rate of exchange between that place and Paris? As I shall write by tomorrow's post to young Mr. Rutledge at London, I should be glad to let him know how the money may be paid to him in London, as I beleive he is anxious on that subject. I have the honour to be with much esteem Sir Your most obedient humble servt.,

TH: JEFFERSON

PrC (DLC).
The BILL OF EXCHANGE drawn by Rutledge was enclosed in a (missing) letter from John Rutledge to TJ of 19 Jan. 1788, instructing him to employ the proceeds for John Rutledge, Jr. (see TJ to Rutledge, 17 July 1788).

From Giuseppe Chiappe

Excellence   Mogador Le 26e: Fevrier 1788

Je profitte de l'occasion en droiture pour Marseille voÿe de Mer, et à l'adresse de ces Messieurs Cathalan, pour Joindre Copie de ma précédente que J'ay eû l'honneur d'écrire à Votre Excellence par la voye de Salé aux Soins du Consul Général de France, Monsieur du Rocher, qui m'assure l'avoir acheminée et Je ne doute nullement qu'elle ne soit parvenue à Votre Excellence. Il n'est rien arrivé depuis de remarquable si non que le Départ du Capn. Joseph West pour la Martinique avec 60. Mules. Un Mesire Tunisien s'est presenté à la Cour de la part de cet Bay là pour obtenir de Sa Majesté Impériale 500 quinteaux de Cuivre, ce qui Luy a été accordé par le Roy, et il n'attend que le Batiment qui doit les charger, et on assure que Sa Majesté Impériale en envoyera 1000. quinteaux en *Présent au dit* Bay de Tunis pour la *bonne armonie* qu'ils conservent entre Eux; Sa Majesté Impériale a fait écrire partout que, au cas que au Moy de May prochain il ne vienne de Hollande un Ambassadeur avec des Présents, ou sans, de la part de SS.HH.CC. pour sçavoir s'ils sont en guerre ou en Payx avec Luy, il envoyerra Luy même un Ambassadeur avec Cinq de ses Frégattes pour être informée des dispositions de SS.HH.CC. envers Luy, lesquelles étant favorables le dit Ambassadeur s'en retournera, et au contraire il passera en droiture avec les Cinq Frégattes en Amérique, où toute prise qu'Elles puissent faire sur les Hollandois, il en sera disposé de conformité aux ordres généreaux et illimités reçus préalablement leur Départ, sans rapporter même les dittes Prises dans ses Ports. C'est qui s'offre de notitier Votre Excellence, et tousjours rempli de la plus grande considération, J'ay l'honneur de me répéter de Votre Excellence Vre très Humble & très Obeissant Serviteur,

GIUSEPPE CHIAPPE

RC (MoSHi); endorsed. Enclosure: Chiappe to TJ, 27 Dec. 1787.

To William Macarty

SIR   Paris Feb. 26. 1788.

I have received your favor of Feb. 18. and communicated it to the Marquis de la Fayette. We both suppose the suppression of the India company so probable, and the decision of that question so near, that that will enable us to give you the answer you wish for. The decision will certainly take place in a few days. We suppose that were the proposition to be made to the government at present, it's success would be an impossibility. The clause in the late arret, which gives us the rights of native subjects in their East India possessions, is a gift of nothing as long as that company subsists. It was only on the prospect of their suppression that that clause was asked. As soon as a more decisive answer can be given you may rely on hearing from me, as well as on all the dispositions possible to serve you. I am with much esteem Sir Your most obedient & most humble servt.,   TH: JEFFERSON

PrC (DLC).

To Jean-Armand Tronchin

SIR   Paris Feb. 26. 1788.

I should with great chearfulness have done any thing I could for the manufacturers of Bourges, had any thing been in my power. To this I should have been induced by justice to them, and a

[627]

desire to serve whomsoever you befriend. This company is part of a great mass of creditors to whom the United states contracted debts during the late war. Those states, like others, are not able to pay immediately all the debts which the war brought on them; but they are proceeding rapidly in that paiment, and will perhaps get thro it more speedily than any nation ever did before. You will have seen in the public papers the progress they are making in this matter. They proceed in this by fixed rules from which it is their principle never to depart in any instance, nor to do on any account for any one person what they will not be able to do for all others claiming on the same grounds. This company should engage the French consul or some other person on the spot to be always ready to present their claim whenever any thing can be received on it according to the order of paiment established by Congress. I suppose that the interest might have been annually received. With respect to what they call the reduction of their debt from it's nominal sum, it is not a reduction of it, but an appreciation at it's true value. The public effects of the United states, such as their paper bills of credit, loan office bills &c. were a commodity which varied in it's value from time to time. A scale of their value for every month has been settled according to what they sold for at market, in silver or gold. This value in gold or silver with an interest of six per cent annually till paiment is what the United states pay. This they are able to pay: but were they to propose to pay off all their paper, not according to what it cost the holder in gold or silver, but according to the sum named in it, their whole country if sold, and all their persons into the bargain might not suffice. They would in this case make a bankruptcy where none exists, as an individual would who, being very able to pay the real debts he has contracted, would undertake to give to every man fifty times as much as he had received from him. The company will receive the market value of the public effects they have in their hands, and six per cent per annum on that; and I can only repeat my advice to them to appoint some friend on the spot to act for them whenever any thing can be received. I have the honour to be with sentiments of the most perfect esteem and respect Sir Your most obedient & most humble servt.,   Th: Jefferson

PrC (DLC).

[628]

From John Trumbull

Dear Sir   London 26th Febry. 1788.

Your letter of the 20th. came to my hands this moment with the welcome news of Mrs. Church's trunk. I shall probably find it at the Bureau de Diligence this evening. I have written from Boulogne and this an account of our suite of adventures. The moment we have any account of the Count de Moustier I will communicate to you. There is however no reason even yet for anxiety. A Ship, which left this port the middle of October, arrived in Boston after 84 days; others which saild soon after were not arriv'd the 20th. January. Allowing him therefore as slow a passage, He may be regarded as safe, even tho' He should not be arrivd at the sailing of the English Febry. packet.

I have seen Oldham on the subject of the Tea Vase. He seems to think there will be difficulty in adapting it to your wishes; that no improvement in point of Elegance can be made without a sacrifice of convenience. He is to th[ink] of it, and I am to see him again.

The Odometer may be made at Watkins's, Charing cross, but they are not kept ready made because the exact diameter of the wheel to which they are to be applied must be known, as this is the basis of their calculation. If you order one, you must remember this and be attentive likewise to decide the measure, whether it be French or English; that fitted to the Wheel will cost about Eight Guineas. They are likewise made to be fixed on the inside the carriage. But these are extremely liable to get out of order, and cost double that Sum.

I have order'd your Taylor to make the four pair of breeches. He wonders that you make no mention of Waistcoats. If it be an omission in your memorandum you will give your further Orders in your next. They will be finish'd immediately and you will probably receive them by Mr. Rutledge in two or three weeks.

A Chariot perfectly neat simple and elegant, if painted plain and with brass harness will cost you at one of the best Shops in Town, about 130 Guineas; with plated harness 142; if you choose any recherché in the painting or Varnish, more in proportion. It can be finished in five weeks from the receipt of the Order.

Mrs. Adams had sent you by Mr. Parker, the morning before I mention'd your commission, the ballance of her account. Smith has written and writes again today, on the subject of his, which is according to him within a few shillings of a Ballance. But this will only give you the trouble of sending me a draft on Mr. Grand's correspondent for the trifle I may expend for you. In my last I beg'd you to direct how much I am to pay Brown for Mr. Adams's picture. For your's He says you gave him ten pounds. I suppose he hopes the same for this.

I am with much respect Your gratefull friend,

JNO. TRUMBULL

Mr. and Mrs. West present their Compliments and beg for the trouble of forwarding this to Mr. Bar[rett?]

RC (DLC); MS faded. Enclosure missing, possibly a letter to Nathaniel Barrett.

From André Limozin

Le Havre, 27 Feb. 1788. Acknowledges TJ's letters of 14 and 21 Feb. and thanks him for intelligence on political matters; has received two boxes by the diligence from Paris, one on 2 Feb. and the other 12 Feb.; has shipped both on the New York Packet, consigned to James Madison; is afraid one of the packages was not from TJ and, therefore, cautions TJ, in future, to order his servant to write TJ's name on the direction in order to avoid mistakes which are "very dangerous and disagreable"; encloses bills of lading and accounts of expenses, one of the latter for 12.^{tt} 18, for the two packages sent to New York, and the other for 59.^{tt} 1.13, for four barrels of fruit received from New York, all of which were rotten when they were received, and a case of trees which have been forwarded to TJ. Capt. Butler, of the ship *Bowman*, has gone to Dunkirk where the owners of his cargo have ordered him to unload. The bust of Lafayette will be forwarded to Norfolk by some other ship.

RC (MHi); 4 p.; endorsed. Tr (DLC: Short Papers); enclosed in Limozin to Short, 13 Mch. 1788, in a covering letter asking for further information about the two boxes which were sent to Madison. The enclosed bills of lading have not been identified; the two statements of account are in MHi. See TJ to Limozin, 21 Aug. 1788.

To Lormerie

MONSIEUR   à Paris ce 27me Fevrier 1788.

M. le Comte de Doradour réside à Issoir en Auvergne, au chateau de Serlan.

Je viens de recevoir de M. Claiborne une lettre où il me dit qu'il est près de vous donner toutes les confirmations possibles de vos titres pour les terres achetées de M. Blackden.

Les recherches historiques et politiques sur les etats unis est une bonne ouvrage, écrite par M. Mazzei, et on peut se confier avec une certitude entière à ses faits.

Je n'ai point des nouvelles récentes sur le progrès de la nouvelle constitution, ni sur la guerre des sauvages. Aussitôt que j'en aurai, j'aurai l'honneur de vous en faire part, ayant celui d'être avec une considération tres distinguée Monsieur votre tres humble et très obeissant serviteur, TH: JEFFERSON

PrC (DLC).

To John Rutledge, Jr.

DEAR SIR   Paris Feb. 27. 1788.

I received from Mr. Rutledge, your father two days ago the inclosed letter with a bill of exchange on the house of Berard & Co. for 2400 livres. This company being established at Lorient I have sent the bill there for their acceptance. It is paiable at 30. days sight. I have desired to know of them whether it would be convenient to them to pay it at London when it becomes due. And I suppose from what a person here told me who is connected with their house that they will be willing to order paiment at Sr. James Harris's in London. Be so good as to inform me whether you would chuse paiment in London or where else, and I will have it arranged according to your convenience. When you to return to Paris I will trouble you to ask of Mr. Trumbull some little articles of clothing he is to have made for me in London. With many wishes for your health and happiness I have the honour to be Dr. Sir Your most obedient humble servt., TH: JEFFERSON

PrC (DLC). The enclosed letter has not been found, but it must have been one from John Rutledge to his son, dated about 19 Jan. 1788, the date of the (missing) letter from Rutledge to TJ in which it and the BILL OF EXCHANGE were enclosed.

To Thomas Mann Randolph, Jr.

DEAR SIR   Paris Feb. 28. 1788.

Your favour of April 14. 1787. gave me reason to hope we should have seen you here this winter. That being nearly passed over I am apprehensive you may have changed your plan. Or perhaps you have chosen first to finish those courses of lectures which are to make a part of your education. This is certainly wise, but I hope you will not be diverted altogether from your purpose of coming here. I troubled you with a letter on the 6th. of July last in which I ventured some ideas on the best mode of passing your time for 3. or 4. years to come. On the 11th. of August I took the liberty of suggesting the same ideas to your father. I have not heard from him since, but presume you have. In any event I shall be pleased to know your ultimate decision and happy to be useful to you in whatever line you may chuse to proceed.

I must take the liberty of troubling you with the execution of a commission for me. I am making a collection of all the Greek authors, and of those editions of them which do not exceed the octavo size. I know that many of them have been printed at the Oxford press, and by the Foulis' in Glasgow, and probably at other presses also of Great Britain. I wish to have a catalogue of all the 8vo. and smaller editions of them which have been printed in Great Britain, specifying whether they have translations or not, what is their price, and what works of the author they contain if they contain not the whole. I presume that any well informed bookseller can readily make out a catalogue of these editions. Will you be so good as to get some one to do this, and to undertake yourself the trouble of forwarding it to me? I shall be happy to hear from you at all times, and am with great sincerity Dr. Sir Your affectionate humble servt., TH: JEFFERSON

PrC (ViWC).

From Capellen

MONSIEUR   Paris le 29. fevrier 1788.

Je me suis presenté hier avec Mr. van Staphorst à vôtre Hotel avec intention de vous présenter mes homages, et pour Vous prier de m'accorder des Lettres de recommandation à vos Amis en Amerique, en faveur de mon Ami Mr. François Adrien van der Kemp, victime très remarquable de la persécution existante en Hollande, qui se propose de s'établir avec Sa Femme et ses Enfants parmis vos dignes et respectables Compatriotes à New York ou en Albanie. Son intention est d'entreprendre ce voiage vers la mis Mars par l'Angleterre. Je m'intéresse beaucoup au sort de mon dit Ami, qui s'est constamment conduit en vrai ami de la Liberté. Et son zèle et ses talents ont contribués à faire déterminer l'opinion publique pour ce que tout vrai Hollandois a taché d'obtenir, mais dont nous avons été frustré faute d'avoir été soutenus à tems par la même Puissance qui a si noblement secondés vos efforts et vos succès. Je me flatte, Monsieur, que vous voudrez bien me procurer l'avantage, l'occasion se présentant, de faire votre connoissance personelle. Soyez en attendant assuré, que j'ai l'honeur de me nommer, avec la considération la plus distinguée Monsieur Votre très humble et très obeiss: Serviteur,   LE BON. DE CAPELLEN

RC (DLC); endorsed.

Baron van der Capellen van de Marsch, an exiled Dutch patriot who lived in Paris after 1787, is not to be confused with Baron Capellen de Pol, who died in 1784. For Capellen's relations with Francis Adrian van der Kemp, see H. L. Fairchild, *Francis Adrian van der Kemp* (New York, 1903), p. 103-6.

From William Stephens Smith

MY DEAR SIR   London Feby. 29th. 1788.

I wrote you last fryday's post and by Mr. Parker on Saturday. In the former, I find I left out, on the credit side, the 2 pr. of shoes which Mr. Short paid for, amounting to 13/4, which deducted from the £1.10.7 which I make the ballance between us, reduces it to seventeen and three pence.

Mr. Adams setts off this morning for the Hague to take leave in person of their High Mightinesses and the Prince of Orange.

Give my best regards to Mr. Short and believe me sincerely your most obliged Humble Servt.,   W. S. SMITH

RC (MHi); endorsed.

From Lamarque & Fabre

[*Paris, Feb. 1788*] In 1780 their firm, "fournisseurs des Troupes," delivered to Commodore Gillon, agent for the state of South Carolina, some clothing for soldiers, payment for which was to be made before Gillon left for America. There is still due on that account 26,000 livres principal, plus seven years interest which the state promised to allow. Would like to know whether the state has determined the terms of settlement; whether payments will be made in Europe; and on what dates they will be made; ask TJ to inform them what steps the state of South Carolina has taken to settle this long-standing debt.

RC (ViWC); 1 p.; in French; written in the 3rd person; at head of text: "Mémoire"; undated but assigned to this date because the only entry in SJL is Index for a letter from Lamarque & Fabre is dated: "88 F." There is no entry for a letter to this firm. Enclosure: Although there is no mention of an enclosure, another undated "Mémoire" (MoSHi, 2 p.) may have been sent with this; it states that on the recommendation of Lamarque & Fabre the firm of Chrestien & Co. furnished some cloth for Commodore Gillon in 1780; they did this only after consultation with Dr. Franklin, who confirmed the authenticity of Gillon's position; in payment of their account Chrestien & Co. received four bills drawn to their order, totalling 16,827 livres; all four bills were protested; they then sent the bills to a merchant in Philadelphia for collection; when the bills were presented to the state authorities they acknowledged them and promised to pay them with interest; in spite of all this Chrestien & Co. have received nothing. On Gillon's affairs, see TJ to Castries, 19 Apr. 1787, note.

From Charles Bellini

Williamsburg, 1 Mch. 1788. Received TJ's letter of 29 May 1786 by Paradise, who is a valuable acquisition as a friend to every person of intelligence; regrets that his adverse circumstances and the constant infirmities of his wife prevented him from showing Paradise the civilities he deserved. Mr. Wythe communicated a letter he had received from TJ which mentioned a lens that TJ was sending Bellini through Wythe to help his eyes, now almost useless without assistance. The box of books in which the lens was sent has not yet arrived and may be lost but he thanks TJ for his thought of him. Wishes the ocean did not separate them, but must not dwell on that subject because it gives him too much pain. His wife sends her compliments to TJ and his daughters, especially to her godchild. Encloses a letter for Mazzei of the same date.

RC (DLC); 2 p.; in Italian; endorsed. The enclosed letter for Mazzei has not been found.

Mrs. Bellini may not have employed the word GODCHILD in its literal sense, and may only have meant "favorite." She was evidently referring to Mary Jefferson, who was born in 1778.

From Joseph Bernard

MONSIEUR   à Marseille le 1 mars 1788

Je fis Copier les observations météorologiques depuis 1779 jusques à 1786, ainsi que vous L'aviés désiré. Lorsque le Travail fut terminé, j'en prévins M. l'abbé papon. Comme je n'eus point de Réponse sur cet objet, je crus que vous n'étiés plus à paris. J'ai été détrompé par M. Cathalan. Je lui ai remis Tout de suite Les Cayers d'observations de 7 années, et il s'est chargé de vous les faire parvenir. Je vous prie de vouloir bien m'excuser. Ma négligence n'a été qu'apparente, et j'exécuterai Toujours avec empressement Les ordres que vous voudrés me donner.

Je suis occupé de La rédaction d'un travail étendu sur l'histoire naturelle de mon païs. Les objets de Culture Les plus importans seront traités avec Soin et présenteront des vues utiles pour Toutes

Les Con[trées] qui, ayant le même climat que La Provence, seront susceptibles des mêmes productions. Les mémoires sur le figuier, sur l'olivier, sur le câprier, &c., sont sur le point de paroître. Je serois infiniment flatté si vous vouliés permettre que votre nom honorat la liste de mes Souscripteurs et si vous trouviés ensuite à mes observ[ations] Le Caractère d'utilité que j'ai voulu Leur donner.

Je suis avec un profound Respect Monsieur votre très humble et très obeïssant Serviteur, BERNARD

RC (DLC); endorsed.

Joseph Bernard, was an astronomer, naturalist, and agronomist, director of the observatory at Marseilles, and permanent secretary of the Marseilles Académie, whom TJ met in 1787 while he was in Marseilles (communication of Louis Bergasse to Howard C. Rice, Jr.; see also TJ to Bernard, 12 Aug. 1788). The CAYERS D'OBSERVATIONS that Bernard sent to TJ through Cathalan were listed in the 1815 catalogue of his library as "Meteorologie de Marseille. 4to. M.S. 1779-1786," which, according to Sowerby, No. 656, is no longer extant.

From Madame de Bréhan

New York March the first 1788.

I have suffered, Sir, a great contrariety not to be able to keep the engagement which I had taken with you, to give you, at our arrival, an account of our passage, which has been long and tedious. I have had at every moment the painful thought that my Brother could not support the end of the voyage. He is arrived in a pitiful state, and nevertheless has been recover'd. As to me I was tolerably well when we disembark'd, but two, or three days after I had been here, I caught a violent cold which obliges me to keep still my room. You see, Sir, that my stay in this country has not been, till now, very pleasing and that I cannot tell you what I think of it; besides, all is at present in a combustion, and every body who takes a sincere interest for the inhabitants of this country must wish ardently to see a favorable change in the constitution. If there were many Jeffersons, many Madissons, every thing, I believe, would go better. We have had the pleasure of forming the acquaintance of Mr. Madisson just long enough to regret his loss. We have very often spoken of our dear Mr. Jefferson whom I would be glad that circumstances could call soon back to this country.

I send you, Sir, my best wishes, my best compliments and the new assurances of my tender friendship. I hope, Sir, that you will preserve yours to me, you know how much I value it.

[635]

Since we are here, we have not yet had news of anibody, this want of information of every thing which interests, is very sad.

Be so good, Sir, as to recall me to the remembrance of Mr. Short and to tell him that I shall have the pleasure to write to him by the first paquet boat.

RC (DLC); unsigned; endorsed by TJ: "Brehan Mde De."

From James Swan

SIR   Roüen 1 March 1788.

I have had the honour of receiving your Letter of the 9th. Ulto. and thank you for the politenesses expressed in it for Mrs. Swan and myself. It shall be our wish to endeavor always to merit them; and I hope to have the happiness of presenting her to you sometime in the approaching Summer.

Before my departure and it has been so for two years, my friends General Knox, Mr. King and many others engaged their particular interest in my favor (and of General Washington if in administration, at whose house I resided when in Virginia January 1787) for a Consulship in Europe; and if in my nomination to the Southern ports in France, particularly Marseilles.

The want of efficient funds has deterred Congress from making a Consular establishment and the prospect of an alteration taking place in, if not wholly a new, Confederation, by which more power might be lodged in the Federal Government, has likewise greatly tended to promote that delay. Finding much time on my hands— being wholly out of Mercantile business—having contracted a great attachment for Havre; regarding the climate as more healthy than that of Marseilles because more cold; and being acquainted with many, or most all the Officers of Government and the Merchants, having had particular Letters to the Intendant General, to the chief of the Class and to others, I think I could be of as much service to America in that as in any other port in France; and wishing very much to promote the particular interest of the northern parts of America, the Manufactures and Trade of which are most suitable to this quarter and there being no Consul, or Vice Consul, nor other officer there under the United States, I beg leave to propose to Your Excellency, giving me a Brevet, as Consul or Vice during the absence of Mr. Barclay, or untill one shall be appointed by Congress. There has a glaring instance just happened, of the necessity of such an appointment. A Boston Ship, upon freight, consigned to no particular house, was in want of some money to fit her out. The owners being unknown and no consul who could authenticate the place of her resort or where belonging, or the Owners, the concern will become great sufferers for want of a Certificate and Official Credance. I shall expect no benefit at present, but the little respect which might result from it. Should Your Excellencie's opinion or determination correspond with my request, and it be necessary for me to go to Paris (altho' I did not intend it till I could speak french perfectly) I will wait your commands.

Does your Excellency know whether the Marquis de la Fayette is at paris or not? I have written him twice, the last time requesting his obtaining the original or copy of a memorial upon the trade of America with France, which I addressed to him about two Years ago. It was translated by Mr. Consul General de la Tombe into French and transmitted to the Mareshal de Castries. As I want to make additions to it, opposing with truths, the false sentiments against America, which a Mr. Burnett from Paris has lately published, with remarks upon the regulations made since by the French Government in favor of American articles, and with some Observations founded upon a view I've had of the manufactures in this province. But I've not heard from him.

I have the honor to be with the most perfect respect & esteem Your Excellencies Most obedient & very humble Servant,

JAM. SWAN

Any Letters addressed to M. Quesnel, Commissary de la Marine, here; or to Messrs. Magon la forest & co. at Havre, will reach me.

RC (DLC); endorsed.
For a note on the MEMORIAL UPON THE TRADE OF AMERICA WITH FRANCE, see Swan to TJ, 31 Jan. 1788.

To John Adams

DEAR SIR   Paris Mar. 2. 1788. Sunday

I received this day a letter from Mrs. Adams of the 26th. ult. informing me you would set out on the 29th. for the Hague. Our affairs at Amsterdam press on my mind like a mountain. I have no information to go on but that of the Willincks and Van Staphorsts, and according to that something seems necessary to be done. I am so anxious to confer with you on this, and to see you and them together, and get some effectual arrangement made in time that I determine to meet you at the Hague. I will set out the moment some repairs are made to my carriage. It is promised me at 3. oclock tomorrow; but probably they will make it night, and that I may not set out till Tuesday morning. In that case I shall be at the Hague Friday night. In the mean time you will perhaps have made all your bows there. I am sensible how irksome this must be to you in the moment of your departure, but it is a great interest of the U.S. which is at stake and I am sure you will sacrifice to that your feelings and your interest. I hope to shake you by the hand within 24. hours after you receive this, and in the mean time am with much esteem & respect Dear Sir Your affectionate friend & humble servt, TH: JEFFERSON

PrC (DLC).

To Brack

à Paris ce 2me Mars 1788.

Je vous dois mille et mille remercimens, Monsieur, pour les peines que vous avez bien voulu vous donner sur ces malheureuses gazettes et brochures. Le nommé Petit est mon domestique, et le même qui a si souvent eu l'honneur de vous parler sur cette affaire. Le paquet I. venant de Calais sous acquit portant No. 119. marqué R. a été véritablement retiré par lui. Mais c'est ça une paquet qui m'est venu de Londres. Au lieu que celui que nous cherchons est venu de l'Amerique, est arrivé à Havre, d'où ce m'a été adressé par M. Limozin au mois d'Aout ou 7bre. passé. Le nommé Petit l'a bien vu à la Douane. Si ce n'étoit que des gazettes, Monsieur, je n'aurois pas osé vous donner tant de peine. Mais il y a avec les gazettes des brochures qui me sont intéressantes et pour leur matière, et parce qu'elles font partie d'une suite. Mais si les renseignemens actuels ne peuvent pas les recouvrer, assurément, Monsieur, je les abandonnerai avec plaisir plutôt de vous coûter encore des recherches ladessus. Agréez, je vous en prie, toutes mes remercimens pour vos bontés, et les assurances des considérations tres distinguées avec lesquelles j'ai l'honneur d'etre Monsieur votre tres humble et tres obeissant serviteur, TH: JEFFERSON

PrC (DLC).

To C. W. F. Dumas

SIR   Paris March. 2. 1788.

Being informed that Mr. Adams was to leave London on the 29th. Ult. for the Hague, I have determined to meet him there. But lest he should have finished his business and be gone before I can get there, I write the inclosed to press him to await an interview, and send it by the post which will be 24 hours before me. I take the liberty of putting it under your cover, as you will certainly know where Mr. Adams is to be found. It will be an additional gratification to me to be able to assure you in person of those sentiments of esteem and attachment with which I have the honour to be Sir Your most obedient & most humble servt,

TH: JEFFERSON

PrC (DLC). Enclosure: TJ to John Adams, same date, q.v.

To Montmorin

SIR   Paris Mar. 2. 1788.

The account of the loss of the Count de Moustier, which circulated for some time, tho' destitute of foundation, left in all minds a painful anxiety to hear of him. I have the happiness to inform your Excellency that news of his safe arrival in America has been received at London by a ship which left New York on the 16th. of January. Incertain whether you may have received this information thro' any other channel, and desirous of shortening your moments of uneasiness on the subject, I take the liberty of communicating it to you.

I have the honour to assure you at the same time of those sentiments of respect and attachment with which I am very sincerely Your Excellency's most obedient & most humble servant,

TH: JEFFERSON

Pr (DLC). See TJ to Short, 29 Mch. 1788.

To Stephen Cathalan, Jr.

SIR   Paris Mar. 3. 1788.

Being called to Holland at a very few hours warning I have only time to notify you that I shall be absent from this place three or four weeks to come. In the mean time should any thing pressing occur, Mr. Short my secretary will attend to it.

I have paid Sr. John Lambert according to the account you sent me for the articles you were so kind as to procure for me. All have come safely except the oil of which I have never heard. Perhaps they may have omitted to send it from Aix. If you can give any information to Mr. Short as to the carriage by which it came, he will have a search made to see if it is here. I have the honor to be with great esteem to yourself & the family Sir Your most obedt. humble servt, TH: JEFFERSON

PrC (DLC).

I HAVE PAID SR. JOHN LAMBERT: A receipt (DLC) for 272^{tt} 5, dated 2 Mch. 1788, probably signed by Lambert's servant, acknowledges payment "pour le compte de Monsieur Ete. Cathalan"; TJ entered the following in his Account Book under 2 Mch.: "[pd Petit] for Sr. John Lambert for Cathalan, fruits, oil &c. 272-5." This account was probably enclosed in a (missing) letter from Cathalan of 2 Feb. 1788, recorded in SJL Index.

To André Limozin and Others

SIR   Paris Mar. 3. 1788.

Being called to Holland at a very few hours warning I have only time to notify you that I shall be absent from this place three or four weeks to come. In the mean time should any thing pressing occur, Mr. Short, my secretary will attend to it.

I have the honour to be with great esteem Sir Your most obedt. humble servt., TH: JEFFERSON

PrC (DLC); at foot of text: "M. Limozin M. Carnes M. Bondfeild."

From Robert R. Livingston

New York, 3 Mch. 1788. Introducing Mr. Kissam "a young gentleman of the profession of the law" who has very respectable connections.

RC (NNP); 2 p.; endorsed.

To William Macarty

SIR   Paris Mar. 3. 1788.

Being called to Holland on a very few hours warning I have only time to notify you that I shall be absent here for three or four weeks to come. I shall see the Marquis de la Fayette to day and will get the favor of him to attend to the issue of the affair of the East Indies, and to communicate it to you.

I have the honour to be with very great esteem Sir Your most obedt. humble servt,   TH: JEFFERSON

PrC (DLC).

To Montmorin

SIR   Paris Mar. 3. 1788.

Having received information yesterday that Mr. Adams was gone to the Hague for a few days, and there being a great necessity that I should have an interview with him before his departure, I have concluded to set out for that place immediately. This will occasion me an absence of three or four weeks, during which, should any thing material occur Mr. Short, my secretary, will be here. He is the same person from whom your Excellency was so good as to receive communications during my absence the last year, and for whom I will beg the same indulgence now, should any occasion arise.

I have the honour to be with sentiments of the most perfect respect & attachment Your Excellency's most obedient & most humble servt.,   TH: JEFFERSON

PrC (DLC).

From Abbé Morellet

MONSIEUR   lundi 3 mars 1788.

Le commissionnaire qui m'apporte la planche s'en va sur le champ sans que je lui parle et sans que je puisse vous addresser ma reponse et mes remercimens. Je vous en dois beaucoup pour les soins et les peines que vous aves prises. Sans la complaisance que vous aves je me serois trouvé avec 300 exemplaires de votre ouvrage sans cartes et par consequent non vendables. Avec la planche revenüe je les completerai et je viendrai à bout de retirer mes frais car avec la juiverie de nos libraires c'est tout ce que je pourrai faire quoique l'ouvrage se soit bien vendu. Vous venes de faire encore une depense pour le retour de cette planche que je dois vous rembourser si vous aves la complaisance de me donner la note des frais. Je suis toujours si sedentaire et si occuppé que je suis forcément privé du plaisir que j'aurois à aller m'entretenir avec vous. Quand le tems sera devenu un peu plus supportable je me dedommagerai. J'ai appris avec une grande satisfaction par Mr. Grant que le bruit qui avoit couru de la mort de notre respectable ami n'est pas fondé. Rappelles moi je vous prie à son souvenir en lui ecrivant. Je lui ai envoyé quelques papiers sur la fin de l'année derniere et j'aurai peut etre quelque réponse de lui. Je lui souhaitte bien de tout mon coeur une prolongation de vie sans douleur. Agreès les assurances du respectueux devouement avec lequel je suis Monsieur Votre très humble et très obeissant Serviteur,

L'ABBÉ MORELLET

RC (DLC); endorsed.
NOTRE RESPECTABLE AMI: Benjamin Franklin.

From Parent

MONSIEUR   a Beaune ce 3 mars 1788

Je vous prie de vouloir bien payé ma traite Sur vous de quatre cent quarante une livres Dix Sols, qui est du montant du vin que je vous ait fait passé; elle est du premier mars à trois jours de vüe à Monsieurs Paschal et fils de Notre ville de Beaune, ou à leur ordre, et je vous seré bien obligé de votre Complaisance et j'espère que vous Seré Comptant du vin. Monsieur, je vous prie de vouloir bien m'en procurer quelque bonne Maison, Si cela ce trouve par hasard je vous seroit bien obligé de me les procuré. J'ay Payé les deux feuillette à Monsieur Bachey, et je crois qu'il pourroit peut estre Remettre l'autre feuillette. Je suis tres Sincèrement Monsieur Votre tres humble et tres obeissant Serviteur,

PARENT

C'est pour Solde de tout Compte jusqu'à ce jour.

RC (MHi).

To Schweighauser & Dobrée

GENTLEMEN   Paris Mar. 3. 1788.

I have at length been able to recover your papers, which had been mislaid at the bureau of the Diligence. Being called to Holland at a few hours warning I have only time to assure you that this settlement shall be one of my first occupations on my return, and that I am with great esteem Gentlemen Your most obedt. humble servt., TH: JEFFERSON

PrC (DLC). This is no doubt a reply to a (missing) letter recorded in SJL Index as dated 23 Feb. 1788.

To John Trumbull

DEAR SIR   Paris Mar. 3. 1788.

Being obliged to set out for Holland at a very few hours warning I have only time to notify you that I shall be absent hence three or four weeks. I trouble you with a letter on which I know not how to put any address particular enough to find the gentleman who is at Edinburgh. If you can supply it by enquiry and forward it, I will be obliged. My affection to our two friends Mrs. Church and Mrs. Cosway. I am with very great esteem Dr. Sir Your friend & servt,   TH: JEFFERSON

PrC (DLC). Enclosure: Evidently TJ to Thomas Mann Randolph, Jr., 28 Feb. 1788, q.v.

From Goldsmith

Lyons, 4 Mch. 1788. Has returned a small volume, *"La Suite de L'ami d'enfans,"* which belongs to TJ and was left at Goldsmith's lodgings in Paris; offers his services in Lyons, where he has established a "warehouse of my own, of the English goods"; resides there at the "Hotel and Rue de quatre Chapeaux."

RC (DLC); 2 p.; endorsed.

From Stephen Cathalan, Sr.

Marseilles, 6 Mch. 1788. Introduces his friend, John Turnbull, to whom he is indebted for the "acquaintance and Friendship of Robt. Morris," as well as most of his American friends, and without whom his son "had never spocke English"; Turnbull, who, with his wife, will be in Paris a short time, will deliver "the Seven years meteorological observations made by Mr. Bernard, of our observatory."

RC (DLC); in the hand of Stephen Cathalan, Jr., signed by his father; on page 2 of MS TJ jotted down the heads of subjects covered in his reply to this letter (see TJ to Cathalan, 20 May 1788). For a note on the METEOROLOGICAL OBSERVATIONS . . . BY MR. BERNARD, see Bernard to TJ, 1 Mch. 1788.

From Francisco Chiappe

Mogador, 6 Mch. 1788. Acknowledges TJ's letter of 15 Sep. 1787; has delivered to the Emperor the letter from Congress and the ratification of the treaty; has not yet obtained a reply, but will use his connections at court to do so when he returns to Morocco; is not sending copies of the Emperor's letters granting favors to Americans because his brother has done so; but will inform TJ of other affairs of interest to America as they occur. Has not delivered the letter to Taher Fennish because Fennish has been in Constantinople; will do so as soon as he returns. Suggests that TJ write him in French to eliminate the need of seeking an interpreter, and that he send his letters through the American agent at Cadiz who will forward them through the Venetian consul general to Mogador or Tangier, both measures for the sake of secrecy.

RC (MoSHi); 2 p.; in Italian; endorsed.

From Giuseppe Chiappe

EXCELLENCE   Mogador Le 6e: Mars 1788

J'ay eû l'honneur d'écrire à Votre Excellence voye de Terre et de Mer le 26e: passé; et pour l'informer ensuite de ce qui se passe, et regarde plus particulièrement les affaires de la Bienheureuse Nation de l'Amerique, Je m'empresse d'expédier un Courrier à Tanger pour que la présente parvienne à Votre Excellence le plus tôt possible. Sa Majesté Impériale a fait publier dernièrement, Je ne scaurois par quel mécontentement, que les Anglois ne reçeuvront plus de ses Ports de l'Arache, Tanger et Tetuan aucunne provision, ni ne pourront non plus même decendre à terre dans les Ports susmentionés. Comme Je ne manque pas à la Cour de nombre d'Amis qui sollicitent pour moy la continuation des faveurs que S.M.I. paroit disposée d'accorder aux Americains, il a plû à sa ditte S.M.I. de les distinguer dans cette occasion par une grace singuliaire qui éclatte dans les Lettres que Je viens de reçevoir, et dont Je joins à Votre Excellence Copie exacte traduite de l'Arabe pour en faire usage de conformité aux intentions amicales de S.M.I. envers toute la Nation Américaine, et Je ne doute nullement que Votre Excellence voudra les faire notifier pour que un chacun de la ditte Nation en profitte, ce qui concurrira à une plus étroite réciproque correspondence, et J'ay l'honneur d'être très-profondement De V.E. Le très-Humble & très-Obeissant Serviteur,

GIUSEPPE CHIAPPE

[644]

RC (MoSHi); endorsed. Enclosures (RC: MoSHi; Tr in the hand of William Short, accompanied by a translation in the hand of Isaac Pinto, in DNA: PCC, No. 87, II; PrC of Short's Tr in DLC): Italian translations of communications from the Emperor of Morocco: (1) To Giuseppe Chiappe, 29 Feb. 1788, informing him that "the Americans are not included with the English because they are independent of the English government, and for that reason we ordain that any American Vessel arriving, whether of War or a Merchantman, and which may be in want of refreshments, they may take them in freely, estimating her, in the number of all the other nations who are at Peace with us, and after that if any of these Vessels shall arrive which bring Merchandise, we ordain that they be regulated at the rate of 5. pr. Ct. which we grant to the American Nation for the term of three years," and requesting him to inform the Americans to this effect. (2) To same, 2 Mch. 1788, informing him that orders to carry out the decision set forth in his communication of 29 Feb. have been sent to all the ports of Morocco. (3) To Francisco Chiappe, same date and conveying the same intelligence as no. 2.

From Maria Cosway

London 6 of March

I have waited some time to trie if I could recover my usual peace with you, but I find it is impossible yet, therefore Must adress Myself to you still *angry*. Your long silence is impardonable, but what is the Name I Must give to————Mr: Trumbull and Mrs: Church not bringing Me a letter from you? No, My war against you is of such a Nature that I cannot even find terms to express it. Yet I will not be in your debt. I think it a great One since it is to acknowledge *one* letter from you, *One* and *short*, however I beleave that realy you know how I value every line which comes from you, why will you add scarcity? But I begin to runn on and my intention was only to say, *nothing*, send a blank paper; as a Lady in a Passion is not fit for Any thing. What shall you do when you will be Much farther, I can't bare the idea.—Will you give Mr: Trumbull leave to Make a Coppy of a certain portrait he painted at Paris? It is a person who hates you that requests this favor. If you want private conveiance to send me a letter there are many. Ask Abbe Piattoli, Madme: de Corney, and Many others. Tho' I am angry I can hardly end My letter. Remember, I do you justice by not thinking of you now.—

RC (MHi); unsigned; endorsed by TJ: "Cosway Mde." Full date established from entry in SJL Index for a letter of 6 Mch. 1788.

The ONE AND SHORT letter from TJ was evidently that of 31 Jan. 1788, wherein he spoke of WANT OF PRIVATE CONVEIANCE TO SEND . . . A LETTER.

[645]

From Montmorin

A Versailles le 6. Mars 1788.

J'ai communiqué, Monsieur, à M. le Comte de la Luzerne le mémoire que vous m'avez fait l'honneur de m'adresser en faveur du nommé Gross, américain, détenu comme otage à Dunkerque depuis 1782. Je joins ici une copie de la réponse que j'ai reçue de ce Secrétaire d'Etat, ainsi que de toutes les pièces dont elle est accompagnée. Je ne doute pas que vous n'adoptiez l'avis de M. de la Luzerne sur les raisons qui s'opposent à la liberté du nommé Gross.

J'ai l'honneur d'être très sincerement, Monsieur, votre très humble et très obéissant Serviteur,

Le ct De Montmorin

RC (DLC); in a clerk's hand, signed by Montmorin. FC (Arch. Aff. Etr., Paris, Corr. Pol., E.-U., vol. 33; Tr in DLC; the MSS from which the enclosures were made are in same). Enclosures (DLC): (1) Tr of La Luzerne to Montmorin, 24 Feb. 1788, stating that he had transmitted TJ's memorandum concerning Gross (enclosed in TJ to Montmorin, 6 Dec. 1787, q.v.) to an officer of the admiralty at Dunkirk; that from the enclosed reply the memorandum is not accurate; and that, therefore, it will be impossible to set Gross free. (2) Copy of a letter enclosed in the foregoing from an officer of the admiralty at Dunkirk to La Luzerne, 11 Feb. 1788, stating that Gross has not been held at the expense of the king, but that the advances for his maintenance have been made by a certain Michelon, a merchant of Dunkirk, and enclosing (3) Michelon's statement to the officer of admiralty, 6 Feb. 1788, to the effect that Gross is being retained on his behalf; that he has made all advances for his maintenance; that he has sent a bill of ransom to the British government to recover the money involved and expects a favorable reply thereto; and that, consequently, it would be unjust to liberate Gross at this time.

From William Short

Dear Sir   Paris Feb. [i.e. Mch.] 6. 1788

The first post day for the Hague, since your departure, will be to morrow. This letter will then set out and carry agreeable news of the health of your daughter. She has continued mending uniformly since the favorable turn of her disorder of which you were a witness, and this morning when I was at the Convent I learned that nothing remained of the indisposition except a necessary weakness. Miss Jefferson told me she should write to you. I am to send for her letter this evening and shall inclose it in this. From her you will receive probably more exact details respecting all three of the young ladies.

I am told this morning that the Amsterdam Gazette mentions

[646]

Dr. Franklin's death as a matter to be questioned and as being communicated by a vessel just arriving there from Philadelphia. Is it true that such a vessel has arrived there?

A new book has appeared this morning that occupies already all Paris—that is to say all the Novelty readers in Paris. It is Mr. Necker's book, on the importance of religious opinions, one vol. in 8vo. very thick, I think upwards of 500. pages. In an advertisement at the beginning he takes notice of M. de Calonnes last memoire and promises to answer it victoriously and support by incontestable evidence the truths of the *compte rendu*. To this advertisement he has put his name.

I hope you are now as far advanced in your journey as you hoped to be and that I shall have the pleasure of hearing that you arrived there well, and in time to meet Mr. Adams. Adieu, my dear Sir and believe me with sentiments of the most perfect sincerity Your friend & servant, W. SHORT

RC (DLC: TJ Papers). PrC (DLC: Short Papers). No letter from Martha Jefferson of this date has been found, nor is such a letter recorded in SJL Index; but see Short to TJ, 9 Mch. 1788.

The NEW BOOK was Jacques Necker's *De l'Importance des Opinions Religieuses*, [Paris], 1788, reviewed in the *Journal de Paris*, 22 Mch. 1788; see Short to TJ, 9 Mch. 1788. Sowerby, No. 1520. It was Mary Jefferson who was ill; the other of the THREE . . . YOUNG LADIES was Catherine Church.

From John Trumbull

DR. SIR   London 6th. March 1788.

Mr. Rutledge is so good as to take charge of the Breeches which you order'd. I mention'd in my last, your taylor's guess with respect to the Waistcoats.

Brown is busy about the pictures. Mr. Adams's is like. Your's I do not think so well of. They, with the Polyplasiasmos, shall come by the diligence.

Mrs. Church's trunk is arriv'd safe. The Story will be to me a lasting eulogy of French honesty. If I had left it so carelessly at an English Inn, I doubt whether its fate would have been similar. She desires to be remember'd by you with Affection. Mrs. Cosway's love to you, and his too. She is angry, yet she teases me every day for a copy of your little portrait, that she may scold *it* no doubt.

I beg you will remember me to the little Family at Pantmont, to *my Goddaughter* especially. I hope she is happy and studious. I am Dr. Sir Your's gratefully, JNO. TRUMBULL

RC (DLC); endorsed. For Mather Brown's portrait of TJ, see Vol. 1, frontispiece, and for that of John Adams, see illustration in this volume.

From John Bondfield

SIR
Bordeaux 7 Mars 1788

I am honord with your favor of the 22 february ulto. inclosing a Letter for President Pichard which I have forwarded to him at Liburn, the residence of our Parliament. The last post brought me a Letter from Mons. Lambert de frontignan advising his having forwarded to my care two Cases of his Wine for Mons. Le Cte. de Moustier at N. York.

To avoid troubling Mess. Elie Lefebre at Rouen I address the wine shipt by the Actif to Mons. Montfort being in that particular line of receiving and forwarding Goods to Paris. Ere this I expect the wine is with you. In future please to transmit me the Passport which will accompany the wine all the route from hence to Paris.

A Memorial from Rouen against some part of the arret has been sent to our Chambre of Commerce which they have under consideration.

Had the Duties on the Imports been at fixt rates and not *ad Valorum*, being an arbitrary Estimation, it would have avoided difficulties that we shall not cease to have with the Officers of the Douannes. Our Tobaccos are all sold, not a hogshed remains for sale. The farmers have purchased about 1000 hogd. that was on hand, the first that comes in will arrive to a good market. The Smugglers that resorted to Lorient of late found it their advantage to come here. This has caused a considerable decrease of Trade at Lorient, but what Lorient has lost Bord. has gain'd which to the nation becomes the same.

Private Interest as in most communites counter act public measures, when Admin[is]tration after mature deliberation have addopted a system that in some points may appear defavorable to a certain Class, but beneficial to the community at large (unless representations demonstrative of error in the pursuit) firm and unalterable perseverance works by imperceptable progression the point in view, hasty precipitate measures are generaly to satisfy private Interests which frequently sacrifice all other.

Administration appears fixt in their Ideas of the National advantages, that will result from the Trade of America. The Indulgences granted and protection given will bring it about. England sets every Engine to work to counter act the Measures. Their Agents, factors, and private Subjects settled in the Ports of the Kingdom form societies which with their conections with England form chains and preserve within their Circle the Trade discouraging all in their Power the Introduction of conections of the Americans with the french. In this they Act their part it is for others to act theirs.

France has very lucretif foreign branches of Trade. Her West Indies are inexhaustable resourses, they Aliment a Navigation the most profitable known, the Imports and Exports are extraordinaryly extensive, so long as they can retain their Exclusive Monopoly, they hold tributary the other Powers. England by forced and fictious resourses supports a Numerous Navigation. The supply of Coals from Newcastle to London, the great nursery of her Seamen, is a forced Trade. There are Coal Mines within 10 Miles of London that would amply supply that demand. Was france to Cast her Views in the same line she has ample measures. The supply of fire wood from New England for the supply of Paris would employ more Shiping, and the price paid by the Parisiens for their fire wood would allow to the Ships employ'd in that Navigation a greater freight than the Coliers obtain.

As a Cityzen of America, foreign Navigation in the present state of that Country is it the Interest of the States to be pursued to a certain extent. Other employment do they not offer more substantial advantages. The situations of Europe and America are very diferent. In Europe every Empire Kingdom and State are surrounded by powerful Neighbours who with unremitting attention watch the moment to improve the least relaxation. The Cord of Industry is perpetually stretcht. Power, show, Luxery, under Thousand Shapes, by Silent progression are become no longer fictious wants, but indispensable. America has not a neighbour. By the feoderal Convention the parts form the Body, Canada the only people on the Continent to exite attention. Whenever the States judge it her Interest to incorporate that Province has only to intimate her intentions to work the revolution, America having no cause to exert forced measures which in Politics as in Mecanicks are but tempory resources and frequently weaken the Machine. By giving to the different branches and departments protection every nessessary success will timely be brought about.

It is incumbent on france to watch the motions of the Rival powers and addopt every measure to draw to her Ports the Western Trade which in every light merrits her pursuit by rendring the Northern Nations tributary and encreasing her Navigation. No Expense or pains ought to be spared on her side even Sacrifices by bounties would be prof[itable] and they appear to Act in Consiquence. The Mercantile Board in General are not indowed with

Mercantil spirrit or Intelig[ence.] The next race now springing will make some progress. A different System of Education which is at present carefully inculcated will influence much in favor of Trade and Navigation.

The memorial from Lorient contre les fermiers contains many sensible remarks. I could wish to trans[mit] you Monthly returns of our Imports and Exports to enable you to form a Ballance of our Trade but this cannot be brought about until by Consular Powers I am impowered to oblige the Captains of all American Ships before they make their Entry to present to me their Registers and State their Cargoes, as is the use in all Ports where resides foreign Consuls. With respect I have the Honor to be Sir your most Obedient Humble Serv., JOHN BONDFIELD

RC (DLC).

From John Page

Rosewell March the 7th. 1788

You will pardon my long Silence my dear Jefferson when I tell you that in Addition to the many Reasons which I have given in my former Letters and which might be repeated here, I have to add that of the long Indisposition, and at length the Death, of my beloved Wife. It is true, she has been dead almost fourteen Months but many of these Months have passed off like a Dream, and the others have been insufficient for my Attention to my distressed Family and Mr. Burwell's and my own perplexed Affairs. Were not this my unhappy Case, I should long since have thanked you for your many valuable Presents, and particularly for your Notes on Virga. I sincerely thank you, and the more so, as you have continued your Proofs of Friendship to me (as I find by your Letter to Mr. Wyth in which you mention sending me more Books and amongst them your new Edition of The Notes on Virginia) when I must have appeared to have forfeited all Pretensions to a Continuance of your Attention. I have long wished for a leisure Hour to write to you, but really could not command one till now; when by means of an uncommon spell of severe Weather, and a deep Snow, I am caught at Home alone, having left my Family at York, to attend on the Election of Delegates to serve in Convention in June next. I came over, offered my Services to the Freeholders in a long Address which took me an Hour and an half to deliver it, in which I explained the Principles of the Plan of the fœderal

Constitution and shewed the Defects of the Confederation declaring myself a Friend to the former, and that I wished it might be adopted without losing Time in fruitless Attempts to make Amendments which might be made with more probability of Success in the Manner pointed out by the Constitution itself. I candidly confessed that I had been at first an Enemy to the Constitution proposed, and had endeavoured to fix on some Plan of Amendments; but finding that Govr. Randolph, Col. Mason, and Col. Lee differed in their Ideas of Amendments, and not one of them agreed with me in Objections, I began to suspect that our Objections were founded on wrong Principles, or that we should have agreed, and therefore I set to work, and examined over again the Plan of the Constitution; and soon found that the Principles we had applied were such as might apply to the Government of a single State, but not to the complicated Government, of 13, perhaps 30 States which were to be *united*, so as to be *one* in Inter[est] Strength and Glory; and yet to be severally sovereign and independent, as to their municipal Laws, and local Circumstances (except in a few Instances which might clash with the general Good); that such a general Government was necessary as could command the Means of mutual Support, more effectual[ly] than mere Confederacies Leagues and Allian[ces,] that is, a Government which for fœderal Purposes should have all the Activity Secresy and Energy which the best regulated Governments in the World have; and yet that this should be brought about without establishing a Monarchy, or an Aristocracy, and without violating the [just] Principles of democratical Governments. I say I confessed, that, when I considered, that this was to be the Nature of the Government which was necessary to be adopted in the United States I found that the Objections which might be made by a single State thus governed, would not apply to this great delicate and complicated Machinery of Government, and that the Plan proposed by the Convention was perhaps the best which could be devised. I have run myself out of Breath in a long winded Sentence, and lost a deal of Time in telling you what I might as well have said in three Words, vizt., that after all my Trouble the Freeholders left me far behind, Warner Lewis and Thos. Smith on the Lists of Candidates. I had however this Consolation, that I was not rejected on Account of my Attachment to the Constitution, for those two Gentlemen openly avowed the same Sentiments which I had declared in my Address to the People. Many of my Friends were very much mortified at the Disappointment we met with, and thought they comforted me by telling me of the extreme badness of the Weather which they said prevented many Freeholders from attending on the Election. But I comforted myself with the Reflection that I had adhered to my Resolution of treating the Freeholders like freemen; having never insulted them upon such Occasions by Solicitations and Caresses; and that they would now see clearly the Impropriety of engaging their Votes; and I comfort myself now, with the Reflection, that I shall have a little more Leisure to attend to my Affairs and to my Friends. I came Home that Night alone to prepare some of Mr. Burwell's and my own Papers for Business the next Day, when I was caught by a heavy Snow which is still 9 Inches deep. That was Monday (our Court Day being now the 1st. Monday) and this is thursday at Noon. The Thermometer has not been above 30 till yesterday, and now it is but 41 above 0 and the Wind has been high at N.W. ever since Monday Morning. This mention of the Weather leads me to tell you that we have had a worse Winter than I ever saw. More Snows, and more frequent, and greater sudden changes from warm to cold than can be remembered. The Thermometer has frequently been below 22, and once or twice as low as 17, but we seldom have had more than 4 or 5 very cold Days without a Change to warm Weather. On the 15th. of Jany. York River was frozen over opposite the Town, but the next Day the Thermometer rose 24° with a South West Wind which produced a very great Thaw and apparently Summers Heat. I have not been at Leisure to keep a Journal of the Weather for a long Time past but our Friend Jameson has promised me to go on with his. The last Summer was the coolest ever known here, which I attribute to the great Quantities of Ice which drifted into the Seas on the American Coasts, into a lower Latitude than I ever heard of, and much later in the Season than I believe we have any Account of for "the Brig Jolly Tar on the 10th. day of June in Lat. 43°:4′, long: 51°:8′ W. ran against a large Island of Ice, which carried away her Bowsprit and Foremast." This is extracted from Mr. Wm. Anderson's Letter to me dated London July 20th. 1787 giving me an Account of receiving my Tobacco safe by the Jolly Tar notwithstanding the shock she had received. I confess I suspect that such Circumstances may often attend cool Summers; but that if the Merchants Ships are not injured by them, the Phænomenon an Island of Island[1] is unheeded and Philosophers hear nothing of it. Mentioning Mr. Anderson reminds me of Mr. Mat: Anderson, and he, by an Association of Ideas, of the Farmers General, and their Contract. Would it not be better to procure Permission for Congress, or the States to ship the public Tobacco, upon the same Terms to France that R. Morriss does, than to abolish such Contracts as his? Or, granting that no more Tobacco should be received in Taxes, does not that, on such Contracts secure to the Planters of the States the certain Sale of 20000 Hhds. Tobacco pr. Annum which will be shipped to France, that Country, which, from its Situation with Respect to England, and the contracted Scale of their Commercial Affairs, especially in these States, would probably purchase the Tobacco it would have Occasion for, in London, rather than in America? And though it may be said that they, the London Merchants, must purchase it in America, yet, would not this be a Means of throwing 20,000 Hhds. into a Channel of Trade which is, and has ever been the most disadvantageous that can be conceived? The fatal Business of Consignments would be encreased. When Morriss' Agent purchases here, he is obliged to pay Cash or Bills, by which means whoever wants either may receive it, for his Tobacco. It is generally supposed that his Agent lowers the Price of our Tobacco. His Practice certainly has that Tendency. But I have often known him to give 5 pence per. Ct. more in Specie than the Merchants in Richmond would allow in Goods and Cash. But there is no telling what would be the Price of Tobacco were Remittances made in Specie as they would be, did not this Agent furnish so many Bills of Exchange for that Purpose; and did he not constantly keep by him, and in the Hands of his Deputies very large Sums of Money and I may add were we to depend upon british Purchasers, who have such Consignments as to care but little about Purchases; or on french Merchants, who would be more likely to barter their Goods for our Tobacco than to purchase it with Specie or Bills of Exchange. I humbly conceive therefore that your Plan of abolishing the Farmers General would rather be prejudicial than otherwise under the present Disposition of our Peoples Minds and the Circumstances of the Country. Had our Country men broken off the Dependance on the Merchants of Britain, by turning away from the Extravagance which you so justly complain of, in your last Letter; had they Learned Industry, and united in proper Measures to encourage Manufactures to lessen the Price of Imports, and to encrease that of their Staple Commodities, then I should wish you had succeeded in your Attempt.— But enough of this, and indeed I may say enough of such a Scrawl, and might immediately put an End to it, were I not bound to acknowledge the Receipt of yours by Mr. Paradise. I am much obliged to you for your Introd[uction] of him. He supports the Character you gave him wherever he goes. We think him a great Acquisition to our Country and to Wmsburg. in particular. He has lately received a severe Shock by the Account of his Daughter's Death in England. Mr. Paradise was a great Relief to Mr. Wyth who had lost his Lady. Mentioning Mr. Wyths Loss reminds me of the many Husbands who have been bereaved of their Wives in the Course of a Year. Mr. Harrison of Brandon, his Namesake of Richmond, R. Bolling of Petersburg, Mr. Carter of Nomony, and St. Ge. Tucker mourn with Mr. Wyth and myself our similar Fate, and several others have lost their Wives with whom you had no Acquaintance. Your Acquaintances in, However, Gloster vizt. Fontaine, F. Willis and W. Lewis and their Families are well. If you ever see Mazzei, tell him that as this is the first Letter I have written to you since he left us I hope he will not think himself slighted. When you write again let me know particularly how the Young Ladies your Daughters are, and our Friend Mr. Short. Remember me affectionately to them, and believe me sincerely yrs.,

John Page

RC (DLC).
YOURS BY MR. PARADISE: See TJ's letter to Archibald Cary and others of 29 May 1786. YOUR LAST (not technically TJ's last): 4 May 1786.
¹ Thus in MS; Page meant to write "an island of ice."

From David Ramsay

DEAR SIR   Charleston March 7th 1788

Mr. Walters an ingenious botanist of this country has desired me to forward to you a sample of a new grass he has discovered and from which he expects much. His newspaper description thereof is inclosed. He is an ingenious man and a curious botanist. I have transmitted the whole to London under cover to my nephew John Ramsay who lately sailed for Europe to prosecute medical studies. At his departure from this place on the 20th of January 1788 I gave him a letter to you supposing that he might some time or other visit Paris. If he should I request the favor of your notice of him as a young man of virtuous principles and fond of acquiring useful knowledge. I have never seen nor heard from the Parisian book seller who undertook the translation of my history. When the money becomes due to me on that account, if it is paid to my nephew or his order, his receipt shall be a full discharge on my account. I shall draw no orders nor do any thing in the matter but only say that I will confirm any receipt my nephew may give on an offered payment of any thing that may be due to me.

Our State convention is to sit in May when I hope they will confirm the proposed federal constitution. Some opposition may be expected here but I trust there is a decided majority in favor of it. With the highest Sentiment of respect and esteem I have the honor to be your most obedient & very humble Servt,

DAVID RAMSAY

RC (DLC); endorsed. Recorded in SJL as received 4 Jan. 1789. Enclosure missing.

MR. WALTERS: Thomas Walter, botanist and agronomist, devoted the greater part of his life to the study of the plant life of South Carolina. A grass discovered by Walter in 1786 was taken to England by John Fraser and was known there as "Fraser's Carolina Grass." Walter died in Jan. 1789 (DAB; W. R. Maxon, *Thomas Walter, Bota-* *nist, Smithsonian Miscellaneous Collections*, XCV, No. 1 [Feb. 1936]; "Fraser's Carolina Grass," *Gentleman's Magazine*, LIX, Pt. 2 [1789], 872-3). This letter was enclosed in John Ramsay to TJ, 22 Nov. 1788, q.v., but the grass seed was mislaid and apparently never reached TJ. No letter from David Ramsay to TJ of 20 Jan. 1788 has been found and none is recorded in SJL Index.

To Capellen

Rotterdam Mar. 8. 1788.

SIR

It was not in my power to write the letter for Mr. Van der Kemp the evening before I left Paris; and it is not till I arrive here that I have found one moment of leisure. Not knowing in what state of our Union he may chuse to settle I am not able to know to what persons he may be usefully and directly addressed. I give him therefore a letter to Mr. Madison, my most particular friend, now a member of Congress at New York. Whenever M. van der Kemp shall have made up his mind as to his settlement in America, Mr. Madison will be able to give and to procure for him the best introductory letters possible. His influence will be zealously used and omnipotent in it's effect. I am happy, while serving a worthy man, to have the additional gratification of doing what is pleasing to you, and to assure you of those sentiments of respect and attachement with which I have the honour to be Sir your most obedient & most humble servant,

TH: JEFFERSON

PrC (MHi). The existence of this and other press copies of this period proves that TJ carried his small copying press with him on the journey to Holland, just as he had on his trip of the previous year to Southern France (see, for example, TJ to Martha Jefferson and to Short, both dated 21 May 1787).

To James Madison

DEAR SIR   Mar. 8. 1788.

The bearer of this letter is Mr. Francis Adrian Van der Kemp one of the late victims of patriotism in Holland. Having determined to remove himself and his family to America, his friend the Baron de Capellen, another of those expatriated worthies, has asked of me to give letters of introduction to Mr. Van der Kemp, recommending him for his extraordinary zeal in the cause of liberty, his talents, and his sufferings. These motives, together with a respect for the very estimable person who recommends him, induce me to ask for him your civilities and your services. Uninformed of the part of our country in which he may chuse to settle, I am unable to address him to the particular persons into whose society he may wish to enter. But when he shall have decided on the place of his settlement, you will be able to give, or to procure for him, such letters as may be accomodated to his views. In doing this you will add to the many motives of obligation and esteem with which I am, Dear Sir, Your affectionate friend & humble servt,

TH: JEFFERSON

RC (DLC: Madison Papers). PrC (DLC: TJ Papers).

From Angelica Schuyler Church

London March 9. 1788

I send by Mr. Rutledge some views in Ireland for Miss Jefferson. They are wild and Romantic. I should like to see them, but prefer seeing those of my own country first, because I should find there an agreeable guide, or rather if I may say what I hope, an amiable friend, whose society would improve my mind, and give me a relish for simple and happy amusements. I am very much afraid that the vase cannot be impresed in the manner you wish. Will you like to have it as it is? Do not beleive that I have not written to you before because I wanted Inclination. It was from a diffidence, that only serves to convince me of the respect and esteem you have inspired. My Love to the Young Ladies. I will not thank you for your kindness to Catherine. I feel it. Adieu Sir and beleive that I am sincerely your friend,

ANGELICA CHURCH

RC (MHi); endorsed.

From La Blancherie

MONSIEUR   Paris le 9 mars 1788.

Je suis dépositaire d'un mémoire pour M. Franklin. J'ai l'honneur de prier votre Excellence de me faire savoir si Elle voudrait bien Se charger de l'envoyer; l'auteur et moi vous aurons beaucoup d'obligations. J'espère que le bruit qui s'est répandu de la mort de M. Franklin est dénué de fondement et que ses jours se prolongeront encore pour le bonheur d'une multitude d'hommes et la gloire des Sciences. Je vous dois beaucoup de remerciemens, Monsieur, pour la peine que vous vous êtes donnée Relativement à ma Correspondance avec M. Adams. Des Personnages tels que vous l'un et l'autre, je ne puis attendre que justice et munificence. Je serais bien heureux si j'avois l'occasion de vous prouver également mon dévouement et ma reconnaissance.

Je suis avec respect Monsieur Votre très humble et très Obéissant Serviteur,   LA BLANCHERIE

RC (DLC).

From William Short

DEAR SIR   Paris March 9. 1787 [i.e. 1788]

My letter by friday's post has not yet reached you and still I despatch this that there may be as little interval as possible between the times of your hearing from your family in the convent. I have sent regularly to enquire about the health of Miss Polly and have as regularly received for answer that she was better. At present they are gone to enquire and to ask Miss Jefferson for the letter she is to write you. If she sends it to me I shall inclose it as I did the former one. From her you will learn l'etat actuel. The intelligence will thus be the most authentic, and in the same time communicated in the manner the most agreable possible. You may certainly free yourself at present from any uneasiness on account of an illness which could not be less than alarming to a parent.

Nothing new has occurred since your departure worthy of communication. A letter has been sent here from Versailles countersigned, Montmorin. It will be kept for you with several others which have arrived until you return.—The Packet has not yet arrived.—M. de Brehan called on me some days ago to get particular information respecting the account of his lady's arrival in

[657]

America. He is a *vieux bon homme ayant l'ouie dure*. I comforted him very much by confirming the account. He seemed to be really pleased and I dont doubt was as much so as he seemed to be.

Your wine man Parent has drawn on you for 441^{lt} 10s. I have given the money to Petit to go and pay the bill, being out when it was sent here.

Mr. Necker's book has put all the minds in a fermentation. I have heard more religion talked and discussed since the appearance of this book than in three years before. I believe it will work a contrary effect from what the author intended, for I may say also that I have heard more atheism avowed within these three days than during my whole life before. Adieu my dear Sir and believe me with sincerity Your friend & servant,   W. SHORT

P.S. Miss Jefferson has just sent me word by the Commissiare that she shall not write by this post, that Miss Polly is much better and indeed well. The Commissiare saw her (Miss Polly) and says she was quite gay and cheerful—a good sign of health.

RC (DLC: TJ Papers); endorsed by TJ, in part: "recd at Amstdm Mar. 15." PrC (DLC: Short Papers).

From William Frederick Ast

〚*10 Mch. 1788.* Recorded in SJL Index. Not found.〛

From Monfort

Rouen, 10 Mch. 1788. At the request of Mr. Bondfield, has forwarded to TJ at Paris, by water, 5 cases of wine containing 50 bottles each; in spite of the rising of the waters of the Seine the boat should not be late; encloses statement of his disbursements at Rouen in the amount of 60.^{lt} 5; the bargeman will receive payment for this in addition to his own charges of 3^{lt} per case.

RC (ViWC); 3 p.; in French; endorsed. Enclosure (ViWC).

From Martin Oster

〚*10 Mch. 1788.* Recorded in SJL Index. Not found.〛

To William Short

DEAR SIR   The Hague. Mar. 10. 1788.

After two days of prosperous journey I had a good gleam of hope of reaching this place in the night of the third day. In fact however I got on the third day only to within 8 hours land journeying and the passage of the Moerdyke. Yet this remnant employed me three days and nothing less than the omnipotence of god could have shortened this time of torture. I saw the Saturday passing over, and, in imagination, the packet sailing and Mr. Adams on board. And it was not till Sunday my anxieties were ended by finding him here. We are setting out this morning for Amsterdam, where if we fail in the principal object, I shall at least have the solace of easing my own shoulders of the burthen.

I was at Rotterdam the evening of the prince's birthday. The illuminations were the most splendid I had ever seen and the roar of joy the most universal I had ever heard. My journey has been little entertaining. A country of corn and pasture affords little interesting to an American who has seen in his own country so much of that, and who travels to see the country and not it's towns. I am as yet totally undecided as to the time and route of my return. In the mean time be so good as to let me hear from you often. Address your letters to Messrs. Willincks & Van Staphorsts and accept assurances of the esteem & attachment with which I am Dear Sir Your affectionate humble servt,

Th: Jefferson

PrC (DLC).

From John Paul Jones

SIR   Copenhagen March 11th. 1788

I have been so much indisposed, since my arrival here the 4th. from the fatigue and excessive cold I suffered on the Road, that I have been obliged to confine myself almost constantly to my Chamber. I have kept my Bed for several Days; but I now feel myself better, and hope the danger is over.

On[1] my arrival I paid my respects to the minister of France. He received me with great kindness. We went five days ago to the minister of foreign affairs. I was much flattered with my reception and our conversation was long and very particular respect-

[659]

ing America and the new constitution of which I presented a copy. He observed that it had struck him as a very dangerous power to make the president commander in cheif. In other respects it appeared to please him much as heading to a near and sure treaty of commerce between America and Denmark. It was a day of public business and I could not do more than present your letter. I shall follow the business closely.

In a few days, when I am reestablished in [my][2] Health, I am to be presented to the whole Court, and to Sup with the King. I shall after that be presented to all the Corps Diplomatic and other persons of Distinction here. I am infinitely indebted to the Attentions I receive from the Minister of France. I made the inquiry you desired in Holland, and should then have written to you in consequence, had I not been assured by authority[3] that I could not doubt, that Letters had been sent you on the Subject, that could not fail of giving you satisfaction. Mr. Van Staphorst was very obliging. At Hambourg I ordered the smoak'd Beef you desired to be sent to you, to the care of the American Agent at Havre de Grace. You have nothing to do but receive it, paying what little charges may be on it.

My ill Health and fatigue on the Road hindred me from preparing the extract of the Engagement. When you see Mr. Little Page, I pray you to present my kind Compliments. It is said here that the Empress confides the [chief][2] command of her Fleet that will pass the Sound to Admiral Greg and that he means to call at an English Port to take Provisions &c. The Hambourg Papers, I am told, have announced the Death of Dr. Franklin. I shall be extremely concerned if the Account prove true. God forbid. The departure of the Post obliges me to conclude. I am, with a deep sense of your kind attachement, Sir, Your most obedient and most humble Servant,

PAUL JONES

Dupl (DLC: John Paul Jones Papers); in Jones' hand, signed; partly in code and decoded by TJ interlineally. RC (same); same passage coded but in a different code, and only partly decoded by TJ (see Jones to TJ, 20 Mch. 1788).

[1] This entire paragraph is written in code and has been decoded by TJ interlineally, employing Code No. 12.
[2] This word in brackets (supplied) is in RC but not in Dupl.
[3] At this point Jones put an asterisk and, in the margin of Dupl, wrote: "M. Van Staphorst."

From Collow Frères, Carmichael & Co.

Le Havre, 12 Mch. 1788. Acknowledging TJ's letter of 15 Feb. and expressing the hope that the new regulations for trade "may be the means of establishing the most permanent and friendly Intercourse between the two Countries." The wine for Donald has arrived and will be shipped to him by the first opportunity; hope to send the bust of Lafayette at the same time.

RC (MHi); 2 p.

To John Jay

Sir   Amsterdam Mar. 13. 1788.

Mr. Adams having announced to our bankers here his approaching departure from Europe, and referred them to me for counsel on our affairs in their hands, they sent me a state of them, and of the difficulties which were pressing at the moment, and impending more seriously for the month of June. They were urging me by almost every post on this subject. In this situation, information of Mr. Adams's journey of leave to the Hague reached me on the day of his arrival there. I was sensible how important it was to have the benefit of his interference in a department which had been his peculiarly from the beginning, and with all the details of which he was as intimately acquainted as I was little so. I set out therefore in the instant, joined him at the Hague, and he readily concurred with me in the necessity of our coming here to confer with our bankers on the measures which might be proper and practicable. We are now engaged on this object, and the result, together with a full explanation of the difficulties which commanded our attention, shall be the subject of a letter which I shall do myself the honor of writing you by Mr. Adams to be forwarded by Colo. Smith who will go in the English packet. I avoid further particulars in the present letter because it is to pass thro' the different post-offices to Paris. It will be forwarded thence by Mr. Short, whom I have desired to do himself the honour of writing to you any occurrences since my departure which may be worthy of being communicated, by the French packet of this month.

I have the honor to be with sentiments of the most perfect respect & esteem Sir, Your most obedient & most humble servant,

TH: JEFFERSON

RC (DNA: PCC, No. 87, II); addressed. PrC (DLC). This letter, enclosed in TJ to Short, 13 Mch. 1788, was transmitted by Short to Jay in his own letter of 18 Mch. 1788, q.v.

From Moustier

MONSIEUR   à Newyork le 13. Mars 1788.

La navigation cet hiver a été tellement contrariée que tous les navires destinés pour ces côtes s'en sont plus ou moins ressenti. Notre paquebot du 25. Xbre. est vainement attendu depuis longtems. Voilà comme souvent les spéculations des hommes sont trompées. Je l'ai assez éprouvé pour ma part quant à l'accueil que je m'attendois qu'un Ministre du Roi de France auroit dû trouver dans ce pays-ci après les liaisons intimes qui ont existé pendant un tems entre nos deux Nations. Il y a à la verité quelques individus qui savent éprouver les sentimens qui sont toujours chers à des âmes nobles, la reconnoissance et la confiance; ils ont aussi le bon esprit de savoir aprécier les véritables interêts de leur patrie. Mais aujourdhui ces individus ne l'emportent pas dans la majorité du peuple Américain. Je dois du moins le présumer d'après ce que j'ai remarqué de la part des Assemblées qui le représentent et agissent en son nom. Vous êtes sans doute informé, Monsieur, des procédés de l'Assemblée de votre Etat qui paroit avoir adopté à notre égard une conduite bien différente de celle qu'il a suivi autrefois. Je ne vous parlerai pas du discours dicté au Président du Congrès par cette Assemblée Souveraine, aux yeux des Etrangers, quoique bien éloignée de l'être de fait. Vous l'aurez lû et malheureusement il l'aura été dans tout ce Continent et en Angleterre. Malgré le peu de motifs que j'ai de me louer des manières de beaucoup de gens ici, j'ai cependant eû soin d'éviter ce qui auroit pû marquer trop ma sensibilité. En conséquence, j'ai renoncé au plan que j'avois fait de rendre mes visites de Cérémonie aux membres du Congrès par Députation collectivement. J'ai suivi l'étiquette prescrite au pied de la lettre. Mais j'avoue que je trouve cette étiquette si peu convenable à plusieurs égards, que si elle n'est pas changée, j'opinerai pour que je ne sois pas remplacé par un homme de mon caractère ni de mon état, parceque j'avoue qu'il est dur d'être humilié et de débuter par des dégouts. Vous voyez, Monsieur, avec quelle confiance je m'explique avec vous. Elle est une suite de l'estime et de l'affection bien sincères que j'ai conçues pour vous. Je suis sûr que vous serez moins étonné que fâché de ce que j'ai l'honneur de vous mander. Je me donnerai bien de garde de me laisser guider dans ma conduite par aucune espèce de ressentiment personel; je tacherai au contraire de suivre autant que je le pourrai les premières impulsions que j'avois reçues en faveur des

[662]

Américains avant de venir parmi eux. Cependant il faudra bien que je compte quelquefois avec des gens qui comptent toujours et souvent d'une manière bien étrange. Par exemple, est-ce bien noble et bien juste, même politique, de publier qu'on ne doit point de reconnoissance à la France pour être venue au secours des Américains? Est-ce bien sage de prétendre qu'Elle a aujourdhui besoin d'eux et qu'eux n'ont pas besoin d'Elle? Enfin, que dois-je penser de gens qui interprètent mon empressement à me rendre parmi eux, à ce même besoin, qu'ils prétendent naître de l'embarras où se trouve le Royaume et de la crainte que nous avions de l'Angleterre? Que les tems sont changés! Il faudroit qu'il y eut dans une Assemblée à qui on laisse jouer le role de Souverain, en paroles, des personnes capables de juger les vrais intérêts de leur patrie et de parler en conséquence quand il est bien prouvé qu'on est trop foible pour agir. J'attends les changemens qui réuniront pour le bonheur des Etats Unis, que je désire bien sincèrement, le pouvoir, les lumières et la sagesse. Nos intérêts communs ne pourront qu'y gagner. Je dis *communs*, car c'est le mot propre; s'ils sont négligés d'un côté, il faudra bien les abandonner de l'autre. Je me propose de les mettre dans une balance bien exacte pour démontrer ma proposition. Ma satisfaction sera de former une union que j'avois crû toute formée. En attendant, je trouve piquant d'avoir sacrifié, par un trop grand empressement interprété à mon propre désavantage, ma santé, mes intérêts et les agrémens de la société et d'un séjour qui me plaisoit. Certainement, si je m'étois attendu à l'effet qu'a produit mon arrivée ici, je serois encore à Paris. Je n'aurois pas à ajouter aux peines que j'ai éprouvées, celle de voir qu'un climat rigoureux a attaqué la santé d'une personne qui m'est chère et qui se trouve confinée dans son lit, dans un pays où Elle est totalement étrangère quant à son origine et aux usages. Nous parlons souvent ensemble de vous, Monsieur, et nous regrettons bien de ne pas vous posséder dans votre propre pays où il seroit à désirer que vous eussiez beaucoup d'imitateurs. Nous n'avons joui qu'un instant d'un homme que nous n'avons connu que pour le regretter. Pour moi particulièrement j'avois besoin de pouvoir placer ma confiance et je doute que je puisse de longtems en trouver l'occasion.

Le dérangement de la santé de ma soeur, la petitesse de ma Salle à manger et le peu de commodité de ma cuisine, m'ont empêché jusqu'àprésent de rendre les dîners auxquels on a bien voulu m'inviter. J'en ai d'autant plus de regrets, que personne n'est plus sensible que moi aux égards et n'a plus d'envie de répondre aux bons procédés. J'espère que le changement de saison et de maison me procurera la facilité de suivre mon inclination à cet égard. En attendant que je puisse suivre pour les invitations l'étiquette qui règne ici jusqu'à la table, j'ai commencé à essayer du genre plus sociable d'avoir de petits dîners auxquels je prie verbalement, pour qu'ils ne puissent passer que pour des *Family dinners*. Il y a quelques personnes, et entre autres votre compatriote le Président du Congrès, à qui ce genre là paroit convenir. J'ai déjà prévenu que, même quand je donnerois des dîners de cérémonie, je réclamois la permission de me soustraire à l'usage pénible pour un maître de maison de rester le dernier à table. J'ai assez de voix en ma faveur pour m'autoriser à me lever pour passer dans le sallon avec ceux qui peuvent gouter la société sans avoir besoin d'être armés d'un verre. Pour éviter la mauvaise plaisanterie que ce seroit l'économie de quelques bouteilles de vin qui me feroit prendre ce parti, j'établirai liberté plénière pour les amateurs, de rester à table pour y être en véritables démocrates. Je compte pour rien le tort qu'on prétend que je me fais en perdant l'occasion d'entendre Messieurs les Américains parler à coeur ouvert de toutes leurs affaires. J'espère qu'un jour, quand ils me connoîtront mieux et quand il y aura des esprits éclairés à leur tête comme il y en a déjà eû, qu'il n'y aura pas besoin de nous animer réciproquement par le vin pour traiter nos affaires. Je ne veux rien d'eux par surprise, mes vues sont assez bonnes pour que je puisse les montrer à toute heure. Je voudrois que nous en vinssions tous là. Alors nous prendrions notre tems pour les affaires et nous en aurions pour le plaisir sans mêler tout celà ensemble pour rendre la société ennuyeuse et les affaires indigestes. Si je prends la liberté de changer chez moi quelque chose aux usages reçus, c'est surtout parceque je crois qu'il n'y a qu'à y gagner pour les Américains même, qui jusqu'àprésent n'ont pas encore des usages particuliers à eux, mais qui suivent ceux qu'ils ont reçus des Anglois, ainsi que leurs loix et leurs principes, en quoi il est cependant très aisé et très nécessaire *to improve*.

Je ne sais si l'on s'aperçoit ici de ma délicatesse à tant différer de parler de ce qui nous est dû. Je prouverai du moins par mon long silence là dessus, quoique mes instructions ne le portent pas, que ce n'est point un huissier, mais un Ministre plénipotentiaire de confiance de la part de sa Cour et connu pour être bien intentionné en faveur des Américains, qu'on leur a envoyé. Je désire que ceux, qui avec aussi peu de fondement ont attribué ma prompte venue à la détresse du Royaume, ne soient pas dans le cas de sentir trop vivement celle des Etats Unis. Je voudrois qu'ils pussent au moins nous imiter dans l'exactitude à acquitter nos engagemens et qu'ils eussent des ressources aussi grandes et aussi faciles. Mais puisque malheureusement ils ne les ont pas, je voudrois du moins qu'ils pussent sentir qu'il leur convient d'avoir pour amie une Nation qui les a et qui ne demande pas mieux que de contribuer à leur prospérité après la guerre, comme elle a contribué à leurs succès pendant celle qui lui a couté tant de sang et d'argent répandus pour eux sans avoir gagné leur reconnoissance.

J'attendrai pour faire quelques courses dans l'intérieur que la santé de ma soeur soit rétablie et que j'aie fait mon déménagement. J'entrerai au mois de Mai dans une maison oû je serai beaucoup mieux logé que je ne m'y étois attendu. Mais j'y serai comme l'oiseau sur la branche, puisque nous ne savons pas où ira le Congrès ni même ce qu'il deviendra. Sera-t-il métamorphosé en un corps plus puissant, ou sera-t-il dissous? Voilà la grande question dont nous aurons la solution dans quelques mois. En attendant je fais des voeux bien sincères pour que tout aille pour [le] mieux.

J'ai l'honneur d'être avec un très sincère et parfait attachement, Monsieur, Votre très humble et très obeissant Serviteur,

LE CTE. DE MOUSTIER

RC (DLC); endorsed. In DLC: TJ Papers, 37: 6376, there is a note in Remsen's hand (but bearing a brief calculation in TJ's hand of unknown significance) reading as follows: "Count de Moustiers *first* letter to Congress after his arrival, (enclosing his letter of Credence and the Chevr. de la Luzerne's letter of Recall) is dated February 4, 1788. He had his Audience the 26th of February 1788." The above outpouring to TJ reveals how quickly he discovered that his circumstances in New York were uncongenial. See notes to TJ to Mrs. Adams, 30 Aug. 1787, and TJ to Jay, 8 Oct. 1787.

To William Short

DEAR SIR   Amsterdam Mar. 13. 1788.

I received yesterday your favor of the 6th. with the agreeable information of the convalescence of my daughter, for which I thank you. I expect we shall be able to leave this place on the 19th. What route I shall take will depend on information not yet received relative to the roads, and partly too on the weather's becoming milder than it now is. So that at present I can only ascertain the limits of my return to Paris to be from the 1st. to the middle of April. I inclose a letter for Mr. Jay to go by the packet. It contains nothing more than a general idea of the cause of my coming here, and a reference for details to the letter which I shall write by Mr. Adams to go by Colo. Smith in the English packet. But I have mentioned to Mr. Jay that if there is any new occurrence at Paris worth communicating you will be so good as to write it. In my letter to you from Leyden I desired you to address to me to the care of Willincks & Van Staphorsts. It will be of no avail however to write to me after your receipt of the present, as by that time I shall be leaving this place. Things in this country appear established beyond the reach of every thing short of full conquest. Be so good as to mention this to the M. de la fayette, to remember me to my daughters and to be assured yourself of the sincere esteem & attachment with which I am Dear Sir Your affectionate friend & servt, TH: JEFFERSON

RC (ViW); endorsed. PrC (DLC). Enclosure: TJ to Jay, this date. MY LETTER FROM LEYDEN: An error for TJ's letter from The Hague, 10 Mch. 1788.

From C. W. F. Dumas

MONSIEUR Lahaie 14e. Mars 1788

J'espere que l'incluse, reçue en ce moment, 4 h. après midi, vous portera de bonnes nouvelles de la santé de Madle. Jefferson, comme j'aime à supposer que la précédente que j'ai eu l'honneur de vous acheminer mardi passé, vous en aura appris de bonnes aussi.

J'ai eu enfin la satisfaction d'être assuré positivement, et de très-bonne part, que l'on s'en est tenu ici à la mauvaise humeur témoignée contre moi dans certaine réponse faite à S.E. Mr. Adams; qu'on n'a point écrit directement, et qu'on n'écrira pas, n'ayant rien à alléguer à ma charge. On m'a dit aussi, que plusieurs Membres n'ont nullement approuvé cet éclat de mauvaise humeur, et encore moins certaine bassesse et vilainie qui a eu lieu à mon égard depuis peu, contre l'usage le plus constant. J'en suis tout consolé. Je n'ai pas à en rougir moi. Ayez la bonté, Monsieur, de faire part de tout cela à S.E. Mr. Adams, avec mes respects.

Si je reçois une autre Lettre mardi prochain, et si Votre Excellence n'est pas de retour ici ce jour là, faut-il envoyer la Lettre comme celle-ci, ou la garder ici? Si votre Excellence veut me diriger là-dessus par un mot, je serai plus sûr de ne pas mal faire en tout cas.

Je suis avec grand respect, de Votre Excellence, le très humble & très-obéissant servit., C W F Dumas

RC (DLC); endorsed by TJ, in part: "recd at Amst. Mar. 17." Enclosure: Short to TJ, 9 Mch. 1788.

From Lanchon Frères & Cie.

L'Orient, 14 Mch. 1788. Their enquiries to TJ in December were promptly answered by the government's decree on trade with the U.S., except for information concerning the price the farmers-general are required to give for tobacco; without a set price the resolve is of little avail. "The promises Contained in Mr. Lambert's Official letter of the 29th. Decr. . . . has suggested the idea to some of Our New England friends of opening a new Branch from their States to this country with Salt provisions of Butter Beef and Pork in which they say they can rival the Irish for quality and Cheapness." To further this idea it has been suggested that France supply her navy with American instead of Irish provisions because supplies from the latter source have been impeded by strained relations between England and France. Having been charged with presenting this matter to the U.S. consul general or TJ and there being no consul general, they have no choice but to trouble TJ.

RC (ViWC); 2 p.; endorsed.

From Parish and Thomson

〚*14 Mch. 1788.* Recorded in SJL Index. Not found.〛

From William Short

My dear Sir   Paris March 14. 1788

I am now in daily expectation of the pleasure of receiving a letter from you and hope it will bring us an account of your safe arrival at the Hague and of your having found there Mr. Adams.— You recollect without doubt the extract in the Mercure, from Mazzei's book, where it was said, 'qu'il y a vingt dieux, ou qu'il n'y en a qu'un &c.' In consequence of it Pankcoucke is *decreté d'ajournment personnel* and Rollin the *censeur* is displaced.

The Packet has not yet arrived, and a report has prevailed for some time, that in consequence of the enormous sums which they cost they were to be suppressed immediately. It was even said that the one destined to sail the 25th. of this month would be stopped. Yesterday morning however Count D'Houditot came to the pension opposite to us and told young Crevecoeur that the Packet of the 25th. would certainly sail. As to the suppression in future he knew nothing. I fear however it will end there, for it is said the Packet boats under the present administration form an object of expence worthy attention.

The Messenger has this moment returned from the convent, whilst I was finishing the last sentence; he says Miss Polly is perfectly well, so that you may consider her at present as on a footing with the other two pensionnaires, who I hope will continue as you left them.

Mde. de Corny complained to me that you had not answered her letter which she wrote by your commissionaire the evening before your departure. She asked your permission to visit your daughters and to take them out of the convent sometimes. She wished particularly to bring them here one of the days of Longchamp. Elle en veut furieusement á Mr. Adams. Il la poursuit, dit-elle, partout. C'est lui qui la prive de sa chere Angelique plutot qu'elle ne serait partie sans lui. C'est lui également qui la prive de vous. Elle est bien malheureuse. Elle va vous écrire pour vous prier de revenir le plutot possible auprès d'elle.

Mr. Parker set off soon after you for Amsterdam. I learned it two days ago only from Mr. Barrett. He says however, and Mr. Appleton also, that Mr. Parker sent here the day of his departure to take my commands for you, but the old porter certainly forgot that amongst his other *oubliés*, as I never heard any thing of it. Adieu my dear Sir & believe me with sincerity your friend & servant,

W SHORT

RC (DLC: TJ Papers); endorsed by TJ: "Short Wm. recd at Amstdm Mar. 18." PrC (DLC: Short Papers).

THE EXTRACT IN THE MERCURE from Mazzei's *Recherches Historiques* appeared in the *Mercure de France* for 23 Feb. 1788. It was in reality a summary, with comments by the reviewer who quoted (in Mazzei's translation) from TJ's *Notes of Virginia* that part pertaining to religious freedom: "The legitimate powers of government extend to such acts only as are injurious to others. But it does me no injury for my neighbor to say there are twenty gods or no god (IL Y A VINGT DIEUX, OU QU'IL N'Y EN A QU'UN &c). MDE. DE CORNY'S letter, evidently written on 2 Mch. 1788, has not been found. For an account of the traditional springtime "Promenade de Long-champs" during Holy Week, see Thiéry, *Guide des Amateurs*, I, 25; Mercier, *Tableau de Paris*, II, ch. 122.

From [Nicolas?] van Staphorst

[Amsterdam, ca. 14 Mch. 1788]

Mr. Van Staphorst's compliment to Mr. Jefferson, and is sorry he cannot for the present assure, that what he will inform Mr. Jefferson about the quantity of *pure* Silver in a Gulden is exactly right, because he has taken it from a Book, of which authority he is not certain, in this case, but he will endeavour to ascertain it to morrow. $23^{67}/_{31}$ florins or Guldens must weight one Mark troys of 5120 Azen, and the pure Silver 10 penny 22½ grain. The proportion between this weight and the french is 760 Dutch oncen = 762.8 french ones.

RC (MHi); addressed; without date, which has been assigned from the following note, in an unidentified hand, on the verso of the address leaf: "The Balance actually in favor of the United States this 14 March 1788 is ƒ79268.2.8 Guilders and there are 590 Bonds remaining on hand." There are various calculations in TJ's hand on the recto of the address leaf.

From Lucy Paradise Barziza

EXCELLENCE   Venise 15me. de Mars. 1788.

Ce n'est pas de ce Moments que je vous dois la plus forte reconoissance pour les bienfaits que ma famille a toujours recu de vous. Mon Père jouisse de son état par vôtre ouvrage, et n'avons personne au Monde que nous soyons si redevables comme à vôtre Excellence. Les dernieres traites de bonté, que vous avez eut, en recommendant aux états Units de L'Amérique Mon Père, avec des expressions si forte, ce qu'il lui a porter tants des faveurs, et distinction en Virginie, achève de nous lier à vôtre cher personne, par des Noeuds inebranlables; en effet Mon père m'ecrit avec un excess de tenderesse, et gratitude envers vous qu'on ne peut pas mieux. Agréez encore mes plus sincere remerciments, souhaitant de pouvoir vous témoigner par quelques services les sentiments de mon coeur. Dieu m'a fait le bonheure de me marier avec une personne, dont l'état, leur raports, et le genie me rende la femme la plus heureuse, et d'après la preuve d'un Année entière je me trouve si contente, que je ne changerai mon sort avec celle de la reine. Il n'y a que deux Mois que j'ai obtenu une fille, l'objet de ma tenderesse, après son père. Je sais que mon époux vous écrit, et si jamais vous l'aurai à bien connoitre, je suis sur, que vous lui donnerai vôtre Amitié.

[669]

Nous aurons toujours besoin de vôtre protection que j'implore, et que nous tacherons de ne la démériter jamais. Dans cette esperance je suis, avec autant de respect que d'attachement, De Votre Excellence très humble et très obeissante servante,

LUCY BARZIZA NÉE PARADISE

RC (MHi); endorsed by TJ: "Paradise Lucy. Countess of Barziza."

From Barziza

Venice, 15 Mch. 1788. The news received in a letter from his father-in-law, John Paradise, dated 22 Nov. 1787, from Virginia, gives him an opportunity to write to TJ to express his thanks for the singular favors TJ has bestowed on Mr. Paradise; is convinced that TJ is the most gracious and obliging person in the world; hopes that, because of his connection, he may share TJ's friendship and that he will merit it on his own account.

RC (DLC); 2 p.; in French; endorsed by TJ: "Barziza. Count."

To C. W. F. Dumas

SIR   Amsterdam March 16. 1788.

I return you many thanks for your kind attention in forwarding my letters. I shall probably remain here till Thursday or Friday next, and will therefore pray you to forward hither any which may arrive before that time. None I believe will come after that, as I have let Mr. Short know I should be gone. Since my arrival here I have had some thought of making a tour up the Rhine instead of returning directly to Paris. In that case I shall be deprived of the pleasure of seeing you at the Hague as I had fully promised myself. I am not yet decided: but should I conclude to go by the way of Utrecht, Nimeguen &c. I shall do myself the honour of writing you a letter which may answer the purpose of tranquilising your family as effectually as the interview which I had hoped to have had. I have the honour to be with sentiments of great esteem & attachment Sir Your most obedient & most humble servt,

TH: JEFFERSON

PrC (DLC).

To John Jay, with Enclosures

SIR   Amsterdam March 16. 1788.

In a letter of the 13th. inst. which I had the honor of addressing you from this place, I mentioned in general terms the object of my journey hither and that I should enter into more particular details by the confidential conveiance which would occur thro' Mr. Adams and Colo. Smith.

The board of Treasury had, in the month of December, given notice to our bankers here that it would be[1] impossible for them to make any remittances to Europe for the then ensuing year, and that they must therefore rely altogether on the progress of the late loan. But this, in the mean time, after being about one third filled, had ceased to get forward. The bankers, who had been referred to me for advice by Mr. Adams, stated these circumstances, and pressed their apprehensions for the ensuing month of June, when 270,000 florins would be wanting for interest. In fine, they urged an offer of the holders of the former bonds to take all those now remaining on hand, provided they might retain out of them the interest on a part of our domestic debt, of which they had also become the holders. This would have been 180,000 florins. To this proposition I could not presume any authority to listen. Thus pressed between the danger of failure on one hand, and an impossible proposition on the other, I heard of Mr. Adams's being gone to the Hague to take leave. His knoledge of the subject was too intimate to be neglected under the present difficulty, and it was the last moment in which we could be availed of it. I set out therefore immediately for the Hague, and we came on to this place together, in order to see what could be done. It was easier to discover, than to remove the causes which obstructed the progress of the loan. Our affairs here, like those of other nations, are in the hands of particular bankers. These employ particular brokers; and they have their particular circle of money lenders. These money lenders, as I have before mentioned, while placing a part of their money in our foreign loans, had at the same time employed another part in a joint speculation to the amount of 840,000 dollars of our domestic debt. A year's interest was becoming due on this, and they wished to avail themselves of our want of money for the foreign interest, to obtain paiment of the domestic. Our first object was to convince our bankers that there was no power on this side the Atlantic which could accede to this proposition, or give it any countenance.

They at length therefore, but with difficulty receded from this ground, and agreed to enter into conferences with the brokers and lenders, and to use every exertion to clear the loan from the embarrasment in which this speculation had engaged it. What will be the result of these conferences is not yet known. We have hopes however that it is not desperate, because the bankers consented yesterday to pay off, and did actually pay off the capital of 51,000 florins which had become due to the house of Fizeaux and company on the first day of January, and which had not yet been paid.

We have gone still further. The Treasury board gives no hope of remittances till the new government can procure them. For that government to be adopted, it's legislature assembled, it's system of taxation and collection arranged, the money gathered from the people into their treasury, and then remitted to Europe, must enter us considerably into the year 1790. To secure our credit then for the present year only, is but to put off the evil day to the next. What remains of the last, even when it shall be filled up, will little more than clear us of present demands, as may be seen by the estimate inclosed. We thought it better therefore to provide at once for the years 1789. and 1790. also; and thus to place the government at it's ease and our credit in security during that trying interval. The same estimate will shew that another million of florins will be necessary to effect this. We stated this to our bankers, who concurred in our views, and that to ask the whole sum at once would be better than to make demands from time to time so small as that they betray to the money holders the extreme feebleness of our own resources. Mr. Adams therefore has executed bonds for another million of florins: which however are to remain unissued till Congress shall have ratified the measure; so that this transaction is something or nothing at their pleasure. We suppose it's expediency so apparent as to leave little doubt of it's ratification. In this case much time will have been saved by the execution of the bonds at this moment, and the proposition will be presented here under a more favorable appearance according to the opinion of the bankers. Mr. Adams is under a necessity of setting out tomorrow morning: but I shall stay two or three days longer, to attend to, and to encourage the efforts of the bankers to judge and to inform you whether they will ensure us a safe passage over the month of June.

Not having my letters here to turn to I am unable to say whether the last I wrote from Paris mentioned the declaration of the emperor that he should take a part in the war against the Turks. This declaration appeared a little before or a little after that letter, I do not recollect which. Some trifling hostilities have taken place between them. The court of Versailles seems to pursue immoveably it's pacific system: and from every appearance in the country from which I write we must conclude that it's tragedy is wound up. The triumph appears complete and tranquillity perfectly established. The numbers who have emigrated are differently estimated from 20. to 40. thousand.

A little before I left Paris, I received a piece of intelligence which should be communicated, leaving you to lay what stress on it it may seem to deserve. It's authenticity may be surely relied on. At the moment of the late pacification, Spain had about 15 ships of the line really ready for sea. The convention for disarming did not extend to her, nor did she disarm. This gave inquietude to the court of London, and they demanded an explanation. One was given which they say is perfectly satisfactory. The Russian minister at Versailles getting knolege of this, became suspicious on his part. He recollected that Spain during the late war had been opposed to the entrance of a Russian fleet into the Mediterranean, and concluded, if England was not the object of this armament Russia might be. It is known that that power means to send a fleet of about 24. ships into the Mediterranean this summer. He went to the Ct. de Montmorin, and expressed his apprehensions. The Count de Montmorin declared that the object of Spain in that armament was totally different; that he was not sure she would succeed; but that France and Spain were to be considered as one, and that the former would become guarantee for the latter that she would make no opposition to the Russian fleet. If neither England nor Russia be the object, the question recurs, who is it for? You know best if our affairs with Spain are in a situation to give jealousy to either of us. I think it very possible that the satisfaction of the court of London may have been pretended, or premature. It is possible also that the affairs of Spain in South America may require them to assume a threatening appearance. I give you the facts however; and you will judge whether they are objects of attention, or of mere curiosity.

I have the honor to be with sentiments of sincere esteem & respect, Sir, Your most obedient & most humble servt.,

TH: JEFFERSON

[673]

P.S. I enclose herewith an extract of a letter from the Ct. de Vergennes to the French Ambassador at the Hague which will make a remarkeable chapter in the history of the late revolution here. It is not public, nor should be made so by us. Probably those who have been the victims of it will some day publish it.

RC (DNA: PCC, No. 87, II); endorsed by Charles Thomson: "Letter 16 March 1788 Mr T. Jefferson Read 22 May 1788 23 May Referred to Mr Baldwin Mr Duane Mr Otis Mr Kearny Mr Carrington." PrC (DLC).

[1] At this point TJ deleted the word "altogether."

ENCLOSURE I

SUMMARY OF FUNDING OPERATION EXECUTED BY ADAMS
AND JEFFERSON IN AMSTERDAM, MARCH 1788

		florins	
1788. Fizeaux & co. their capital & 3. months interest		51,637.10	
Virginia, an advance from their fund to be replaced	29,765^{tt}		
Grand, advances to be replaced	49,180^{1}	35,600	
Gateau, balance due him for a medal about	2,000^{tt}	900	
Mr. Short^{2} arrears of salary due to him about	5,000		
Mr. Ast (late Secy. to the Consulate) do.	3,000	3,600	
Mr. Dumas, do.		12,500	
Foreign officers, 3 years arrears of interest	136,960^{tt}-14-6	61,700	
Captives at Algiers^{3} say about		60,000	
legations^{4} from April to December, 9 months		36,000	
June interest		270,000	531,937.10
1789. legations for the whole year @ 4000 florins a month		48,000	
Foreign officers	45,653^{tt}.11.6	20,540	
Medals about		20,000	
February interest		80,000	
lottery on same loan, paiable at same time		70,000	
June interest (supposing the loan of 1787. filled)		300,000	538,540.
1790. legations for the whole year		48,000	
Foreign officers	45,653^{tt}.11.6	20,540	
February interest		80,000	
June interest (supposing the loan of 1788 half filled in 1789)		325,000	473,540
			1,544,017.10

florins

Cr. 1788. Mar. 14. by cash in hands of
        the bankers this day   79,268.2.8
    by nett proceeds of 590.
        bonds of 1787. remain-
        ing @ 920f each.   542,800
    by do. of 1000 bonds of
        the loan now proposed
        @ 920 each   920,000   1,542,068.2.8
    Deficiency   1,949.7.4[5]

                          1,544,017.10[6]

MS (DNA: PCC, No. 87, II). PrC (DLC). Dft (DLC). Another copy was sent to the Commissioners of the Treasury in TJ's letter of 29 Mch. 1788. The more important variations between MS, Dft, and Tr sent to the Commissioners are noted below.

1 These two items are bracketed in Dft and "36,000" written in margin.
2 In Dft "5,943.4" is written in margin beside this item.
3 Instead of the words, "Captives at Algiers," Dft reads: "a particular purpose committed by Congress to Th:J." This would seem to indicate that the Dft was a working copy which TJ employed in the negotiations with the Amsterdam bankers and that he did not wish to specify the object embraced by this item. Tr sent to Commissioners reads: "redemption of captives." See note to Montgomery to TJ, 15 Oct. 1787.
4 Tr sent to Commissioners reads: "legations and little expenses from Apr. to Dec. about 4000 florins a month."
5 Dft and Tr to Commissioners read: "1947.7.4."
6 Following this point, Tr to Commissioners reads: "Errors which were not noted at the time of making this estimate, and which are to be corrected. 1. The commission of the bankers on their paiments is not charged. 2. The articles stated in livres are extended in florins banco, whereas the loans being in florins courant, these should have been also."

ENCLOSURE II

Extrait de la depeche de Monsieur le comte de Vergennes à Monsieur le Marquis de Verac, Ambassadeur de France (à la Haïe) du 15. Mars 1786.

Le roi concourera autant qu'il sera en son pouvoir au succès de la chose, et vous inviterez de sa part les patriotes à lui communiquer leurs vues, leur plan et leurs envieux. Vous les assurerez que le roi prend un interêt veritable à leurs personnes, comme à leur cause, et qu'ils peuvent compter sur sa protection. Ils doivent y compter d'autant plus, Monsieur, que nous ne dissimulons pas que si Monsieur le Stadhoulder reprend son ancienne influence le systeme Anglois ne tarderoit pas à prevaloir, et que notre alliance deviendroit un etre de raison. Les Patriotes sentiront facilement que cette position seroit incompatible avec la dignité comme avec la consideration de sa Majesté. Mais dans le cas, Monsieur, où les chefs des Patriotes auroient à craindre une scission, ils auroient par devers eux le temps suffisant pour ramener ceux de leurs amis que les Anglomanes ont égarés, et preparer les choses de maniere que la question de nouveau mise en deliberation soit decidé[e] selon leurs desirs. Dans cette hypothese, le roi vous authorise à agir de concert avec eux, de suivre la direction qu'ils jugeront devoir vous donner, et d'employer tous les moyens pour augmenter le nombre des partisans de la bonne cause.

Il me reste, Monsieur, à vous parler de la sureté personelle des patriotes. Vous les assurerez qu'en tout etat de cause, le roi les prend sous sa protection immediate, et vous ferez connoitre partout où vous le jugerez necessaire que sa Majesté regarderoit comme une offense personelle tout ce qu'on entreprendroit contre leur liberté. Il est à presumer que ce langage tenu avec energie en imposera à l'audace des Anglomanes, et que Monsieur le Prince de Nassau croira courir quelque risque en provoquant le ressentiment de sa Majesté.

Tr (DNA: PCC, No. 87, II); accompanied by an English translation by John Pintard, printed in *Dipl. Corr., 1783-89*, II, 137-8. For TJ's considered opinion of this letter, see his Autobiography, Ford, I, 101-7.

From Brailsford & Morris

Charlestown, S.C., 17 Mch. 1788. Enclose a bill for 726 livres tournois, drawn by the French consul, Petry, on Petry at Paris, subject to the order of the Agricultural Society; it is intended for purchase of "Olive, and other Fruit trees"; have written Bérard asking him to remit £300 to TJ for the use of John Rutledge, Jr.

RC (DLC); 2 p.; at foot of text in TJ's hand: "bill accepted May 30. 1788."; endorsed.

From William Short

MY DEAR SIR   Paris March. 17. 1788

I cannot let the post go off without sending you some intelligence of your little family at the convent. Few words will convey it as there is only to say that they are all perfectly well. This is the answer which I get from the convent when I send there. It shews that Miss Polly whom you left sick is at present classed with those whom you left well.

The Packet has not yet arrived. It is the first instance I think of so great a delay. Mr. Rutledge arrived here a few days ago from London. He brings no late intelligence at all from America, except as to his own State. He tells me he has letters from thence of the 20th of Jany., that the Assembly was about meeting and it was not doubted the first thing they did would be to recommend the appointment of a convention.

I forgot to mention to you in my last that Mde. la Marquise de la Luzerne died here almost suddenly about the end of the week before last. It will be a very unexpected piece of intelligence to the Ambassador, who does not know that she was indisposed.

Colo. Ternant has returned here. I have not seen him, but am told he was much displeased with London himself, and says the

Ambassador also was not too content. Neither the one or the other ventured to wear the ribbon of Cincinnatus whilst there, and I should have hoped he would not have resumed it on his return; but I suppose he took courage at Calais, for he has it at present.

I am very anxious to receive a letter from you. I had supposed there would have been time enough for one to arrive here by this time, and particularly if you had reached the Hague as soon as you expected. I still hope however that you got there well and safe and in time to meet Mr. Adams.

Adieu my dear Sir and believe me with the most perfect sincerity your friend & servant, W SHORT

RC (DLC: TJ Papers); endorsed: "Short Wm recd at Amstdm Mar. 2[2?]." PrC (DLC: Short Papers).

NEITHER THE ONE OR THE OTHER VENTURED TO WEAR THE RIBBON OF CINCINNATUS WHILST THERE: See Smith to Short, 22 Feb. 1788, whence this information was drawn (quoted in note to Smith to TJ, 22 Feb. 1788).

From Peter Carr

DEAR UNCLE   Williamsburg—March. 18—1788

Mr. Paradise being about to sail to Europe in a few days, furnishes me with an opportunity of informing you of my progress and situation. In my letter of the 10 December I acquainted you, that from the want of money I had been obliged to stay in Goochland, some time; soon after the date of that, I was fortunate enough to receive some, and return'd to this place immediately. Mr. Wythe advised me to begin the study of the Law, reading it two or three hours every day, and devoteing the rest of my time to the languages, history and Philosophy; but that you may know how I imploy every hour of the day I will give it you in detail. I rise about day, and take a walk of half an hour to shake off sleep, read law till breakfast, then attend Mr. Wythe till 12 oclock in the languages, read philosophy till dinner, history till night, and poetry till bed time. Mr. Paradise has lately presented me with the history of Greece by Gillies, together with Priestley's historical chart, each of which I shall endeavour to use in such manner as to merit them. The Books you mention in your letter to Mr. Wythe have never yet come to hand, when they do I hope to profit by those, which you mention are for me. My mother and family are well, and desire to be remembered to yourself and daughters. Accept of my sincere wishes for your health and welfare, and believe me to be your Dutiful and affectionate nephew, PETER CARR

RC (ViU); endorsed.

To Van Damme

ce 18me. Mars. 1788.

4184. Strabo. Lugduni. Gabr. Coterius. 1559. 2.vols. in 16s.

4771. Arrianus. Gr. Lat. Raphelii. Amstelodami. Wetstenii. 1757. 8vo.

4856. Appianus Alexandrinus. Gr. Lat. Tollii. Amstelod. 1670. 2.vols. 8vo.

4909. Savillii Commentarius in Taciti historias. Amstel. Elzevir. 1649. 12mo.

2092. Vitruvius Philandri &c. Amstelod. Elzevir. 1649. fol. 2. exemplaires.

2572. Aristophanes Gr. Lat. Scaligen et Fabri. Amstel. Ravestein. 1670. 16s.

1268.[1] Seneca philos. et Rhetor. 3.vols. 8vo. Elzevir. 1672.

1804. Celsus. 16s. Lugduni. Tornaesius. 1549. 1544.

Apicius Coelius de opsoniis. Listeri. Amstel. 8vo.

2683. Virgil. Sedani. 12mo. 1625.

4107. Alciphronis epistolae. Gr. Lat. 8vo. Lipsiae. 1715.

4109. Aristenaeti epistolae. Gr. Lat. Sambuci. Paris. 1610. 8vo.

4118. Plinii epistolae Elzevir. 1640. 12mo.

4122. Symmachi epistolae. Lugd. Batav. 1653. 12mo.

4123. Abelardi et Heloisae epistolae. Lond. 1718. 8vo.

163. Van Dale super Aristae

3362[2] Van Dale dissertationes. 4to.

Traduction des Annales Belgiques de Grotius, en Anglois, Italien ou Francois.

Morelli Dictionarium Graeco-Latino-Gallicum. petit in 8vo. 1. vol.

Dictionary. Dutch & English.

Monsieur Van Damme est prié de la part de Monsieur Jefferson de lui procurer les livres, et les editions notées ci-dessus, si cela se peut faire à des prix assez raisonables, et de les faire passer à Paris à son adresse, qu'il a l'honneur de mettre au bas de cette note.[3] Il lui fera toucher son argent toujours chez Messieurs Nicholas & Jacob Van Staphorsts, banquiers à Amsterdam.

les Numeros sont de Debeurre

RC (Meermanno-Westrenianum Museum, The Hague). PrC (DLC).

In a collection of trade cards, addresses, tavern bills, &c., accumulated during TJ's trip to Holland and Germany (MHi) there is a card in the hand of Van Damme which reads: "Addresse. Pr. van Damme, Libraire, A Amsterdam." LES NUMEROS . . . DEBEURRE: The numbers in TJ's list of books correspond to those in Guillaume-François De Bure, *Bibliographie Instructive: ou Traité de la connoissance des livres rares et singuliers,* 10 vol., Paris, 1763-82; his listing of the volumes desired is drawn in greatly abbreviated form from De Bure's descriptions of the volumes under these numbers. Several errors have been corrected below but variations in spelling have not been noted. In the RC there are check marks drawn before each of the numbers representing the volumes which were sent to TJ by Van Damme with his letter of 25 June 1788, q.v.

1 An error for De Bure No. 1288, which describes the edition of Seneca listed here.

2 Written below this number, in another hand, is the number "1743", and following the description, in the same hand, "Nm: 263" (the latter possibly referring to the number of the same item in a Van Damme catalogue);

neither No. 3362 nor No. 1743 in De Bure refers to Van Dale, but De Bure No. 5743 is a description of Van Dale, *Dissertationes de origine ac progressu Idololatrie & Superstitionum,* Amsterdam, 1696, 4to., which may have been the volume intended. However, the preceding item, "No. 163," is inserted in RC in TJ's hand in another ink and does not appear in PrC; therefore, this may be TJ's correction and clarification of the original listing, the entry for De Bure No. 163 being: "Antonii Van Dale Dissertatio super Aristea de LXX. Interpretibus. . . . *Amst. Wolters, 1705. in* 4°." This volume was sent to TJ in June 1788 and is the only work by Van Dale listed in the Library Catalogue, 1815.

3 At foot of text TJ wrote: "Monsieur Jefferson, ministre plenipotentiaire des etats unis d'Amerique à Paris."

From C. W. F. Dumas

MONSIEUR   La haie 18e. Mars 1788.

En réponse à l'obligeante Lettre de Votre Excellence, d'avanthier, je recevrai avec bien de la reconnoissance la Lettre qu'Elle me destine pour m'aider à tranquilliser ma famille; et après elle mon bonheur seroit complet, si les projets de Votre Excellence Lui permettent de repasser ici, et de me mettre par là à même de Lui présenter mon Epouse, et de lui faire entendre de sa bouche respectable la confirmation de ce qu'Elle voudra bien m'écrire là dessus. Indépendamment de la satisfaction personnelle que nous causeroit la présence de Votre Excellence, je m'intéresse trop à votre conservation et bien-être, Monsieur, pour Vous cacher la peine que me feroit de savoir Votre Excellence exposée dans un voyage, dont je connois parfaitement les routes dangereuses, pour avoir pensé y périr. Mauvaises en tout temps, elles sont affreuses dans cette saison. La débâcle du Rhin, tous les jours et subitement à craindre (or vous devez le passer entre Utrecht et Nimegue, et rouler ensuite sur une digue étroite, escarpée et mauvaise, et puis le passer encore à Dusseldorp et à Cologne) m'inquiète pour Votre Excellence. Quelleque soit après cela la résolution de Votre Excellence, et s'il étoit décidé que nous n'eussions pas la consolation, mon Epouse de faire votre connoissance, Monsieur, et moi de vous revoir, nous prions Dieu de vous prendre sous sa garde, et de vous accorder le voyage le moins incommode et le plus agréable possible.

[679]

Et je suis avec le plus respectueux dévouement, de Votre Excellence Le très-humble & très-obéissant serviteur,

C W F Dumas

RC (DLC); endorsed by TJ: "Dumas. recd Amstdm Mar [. . .]."

To Geismar

Amsterdam Mar. 18. 1788.

Having been called hither, my dear friend, by business, and being somewhat at liberty as to my return, I propose to go along the Rhine as far as Strasburg before I turn off to Paris. I shall be at Frankfort probably between the 1st. and 5th. of April. If your residence is still at Hanau, I know you will meet me at Frankfort. I shall be at the Rottinhouse tavern. As I may be a little earlier there, or a little later than I expect, if you will lodge there a note of your address, I will contrive to see you. This pleasure has had it's share in determining my return to Paris by this route, tho' I am very apprehensive you will have removed with your court from Hanau to Cassel. In that case I must fail in this effort to see you, and be contented to preserve for you in absence those sentiments of sincere attachment and esteem with which I am, my dear Sir Your affectionate friend & servant,   Th: Jefferson

PrC (DLC).

From John Paul Jones

Copenhagen, 18 Mch. 1788. Was presented at court the previous day by the French minister, La Houze, and had a "polite and distinguished reception"; talked with the queen, who has "a dignity of Person and deportment, which becomes her well, and which she has the secret to reconcile with great affability and ease"; the princess royal commands "that homage which artless Beauty and good nature will ever command." All members of the royal family spoke to him but the king, "who speaks to no person when presented"; the prince royal, who is "greatly beloved and extremely affable," asked pertinent questions about America; Jones was "invited to sup" with the royal family, ministers of state and foreign ambassadors. The report of the death of Dr. Franklin is generally believed and much lamented. "*I have had a second conference with the minister of foreign affairs but nothing is yet done. I will press him to conclude.*" Knows he made at least one mistake in the code of his last letter but has been so busy with his social engagements that he has not had time to compare the whole letter.

RC (CtY); 2 p.; endorsed in an un-identified hand, in part: "No. 82"; partly in code. Dupl (DLC: John Paul Jones Papers); the sentences written in code (italicized and quoted above) were decoded interlineally by TJ, employing Code No. 12 (see Jones to TJ, 20 Mch. 1788); printed in Sherburne, *John Paul Jones*, p. 292-3; *Dipl.Corr.*, *1783-1789*, III, 716-17.

DEATH OF DR. FRANKLIN: At this point in Dupl Jones placed an asterisk and then wrote in margin: "it is now happily contradicted."

William Short to John Jay

SIR   Paris March 18. 1788.

I have the honor of inclosing for your Excellency a letter forwarded to me here from Mr. Jefferson at Amsterdam. From it you will learn the cause of his journey to that place. It would be therefore impertinent in me to trouble you with a repetition of it. The same reason should induce me to be silent on the subject of the treaties which have been negotiating for some time between the United Provinces and Prussia and the same U.P. and England.— Mr. Jefferson being on the spot will probably give your Excellency much better and more recent information than I can. Many letters from Holland say that these treaties are signed and yet the Minister of foreign affairs affirmed the day before yesterday that he had recieved no account of it. There is no question that the treaty with Prussia is or will be very shortly completed. Yet that with England may very probably meet with obstacles. The possessions of the two nations in the East Indies is the ostensible difficulty. Yet there is another less in sight, but which perhaps has more weight. It is the influence of the court of Berlin in the United Provinces. It seems the policy of that court to prevent their High Mightinesses taking engagements with England and that for a variety of reasons which will naturally present themselves to your Excellency. But above all because whilst they hold Holland in their own hands and are at liberty to throw her either into the English or French scale, they are a power much more to be feared and consequently much more to be courted by France. And it is the friendship of France which Prussia must desire in the end, whatever imprudent measures she may have adopted from a momentary impulse. It is under this point of view that the treaty between the United Provinces and England may be considered as the thermometer by which to measure the future political relations between the courts of Berlin and Versailles. These considerations induce many people to suppose that if there is a treaty concluded between the United Provinces and England it will only be a formal one.

[681]

The war between the two empires and the Turks seems too far advanced at present to be stopped in its infancy. The Emperor has at length made a formal declaration of war and hostilities have immediately followed it. In the principal skirmish the Turks have been successful. Yet if it were possible that no other powers should interfere it would seem inevitable that they would be driven out of Europe. The two imperial armies are approaching Belgrade on one hand, and Oczakow on the other. It is supposed these two places must soon yield and then there will be nothing, if you except famine and the plague, to prevent the troops marching immediately to Constantinople.

The various reforms in the finances of this country are going on still, but with much less effect than had been at first hoped. It is found that Majesty and Ministry who are omnipotent in all other directions, become weak when opposed to the hydra of abuses. The suppressing an abuse in one department raises up two or three in another. And I am assured that some reforms have cost more than the abuse intended to be reformed. It is probably from taking articles of this sort into the account, that some calculators prove that the finances of France (supposing there should be no war and the present system should remain) will be in no better condition in the year 1791. than at present. The truth is that the finances of the Kingdom must necessarely be ameliorated though in a degree far inferior to the expectations of many. The assembly of the States general will form an aera from which we may count some stability in their finances. And then calculations may be made with certainty as to the time of the nations exonerating itself from debts and incumbrances which have forced it to submit to injuries and abandon its friends.

The Parliament of Paris presented to the King a few days ago their remonstrances which have been so long preparing against the use of *Lettres de cachet*. The banishment of the Duke of Orleans and two members of the Parliament are the ostensible motives of these remonstrances. But they take occasion to recall to the view of Majesty principles of justice and liberty which have been long lost sight of in most parts of Europe. These are seeds which are sown now, but will probably produce no fruit before the States general of the nation have ingrafted them on a constitution.

The result of the proceedings of the Council of war will be made public, it is said, in a few days. As yet it is not decided whether there will be a council of Marine. The Count de la Luzerne is against, the principal Minister for, it. If he insists, it must take place. Many think that it is already decided on. And a list of its members is handed about in public. But these members themselves, among whom are the Marquis de Bouillé and Marquis de la fayette, are not sure of its being true.

The arrêt of the King's council for the encouragement of American commerce has been violently attacked as your Excellency knows, and suffered a slight alteration. No other change I believe will be attempted. The extreme jealousy of the ministry with respect to our fisheries, is kept alive and augmented by some Americans settled at Dunkirk, who flatter them with the idea of employing seven thousand French fishermen in that business, provided a proper encouragement is given them, or in other words, provided other nations are properly discouraged. This hope will probably do injury to the American commerce without rendering service to the French fisheries.

The Packet boats between Havre and New-York will, it is thought, be discontinued. It is unquestionably the plan of the principal Minister at present, insomuch that I think this which sails the 25th. of the month will be the last. The expence which accrues on their account is given as the reason.

I heard yesterday that a person of the name of Cezaux, who had considerable demands against Congress for supplies furnished in Canada, is publishing a memorial in which he intends to accuse them of a want of good faith. His object, it is said, in this publication is to interest the French Ministry in his behalf, and to endeavour to get them to be a kind of security to him for the repayment of his advances. This is the account given me by a friend of the advocate employed to draw up the memorial, and who, he says, had a good deal of conversation with Mr. Jefferson on the subject before his departure for Holland. Mr. Jefferson never mentioned any thing to me on the subject, so that I know not what credit is due to the information given me. Still however as such a memorial might make an unfavorable impression with those who read little and think less I have desired it might be suspended until the return of Mr. Jefferson. My informant promised me he would endeavour to have it done.

I have been in some measure emboldened to trouble your Excellency with so long a letter, by the goodness with which you were pleased to answer a former one. I will only add to this at present by begging you to be assured of the happiness it will afford me to be honored Sir with any communications, or orders you may please to give me. I have the honor to be with sentiments of the most profound respect Your Excellency's most obedient & most humble servant,

W: SHORT

RC (DNA: PCC, No. 87, II).

From Collow Frères, Carmichael & Co.

Le Havre, 19 Mch. 1788. The ship *Portsmouth*, Capt. Oldner, arrived with tobacco from Virginia the previous night and will proceed to Dunkirk immediately to unload, "Tide Wind and Weather permitting"; the wine for Mr. Donald will be sent by the vessel since she will return to Virginia immediately. Have written to Limozin about the bust of Lafayette but it has not yet arrived. There are some trees for TJ on board the *Portsmouth* directed to the care of Limozin; enclose two letters which also arrived on that ship; any letters to be sent to America on her return voyage may be addressed to Debacque Frères at Dunkirk.

RC (MHi); 3 p. The enclosed letters have not been identified.

From Collow Frères, Carmichael & Co.

Le Havre, 20 Mch. 1788. Patrick Parker, a passenger on the *Portsmouth*, has just delivered the two enclosed letters. Mr. Limozin had been informed by several messages of the necessity of taking the trees for TJ from the *Portsmouth* during the day because the ship would sail in the evening; they would have landed the trees themselves if they had not thought Limozin would consider their interference officious. In the evening the captain sent a message that the trees were still on board and that "the Ship was laying on the ground heeling so much that they could not be got at." When the ship floated it was so dark, no lights being allowed in the harbor, that the trees could not be obtained. Limozin then took the pilot, who was to carry her out to sea, out of the ship, "telling him the Trees belonged to the King and that he would have him punished if he dared to carry the Ship away." They were forced to protest the detention because of their duty to Mr. Donald, and Limozin was "obliged to explain the Matter to the Pilot, well knowing that he must have been answerable for the Consequences which were likely to ensue from a full loaded Ship laying with her Topmast up, another Tide upon the Ground." Fearing, from Limozin's "abusive Language," that he will prejudice TJ by a different representation, they are troubling TJ with the true account. Captain Oldner will forward the trees from Dunkirk; the wine for Mr. Donald has been shipped and bill of lading is enclosed; if TJ will send the amount of his expenses in connection with this transaction, they will reimburse him.

RC (MHi); 4 p.; endorsed. Enclosures not found.

[684]

From John Paul Jones

Sir   Copenhagen March 20. 1788.

I embrace the occasion of a young Gentleman, just arrived here Express from St. Petersburg, and who sets out immediately Express for Paris, to transmit you the foregoing Copy of my last of the 18th. I have written to *Norway*[1] and expect a satisfactory Answer. *The minister of France is surprised to have had no object from Versailles respecting me.* I pray you and so does *he* to push that point immediately. *The minister of foreign affairs will receive me on Saturday.* Please to present my kind compliments to *Littlepage*. If there is any thing new from that quarter, you will no doubt communicate it.

I am sincerely, Yours in haste,   PAUL JONES

NB. The Cyphers in the Original Letters are all corrected in the Copys, and the Numbers that were at first erronious, are now *underlined*.

RC (DLC: John Paul Jones Papers); partly in code. Although this letter has the word "Copy," in Jones' hand, at the head of the text, as do the duplicates of his letters to TJ of 11 and 18 Mch. 1788 which are written on the same sheet as the above, it is probable that this is the only copy of the letter of this date sent to TJ.
THE OCCASION . . . FOR PARIS: Jones' letter of 25 Mch. 1788, q.v., is written on the same sheet of paper as the above. It is probable therefore that before

Jones sent this letter and the copies of his letters of 11 and 18 Mch. he received information from Paris that TJ had gone to Amsterdam and therefore transmitted this letter with his letter of 25 Mch.

[1] This and the following words in italics, with the exception of "underlined" in the postscript, which is underscored, are written in code and were decoded interlineally by TJ, employing Code No. 12.

From Thomas Mann Randolph, Jr.

[*20 Mch. 1788.* Recorded in SJL Index. Not found.]

From François Boissel

MONSIEUR   Le 21 Mars 1788.

J'ay Lu, dans L'introduction de L'importance des opinions religieuse de M. Neker, que la philosophie d'àprésent s'occuppoit de la recherche des moyens de s'assurer si les hommes ne pourroient pas se bien conduire et se très bien gouverner, sans aucun espèce de Culte, ni prêtres, ni Eglises, ni temple par conséquent.

[685]

Et hier, au soir, un vieux Anglais m'apprit au licée que, dans une des provinces des etats unis de l'amérique, qu'il m'a nommé, si je m'en souviens bien, la Virginie, ces moyens étoient deja mis en pratique et que touttes les Eglises, les temples, les maisons des ministres tomboient en ruine. Cet anglais même me demanda mon avis sur cette question, comme partie intéressée, à Ce qu'il m'a paru, en présence de plusieurs jeunes abbés. Ce qui m'obligea de Luy répondre que comme Chrétien je devois penser pour la Néga-tive; mais que la philosophie d'aujourdhui avoit de puissantes raisons pour L'affirmative.

Comme vous êtes, Monsieur, le député de Ces etats dont la position, quelque Critique qu'elle soit, me paroit infiniment plus heureuse que Celles des peuples de touttes Les autres parties du globe terrestre, à Cause qu'elle Les rend maîtres de profiter de plus de soixante siècles d'expériences et de touttes Les Lumières acquises pour s'établir un ordre moral ou social dont Les fonde-ments ne seront point assis, Comme les Nôtres, sur les erreurs, les impostures, la Férocité, la superstition, les fictions, les révélations; les visions, la Stupidité, les Chimères, l'orgueil, la bassesse, et l'Egoïsme du fanatisme oriental, mais bien mieux sur les vérités que L'expérience de tant de siècles, ont dû nous faire acquérir, dans la morale comme dans la phisique. Je vous supplie, Monsieur, d'aggréér L'offre que j'ay L'honneur de vous Faire d'un manuscrit pour en prendre Copie, essentiellement rélatif à la position actuelle des etats unis et aux intérêts Les plus précieux de votre Nation, Comme de la nôtre qui n'a pas Le même Bonheur de La Liberté du choix du bien et du mal.

Je vous supplie de Croire, Monsieur, que je n'ai d'autre vüe, dans Cette offre, que de vous mettre à même d'accélérer l'établissement d'un ordre, dans votre patrie, qui la mettra à Couvert pour jamais des maux qui ont désolé et désolent Encore touts Les peuples, même les plus Eclairés, par une suite nécessaire de L'ordre mer-cenaire et homicide, originairement établi par Les imposteurs de L'orient. La grâce que je vous demande, Monsieur, C'est de me garder le Secrèt et de charger la personne que vous envoyez chéz moy, de me donner un Reçu de mon manuscrit, signé de votre main.

J'ay L'honneur d'etre très Respectueusement, Monsieur, Votre tres humble et tres obeissant serviteur,   BOISSEL
        paris rüe Baillif maison de Made. tramblon au 3e.

RC (DLC); endorsed. There is no indication that TJ an-swered this letter or that Boissel ever wrote to him again. Boissel published

Le Catechisme du Genre Humain (Paris, 1789) which argued for an egalitarian society to be achieved by a general revision of methods of education which, beginning in infancy, would condition the citizen against tyranny imposed by aristocracy, priestcraft, or the civil magistracy. In a note by the author published in the second edition (Paris, 1792), Boissel wrote: "Cet ouvrage fut mis à l'impression trois mois avant l'enlèvement de la bastille. Puissance du ciel, qui venoit d'affranchir la nation françoise du plus honteux esclavage et des persecutions infernales des monstres de l'humanité, ses tyrans, achevez votre ouvrage; que ce triomphe, pour sa liberté, ne soit pas séparé du triomphe de la véritable lumière, sans laquelle l'homme ne sauroit en faire usage que pour son malheur!"

To Van Damme

Vendredi. 21. Mars. 1788.

M. Jefferson prie M. Van Damme d'ajouter encore à sa catalogue

1788. Hippocratis opera omnia. Gr. Lat. Van der Linden. 2. vols. 8vo. Lugdun. Batav. 1665.

Mr. Jefferson ne partira pas d'Amsterdam avant le Mardi prochain. Il sera charmé de scavoir quel progrès M. Van Damme aura fait dans ses recherches pour les livres dont M. Jefferson lui a donné la catalogue.

RC (Universiteits-Bibliotheek, Amsterdam); addressed.

This note supplements TJ's letter to Van Damme, 18 Mch. 1788, q.v.; a full description of this volume is found in De Bure, No. 1788, where it is described as being rare and much sought after. This item was included in the books sent with Van Damme's letter of 25 June 1788, q.v.

From La Boullaye

Paris, 22 Mch. 1788. Acknowledges TJ's letter of 18 Feb. 1788; is pleased to inform him that, after consultation with the controller general, Barrett's request for refund of extra duties paid on oil imported into France will be granted, and that this decision has been communicated to the farmers-general.

RC (DLC); 1 p.; in French.

From Francis Coffyn

Dunkirk, 23 Mch. 1788. Informs TJ of the arrival of the ship *Portsmouth,* "on board of which Coll. Banister of James River near Petersburg, ship'd four Cases young Trees," which were assigned to Limozin at Le Havre but could not be unloaded there because of the short time the ship stayed in that port; will take the trees to his house to await

TJ's orders; fears it would be dangerous to ship them by land; suggests sending them to Rouen to be forwarded from there by water.

RC (MHi); 2 p.; endorsed.

To Van Damme

23me. Mars 1788.

Vol. 1.

pa. 7. Admiranda narratio &c. Virginiae. a Thomâ Harriot. fol.

9. Aesopi Phaedri, Aviani, Abstemii fabulae. Gr. Lat. Francofurti. 1610. 8vo.[1]

52. Bentivoglio della guerra di Fiandra. Cologna. Elzevir. 1635. 3.v. 12mo.

56. Biblia Tremellii et Junii et Testam. novum Bezae. Amstel. 1628. 12mo.

150. Dictionarium Latino-Graeco-Gallicum Morelli 8vo. (c'est le meme qui est mis sur l'autre catalogue)

157. Diodorus Siculus. Graecé. Basileae. 1539. 8vo.

215. Frontini stratagematum. Lugd. Bat. 1675. 12mo. Frontino. Astutie militare. Venetia. 1537. 12mo.

220. Gellii Noctes Atticae. Elzevir. 12mo.

233. Grotii Mare Liberum. Lugd. Bat. 1633. in 16s.

237. Halicarnessei (Dionysii) antiquitates. Lugd. 1555. 2.v. p. in 12.

282. Historia delle guerre esterne de Romani d'Appiano Alessandrino. in 12.

284. Hobbes de cive. Elzevir. 1669. 12mo.

292. Hippocratis aphorismi cum Celsi sententiis. Lugd. Bat. 1732. in 16s.

310. Juliani opera. 1583. 8vo.

Vol. 2.

pa. 29. Lucretius. Amstel. 1626. in 16.

72. Miscellaneous works of Middleton. 5.vols. 8vo.

84. Neubrigientis (Gulielemi) rerum Anglicarum. Antverp. 1567. 8vo.

111. Orang Outang by Tyson. 4to.

148. Polybius. Lugd. 1548. p. in 12.

217. Seldeni mare clausum. Elzevir. 1636. in 12.

223. S'il est permis de faire arreter un Ambassadeur &c. 1745. p. in 4to.

235. Strada de Bello Belgico. Romae 1648. 2. vol. in 12.

237. Suetonius cum notis diversorum. Amstel. 1700. in 16. ou celui de Pontanus Amstel. 1627. in 16. s'il est plus beau.

287. Vetus testamentum graecum. Cantab. 1666. 12mo.

303. Voyage d'un Francois exilé pour la religion dans la Virginie et Marilan. 1687. in 12.

304. Voiage de la Louisiane. par le p. Laval. 4to.

307. Les voiages de la Nouvelle France par le Sr. de Champlain. 1632. 4to.

M. Jefferson prie M. Van Damme de lui procurer encore les livres ci-dessus qu'il a trouvé sur la catalogue que M. Van Damme lui avoit preté. Il souhaiteroit aussi d'acheter une exemplaire de la catalogue. Il seroit bien aise de voir cette collection s'il etoit possible, parce qu'il trouve sur la collection encore d'autres livres, qu'il lui faudroit voir pour se decider de leur achat.

RC (Meermanno-Westrenianum Museum, The Hague); addressed. PrC (DLC).

The catalogue to which this letter refers has not been identified further than that it was for a collection of books which was to be sold at public sale the following September. There are check marks in the margin of RC before page numbers 215, 220, 233, 284, 292 of vol. 1, and 217, 235 of vol. 2; these items were sent to TJ with Van Damme's letter of 25 June 1788, q.v.

[1] PrC has the following written between page references 9 and 52; this item is deleted in RC: "18. Anacreonte. Gr. Lat. Ital. Venezia 1736. 4to."

From C. W. F. Dumas

The Hague, 23 Mch. 1788. Hopes TJ received the last letter he forwarded from Paris; saw Adams when he passed through The Hague again and learned through him of Adams' and TJ's kindness in arranging for the payment by the U.S. bankers in Amsterdam of the arrears in funds due him; the Van Staphorsts have just confirmed this information. Has attached to the enclosed letter for the U.S. foreign office a statement of his account and sends a duplicate of the account for TJ. Understands that TJ's journey to Germany is certain; is distressed that he will be deprived of seeing TJ again; had hoped that personal acquaintance with TJ would induce Dumas' wife to forgive him for all she had suffered in their troubled situation; hopes for the restoration of her health which has been disturbed by a nervous ailment; is counting on the letter which TJ has promised which he hopes will console her; hopes TJ has a pleasant journey.

RC (DLC); 2 p.; in French; endorsed by TJ: "Dumas. recd at Amstdm. Mar. 27." FC (Rijksarchief, The Hague, Dumas Letter Books; photostats in DLC); varies slightly in phrasing from RC. Enclosure: Dumas to John Jay, 23 Mch., informing Jay that TJ and Adams had made provision for payment of the arrears due him, and enclosing a statement of his account (the letter to Jay is printed in translation in *Dipl. Corr., 1783-89*, III, 611; the enclosed statement of account has not been found).

From John Paul Jones

Copenhagen, 25 Mch. 1788. Is sending the present letter in care of the Van Staphorsts at Amsterdam. "My mission here is not yet at an end, but the minister has promised to determine soon and I have wrote to claim that promise."[1] Before receiving this letter TJ will have been informed by Simolin that TJ's "proposal to him, and his application on that Idea, have been well received." Jones has received a flattering letter from Baron de Krudener on this matter; there "seems, however, to remain some difficulty respecting the *letter* of Monsieur de Simolin's proposal though it is accepted, *in Substance*, with an appearance of great Satisfaction." He finds it necessary to depart directly for Petersburg, through Sweden; future letters should be sent to the French minister there or given to Simolin, whom he thanks for his good offices; is also grateful to Littlepage.

RC (DLC: John Paul Jones Papers); 2 p.; written on the same sheet as Jones to TJ, 20 Mch., q.v.; partly in code; full text printed in Sherburne, *John Paul Jones,* p. 293-4.

[1] This sentence is written in code and was decoded interlineally by TJ, employing Code No. 12.

From La Blancherie

MONSIEUR   Paris 25 mars 1788.

J'eus l'honneur de vous écrire dernierement pour savoir si vous voudriez bien vous charger de faire passer un pacquet qui m'avait été remis, à M. franklin. J'ai trouvé une occasion pour le lui faire parvenir avec la Collection des feuilles de cette année dont je lui fais l'hommage. L'Etablissement, l'ayant eu pour juge et ayant obtenu son approbation publique; J'ai pensé que vous ne trouveriez pas mauvais que je lui en fisse passer la suite sous votre adresse. Dans le cas où cela serait indiscret, je vous prie de m'en faire donner avis et j'userai d'une autre voye. Il m'est venu dernièrement d'Angleterre des titres de Livres nouveaux, parmi lesquels j'en trouve un Sur la Virginie ayant pour auteur *Son Excellence Monsieur Jefferson.* Si, comme je le suppose, vous êtes cet Auteur, Je Supplie votre Excellence de vouloir bien me confier pour quelques instans un exemplaire de cet ouvrage afin que j'en fasse rendre Compte dans la feuille. Je serai Charmé d'avoir Cette occasion de vous rendre un hommage public. Permettez encore que je vous prie de me faire savoir si vous avez reçû de M. Adams une réponse relative à ce qu'il doit à l'Etablissement de la Correspondance. Les Nouvelles d'Angleterre m'apprennent qu'il part bientôt pour l'Amérique. Il serait plus commode pour nous de terminer pendant qu'il est dans nos contrées. Je puis lui faire présenter Son engagement à Londres et faire tirer une lettre de Change sur lui, moyen que plusieurs associés m'ont déjà indiqué. Etant obligé de rendre mes Comptes pour les Années passées, je serais répréhensible du déficit qu'on remarquerait à l'article de M. Adams, car il ne pourrait être attribué qu'à mon insouciance pour réclamer la bagatelle dont il est redevable.

Je Suis avec Respect Monsieur Votre très humble et très Obéissant Serviteur, La Blancherie

RC (DLC); endorsed.

From Stephen Cathalan, Sr.

Marseilles, 26 Mch. 1788. Has received TJ's letters of 3 and 4 Mch.; hopes TJ has safely returned from Holland; is surprised the oil has not arrived; thanks TJ for paying Lambert. Bernard of the observatory has sent meteorological observations covering seven years, in accordance with TJ's wishes; they have been given to John Turnbull, who will be in Paris about 15 Apr. Bernard has left to Cathalan's discretion what is to be paid the copyist; he, not knowing what is reasonable, will leave the determination to TJ but suggests 5 Louis, part of which, he assumes, will go to Bernard. The arrêt of 29 Dec. 1787 has not been registered and the farmers-general have not been officially informed of it, though it has been published in all the newspapers. Has not sold one barrel of fish oil and fears it "will be a bad affair"; as for tobacco, the farmers have said nothing and they pay very little attention to Lambert's letter; however, they "must soon prove the purchase of 4666 hhgs."; most of the tobacco in northern ports has been sold for exportation so it is expected the farmers will be obliged, in the next four months, to buy all the 1350 hhds. here; hopes TJ will push the farmers, in the next month, to show their purchases since 1 Jan. The price of wheat in America is encouraging for shipment to the Mediterranean; this will necessitate protection against the Algerines; Philadelphia or New York wheat would now bring 28^{tt} for 250 lbs.; the farmers would pay 33^{tt} for Virginia wheat delivered at Cette but the holders want more. Has no news from Barclay; Cathalan's family present their respects to TJ.

RC (DLC); 4 p.; in the hand of Stephen Cathalan, Jr., signed by his father; endorsed.
No letter from TJ to Cathalan of 4 Mch. has been found nor is a letter of this date recorded in SJL Index.

From Geismar

à Hanau Ce 26 de Mars 1788

L'expression, Mon Cher Ami, est au dessus de ce que je sens du plaisir de Vous revoir. Je me réserve donc tout à notre entrevue,

[691]

persuadé que la Main Serrée de l'Ami sincèr dis plus que toutes les plumes de l'univers peuvent exprimer. J'ai donné ordre à l'aubergiste de la Maison rouge qui Vous remettra celle-ci de m'avertir d'abord de Votre arrivée. Si donc Vous voullés me dire quelques Mots, donnés les à Lui et il me les remettra, ou par une Occasion ou par estaffette, et peu de Moments après Vous me verrés à Vous témoigner de bouche les Sentiments d'Amitié qui me lient à Vous. LE MAJOR DE GEISMAR

RC (DLC); endorsed by TJ: "Geismar recd at Frankfort."

On a separate sheet (DLC) there is the following address, in Geismar's hand: "A Monsieur Monsieur le Baron de Geismar Capitaine et gentilhomme de la Cour au Service de S: A: Sme. Monseigneur le Land Grave et Prince Hereditaire de Hesse Cassel à Hanau pres Francfort sur le Main." This slip of paper was probably left with the above letter for the instruction of the innkeeper in summoning Geismar on TJ's arrival.

To John Paul Jones

SIR   Amsterdam Mar. 27. 1788.

I arrived at this place on the 10th. inst. and expected to have staid here a week only. Since the expiration of that week I have been in constant expectation of leaving it within 2. or 3. days. Such is my expectation at this moment; so that any letter you may be so good as to write me after the receipt of this will find me at Paris. Any one written before that will be unanswered till I get back. I wish I had known on my arrival here that I should have staid so long, as I might have written to you and got an answer here.

The January French packet and February English one being still due we have no news from America later than the 16th. of January. Our information is not sure that the Count de Moustier had then arrived there. Such a report has gone about. The January French packet was not arrived at Havre on the 17th. of March, when she should have been out eight weeks. There has been a rise lately of 10. per cent in the English bank stock. I do not know whether it has extended to other stock. The government of that country refuse to receive or furnish refreshment to the Russian squadron destined for the Mediterranean. I am with very great esteem Sir Your most obedient humble servt,

TH: JEFFERSON

PrC (DLC).

To André Limozin

SIR   Amsterdam Mar. 27. 1788.

Messieurs Van Staphorst will forward from this place to Havre two boxes for me, which I have taken the liberty of addressing to your care. One contains iron ware which cost here 13. gilders, and I suppose must pay duties accordingly. The other contains cups for tea, coffee and chocolate of East India porcelaine. This being prohibited, I must leave to you the method of conveying it to my house at Paris, either over the walls of your town or through them as you see best. I could obtain a passport for it, but it is too small an object to trouble the minister on, having cost here only 24 gilders. If it could pass by paiment of duties, I should pay them cheerfully: but I apprehend it is prohibited altogether. Perhaps it could be reported as glass or some other dutied article.

My absence from Paris will be longer than I expected. It will still be a month before I shall be there. In the mean time should any plants arrive for me, be so good as to forward them on to Mr. Short either by the Diligence or the roulier according to their size. I have the honour to be with much esteem Sir Your most obedient humble servt,   TH: JEFFERSON

PrC (MHi).

To John Trumbull

DEAR SIR   Amsterdam Mar. 27. 1788.

I wrote you a line just as I was taking wing from Paris for this place. I expected to have staid here a week, and have been here three already, and know not yet the term of my stay. I hope however to get away in three or four days. I intend to make my return somewhat circuitous, in order to see what I have not yet seen. This renders the moment of my arrival at Paris incertain. In the mean while, the little balances I expected you would receive for me turning out less than I had calculated, you will be so good as to take one half of the inclosed bill of exchange to be applied as wanting to the purposes I had troubled you with. The other half, being £15. I will beg the favor of you to pay for me to Mr. Stockdale on account, letting him know at the same time that any letters he may have written to me since the last of February will be unanswered till I get back. The substantial answer however is that which you will give him as above desired.

[693]

Will you consult with some Amateur in classical reading to know who is the bookseller for classical authors in London, the most curious and copious, of whom one may get the particular editions they would wish, and send me his address? Give my love to Mrs. Church and Mrs. Cosway. Tell them they will travel with me up the Rhine, one on each hand, and for this I shall be indebted, not to any goodness of theirs, but to my own imagination, which helps me on cheerily over the dull roads of this world. God bless them and you, and Adieu. Yours affectionately,

TH: JEFFERSON

P.S. I must trouble you to send me from Mr. Woodmason 2. sets of wetting and drying books, 2 brushes and a ream of quarto copying paper of the best quality. Be so good as to notify it to Mr. Short that he may have it demanded at the bureau of the Diligence.

PrC (DLC). PrC of a Dupl (DLC); at head of text in TJ's hand: "Copy."

The two SETS OF WETTING AND DRYING BOOKS were for use in connection with TJ's copying press. Both were made up of coarse blotting paper, the former for moistening with BRUSHES so that, when a sheet of the thin COPYING PAPER was placed in contact with the letter or document being copied and both were inserted between the leaves of the WETTING BOOK, a reverse offset impression resulted from the moisture and pressure; this impression could be read *through* the copying paper. The DRYING BOOKS were for removing most of the moisture that the letter copied had absorbed in the process, so that it could be folded, sealed, and posted. With the introduction of envelopes the need for the drying book was eliminated.—The original of this letter was sent through the Van Staphorsts and was returned because of insufficient address. Trumbull wrote TJ on 23 May that he had not received it and TJ forwarded a duplicate in his reply of 28 May 1788. Trumbull received the original and its enclosed BILL OF EXCHANGE on 20 June 1788. What appears to be a duplicate of the bill of exchange—"Second of Exchange (first not paid)"—is in DLC: TJ Papers, 38:6549; it is signed "Nic & Jac. van [Staphorst]," dated 28 Mch. 1788, and drawn in favor of TJ for £30 sterling on Messrs. Charles Herries & Co. of London, being endorsed by TJ in Trumbull's favor and having the signature cancelled by being torn away. Its presence in TJ Papers indicates that the "First of Exchange" was paid and was evidently the one enclosed in the present letter; see TJ's Account Book, 28 Mch. 1788.

From Bourdon des Planches

[*Paris*] *29 Mch. 1788.* Transmits letters from the son of the late Comte de Grasse to George Washington and the President of Congress requesting that he be admitted to the Society of the Cincinnati; has no doubt this request will be granted if TJ will attach to these letters a word of recommendation; wishes to take the occasion, also, to recall to TJ's memory a request of his own to Congress in Dec. 1786; not having received a reply, fears his request has gone astray; in spite of the gratification an award of his claim would give, does not wish TJ to take up the matter unless there is a possibility of a favorable result.

RC (DLC); 4 p.; in French; endorsed. The enclosed letter from De Grasse to Washington, 11 Mch. 1788, telling of his father's death and asking that he be permitted to assume the honor conferred on his father of membership in the Society of the Cincinnati, is printed in *General Washington's Correspondence concerning The Society of the Cincinnati*, ed. Hume, Baltimore, 1941, p. 324; the letter to the president of Congress has not been found.

For Bourdon des Planches' request of Congress in Dec. 1786, see his letter to TJ, 10 Aug. 1787; George Washington to Bourdon, 8 Jan. 1788 (*Writings*, ed. Fitzpatrick, XXIX, 363).

To C. W. F. Dumas

SIR   Paris[1] Mar. 29. 1788

I have now to acknolege the receipt of your favors of the 14th. 18th. and 23d. inst. I would have preferred doing it in person, but the season and the desire of seeing what I have not yet seen invite me to take the route of the Rhine. I shall leave this place tomorrow morning and probably not reach Paris till the latter end of April. In the moment we were to have conferred on the subject of paying the arrears due to you, a letter of the 20th. of Feb. from the board of treasury was received forbidding the application of money to any purpose (except our current salaries) till June interest should be actually in hand. Being by this letter tied up from giving an order in your favor, I return you the letter you had written Mr. Jay on the supposition that the order for your arrears was given. It has been suggested however that if you could receive bonds of the loan, you could make them answer your purpose, and the Commissioners say this would in no wise interfere with the views of the Treasury board nor the provision for the June interest. I have therefore recommended to them in writing to give you bonds to the amount of your balance if you chuse to take them rather than to wait. I wish th[is] may answer your purpose. I remember that in the conversation which I had the honor of having with you the evening I was at the Hague, you said that your enemies had endeavoured to have [it] believed that Congress would abandon you and withdraw your appointments. An enemy generally sais and believes what he wishes, and your enemies particularly are not those who are most in the councils of Congress, nor the best qualified to tell what Congress will do. From the evidence you have received of their approbation, and from their well known steadiness and justice, you might be assured of a continuance of their favour were they to continue under their present form. Nor do I see any thing in the new government which threatens us with less [firm]-

[695]

ness. The Senate who will make and remove their foreign officers must from it's constitution be a wise and steady body. Nor would a new government begin it's administration by discarding old servants; servants who have put all to the risque, and when the risque was great to obtain that freedom and security under which themselves will be what they shall be. Upon the whole, my dear Sir, tranquillize yourself and your family upon this subject. All the evidence which exists as yet authorizes you to do this, nor can I foresee any cause of disquiet in future. That none may arise, that yourself and family may enjoy health, happiness and the continued approbation of those by whom you wish most to be approved is the sincere wish of him who has the honour to be with sentiments of sincere esteem & attachm[ent] Sir Your most obedient & most humble servant, TH: JEFFERSON

PrC (DLC). Enclosure: Dumas to John Jay, 23 Mch. 1788, enclosed in Dumas to TJ of that date, q.v.

1 Thus in MS.

To William Short

DEAR SIR   Amsterdam Mar. 29. 1788.

I have received from you three letters of Mar. 9. 14. and 17. and written you two of the 10th. and 13th. In the last I mentioned to you that I should leave this place the 19th. but I have been drawn on from day to day by the hope of seeing the business on which I came settled on the basis of positive engagement: and the great object of the month of June appeared so sure that we were about proceeding to immediate paiment of Mr. Grand, the state of Virginia and all smaller claims, when a letter of the 20th. of Feb. from the Commissioners of the Treasury arrived forbidding the application of money to any object (except the diplomatic expences) till the cash for the June interest was actually in hand. No room was left for the bankers to exercise their discretion. The consequence is a delay of all other objects for some weeks, which probably might have been effected instantly without danger to the great one. Indeed I had obtained a positive engagement on that ground. Be so good as to communicate thus much to Mr. Grand.

A letter from Mr. Van Berkel at New York confirms the arrival of the Count de Moustier there on the 18th. of January, and removes all suspense and anxiety on that subject. You know we received a similar account the day before I left Paris which I communicated to M. de Monmorin. It is with infinite affliction that I recollect in the hurry of my departure to have omitted to notify the same to M. Dupont, who had a son embarked in the same bottom. I am haunted with this recollection, and would beg either yourself or Mr. Grand, whichever sees M. Dupont first to let him know that it was neither want of attention nor attachment to him which occasioned it to escape me, but the confusion which attended the setting out on such a journey on so short notice.

I set out tomorrow for Utrecht, Nimeguen &c. and shall pursue the course of the Rhine as far as the roads will permit me, not exceeding Strasburg. Whenever they become impassable or too difficult, if they do become so, I shall turn off to Paris. So also if any thing of importance should call for me at Paris, sooner, you will be so good as to address to me at Francfort and Strasburg poste restante. I will call at the post offices there and be happy to find news from you relative to yourself, my daughters and America. I shall be at Franckfort about the 8th. of April and at Strasburg about the 15th. You shall hear from me on the road.

I inclose you a bill for an hundred Louis. Be so good as to take out of it 600.^{tt} or any other sum you want, and to give the balance to Petit with instructions to pay 600.^{tt} to Panthemont, 60.^{tt} more to my daughter and to apply the rest to the servants' wages and current expences. A quarter's rent (1875.^{tt}) will become due on the 15th. If I should not be arrived when the Ct. de Langeac applies for it, be so good as to desire Mr. Grand to do me the favor to pay it, and I will replace it by my draught on Amsterdam at the end of the month.

My friend Bannister must have been negligent if his plants are not arriving by this time. I have written from hence to Limozin to send them on by the roulier or Diligence the moment they arrive. You will be so good as to mention this to Madame de Tessé, with my respects to her and Made. de Tott. Some few of the plants and seeds I intended for another friend, but it is impossible for me to direct any partition from hence. Therefore I shall present a claim to Made. de Tessé in the autumn. Perhaps Bannister's failure altogether will save her that trouble. Adieu. Yours affectionately,

TH: JEFFERSON

RC (ViW); endorsed. PrC (DLC). Enclosure not found.
I HAVE WRITTEN ... TO LIMOZIN: See TJ to Limozin, 27 Mch. 1788.

[697]

To the Commissioners of the Treasury

GENTLEMEN   Amsterdam Mar. 29. 1788.

Mr. Adams having notified our bankers here of his approaching return to America, and referred them to consult with me in their future difficulties, they, on the receipt of your letter wherein you informed them that your sole reliance for the June interest was on the progress of the late loan, inclosed me a copy of that letter, informing me at the same time that the loan had ceased to get forward, and desired me to say what could be done. They continued to press this matter on me, and they communicated to me a copy of the proposition they had conveyed to you which was that certain persons who had purchased up a part of our domestic liquidated debt would furnish the balance of our last foreign loan on condition they might retain out of it one year's interest of their liquidated stock. So far I had the honour, in my last letter of stating this matter to you as the only persons competent to decide on the proposition. But as your decision might be against it, or might come too late, the bankers urged that something should be determined here. One thing I could easily determine which was that the proposition was totally out of my province. I was filled with anxiety however at the approaching crisis which they announced to be insuperable in any other way. Hearing therefore that Mr. Adams was come to the Hague to take leave, I set out immediately for that place to get him to come on here and join in conferences with the bankers to see what could be done to set the loan in motion again. We came here and our first object was to convince them there was no power on this side the Atlantic to accede to that proposition. At length we prevailed to get them and the brokers to abandon this idea. It would be tedious to give you the details of what passed. It was agreed to push the loan on other grounds. But this appeared not enough. Your letter looked forward to the new government as the only resource for remittance. It was evident that for that to be adopted, it's legislature assembled, system of taxation established, the collection made and remitted, neither this year nor the next would suffice; and that to place the government perfectly at it's ease till this process could be gone through, the years 1789. and 1790. should be provided for as to all our European demands. You will perceive by the inclosed estimate that this will require another million of florins. The bankers joined us in opinion therefore that as Mr. Adams's powers to borrow had not been revoked, he should execute bonds for another million, which should be kept up till the ratification of Congress could be received. This being done, Mr. Adams was obliged to return to England, having first concurred in the absolute necessity of paying Fizeaux demand as the first measure which could give a new spring to our credit. This was paid on the spot therefore, and the bankers and brokers thought that if I waited a few days I might see the effect of this and perhaps aid it. I have now waited twelve days since the departure of Mr. Adams; and tho' the success of this measure has not been as great as was hoped, yet both bankers and brokers from what they learn upon change are become well enough satisfied that the month of June will be provided for. So much so indeed that it was in contemplation to pay out of the monies now on hand, the 2d. to the 7th. articles inclusive of the inclosed estimate, amounting to about 52,000 florins: and we were yesterday to have conferred on this question Whether this paiment could be made without endangering the June demand? One of the houses, and the brokers had given it as their opinion it might be done without danger, and indeed a principal broker had promised me he would raise the money for June on his own account if it should not be raised by the sale of bonds. The other house was hesitating, and your letter of Feb. 20. arrived in the morning of yesterday in time to decide the point, as in that you expressly forbid the applying money to any other purpose till the June interest be provided for. We all hope the delay will not be great. The 2d. article I had before explained to you. You had authorised me as to the 3d. to assure Mr. Grand his advances should be replaced as soon as the bankers should be in condition to do it. The 4th. 5th. 6th. and 7th. articles speak for themselves. As to the last indeed the bankers are of opinion Mr. Dumas will take bonds in lieu of money, as he can obtain it on them from his friends, and that his circumstances absolutely require it; that of course he can be relieved without affecting the object of your instructions, and on this hypothesis I can but think he should be paid with bonds if he will take them. With respect to the 8th. and 9th. articles you will be pleased to consider whether you will order them to take place as soon as the June interest and all the other articles here placed to the year 1788 are secured. I can take no step as to our captives till the money shall be in the hands of such banker as the persons to be employed in the negotiation shall have full confidence in. I shall set out from this place tomorrow, and pursue your future orders as to this last subject, whenever received.

I cannot close my letter without some observations on the transfer of our domestic debt to foreigners. This circumstance together with the failure to pay off Fizeaux loan were the sole causes of the stagnation of our late loan, for otherwise our credit would have stood on more hopeful grounds than heretofore. There was a condition in the last loan that, the lenders furnishing one third of the money, the remaining two thirds of the bonds should remain 18. months unsold, and at their option to take or not, and that in the mean time the same bankers should open no other loan for us. These same lenders became purchasers of our domestic debt, and they were disposed to avail themselves of the power they had thus acquired over us as to our foreign demands, to make us pay the domestic ones. Should the present necessities have obliged you to comply with their proposition for the present year, I should be of opinion it ought to be the last instance. If the transfer of these debts to Europe meet with any encouragement from us, we can no more borrow money here, let our necessities be what they will, for who will give 96. per cent for the foreign obligations of the same nation whose domestic ones can be bought at the same market for 55 per cent? The former too bearing an interest of only 5. per cent while the latter yeilds 6. If any discouragements can be honestly thrown on this transfer, it would seem adviseable, in order to keep the domestic debt at home. It would be a very effectual one if, instead of the title existing in our treasury books alone, it was made to exist in loose papers, as our loan office debts do. The European holder would then be obliged to risque the title paper of his capital, as well as his interest in the hands of his agent in America whenever the interest was to be demanded whereas at present he trusts him with the interest only. This single circumstance would put a total stop to all future sales of domestic debt at this market. Whether this or any other obstruction can or should be thrown in the way of these operations is not for me to decide. But I have thought the subject worth your consideration.

I have the honour to be with sentiments of the most perfect esteem & respect Gentlemen Your most obedient & most humble servant, TH: JEFFERSON

RC (NHi); endorsed. PrC (DLC). Enclosure (PrC in DLC): The text of the schedule enclosed in this letter is essentially the same as Enclosure I in TJ to John Jay, 16 Mch. 1788, q.v. for variations in text.

To Willink & Van Staphorst

GENTLEMEN   Amsterdam March 29. 1788.

Yourselves Mr. Adams and myself have concurred in agreeing that Mr. Dumas's situation required the [immediate payment of the] arrears of salary due to him. These arrears are 11516 florins [according] to an account rendered by him. Had the board of treasury been on the spot they would probably have thought as we do. However their letter of Feb. 20. does not leave a liberty to pay to him this sum of money till the cash for the June interest shall be secured. It has been supposed, and I think it was your opinion, that Mr. Dumas could make bonds answer his purpose, and that these might be delivered to him without interfering at all with the provision for the June interest. I therefore think and should advise you to deliver to him bonds to the amount of 11516. florins, convinced that under these circumstances it will meet the approbation and fulfill the dispositions of Congress and the board of treasury towards Mr. Dumas. I must however add a saving in favour of any objections to his account, should any justly arise, whenever the board of treasury shall settle it, so that this paiment is not to be obligatory on the United states farther than the account shall be found right, which I dare say will be in the whole. I am with very great esteem and respect Gentlemen Your most obedient humble servt,   TH: JEFFERSON

PrC (DLC).

From Madame Duplessy

Paris, 31 Mch. 1788. Encloses invitations for an assembly which she hopes to make useful as well as pleasant; has been assisted in this effort by Mmes. de Sillery and Duborcage; hopes some foreigners will attend.

RC (DLC); 1 p.; in French. Enclosures missing.

Preliminary indexes will be issued periodically for groups of volumes. An index covering Vols. 1-6 has been published. A comprehensive index of persons, places, subjects, etc., arranged in a single consolidated sequence, will be issued at the conclusion of the series.

THE PAPERS OF THOMAS JEFFERSON is composed in Monticello, a type specially designed by the Mergenthaler Linotype Company for this series. Monticello is based on a type design originally developed by Binny & Ronaldson, the first successful typefounding company in America. It is considered historically appropriate here because it was used extensively in American printing during the last thirty years of Jefferson's life, 1796 to 1826; and because Jefferson himself expressed cordial approval of Binny & Ronaldson types.

❖

Composed and printed by Princeton University Press. Illustrations are reproduced in collotype by Meriden Gravure Company, Meriden, Connecticut. Paper for the series is made by W. C. Hamilton & Sons, at Miquon, Pennsylvania; cloth for the series is made by Holliston Mills, Inc., Norwood, Massachusetts. Bound by the J. C. Valentine Company, New York.

DESIGNED BY P. J. CONKWRIGHT

17

4659